he Life Of St. Alphonsus Maria De Liguori: Bishop Of St. Agatha Of The Goths And ounder Of The Congregation Of The Holy Redeemer

Antonio Tannoja

THE LIFE

OF

St. Alphonsus Maria de Liguori,

BISHOP OF ST. AGATHA OF THE GOTHS,

And Founder of the Congregation of the Most Holy Redeemer.

COMPILED FROM THE PUBLISHED MEMOIRS OF THE SAINT,

BY ONE OF THE REDEMPTORIST FATHERS.

BALTIMORE:
PUBLISHED BY JOHN MURPHY & CO.
No. 178 MARKET STREET.
LONDON....C. DOLMAN, 61 NEW BOND STREET.
PITTSBURG....GEORGE QUIGLEY.
Sold by Catholic Booksellers generally.
1855.

S. ALPHONSUS MARIA DE LIGUORIO.

Episcopus et Fundator Cong. S.S.mi Redemptoris

(Cujus festum celebratur 2. Aug.)

PREFACE.

The compiler long since noticed with regret, that there was no Life of St. Alphonsus published in the English language, which adequately set forth the merits of that illustrious Saint, and displayed his many claims to our admiration and respect. In order to supply this deficiency, he undertook, more than ten years ago, a translation of the Life of the Saint from the Italian; but various circumstances occurred to retard its completion. In the meanwhile, he learned with pleasure that such a publication was announced in England, in the series of the Lives of the Saints edited by the fathers of the Oratory; but this work, when it came to hand, though it left nothing to be desired in point of fulness of illustration, did not seem fully adapted to meet the object he had proposed to himself, as its length was so great as to prove an obstacle to its general circulation. As soon, therefore, as his occupations permitted, he resumed his undertaking; but thinking that a compilation from the English Life would answer his purpose better than the proposed translation, he was induced to change his original plan, and to prepare for publication the work which is now presented. While, however, he has attempted nothing beyond a mere compilation, care has been taken to unite completeness with brevity, and he believes that the portrait of St. Alphonsus which is given in the following pages, could not have been rendered more perfect and true otherwise than by the entire reproduction of the voluminous memoirs already published.

There is no occasion to enlarge here upon the merits of the Saint. During a life-time of ninety years, laboriously occupied in the service of God and in the salvation of souls, he exhibited continually such splendid examples of every virtue, that the mere narration of them will be at once his best panegyric, and the most persuasive exhortation to the imitation of his holiness.

Impart then, O Lord, thy benediction to this work, and do thou take it under thy protection, O Blessed among women; that the heroic actions and labors which it records may, in their recital, repeat the result which was the effect and aim of their first achievement, by bringing new honor and glory to the holy names of JESUS and MARY.

BALTIMORE, *Nov.* 1*st*, 1854.

CONTENTS.

CHAPTER XXVIII.

CHAPTER XXIX.

CHAPTER XXX.

CHAPTER XXXI.

CHAPTER XXXII.

CHAPTER XXXIII.

CHAPTER XXXIV.

Life of St. Alphonsus.

CHAPTER I.

Birth and Childhood of Alphonsus.

IN all ages of the world, the Almighty has raised up extraordinary men to supply the wants of humanity; and, incessantly watching over the welfare of his Church, he has, in every succeeding century, provided chosen vessels to defend and edify it. In the eighteenth century, impiety and overstrained rigidity had united to undermine the edifice of the Church. A servile fear had expelled the charity of God; the sacraments, those fountains of life, were abandoned, or turned into derision; the divine Eucharist, the life-spring of Catholic piety, had become an object of dread; and the spirit of Christianity seemed passing away. But the eye of an omniscient Providence watched over it: to confound impiety, to fight against Jansenism, to awaken faith, and kindle love, in its source, the Sacrament of the altar, God gave to his Church and to the world, a man after his own heart, Alphonsus Liguori.

Joseph de Liguori, of an ancient patrician family in Naples, and Anne Catherine Cavalieri, of an equally noble family from Brindes, were the happy parents of Alphonsus. Illustrious by his birth, as also by his military talents, and the public offices which he filled with integrity and prudence, D. Joseph was, moreover, a man of exemplary piety, and by his devotion to the passion of our Lord he obtained many signal graces. His wife was a woman of singular virtue, and descended from parents equally remarkable for their piety and their rank. Devoted to prayer, loving the poor, she practised self-denial and mortification, abstained from worldly amusements, and was to be found most frequently in the house of God.

Alphonsus was born on the 27th of September, 1696, in the vicinity of Naples, at Marianella, where his parents had a country-house, and two days after, he was baptized in the Church of St. Mary of Virgins in Naples. He received the following names: "Alphonsus Mary Anthony John Francis Cosmas Damian Michel-Angelo;" the first of which were given him in memory of his ancestors, the others in honor of the Saints on whose respective days he was born and baptized. From the hour of his birth, he was placed in a special manner under the protection of the Blessed Virgin, that in all his necessities he might find in her an advocate and mother. Shortly after his birth, St. Francis Jerome, of the Society of Jesus, foreseeing with a prophetic eye how dear to God, and how useful to his Church, the infant would become, foretold his future sanctity. He took him from the arms of his mother, and blessing him, said: "This little child will live to a great age, even until ninety years; he will be a bishop, and will perform great things for Jesus Christ." Alphonsus was henceforth regarded as a special gift from heaven, destined to procure the salvation of souls and promote the glory of Jesus Christ.

Contrary to the usual custom among the nobles, the early education of Alphonsus was not confided to strangers; his mother superintended it herself, and instructed her son in the knowledge of religion. The brother of Alphonsus, D. Gaetan, related that every morning after having blessed her children, she made them pray to God, and every evening she assembled them around her, and taught them the elements of the Christian faith, reciting with them the Rosary and other prayers in honor of different Saints. She was careful in preventing them from associating with other children of their age; she wished that grace should anticipate in them the malice of sin, and that they might early be taught to hate it; she therefore took them every week to confess to her own director, F. Thomas Pagano, of the Oratory of St. Jerome. It was thus she guided her dear Alphonsus, and made him truly holy. Above all, she endeavored to kindle in his heart a tender love for Jesus Christ, and a filial confidence in Mary. He was born with a heart so ready to receive the impressions of grace, that piety and love of virtue seemed natural to him. One might say, that in him virtue anticipated age, so early did he show maturity in his devotions.

Even in childhood, he knew not the ordinary amusements of infancy, but placed all his delight in erecting little altars, and celebrating in his childish manner the feasts of different Saints. When he was more advanced in age, and had tasted in the practice of piety the sweets of celestial communication, he might be seen continually presenting himself before God, and pouring out his heart in holy affections before him. Thus he so early began to receive those precious graces which God bestows on souls destined to the highest degrees of sanctity.

At this time, the Fathers of St. Jerome directed a fervent Congregation, having for its object the spiritual welfare of the young nobility. The parents of Alphonsus placed him under their care, when he was only nine years old, and his exemplary conduct and great piety were the admiration of these good Fathers. He came early every Sunday morning to the Congregation, and although so young, he was docile and submissive to the slightest command of the Superiors, attentive and recollected during the devotional exercises, full of a holy avidity for the general instructions, and even over-anxious in his desire to profit by them. He regularly confessed to F. Pagano, and when arrived at the proper age, received holy communion from his hands. It was then an edifying spectacle to see this young child on his knees, hearing mass with singular devotion, and approaching the holy table with the greatest fervor. He prepared himself always by the aid of little books of piety, which he devoutly held in his hands, and never retired without kneeling long to make acts of thanksgiving.

As Alphonsus advanced in age, his mother redoubled her solicitude: not content with all he learned under these excellent fathers, she took care to instruct him herself in the manner of performing his devotions, and acquitting himself of his other duties. She spoke to him of the enormity of sin, of hell which it merits, and of the great displeasure the slightest fault gives to the heart of Jesus Christ. What was most admirable in him, was his constancy in his devotional exercises. When the hour arrived for his joining his mother in some devout practice, he presented himself before her, nor was he less punctual in other pious exercises, which he imposed upon himself.

When he had attained his twelfth year, his prayer was not only more than ordinary, it was sublime; as is proved by the following very remarkable occurrence, related by an eye-witness. The Fathers of St. Jerome were in the habit of taking the young gentlemen of their congregation, every Sunday after vespers, to some country-house for recreation. On one of these occasions, the young people began to amuse themselves with a game called the game of oranges. Alphonsus was asked to join, but excused himself on the plea of not knowing the game: his companions, however, urged him so much, that at length he consented. Fortune favored him, and he gained thirty times running. This success made his companions jealous, and one, older than he, exclaimed in a rage: "It was you who did not know the game, was it!" adding in his anger a very indecent expression. Alphonsus reddened, when he heard it, and with an air of severity turned towards his companions and said: "How is this, shall God be offended for the sake of a little miserable money? Take back your money!" and throwing on the ground what he had won, he turned his back on them with a holy indignation. When evening came, and the young people were to return, he was nowhere to be found. They called him, but they called in vain, and every one went to seek him. But what was their surprise, when they discovered him on his knees, before a picture of the Blessed Virgin which he had with him, and had placed upon a laurel branch. He was quite absorbed, and so ravished in God, that it was some time before he came to himself, notwithstanding the noise his companions made.

To the latest period of his life, Alphonsus continued to acknowledge his obligations to his mother, for the great care she had taken of him during his childhood. "If I must admit," he was wont to say, "that there was any thing good in me, as a child, and that I was kept from wickedness, I owe it entirely to the tender solicitude of my mother." He once said: "At the death of my father, I refused to go to Naples, offering to God the sacrifice of a duty, which nature claimed from me; but when my mother is dying, if I am not otherwise prevented, I shall not have the courage to refuse going to assist her."

CHAPTER II.

Alphonsus applies to Studies.

D. JOSEPH and D. Anna, fearing that in a college the innocence of their son might run some danger, and that intercourse with other young men might tarnish its lustre, would have him continually under their own eyes, sheltered from every occasion of sin, and procured him excellent private masters to teach him belles-lettres. His grammar master was the learned Dominic Buonaccio, a native of Calabria, and a man of piety and irreproachable morals. His master found little difficulty in conducting his education: his naturally happy disposition and inclination for virtue, much abridged the lessons of this good priest, as well in reference to science, as to spiritual matters. His mind was quick and penetrating, his memory faithful and retentive, and he combined great docility with an ardent desire for instruction. With these excellent qualities, he made rapid progress in his studies, and gave great satisfaction both to master and parents.

As the father and mother of Alphonsus wished not only to make their son a man of letters and a good Christian, but also an accomplished gentleman, they took care to adorn his mind with every other species of knowledge necessary to form a distinguished education. He was yet a child, when they gave him masters in drawing, painting, and architecture. He succeeded admirably in all these arts: even in his old age he sketched pictures, sometimes of the infant Jesus, or of the blessed Virgin; and had engraved several of them for the use of his congregation. His father, who was exceedingly fond of music, wished him also to excel in that art, and gave orders that he should apply himself three hours daily to the study of it with a master. Thus before Alphonsus had attained his twelfth year, he touched the harpsichord with great skill. In his later years he regretted the time he had spent in acquiring this accomplishment. "Fool that I have been," said he one day, looking at the harpsichord, "to have lost so much time on that; but it was right to obey my father, he would have it so." He excelled so much both in music and poetry, that even in his old age he wrote and composed wonderfully well. This his talent is apparent in the numerous hymns he composed, among which are many that force us to recognise in them the hand of a master. D. Joseph, ambitious of seeing his son distinguish himself in the magistracy, by the talents with which he was adorned, wished him, when his philosophy and other studies were finished, to apply himself to civil and canonical law. He gave him two learned masters, who enjoyed great reputation in Naples. Alphonsus was not less successful in this new career.

Among these numerous occupations, all the recreation he permitted himself to take, was with D. Charles Cito, at whose house he passed an hour in the evening, to play at cards with other young people of irreproachable character, who visited there. The favorite games of the young gentlemen were tersillio, ombre, and such like, then usual in good society, in which the mind found recreation and exercise, while the morals received no damage. These amusements had very strict bounds, D. Joseph wishing that they might be rather a means of advancing, than retarding, him in his studies, and that the short relaxation might enable him to resume them again with renewed vigor. He was always displeased, when his son stayed beyond the appointed time; for it sometimes happened that Alphonsus was rather late. On one of these occasions, wishing to mortify him, he removed all his books from his table, and substituted for them packs of cards. Alphonsus felt this mortification most sensibly, and nothing else was necessary to make him blush, and strive more punctually than ever, to obey his father's injunctions. In his old age he mentioned, that at the same time he had been very fond of hunting, but had never indulged in it, except on days when he was dispensed from study, adding, that the birds were fortunate that had to do with him, for, notwithstanding all his endeavors, he rarely killed one. Such were the useful and interesting occupations of the young Alphonsus; and we believe his parents were wise enough to interdict other accomplishments usually taught, and regarded by worldly persons as indispensable. They looked upon dancing as an amusement perilous for the soul, and on fencing, as exposing both soul and body to many dangers.

Alphonsus devoted himself so successfully to the study of jurisprudence, that before his sixteenth year he was master of it. He received his degree on the twenty-first of January, 1713, amidst general applause, having previously obtained a dispensation of three years and nine months, being little more than sixteen years old. He might from that time be seen constantly before the tribunals of Naples, listening with an ardent avidity for instruction to the numerous decisions of the counsels, so much respected in that town. At first his father placed him with Peronne, a celebrated advocate, after whose death he was placed with another jurisconsult not less esteemed, called Jovene. It was about this period that he began to deny himself all kinds of amusement, and even to renounce the agreeable society in the house of D. Cito. He associated only with the president, Dominic Caravita, a man as pious as he was learned, and inferior to none in the science of civil and canon law. His house was then a kind of academy for studious young men, where the most virtuous and learned in legal matters used to meet. The president did all in his power to render them skilful in discussing points of law, and in the choice of proper words. Every evening he held conferences, in which they treated the most difficult questions, while the president adopted or rejected their conclusions.

CHAPTER III.

Alphonsus follows the Profession of Law—His Father's project of marrying him.

ALPHONSUS had not yet attained his twentieth year, when he saw himself surrounded by numerous clients, and seated before the tribunals, side by side with the most distinguished advocates. His father's family, at that time, had many friends and relations among the principal senators. These men of quality, knowing the talents and good conduct of Alphonsus, and his desire of advancement, united all their endeavors to procure him distinguished clients, and he himself knew so well how to gain public esteem, that in a short time the most important causes were confided to him. The rules by which he regulated his conduct as a lawyer, cannot be too generally known; for if they were imitated, the whole face of society would be renovated. They were as follows:

1. Never to accept unjust causes, as being pernicious to conscience, and hurtful to honor.

2. Never to defend a cause by illicit and unjust means.

3. Never to burden clients with superfluous expenses.

4. To defend the causes of clients with the same care as one would his own.

5. To study carefully the details of a process, in order to draw arguments from them that may effectually help the defence.

6. To implore the assistance of God in order to succeed, because he is the protector of justice.

7. If the dilatoriness and negligence of a lawyer prove prejudicial to clients, he must reimburse the loss caused in this way, otherwise he sins against justice.

8. A lawyer must not undertake causes which surpass his talents or his strength, or for which he foresees that he will not have leisure to prepare his defence.

9. Justice and probity should be the characteristics of a lawyer, and he ought to preserve them as the apple of of his eye.

10. A lawyer, who loses a cause by negligence, contracts the obligation of making up all the losses of his clients.

11. In the defence of a cause it is necessary to be truthful, sincere, respectful, and reasonable.

12. The qualities requisite for a lawyer, are knowledge, diligence, truth, fidelity and justice.

Guided by such rules, it is not to be wondered at, that he gained an ascendancy over all hearts, and so enchanted his audience when he spoke, that not only the judges, but even his adversaries, often ranged themselves on his side. Such must ever be the ultimate effects of truth and honor.

If Alphonsus desired to strike out a brilliant path for himself as a lawyer, he was no less anxious to increase in virtue and render himself dear to God. Two years after receiving the gown, he advanced from the Congregation of young nobles to that of doctors, established in the same house of the Fathers of the Oratory. Besides frequenting the Congregation, he often visited F. Pagano, his spiritual director, whom he regarded as his guardian angel. To him he exposed all his doubts and fears, and he never deviated from his counsels; and thus, far from relaxing in his piety and devotion, he daily made more and more progress. He frequented the sacraments, he visited the sick in the hospitals, and loved prayer, to which he joined the mortification of his passions and his senses. He never went to the law-courts, before he had heard Mass, and finished in the church his other devotional exercises.

While Alphonsus gave himself to piety with so much assiduity, his father was at the same time anxious to confirm him in these dispositions. He wished him annually to make with him the spiritual exercises in the house called Conocchia, kept for this purpose by the Jesuits, or in the house of the Missionaries of St. Vincent of Paul. Alphonsus afterwards spoke of these retreats, as having made a great impression upon him, and of his having drawn from them the most salutary fruits. One of the most precious of these was an especial love for the holy virtue of purity. During the whole period of his youth, no one ever remarked, in his conversations with young companions, a sign, or a word, that could indicate a shadow of impropriety. Every thing about him proclaimed his modesty, by which he edified all around him. He was so jealous for the conservation of this virtue, so dear to the Son of God, that, as his brother D. Gaetan related, in order to prevent during his sleep even any involuntary movement contrary to it, he put his hands, when going to bed in the evening, into a kind of etui made of paste-board. Afterwards, he used to sleep, holding a cross of wood in his arms, which he did to the end of his days.

A life so exemplary could not fail to produce the most abundant fruits; and although all the good resulting from it in the edification of others, will only be known in heaven, yet it has pleased Providence, that one instance should be upon record—the conversion of a slave in his father's house. D. Joseph, as commander of the galleys, had several slaves in his service; one of them was selected to wait upon Alphonsus. He soon after manifested an inclination to become a Christian, and when asked what had made him think of such a thing, he replied: "The example of my young master has made a great impression on me; for it is impossible that that religion can be false, which makes him lead a life so pure and holy." F. Mastrilla, of the Congregation of St. Jerome, undertook to instruct him; but soon after, he became sick and was sent to the hospital. One evening he expressed a great desire to see F. Mastrilla immediately. Upon his arrival, he requested to be baptized, saying: "I have seen our Lady, St. Joseph, and St. Joachim, and they have told me I must be baptized now, because they wish to have me in Paradise." The priest replied that his illness was not dangerous, and besides, that he was not sufficiently instructed. "Let your reverence interrogate me," replied the slave, "for I am prepared to answer all your questions." In fact, he replied with the utmost precision and accuracy to every question. He was baptized, and then told to repose a little after the fatigue. "This is not a time to rest," he said, "for I must go immediately to Paradise." In about half an hour this poor slave, his countenance radiant with joy, surrendered his pure soul into the hands of his Creator.

Alphonsus was now approaching his twentieth year, and, seeing the progress he daily made in the career of the law, every one prognosticated, that with such distinguished talents, and such powerful family interests, he would soon attain the highest dignity in the magistracy. These rare prerogatives, enhanced by all the qualities that could be wished for in a young nobleman, and joined to irreproachable conduct, made the first families in Naples anxious for him to form a matrimonial alliance with their daughters. Among all the parties who presented themselves, the choice of D. Joseph fell upon D. Theresa, a rich heiress, who was also nearly allied to the family, the only daughter of D. Francis de Liguori, Prince of Presiccio: he expected thereby to acquire for Alphonsus a considerable fortune. The prince regarded it as an honor for his daughter to become the wife of such a young man, and the affair was considered as arranged. As for Alphonsus, he took no part in the matter, and showed not the least intention of marrying. While this affair was in progress, the mother of the princess, contrary to all expectation, became pregnant, and this incident changed immediately the designs of D. Joseph, who no longer found in the marriage the advantages he had originally contemplated for his house. His ardor cooled, and when she was brought to bed of a son, he withdrew himself entirely. At the end of a few months, the infant died, and the father of Alphonsus began again to frequent the house, and to speak of his original proposals. Although they felt themselves aggrieved, the prince and princess were willing to renew the negotiations; but Theresa would not listen to these new proposals. "When my brother was alive," said she, "I was not considered a suitable match for Alphonsus de Liguori; but now he is dead, they think it advisable—it is my fortune they seek, and not myself. I know enough of the world; and now I wish to have nothing more to do with it. I desire to take Jesus Christ for my spouse." She entered into the convent of the Nuns of the Holy Sacrament, or of St. Mary Magdalene de Pazzi, and took the veil on the eighth of March, 1719. This rupture between Alphonsus and Theresa was an arrangement of Providence, to withdraw both of them from the dangers of the world. Theresa, from the moment she entered the convent, gave herself entirely to Jesus Christ, and spared no sacrifice in order to please Him. Her life was short, but full of merits, and she died in the odor of sanctity, the 30th of October, 1724. Soon after her death, Alphonsus, at the request of the Superior of the convent, wrote the edifying life of her, who had been intended for his wife.

A circumstance occurred about this time which shows the perfect submission of Alphonsus to his father. One evening there was at the house a party of ladies and gentlemen, and it happened that one of the domestics showed stupidity in attending to the guests. D. Joseph scolded the servant, and reproached him with his inattention: it was an involuntary fault, yet he did not cease to express his displeasure with him as he went and came. Alphonsus was sorry for the man, and said to his father: "What a noise you make about it, my father: when once you begin, you can never end." This speech displeased D. Joseph, who so far forgot himself, as to give his son a blow in the face. Alphonsus was confused, but said not a word, and, deeply humiliated, withdrew immediately to his room. The hour of supper came, and as he did not appear, his mother went to call him, but found him bathed in tears, deploring the want of respect he had shown towards his father. He confessed how wrongfully he had acted, and begged she would intercede for him, and obtain forgiveness. Accompanied by his mother, he went to his father, and asked him to forgive him. D. Joseph, affected by his submission and repentance, embraced and blessed him; and if the fault of his son had wounded him, he was more touched and consoled by seeing him so sincerely humble.

Alphonsus had never ceased to distinguish himself in the practice of virtue; nevertheless, he confessed in his old age, that, at this period of his life, his piety became cold, and that he was in danger of losing his soul and his God. His father obliged him to accompany him into society; he frequented the theatres; and often, although always out of obedience, he took part in a private play. Added to these, though innocent, yet dissipating, amusements, were the applauses he received on all sides, the proposals of marriage, the compliments which were showered upon him by ladies and their relations: in short, every thing flattered his passions, his heart was tainted, and he lost his first fervor. In this state of spiritual coldness, the slightest cause was sufficient to make him omit some one of his pious practices: he has said himself, that if he had remained much longer in this dangerous position, he could not have avoided soon falling into some great sin. But the watchful eye of Providence failed not to send him timely aid, and, with a peculiar and paternal care, made him enter into himself.

Alphonsus was on terms of the most intimate friendship with D. F. Cape-Celatro, Duke of Casabona, a young man of his own age. The young nobleman, alarmed at seeing his friend beginning to be negligent in the service of God, and wishing to rekindle his own fervor, proposed that he should join him in making a retreat during Lent, in the house of the Missionaries of St. Vincent of Paul. Alphonsus, with his friend and some others, went there on the twenty-sixth of March, 1722. He was among those who profited most. Grace knocked at the door of his heart, making him feel how he had fallen from his first fervor: he saw, that, in following the world, he was pasturing on vanity, and that he was loving God but in an imperfect manner. The Divine Light penetrated his soul at a propitious moment. He deplored his tepidity, and made a solemn promise to God to quit that mode of life, which he had so inconsiderately engaged in, and over which he lamented and wept. He always acknowledged, that this retreat had been for him one of the greatest blessings he had ever received from the Divine Majesty, and often said, that, under God, he owed it to his friend Cape-Celatro, that he had not been the slave of the world and a prey to his own passions.

From the manner in which he sometimes spoke of this period of his life, we might be led, at the first glance, to imagine he had lost his innocence; but it was not so. The Saints always speak in exaggerated terms of their faults; and besides, we have the testimony of many who directed his conscience, that he had never committed a mortal sin. On one occasion, speaking of himself, he said; "I have frequented the theatres; but thanks be to God, I never committed even a venial sin there, for I went to hear the music, which absorbed all my attention, and hindered me from thinking of any other thing." Even at this time, every one regarded him as a young man of pure and irreproachable manners; and one of his intimate friends, on being asked whether he had ever perceived any lightness in his conduct, replied, bowing his head respectfully: "No, he was always a most virtuous young man: I should blaspheme, if I said otherwise." Among many other fruits which Alphonsus gathered from this retreat, was an especial and tender confidence in Jesus present in the Blessed Sacrament. Besides approaching thenceforth the holy table several times a week, he went every day to visit the Holy Sacrament in the Church where the forty hours' adoration was made, and there he remained, not a few minutes, but for hours, in contemplation, edifying every one around him. He often purchased flowers to adorn the altar of his parish church; and preserved during his whole life this devotion for ornamenting altars, procuring the rarest seeds, and cultivating them himself to embellish the altars of the churches of his Congregation. This same practice he recommended to the Rectors of the houses, for he loved to see the altars ornamented with the finest flowers. The following year, in March, 1723, his father being in Naples, they withdrew together to the house of the same Missionaries to make another retreat. He received more graces, and was confirmed in his resolution of observing celibacy, which he had made during the last retreat, and of consecrating himself more than ever to God: he determined to yield his birth-right to his brother Hercules, although he had not yet decided to abandon the law.

D. Joseph, ignorant of all this, projected another treaty of marriage with the daughter of Dominic del Balso, Duke of Presenzano, an amiable and noble lady, and, without consulting his son, he made proposals to the Prince, who at once agreed to them. This displeased Alphonsus; but fearing to offend his father, who he knew would be very indignant at his refusal, he frequented the house of Presenzano, although very unwillingly; and he often said afterwards, that in the midst of amusements there, he felt as upon thorns, and thought only of the moment when his martyrdom would end. When D. Joseph saw the indifference of his son, he did all in his power to overcome it;

but Alphonsus excused himself by saying that weakness in his chest, and tendency to asthma, warned him not to think of marriage. His father attributed all these excuses to bashfulness, and continued to take him often with him to the house of the Duke; and, not to displease his father, Alphonsus accompanied him thither, but occupied himself with anything but striving to please the lady, taking part in the conversation with so much modesty and reserve, that no one could suspect what was passing between the families. On every occasion he behaved with the greatest circumspection. It happened one evening at the Duke's house, that he was invited to play the harpsichord: he willingly consented, when the young lady proposed to accompany him in a song: she rose and stood near him, turning her face towards him. Alphonsus immediately turned his head to the other side, and she, thinking it accidental, moved round: no sooner had she done so, than he again turned from her. The young Princess, perceiving the truth, was offended, thinking his indifference proceeded from contempt; and turning to the company, she said: "It would seem the young gentleman has suddenly become moon-struck;" and so saying, she withdrew. Alphonsus was much mortified, but the others were edified by his admirable modesty. Yet D. Joseph did all he could to hasten the marriage, while Alphonsus continued to excuse himself on the plea of bad health. Seeing at length that his excuses were unavailing, he opened his mind to his mother, begging her to persuade his father to cease his importunities. D. Anna was vexed at her son's determination, and tried to persuade him of the advantages he would derive from his father's arrangements, and the displeasure his refusal would cause him. But he expressed his resolution to throw all possible difficulties in the way of his father's negotiating any marriage for him. At last the young lady herself, seeing his coldness, declared her unwillingness to marry a young man who would hardly look at her.

CHAPTER IV.

Alphonsus retires from the Bar, and resolves to quit the world.

THINGS were in this state, when God, who had other designs for Alphonsus, changed the aspect of affairs, and demolished at one blow all the worldly hopes of D. Joseph for his son. The tribunals of Naples were at this time occupied with a feudal process of great importance between the Grand Duke of Tuscany and one of the most powerful nobles of the realm: about six hundred thousand ducats depended on the decision. Alphonsus undertook the cause of the nobleman, and after an entire month passed in the most careful study of the case, he believed he had discovered facts so evident, and reasons so strong, that they could not fail to gain a decision in favor of his client. Notwithstanding he had carefully examined over and over the details of the process, he was completely mistaken regarding the sense of one document, which constituted the right of the adverse party. The advocate of the Grand Duke perceived the mistake, but he allowed Alphonsus to continue his eloquent address to the end; as soon, however, as he had finished, he rose, and said with cutting coolness: "Sir, the case is not exactly what you suppose it to be: if you will examine this paper attentively, you will find there precisely the contrary of all you have advanced." "Willingly," replied Alphonsus; "the decision depends on this question"—whether the fief were granted under the law of Lombardy, or under the French law. The paper being examined, it was found that the Grand Duke's advocate was in the right. "Yes," said Alphonsus, holding the paper in his hand, "I am wrong, I have been mistaken." A discovery so unexpected, and the fear of being accused of unfair dealing, filled him with consternation, and covered him with confusion, so much so, that every one saw his emotion. It was in vain that the President Caravita, who loved him, and knew his integrity, tried to console him. Alphonsus would listen to nothing, but, overwhelmed with confusion, his head sunk on his breast, he said to himself: "World, I know thee now: courts of law, never shall you see me again." He withdrew to his own house, incessantly repeating to himself: "World, I know thee now;" and shut himself up in his chamber. His father was absent, and his mother did not notice his distress. When the dinner hour came, they called him in vain; they knocked at his door; he said he would eat nothing; they insisted, but he would not reply. The hour of supper passed in the same manner. Next day, when D. Joseph returned, his wife recounted to him her vexation; he immediately went to his son's room, but was refused admittance. It was not until the third day, that, overcome by his mother's tears, he consented to open his door. They pressed him to eat, and with difficulty persuaded him to take a slice of melon, which, as he afterwards declared, seemed to him more bitter than gall.

When rest had calmed his spirit, he took leave of his clients,* renounced his intimacies, and lived in the house of his father the life of a hermit. Grace daily gained more empire over his soul, and his greatest pleasure was to spend his days partly in the Church and partly in the Hospital of the Incurables, or if he did remain at home, it was to meditate on the lives of the Saints, to converse with God, and to read books of devotion. These occupations daily gave a new charm to his soul; but it was, above all, in the presence of his Divine Saviour, in the churches where they made the forty hours' adoration, that he enjoyed a foretaste

*This accident, however, was not precisely the cause of his leaving the bar; it was rather the occasion of his doing so at this time. For, on several occasions, he had spoken to his friends in such a manner, that it was evident he had already resolved to quit the profession on account of its difficulties and dangers. He said one day to D. Joseph Cape-Celatro: "My friend, our profession is too full of difficulties and dangers; we lead an unhappy life and run risk of dying an unhappy death. For myself, I will quit this career, which does not suit me; for I wish to secure the salvation of my soul."

of Paradise, and often he was so absorbed as to be unconscious of all around.

This behaviour of Alphonsus was for D. Joseph a subject of the greatest affliction: he imagined his son was out of his mind and had become good for nothing. "What project can he be meditating?" said he to his wife; and D. Anna, sharing his uneasiness, could throw no light on the subject. A few days after the events we have related, D. Joseph brought to his son a process, which interested the family, desiring him to examine it the next day. "Give it to some other person," replied Alphonsus; "the tribunal is no longer a place for me; henceforward I will occupy myself only with the salvation of my soul." This reply, which D. Joseph hardly expected, fell on him like a thunderbolt, and he burst into tears. His wife tried to console him, and to persuade him, that after the crisis should be past, their son would return to his former occupation; but he would not believe it; "No," he said, "Alphonsus is too obstinate, he will not change his resolution."

God, who wished to withdraw him entirely from the world, and take complete possession of his heart, prepared another trial for him. It was on the 28th day of August, a day ever memorable in the annals of Alphonsus, that the birth-day of the Empress Isabella, the wife of Charles VI, was celebrated. There was a grand fete at the court, and D. Joseph wished to assist at the ceremony of kissing hands, and ordered his son to prepare to accompany him. He coldly excused himself; but his father continuing to insist, he replied shortly: "What would you have me do there?—all that is vanity." Irritated by this answer, D. Joseph said in a transport of rage: "Do what you will, and go where you will!" Alphonsus, seeing his refusal had provoked his father, felt some scruple, and replied: "Do not be annoyed, my father, I am ready to go with you." D. Joseph, however, was too angry to listen to him, and only continued to repeat: "Go where you will, do what you will!" and turning his back, he left the room, and stepping into his carriage, drove straight to his country-house, overwhelmed with chagrin. Alphonsus, greatly distressed at witnessing the vexation of his father, exclaimed: "My God, if I resist, I do wrong, if I consent, I do worse; I know not how to act!" In great affliction, he left the house, and went to the Hospital of the Incurables, in the hope of finding some consolation. Almost overpowered with his own sorrows, he was striving to assuage the miseries of others, of the poor and needy, when in a moment a light shone around him, the building seemed to be overthrown, and he heard a loud voice saying to him: "Forsake the world, and give thyself entirely to Me." Awed and astonished by what had occurred, he nevertheless continued assisting the sick; but when he was about leaving the hospital, and had reached the staircase, the house again seemed falling around him, and he heard the same voice, saying: "Forsake the world, and give thyself entirely to Me." He stood still, and then, like another St. Paul, gave himself up to the divine call. Weeping, he exclaimed: "Lord, I have too long resisted thy grace; here I am, do with me what Thou pleasest." He quitted the hospital, and proceeded to the church of the Redemption of Captives, dedicated to the Blessed Virgin, a favorite resort of his, because of a magnificent image of the Virgin which was there. He cast himself at the foot of the altar, imploring the assistance of his Divine Mother. Strengthened by her aid, he renounced the world, promised to give up his birth-right, and offered himself a perfect sacrifice to his Saviour and his Blessed Mother, solemnly engaging himself to enter into the Congregation of the Oratory of St. Philip Neri; and drawing his sword, he laid it on the altar of our Lady of Mercy, as a pledge of his fidelity. He never ceased to call this day the day of his conversion, nor ever afterwards visited Naples, without going to this church to return thanks to his divine benefactress. On the evening of this memorable day, Alphonsus went to his confessor, F. Pagano, and confided to him what had happened, declaring his resolution immediately to join the Fathers of the Oratory. "This is not a thing to be decided hastily," said his director, "I must think it over during a year, before I give you a reply." "A year!" cried Alphonsus, "I will not wait another day." Pleased with his fervor, F. Pagano said they both should recommend the important affair to Jesus and Mary.

For three days after these remarkable events, he tasted no food; he would do penance for not having sooner obeyed the call of grace. In the mean time his soul was filled to overflowing with the manna of heaven. His father, on returning from his country-house, having heard of his son's refusal to eat, was extremely vexed, and again began to importune him on those points on which their views were so opposite. He urged him, with all a father's tenderness, to resume his place at the bar, pointing out to him the loss his refusal would occasion to himself and the whole family; but when he saw he made no impression, he relapsed into anger. These scenes were repeated daily, and those only who have experienced them, can fully comprehend how they rend the heart; but Alphonsus continued firm: he daily saw his director, who, with the other fathers, advised him to proceed slowly, hoping for a favorable turn in his father's sentiments. It happened one day, that D Joseph, very much provoked at the thought of his son's splendid talents being lost in inaction, and at what he considered the inutility of his present mode of life, said to him in the bitterness of his heart: "Would to God that I were removed from this world, or that you were withdrawn from it; for I have no longer the courage to look at you!" The expression of such feelings quickened the resolution of Alphonsus. "Am I," said he to himself, "an object of such horror to my father! Then God is my only friend; from henceforth I must be satisfied with him alone!" He then renewed his vows, offering himself without reserve as a living sacrifice to the Lord. He had not yet declared his intentions to his father, but summoning courage he said to him soon after: "My father, I see how much you grieve on my account, and yet, I must assure you I am no longer for the world. Inspired by God, I have formed the resolution of entering the Congregation of the Fathers of the Oratory;

I beseech you not to be offended, but to give me your benediction." At these words, his father stood motionless with consternation, and then bursting into groans and lamentations, he withdrew to his chamber, plunged in profound grief. The devil, finding himself vanquished by the resistance of Alphonsus to the storm, determined to undermine his resolution by the more dangerous temptations of the heart; and from this time his father employed the most tender entreaties, the tears, and the mediation of friends. He engaged on his side F. de Miro, who, supposing Alphonsus was merely influenced by a melancholy humor, urged on him the propriety of employing his talents for the honor of his family, of considering the interest they possessed with the Austrian Court, and the brilliant prospects of his brother, which would be so entirely overcast, if he persisted in his present plan: he finished by affirming it was no divine inspiration which guided him, but an illusion of the devil. Alphonsus remained firm, and when de Miro insisted, he replied: "Rev. Sir, be assured, I am convinced God calls me out of the world. He wishes me to embrace the ecclesiastical state: I ought, and I will, respond to the call of God, and not to the wishes of my father." D. Joseph employed other friends to intercede with him, but his constant reply was: "God has called me, I cannot resist Him." Mgr. Cavalieri, his uncle, being then in Naples, Alphonsus applied to him for protection and support. When his parents endeavored to engage this learned prelate on their side of the question, he replied: "Have not I renounced the world and my right of primogeniture to secure my salvation? how, then, could I advise your son and my nephew to do the contrary, without risking his salvation and my own?"

CHAPTER V.

Alphonsus enters the ecclesiastical State.

IN the midst of these trials, Alphonsus had many defenders of his cause; his uncle the bishop, another uncle, the canon Peter Gizzio, and several ecclesiastics, who succeeded at length in obtaining a reluctant consent from his father, that he should enter the Congregation of the Oratory. After this forced acquiescence, he could not avoid presenting his son to the Archbishop of Naples, Cardinal Pignatelli. His Eminence was struck by the resolution of Alphonsus: "What," said he, "it is your son who wishes to become a priest?" "It has pleased God it should be so," replied his father, while the tears stood in his eyes; "it is but too true that he has taken this resolution." Even after this decisive step, he continued to throw difficulties in the way. He would not supply him with money to furnish his ecclesiastical dress: Alphonsus, however, found means to get what was necessary, and suddenly appeared one day clad in ecclesiastical costume. At this sight, D. Joseph uttered a piercing cry, and threw himself on his bed, overcome with grief. For a whole year after this occurrence, he never once spoke to his son. D. Anna recognised the will of God, and cheerfully submitted to it, doing all in her power to soften the feelings of her husband, and justify the conduct her son had pursued. The world in general condemned him: the lawyers and senators who were formerly his friends, now accused him of egregious folly; the president de Maio, in particular, passed him as a person unworthy of notice.

But if God generally tries by the loss of friends those whom he calls, he as surely recompenses the sacrifices made for him, a hundred fold. One of the first fruits of Alphonsus' sacrifice, was the friendship of the Rev. Joseph Porpora: this priest had often been edified by his devotion, when he saw him prostrated for hours before the Blessed

Sacrament, but without knowing him. At length he saw him in the ecclesiastical dress, and soon discovered who he was. He wished to make his acquaintance, but was restrained by a feeling of human respect. One day, however, seeing him conversing with an intimate friend, the Rev. John Mazzini, he felt such an ardent desire to share his friendship, that he could no longer restrain himself, and, darting suddenly forward, exclaimed: "And I also, I wish to belong to you." From that moment they seemed to have but one heart and one soul, every day they met together before the Blessed Sacrament, and mutually excited each other to advance in the path of perfection.

After Cardinal Pignatelli had given Alphonsus the ecclesiastical habit, he attached him to the parish of St. Angelo. He immediately went to offer his services to the curate of the church, and every day afterwards he might be seen serving at mass, and on feast-days assisting at every ceremony. His devotion and modesty at length turned the tide of public opinion, and those who had proclaimed him a fool, now spoke loudly in praise of his generosity in sacrificing such brilliant prospects for the love of God. But that which excited the greatest admiration, was to see him on Sundays perambulating the parish, singing hymns, and carrying the crucifix, to assemble the children together, and lead them to the church to be catechised: nothing contrasted so strongly with the remembrance of the advocate, who so lately had electrified the tribunals by his eloquence. Above all, he was most indefatigable in instructing and preparing them for their first communion.

But as virtue only is not sufficient for a preacher of the Gospel, Alphonsus at the same time applied himself with ardor to the studies befitting his new position: he frequented the company of the most learned ecclesiastics, receiving daily lessons from D. Julius Torni, one of the most eminent theological professors, who was afterwards elevated to the episcopacy. His musical and poetical talents he employed in composing sacred hymns for the use of the people, and soon had the satisfaction of seeing them replacing dangerous and loose songs. From the time he assumed the clerical habit, his mode of life became stricter than ever. Prayer and study occupied him alternately: he mortified his senses, refusing them every species of indulgence. He fasted, used the discipline, wore hair shirts, and practised all kinds of penitential exercises, in order to follow more closely the steps of his Divine Master, and to keep his body under subjection. Every Saturday he fasted on bread and water, in honor of the Blessed Virgin; his clothes were as plain as possible; for some little time, to please his father, he allowed himself to be followed by a footman, but soon disembarrassed himself of this encumbrance. Thus bidding adieu to the vanity of time, and enriching his soul with treasures for eternity, he became the edification of the whole city.

A year after Alphonsus had assumed the ecclesiastical habit, he received the tonsure from the hands of Mgr. Mirabello, Archbishop of Nazareth, on the 23d of December, 1724. On the 23d of September following, he was promoted to minor orders, with a dispensation, and in December succeeding, was made subdeacon by Mgr. Javitti, bishop of Satriano. He then entered as novice in the Congregation of the Missions. There he applied himself, with remarkable diligence, to the observance of all the rules and practices of piety; he accompanied the missionaries in the country, catechising the children. But he did not confine his assistance to this Congregation; he frequented the house of the Fathers of St. Vincent of Paul, and he associated himself to a Congregation called that of the White Monks, proving his zeal in endeavoring to procure the aids of religion for condemned criminals. We give here the rules, which guided him as a candidate for the priesthood:

1. The cleric, in order to sanctify himself, ought to frequent the society of holy priests, to be edified by their good example.

2. He ought to spend at least one hour daily in mental prayer, in order to live in fervor and recollection.

3. He ought to visit frequently the Holy Sacrament, particularly where it is solemnly exposed.

4. He ought to read the lives of holy priests, to furnish him with rules for his conduct, and excite him to imitate them.

5. He ought to honor the most holy Virgin Mary, the mother and queen of the Church, and consecrate himself particularly to her service.

6. He ought to take the greatest care of his reputation in all things, sustaining the honor of the ecclesiastical state.

7. He ought to fly worldly conversation, to avoid familiarity with laymen, and particularly with females.

8. He ought to be obedient to his superiors, fulfilling their commands, because it is the will of God.

9. He ought to wear the cassock and the tonsure, to be modest without affectation, fastidiousness, or severity.

10. He ought to be quiet and gentle in the house, exemplary in the class, and edifying in the church, particularly during divine service.

11. He ought to confess every eight days, and communicate still oftener.

12. In short, he ought to have negative sanctity, that is to say, to live free from sin, and he ought to have positive sanctity, namely, to practice every virtue.

CHAPTER VI.

Alphonsus is ordained Deacon and Priest. His first Labors, Zeal, and Success in the pulpit and the confessional.

EDIFIED by Alphonsus' holiness of life, the Cardinal Archbishop, by dispensation, gave him deacon's orders on the 6th of April, 1726; and, satisfied with his zeal and talents, gave him permission to preach in all the churches of Naples. It was in the church of St. John at the Latin Gate he preached his first sermon, from these words of

Isaias: "O that Thou wouldst bend the heavens, and come down . . . . the waters would burn with fire," (ch. lxiv, 1-2;) and the fire of his eloquence was directed to show the amazing love of Jesus Christ towards us, and our monstrous ingratitude towards God. Such was the effect of this sermon, that invitations to preach poured in upon him from all quarters: his usual subject was the dogma of the Eucharist, and it rarely happened, that he did not preach in the church where the Blessed Sacrament was exposed. The Fathers of the Mission sent him also into different parts of the kingdom, where he attacked vice with such eloquence, that he did much to promote the glory of God in the salvation of souls.

Overcome by constant exertion, his body sank under it, and he became so ill, that the physicians lost hope, and one night they sent in haste for a priest to administer the last sacraments. In this extremity he placed all his confidence in the Blessed Virgin, and eagerly asked them to bring the large statue of our Lady of Mercy, from the church in which, at the foot of this statue, he had renounced the world and consecrated himself to God. They brought the miraculous statue without delay, and placed it before his bed: his prayers were heard, he immediately felt better, and was pronounced out of danger.

On the 21st of December in the same year, he was elevated, again by dispensation, to the priesthood, and if he before burned with zeal to promote the glory of God, from henceforth this fire seemed to consume him; descending from the altar, he might be seen rushing like a lion on his prey, to attack the strongholds of Satan. The Cardinal, struck by the prodigies of grace which he operated, appointed him to give spiritual exercises to the clergy of Naples, and his Eminence had good reason to congratulate himself on his choice, because of the numbers who attended, and the benediction poured out on his labors.

Every where he was now sought after, curates desired him to preach in their churches, Congregations besought him to give spiritual exercises, and many monasteries desired with avidity to participate in the fruits of his powerful eloquence. Animated only by the Spirit of God, he preached Christ crucified, and far from studying fine phrases and eloquent expressions, he avoided with the utmost care the vain ostentation of a superfluous erudition. To a style simple and popular, he knew how to add all that was solid and energetic. What rendered his eloquence most persuasive was his modesty, his recollection, his profound humility, and his contempt for the world. Nicolas Capasso, a man celebrated for his learning and talent for satire, used to attend these sermons; on one occasion Alphonsus met him, and said, laughing: "I see you always at my sermons, you are probably about to publish some satire against me." "No," replied the other, "when I go to hear you preach, I listen with pleasure, because I see that you forget yourself in order to preach Christ crucified."

His time was fully occupied, either in the city of Naples, or the adjoining districts, where he was frequently sent on mission with the Fathers of the Congregation, and he was never known to excuse himself for want of time, or negligently to fulfil any duty to which he was appointed. The Congregation enjoyed a benefice attached to a chapel, for which the testator had made it a rule, that it should be served by a single individual, and that the person appointed should be the most indefatigable of the Institute; and although Alphonsus was the last who had been admitted, he was chosen by universal consent to undertake the charge. It was about this time that his father happened to pass before a church, and hearing the voice of his son preaching, he felt an irresistible feeling of curiosity to enter and listen; before long he was moved to tears, and touched to the heart at the recollection of his violent and harsh conduct towards him; full of such thoughts he returned home, and scarcely had Alphonsus entered the house, when he ran to his room, and embracing him tenderly, said: "O my son, what do I not owe you; it is you who have to-day taught me to know God! I bless you—I bless you a thousand times for having embraced a state so holy and so agreeable to God."

Notwithstanding his incessant labor to promote the salvation of others, he did not neglect his own; every day he consecrated some hours to meditation, without including the time spent in reading the lives of the saints, which he used to call "the Gospel in practice." Every morning he said mass with so much devotion, that it occupied a considerable time, besides long preparation, and returning thanks afterwards. Not a day passed without his visiting Jesus Christ in the church where the forty hours' adoration was made, and there he might be seen, sometimes for hours, contemplating his divine Redeemer: never forgetting the "quiescite pusillum," the repose which Jesus Christ recommended to his apostles, he from time to time suspended his apostolical labors to "enter into his chamber, shut the door, and commune with his God."

He had, as we have already seen, contracted an intimacy with several priests, whose views and feelings were in accordance with his own. In order to tighten the bonds of charity more and more, one of them, D. de Alteriis, gave a country house, where there was an oratory, in which was placed a beautiful statue of the Virgin. Once a month they retired thither, to spend three or four days in penitential exercises. Their repasts were simple, and a little statue of the Infant Jesus was placed as if presiding at the table, to whom each one made an offering of part of the food which was served him. Their recreation was singing hymns, before they again resumed their holy meditations. They afterwards occupied a house still more retired and solitary, where they employed themselves, with unceasing satisfaction, in the care of their souls, and renewed the fervor of their spirit.

Alphonsus had been one year a priest, when he received from Cardinal Pignatelli faculties for hearing confessions. No sooner was he seated in the confessional, than he saw himself surrounded by persons of every rank and condition; he received all with unexampled charity; he was the first to take his place in the confessional, and the last to leave it. It was his invariable opinion, that the office of confessor is more profitable to souls, and less apt to produce vain glory in the priest, than any other priestly function. For by confession, sinners are immediately reconciled to God, and the grace of Jesus Christ is applied to them superabundantly. Severe towards himself only, he treated the greatest sinners with inexpressible meekness, and, without excusing the sin, was full of compassion for the sinner, when, sincerely repenting, he wished to make his peace with God; and the more a soul was sunk in vice, the more compassionate was his manner, in order to draw it from the fangs of Satan, and lead it into the arms of Jesus Christ. In his old age he said, that he did not remember ever having sent away a single sinner without having succeeded in reconciling him to God, much less of ever having treated one with harshness and rigor. He received all sinners with kindness, instilling into them a great confidence in the blood of Christ shed for them, and pointing out to them the way of withdrawing from their sins. "If the sinner is repulsed," he used to say, "he will never resolve to abandon his sin." "Let us give to penitents," said he, "the penance they will perform willingly; but let us beware of loading them with obligations they would accept with repugnance, and afterwards abandon easily. The penance ought to be such as to inspire horror for the sin, but not for the penance." Thus he frequently enjoined the penance of returning to confess, of frequenting the sacraments, of hearing mass daily, of meditating on the passion of Christ, or on some eternal truth. For this purpose he composed a small collection of meditations, and gave them often to his penitents. He also imposed, as penances of obligation, to visit daily the Blessed Sacrament, or some image of the Virgin Mary, to recite the Rosary in her honor, and he persuaded the heads of houses to recite it regularly with their family. As to fasting, disciplines, and penances of this kind, he might counsel them occasionally, but never commanded them. "If the penitent be contrite," he said, "he will do these things of himself, otherwise he will neglect the penance, and relapse into sin, if it be made obligatory." Thus he daily gained a multitude of sinners, who had long lived in disorder and vice.

He often went to preach in the market-places and at the Lavinaro, where the dregs of the people of Naples are to be found. He delighted in seeing himself surrounded by the lowest, the lazaroni, and such like; he enlightened them, instructed them, and disposed them to receive grace through the sacraments. Many of those who had been great sinners, conceived under his direction such a lively horror of sin, that they became instant in prayer, and burned with an ardent love for Jesus Christ. Among the almost innumerable conversions of which he was the instrument, two, in particular, deserve to be mentioned.

The first is that of Peter Barbarese. He was a poor school-master, who taught reading and writing, but his heart being full of evil thoughts, instead of enlightening his scholars, he corrupted their will. He attended a sermon of Alphonsus, which moved him to contrition; entering into himself, and full of repentance, he threw himself at his feet, forsook sin, and embraced a life of penitence. Regenerated by grace, all his endeavors were now directed to inspire his pupils with the greatest horror of sin. He assembled them every morning at an early hour, and conducted them to church to hear mass, after which he made them meditate on some eternal truth, suggested to them holy resolutions, and finished by reciting the acts of faith, hope and charity. Again in the evening he took them to visit the Blessed Sacrament and the Blessed Virgin. He wished also that they should go weekly to confession, and prepared the elder ones for making their first communion. He was careful in instructing them to make acts of faith previously, and thanksgiving afterward, and began a practice still in use in Naples, of the more advanced instructing, and attending to, the others on such occasions.

The other was that of Lucas Nardone: this man had led an irregular life as a soldier, had often deserted, and at length was about to be condemned to die, when some one obtained his pardon. He was, however, chased from the army with infamy, and lived covered with shame, and loaded with sin. He one day heard Alphonsus preach, and touched by grace, sought an audience. He was received with open arms, encouraged, consoled, and led to the right path, and soon became, as it were, a furnace of divine love, gaining many souls to Christ by dragging them from the toils of Satan.

The following is an instance of the unction Alphonsus' simplest words had, powerfully to move sinners to repentance. A gentleman had detailed to him in confession the greatest crimes with the utmost indifference. When he had finished, Alphonsus asked him if he had nothing more to say. "Nothing, that is all," he coldly replied. "What," answered Alphonsus, "that is all! now do you not see that the only thing wanting to complete your career, is to put on the turban and become a Turk? what more could you have done than the crimes which you have just confessed? Tell me now, my child, what evil has Jesus Christ done to you?" These words, pronounced with the force of ardent zeal, went directly to the heart. "Have I, then," said he to himself, "committed such sins, that I cannot commit greater?" and penetrated with the deepest contrition, he bewailed his past disorders, placed himself in the hands of Alphonsus, and led ever afterwards a most exemplary and devout life.

The means Alphonsus employed to lead his penitents to perfection, may be reduced to two, meditation or prayer, and mortification. He affirmed there could be no true prayer without mortification, and to practice mortification, the spirit of prayer was indispensable. He prescribed prayer, saying, "He who prays will certainly be saved, and he who neglects prayer will as certainly be damned." But above all remedies, he prescribed frequent communion, and daily visits to the Blessed Sacrament, particularly in the church where it was exposed for the forty hours' adoration. He exacted besides, a filial confidence in the Divine Mother Mary, he wished that all should daily recite the Rosary in her honor, visit some church where her image was placed, and have a picture of her at the head of their bed. He required of all his penitents to communicate at each of her feasts, and was careful to propose some devotional practice for each of her Novenas. He recommended to others to fast, as he practised it himself, every Saturday in her honor, and on the eves of all her feasts.

Although he preferred to devote himself to the service of the poor, and of the lower class of the people, he did not refuse to direct those of higher rank, considering the great influence they possess over others, for evil or for good. Around his confessional might be seen persons of all conditions, and the highest did not disdain to await their turn with the lowest, submitting willingly to any inconvenience, rather than not have him for their director.

CHAPTER VII.

Alphonsus establishes public Meetings for the advancement of his penitents, and the instruction of poor people in general.

CROWDS coming thus from every quarter to obtain the benefit of his direction, and as he had no time to give many fervent souls the instructions he judged necessary, to advance them in the way of perfection, he thought of assembling them for instruction, in some solitary place, during the summer evenings, and first chose a spot near the convent of the bare-footed Carmelites, afterwards, beyond the convent of St. Angelo, and, at last, fixed on a site before the church of the Star, which belongs to the Minims. The assembly consisted not of the noble, but of the poor, who came, after their day's work, from different quarters of the city, some a considerable distance. Other priests also took part in the good work. In this assembly, composed of persons low in the eyes of the world, but great in the sight of God, Alphonsus daily preached the truths of religion, showing them the horrible nature of vice, and the sublime beauty of Christian virtue. The other priests spoke alternately to the people, pointing out to them the different degrees of the love of God and our neighbor, showing them the necessity of mortifying the flesh and of self-denial, if they would advance in perfection, and the misery produced by unrepressed passion. At other times they would talk of imitating Christ crucified, and propose for their example the life of some Saint, thus exciting them to virtue. There were some individuals, residing in the neighborhood, to whom these meetings seemed not a little strange, and because they were new, they took it for granted they must be evil. In the hope of confirming their suspicions, they concealed themselves behind their windows, to hear what was going on. Now, some of these poor people were so anxious to do penance, that they fasted rigorously, and one evening a poor artisan was pointed out to Alphonsus, who ate nothing but raw vegetables and roots, though obliged to work hard to support his family. He began to reprove him for this excess, when D. Joseph Porpora took up the word and said: "God wills that we should eat in order to live;" and added, laughing, "if any one gives you four cutlets, you will do well to take advantage of it." The multitude were much amused at this, and began to laugh, each one passing the joke to his neighbor. The listeners, hearing the words "cutlets, eating," thought the people were an assemblage of libertines; and, going still further, came to the conclusion that they must be a club of Molinists, and a band of heretics. They reported the matter to Cardinal Pignatelli. As the accusation referred to nocturnal assemblies, and the circumstances seemed equivocal, his Eminence supposed they must be evil-disposed persons, and he was confirmed in this opinion, in consequence of several small bands of Lutheran soldiers having formed themselves in different parts of the town, some of whom had already been seized. Information was conveyed to the Governor, who ordered a captain of the guard to disguise himself, and go to one of the meetings. They were then in the middle of the Novena of the Nativity of our Lady, and Alphonsus, in proposing some pious practices in honor of the infant Mary, made use of certain expressions, which seemed mysterious and suspicious to the captain. In consequence of his report, the Governor and the Cardinal were persuaded it could be nothing good, and ordered both priests and laymen to be arrested. Next morning, Alphonsus, happening to be at the palace of the Cardinal, heard of the affair and the proposed arrest, and not doubting it was his own meeting, he hastened to warn his penitents not to assemble at the usual place. It was impossible, however, to warn every one, and those who lived at a distance, came as usual, among whom were the two formerly mentioned, Peter Barbarese and Lucas Nardone. The poor people had scarcely arrived, when they were surrounded by archers and sergeants, and carried off to the guard-house; from whence the two prisoners, escorted each by an archer and a sergeant, were conducted before the Procurator of the court. The good penitents took the matter calmly: "Comrade," said Nardone to the other, "this piece of politeness is perhaps not much to your taste." "On the contrary," replied Barbarese, "I am well satisfied; Jesus Christ was bound with ropes, and we are treated much more civilly, only a simple cord at the arm." The Procurator having ordered them to declare what they did at the place of the Star, they replied, that they were poor ignorant people, who came to receive instruction from D. Alphonsus de Liguori and other priests. When the Procurator heard the name of Liguori, he exclaimed: "God forgive you; you have alarmed the two courts, the ecclesiastical and the civil!" They were then conducted to the house of the Governor, where the mention of the name of Liguori was at once sufficient to establish their innocence. While the Governor questioned them about the pious practices which they were taught, they heard the sound of bells announcing that the holy Viaticum was being carried through the street; at once the two prisoners turned their backs on the Governor, and ran to prostrate themselves at the balcony, crying out: "It is our Lord, it is our Lord!" The Governor asked no more questions, but dismissed them with tears of tenderness and consolation.

Alphonsus, when he heard what had happened, went next day to the Cardinal, acknowledging himself as the author of the mischief, and alone deserving of punishment. His Eminence soon quieted him by expressing his satisfaction at the good he had done, but notwithstanding advised him to discontinue these meetings. "The times," he said, "are too critical: we must be careful that wolves may not cover themselves with sheep's clothing, to do mischief under the shadow of your name."

Alphonsus did great good in Naples by these conferences, and many of those who had attended them, ever after led the lives of saints. Some entered into religion, while others remained in the world, to embalm it by the odor of their virtue. The two most remarkable were Anthony Pennino, who sold eggs through the town, and found means, while pursuing his avocation, to draw many souls from perdition. After his death he appeared to several persons and converted them. The other, Leonard Cristano, went through the streets with his ass, and sold chesnuts; both of them performed miracles during their life and after their death.

The triumph of the devil seemed complete when these meetings were put down, but here, as elsewhere, he found himself defeated. Convinced by experience how useful they had been, Alphonsus suggested to Peter Barbarese and a few others, that they should give instruction to the lazaroni and other people of the same class, in suitable places removed from public observation. Peter, thus encouraged, began to instruct the little porters or errand boys, in the shop of a barber. A priest who saw the good he was doing, advised him to meet his little flock in a neighboring chapel; he did so, and every evening about sixty young people attended, without counting those of a more advanced age. Lucas Nardone, and several others, pursued the same course, so that in different quarters of the town, the penitents of Alphonsus were busy in drawing souls from destruction, and winning them to Jesus Christ. He, on his part, was careful to visit and superintend these meetings, animating them to pursue the great work of their salvation, and leading them to the love of the cross.

One evening, Canon Romano was taking a walk in the neighborhood where Peter Barbarese taught the most numerous of these assemblages, when a friend met him, and said: "Come with me, I wish to give you an agreeable surprise;" and led him to where Peter was instructing his hearers. Delighted with what he had seen, Romano could not resist detailing the whole to Cardinal Pignatelli, who was so pleased at the good that was done, that he suggested to the Canon, that he should instruct the people himself. Peter willingly resigned his place, and immediately commenced assembling in another house more lazaroni and porters. The meetings began to multiply, and at length, in almost every quarter of Naples, the fervent penitents of Alphonsus might be found, instructing and catechising the ignorant. In after times, he never came to Naples without visiting these favorite meetings, exhorting them to perseverance in the service of God, and in gaining conquests to Christ. Thus Alphonsus was consoled by the thought, that the overthrow of one good undertaking had been the very means of producing another much more extensive, and still more agreeable to God. The work continued to increase, and before long, these meetings, protected by the Cardinal himself, ceased to be held in shops and private houses, and were transferred to public oratories and churches. In 1834, they amounted to a hundred, numbering each about three hundred persons, and the good they produced among the working classes was incalculable. The most zealous priests are attached to them, and the Archbishops of Naples find them invaluable. Barbarese lived to an advanced age, and so did Nardone, both persevering to the end in their pious labor. After the death of Barbarese, his body retained such an appearance of life, that for some time they hesitated to bury him. He left behind him a great reputation for sanctity, as did also his fellow-laborer, Nardone. Alphonsus occupied himself also in establishing schools for women; a well educated lady was placed at the head of them, to direct the others, and he himself visited them from time to time; but this good work did not last long.

CHAPTER VIII.

Alphonsus retires into the Chinese College, and gives missions in the country.

IT was against his will that Alphonsus continued to live in the house of his father; he longed for a solitary cell, where, retired from the world, he could enjoy that calm and delicious peace, to be found only in solitude. God soon furnished him with an occasion. A celebrated missionary, D. Matthew Ripa, had lately returned from China; he had brought with him a Chinese Doctor, and four young men full of zeal, with the intention of founding at Naples a college for the Chinese. God blessed the enterprise, and on the 14th of April, 1729, they opened the house of the Chinese Mission, with the consent and authority of Pope Benedict XIII. Alphonsus, considering the excellence of this institution, the rare merits of its founder, and the great fervor which reigned there, with the poverty and privation which they endured for love of God, formed the resolution of joining F. Ripa, and sharing, as a pensioner of the house, in the fervor which animated this new society. He entered the college about the middle of June, 1729. A resolution so unforeseen vexed his father extremely, who deeply regretted the loss of the society of one whom he now considered less as a son, than as an angel sent him by God. Painful as the separation was, he had not, however, the courage to oppose so laudable a design.

No sooner did Alphonsus find himself in the college, delivered from the surveillance of his parents, than he gave himself up to the practice of mortification with more freedom and ardor than ever. He was clothed in sackcloth, and wore chains of iron; several times a day, he took the discipline until the blood flowed. The wretched food which he ate was not sufficient for his love of mortification, but he added to it bitter ingredients, such as myrrh, aloes, and wormwood. He ate but little, or not at all, of the fruits of which the others partook, and fasted every Saturday on bread and water, and generally ate in a kneeling position, or sitting on the floor. In his chamber he would not allow himself a chair, but stood while he studied, holding his book in his hand, and keeping little stones in his shoes. Mgr. Coppola, Bishop of Cassano, said, that his penances surpassed even those of St. Peter of Alcantara. Besides, he never exempted himself from the privations imposed upon all the members of the community, and indeed the new-born Congregation wanted not for opportunities to practise poverty. Although their rule limited them to the use of vegetables and a little boiled meat, they frequently had no meat at all, and often the scraps which appeared on their table were stale; and when these failed, they had ordinarily but a salad of mushrooms. Sometimes they could only afford to buy bones, from which they strove to extract a miserable soup. During Lent they scarcely ever had fish, a pilchard with their vegetables was a feast to them, and when they did buy fish, it was always the cheapest that could be found. They sowed beets in a little plot of ground attached to the house, and for months they lived on these roots, varied occasionally with a few pears. Their evening repast usually consisted of the remnants of dinner, boiled with a few coarse biscuits; their bread in general was of the coarsest kind. And so far from ever showing the slightest repugnance to all this, Alphonsus on the contrary rejoiced in it, and encouraged the others to suffer with pleasure, that they might become more holy and agreeable to God.

In the meanwhile he continued to draw new strength from prayer, and the examples of the saints. Besides the meditation of the community, he daily spent an hour and a half, at least, before the Blessed Sacrament in the church where the forty hours' adoration was held. He spent whole nights in watching, sometimes in his room, sometimes in the church, before the Blessed Sacrament. And the little rest he granted to nature was given grudgingly, and not without many contrivances to render it as little agreeable as possible; he often lay on the bare ground, or on a hard board. It might naturally be supposed, that amidst these bodily austerities undertaken and endured from pure love of God, his mind would be enjoying that foretaste of heaven which nothing worldly can give; but it was not thus with our Saint; God permitted him to feel the nature of our Saviour's anguish, when he exclaimed, "My God! my God! why hast thou forsaken me?" His heart enjoyed no consolation. He was deprived of all those favors which render every trial light and easy. He believed he had lost all devotion for mass, his prayer was arid; he sought God, and found him not. "I go to Jesus," he said, "and He repulses me. I have recourse to the Blessed Virgin, and she listens not to me." All he did at this time was done by the mere light of faith, which made him resolute in seeking to please God in all things, without being impelled either by the hope of heaven or the fear of hell. During the time he remained in this college, he continued to give the greatest proofs of his zeal. Crowds came to the church to confess to him; every Friday he discoursed on the glories of Mary, and recited with the people the chaplet of her sorrows. He celebrated several Novenas in the course of the year, during which he preached in honor of the Blessed Virgin, or the holy family, the titular patrons of the college. Every year he gave retreats, to the great benefit of the crowds who thronged the church during those holy exercises. He scarcely took time to eat; and often before his meal was over, numbers were waiting for being heard in confession. In the evenings, after the exercises of the forty hours' adoration, he used to enter the church with a train of penitents, whose confessions he heard until late. F. Ripa, in his memoirs of the Congregation, writes thus of Alphonsus: "We have for pensioner the noble D. Alphonsus de Liguori, a priest eminent not for his birth only, but for his excellent conduct and general qualifications as a missionary. Although not aggregated to the mission, he has nevertheless the desire, and holds himself ready, to go to China, as he has more than once declared to his director. Assured of his zeal and his talents, I gave him the entire care of the church, and in all that regards the pulpit and the confessional, he has acquitted himself to the great advantage of souls."

It would be impossible to enumerate the number of obstinate sinners, old in crime, whom he reclaimed, kindling within their obdurate hearts a tender love towards their Saviour. He possessed a peculiar gift, in the confessional, of inspiring his penitents with compunction, and scarcely had they knelt at his feet, when they felt their hearts touched with sorrow for their sins. He converted a celebrated courtesan, who was afterwards eminent for her sanctity, and many who had lived ordinary good lives, became, under his direction, models of perfection. He also induced a number who were occupied in worldly pursuits, to renounce the world and consecrate themselves to God. The first sermon he preached, when once giving a retreat, inspired fifteen young persons with the resolution of giving themselves to the service of God.

We will relate more fully one instance only of a very remarkable conversion of this kind. A young lady, named Mary, was a source of great anxiety to her pious mother, as her heart and mind were filled with the world, to the exclusion of every thing serious. She besought Alphonsus to pray for the conversion of her daughter; he did so, and the young girl seemed to be reformed; but before long she became more giddy and thoughtless than ever. Again the poor mother had recourse to Alphonsus, who, at her earnest entreaty, spoke seriously to the girl, strongly representing to her the danger of her position; and she, touched to the quick, retired to a corner of the church, and began bitterly to bewail her sins. Alphonsus, seeing this, before he quitted the confessional, called her back: "Mary," said he, "will you sincerely give yourself to God?" "Yes," she instantly replied. "But without reserve, and with your whole heart?" he continued. "Without the slightest reserve, with my whole heart," said the girl with much energy. "Then," said he, "go instantly, cut off your hair, and become a Carmelite." She obeyed, took the religious habit, persevered, and, after her death, was invoked by many, and worked several miracles.

At this period of his life, his labors were so incessant and multifarious, that we can scarcely conceive the possibility of one individual accomplishing the half he performed. Preaching in various churches in Naples, giving retreats, hearing confessions, and going on missions to the neighboring towns,—he yet found time for all, without encroaching either on his studies or devotions. In the year 1729, a frightful epidemic ravaged the city of Naples; he profited by this occasion to sacrifice himself more and more; and amongst the brothers of the Congregation of Apostolical Missions, he was ever the first in anointing the sick. Besides, he opened a mission in the large church of the Holy Spirit, and took advantage of the time, to withdraw souls from the power of Satan. In consequence of his great fatigues, he was seized the following year with a pulmonary complaint, which brought him to the gates of death, but again his beloved Mother performed a miracle in his favor. About this period, his life was also exposed to a danger of a different kind. He was sitting with the other fathers during recreation, when a tremendous thunder-storm came on, and a bolt fell in the midst of them. F. Ripa was wounded in the throat, while Alphonsus and others fell down senseless; they soon recovered, however, to thank God for their escape, and devote themselves with renewed zeal to his service. They were saved by an evident interposition of Providence.

In the spring of the year 1731, the Puglia and the neighboring provinces suffered exceedingly from an earthquake

The bishops, that the opportunity might not be lost for calling the people to repentance, invited the brothers of the Propaganda. On this occasion, Alphonsus, as usual, produced a miraculous effect, and many were reclaimed and converted. The town of Foggia had been almost reduced to a mass of ruins; but the God who smote them, would also comfort them, by giving them a miraculous proof of his love. They venerated in this town a very old and miraculous picture of the Virgin, the colors of which being almost obliterated by age, it was glazed, and covered with a curtain. The people, terrified by new repeated shocks of the earthquake, came in crowds to place themselves under the protection of the mother of mercy. On the morning of the 22d of March, while the multitude were kneeling before this picture, the Blessed Virgin showed herself to them under the appearance of a young woman, and this miraculous manifestation was repeated for several days, and seen by crowds, who came to venerate the picture. This apparition made a great noise throughout the kingdom, and when their mission was finished, Alphonsus and his companions went to visit the miraculous picture. The bishop, Mgr. Faccola, insisted he should give a Novena in honor of the Blessed Virgin; at first he refused, having no permission from his superiors to prolong his stay, but at length he yielded to the circumstances of the time and the urgent entreaties from all sides. The concourse of people was such that the greater part could not enter the church; they therefore erected a pulpit at the door, at the side of which was exposed the miraculous picture. The effects were extraordinary, and beyond description; great as was the number of priests, they were not sufficient to hear the confessions of crowds, who, touched to the quick by the discourses of Alphonsus, turned from their wickedness and wished to be reconciled with God.

There happened to him, during this Novena, a very remarkable event. His delight was to remain near the miraculous image, from which he could hardly turn himself away. One day, when the people had withdrawn, and the image was replaced in the church, he got up on the altar to examine it more nearly; but scarcely had he placed himself in front of it, when he fell into an ecstasy, which lasted nearly an hour. The Virgin would fully satisfy his devotion, crowning his happiness by showing to him her face radiant with celestial beauty. When the vision disappeared, he descended from the altar, inebriated with joy, intoning the "Ave Maris Stella," in which he was joined by about thirty persons who had witnessed the occurrence. He afterwards attested having seen the Virgin Mother under the appearance of a young girl of thirteen or fourteen years of age, wearing a white veil, and moving from side to side. The next morning, he described his vision to a painter, and the picture drawn at the time is still preserved at Ciorani. On returning to Naples in the middle of the month of May, the Canon D. Julius Torni, whether he really blamed him for giving a Novena at Foggia, or whether he would only try his humility, reprimanded him strongly in presence of all the Congregation. Alphonsus did not attempt to excuse himself, he did not speak; but, on the contrary, rejoiced to see himself mortified before such a respectable assembly.

CHAPTER IX.

Alphonsus is called to found a Congregation of Missionary Priests.

ALPHONSUS being exhausted and worn out by his labors in the provinces, his friends began to have serious apprehensions for his health, and accordingly it was determined he should retire to the country, until he should recover his strength. The place fixed upon, was a hermitage in the neighborhood of Amalfi, situated on a hill near the sea. He was accompanied by Joseph Jorio, John Mazzini, Pansa, and two others. When they had arrived at Amalfi and went to pay their respects to the Archbishop, they met the Vicar-General, who strongly urged them to change their plan, and go to a hermitage near Scala, where they would be at the same time useful to the poor goatherds of the neighborhood, who were destitute of spiritual aid. The proposal was willingly agreed to, and they established themselves at St. Mary of the Mount—this was the name of the hermitage. They had obtained permission to keep the Blessed Sacrament in the hermitage, and while Alphonsus was recovering strength of body, he gained new strength to his soul in the presence of his beloved Saviour.

They began to catechise the poor shepherds and goatherds, with the other inhabitants of the country around, and heard their confessions; and this sojourn in the country became an uninterrupted mission, which produced abundant fruits. It was now that Alphonsus became acquainted with the extreme destitution of the people scattered over the country, who often lived without the knowledge necessary for salvation; many, being without the sacraments and the word of life, had to be instructed in the first rudiments of faith, before they could make their confession. He was soon invited by the inhabitants of Scala, and the bishop, to preach in that town. He accepted the invitation, and preached one sermon, which produced all the effect of a regular mission. It was on the Sunday following the Octave of the Blessed Sacrament; he urged upon them such strong motives for loving Jesus in His Sacrament, and for detesting sin, that the whole congregation were dissolved in tears, and their sobs and groans resounded in the neighborhood. The superior of the nuns of St. Saviour besought him also to preach in their church, which he did with his usual success, and the bishop was so delighted, that he engaged him for a Novena, to be celebrated in the Cathedral for the feast of the Holy Redeemer, in the month of September.

He continued to labor among the good shepherds of St. Mary of the Mount, until September, when he returned to Scala, accompanied by John Mazzini. During the Novena he gave a retreat to the nuns of St. Saviour. This was the moment God had chosen, to make known his will to him. There was in the Convent a nun of great sanctity, possessed of supernatural gifts. Alphonsus had often besought God, even with tears, to choose some one to labor with efficacy among the abandoned people of the country: the nun knew nothing of what was passing in his mind; but on the 13th of October, she saw in a vision a new Congregation of priests, who were employed in the care of thousands living in villages and scattered hamlets, destitute of spiritual aid; she saw Alphonsus at the head of this Congregation, and heard a voice which said: "This is the man I have chosen to be the instrument of my glory in this great work." A few days after, she told him, in the confessional, of the vision she had had, and of the designs God had upon him. Fearing it was but a vain illusion, notwithstanding the remarkable conformity between her vision and his own thoughts, Alphonsus reproved the nun, and treated her as a visionary. She humbled herself before him, but persisted, and the more he repulsed her, the more she assured him that God had chosen him to be the instrument of his mercy towards the inhabitants of the country.

On his return to the house, F. Mazzini, seeing his trouble and agitation, asked the cause. He hesitated to tell him, when Father Mazzini said: "I know you have had a dispute with one of the nuns, for I heard you speaking loud." Yielding to his friend's desire, Alphonsus told him what the nun had said; and far from treating it lightly, Mazzini did all in his power to persuade him of its truth. The sanctity of the nun was undoubted. "Besides," argued his friend, "an institution of the kind is much wanted in this kingdom, and who knows what designs God may have upon you?" "I approve much of such an institution," said Alphonsus, "and I foresee the glorious fruits of it, but what can I do myself? Where are my companions?" "Here am I for one," answered Mazzini, "and I am sure other priests will be found willing to consecrate themselves to a work which must contribute so much to the glory of God!" In the meanwhile, Mgr. Falcoja, Bishop of Castellamare, arrived at Scala; he was a prelate of eminent sanctity, and skilled in the science of spirituality, and the Bishop of Scala was not inferior to him. The presence of these two saintly men raised Mazzini's hopes, and he urged Alphonsus to consult with them. He accordingly told them all, and after several days spent in narrowly examining the subject, they both agreed that the inspiration came from God; the vision of the nun strengthened their confidence, she being a person peculiarly favored by God, whose sincerity and love of truth were undoubted. This nun, sister Mary Celeste Castarosa, died the 14th of September, 1745, at the Convent of St. Saviour, at Foggia; her body is still entire and uncorrupted. The nuns open the coffin and clothe the body anew, every time any of the sisterhood dies.

Alphonsus returned to Naples, and immediately opened his whole heart to his own spiritual director, F. Pagano. This sage director, after a careful consideration of some days, hesitated not to declare his opinion, that such an undertaking could not fail to promote the glory of God and the salvation of souls; but doubting his own judgment, he advised Alphonsus to consult with more enlightened persons. He accordingly spoke with F. Vincent Cutica, superior of the Mission of St. Vincent of Paul, and F. Manulius, a Jesuit, both of whom were much venerated in Naples. Their opinions coincided with that of F. Pagano, viz. that it was the will of God, and they urged him to respond to the call of Heaven. Still unconvinced, he consulted others, eminent for their sanctity and wisdom, and finding all of the same mind, he could no longer doubt, and taking courage, he gave himself unreservedly to God. But a work which was intended by God to promote the salvation of souls, not in Italy only, but in all other kingdoms of Europe, and in America, could not fail to stir up all the powers of hell, to accomplish, if possible, its overthrow, yea, even to prevent its being begun.

As soon as Alphonsus' determination was known, all Naples seemed to be in arms against him. Some said that he was mad, and that his brain must be affected; others treated him as a fanatic and a visionary; some affirmed it was pure pride, and that he had been spoiled by too much praise. It was in the College of the Chinese he found his greatest adversaries; his companions there loaded him with blame and ridicule. F. Ripa, who was then at Rome, did, on his return, all in his power to convince him that his plans were impossible, and useless, even if they should succeed. Seeing, however, that all his endeavors to dissuade him were in vain, he chose to believe with the others that his head was affected, and that he was the victim of some delusion, and reproached him both privately and publicly with what he called his extravagance. The Fathers of the Propaganda also ranged themselves against him. Having heard of the vision of the nun, they imagined it was the sole basis of his enterprise, and were shocked at his allowing himself to be led away by what they called the reveries of a young nun. But what afflicted Alphonsus most of all, was, that these opinions were taken up by his uncle Matthew Gizzio, Rector of the Seminary, and by the Superior of the Propaganda, Julius Torni. They assailed him on every side, while he only replied that he would do nothing disapproved of by his director. "It is not God who directs you," said his uncle, "but you blindly follow the reveries of a nun, and do you not see that you are the victim of an illusion?" "I do not regulate my conduct by visions," he meekly replied; "I regulate it by the Gospel." On another occasion his uncle jeeringly asked him if he ever expected to realize his schemes. "He who trusts in God," replied he, "can do all, and should hope all." At last his uncle went so far, that, in the presence of some other canons, he treated him as a fool whose brain was turned by self-conceit. One day as Alphonsus entered the sacristy of the cathedral, several persons of consequence began to abuse him before others in authority, who happened to be present. "Keep to your word now," said they, "and make haste to show the Church those new institutions and foundations which you have promised her." Alphonsus said nothing, but bowing his head, humbled himself interiorly.

After some time, his uncle insisted that he should take advice from F. Louis Fiorillo, a learned and pious Dominican, by whom he himself was guided. At first he declined, but on his afterwards repeating to F. Pagano what had passed, he urged him to follow his uncle's advice, saying, that he would consider F. Fiorillo's decision as the voice of God. Alphonsus had never seen F. Fiorillo, but soon after, he met him one day at his uncle's; the moment F. Fiorillo saw him, he exclaimed, as it were, by inspiration: "God is not yet satisfied with you; He wishes you to be altogether His, and expects great things from you." Alphonsus took him aside, and told him of his desire to consult him, and a time and place of meeting was agreed upon.

He now began to perform the most severe penances, praying continually that the Father of lights would enlighten His servant F. Fiorillo, on whose decision the affair seemed to depend. He recommended himself to the prayers of many holy persons, but above all to the nun at the monastery of Scala. All the convent joined with her; they prayed, they fasted, they gave themselves the discipline for half an hour each day; all united to beseech God to enlighten his directors. A singular fact now occurred: several of the nuns, yielding to the opinion of some ill-disposed persons, believed that God would not establish the Congregation. One day, while they were disputing about it with the nun who had had the revelation, she cried out in an ecstatic transport, "God wills this work, and you will see it accomplished!" "Yes," replied a nun more incredulous than the others, "I will believe it when Sister Mary Magdalene is cured." This sister had been deranged for several years, but from that moment she perfectly recovered her senses.

When Alphonsus had made known all to F. Fiorillo, the man of God replied: "In a similar conjuncture, St. Lewis Bertrand asked six months from St. Theresa to reflect, before giving an answer; I would ask the same from you." "Not six months only," said Alphonsus, "take a whole year." Some days after, he met him again, when the venerable Father embraced him with joy, saying, "Go, take courage, this work is divine; throw yourself into the arms of God, as a stone which falls from the mountain in the valley. You will encounter contradictions, doubtless, but place your confidence in God, He will help you." At this time, however, F. Fiorillo had many good works on hand, and fearing to scandalize the clergy, who might overturn them, he begged Alphonsus to conceal his approbation, and not to visit him again. Satisfied now that he was acting according to the will of God, he feared no farther contradiction, and began in earnest to look about for companions.

In the meanwhile the Missionaries of the Propaganda blamed him every where, and would not bear to hear him spoken of as one of them. The Canons Torni and Gizzio were extremely annoyed by the slur which Alphonsus' project seemed to cast upon the Propaganda. They hoped that F. Fiorillo would never approve of it, and that at last F. Pagano himself would oppose it. Meeting Alphonsus one day, and finding him unaltered in his views, they attacked him more violently than ever. Alphonsus meekly replied: "Say what you will, uncle; I assure you I am not acting in consequence of such visions, but am ruled by the word of God, and guided by those on whom I ought to rely." In circumstances such as these, his embarrassment was great; he was bound not to betray F. Fiorillo, who was then absent from Naples; and on the other hand, the astonishment and scandal augmented every day. F. Pagano advised him not to keep the secret any longer; so also did the Bishop of Cassano, and Mgr. Amato, Bishop of Ischia, whom he consulted on the subject. When he came to see the two Canons, hardly had he entered the house, when they attacked him again. "Are you not ashamed of yourself, scandalizing all Naples by your obstinacy, and acting in opposition to F. Fiorillo? How can your conscience permit such a thing?" Then Alphonsus calmly, but firmly, replied: "You are deceived in supposing that I act contrary to the advice of F. Fiorillo; my conduct is the result of the counsels he has given me." He had provided himself with a copy of the letter Fiorillo had written to him on the subject, and as he ceased speaking, he placed it in his uncle's hands. Great was the confusion of both Gizzio and Torni. "But this is not sufficient," said Torni, "I would see the original." Alphonsus gave it to him. "Now," said he, holding it in his hand, "I want no other testimony; this is sufficient for the honor of my Congregation."

After this, Alphonsus expected to have peace, as he could no longer be blamed for acting contrary to the opinion of wise directors; but the enemy of mankind would not yield without a farther struggle. His brothers of the Propaganda refused to be reconciled with him, and threatened to turn him out of their Congregation. But Cardinal Pignatelli, although he had been prejudiced against Alphonsus, no sooner discovered the truth, than he warned the Canon Torni to beware how *he took* any steps against Alphonsus de Liguori. F. Ripa, on the other hand, although now persuaded that he acted in accordance with the advice of F. Fiorillo, ceased not to accuse him of visionary schemes. He believed himself justified in opposing plans which would remove him from Naples, where he was certain to be most useful, and above all, useful to the Chinese College; besides, some of his most distinguished subjects were inclined to follow Alphonsus. He quarrelled with F. Pagano and F. Fiorillo, and wrote a very bitter letter to Mgr. Falcoja, whose reply is too admirable to be omitted here:

. . . . . . "You know," he wrote, "that it does not belong to a spiritual Father to give his penitents any vocation which may happen to please himself; this gift belongs only to that divine Providence, who has many niches in Paradise for the statues He fashions upon earth, and on earth He establishes different studios, and is daily opening new ones, where those rational statues are to be moulded to perfection according to His most holy will, that they may be prepared for their position in everlasting glory. . . . It is not the province of a spiritual Father, to do any thing else than to approve or disapprove. When a soul is faithful to God and His holy words, 'He who heareth you, heareth me,' we may believe that she cannot go astray. You may argue that a spiritual Father can be deceived; but I would reply that God, who is always faithful, will not fail to make known His will to those whom He has appointed to enlighten others; for if it were not so, what assurance could we have in deciding on what was God's will? Now, inasmuch as Alphonsus has followed this rule, he cannot go astray. I see from your letter, that you judge and condemn me, as one who would overthrow your Congregation, and ruin a valuable work which owes all to your labors: but fear not. Is the arm of the Lord shortened? Is He not able to sustain your Congregation and many others at the same time? Let God perform His own work; for a work which comes from Him may aid, but cannot destroy, another equally divine. But this enterprise, you say, will dissipate itself; if you say true, then you lose nothing; but according to my view of the case, this enterprise comes from God, and it cannot perish, if he, who is charged with it, continue faithful; those therefore, who oppose it, set themselves in opposition to the will of God.

"But you say, this new work will take away some of your most valuable subjects. I wish, my dear Father, you would put a little more confidence in God, and less in man. The Congregation of Pious Workers had scarcely been established, when four of their most excellent members left them, and founded four different Congregations. Notwithstanding, the venerable Fathers, Charles Carafa and Anthony de Colellis, were not annoyed by fearing that their Congregation would be ruined; the contrary happened, it increased more and more by the arrival of other men, whom the Father of the family sent to replace those who had left. Be persuaded, that the work of Alphonsus is no suggestion of the devil, but on the contrary, that the devil opposes it as the will of God, as he has done on a thousand other occasions, when he foresaw that an institution would have the effect of destroying his empire in the world."

It seems incredible, yet it is true, this letter produced no effect on F. Ripa, who continued to blame Alphonsus for his inconstancy, and even in his Memoirs of his Congregation, complains bitterly of him and all who had any hand in approving or forwarding his projects.

When the Fathers Fiorillo and Pagano saw that the tempest, instead of abating, rather increased, they began to fear for the success of their own immediate affairs, if they continued to bear the blame of giving counsel to Alphonsus. They therefore strongly urged him to put himself entirely under the direction of Mgr. Falcoja, a man of undoubted wisdom and sanctity, and held in great consideration by all Naples. The feast of the Assumption approaching, Alphonsus resolved to apply for aid to his blessed Mother, and made the Novena of the feast in the church so dear to him, the church of the Redemption of Captives, where her statue was exposed during those nine days. The divine Mother listened to her favorite child, and enlightened him regarding the course he ought to pursue. He placed himself in the hands of the holy prelate, promising to do nothing without his advice, and never was a child more obedient to a parent.

The Canon Torni came also back to the charge, as he could not bear the idea of Alphonsus' services being lost to Naples. Having no hope of directly succeeding in opposing him, he began an indirect attack, in his quality of Superior of the Congregation of the Propaganda. He gave him the charge of several important matters, trusting that, when he saw the good he was doing in Naples, he would give up the idea of going elsewhere. In the beginning of October he commanded him, in the name of the Cardinal, to give a retreat to the clergy of Naples. He obeyed his Superior, notwithstanding his repugnance to appear before those, many of whom had treated him so unjustly, and God poured out His benedictions on his labors more abundantly than ever. The Cardinal himself attended, and was so moved, that he exclaimed, "We may easily see he is a vessel of election, for the Holy Spirit speaks by his mouth." After this retreat, he was sent successively to three other churches to give Missions, when, as before, multitudes from all quarters flocked to hear him, and crowded round the confessionals. But notwithstanding all this abundant harvest, Alphonsus was longing for the moment when the arrangements would be completed for him to commence his new Congregation. Mgr. Falcoja, however, seeing that the storm still continued to rage, wished to put his constancy to farther proof, and delayed to give him his parting benediction; but those days of delay seemed ages to Alphonsus.

Many were the contradictions and annoyances he experienced during the last days he remained, particularly from F. Ripa and his uncle Gizzio. Because they loved him, they thought they had a right, forcibly to withdraw him from an enterprise they considered extravagant. God, in his impenetrable Providence, sometimes permits his servants to fall into similar mistakes; it may be, to keep them humble, and as a means of advancing the sanctity of both parties. In after time, those who had opposed him now, lauded his enterprise, when they saw the blessings of heaven accompanying his work.

In spite of the outcry made against Alphonsus by many influential individuals, there was still a number of zealous priests who declared their willingness to accompany him on his arduous mission. One of his first companions was D. Vincent Mandarini, a noble Calabrian. He was, like Alphonsus, a pensioner in the Chinese College, and an excellent theologian. The second was Don Janvier Sarnelli, son of the Baron of Ciorani, also one of the Chinese College, of great talents, both natural and acquired, besides being a man of eminent virtue. The third was D. Silvester Tosquez, a gentleman of the town of Troja, still a secular, and a great friend of Mandarini; he was an excellent man, and well versed in jurisprudence and theology.

His other companions were men equally estimable and enlightened, seven in number. Mazzini would have joined him at first, had not his director insisted on his delaying, in order to prove his vocation. A gentleman named Vitus Curzius, whose vocation was evidently miraculous, was the first who joined him in quality of lay-brother. He had been secretary to the Baron of Vasto, and was very intimate with Sportelli, one of the companions of Alphonsus, still a secular. Sportelli had not communicated to him his design of quitting the world, when one day Curzius told him a dream he had had the previous night. "I thought," said he, "that I stood at the foot of a high and steep mountain, which many priests were trying to ascend. I wished to imitate them, but at the first step I took, I fell backward. Not willing to give up the attempt, I tried to mount several times, but to my great annoyance, I always slid back, until one of the priests, taking compassion on me, gave me his hand and helped me to ascend." In the course of the day, as they were walking together near the Chinese College, they met Alphonsus, when Curzius, who had never before seen him, turned in astonishment to Sportelli, exclaiming, "There is the priest who gave me his hand last night." Sportelli saw the mystery of the dream, and told him that this was Alphonsus Liguori, who was about to found a new Congregation of missionary priests, and mentioned his own intention to join him. The young man instantly recognized the divine will, and unhesitatingly declared, that he wished to be of the number, as a lay-brother.

CHAPTER VII.

Alphonsus establishes his Congregation at Scala. It undergoes a severe trial.

AFTER having received the benediction of the Fathers Pagano and Fiorillo, Alphonsus, without acquainting either friends or relations, hired a miserable donkey, and departed from Naples on the 8th of November, 1732, directing his steps towards the town of Scala. The day on which he left Naples, he completed two sacrifices; the definitive renunciation of all the splendors of the world, and the entire disruption of the ties of flesh and blood. This last completed the numerous sacrifices he had already made. Since the month of August, he had quitted the Chinese College, and returned to his father's house, for the better arranging of his affairs. D. Joseph, who loved him less as a son than as a spiritual father, was miserable at the thought of losing him, and one day he entered his room, when he had laid down to take a little repose, and throwing himself on the bed beside him, pressed him in his arms and exclaimed: "My son, why will you abandon me? My son, I do not deserve that you should cause me so much misery." Taken by surprise, Alphonsus suffered most intensely, and this scene lasted during three hours, his father holding him in a close embrace, repeating always, "My son, do not abandon me." He afterwards spoke of this trial, as the most terrible he had ever had to endure.

On arriving at Scala, he was joined by only eight of his companions; Sarnelli and Tosquez were obliged, from certain circumstances, to delay. The dwelling prepared by the Bishop, Mgr. Santoro, accorded in every respect with their wishes—it was an hospice belonging to a convent, almost destitute of furniture, small and inconvenient; besides a small oratory, there were only a parlor, and three little rooms containing palliasses and scanty coverings, with a few earthen dishes for the table and the kitchen.

The day after their arrival, they assembled in the Cathedral, and after a long meditation, chanted the mass of the Holy Spirit, thanking God for the establishment of a Congregation so ardently desired, and asking for His benediction upon the work. They gave it the name of "The Holy Saviour," placing it under the protection of the Chief of all Missionaries. They now applied themselves sincerely to prayer and penitence; their hearts overflowing with love to God, they embraced every opportunity of mortifying themselves; they wore sack-cloth, and small chains with sharp points. But it was at the hours of repast, those hours when the world seeks after sensual enjoyments, that these holy men signalized their love of mortification. Some kissed the ground; others knelt, and remained for a length of time with their arms extended in form of a cross, before eating; another made the round of the refectory, kissing the feet of each of his brethren. They ate kneeling, or sitting on the floor, while others, to make the moments of eating still more uncomfortable, hung a heavy stone round their neck. Their poor and scanty food they seasoned with bitter herbs; many would not taste meat, or abstained from fruit. Their food was of such a quality that the poor hesitated to accept what they left. Vitus Curzius was cook, and as he knew nothing of cookery, he spoiled every thing he attempted to prepare.

Such was the life these missionaries led at Scala. As for Alphonsus, he occupied himself with God only, "instant in prayer," reading the Lives of the Saints, or laboring to save souls. His application was constant; and besides Mass with a long thanksgiving, and the general prayers of the community, he spent hours in adoration before the Blessed Sacrament. He carried his austerities to such an excess, that the utmost the others could do, seemed as it were nothing. He sometimes seasoned his food with such herbs, that those who were near him could hardly endure the smell; and not content with wearing sack-cloth, chains, and crosses armed with sharp points, he gave himself the discipline twice a day. The care he bestowed on his own perfection and that of his companions, did not hinder him from attending to the people of Scala. He introduced the custom of giving a meditation in the Cathedral, every morning, and making visits to the Blessed Sacrament and the Virgin Mary, every evening. Every Thursday, he gave a sermon with exposition of the Blessed Sacrament, and every Saturday, he preached on the glories of Mary. On Sundays and feast days, he instructed the people on their individual duties, and catechized them. He established two Confraternities, one for gentlemen and another for artisans, and two others for the young people of both sexes; and every Sunday, each of these Confraternities received a particular instruction. Scala was in a short time thoroughly reformed, to the great satisfaction of Mgr. Santoro. Seeing himself so well seconded by the zeal of his companions, Alphonsus gave missions to the different towns and villages round about, so that the renown of the new Congregation began to spread every where, and bishops were constantly beseeching their assistance for their flocks, while many even offered them establishments in their dioceses.

The Fathers of the Propaganda, instead of becoming reconciled to the step taken by Alphonsus, showed themselves more and more embittered against him, continuing to load him with contempt and ridicule. Their conduct deeply wounded Alphonsus, and he was grieved to see pious and zealous servants of God partaking in all the prejudices of the world, and rather exciting than preventing them. Persuaded that honor and purity, with rectitude of judgment, are the true riches of a minister of God, and seeing his ancient brethren striving to despoil him of them, he complained in a letter to the Canon Torni, who sent him a reply full of the most friendly assurances.

But the peace he had found in the friendly behaviour of Torni, was soon attacked, by the renewed violence of the other members. They clamored against Torni, and insisted, that he should expel Alphonsus, and deprive him of the chaplainship. He was forced to yield, and on the 20th of February, 1732, to the great joy of all, they affixed to the door this announcement: "According to the order of our Superior, on the 23d instant there will be a general investigation on the following questions: Whether the brother D. Alphonsus de Liguori should be expelled from the Congregation? And whether he ought to be deprived of his chaplainship?" Torni had yielded, only to prevent the vexatious proceedings going farther, and secretly informed the Cardinal of what was about to be done, expressing his opinion of its injustice. The Cardinal was exceedingly vexed, but he would not hinder the convocation. "Let them deliberate," he said, "but fear nothing; I will provide for the result, and settle every thing in the most expedient way." The Congregation assembled on the appointed day, animated with incredible rancor. In order to prevent any interference in his favor, they proceeded secretly with the scrutiny, and his expulsion was unanimously decided upon. But they could not register this decree, the Cardinal having forbidden any steps to be taken against Alphonsus, without his knowledge. The Superior and some of the principal members went to the Cardinal, to tell him what had been done. His Eminence was much displeased. "Why," said he, "do you proceed to such extremities? either God will bless the enterprise of Alphonsus, and it will prove a glorious thing for you, or He will overthrow it, and then all that could be said would be, that it was a good work, though it had proved unsuccessful. In any case, I do not see how you can find dishonor in it." He concluded by saying, "I am Superior of this Congregation, and I desire that Alphonsus de Liguori be reinstated, and that he continue to enjoy his chaplainship; and I forbid any steps being taken against him, unknown to me." This firm conduct arrested the flame, but did not extinguish it. The deputies retired, silenced and disconcerted, but still determined never to recognise him as a member of their Congregration.

The storm was thus subsiding in Naples, and Alphonsus was living in Scala, in profound peace, when God wished to try his servant still more severely, by permitting discord to arise in the bosom of the new-born Congregation itself. Alphonsus wished that the new Congregation should be occupied only in laboring to promote the sanctification of clergy and laity, giving them spiritual exercises in convents, and procuring also the salvation of destitute souls, particularly in the country and small hamlets, by means of missions. Mandarini proposed that, besides the missions, they should occupy themselves in teaching; but Alphonsus opposed this, because the Jesuits and other religious orders supplied this want. He added, that the spirit of the Institute finding itself divided between two objects so different as teaching and giving missions, both would be fulfilled in an imperfect manner, since there would be too few laborers to undertake both branches. The others had each his individual opinion, and D. Tosquez, going still farther, insisted, that, as the end of the institution was to imitate Jesus Christ, it was necessary to be dressed in a dark red cassock and a mantle of celestial blue, as these were the colors our Saviour is said to have worn. Some disliked the recitation of the office in common; others objected to sleep on straw, as also to other austerities to which they would not submit. They disliked practising poverty in all its rigor, and the perfection which community life exacted, yet it was to community life that Alphonsus principally held. Tosquez went into a contrary excess, and would embrace the reform of the most austere mendicant order, insisting that each should sell every thing he possessed, and lay the price of it at the feet of his Superior.

Alphonsus approved of establishing a choir, though without chant, as being a good means of reciting the office well. He insisted on the vow of poverty, because without it the spirit of Christ would be wanting, and it would be impossible to observe the common life, which is the mother of poverty. "If," said he, "the words *mine* and *thine* are found among the brethren, great inconvenience will result; they will go on the mission not for God, not to gain souls to Christ, but for emolument and for themselves;" all these opposing sentiments could not fail to disturb his serenity; he spoke, he supplicated, in vain; they shut their ears to all he said. Fearing a total shipwreck, he had recourse to prayer, while at the same time he neglected no human means. He consulted Mgr. Falcoja, F. Pagano, and the Canon Torni, who all looked upon it as a stratagem of the devil. They decidedly opposed Mandarini's plan of teaching, notwithstanding which, all the others joined him in sustaining this point. These discussions lasted long. Mandarini persisted in his scheme for teaching, and thought Alphonsus ought to yield, because the others were of his opinion. He remained firm, however, and at length all left him but Sportelli, and founded a house at Tramonti; where they opened schools for youth, and formed a separate Congregation called of the Most Holy Sacrament.

This separation is supposed to have taken place about the month of March of the year 1733, four months after they had met at Scala. Although Alphonsus thus saw himself abandoned and almost alone, he placed his confidence in God only, and the result proved the wisdom of acting thus. Though he had endured the blow caused by these divisions with all the strength of a soul which rests on God, he did not the less feel a bitter sorrow. God sustained him on the one hand, but on the other, the devil assailed him with suggestions full of despair. He stood balancing between a confidence in God, which never deserted him, and a diffidence in himself, which bowed him to the earth. In the midst of his affliction, he thought of Mgr. Falcoja. He sought him at Castellamare, certain of finding strength and consolation, and trusting with his assistance to weather the storm; but God would not give him this comfort: he found the bishop disgusted with the whole affair, and was received with marked coldness. Before he had time to explain the object of his visit, the bishop addressed him in these words: "Vultis et vos abire—God has no need of you and your companions; if it be His will that this work should go on, He will raise up other laborers to fill your place." For a moment, Alphonsus stood stupefied by this reception, so different from what he had expected; but immediately regaining courage, he said: "My Lord, I am well convinced that the Almighty has no need of me, or of my labors; notwithstanding, I believe it to be His will that I should proceed in this work, and singly and alone as I am, I shall yet succeed." He continued: "I have not left Naples, I have not renounced the world, to gain the glory of founding a new order, but to do the will of God and promote His glory." This reply touched Mgr. Falcoja deeply, who, suddenly changing his manner, said: "Put your confidence in God, and he will certainly bless your good intentions."

On the whole, he returned to Scala much comforted by this interview; but the devil would not leave him in peace. D. Sportelli was often necessarily absent, and when Alphonsus found himself alone on this desert mountain, disgust, anxiety, and depression, assailed him more strongly than ever. He knew whence those temptations came, and one day when they were at their height, he threw himself on his knees, and solemnly vowed to consecrate himself irrevocably to the salvation of destitute souls, even if he should remain altogether alone. God evidently blessed this heroic action; from that moment his fears and anxieties vanished, and he felt himself filled with courage, hope, and consolation. Even in his old age, he could not remember, without a shudder, the terrible struggle he had then sustained; and he said to F. Dominic Corsano, his director, that this, and his separation from his father, were the two most dreadful trials he had ever undergone.

He had also, not without reason, dreaded the effect this rupture would produce in Naples. No sooner was it known that the new founder was abandoned by his companions, and that the society was dissolved, than every one laughed at and ridiculed the whole proceeding, condemning the fanaticism of the pretended head of the Congregation, who had blindly lent himself to the dreaming fancies of a woman. They went the length of affirming, that the Pope himself had interfered, and forbidden the establishment of such a Congregation. Even the pulpits resounded with anathemas; the preachers pretending to show, by these events, to what an extent even the most favored individuals can go astray, when they allow themselves to be caught in the snare of the devil, and to forget the precepts of humility. At this crisis, even his friends were silenced by their own share of the contempt and mockery which they received. F. Fiorillo alone saw that all this was the work of the devil, and continued to be convinced that God would uphold his own work. Cardinal Pignatelli pitied Alphonsus, but did not condemn him. "There was nothing reprehensible in it," he said, "but who can know the judgments of God?" and touched by the embarrassment in which Alphonsus found himself, he desired the Canon Torni to recall him to Naples.

Every one can imagine the reception Alphonsus had to expect in this city, and how much it must have cost him to return at such a moment. On all sides he saw himself condemned and turned into ridicule. The Canon Gizzio refused to see him or hear his name mentioned. F. Ripa would have nothing to do with him, and it was the same with many others, who had once held him in the highest esteem. He went to the Cardinal, accompanied by the Canon Torni. This wise prelate was afflicted to hear of the number of lies that had been circulated against him. The Canon, who wished to retain Alphonsus at Naples, remarked, that if this work had been pleasing to God, He would not have withdrawn the means of carrying it into execution; and that surely he could be more useful at Naples, than elsewhere. But Alphonsus replied with entire confidence: "We have reason to be convinced that the devil is the author of what has happened at Scala; but it must not be said that I have allowed myself to be conquered, because the demon has come across my path. If my first companions have deserted me, that is no reason why other zealous priests should not be found; but be that as it may, I do not hesitate, even alone, to sacrifice myself for the good of the destitute souls scattered through the villages and hamlets of this kingdom." The Cardinal could not help admiring the heroism of this speech, and turning towards the Canon, he said: "It will not do to abandon Scala just yet; let us have recourse to God in order to know His holy will." Then encouraging Alphonsus, he continued: "Trust in God, put no confidence in man, for it is God who will help you." He approved his constancy, and advised him against a reunion with those who had separated themselves from him.

Consoled by the sentiments of the Cardinal, Alphonsus returned to Scala full of hope and confidence, while the opinions expressed by his Eminence disconcerted those who railed against him, and reduced them to silence. At Scala their number consisted of three, D. Sportelli, who was still a layman, Vitus Curzius, the lay-brother, and himself. In this solitude, Alphonsus reposed in the bosom of God, and he soon had the consolation of seeing his convent frequented by new subjects, who aspired to enter the Congregation. Rejoicing to find his hopes realized, he wrote to a friend, in July, 1733, thus: "Our novices think neither of country nor friends, nor even of suffering; all their desire is to love God and perfectly to conform themselves to His will."

About this time, they quitted the hospice for a house called Anastasius, but equally poor with the first. One who saw it, describes it as follows: "There was one small parlor, in which Alphonsus had made an oratory, and erected a crucifix so beautifully carved, that it drew tears from the eyes. The bishop had arranged for the church a square apartment under ground, which looked more like a burial vault than a chapel. Poverty reigned every where in the house and in the church; they had not even a tabernacle for the Blessed Sacrament, and Alphonsus placed it in a box ornamented with ribbons and silk drapery. The altar was also poor, but they embellished it as well as they could with roses and bouquets of artificial flowers. Alphonsus and his companions passed the greater part of the night there, taking a little repose on the bare earth, before the Blessed Sacrament."

CHAPTER VIII.

Alphonsus gives Missions and founds the Houses at the Villa dei Schiavi and at Ciorani. He abandons the former.

AFTER Mandarini and his companions had quitted Scala, the spirit of penance and prayer reigned there as before; all breathed self-denial and mortification, each one feeling himself impelled to imitate Alphonsus, who, as usual, signalized himself among the others. At the side of the house was a half ruined grotto, where every day he submitted his body to the most rigorous penances. There is a tradition among the inhabitants, that while he was in it chastising his body, the Blessed Virgin appeared to him, and bestowed upon him many special favors. Whenever he returned to visit Scala, he went to see his beloved grotto, exclaiming: "O my grotto, my beloved grotto, why can I not enjoy thee now as in times long past!"

Four months had scarcely elapsed since the departure of Mandarini, when Alphonsus found himself in a position to give missions in the neighboring dioceses until the Christmas of that year. In the mean time, he had been joined by the priest Sarnelli, of Ciorani, and in January following, he yielded to his pressing solicitation, and accompanied him to the territory of Ciorani. The inhabitants of this country never lost the remembrance of this first visit. They spent but a few days there, being called by the Bishop of Cajazzo to give a mission in his diocese. The general reformation in manners which followed, excited the most ardent longing for their establishing a house there, but they were not yet sufficiently numerous. At Formicola, in the principality of Columbano, was a house with a church adjoining, extremely well suited for the Congregation. Xavier Rossi, a young nobleman, who had received priest's orders, was most anxious, among others, to see them established in it. He exerted himself to the utmost, sent for an architect to arrange for the necessary alterations and repairs, and soon the work was begun at his own expense. He afterwards, led by a sudden movement of grace, when one morning he served the mass of Alphonsus, and saw in him at the altar, not a man, but a seraph, felt impelled, in spite of himself, to follow him. Alphonsus would prove his sincerity by delay; but he gave so many proofs of strong determination, that he soon admitted him to his novitiate. He became afterwards a corner-stone in the new-born Congregation, and died as a Saint, after having rendered the greatest services.

This foundation exactly suited the views of Alphonsus, being situated on the confines of four dioceses, surrounded by a great number of villages, and a thickly peopled country. At the beginning of March, the building was so far advanced that they could inhabit it. Four apartments level with the ground, rèsting against the church, were given to the missionaries, and four chaplainships were assigned to them, with a revenue from each, of one carlino a day, that is, about nine cents of our money. This was certainly but little with which to found an establishment of missionaries; but Alphonsus looked out only for souls, and contented himself with a small and poor house, distinguished from others only by a belfry, after the example of St. Theresa, whom he loved to imitate. No sooner was the house established, than he undertook different good works to promote the salvation of the people in the neighborhood, and gave frequent missions. While the building continued to go on, the people eagerly assisted in the work, and even some of the neighboring nobles might be seen mingling with the others in carrying materials. Alphonsus was the first to set the example, laboring like a simple workman, and when the gentlemen insisted on his stopping, he replied: "This is nothing, I wish to have my share of merit with the others." It happened one day, that a poor woman was carrying a large stone, when another equally large fell from the building upon her head; every one thought that the blow was mortal, but Alphonsus, who saw the accident from a distance, entered the church, and addressed himself to the Blessed Virgin: his prayer was heard, the woman rose up unhurt.

Alphonsus remained until the month of August, and here he had the happiness of receiving John Mazzini, who had so long been wishing to join him. Such was his opinion of this Father's virtue and wisdom, that he immediately made him rector of the new house. At the same time, a talented and promising subject was, though yet a cleric, taken from him by violence. Michael d'Alteriis, of Panecocoli, near Naples, had retired into the Congregation without the consent of his father, who was so much irritated at this, that he sent armed men to the house of the missionaries, to take his son away by force. Alphonsus, persuaded of the divine vocation of the young man, saved him from their hands by sending him away during the night. His father and other relatives were so full of resentment at this, and made such a noise, that the Cardinal, to prevent worse consequences, counselled Alphonsus to send the young man back to his family. Alphonsus obeyed, saying: "This violence will cost them much." And in fact, scarcely had Michael returned, when his eldest brother became sick and died. The unhappy father recognized in this the hand of God, and said: "I have taken one from God, and God has now taken the other from me." God however, blessed Michael, who in leaving had but obeyed his director. He returned to the Congregation afterwards, and after having labored in it zealously and indefatigably, he died in the odor of sanctity.

The life which Alphonsus led with his brethren in this new house, "The Villa dei Schiavi," was equally admirable with the life he had led at Scala. An eye-witness reports, that every day he ate on his knees, with a heavy stone hung round his neck; his food usually consisted of a simple pottage, seasoned with bitter herbs, he never drank wine: besides taking the discipline in common, he took it privately every day, and the walls of his room were covered with blood; the hair cloth he wore was so heavy, that he could hardly walk; his sleep was short, a stone served him as a pillow, and his straw mattress was so thin, that he might be said to sleep on boards. His humility was extraordinary, before and after meals, he kissed the feet of all; he never used a razor, but cut his beard with a pair of scissors; his cassock was so worn and mended, that the original form could hardly be recognized; he never went on horseback, but always on foot or on a mule, which he said was good enough for him. A profound silence was generally observed in the house, and the hour of recreation after their frugal meal, was still an uninterrupted conference on spiritual subjects. Such was the mode of life led by Alphonsus and his companions, and, besides the three meditations which they made every day, he was continually in prayer, and spoke only when it was absolutely necessary. When their new foundation was sufficiently consolidated, Alphonsus returned to Scala. The good that had been done during his absence by Doctor, now Father, Sportelli, gave him great consolation, which was increased by finding many candidates for the novitiate, awaiting him with impatience. In the course of the autumn, he gave several missions in the neighborhood and elsewhere. In January, 1735, he returned to the territory of Cajazzo, visiting the house of the Villa dei Schiavi, where he remained some time. At the request of Mgr. Santoro, he consented, rather unwillingly, to preach the Lent in the Cathedral of Scala, when he also gave a retreat in the parish of St. Catherine, and another to the nuns of St. Cataldo.

At this time, the Curate of the territory of Ciorani, having learned the good that was done in the neighboring parishes, both he and his flock desired ardently to see a house of the missionaries established among them. No one entered more into the spirit of this plan than the brother of F. Sarnelli, D. Andrew. He persuaded the Baron, his father, of the immense advantages that would result, and set himself about to procure the means of carrying it into execution, and by the month of April, he had received a sufficient rent for their maintenance. After an agreement was made with the Archbishop of Salerno, Alphonsus, with Fathers Mazzini and Rossi, came to Ciorani in the month of May, 1735. Four miserable donkeys formed their equipage, but an immense concourse of people awaited them at the entrance into the barony, with the Curate and his clerics. Arrived at the parochial church, at the sight of such a multitude, Alphonsus mounted the pulpit, and taking for the subject of his discourse the motive of his coming—the salvation of their souls—he preached with such powerful effect, that every heart was penetrated with compunction. On the evening of the next day, he opened the mission. The people ran thither in such crowds, that the church, though spacious, could not contain them. At the sight of Alphonsus, so poor, so humble, so full of the spirit of God, no one could resist him; the hearts of all, even of the most abandoned, were touched, and the conversions were innumerable.

The habitation which the Baron had given the missionaries, besides a sort of cellar, which served for a kitchen, consisted only of two large rooms. After a while he gave them two other apartments, but in passing from the one to the other, they were obliged to cross an open court, which was a great inconvenience, particularly in winter; besides, these places had only planks for the exterior wall, through the chinks of which the cold wind entered. In addition to these annoyances, they were situated above a public house and a prison, a neighborhood not exactly suited for men of prayer and retirement. In one of these rooms, Alphonsus erected a small oratory, reserving the three others for their own use. The furniture of the whole was miserable enough, and, so far from having superfluities, absolute necessaries were wanting. He and his companions rejoiced in these discomforts, their oratory being for them a little heaven. It was there, during the night, oftener than during the day, that Alphonsus poured out his soul into the bosom of God. After the missions, they established the same pious practices and confraternities as at Scala and Villa dei Schiavi. The exercises were made in the parochial church, but the concourse of people being every day as great as on feast days, the missionaries had scarcely time to eat or sleep. As the people came very early in the morning, and disturbed the poor old Curate, Alphonsus was at the expense of repairing the old church of St. Sophia, annexed to the signorial palace, and met the people there. As all the inhabitants of the neighboring villages could not come to Ciorani, he sent missionaries, on Sundays and feast days, to the great comfort of the sick and the infirm. It was not long before the barony was completely reformed. The inhabitants began to resemble the first Christians. Quarrels and hatred were banished; the language and behaviour of the young men became pure; the young women no longer sang loose and profane songs, but pious canticles which Alphonsus composed himself. When the inhabitants met, they saluted each other, saying: "Praise be to Jesus and Mary." No more imprecations were heard, the public house in the village was deserted, and all improper games were forbidden.

Tosquez and Mandarini now began to recognize the pernicious effects of their divisions. Although they had got the approbation of the sovereign Pontiff for their establishments, they were not successful, and continually wrote to Alphonsus on the subject of a re-union. Having weighed the matter maturely, he at length wrote a definite answer. "It is true," he said, "that it promises much, but I doubt whether these promises would ever be realized. First impressions are not easily effaced, and what we retract to-day, we recommence to-morrow, and when the spirit is cooled, the fairest promises are forgotten." Above all, he remembered the advice of Cardinal Pignatelli against this re-union, and the affair was forever broken off.

The Archbishop of Salerno, struck by the good which was done by the missions, and the very small expense necessary to lodge the missionaries, since they were content with a morsel of bread and a corner in the sacristy, gave Alphonsus license to go where he wished, commanding the curates, at the same time, to show them every respect and attention. Notwithstanding, there were some who received them with an ill-grace, and even repulsed them. On one occasion, Alphonsus had fixed the day for giving a mission in a parish: on his arrival the curate met him, and without asking him to dismount from his ass, refused to permit him to give the mission; but fearing to offend the Archbishop, he tried to palliate his conduct, by mentioning a future period when the mission might be held. Alphonsus calmly answered: "Your Reverence believes the mission can be held at that time; but I assure you, you will not be in a condition to receive me then." The curate did not understand these words; but before the time appointed, although in the prime of life, he had paid the debt of nature.

In consideration of the inconveniences of their habitation at Ciorani, the Baron gave up to the missionaries a building in another part of his property, and added some ground for a garden. No sooner was this done, than men and women came from all quarters to assist. Some carried stones and wood, others constructed a furnace to make bricks, and the sons of the Baron, with the curate and priests, labored almost as hard as the people, and the building advanced as if by enchantment.

One might say that the practice of the holy exercises was brought to perfection at Ciorani; for in spite of the annoyances of the locality in which they dwelt, many persons, both priests and laymen, came to place themselves under the direction of Alphonsus. Many persons of quality, belonging to San Severino and the neighborhood, seeing the effect produced upon others, ardently desired to have a kind of mission for themselves. As the Baron Angelo was then in Naples, Alphonsus obtained permission to give the mission in the great hall of the castle, and also that those gentlemen who were too far distant from home, might remain all night. Many ecclesiastics assisted at this mission, and the fruits were seen in their redoubled ardor for the souls of men; while the gentlemen returned home to edify all by the reformation of their lives and manners. It was in this retreat that the young priest Andrew Villani, a descendant of the Dukes of Sacco della Polla, convinced that the world is deceitful and full of snares, took the resolution of quitting it, and consecrating himself to God in this new Congregation. He afterwards became a model of sanctity, and a foundation stone in the new-born Congregation.

Alphonsus took every care to make the people love the holy exercises, and all rejoiced in the good they produced. Many ecclesiastics came during the year, but chiefly in Lent, to make retreats; and magistrates, nobles, and princes, came also, besides many prelates with their clerics. He attached the greatest importance to the holy exercises of a retreat, for all conditions of men, and the fruits which always accompany them prove his wisdom.

While such glorious works were progressing, the devil could not look quietly on; accordingly he had, even before the foundation was approved of, excited the jealousy of some neighboring curates, who, joined by some mendicant friars, beset the Archbishop, who began to doubt whether he ought not to suppress the house. But in the end they became quiet, and the Archbishop definitely authorized the foundation, on the 12th of December, 1735. By this time F. Sarnelli, out of an injudicious zeal, and too great an anxiety for the support of the Congregation, suggested to the Archbishop, that as so many curates profited by the labors of the missionaries, each should contribute a trifle towards their support. The parties interested keenly opposed the measure, and not only did they look upon Alphonsus with an evil eye, but they set themselves by all means to have the missionaries chased out of the territory. The Curate of Ciorani was asked to lend his aid, but the good old man replied: "What! these holy priests who labor incessantly in my parish, would you have me deprive my people of such great help?" They then reported to the Archbishop, that under pretence of zeal and devotedness, they only sought to enrich themselves at the expense of the legitimate pastors, and that they ought to be immediately expelled from the diocess. The Archbishop smiled at this and said: "I know Alphonsus de Liguori; he and I resemble each other in reference to fortune: I know he has quitted the world not from necessity, but from choice, and that if he has any anxiety, it is not about temporal interests, but to gain souls and secure his own salvation;" and declared that he took the missionaries under his own immediate protection, as the work to which they had devoted themselves was most advantageous to the souls confided to his care. This storm having abated, those who were most opposed to Alphonsus were the first to profit by his labors; he gave missions in the different parishes; and the fruits of his zeal were as abundant as ever.

In the course of the retreats he gave about this time, a striking event occurred to prove how God watched over him and protected him. Speaking one day of the enormity of sin in priests, he concluded by quoting the words of St. John Chrysostom, "In sacerdotio peccasti, periisti." At these words, an ecclesiastic replied, to the great scandal of all who heard him: "Nego consequentiam." This miserable man soon experienced the consequence: next morning, as he began at the foot of the altar the psalm, "Judica me Deus," he dropped down dead.

In the course of the year 1737, Alphonsus, at the pressing entreaty of the Superior of the Propaganda, who for fear of his refusing had addressed himself to Mgr. Falcoja, his director, went to Naples for the mission to be opened in the church of the Holy Spirit, on the 26th of October. It has been said that a volume might be filled with the conversions he made on this occasion. After this mission, without taking any repose, he proceeded immediately to visit Amalfi, and thence went to Masuri. In this place, a poor woman whose son had been assassinated, had constantly refused to pardon the murderer, though the most influential persons had besought her to do so. She went to hear Alphonsus preach, and was so touched by the sermon, that, the same evening, she brought a written declaration that she pardoned the criminal, and publicly laid it at the foot of the crucifix. Throughout the neighborhood he gave missions, which reclaimed multitudes of sinners, and impelled the virtuous to strive after a higher degree of sanctity.

At this time he was called by Mgr. de Liguori, his uncle, to St. Lucy, in the diocese of Cava. The inhabitants were very immoral in their lives, but "where sin abounded, grace did much more abound." Abuses were extirpated; nothing was spoken of but pardoning injuries, making restitution, and repairing scandals; and so well did he convince them of the merit of chastity, that upwards of fifty young ladies protested they would no longer think of marriage, but would consecrate themselves to God. They carried their resolve into execution, and united themselves into a Congregation, under the direction of a zealous priest, and were soon joined by many others, attracted by their noble example.

At this time, the buildings at Villa dei Schiavi were nearly finished, and the missionaries had already begun to give retreats. They were visiting the country around, extirpating sin and planting virtue. A Congregation of artisans had been established, which already numbered more than two hundred members, whose zeal and fervor made them missionaries throughout the neighborhood. The frequentation of the Sacraments became general, and many individuals were arriving at a high degree of prayer. But all at once, a storm arose, withering those blossoms which promised such abundant fruits for eternity. There were in the country certain individuals who could not bear to have their vices censured, among others, a man who led a life openly immoral: not enduring to have his conduct animadverted upon, and doubtless instigated by the devil, he conspired the ruin of the missionaries. All the wealth of this house consisted of the four chaplainships, which brought each a carlin a day; under pretext of defending the interests of the priests of the country, this man began to declaim aloud against the missionaries for coming thither to eat the bread belonging to the inhabitants, and getting money by extra masses, to which the legitimate pastors had a right. Pecuniary interests being thus brought into play, the clamor became general, and the most gross and injurious expressions were employed against them. The calumnies augmented, and, at length, their morals were attacked. Alphonsus himself was pointed out as one who made a traffic of his pretended sanctity. They went so far as to say that the missionaries intrigued with a woman, and received her into the convent by night; and this wretched creature lent herself to the calumny, defaming Alphonsus even more than the others, and showing presents, which she pretended to have received from them. These calumnies made little impression upon Alphonsus; he knew that persecution always accompanied works undertaken for God; and contented himself with prescribing to the community still more circumspection, and more frequent recurrence to prayer. The wicked man and his accomplices at last succeeded in prejudicing the Baron himself. Alphonsus, seeing the storm thus increasing, went to the Baron, to claim his protection; but it was too late, as soon as he saw him approach, he permitted these words to escape: "What have we here, one of those filthy hermits?" and immediately dismissed him with still greater contempt.

This scene was soon reported, and filled the enemies of Alphonsus with joy. They now no longer confined themselves to outrageous words, they took bolder steps, and solicited the tribunals of Naples to interfere in various ways, though without success. They at last had recourse to open violence. One of the lay-brothers, going in the morning to the church to sound the Angelus, was met by one of the wardens, accompanied by several people; they forced the keys from his hands, locked the church, and sent him back to the house, loaded with reproach. But fearing the people might take part with the missionaries, and force open the door, they placed persons with loaded muskets on the belfry, to prevent approach. They also besieged the house, and without exception interdicted all communication with those within. This situ tion becoming every day less endurable, the missionaries determined to abandon the place: the bishop wept with regret, the poor people were not less disconsolate, and the surrounding villages were in mourning. On the night of the 10th of June, 1737, they shook the dust from their shoes, and left the Villa. God did not permit this wickedness to go unpunished. The wretched woman who had accused Alphonsus and his companions, had her tongue eaten by worms, and was reduced to such a condition, that she could not receive the sacraments; she was seized with the most dreadful remorse of conscience, and publicly avowed that all she had said was but an infamous calumny. One individual, who had joined in the conspiracy, died soon after in despair, uttering the most frightful cries. Another, one of the principal persecutors, terminated his life in the most terrible convulsions, and howling like a maniac. A third, who had sought out the false witnesses and written down their testimony, had his hand withered, and his only son died soon after: he then became an idiot and expired in great misery. A fourth, who had been bribed to attest all the calumnies, died in impenitence. A fifth, a healthy young man, fell down dead immediately after the departure of Alphonsus. The chief instigator alone seemed to have escaped. He remained deaf even to a warning sent him from heaven. For scarcely had the missionaries quitted the Villa, when a tremendous storm arose: the lightning flashed, and a thunderbolt fell at the feet of this man, as he sat in his room: it stunned him, and for some little time he remained without sense or motion. When he came to himself, he would not recognise the warning: but before long he fell into disgrace with his prince, was ill-used and persecuted, and within a year, he was found, one morning, lying dead under his bed, and bathed in blood.

CHAPTER XII.

Apostolic Courses of Alphonsus. He abandons Scala. Missions in various places and Dioceses, especially in that of Naples.

ALPHONSUS continued to give missions throughout the country, every where reaping the most abundant harvest. But it was in the Barony of St. George, at the little village of Ajello, that God poured out the most extraordinary graces. Scandals disappeared, taverns were deserted, and the churches filled. Here he established, as usual, many devotional exercises, and there was not a house in which they did not say the Rosary in common. It was also at this place, that the Blessed Virgin was pleased to give to Alphonsus a public testimony of her love. One evening, while he was preaching on the glories of Mary, and exciting the people to honor her, he was ravished in ecstasy and raised some feet above the pulpit; at the same time rays of glory proceeded from a statue of the Virgin, and rested on the head of her chosen servant.

Shortly after, he visited Castellamare, a town which was in great want of spiritual succor, its maritime commerce bringing strangers from all parts, which necessarily corrupted morals. He took with him nine companions, and remained long, because of the great necessity of the people. Multitudes were converted, among whom were many unfortunate women; smuggling was discouraged; and the magical practices in use among the sailors were abolished. The whole town breathed an air of devotion, the churches were crowded, and the Sacraments frequented.

By this time the new house of Ciorani being finished, and the small church erected, they abandoned that of St. Sophia. It was dedicated to the Blessed Virgin, and in it Alphonsus placed that beloved statue of her, before which he had so often poured out his heart in those retreats which he made with his companions at Naples, in the house of D. de Alteriis. The conveniences afforded by the new house, drew strangers there at all times, candidates for ordination, numerous ecclesiastics and laymen, especially in general missions, so that Alphonsus and his companions had often to sleep on the floor in a common apartment. At the death of the Bishop, the Archdeacon, D. Francis de Vicariis, who succeeded him in March, named Alphonsus Grand Penitentiary of the archdiocese, which increased the concourse of visitors, and was a new occasion for the exercise of his zeal.

Rejoicing at the establishment of this house, Alphonsus exerted himself to make the rules strictly observed, for the inconveniences of the former habitation had made this impossible. The deserts of Nubia and Thebes perhaps never counted among their cenobites contemplatives, such as were seen in the house at Ciorani. Penitence and mortification were the two virtues to which they attached themselves most, as the necessary preparation for prayer and contemplation. If there were brethren who did not excel, the example of their Superior and model, Alphonsus, drew them after him in spite of themselves.

If on his part Alphonsus was doing all in his power to establish the Congregation, the devil was as busy in attempting to destroy it. Until then they had had no house at Scala. Alphonsus, in concert with the Bishop, thought of erecting one; but scarcely had they put their hand to the work, when a general commotion ensued. Several individuals, having learned what had happened at the Villa, began in their turn to murmur and to excite others, by putting forward the same motives, so that soon jealousy, aided by interest, caused many to regard the missionaries with bitterness. Alphonsus, warned by what had happened at the Villa, wished to shun new misfortunes, and, without loss of time, removed from Scala. This was a blow deeply felt by Mgr. Santoro. The good lamented, but the envious triumphed, when on the eve of St. Bartholomew, the 24th of August, 1737, the missionaries left the town. It was reported that on the night when they departed from Scala, there was heard throughout the town a noise made by evil spirits shouting and dancing. They celebrated a great victory, the departure of the missionaries arresting the good they had been doing; for to the scandals that had once been so common, had succeeded a horror of sin; even the porters had been reformed, they often approached the holy table, and frequently might be met in groups carrying their burdens, and reciting the Rosary, or singing the hymns which Alphonsus had taught them. Two years after, the Pious Workers went to preach a mission there, when one of them declared, that they had not found among the people one voluntary venial sin, and that all sorts of pious practices were already established. On the 28th, a violent storm destroyed the harvest, which in that country consists of chestnuts, on which the poor chiefly live. Many considered this as a punishment of the wickedness of those who had forced the missionaries to retire, and of the weakness of the greater number, who had not opposed it. Alphonsus, however, did not forget Scala; he sent some of his missionaries to give the novena of the Crucifix, that the nuns might not be deprived of their religious exercises.

The fields in which Alphonsus labored during the following autumn and winter, were not less fertile in the fruits of salvation. He preached penance in many districts, and at Castaglione the concourse of people was so great, that they passed the night in the church. The same thing occurred at Coperchia, near Salerno. The year 1739 was opened by a mission in the village of Prepezzano. The name of Alphonsus had become so celebrated in the diocese of Salerno, and such wonders of grace were operated by him, that persons frequently came a distance of seventeen miles to confess to him. At Calvanico, besides the most wonderful fruits produced in the people, the ecclesiastics, to whom, as was usual, he also gave the exercises, were so animated with fervor, that some of them followed in his suite to assist at the missions, a practice which is now not unfrequent. Having during the summer returned with his companions to Ciorani, to give a little relaxation to a body overpowered with fatigue, and refresh his spirit in retirement, he issued forth again with renewed strength and redoubled vigor to attack the strongholds of Satan. In the beginning of 1740, accompanied by eleven missionaries, he overran the country, shedding the benedictions of Heaven on many villages where great disorders had previously reigned. After the spring missions, he returned again to Ciorani, to regulate the affairs of the Congregation, and reanimate his brethren by his example in the observation of the rules.

The country of St. Severino suffered, during the summer of this year, from great drought. To obtain the divine mercy, the inhabitants of Acquarola invited Alphonsus to give a mission towards the end of July: their fervor was great during the exercises, and one day Alphonsus foretold, that, at a time specified an abundance of rain would fall. The day came without any appearance of rain, when all at once a very small cloud was seen above Salerno. When Alphonsus saw it, he extended his arms, as if to invite its approach, and then, prostrating himself on the ground, he besought the divine mercy in behalf of the people; and all at once the air was obscured by clouds, thunder was heard, the lightning flashed, and during five hours the rain fell in torrents.

In the autumn of the same year, he again gave missions in many villages with his usual success, as also in the beginning of 1741. Among the number of those converted, were bandits and murderers. Many priests, who had been cold and indifferent, gave themselves fervently to God, a circumstance which always rejoiced Alphonsus, who used to say: "The conversion of a priest gives more glory to God, than that of a hundred seculars. No layman, however holy, can perform the good done by a priest."

A zealous priest of Nocera, who used to frequent Ciorani, resolved, if possible, to have a house established in that town. He knew that the Dean of the place had resolved to endow a house of missionaries; he therefore spoke to him and to the principal inhabitants, of the virtues of Alphonsus and his companions, and arranged that they should give a mission there. It had the greatest success, and every one designated Alphonsus as the "Apostle." He certainly enjoyed many supernatural gifts: he knew how to touch all hearts: he had the spirit of prophecy and the gift of healing, often curing fevers and other diseases, by making the sign of the cross. He lodged in the house of the aforesaid priest, whose mother was subject to convulsions from an excessive pain she had in her arm. She wrapped herself in a shirt belonging to Alphonsus, full of faith in his sanctity, and was immediately cured. All this made the people more than ever anxious to have the missionaries established among them. Plans were formed, but the designs of Providence were not accomplished until a later period.

It was on the 18th of April in this year, that God called to himself the first member of the Congregation. He was a lay-brother, Joachim Gaudiello: he died in transports of joy, exclaiming: "It is I who will carry the standard." All the virtues seemed to have taken up their abode in this excellent subject. They had neglected to take his portrait, and eleven days after his death, in the hope that his body was still uncorrupted, they opened the coffin, and found their expectation justified: his body was flexible and entire, as if still alive.

Providence had destined a new field for Alphonsus to cultivate in the spring of 1741. His Eminence, Cardinal Spinelli, having become Archbishop of Naples, by the death of Cardinal Pignatelli, invited him to supply the great necessities of his diocese, and persisted in claiming his services, so that at last he was obliged to yield. That his other missions might suffer as little as possible, Alphonsus only took from his own Congregation the Fathers Sarnelli and Villani, but chose the elite of all the Congregations in Naples to assist him, and above all, the best missionaries of the Propaganda. The Cardinal wished it should be so, in order that the others might learn from him to conduct missions with more success. He placed at his disposal a country-house in the Barra, to which the missionaries might retire to recruit after their fatigue. On this occasion, the Superior of the Propaganda pretended that, his Congregation having a pre-eminence over all the Congregations in Naples, to him belonged the right of deciding who should be the chief; but the true motive of his opposition, was the unwillingness of the members of the Propaganda to submit themselves to a man, whom they had so lately wished to expel. The Cardinal, when they complained, replied: "I am your Archbishop, and I am Superior of the mission, as well as of all other Congregations in the diocese, and since the missions depend on me, I am the person to appoint the chief."

It was in the month of May these missions commenced at Fragola, where Alphonsus opened three at once in three parochial churches, and where, besides the divers pious practices and exercises he was wont to establish, in order that the good done might be lasting, he instituted conferences, to be held every eight days, in which were discussed different cases of conscience, in order to render the priests more skilful in the confessional. After the mission of Casal Nuovo, which lasted till June, he dismissed the Neapolitan missionaries, and notwithstanding the heat of the summer, he remained with his own at St. Angelo, where they continued to preach and hear the confessions of crowds, who came from all quarters. On feast days, he went himself, with his brethren, into the neighboring hamlets, exhorting the people to penance.

On these missions, they followed the same rules which had been established for the interior of the Congregation. The most common bread only was permitted, Alphonsus holding the maxim, that the people would be gained rather by example than by words. When they wished to supply his table with rare dishes, he sent them away, although his guests were often Canons from Naples, and other persons of distinction. At Christmas, they expected some relaxation in these rules, but they were mistaken. Certain persons attached to the service of the Cardinal, said to him on their return: "Your Eminence is, perhaps, not aware, that Alphonsus gave us a treat on Christmas; he made them serve several additional force-meat balls, on that occasion, at the risk of ruining his household economy." He allowed the other missionaries to travel in a carriage, because they were not accustomed to do otherwise; but he and his brethren would only make use of asses.

In the beginning of November, the missionaries met again, and recommenced their pious labors. During the Holy Week of 1742, although in the service of Mgr. Spinelli, Alphonsus could not refuse going to Nocera, to give the exercises in honor of the Holy Sacrament, in the great church of Corpus-Christi; the effects of which were most consoling.

The Cardinal, considering the abundant blessings Alphonsus and his missionaries produced, proposed to establish them in the Barra situated in the centre of his diocese. But this was far from according with the views of Alphonsus, as he explained to his Eminence: "When my missionaries," said he, "will be settled at the Barra, and have ladies and gentlemen for their penitents, will they be very willing to leave this place for the hamlets and the mountains? And who knows but, fascinated by their noble penitents, they may fix themselves at Naples for the greater part of the year?" He continued: "Your Eminence is not in want of able workmen at Naples to employ in the care of the diocese, but other Bishops have not this advantage; it is not from Naples we can draw missionaries for villages and remote hamlets."

During the octave of Easter, he again began the missions in the country, and during the season, besides spiritual exercises, he gave more than seventy missions. An eye-witness, speaking of the effect of his labors, says: "Were I to report all the facts in particular, they would fill volumes. In the diocese of Naples, the Father D. Alphonsus banished scandals and abuses without number. No more indecencies were committed in the church; women no longer dressed in a manner to give scandal, and occasion the weak to sin. . . . Taverns were no longer frequented, certain dances and pastimes, formerly in use, were abolished; pious canticles replaced the licentious songs so common during the harvest and vintage." If Alphonsus operated wonders on the morals of the people, it was due to his extraordinary labors and fatigues: his body and his mind were continually in action; no one could understand how he managed to do what would have overpowered any one else; people said he lived by miracle; he often preached twice, sometimes three times, in one day; but he preached even more by his example. He ate little, and the time he gave to sleep was short. In long journeys, and during the exercises of a mission, whatever his fatigue might be, he never lessened his bodily austerities, never gave himself the least solace. He always travelled on an ass, and those who did not know him, often mistook him foi a domestic. One day when he preached at the opening of a mission, the peasants, struck by the beautiful words which they heard, said to each other, "Well, if the cook can preach in that manner, what will it be when the others begin?" He always reserved for himself the worst bed and the most incommodious chamber. Every thing came well to him, provided he were mortified and humiliated. At Casal Nuovo, he gave up to his companions the only three rooms that could be had, and kept for himself a miserable ruin, long uninhabited.

When the heat of summer had increased, and the harvest time was at hand, Alphonsus sent his missionaries in small numbers, and for a few days only, to those places where missions had already been given. These renewals of missions, which he originated, they having been unknown before him, produced much fruit. They re-animated the fervor of the confraternities which had been established, confirmed the people in their pious practices, raised those who had fallen, and encouraged those who persevered. During this summer, he labored incessantly to promote devotion to the Mother of God, giving retreats for nine days preceding any of her feasts. He was also the originator of these

Novenas, now so common in Naples and other places, which continue to produce such benefits to the souls of all who engage in them. After terminating his labors in the Barra, he returned, in the beginning of July, for a short time, to Ciorani.

CHAPTER XIII.

Alphonsus, with his Companions, makes the three Religious Vows. He founds the House of Nocera. Oppositions he encounters.

HITHERTO Alphonsus and his companions had lived together without binding themselves by vows. All was free and spontaneous; but, considering that in a society the spirit of religion decays rather than increases, Alphonsus determined to retain and fix the spirit of piety by vows, and form his Congregation into an apostolical community. He represented to his companions the merit they would acquire before God, when by vows, they should have sacrificed their own will, and despoiled themselves of worldly wealth: "The renouncement of our own will," he said, "procures more glory to God than all the good works we could do from our own choice. A delicious fruit gives pleasure to him to whom we present it; but, if with the fruit we give also the tree that produces it, the offering acquires an infinitely greater value." "The vow," he added, "will be as a buckler in the hand of the missionary against the devil and his own inconstancy; it will confirm him in his vocation to the service of God; it will be to him as an anchor to preserve his vessel beaten and tossed by the winds." The most of his companions needed no importunities to induce them to make the generous sacrifice; on the contrary, they never ceased to urge him to put it into execution. The measure being resolved upon, Alphonsus thought only of the engagements by which the members of his Congregation should be bound.

It was determined that each, in preserving his wealth, should renounce the temporary use of it. He determined that they should bind themselves to accept no ecclesiastical dignity, no title, employment, or benefice, out of the Congregation; and that they should refuse every thing of the kind, unless commanded by the Pope himself to accept. He prescribed a life in common, without distinction of merit or rank, in order to unite them closely in God, and bind them together by the disinterested ties of charity. After having, by these rules, banished interest and cupidity, he desired above all, to unite the hearts of all by the vow of obedience to the will of one Superior, this virtue of obedience being the guarantee for the existence of a religious house. "When obedience and subordination are wanting," he used to say, "a true religious cannot live, and what would have been a Paradise by concord, becomes a Hell by diversity of feeling and sentiment." He established by unanimous consent, that every one, on the termination of his novitiate, should take the vow of living and dying in the Congregation; but in case of a sufficient cause to act otherwise, dispensation could be obtained, only, however, from the sovereign Pontiff or the Superior General, whilst the Congregation would be always free to send away any one whose conduct should not be edifying, and who should be incorrigible.

Always distrusting his own light, he recurred frequently to God, and consulted with many pious persons, above all, with Mgr. Falcoja. All approved of the plan submitted to their consideration; and at length it was resolved to proceed to the profession on the day of St. Mary Magdalene, the 22d of July, 1742, after three days passed in retreat, constant prayer, and the most rigorous silence. As the Institute was not yet confirmed by the Pope, and Alphonsus had no legitimate character of Superior, they agreed to make their vow of perseverance to Mgr. Falcoja, in his quality of Bishop, as he took such a deep interest in the Congregation. The joy was unanimous, and Alphonsus, after having returned thanks to God, and animated his brethren to be faithful, departed with F. Villani for the Barra.

Although Alphonsus saw the great good which resulted from his mission in the diocese of Naples, and the extreme satisfaction of the Cardinal, it was yet with regret that he labored there. He thought continually of the want of so many other places, reflecting that the good could be as easily done by the numerous zealous and pious missionaries the Cardinal had at his own disposal. He prayed, he disciplined his body, and exhorted his brethren of Ciorani to join with him in prayer, that he might be delivered from Naples. Unhappy as he was on this subject, he would not displease the Cardinal, yet it was impossible to remain much longer in his present condition. He applied to the Canon James Fontana, a man of much merit, who had a great influence with the Cardinal, and explained to him his anxieties on the subject, requesting him to speak with his Eminence, in order, if possible, to obtain his consent to withdraw from these missions. The Cardinal was much annoyed, when the Canon first spoke with him, and declared that if Alphonsus left, he would discontinue the missions altogether. Fontana persisted however, and in the end persuaded him, that the missions could be carried on successfully without Alphonsus. But it was only on condition that F. Sarnelli should be left to superintend them, that the Cardinal at last consented to part with Alphonsus. This arrangement being made, F. Sarnelli remained at Naples until 1748.

Alphonsus took leave of the Archbishop, on the 3d of July. Mounted on a sorry mule, he traversed the streets of Naples with F. Villani, and alighted at the gate of the archiepiscopal palace; some were edified by his humility, while others mocked at him and laughed. He placed himself in an obscure corner of the ante-room, which was filled with gentlemen and dignified ecclesiastics. In a few minutes, the Cardinal came out himself, went straight to Alphonsus, took him by the hand, and led him into his chamber. He spoke of the missions, the good they had produced, and thanked him for the zeal he had shown in the cause, and testified the greatest regret at losing him. Alphonsus, on his part, thanked him for the favors he had received, and begged his continued protection for the Congregation. He then proceeded to Barra, where he had promised to make the novena of the Assumption, and afterwards, accompanied by F. Villani, returned to Ciorani.

The projects of the Dean of Nocera now began to take effect. Clergy and laity were equally desirous to have the Congregation established there, and the Bishop, Mgr. Dominicis, sighed for the day of their arrival. The Dean Contaldi gave the house and furniture, promising to give at his death a further legacy of three thousand ducats. He expressed his intention of living in the house with them; while they, on their part, promised to care for him as if he were one of themselves. All was finally arranged, to the great satisfaction of the inhabitants, in October, 1742. F. Sportelli was made rector, and the Fathers Mazzini and Jourdan, were appointed to be with him.

Having disembarrassed himself of Naples, Alphonsus set about giving missions in the destitute parts of the country. Here, as elsewhere, his ardent zeal and apostolic labors were crowned with the most astonishing success. God also furnished him occasions for exercising patience, meekness and humility. In one of the numberless villages where he gave missions, he obtained with great difficulty a lodging in a monastery, where the Archbishop had ordered him to be received. The Superior received him with a very bad grace, and took leave of him still more rudely. As soon as the mission was terminated, he turned him out of the monastery, notwithstanding his being attacked by fever in consequence of fatigue; he left the place without uttering a word of complaint. By order of the Archbishop, he went to St. Thecla, although he was scarcely convalescent. Here also he was rudely received by the Curate, who pretended he could not lodge him, and that he had sent a message to tell him so. Alphonsus tried in vain to calm his bad humor, and at length a notary, who was present, indignant at such a behaviour, gave him and his companions accommodation in his own house. This mission was attended with great results. Again at Correa, the Curate would not have a mission there, although the Archbishop of Amalfi had commanded it, and when Alphonsus arrived, he was refused admission to the house. Without being disconcerted, he quietly took refuge in a corner of the church. A gentleman, who witnessed the proceeding, received the missionaries into his own house, and this mission also had wonderful success.

While Alphonsus, after the course of these missions, always more and more disgusted with the world, did penance at Ciorani, and labored for the salvation of men, the world did its best to attract him again. His father, D. Joseph, could not endure the thought, that his brilliant talents should be employed in the country among poor peasants and shepherds; he wished to see him occupy a dignified position in the Church. To obtain this, he employed every artifice, but Alphonsus, on his part, was invulnerable to all attacks. "Speak no more to me," he wrote to him, "on the subject of the episcopate; even if you succeed in obtaining a bishopric for me, I will instantly refuse it. We have a rule in our Congregation to refuse all such dignities." D. Joseph desired to see his son raised to dignities in this world, while Alphonsus only wished to see his father obtain great glory in heaven. He wrote to him about this time as follows: "I beseech you, my dear father, to keep yourself more closely united with God. Confess often, and have your accounts ready, for our Lord will come at an hour when we least expect. Think of your advanced age, for who knows how soon you may be called from this world? That day will come, whether we watch or not: I recommend you to hear mass every day, for I fear much for your eternal salvation. I hope the Virgin Mary will assist you, but without your cooperation she will do nothing."

While affairs were prospering at Nocera, Mgr. Dominicis obtained the sanction for the establishment of the house, and in July, 1743, he issued the letters of authorization. As there was not yet at Pagani a house and church suitable for the new missionaries, the bishop granted them, in the mean time, the church of St. Dominic. When the first stone of the new establishment was laid, the chapter of the cathedral and the four curates of the Dean attended, the Dean himself giving the benediction. The construction was hardly commenced, when materials flowed in from all quarters, as if by miracle. Men and women strove to rival each other in contributing towards its erection; they labored with their own hands; ladies of quality, gentlemen, all united to hasten the progress of the work. Married, as well as unmarried, despoiled themselves of their jewels and ornaments to contribute towards the establishment, and the seven communes voted one hundred ducats.

About this time, when the people of Angri found out the good Alphonsus was doing everywhere, they insisted on having a mission, the place containing about five thousand souls. He went there in the month of November, and was received as an Apostle, each striving to procure some object that he had worn or touched. He lodged in the house of Laurence Rossi, whose daughter obtained from a lay-brother a pair of stockings tinged with his blood. She preserved them very devoutly, but a religious reproving her for doing so, Alphonsus being still alive, she gave them away to a poor man whose legs were swollen with dropsy. Some days after, he returned to the house entirely cured, and when she expressed her astonishment, he replied: "From the time you gave me the stockings, the swelling has disappeared." Alphonsus gathered in this mission the most wonderful fruits. They calculated there were in this place one hundred and twenty-eight women of the town; but when the mission was finished, there was no longer one, all had been reformed. More than three hundred young girls bid adieu to the world, and embraced the religious life, and a priest whose life had been scandalous, became a sincere penitent.

He had not yet been in the centre of the town of Nocera. But as soon as they heard the wonders he had accomplished at Angri, they solicited him to preach in the church of St. Matthew, a parish containing about six thousand souls. He exhorted the faithful of the parish to erect a statue to our Lady of Dolors, in the church. Immediately the women brought every thing they had most precious in gold and silver; the offerings were so numerous that a considerable sum remained, which was given to the poor. During this mission, the most glorious Virgin testified also her love for him by operating the most extraordinary conversions at his intercession. The evening he arrived, an unfortunate young man arose during the night to engage in a sinful transaction. He had a repugnance, however, to commit sin with the scapular about his neck: he took it off to place it in a hole in the wall, but when he extended his hand, he felt himself drawn back, and fled from the spot in terror. The following night the Blessed Virgin, wishing to recompense the slight homage paid to her scapular, appeared to him in a dream. "Miserable being," she said, "thou hadst respect for my scapular, and thou hadst no horror for offending my Son; to-morrow F. Alphonsus will come here to give a mission, go to confess to him, and amend thy life." The young man had never heard of Alphonsus, and knew nothing of the mission; but next morning he went to find a kind of fortune-teller, to have his dream interpreted, but before he opened his mouth, this person addressed him with: "Do you not know that F. Alphonsus has arrived to-day to give a mission?" When the young man heard the words "Alphonsus," and "mission," he was thunderstruck; he ran in haste to the dwelling of Alphonsus, and recounted to him the whole story. "So then," said Alphonsus, his eyes filling with tears, "our good Mother has sent you to me." He reconciled him with God, and his life ever after was most edifying.

When they opened the mission at Ciorani, they found the house much too small to receive the numbers of clergy and laity who came to make retreats. Alphonsus, therefore, at the suggestion of the Archbishop, proposed to extend the buildings, but F. Rossi, who was Superior, differing from him in opinion, because of their want of funds, "My father," said he, "we ought not to build as seculars do, who begin by amassing money, and then set to work; we ought to follow an opposite rule, we ought first to build, and afterwards expect from Providence what is necessary." F. Rossi obeyed, and animated by the confidence of Alphonsus, he began with only one sequin in his pocket, but he had never cause to regret his obedience, for, independently of his own liberality, the Archbishop wrote a circular to incite all the diocese to contribute towards the work. In consequence, considerable sums were forwarded to them, and these were not confined to the diocese. There happened also two remarkable instances of Providence. One day, F. Rossi being dispirited because of the expense, a young man presented himself to be received into the Congregation as a lay-brother, and F. Rossi admitted him provisionally. In withdrawing to prepare for admission, he put into the hands of the father some pieces of money wrapped up in a paper, asking him to say mass for him. The paper seemed to contain about ten shillings; but what was his surprise on opening it, to find a hundred gold ducats. He immediately sent after the young man, but he could not be heard of, and never was seen again. On another day, Alphonsus called together the young students, and ordered them to get up a petition to Jesus Christ in the Most Holy Sacrament, for the success of the newly begun building. When it was signed, he deposited it in the tabernacle, adjoining his own petition to that of the young clerics. Scarcely had he done this, when he was called to Naples, to vote for several gentlemen who wished to receive the order of Knighthood, at the seat of Porta Nuova. He instantly set out on a wretched mule, and arrived at Porta Nuova. On attempting to enter, the guard mistook him for some vagabond, and rudely repulsed him. His clothes were shabby, his beard unshorn, and his hair in disorder; he smiled at the mistake, and waited quietly until the chevalier in waiting perceived him, and advanced to meet him, not with the usual forms of salutation, but respectfully kissing his hand, to the great astonishment and confusion of the guard. On this occasion he received a present so considerable, that it sufficed to finish the building.

About this time, D. Joseph Liguori came to Ciorani to visit his son. He admired the edifying life they led, the silence which reigned, and the odor of sanctity which pervaded every thing. It filled his mind with thoughts of eternity, and detached his heart from worldly things. He felt a holy envy at the happiness of his son's life, pressed him to his bosom, and blessed the Lord for the benediction showered upon his house. He prolonged his stay at Ciorani, and every day more taken with the humble and peaceful life of the fathers, he took the resolution of forsaking the world, renouncing his rank, and living under the direction of his son, as an humble lay-brother, and besought admission with tears in his eyes. But Alphonsus, though delighted with the humility of his father, nevertheless, dissuaded him from his purpose, assuring him that it was not the will of God he should leave the world, but remain in it to edify by his example. He returned to Naples an altered man. Not content with being a pious and exemplary nobleman, he wished to become a saint; he lived like a fervent anchorite, praying in the church, meditating and reading the lives of the saints at home. He kept up a regular correspondence with his son, following his counsels in all that concerned his salvation.

The sun still shone which had enlightened with its beams the birth of the house of Nocera, but about this time it became obscured by clouds, and serious alarms succeeded to the dawn of its morning hopes. The devil feared the increase of a work so contrary to his designs, and attacked it immediately through the envy that began to fill the hearts of some in the neighborhood. They succeeded in alienating the minds of many, and diminishing the respect in which the public had held the missionaries, which ended at last in irritation and contempt. Some priests, with the gentry, continued to favor Alphonsus, but the fire was too strong to be put down by such feeble means. Twenty-five curates entered into a league with other priests; the religious mendicants of Nocera and Pagani joined them. They invited the fathers of Mount Olive, of the order of Citeaux, and those of Montevergine, to join the crusade, but they were horror-struck at the proposition. There remained but two of the curates of Pagani not opposed to the missionaries. When the plot was formed, the first move was to endeavor to prejudice the king, but God made known his displeasure in a singular manner. They employed a celebrated advocate to write out a memorial of their grievances; he took up a pen, it would not write; he tried a second and a third, but all to no purpose; he at length succeeded in writing a page, but when about to turn over the leaf, instead of throwing sand upon it, he lified the ink by mistake, and blotted all he had written. Struck by these mysterious accidents, he exclaimed: "Employ whom you will, but as for me, I will have nothing more to do with any business against these missionaries," and so saying, tore the paper in pieces. This fact made great impression on people of sense, but none on the enemies of the missionaries. They employed another advocate, and God permitted the affair to proceed. In order to gain their end with the king, they would fain have persuaded the bishop to concur in their views, but their efforts were vain. Indignant at their wicked designs, he shut his ears to all their representations; and to show how much he esteemed the missionaries, he, in spite of the malcontents, chose one of them for his own confessor, and when he visited his diocese, caused two of the fathers to accompany him to preach to the people and fill the other offices.

In spite of this check, the courage of their enemies was not abated, but rather increased. The friendship and protection of many excellent priests and wealthy gentlemen of the neighborhood, did not prevent them giving themselves up to all sorts of excess. If any of the fathers appeared in the town, he was assailed with taunts and loaded with insults. One day, while preparing to say mass in the parochial church, one of them had the amice pulled out of his hands. The lay-brothers had their share in these outrages whenever any of them appeared in the street. The Brother Anthony de Lauro, being one day digging in the garden, a man passing on the other side of the hedge, began to abuse him grossly; the brother continued to dig, as if he heard nothing, and this so irritated the man, that he jumped into the garden, ran up to him, and gave him a violent blow on the face. The holy brother showed no resentment, but knelt down and offered the other cheek; the man withdrew, covered with confusion. During the silence of night, they would come howling under the windows, singing indecent songs and using violent language. Alphonsus was then at Ciorani, but as soon as he heard what was going on at Nocera, he came thither with all speed. But how different was his reception now from what it had formerly been! A person came to the house and addressed him as a vagabond, accusing him of coming with his companions to seduce the inhabitants, to eat the bread of their children, and that being but miserable wretches, banished from their own country, they had thrown themselves on this country to devour it. At these odious words, Alphonsus humbled himself, but his humility redoubled the audacity of his adversary, who continued abusing him a long time. The petition addressed to the king had no success; he knew too well the merit of Alphonsus and his disciples, to allow himself to be deceived. No more success had another, addressed to the Viceroy, during the absence of the king in the Abbruzzi, his ministers knowing the probity of the missionaries and the favorable disposition of the king. Being thus defeated, they began to seek help in Nocera itself. They went to Contaldi, on whom Alphonsus leant, and who had aided him in the establishment at Pagani. Vice assumed the appearance of virtue so successfully, that he allowed himself to be gained, and began to repent of what he had done for Alphonsus. Knowing from what had happened at the Villa, that they were threatened with a similar misfortune, Alphonsus inquired diligently to know the will of God; he went to Naples to consult with those enlightened and pious friends, by whose advice he was guided in his difficulties. He went also to Castellamare to consult Mgr. Falcoja, and while they were talking, the bishop suddenly casting his eyes on a small statue of St. Michael, exclaimed: "It is the devil, it is the devil; hold firm, and continue to fight; God and St. Michael will protect you." He then advised him to dedicate the house and the church to the archangel Michael.

The tempest, far from abating, continued to rage with redoubled violence at Pagani. Alphonsus prayed and mortified himself, he besought the prayers of many holy souls, particularly of religious houses, and ceased not to go on with the missions wherever he was asked. His enemies continued their hostilities, and not content with attempting to ruin the house at Pagani, they desired to blot out the Congregation from the face of the earth. But their continual intrigues, their daily cavilings, at length aroused the zeal of several gentlemen of Nocera, Pagani, and other places in the neighborhood, who boldly declared themselves in favor of Alphonsus and his companions, and soon there was hardly one respectable family who did not take their part. The three general, and seven special syndics of the seven municipal communities of the district of Nocera, convoked therefore an assembly of the inhabitants, where all the communities, with the exception of those of Pagani, decided that the missionaries should be defended and upheld. When this manifestation of good feeling was reported to Alphonsus, he burst into tears at finding the good he had done among them appreciated by the most important class. But by this his enemies became more and more embittered, and in the beginning of June, 1744, they attacked him both at Naples and Rome: chiefly attempting to prove that the existence of the Congregation was contrary to civil and canon laws. When Alphonsus saw that with the branches they would destroy the roots also, he recalled the ancient spirit which had animated him at the bar, and with the civil law in his hand, he collected the means of defence, established the reasons which proved the rights of their cause, and showed in what circumstances a convent could be called lawful or illegal. At Rome, he knew equally well how to reduce his enemies to silence, confounding them by bulls of Sovereign Pontiffs, and by the authority of canon law. As to the calumnies against the lives of the members of his Congregation, he would not notice them, for they were sufficiently contradicted by public notoriety. The memorials he produced pleased the Sovereign at Naples, and obtained favor with the Pope and the Cardinals.

After having been defeated in this attempt, they had recourse to the Sacred Congregation of Bishops and Regulars; but the gentlemen of Pagani, Nocera, Corbara and St. Egidio, no sooner learned of this new attack, than they armed themselves to defend Alphonsus. Thirty-six of them undertook, the 16th of July, 1744, to charge themselves with the conduct of this affair at Rome, and to procure an advocate and procurator. At the same time, several curates, the chapter of the Cathedral, the clergy of Nocera, and twenty-three ecclesiastics of Pagani, declared themselves to the Pope, in favor of Alphonsus. Benedict XIV then occupied the Holy See, and hearing thus of an institution lately established in the Church, he wished to inquire into the merits of its founder. He accordingly instructed Cardinal Spinola to obtain exact information from the Bishop of Nocera. In consequence of this, Mgr. Dominicis replied the 3d of August. After having shown that the complaints of the malcontents were unfounded, and after having combatted their calumnies, he proceeded to the most important point, that is to say, the end for which Alphonsus proposed to found the Congregation, and finished by an eulogium on his sanctity, and the high estimation in which he was held by the Cardinal Archbishop of Naples and many other bishops.

The bad success of this last attempt was not sufficient to make the malcontents renounce their enterprise. They got possession of the royal decree, and by bribing the underlings of office, they altered the words from "the king permits the erection of a house with a church," to "the king permits the erection of a house without a church," and with this in their hands, they hastened to the commissary of the king, who was persuaded that Alphonsus in building a church had gone beyond his limits. On the 16th day of July, the commissary despatched an order to Nocera, to discontinue the building at Pagani. This time, the wicked triumphed, and Alphonsus was in great embarrassment, not knowing how to proceed. He sent F. St. Severino to Naples, to the Minister of State, the Marquis Brancone, to inform him of the obstacle, and request his assistance to remove it. The Marquis was astonished when he heard of this, for he remembered that the king had expressly given leave to build a church. He ordered one of the clerks of the bureau to produce the register, and wrote in it with his own hand, "a house with a church," saying with a tone of severity, for he suspected the fraud that had been committed, "I know the intention of the king," and ordered him to go instantly to inform the commissary, and tell him the true state of the case. It was necessary to submit, and on the 21st of July, an order was transmitted to the Syndic of Pagani, to permit the progress of the building.

In spite of all their successive defeats, the malcontents were not proof against a new temptation, which, like their former fraud, turned to their own confusion. Beaten at Naples, repulsed at Rome, they appealed to the tribunals. Contaldi would not appear against them in person, but a process was commenced in the name of his sister, to compel the missionaries to abandon the house. She forced herself unexpectedly into the house, accompanied by twenty other persons and two notaries, before whom she declared that the house was her property. Alphonsus, when he heard of this, came immediately to Nocera to consult on what was to be done, when the bishop and other friends advised him not to yield. A celebrated advocate undertook the cause, and the pretended proprietorship of the sister was soon exposed, to the confusion of those who had attempted to play off such a trick. But their resentment, far from being checked, exhibited itself in every thing that could cause annoyance to the fathers. One day, a person of rank, belonging to the clergy, said to Alphonsus: "If you will act the thief, and rob people by force, why do you not go to the highways." "Blessed be God," meekly replied Alphonsus, "I have left my house to be treated as a robber at Nocera!"

In the month of August, they made another attempt at Rome, but warned by experience, they no longer attacked Alphonsus, but confined themselves to defaming his companions. This roused all the most respectable inhabitants of Nocera and Pagani in their favor. The three general Syndics took upon themselves the expense of defending the Congregation at Rome. On the other hand, Benedict XIV, again charged Cardinal Spinola to make new inquiries of Cardinal Spinelli at Naples, and also of the Archbishop of Salerno, Mgr. Rossi. All this was the work of Providence, in order that the Congregation might become known to the Sovereign Pontiff and the world at large; in reality, the brilliant testimony rendered by these two dignitaries of the Church, hastened the approbation given by the Court of Rome in favor of the new Institute.

In the mean time, Mgr. Dominicis attempted to arrange the affair by arbitration; the proposal was agreed to by both parties; but when Contaldi stated that he would take upon himself the debts contracted, provided the missionaries evacuated the premises and quitted Pagani, and, if they would not, he would shut up the church of St. Dominic, and force them to live as simple individuals, the bishop in the greatest indignation broke up the meeting, and turning to the fathers said: "Prosecute your cause at Rome and at Naples, trust in Cardinal Spinelli; God will protect you." Mgr. Dominicis died on the 22d of August of this year, and to the great dismay of the disaffected, he was succeeded by Mgr. Volpe, who was equally well disposed towards the missionaries as his predecessor had been.

CHAPTER XIV.

Alphonsus founds the Houses of Iliceto and Caposele, and establishes a Novitiate. His first Publications. He seeks to have his Congregation approved by the King.

WHILE the house of Pagani was thus agitated by the tempest, and Alphonsus with his companions, drank, during eight months, the bitter chalice of tribulation, God opened a new field to him, destined to receive seed no less productive than that which had hitherto been sown. The prince of Castellaneta, D. Matthias Miroballo, of Aragon, besought Alphonsus to visit his fief of Iliceto, to give the inhabitants the instruction and consolation of which they were so much in want; the Bishop of Bovino, Mgr. Lucci, dispatched at the same time a canon of his Cathedral, James Casati, to join in the invitation. Alphonsus, acceding to the demand, arrived there with his companions, on the 12th of November. This mission had the usual success. But the Canon had a further object in view. At the corner of a wood, called the Vallin-Vincoli, on a small elevation, stood an ancient church, dedicated to the Virgin, under the title of Mary of Consolation. It had once belonged to the Augustinians, and in the church was a large painting of the Virgin Mary, for which the faithful of the neighborhood had a great devotion. There the Canon had resolved on establishing a community. Alphonsus however hesitated to accept the proposal, because the distance between the church and any inhabited place was very considerable; but when visiting the picture, he was so captivated, that the Fathers Cafaro and St. Severino easily persuaded him to accept the offer, to the great joy of all the people, and to settle there at once. Near Iliceto there were vast domains of the crown, where thousands of men were employed in keeping flocks and herds, and cultivating the ground; a great number of whom rarely received any spiritual assistance, and, even on feast days, had seldom an opportunity of hearing mass. Touched by their destitution, Alphonsus sent his companions out in different directions, to distribute to them the bread of life; and he looked forward to the house of Iliceto becoming the place from whence these abandoned people would derive spiritual succor in time to come. His Majesty gave his approbation for this new house, on the 9th of January, 1745.

Having arranged the affairs of this house, he assembled his companions, and departed towards the end of the same month, for Madugno, where D. Dominic Fiori, professor of music in the Cathedral of Naples, had invited him to give a mission, being determined to found a house in this his native place, having himself no heir to succeed him. This mission was a difficult one, and cost much labor and fatigue; it lasted forty days, so great were the wants of the inhabitants. It was in this mission, that Alphonsus, one morning, while celebrating mass in the church of a monastery, was raised several feet from the ground, as the religious attested. As for the foundation of a house in the place, he advised Fiori to make arrangements with the fathers of St. Vincent of Paul, having heard that the king had granted them an establishment in the neighborhood, and not wishing to interfere with this foundation.

After their return from Madugno, Alphonsus and his companions suffered much in their new establishment at Iliceto. Besides their voluntary penances, they experienced on all sides suffering and affliction. A priest who was there during that winter, said in a letter, "the bread was of rye, mixed with bran, black as a coal, and ill baked, and sometimes they had none at all, and were obliged to accept the charity of an old man, who lived on the produce of his goats and the culture of a small field near his cottage. For pottage, they had a species of broth or panada, or bruised beans, so old that they had the color of bread. They never tasted meat, except when some sheep or cow died of exhaustion. They had no fruits but wild chestnuts or crab apples. They rarely had wine, and then but in small quantity, and very bad. On feast days, they had a large cake made of the same flour as the bread, but seasoned with a little cheese and salt, for sugar or pepper were luxuries they could not afford. They had no linen, and no money to buy it. They were almost shirtless, and could only change once in two or three weeks. There never was a religious house where greater poverty reigned: their clothes were ragged and patched. . . . The house was an old convent, suppressed during the pontificate of Innocent XI, and but a mass of ruins. The wind blew more keenly within than without, the walls were full of cracks, the partitions brick without mortar. The windows were of oiled paper instead of glass. The roof was bad, the cells without ceiling, so that the snow covered the beds during winter; in short, the misery was so great, that one of the fathers lost courage, and returned to the world." Among all these miseries, or rather in consequence of them, Alphonsus had the misfortune to lose his dear Vitus Curzius. During the month of July, he was sent out to beg for a little corn. Although the good brother was unaccustomed to traverse the country during the burning heats, he nevertheless obeyed cheerfully; but one evening, being refused a lodging where he had applied for one, he slept in the field, and, during the night, was seized with a violent fever. Not being able to drag himself to his convent, he was taken into the house by a charitable priest, and after forty-nine days of intense suffering, went to receive the reward of his labors in the mansions of the blessed. This death afflicted Alphonsus deeply, though he was consoled on the other hand, by the reflection that he had died rich in merits and virtues. An abridgment of his life has been written by Alphonsus himself.

The fury of the disaffected of Pagani was not abated, and new plots were invented to ruin the missionaries. Contaldi, finding himself disappointed in obtaining his object through the instrumentality of others, threw off the mask, and openly attacked them. Scarcely had Alphonsus returned from the Pouille, when he openly revoked the donation he had made in their favor, and in concert with his sister, called them to appear before the council of the king. Not knowing how to justify his steps, he pretended that the missionaries had deceived him in usurping the title of Congregation, when they had neither been recognised by the king nor the Pope; he demanded, in consequence, that they should be forbidden to build, protesting that he had made the donation not for a religious community, but for a college of priests. But the royal council, having sent an auditor to verify the facts, the claims of Contaldi were found insufficient, and on the 11th of January, 1745, the auditor, in the name of the council, confirmed the missionaries in the possession of the property, the donation being found valid and inviolable.

This disappointment did not abate his animosity. He presented a claim to the king, filled with malignity rather than reason. But the Syndic of Pagani and three other Syndics, undertook the defence, and the indubitable integrity of Alphonsus and his companions, made his Majesty withstand all his numerous attempts against them. It was plain, however, that these men acted entirely at the instigation of the devil. For they introduced two barrels of gun-powder under the foundation of the house, and had not one of their accomplices, stung by remorse of conscience, revealed the plot, the whole would have been destroyed. From that moment, they were obliged to keep a strict watch nightly. Alphonsus was then at Iliceto, and far from being discouraged by this barbarous attempt, his confidence became greater from having escaped so many imminent dangers. Until now, the fathers had lived under the same roof with Contaldi, and were, therefore, placed under a continual restraint. At last, on the 24th of September, 1745, they resolved to remove to the new building, without heeding the risk they ran from damp and other inconveniences. When Alphonsus, at Iliceto, heard of their installation, he rejoiced exceedingly, and wrote to urge them to a stricter observance of the rule, which had been somewhat interrupted by all the previous proceedings, assuring them that God would bless them and make them become saints, only inasmuch as they observed the rule in its strictness.

The malcontents, provoked to see them established in their new house, again conspired against them, and obtained an order from the council, forbidding them to do any thing new. Their intention was thus to interdict their entrance into the church of St. Dominic, where they had till now, exercised their ministry, and to prevent the completion of the little church yet in progress of building, hoping that by depriving them thus of every opportunity of performing the functions of their ministry, they would force them definitely to abandon the foundation. Informed of all this, on the evening before the day on which they expected to receive the formal orders, Father Sportelli besought some gentlemen of Nocera to detain the king's officer for one night only. This was done, as he had desired, and during the night he sent for the workmen, and in spite of the protestations of the architect, he boldly took away the props, smoothed the earth, erected a portable altar, and arranged, as well as he could, a sort of confessional. They ornamented the altar and the walls with hangings and tapestry, placed garlands and artificial flowers about it, and having, the evening before, obtained permission to bless the church, at day-break, he celebrated mass, preached, confessed, and gave communion to the people. During the proceedings, the officer arrived, followed by a crowd, and calling for F. Sportelli, and those of the household, he declared to them by order of the king, that no one must have the temerity to attempt any thing new, at the risk of incurring the penalties mentioned in the decree. "We will do nothing new," replied F. Sportelli, "and we will conform to the order you bring, but I protest that this edifice is a church; the Holy Sacrifice has been celebrated in it, we have preached in it, and in it the holy sacraments have been administered to the people." Thus they were outwitted in their attempt, and hell had to yield the victory.

While Alphonsus was at Iliceto, another circumstance occurred to second his zeal for the salvation of the people. Benedict XIV, convinced of the great good produced by missions, conceived the project of reforming, by means of them, the whole kingdom of Naples. By a brief dated the 8th of September, 1745, he delegated Cardinal Spinelli to superintend this work, with full powers to send whom he would. Many bishops, upon this, solicited him to send into their dioceses Alphonsus and his missionaries, to which the Cardinal agreed, well knowing the good they did. When the time of the vintage was over, Alphonsus, having received the necessary commission from the Cardinal, and provided with particular graces from the holy Father, began his mission in the diocese of Bovino. At Foggia, the capital of the Pouille, a terrible example ot divine justice occurred, and served as a powerful warning to sinners. One of the Fathers went through the public places to call the people to the church. Happening to pass before a tavern, he invited the drinkers to take part in the mission. A tipsy fellow, holding up his glass, called out: "My Father, would you like to see what is my mission?" and putting it to his lips, he instantly dropped down dead. Another circumstance which happened, gave a high idea of the sanctity of Alphonsus. One evening he was preaching before the image of the blessed Virgin of Seven Veils, which they had exposed on the altar. When he spoke of the glories of the Mother of God, the people believed they saw an angel rather than a man. A bright ray of light darted from the image, and rested on the countenance of Alphonsus, who, at the same moment, fell into an ecstasy, and was elevated several feet into the air. At this spectacle the people uttered such loud cries of joy, that crowds from a distance ran tumultuously towards the church. More than four thousand persons witnessed this miracle.

In a rich and commercial town, great numbers of charitable persons are to be found. Many purses, therefore, were opened to Alphonsus, who earnestly sought out the most necessitous. Young girls were succored, whose poverty placed them in danger; others were placed in orphan houses. Asylums were procured for repentant sinners, and the aged were assisted in their necessities. Christian charity reigned in all hearts, and the town was delivered from many sources of sin.

During the mission at Troy, one day, when on the point of mounting the pulpit, Alphonsus was told of his father's death. He remained some time in prayer, and then recommended him to the prayers of the people. He had heard of his illness, but was so much occupied in his apostolic labors, that he sacrificed the feelings of nature to his God, and continued the mission. When at St. Agatha, he was seized with fever; but this did not prevent his preaching, and when he appeared in the pulpit, the sight of him alone produced compunction in the hearts of the people. After this mission, he was called to Iliceto, the Canon Casati being dangerously ill. Unable to ride because of his fever, he was obliged to take a carriage, and arrived the evening before the Canon expired. He had left all he possessed to the Most Holy Virgin Mary of Consolation, and at his request was buried in the church, at the feet of the Virgin. Alphonsus, full of gratitude for his donation, celebrated his funeral with the utmost magnificence, and had one hundred ducats distributed to the poor.

From the month of March, 1746, a great drought had desolated the Pouille, and the seeds sown were almost destroyed. The inhabitants of Foggia besought Alphonsus to give a novena in honor of the Blessed Virgin, knowing how much he was beloved by her. He was still at Iliceto, ill of a fever, but when he heard how afflicted they were at Foggia, he immediately set out, and was received as an angel from heaven. The novena had scarcely commenced, when his fever suddenly left him; the rain fell in abundance, the seed was saved, and produced a rich harvest. During his sojourn in this town, God prepared the foundation of another house in the diocese of Conza. The Archbishop, Mgr. Nicolai, regretted to see himself at the head of a vast province in the greatest want of spiritual assistance. When he had learned the services the Congregation had rendered to so many dioceses, he sent immediately the archpriest Rossi, to meet Alphonsus at Foggia. He was by no means anxious to embrace the proposal, circumstances not seeming favorable, but at the request of F. Villani, he consented to give a mission there, in order to see more clearly the will of God. During the mission, on the third of June, he went with several gentlemen to visit the church which was offered him, and which bore the name of Mater Domini. He was pleased with the situation, being in the midst of an archdiocese, surrounded by many other dioceses in great want of spiritual aid.

The Archbishop being then at Calabritto, a few miles off, Alphonsus went to visit him. Mounted on a mule, he arrived at the house of the family del Plato, where the Archbishop was staying. Hearing he was at dinner, he went into a small chapel in a wing of the palace, to say his office. While there, the eldest son came to shut the door, and seeing a man covered with rags, and with an unshorn beard, he took him for a vagabond, who was waiting to beg from the Archbishop, and told him to go out, as he was about to shut the door. "Would you have the goodness to wait until I finish vespers," said Alphonsus. "Go out instantly," said the young man, "it is only yesterday we had a napkin stolen, it would be too much to have another stolen to-day." Alphonsus was forced to go out, and finish his vespers in the street. After some time, he presented himself at the palace, and the Archbishop, hearing of his arrival, came out and received him with every mark of esteem. The young del Plato looked confounded, and his confusion increased, when he found Alphonsus was a noble Neapolitan gentleman, and Superior of a mission. Alphonsus appeared not to notice the young man's confusion, but continued the conversation, and after having arranged a meeting at Caposele, he returned in time for the evening sermon.

God showered down many benedictions on this mission. The humility, the modesty, the contempt of himself, shown by Alphonsus, touched all hearts as much as his sermons. At this time he suffered such violent tooth-ache as to cause convulsions. Notwithstanding this, one evening he spoke for two hours, and at last overpowered by fatigue, he had to be carried home, from total inability to walk. Generally, in his sermons, he seemed to be ravished out of himself, and one evening, while he preached, God made him see in spirit what was passing at Iliceto. "We are occupied here with the mission," he said, "and at this moment the devil is tormenting my poor children at Iliceto." Next morning, a lay-brother came to see him, and spoke with him for three hours of the miseries they were enduring there.

The Archbishop came to Caposele, and arrived during a sermon on the blessed Virgin. He was so much touched that he wept, and determined to assist daily at the sermons. The archpriest Rossi arrived at this time, with several other gentlemen, who resolved on contributing towards the establishment of the Congregation there. All seemed to go well, but it was necessary that the devil should attempt to overturn it. A party among the clergy, addressed to the Archbishop a protestation against the new project. When Alphonsus heard of this, he said: "I like to see opposition, it is a mark that the devil apprehends defeat, but God will triumph." When the Archbishop went to the hermitage, accompanied by the gentlemen friendly to the measure, a priest, a very learned man, who had great influence with both clergy and people, attended to oppose the foundation in the name of the chapter. Having entered the church to visit the Blessed Virgin, as he approached the altar dedicated to the divine Mother, he was struck with apoplexy, and his mouth was twisted on one side. He recognised the just punishment, and turning towards the Virgin, said: "Mother of my God, I protest that I have no longer the intention of opposing the foundation." No sooner had he uttered these words, than he recovered, and his mouth resumed its natural position. He immediately joined the others, and far from resisting, he now seconded the proposal with all his eloquence. On the 4th of June, 1746, the establishment of the Congregation was decided upon. When the news spread at Caposele, that the missionaries were to be established in the diocese, every one testified the most unbounded joy. A noble family in the neighborhood put their forests at their disposal, to supply the wood for the buildings. The inhabitants had another consolation in the fulfilment of the prophecy of St. John Joseph of the Cross, that at the end of twenty years, a devout and zealous community of missionaries would be established among them. The twenty years had just expired.

In Pagani, they were not yet left unmolested. The Grand Council having repulsed them, Contaldi tried to obtain satisfaction from the commissary of the king, and this magistrate, being deceived, had ordered the sequestration of certain rents that had been assigned to them, and that they should be given to others. To embroil matters still more, Contaldi made to a priest who was related to him, a donation of a certain property he had already given to the missionaries, and by these measures ceased not to keep them in continual disquiet. Alphonsus could not see without sorrow the vexations his companions had to endure, but this did not lessen his zeal; he continued to give missions in the country round about, which were always attended with the greatest success, vice disappearing, and virtue reigning in its stead.

Towards the end of December, 1746, Foggia invited him again, and he eagerly yielded to the request; but on his arrival, he found that a theatre with foreign comedians had been opened, and that certain gentlemen had bound themselves to support it. This new occasion of sin grieved him exceedingly, and he did all in his power to engage them to send the comedians away, but without success; upon which he left the town, and when they would persuade him to stay, he replied: "We cannot at the same time serve God and the devil. Foggia will not listen to me, but God will lay his heavy hand upon her, and chastise her for her libertinism." Scarcely had he departed, when the town was shaken with a violent earthquake; they sent after him, but he would not return at that time.

The building of the new house at Caposele was now begun, and carried on with great ardor. On the 1st of May, 1748, the first stone was blessed by Mgr. Amati, and the gentlemen commenced to superintend the different works, each placing himself at the head of a division, and in the evening arranging the work for the next day. The Blessed Virgin deigned to testify her approbation of this establishment, and to show in a special manner, that the missionaries were her children. There lived in a neighboring village a wretched being, loaded with sin, who had for three years been confined to bed by a most painful illness; every night he saw the devil, under the form of a goat, place himself on his breast, and press his throat and his sides until he was almost choked. One morning when he awoke, he saw the Blessed Virgin appear in his chamber, radiant with glory, and accompanied by two angels. "My son," she said to him, "how hast thou still the boldness to live in sin? quickly change thy life; to-morrow thou shalt see my children of the house of Mater Domini. Confess, and repent of thy sins, and Jesus will pardon thee." The vision disappeared, and the sinner felt re-animated, but without knowing what to think of what he had heard, for he knew nothing of the mission, nor of the establishment at Caposele. Next day, he heard the bells ringing, and on asking what it was, they replied that the missionaries had arrived; full of joy, he said he must see one of them instantly. F. Matthew Criscuolo went to him, when he related what had occurred, and made his confession amid torrents of tears. The father asked him if he had been in the habit of practising any devotion to the Blessed Virgin; he replied, that he had made a vow to recite the Rosary daily, and that he had never omitted it. He died during the mission, giving evident signs of a true repentance.

Until now, the Congregation had not had a regular novitiate. Hitherto they had received only clerics, who had, in a manner, been professed before they became novices, subdeacons only being admitted; and these made their novitiate in following Alphonsus from village to village. A year before, they had decided on admitting young men of eighteen, as being less filled with the spirit of the world, and consequently more ready to receive the impressions of grace. Alphonsus then thought of establishing the novitiate in the house of Iliceto, but because of the extreme poverty of this house, the young people were discouraged, looked back, and withdrew their hand from the plough, some even, not having the courage to declare their weakness to F. Cafaro, who was master of novices, fled secretly, escaping by the windows, as the door was shut. Afflicted by the inconveniences of this house, and the inconstancy of the novices, he removed the novitiate to Ciorani, the 1st of February, 1748. God blessed the arrangement, and there were soon twenty novices under F. Villani, whose conduct caused great consolation to Alphonsus.

It was at Iliceto Alphonsus first began to write and publish. Until then he had labored only for the countries in which he was placed, but this was a field too narrow for his burning zeal. He wished that all Christians should profit by the reflections he had made. He had long been groaning over the indifference of men, and their estrangement from the adorable mystery of the Eucharist; he resolved to publish the sentiments with which he was penetrated towards the Beloved of his soul, and arrange them in the form of visits for each day of the month, and as his affection for the most Holy Virgin was only inferior to that he bore to her Son, he published also his sentiments of affection for her, in order to induce the faithful to love and serve her. This little work was every where received with applause, and fully answered the purpose for which it was intended, for before long, almost every one had it in his hands, not only in the kingdom of Naples, but throughout Italy. In 1777, Alphonsus received a French translation of it, taken from the fiftieth Italian edition. Next he published another little work, entitled "Reflections and Affections on the Passion of Jesus Christ." Since he had embraced the ecclesiastical state, he had taken St. Theresa for his special advocate, and often in his spiritual wants had experienced the efficacy of her intercession. Desirous to see her honored, he published several meditations, in form of a Novena, in which were comprised all the beautiful things that could be said in her praise. In order to awaken the Bishops, he composed a little work on the precise obligations of the episcopate, which he transmitted to all the bishops in Italy, many of whom wrote to him, thanking him and complimenting him on the occasion. About this time also, he had publicly proclaimed his opinion regarding certain cases of conscience. This gave offence to a priest belonging to a religious house in the Pouille, who, instead of discussing the subject, wrote to him thus: "Who art thou, who comest out of the woods, with the pretension of making thyself Doctor, and giving laws to others?" And having nothing else to say, he treated him as a heretic, and accused him of condemning vocal prayer. Alphonsus replied, and, having abundantly refuted the falsehood, finished his letter, by thanking his accuser for the advice he had given him, without testifying the least resentment.

When the missions in the Pouille were finished, Alphonsus went in April, 1747, to Ciorani; there he found the novitiate filled with virtuous young men and priests, eminent for learning and sanctity. He then returned to Pagani, where he found the church frequented by persons of all conditions, the pious practices taught by the Congregation existing in all their vigor, and a confraternity of artisans, among whom were found persons eminent for their sanctity. The success of the two houses was a subject of great consolation for him, making him shed tears of joy. But, remembering that the argument constantly brought forward by his adversaries was, that the Congregation was not authorized by the king, in order to deprive them of this pretext and insure the existence of the houses already founded, he resolved on going to Naples, determined, in spite of every difficulty, to obtain the necessary authorization.

Arriving at Naples in the month of June, he immediately addressed himself to the Marquis Brancone, Minister of State. Before he would hear him say a word, the Marquis first announced his determination of making him a Bishop. Alphonsus, confounded by the proposition, said: "If you love me, never again speak to me of such a thing. I have abjured the world; its dignities can only inspire me with horror." He said, besides, so much, that at length the Marquis promised to torment him no more on this subject. After having recommended to him the interests of the Congregation, he addressed himself to the Chamberlain, to obtain for him an audience of the king. He had not long to wait; for one day as he was walking in the cloisters of St. Catherine, occupied in saying his office, he was told the king waited for him. He wore then, as usual, an old patched cassock, and his beard unshaven; it was, however, in this miserable condition, that he ran in all haste to the palace. Introduced to his Majesty, he exposed to him the multitude of souls deprived of spiritual succor, how ardently he desired to remedy such an evil, the zeal with which his companions burned, and the reforms they had already produced in so many dioceses; but that the missionaries could not sustain themselves in a position so precarious, and being daily engaged in struggles which threatened their existence, it was necessary that his Majesty should now recognise their institute for a regular Congregation. He presented to his Majesty the rules of the Institute, explaining them in a few words. The heart of the pious monarch was touched; he took notes with his own hand, and placed the rules, with the petition, in the hands of Mgr. Celestine Guliano, his grand almoner, recommending him to examine them and make his report without delay.

F. Vincent Mandarini, Superior of the Congregation of the Most Holy Sacrament, soon learned what was going on, and more anxious than ever for a re-union, went to Ciorani, and in the name of himself and his companions, offered to embrace unreservedly the rule of Alphonsus, and to submit to his authority. Alphonsus refused to agree to this. "He who has been accustomed to possess and to command, will have much repugnance to see himself poor and deprived of his liberty. To-day, before he makes the vow of obedience, he is ready to sacrifice his own will; but once bound, he will begin to repent of having submitted his opinion to another. You are sincere in wishing to submit to me, but be sure, to-morrow your fervor will yield on reflection; the remembrance of your liberty will torment you and your brethren, and the contagion of insubordination and regret would seize upon my own Congregation. It is thus misfortune would menace two communities, and we ought to guard against this." Thus repulsed by Alphonsus, Mandarini applied to the grand almoner, and through influential persons, persuaded him to endeavor to promote the re-union. The grand almoner represented to Alphonsus, that he ought not to reject the proposal, and on his explaining to him the motives which inclined him to refuse, the almoner cut him short by saying: "I wish it." Although much alarmed, Alphonsus did not give up hope, but doubting his own judgment, he had recourse to prayer, yielding himself entirely to the will of God.

At the same time, he began to look about for some influential person, who would interfere in his favor with the king and the grand almoner. He was often not well received; many refused him an audience, and others listened coldly;

and if he was received once, he was refused admittance when he came again. One day he had with difficulty been permitted, by the valets of a certain prince, to wait in the ante-chamber, when the princess, who knew him, happened to pass. Seeing him so poor and ragged in appearance, she exclaimed: "How dirty you are!" "I do not understand you," said Alphonsus. "Ah, then," she said, turning her back upon him, "you are from Calabria." Many others received him, however, with marks of profound respect; in either case, he was unmoved, always calm and serene.

Notwithstanding all the pains taken by Alphonsus, the grand almoner declared on the 21st of August, against his petition for authorization. This declaration afflicted Alphonsus, yet he did not lose courage. He put his confidence in God, and tried to obtain from heaven what man refused. The different houses of the Congregation commenced regular prayers, masses were said, and they exposed the Blessed Sacrament in the evening. Many religious houses united with them in prayer, while they themselves redoubled their penances and mortifications. Alphonsus went five times to obtain an audience of the almoner, but was always refused. He went a sixth time, and was at last admitted, when he knew so well how to plead his cause, that his Lordship could not refuse promising to protect him. He, in consequence, placed before the king what he considered the advantages that would result from authorizing the Congregation; but in the event of its being authorized, he wished them to unite with that of Mandarini. Upon this point the council of state was divided, and also upon certain other conditions not very satisfactory, so that at last it was decided the affair should stand over, and continue to rest on its present precarious basis. Alphonsus, learning this decision, bowed his head, adoring the will of God, and only said: "Fiat voluntas tua." That night he was unable to sleep. The king regretted this decision, and in order to comfort him, sent a message by the Marquis Brancone, bidding him rest assured of his protection, and continue to labor with the same zeal to promote the glory of God and the good of the state. Mandarini on the other hand, ceased to insist on the union of the two Congregations.

Alphonsus made yet another attempt in favor of the Congregation, but it also fell to the ground. He explained to the king the impossibility of giving missions in many parts of the country where the spiritual destitution was great, because of their own poverty, and the poverty of the people, and requested his majesty to make them some allowance for the purpose. "The demand is just," said the king, "we must try to furnish them with some subsidy." It was accordingly arranged, that they should have the surplus revenues of the chapels of the Castelle de Sangro in the Abruzzi; but the individuals who had the management, pretended there were no surplus revenues; they consequently got nothing.

During his stay at Naples, he devoted himself to every work that could promote the glory of God, and husbanded his time so well, that not a moment was lost. He often went, at the request of the director of the seminary, to animate the young people by his exhortations. He frequently visited convents of nuns, who desired to have the affairs of their conscience regulated by him, and gave retreats in different monasteries. He often visited also the college of the Holy Family, established to promote the conversion of China, delighting to animate the young men with love for Jesus Christ, and zeal for the salvation of souls. But while he was enjoying these delightful labors, a storm was preparing to overtake him. The church of Palermo became vacant in the July of this year by the death of Mgr. Rossi, and his Majesty insisted that Alphonsus should succeed him in that see, saying to Marquis Brancone: "The Pope makes good promotions, but I will make one still better than the Pope." The Marquis was pleased with the election, and applauded it as a divine inspiration, and having sent for Alphonsus, made known to him his Majesty's determination. He was, as it were, thunderstruck, and with tears begged him to return his grateful thanks to the king for the honor he proposed conferring on him, but to explain the vow he had made to refuse all dignities, and the ruin it would cause, were he to abandon his brethren at such a juncture. The Marquis, seeing the affliction of Alphonsus, entered into his feelings, and promised to help him with the king; but the prince would take no refusal. This alarmed Alphonsus; he foresaw the king would be supported by the Pope, and the thought of being forced to accept the dignity, left him no repose by night or by day, and he wrote to F. Cafaro, his director, that he would sooner conceal himself in the depth of the forest, than be made bishop. He wrote at the same time to all the houses of the Congregation to pray for him, and had recourse to many holy souls and religious houses to help him by their prayers, while he redoubled his austerities and penances. During the whole month the king persevered in his resolution, Alphonsus was in a continual fright. At length the Marquis succeeded in persuading his Majesty, that he was far more useful as a missionary, than he ever could be as Archbishop of Palermo; and he consequently abandoned his resolution, though with much regret.

Alphonsus had left Naples to go to Ciorani for a few days, when, immediately on his return, he was requested to preach the Novena of the Assumption in the church of St. John Major. Although unprepared, he had not the courage to refuse, and the result was as miraculous as usual. Each of his sermons occupied not less than one hour and a half. During this Novena, thousands of souls awoke from sin, and penetrated with a lively repentance, returned to God. Towards the end of September, he returned to Nocera.

We ought not to omit here two instances of the true apostolical liberty of Alphonsus, both of which happened during his stay at Naples. The Superior of the Apostolic Mission had invited him to give a retreat. During his discourses on this occasion, he spoke to them of the obligation they were under to make known Christ crucified, and not to preach to make themselves known. He condemned the measured style and far-fetched expressions which some made use of, above all, when treating of moral subjects, or the lives of the Saints. He spoke with vehemence against a celebrated preacher lately dead, who, he said, by his manner of preaching had showed himself an enemy of souls and a traitor to the word of God; and he blamed some among them who strove to imitate him. "Fill your discourses," he said, "with evangelical truths, without embarrassing yourselves with vain ornaments, which produce no fruit, but exhaust the preacher in seeking for them." This language offended some of the young missionaries at first, but afterwards they recognized the truth of what he had said, and were filled with a salutary confusion. At another time, he was celebrating mass in the church of the Fathers of the Oratory; when, turning towards the assistant to give communion, he observed a gentleman seated in the choir with his legs crossed. After having said: "Agnus Dei," and seeing this person still sitting and showing no sign of reverence towards the Holy Sacrament, he exclaimed: "Have you lost the use of your limbs, that you cannot kneel?" The gentleman, quite confused, immediately knelt, but excessively provoked, he began to cough and make different noises until the end of mass, when he ran hastily to the sacristy to ask what wretched priest had said mass; but when he heard the name of Alphonsus de Liguori, he felt greatly ashamed.

At the beginning of the year 1748, Alphonsus returned to Naples. Marquis Brancone then informed him, that the king was dissatisfied, that the council of state had refused his request, and advised him to take advantage of the favorable feelings of the monarch towards him, and obtain a subsidy for the Congregation. Instead of this, Alphonsus presented a new petition to obtain the confirmation of his institute, saying to the Marquis, that he wished for nothing else; a mark of disinterestedness which pleased him, and induced him to present the petition himself to the king; but the political views which directed Tanucci, the then minister, did not accord with the pious views of the king, and again the business fell to the ground.

He was scarcely twelve days in Naples, when he was seized with an asthma so violent that he could not speak, and was almost dead. He was unable to say mass for some weeks, and had to keep his bed, yet, he nevertheless continued to give advice and consolation to those who came to him on affairs of conscience; the house was never empty. Immediately after his recovery, he began again to preach and give spiritual exercises. It was about this time that he became the object of a very malicious calumny. When speaking one day of the extreme goodness shown by our Saviour in the Sacrament of the altar, where he is always ready to give audience, he used the following words of St. Theresa: "It is not thus with kings on earth; they give audience only a few times in the course of the year, and how much it costs one to obtain an audience! And then no one can speak as he would wish to do, nor with the same confidence with which all may go to Jesus Christ in this sacrament, and at any moment." A certain person present construed these words into an insult to the king, and to ingratiate himself with his majesty, added all that his wickedness could suggest, and represented Alphonsus as a man discontented with the king, and who would misrepresent him to his subjects. The accusation was listened to by Marquis Tanucci, who, being unacquainted with his integrity, threatened to banish him from Naples. The affair became public, and Alphonsus was looked upon as a guilty person about to be banished for disrespect to his sovereign. It was not until six days after, that he heard of all this. He went immediately to the Cardinal, to implore his protection, and then to Marquis Brancone, both of whom, convinced of his respect for his sovereign, bade him continue his apostolic labors, and fear nothing, assuring him that the king knew him too well to lend an ear to such a report. They both spoke to Tanucci, who was soon undeceived, and from that time held him in the highest esteem and veneration.

Through Marquis Brancone he obtained another audience of the king, when he strove to convince him of the necessity of his approbation for the new-born Congregation, in order to sustain it against the attacks of its enemies. The king, pleased with all he heard, dismissed him, bidding him take courage and rely upon his protection. Before leaving Naples, he was requested to give a retreat in the barracks at Pizzofalconi, which he opened on the 28th of March. Prince Castropignano assisted with the state major and many other cavaliers. When the prince saw the effect produced on the officers, he besought him to give the spiritual exercises also to the men. He consented, and gave two hours more to the soldiers, although he suffered much from the excessive cold of the church. On the 7th of April, the exercises terminated; scandals had disappeared from among the soldiers, blasphemies were no longer heard, taverns were deserted, and lewd women banished from their quarters. He procured for them books of devotion, and as they could not afford to purchase them, he furnished a little library for them. The effects produced on the officers were still greater, and five among them quitted the service, and entered religious houses.

The Congregation at Nocera was still agitated by the tempest, when an event occurred which brought peace at last to the Community. A Dean in the neighborhood, who had been prejudiced against them, one evening, when he was returning home, was beaten on the head with some sharp instrument by one of his relatives, for having often remonstrated with him because of the irregularities of his life. He was carried into a neighboring convent apparently dying, which when F. Mazzini heard, he ran in all haste to render him assistance, and continued to assist him with the utmost care until he was convalescent. The other fathers were also assiduous in their attention to him, and such was the change produced on his mind, that he could think of nothing but how to recompense their services. His conduct disconcerted the malcontents, and he, in concert with Mgr. Volpe, labored to disabuse the Superiors of religious houses and the few priests who still stood out against them, and peace was shortly restored. The generosity of Alphonsus soon consolidated it. In the month of October, the king's council had decided in his favor, and against Contaldi. Alphonsus, having the tranquillity of the Congregation more at heart than its temporal interests, succeeded in persuading the Bishop to allow him to resign at once the donation made by Contaldi, only requesting him, as a favor, to pay a debt of nine hundred ducats, contracted in building. This disinterested conduct gained him more than ever the esteem of good men, and as for the Dean, he could never cease expressing his admiration; he came to make a retreat at Ciorani, and ever after continued to be a powerful protector of the Institute in every emergency. Mgr. Volpe contributed much to the establishment of peace. A just appreciator of the merits of Alphonsus and his children, he frequented the house, and consulted the missionaries on all occasions of difficulty. He gave audiences in their house. He ordered a great number to come to it for spiritual exercises, to be instructed in the rubrics, or to reform their conduct. The esteem thus shown by the Bishop, ended in conciliating the respect and veneration of their greatest enemies.

After his return from Naples to Ciorani, Alphonsus, invited by the people and neighboring curates, continued his warfare against the strongholds of Satan, in every direction; and with his accustomed success. In October he returned to Naples, not having been able to comply, on his last visit, with all the demands made upon him. He commenced by opening a mission in the church of St. Anna de-Palazzo, in which numbers were converted who had never approached the tribunal of penance, and it seemed as if he had only to cast the net, to receive the miraculous draught of fishes. After this he was sent for to preach penance in the suburb of St. Anthony, to which, on a former occasion, through the endeavors of F. Sarnelli and partially of himself, the unfortunate women of the town had been compelled to withdraw. His labors were not unfruitful; many of these poor creatures, touched by grace, began to detest their crimes; numbers were placed in houses of refuge, others were taken care of by charitable persons; besides, a great number of young girls were saved, who, though not yet engaged in the ways of sin, were preparing for it. He also visited and preached in many houses of religious women, while many, both of the priesthood and laity, daily came to him for instruction and advice, so that he had difficulty in finding leisure to recite his office and perform his other devotional exercises.

Cardinal Spinelli desired him to give a retreat in the cathedral, during which the church could scarcely contain the multitude. An eye-witness has remarked, that eternity only can disclose the wonders of grace then operated, and this even among many professed infidels. At length Alphonsus departed for the country, to distribute the bread of eternal life to the more destitute. At the town of Vietri, a man renowned for his infidelity, went one day into the church, for the purpose, he said, of criticising his sermon. He had not listened long, when entering into himself he recognised his deplorable condition, and full of repentance, detested his former blindness. "The sermons of other preachers," said he, "speak but to the mind; but the sermons of F. Alphonsus penetrate to the heart." He immediately went to confession, and persevered to the end.

CHAPTER XV.

Alphonsus obtains the approbation of his Congregation at Rome. He holds the first General Chapter, and is elected Rector Major. Difficulties with some subjects. Other difficulties in Naples. He publishes his Moral Theology.

ENCOURAGED by the pious disposition of the king, and having obtained for his Congregation the support of so many Bishops, Alphonsus determined to apply for approbation to the Pope. He addressed a petition to Benedict XIV, by the hand of Mgr. Puoti, a prelate whom his Holiness honored with his particular friendship. The Pope ordered at once Cardinal Gentili, prefect of the Congregation of the Council of Trent, to charge Cardinal Spinelli to take information and declare his sentiment on the subject. His Eminence asked for the rules, and gave them to the Canon Simede, and his auditor, the Abbe Blaschi, for examination. All three admired the wisdom with which every thing had been arranged. The Cardinal, however, wished some alterations, viz. with regard to fasting, fearing for the health of the subjects, when undergoing so much fatigue, and then with regard to the number of consultors, wishing to have the number limited to six, instead of twelve, which number Alphonsus had determined upon, to imitate the College of the Twelve Apostles.

When he was thus assured of the approbation of Cardinal Spinelli, every one advised Alphonsus to go himself to Rome, but he concealed his humility under the pretence of his infirmities, and confided the whole affair to the management of F. Villani, who was accompanied by another Father. Many Bishops, besides those in whose dioceses the Congregation was established, wrote to give them favorable testimony at the court of Rome; and they had letters from the most distinguished personages to the Cardinal Orsini, and the Duke of Tora. The general of the the Order of St. Basil, and the missionaries of St. Vincent of Paul, exerted themselves also in their favor, and the Abbot of another religious house gave them great assistance. Cardinal Bisozzi was named Reporter; they had wished for Cardinal Orsini, but Cardinal Gentili, the prefect, said to F. Villani, that by this appointment he secured for them a man of still more weight, and when Orsini was told of it, he remarked: "You have now two instead of one," and afterwards went himself to deliver the request into Bisozzi's hands.

When the rule was presented to the Sacred Congregation, they retrenched, as superfluous, the vow of placing themselves at the disposal of the Pope, to be sent, whenever he should be pleased, to preach to the heathen. "We suppose," said the Cardinal, "that all religious orders are always ready to obey the first signal given by the Holy Father." Besides, Alphonsus, in order to take from his Congregation the means of amassing wealth, having fixed that the rents of no house should exceed the sum of twelve hundred ducats, the Cardinals, though admiring his moderation, fixed the maximum at fifteen hundred for ordinary houses, and two thousand for the house of novices and students, in consideration of unforeseen expenses that might come upon them. They were satisfied with every thing else, and full of admiration for the rule, they unanimously approved it. But the devil would not allow things to proceed without his interference. The auditor of Cardinal Bisozzi, having read the approbation of Cardinal Spinelli, which exalted the great good done by the Institute, and its utility to the kingdom, pretended that this meant it should be confined to the kingdom of Naples. But the Cardinal, having been consulted, said that Alphonsus had not applied to the Pope for the kingdom of Naples only, but to obtain his sanction for the Congregation throughout the whole Church. "It is but just," he added, "that a work of so much magnitude should be universal."

Although all was in train, nothing was yet decreed. At length, towards the end of February, (1749,) F. Villani went to Cardinal Orsini, who said to him: "Be comforted, this morning the Sacred Congregation has had one of the most difficult conferences." "But," said F. Villani, "what cannot be done in the Congregation, might it not be done in the house of the Cardinal Prefect?" "True," said the Cardinal, "and I will go to him immediately, for I have something to say to him that concerns myself." "If you would succeed in your affairs," replied Villani, "begin by speaking of mine." "Depend on it," said the Cardinal, "and since you say so, recommend my business to God with yours." That same day, the decree of approbation was given, and the Cardinal, with his own hand, wrote to inform Villani of the news.

F. Villani being presented to the Pope to thank him for his approbation, and ask the confirmation of it, his Holiness inquired for the decree. He replied that it was annexed to the rule. "That is what I wish to examine," said the Pope. The following day he read the decree and rule. He was particularly pleased to find that the offices of Rector Major and his Counsellors were perpetual. "It is this," said he, "that hinders parties and divisions, so often met with among regulars." Seeing that the Congregation bore the name of the Holy Saviour, and reflecting that there was a Congregation established at Venice, which already bore that name, he wished them to take the title of the "Most Holy Redeemer." The Pope named also Alphonsus perpetual Superior of the Congregation. Hearing of this, Alphonsus wrote from Ciorani to beseech them to obtain for him deliverance from so heavy a burden, expressing in the humblest terms his weakness and incapacity for sustaining such a charge. F. Villani wrote to him repeatedly on the necessity and propriety of continuing Rector. In one of his last letters on the subject, he says: "Since your Reverence is named perpetual Rector, it is necessary to have patience and submit to the yoke. My Father, speak no more on the subject; I believe you are bound by duty, by justice, and by gratitude."

There had been still another attempt made to crush the affair at Rome. A respectable Congregation at Naples, beheld with a jealous eye the success of Alphonsus and his Congregation, and sent with all haste one of its members to Rome to oppose him as much as possible; but he could do nothing. The same institute sent another Father for the same purpose, but he wrote back that he had come too late, for every thing was already concluded to the great satisfaction of both Pope and Cardinals. But if the author of evil could not hinder the Holy Father from giving his approbation, he tried at least to paralyze it. We have already seen that the Sacred Congregation approved the rules and the Institute. Now, the person charged with the arrangement of the minutes, having been gained by the friends of the envoy mentioned above, wrote, "Regula et non Institutum." But the Pope, when the decree was presented to him, seeing the ruse, was very indignant, and taking the pen in his own hand, wrote, "Regula et Institutum," so that, to the confusion of the malevolent, Alphonsus had the satisfaction of receiving from Rome, on the 25th of February, 1749, the confirmation of the Rule and the Institute. When he received this news, he burst into tears of joy, and cast himself with his face to the earth, all the others present following his example. After having in this posture thanked God for his mercies, they rang the bell of the community, when, all proceeding to the church, the Te Deum was chanted, after which Alphonsus exhorted all to correspond to so great a grace, by redoubled fervor in the exact observance of the rule, and in love towards Jesus Christ and his holy Mother Mary.

The approbation of the Institute made a great noise at Rome; they spoke of nothing but the new Congregation of missionaries approved by the Pope, of the fervor which reigned among them, and the great good they did. In consequence of this, a great number of subjects, distinguished for their virtue as well as for their science, applied to be admitted into the order. Two curates renounced their benefices and quitted Rome for Ciorani. About the same time, the Abbot mentioned before, as having been useful in obtaining the approbation of the rule, wished also to be admitted. He was a man of great merit, profoundly versed in science, divine and human. Though Alphonsus had made it a rule never to admit into his Congregation any regular, nor any one who had ever lived in community, yet in consideration of the distinguished merit of the Abbot, and the services he had rendered to the Congregation, he made no difficulty in receiving him. The Pope, by a brief, agreed to, and even encouraged, this determination, and the Abbot, after having, with the consent of Alphonsus, made the vows prescribed by the rule, to Cardinal Orsini, at the feet of St. Peter in the Vatican, laid aside his insignia, took the habit, and departed for Ciorani. When it became known at Naples that the Congregation was confirmed by the Pope, a great many excellent young men and distinguished priests, presented themselves also for admission. The prince of Castellaneta, D. Matthias Miroballo, of Aragon, renewed his solicitation to be admitted, but Alphonsus believed himself bound to refuse him. F. Mandarini again began to solicit a re-union, but he refused again to yield to his entreaties, as also to those of his subjects who requested individually to be received.

In the month of October of the same year, Alphonsus held his first General Chapter. At the opening of it, he invited all the members, through F. Cafaro, who opened the meeting, to accept the rules, and to proceed to a formal election to all the offices in general, and in order that the suffrages might be free, that each one should first divest himself of the office he held. All obeyed, and although the Pope had confirmed him in the perpetual Rectorship, he was the first to give the example, and kneeling in the midst of the chapter, laid down his authority, humbling himself before them, and asking pardon for all that had been amiss in his past conduct. Afterwards, that they might recommend themselves to God, he suggested that all should make a retreat of three days, and above all, he insisted that, in electing the Rector Major, they should vote for him whom before God they thought best qualified to fill the office; in short, he neglected no means for exempting himself of the burden. The rules were read, and all joyfully accepted them, and renewed the vows of poverty, chastity and obedience, with the oath of persevering in the Congregation until death. After the three days' retreat, they proceeded to the nomination of the Rector Major, and at the first scrutiny Alphonsus was unanimously elected for life. He adored the judgment of God, thanked the assembly who deigned thus to honor him, and submitting to the divine will, again took up the heavy burden. They proceeded then to the election to all the other charges and offices, and established the necessary regulations for the novitiate, as also for the house for studies, determining the system and authors to be followed in the teaching of belles-lettres, philosophy, and theology. The chapter finished by appointing the F. Abbot professor of philosophy and theology, for which office his vast erudition rendered him eminently qualified.

It was during the sitting of the chapter, that the heart of Alphonsus, saddened at the temporal poverty in which they were plunged, was gladdened by the determination of some gentlemen of Pagani. They had seen, some months before, the young students walking in the neighborhood, and from their modesty and good behaviour, formed a very favorable judgment of the Institute. They earnestly requested him to transfer the students to the house at Pagani, promising that if the Congregation would not support the expense, they would willingly contribute to it themselves. Alphonsus consented to this, and they all subscribed certain annual sums, and Dominic de Mayo, the Dean, signalised himself among them by his generosity. The Bishop also contributed largely, taking the greatest interest in the education of the students.

When all was regulated for the interior of the Congregation, Alphonsus recommenced in the autumn his course of missions. At the opening of the Jubilee in 1750, Mgr. de Novelles invited him to give a mission at Sarno. God showered abundant graces on this mission in particular. A great number of bravos by profession, placed in the hands of the missionaries their daggers, their pistols, and bayonets, and from that time, embraced a peaceful and pious life. It is on record, that for ten years after this, the taverns were quite deserted. It was during this mission that Alphonsus gave an extraordinary example of submission and obedience. His beard had been clipped with scissors the previous evening, and its irregularities were quite in keeping with his mantle and cassock, both mended in a thousand places. The Bishop, wishing to try him, said laughingly: "Notwithstanding our wish to be economical, a few grani are necessary to have you shaved, so I will pay for you myself;" at the same time, he made a sign to a servant to call a barber. Alphonsus said nothing, and when the barber came, he presented himself to be shaved with the most perfect indifference, although it was eighteen years since a razor had touched his chin.

When he had finished the mission in this town, accompanied by fourteen missionaries, he commenced to go through the whole diocese. During his sojourn at Malfi, in the Pouille, where Mgr. Busti had invited him to preach in his cathedral, Alphonsus learned the happy passage to heaven of F. Cesar Sportelli, his first companion in the Congregation. This loss was a heavy blow to him, but he had to rejoice, because of the circumstances attending his death. A month previous, the saintly Father had foretold the day and the hour of his death, and when one of the Fathers set out to join Alphonsus on the mission, he said to him, "Kiss the hand of our Rector for me, and say to him that, when he shall receive at Malfi the news of my death, he must recommend my soul to Jesus Christ." He died in the odor of sanctity, and God glorified him by many miracles. Six months after his death, when they opened the coffin in presence of the ecclesiastical judges, the body was found uncorrupt, and blood was drawn from his veins.

In the course of his missions in the diocese of Malfi, Alphonsus visited Ripacandida, where there was a convent of Carmelite nuns, strict observers of the rule. He gave them a retreat from which he drew not less profit than he gave. He modified, however, their bodily austerities, in which he wished them to use more discretion, and established some relaxation both for the body and the mind. "I did not believe," he said, "that I should find on this rock such a beautiful flower."

Having returned to Ciorani, he finished and published in the course of this year, 1750, his precious work entitled the "Glories of Mary." It was the fruit of years, in which he had employed himself to choose from among the works of holy Fathers and Theologians, the most conclusive proofs in favor of the prerogatives of Mary, and the fittest to engage the faithful to devote themselves to her service. The applause with which the book was received, and the number of editions through which it has gone, is scarcely to be credited.

The contradiction which so many young men had to encounter who joined the Congregation, induced Alphonsus to write, about this time, a small work entitled "Advice regarding a Religious Vocation," in which he showed that a divine vocation is not to be subjected to the will of relations, and that, when God calls us, we must obey Him. He showed the excellence and advantages of the religious state, which is the most certain way of salvation, and pointed out the means of preserving the vocation. This last point he treated in particular in another little work called "Advice to Novices," to aid them in persevering in their vocation. He presented these two little works to all the novitiates in Naples, and it was every where favorably received. "If," said he, "I can hinder one vocation from being lost, the gain is not little."

[illegible]. Alphonsus was enjoying the greatest happiness in seeing his Congregation approved by the Pope, and each day making new progress, when a sad reverse came to change his joy and consolation into bitterness. The Father Abbot was scarcely settled at Ciorani, when, by the brilliancy of his talents, he had gained the admiration of all the students, and their hearts also by his edifying conduct. He had been sent with twelve of the most talented to Pagani. Besides philosophy, he taught them, with the greatest success, the elements of sacred and profane history, and the learned languages. The Fathers in general rejoiced in his success, but Alphonsus feared that the pre-eminence of belles-lettres would hurt the spiritual advancement of the young men. The commencement with the Abbot had been good, but his fervor did not last; habituated to command, he could not humble himself to obey. The rule became a restraint for him; the want of liberty preyed upon his mind; in his conversations with the young men, he would sometimes disapprove of one thing, sometimes would modify another; and with regard to certain practices of devotion, he would not even suffer them. Other practices of exterior humiliation, were in his opinion but grimaces, which produced no effect, though on his first arrival at Ciorani he had practised them himself, and considered them as being useful for promoting humility. F. Mazzini, being informed of all this, believed he ought to give him a friendly warning, but the Abbot received it with a very bad grace, and ceased not to spread maxims contrary to a religious life. When Alphonsus heard at Ciorani of this sad news, his heart was oppressed. He advised F. Mazzini to be prudent, and wrote at the same time to the Abbot, representing to him the great evil that might result from diversity of opinion in a newly established institute; but seeing that this only embittered him against F. Mazzini, he withdrew the latter from Nocera. Notwithstanding this, things did not take a better turn; he troubled the minds of the students to such an extent, that they formed themselves into two opposite parties. When Alphonsus saw the evil thus grow worse, he summoned the Abbot to Ciorani, in the month of September, 1750, and as they were giving a retreat to the young men preparing for holy orders, he gave him the charge of it, that he might not think of returning to Pagani. The Abbot did not like this, and showed great discontent, when Alphonsus said to him firmly: "Either you must obey, or you are free to return to your own Order." He passed the night in consideration, and then agreed to give the exercises, but declared his intention of leaving the Congregation. He, however, entered into himself and became humble. The Fathers Villani and Cafaro interceded for him, and Alphonsus, not wishing to disgrace him, sent him back again to Nocera. Peace seemed re-established, but it was only a truce. The Abbot recommenced his instructions, and among the students one was of Paul, another of Apollo. Not to compromise every thing, Alphonsus tried another expedient. He recalled him to Ciorani. "Every Congregation," said he, "has an asylum at Rome, why should not we try to establish an hospice there?" And it was agreed to send him there with another Father. But the Abbot, beginning to see the reason why Alphonsus had taken this resolution, was exceedingly displeased, and yielding to the temptation, meditated the ruin of the students altogether. He proposed to them to join with him and go to Rome, where they would found a new institute on a footing altogether different. Four of them, the flower of the whole, determined to follow this new founder. Alphonsus was ignorant of this plot, and engaged in arranging all things for the journey of the Abbot. He was to depart for Naples on the 15th of October; he had already taken leave of his friends; and on the 14th, Alphonsus had made the twelve students come to Ciorani. They arrived in the morning, and the same evening Alphonsus assembled a council, and all at once proposed the expulsion of the Abbot; he was opposed, but the very next day they changed their resolution, when the four young men presented themselves to Alphonsus with staves in hand and mantles under their arms, demanding dispensation from the vows. Alphonsus threw himself at their feet, the tears gushing from his eyes, as he strove to convince them of the snare into which they were falling. Finding them obstinate, he proposed to them to make a retreat of eight days, and after that to make their decision; but all was useless, they turned their back on him, and with an air of contempt, without having obtained their dispensation, they all four departed for Nocera.

There was a circumstance which showed in a striking manner the protection God granted to Alphonsus. The Abbot, in order to justify himself, had drawn up a memorial signed by these four young men, and addressed to the Pope, in which they stated a thousand lies against Alphonsus and the Congregation, which they said was full of grave disorders. Thus he flattered himself he should not only obtain a dispensation for the four students, but that his Holiness would advise them to enter the institute he proposed to form. That same morning Alphonsus sent an order to F. Fiocchi, Rector at Nocera, to inform the

Abbot, in whatever spot he might be found, that he was no longer a member of the Congregation. The Abbot had gone to take leave of the Bishop, and F. Fiocchi followed him and told him the decision that had been come to. He had not the presence of mind to return to the house and remove his papers, and the memorial just alluded to was found in his table drawer: so he was minus his memorial, and fully unmasked.

Such were the consequences of the conduct of a subject who had repaid with ingratitude the high estimation in which he had been held. At Naples, he joined the four students, where he seduced a young priest in the College of the Holy Family, under the pretence that he had already established at Rome his new Congregation, and that the Pope had himself designated the four students as so many apostles to gain the palm of martyrdom among the infidels. But the Abbot soon set out alone for Rome, and abandoned the four young victims without their having the least suspicion of it. Alphonsus on this occasion made of him a prophecy, fulfilled a few years later; he said to one of the Fathers of the same order: "The Abbot has made us weep to-day; a time will come when he will make you weep also." Indeed, he troubled the whole order by dividing the abbeys of the kingdom of Naples from those of the Pontifical States, and making himself be declared by the Pope, Perpetual Abbot in Rome, and commissary-general for life to the abbeys in the Pontifical States, causing many other annoyances to the convents in both kingdoms. Alphonsus attributed the discovery of the plot to the special protection of St. Theresa, for all happened between the first and second vespers of the feast of that saint. Since that time the Congregation has taken her for one of its principal patrons. The affliction of Alphonsus was, however, partly tempered by the return of one of the four young men a few days after, who threw himself at his feet. Some time later, a second followed his example. He received them both as a tender father, and ever after showed them a special affection.

Several of the counsels Alphonsus gave to the young students on this occasion, are still on record: "My dear brethren," he said, "I would earnestly recommend you not to keep your conscience closed, for if these unfortunates who have gone out from us had manifested the state of their souls to their Superiors, they would not now be where they are. Had they declared themselves not to any one indifferently, but to him who holds towards us the place of God, and cannot deceive us, this had not happened." Again: "During a temptation, never take a resolution, whatever the case may be, and however holy it may appear, but go instantly, and discover it to your Superior. When the temptation is upon us, we do not recognise that it comes from the devil. He conceals himself under a veil, and puts before our eyes treacherous spectacles, making us see things, not as they are in themselves, but according to our passions. If we would avoid the snare, we should instantly recommend ourselves to God, and abandon ourselves into his hands." And again: "Sapere, et sapere ad sobrietatem." The Abbot had introduced among the students a forced application to study, but all this afflicted Alphonsus, and he would not suffer it. "I am not sorry," he said, after his departure, "when I see you retrench from your studies and give more time to prayer. We have been called to succor poor destitute souls in the country, for this reason, we have more need of sanctity than of science. If we are not holy, we are exposed to the peril of falling into a thousand imperfections and a thousand impatiences with this sort of people. I repeat once more, if to give to spirituality you retrench something from your studies, far from being sorry, I shall on the contrary experience great consolation." All this must be understood of a forced application, as that introduced by the Abbot to the detriment of the spirit of piety. For nothing can be more strong than the terms in which he recommended, at other times, as also in the rules, the proper application to science, and this as well in regard to the students, as in regard to the priests of the institute. His motto was: "A laborer without science, though he be a man of prayer, is like a soldier without arms." He wrote, at the same time, to all the houses the following circular:

"To my Brethren of the Congregation of the Most Holy Redeemer. Blessed be Jesus, Mary, Joseph, and Theresa.

"My very dear Brethren, you know that I am not afflicted when I hear of some one among my brethren being called to another life. I am touched by it, because I am a creature of flesh and blood; but I am comforted, because he has died in a Congregation of which I am certain all the members will be saved. Neither am I afflicted when one among us, because of his faults, ceases to be a member of the Congregation; I am even consoled by seeing that we are delivered from a sickly sheep that might have infected others. Far less am I afflicted because of persecutions; on the contrary, they inspire me with courage; because if we conduct ourselves well, we are certain God will not abandon us. But that which alarms me is, to learn that there is among us one who is vicious, who is negligent in obeying, and who pays little regard to the rule. My brethren, you know it, some who have been with us, are now out of the Congregation. What will their end be? I cannot tell. But of this I am certain, they will lead a life of continued misfortune, they will live in trouble, and die without peace, for they have abandoned their vocation. . . . In mental prayer, they will be torn by remorse of conscience for having left God, and thus they will abandon it, and then God knows where they will end.

"I beseech you to avoid faults of deliberation, and above all, those for which you have been reprimanded. If correction leads the delinquent to amend, the fault will be nothing, but when he will not amend, the devil employs every artifice to make him lose his vocation.

"By the grace of God, wherever we go on mission we perform wonders, and people say they have never had a mission such as ours. And why? Because we go by obedience, we go in poverty, we preach Christ crucified, and each one is attentive to acquit himself of the charge imposed upon him. I have been deeply grieved to learn that some among you, when on mission, have been desirous of obtaining the more honorable employments, such as preaching or instructing. But what fruit could he produce, who preaches from pride? It is a thing which I have in horror. If the spirit of ambition enters the Congregation, the missions will do little good, or rather they will do none at all."

Towards the end of the autumn of 1750, Alphonsus continued to give missions in different quarters, chiefly in the diocese of Salerno, and at Montemarano, in which place numbers of criminals came to him, touched by remorse, and were placed by him in the right way. The conversion of these malefactors was a subject of great consolation in the town, and still more in the neighboring country.

He had scarcely returned to Nocera, when his heart was pierced by a new sorrow, the departure of an ancient Father whom he loved much, and who was very useful in the missions. Offended by a reasonable and moderate correction from his Superior, he communicated to no person his temptation, and set off for Nocera, believing Alphonsus would give him satisfaction. But reflecting by the way on the inconsiderate step he had taken, and not feeling the courage to present himself before Alphonsus, he directed his steps to his own house. All the efforts of Alphonsus and others, to induce him to return, were unavailing. This happened on the 25th of July, 1751, and as the inconstancy of this Father had produced a great sensation in the Congregation, he again wrote a circular to all the houses on the 27th. Among other things, he says in it: "I pray God that he may immediately chase from among us all those proud and haughty spirits who cannot brook a reprimand. . . . He who refuses to be as potters' clay, to be trodden under the feet of all, let him fly, and let him fly immediately. The Lord will be better satisfied if there remain but two who are truly humble and mortified, than if there remained a thousand who were imperfect. . . . I would impress it also upon the heart of each one of you, never to speak evil of the conduct or any thing else of the Superiors. The indiscreet zeal of some does far more harm than good to the Congregation. Those who are truly zealous, when they remark some disorder or inobservance, let them tell it in secret to the monitor of the house, &c. Be attentive, to take count of the least faults, because they are the little foxes the devil makes use of to devastate our mind, and render us incapable of being solicitous to preserve our vocation. Let us, my dear brethren, sustain ourselves by prayer, and by continual prayer, otherwise we shall do nothing." After the apostolic courses of the year 1751, which were not less fruitful in conversions than the former ones, and having giving missions in the territory of Marianella, where he had first seen the light, he wished to pass through Naples on his return. He alighted at the door of the small hospice given to him by his brother Hercules. When the people saw a man riding on a white ass, his beard neglected, and his clothes ragged and worn, they did not recognise him, but mistaking him for a vagabond, they began hooting and ridiculing him. Alphonsus took it all with great good humor, till a merchant calling out his name, made them understand he was the brother of D. Hercules. It was evening when he arrived, worn out with fatigue; he would not sup, but said to the lay-brother that he would lie down. D. Hercules came to visit him, but fearing to disturb his sleep, he resolved to return in the morning; but when he came, Alphonsus had not yet risen; he returned after a while, and fearing some accident, forced open the door. He found him extended on his bed in a fainting fit, and ran to obtain help. The doctors ordered him to be undressed, and they found his body enveloped in sackcloth, which hindered him from breathing. They bled him, and then he began to come to himself. Seeing that he was discovered, he bitterly complained to the brother for having permitted such a thing. Fatigued and weak though he was, he nevertheless consented to give a sermon to the students of the Archiepiscopal Seminary, and visited several monasteries where he was invited.

This same year a new annoyance had overtaken Alphonsus unexpectedly, which threatened ruin, and caused him great anxiety. It happened towards the end of January that the King, while hunting in the territory of Iliceto, saw the house of the missionaries, which is built on an eminence, and asked one of his courtiers to whom it belonged. "It is the house of F. Liguori's missionaries," he replied, "and they have made a good hit there, having fallen heir to no less than sixty thousand ducats." He referred to the will of the late Canon Curate of Iliceto, which was mentioned above. "Ah!" said the King, "these then are just like the others: scarcely do they begin, when they set themselves to acquire wealth." Deceived by what he had heard, the King conceived an unfavorable opinion of the Congregation; all the court soon knew it, and every one talked of their ambition and the certainty of the order being suppressed. A tempest so unexpected alarmed the whole Congregation. Alphonsus, however, full of confidence in God, said to his brethren: "The Lord will make the Congregation prosper, not by the applause, and the protection of princes, but by means of poverty and contempt, of misery and persecution; when have we ever seen the works of God begin in the midst of applause?" Confiding in the integrity of his conscience, he went to Naples; he found the ministers too much prejudiced against the Congregation; every where they spoke of the wealth the missionaries had acquired. Alphonsus had recourse to the protection of God, and tried to obtain mercy by increased mortifications, exhorting at the same time his brethren to join him in penance and prayer, by reciting in all the houses the psalm, "Qui habitat," and taking a discipline in common, in addition to those appointed in the rule. They multiplied their alms and offered many masses.

In these critical circumstances, their affairs were the object of research to notaries and their subalterns, to ascertain, in consequence of orders from Naples, the acquisitions they had made in the several houses. But his Majesty, who could not doubt the integrity of Alphonsus, was not slow to reflect on the improbability of his suspicions, and said to the Marquis Brancone, that Alphonsus himself should arrange an account of the revenues of the different houses. Alphonsus declared that the house of Ilicето had in all a yearly rent of three hundred ducats, and that the deductions made in consequence of different charges upon it, reduced it to much less; that those of Ciorani and Caposele had each about five hundred ducats of revenue; but that Nocera had only the bare walls, and a small bit of garden ground. The reports made by the local authorities attributed much less to each house than Alphonsus had done, and his great sincerity confirmed the King more and more in the high opinion he had of him. But even when the calumny was exposed, Alphonsus could not get rid of uneasiness, the ministers were yet asking whether or not the Congregation should be suppressed. All were inclined to abolish it, they thought the kingdom had already more than sufficient religious establishments, and rather than to consent to the establishment of new ones, they thought of diminishing those already in existence. Alphonsus was without any human support, but he did not lose courage; he said that the souls of the blessed would defend his cause, and abandoned the interests of his Congregation to the piety of the King and the protection of Providence. He quitted Naples, and withdrew to Nocera to prepare for the missions of autumn and winter, and went to preach penance in the Archdiocese of Salerno. After Easter, 1752, he went to Gragnano, accompanied by twenty-two missionaries. Prodigies of grace were performed, particularly among the malefactors, many of whom were seen depositing their daggers and pistols at the feet of the Blessed Virgin. Among these was a celebrated bandit, who, in the procession to erect the calvary, carried one of the crosses on his shoulders, weeping so as to cause the whole people to shed tears of joy.

In the course of these missions, Alphonsus had written to the Marquis Brancone to intercede with the King. The Marquis embraced every opportunity of speaking with his

Majesty, and at length wrote to Alphonsus that matters were so arranged, that he should come to Naples himself, which he accordingly did as soon as the missions were finished. He presented himself to the King, told him how, for nineteen years, he and his companions had visited the most remote and destitute villages of the kingdom; he told him of thousands that had been converted in his own royal domains; that each year they had given more than forty missions; he represented to him that the Archbishop of Conza and Salerno, and the Bishops of Bovino and Nocera, seeing the good produced, had established houses of missionaries in their respective dioceses, and that the Pope, informed of of what had been done, had approved the Institute for the whole Church; but that it was also necessary that the approbation of the sovereign should be given, to insure the future existence of so great a work. As for the acquiring of riches, as this was the sole obstacle that the ministers could oppose, he opened his heart to the King, showing him how very far he was from wishing his Congregation to become rich. "I am persuaded," he said, "that wherever abundance reigns, the laborer will abandon the axe, and the spade, and seek only repose. I would not wish that opulence should reign in the Congregation. I seek only to procure a modest livelihood, according to the intention of the Pope, and I beseech your Majesty to establish a fixed revenue, beyond which we may not go." He also had recourse to the intervention of the Queen, which he managed to secure through the celebrated Jesuit, Francis Pipi, and Mother Mary Angela of Divine Love, who had been his penitent in the world, but was now Superior of a Carmelite Convent at Caporea, to which the Queen often resorted. He visited also the ministers, to urge upon them the importance of this affair, in promoting the salvation of multitudes of people. He spoke to them with tears, but his illustrious birth and extraordinary merits were not sufficient to protect him from insult. Some rejected him with unpitying bitterness. One minister in particular treated him with the utmost rudeness, and after listening with marked incivility to what he said, almost turned him out of doors. "Do not talk nonsense to me," he said, "and tell your stories to some old woman." Alphonsus bowed his head, and said nothing. On another occasion he said to one of the ministry, "My Lord, I recommend to you the cause of Jesus Christ," who replied in the most contemptuous manner, "Jesus Christ has no cause in the royal chambers."

In the midst of these difficult affairs, which detained him at Naples, he did not forget the work to which he had devoted his life. Even his sojourn in that capital was a continual mission. He gave a retreat in the church of the Pilgrims, during which, besides the conversion of many old in sin, hundreds of infidels abjured their errors. He often preached in the Chinese College, and many convents profited by his labors. When the negociations approached a close, he had many masses said, and multiplied his penances, to force, as it were, the benedictions of Heaven. He made special vows to the souls in purgatory, to St. Joseph, and St. Theresa, and wrote to many monasteries, begging for prayers and novenas. His hope being thus fixed on Him, in whom it can never be confounded, the affair was again proposed in the council, and they were finally approved in November, 1752, on condition that they acquired no new revenues for the future, the king furnishing each priest and lay-brother with about twenty cents (of our money) a day, the surplus revenue being to be distributed to the poor, and the moveables already acquired being to be administerered by the bishops of the dioceses in which their houses were situated, the king not recognising their houses or colleges as ecclesiastical communities. This decree caused great embarrassment to Alphonsus, because he feared the existence of the houses was still insecure; but the Marquis Brancone viewed it in another light, and re-assured him on the subject. Thus was partially fulfilled a prophecy he had made before, writing to Mary Angela of Capua: "I believe," he wrote, "that God will mortify my pride, and that this approbation will not be given until after I am dead." Indeed, it was not until the next reign, after he was dead, that the Congregation was placed on a proper footing.

Towards the commencement of the year 1753, notwithstanding his grave and multiplied embarrassments, Alphonsus published his Moral Theology. In the year 1748, he had, at the request of the Fathers of his Congregation, enriched Busembaum with notes, which they wished to have printed, that they might consult them with facility. At a later period, he enlarged this work, and published it in two thick volumes, which he dedicated to Benedict XIV, who gave it his approbation.

This work was the fruit of a pure zeal for the glory of God and the salvation of souls, and while he labored at it, he never embraced or rejected any opinion without having this double object in view, nor did he ever take up his pen without recommending himself to Jesus Christ and the Blessed Virgin, whose images he had always before him. He was exceedingly careful to avoid the extremes of a relaxed probabilism, or a rigid austerity, both of which are pernicious to souls; but he followed throughout the line of exact equity, equally free from that rigid spirit which turns into precept that which is not, wishing to make every thing sinful, and from that easy and accommodating spirit which gives liberty where there is precept. Attaching himself to no party, he respected all, but above all he revered reason, and made the authority of the Church his law. He several times reproached the decisions of the most rigid theologians with relaxation, and hesitated not sometimes to reject, as too rigid, the decisions of the most indulgent. When he hesitated between two opinions, he left the reader at liberty to choose between them for himself. Whenever he had a difficult case to consider, besides meditation and prayer, he passed entire months in examining different opinions, and when he was not convinced, not satisfied with consulting the Fathers of his own Congregation, he sent to Rome and Naples for the opinions of the best theologians, and principally to the Sacred Congregations which are at Rome, as the organs of the Sovereign Pontiff.

Notwithstanding the favorable reception the first edition of this work met with, he reviewed the whole, to examine it with still more reflection before publishing a second edition, he corrected it in several points, as he himself announces in the preface. The respectable Congregations of Naples, however, did not agree in his retractations, judging that the opinions which he retracted were sufficiently probable. Some also said these retractations were not to his credit. "Let them say what they will," he replied; "I seek not my own glory, I seek only the glory of Jesus Christ, and the salvation of souls." The present time in which we live shows how much and in what manner God blessed his labors and upright intentions, not only in Italy, but in all other countries. The Pope spoke prophetically, when he assured him of universal approbation, this being literally the case in these our times. Benedict XIV had such a high esteem for his wisdom, that on one occasion, when a celebrated Neapolitan missionary came to consult him on a difficult case, this great Pope would not give a decision, but contented himself with replying: "You have the Father Liguori at Naples, consult him."

The King, Charles III, showed during this year how much he was satisfied with the labors of Alphonsus and his companions. A respectable and very ancient order had fallen into decay, and a holy individual, charmed with the zeal of Alphonsus, proposed to his Majesty that he should undertake the reform of it, in order that the Congregation might thus be legally erected into a religious order in the kingdom, to perpetuate the work of the missions. The King and the Queen were delighted with the idea, and proposed to the Marquis Brancone to mention it to Alphonsus. Their plan was, that he and his companions, without abandoning their own rule, should take the habit and the name of the order in question, the ancient religious being permitted to retire in certain of their convents, without being disquieted by the reform. Alphonsus begged the Marquis to give him time to consult with his companions before replying to the King. The project was advantageous in some respects, but they recognised that, besides many dangers and contradictions to which the enterprise would expose them, the work of the missions, instead of progressing, would only be seriously impeded, and that if the King died before every thing was settled, the ancient order continuing to exist, they might find themselves some day neither missionaries nor religious. From these and other powerful considerations, he abandoned all idea of the scheme, although deeply grateful for the favor his sovereign had shown him.

In the month of July, 1753, during the Novena of the feast of Mount Carmel, which, though overpowered by previous fatigue, he had accepted to give at Saragnano, the Virgin, his Mother, showed how agreeable he was to her. They were lodged in the house of a physician named Francis Mari, who had invited them. Twelve Fathers arrived one Thursday immediately before dinner, and as they were not expected, nothing was prepared for such a large party. The physician sent to his neighbors, but as he could get nothing, he requested Alphonsus to dispense with the rule and allow him to serve fowls. "No, no," said he smiling, "give yourself no further trouble, put the meat you have on the table, and God will supply what is wanting." And lo! while they were cutting the meat in the kitchen, they saw the pieces becoming visibly larger, and so much so, that, after the whole party had been abundantly served, a considerable quantity remained. Mari afterwards attested that the meat had increased at least seven-fold. Alphonsus, seeing the astonishment of Mari, said: "In all embarrassments, let us have recourse to God, and never doubt his providence."

The autumn and winter of this year were fruitful in missions as usual. The inhabitants of Resina asked for a mission, but because of its proximity to Naples, Alphonsus refused; the people, however, applied to the King, who laid his command on him and furnished all the expenses himself. They afterwards went into the royal territory of Persano, always at the expense of his Majesty, whose good heart delighted in affording his subjects means of grace. The Marquis Brancone, convinced of the greatness of the work, sent them also frequent subsidies, and many bishops contributed liberally towards the expenses of the mission. Alphonsus had, this year, to mourn over the death of F. Cafaro, who died at Caposele on the 13th of August. He loved and esteemed him, regarding him as a model of heroic sanctity, whose example drew others to sacrifice themselves for God. Prayer and mortification were his two inseparable companions; he was the director of Alphonsus. He besought the prayers of all, that this great support of the Congregation might be spared, but the hour was come, and Alphonsus bowed in submission, adoring the decrees of God. He himself wrote a short abstract of his life.

CHAPTER XVI.

Alphonsus founds a house in the Pontifical States. Various apostolical courses and labors. He founds a house in Sicily.

ALTHOUGH approved by the Pope, the Congregation had not yet entered the Pontifical States. It was in the year 1753, that Mgr. Pacca, the Archbishop of Benevento, to supply the necessities of his vast diocese, applied to Alphonsus for the establishment of a house of the order in it; he was persuaded so to do by his Vicar-General, D. Joseph Fusco. To arrange matters, Alphonsus sent F. Villani, who set out for Benevento with Mgr. Nicolas Borgia, Bishop of Cava, who had offered to accompany him, in order to second the measure. The two travellers experienced a special protection of God's providence. When they set out, the weather was beautiful and calm, but before they had proceeded far, a thunder-storm came on, the lightning flashed, and the rain fell in torrents. Twice within a short time a thunderbolt fell at Mgr. Borgia's feet, without

14

hurting him in the least, nor his companion. At Benevento it was decided they should be established at St. Angelo della Coupola, and to prevent delay, the Fathers were to lodge in the mean time in a country-house formerly inhabited by Benedict XIII, when he was only Archbishop, in which they were established on the 6th of April, 1755. The Archbishop was so charmed with the results of their first labors, a retreat given to the students, regular and secular, and also to a part of the seminarists, and another given in the cathedral during a great drought, that he went to Nocera to visit Alphonsus, and thank him as the author of a work so salutary for the people. He invited him to give a missión at Benevento himself, which he agreed to do in November following. The Archbishop declared that it was to him, after God, he would confide the interests of his diocese, and offered every assistance in his power to promote the building of the establishment.

Alphonsus having now resided at Nocera several years, F. Rossi invited him to give a retreat at Ciorani during Passion Week. As soon as his arrival was known, there was such a concourse of priests and gentlemen, that messengers had to be despatched in different directions, to warn them that there was no more room, but they would not return, and resolved to pass the night before the door rather than not hear Alphonsus. The Prince of Castellaneta was there with twelve officers of his regiment, and many gentlemen, who slept four in a room, or on mattresses in the corridors. The Count d'Aguila was so touched by grace, that hearing one of his soldiers swear by the blood of Jesus Christ, he condemned him to be tied to a pole, three hours morning and evening, by the hair of his head, with a gag in his mouth, for a whole week.

It was at this time a discussion took place between Alphonsus and a polemic, who was displeased by his censures on Muratori for having shown himself too reserved in exalting Mary and speaking of her power. Alphonsus answered his attacks mildly, but at the same time so convincingly, that his adversary, a disciple of Jansenius, set himself all at once to attack his Moral Theology, not sparing his very person. But the moderation with which Alphonsus confounded his adversary, drew upon him the esteem of all Italy.

In the course of the autumn, 1755, Alphonsus went, as he had promised, to give a mission at Benevento. He went by Naples, where he found his mother dangerously ill, but he had the consolation of seeing her delivered from the scruples which had formerly tormented her, and entirely resigned to the will of God. He administered the sacraments to her, and fortified her by his counsels during three days. As he could no longer delay his mission, he asked her parting benediction, and set out for Benevento, consoled by seeing his mother dying the death of the just, and full of joy, that her son left her only to conquer souls for Jesus Christ. He arrived at Benevento accompanied by twenty missionaries. A prelate who was present wrote thus: "It is long since we have seen such truly apostolic men; one can form no idea of the effects they produce. . . . . . . The voice of the holy missionary was weakened by age, and still more by fatigue, but the sight of his zeal was sufficient to soften the hardest hearts and melt them like wax. Benevento has been sanctified, and numerous malefactors, when they saw him there, became models of piety. All souls profited by his labors, so that a general reformation of manners succeeded."

The fruits of this mission were so great that the renown of it reached Rome, and Cardinal Orsini wrote to Alphonsus, that the Pope had been so satisfied with what he had heard, that he spoke himself to the Duke of Cerisan to obtain from his Majesty an exequatur to the brief of approbation given to the Congregation.

It was at this time that to render priests, particularly those in remote parts of the country, more skilful in hearing confessions, Alphonsus published his Moral Theology in Italian, in three volumes, giving it a new but abridged form, and adding three interesting appendices for the direction of souls. The work met with great applause at home, and when it became known out of Italy, and the demand for it in foreign countries increased, he wrote a similar one in Latin under the title of "Homo apostolicus."

Different affairs connected with the Congregation obliged him to go to Naples towards the end of February, 1756. The Cardinal Sersales, who knew the talent God had given him of touching hearts, besought him to give the spiritual exercises in a hall of the palace to the ecclesiastics. He expected only the young students, but as soon as he was known to be there, there ran thither such multitudes of canons, missionaries, and entire religious communities, that the number of those who attended was not less than a thousand. His Eminence assisted, and experienced indescribable satisfaction in seeing such a concourse of penitents. Alphonsus on this occasion saw canons, superiors of orders, and even bishops, pressing to the door of the saloon, in order to kiss his hand; but he humbled himself interiorly, and enveloped himself in his mantle to escape observation.

When the Cardinal saw the effect he had produced on the young people of the seminary, he insisted on his returning to preach to them once a week, to confirm them more and more in the good resolutions they had formed. The directors of the seminaries in the town and in the diocese also entreated him to grant them the same favor, so that he often preached two and three times in one day.

The disorders of which Naples, like all other capitals, was not free, caused much pain to Alphonsus; but above all, the increase of homicide, caused by the doctrines of the materialists and deists propagated in Italy. Deploring the sad consequences which he foresaw would accrue from these doctrines to the Church and the State, he pointed out to the Cardinal the great evils produced by the introduction of impious books, which passed from Naples into the provinces, and urged him to remonstrate with the King and the ministers on this subject. To inspire the people with horror for such productions, he spoke openly from the pulpit, condemning, as guilty of grave sin, those who sold such books, and also those who kept them in their houses;

he spoke also to the most respectable ecclesiastics and confessors, advising them to devise means to warn the faithful against the artifices of impiety. He also published his learned treatise of the defence of Religion and of the State, against the materialists and deists; a work which was well received, and found to be particularly useful against the sophists who tried to pervert the minds of the people and sap the foundations of their faith.

Alphonsus returned to Nocera in Holy Week, 1756, but scarcely had he reached the house, when he was called away by the queen-mother, who wished to consult him on affairs of conscience. The court was then at St. Lauro. The nuns of the monastery of St. Lauro wished to obtain a piece of his clothing. They hit on the following expedient. They invited him to visit a beautiful reliquary they preserved in their church, and begged him to give it to each of them to kiss, and while he bent forward for this purpose, one of the pensioners came behind and cut a large piece off his mantle. In the evening, as it was cold, he spread it over his bed; but finding it very short, he said to F. Galdieri, who had accompanied him: "This mantle is not mine; is it yours?" "It is your own," replied the Father; "the Nuns have played you that trick." "Yes," he replied, in confusion, "I see now; I could not comprehend how, in walking, I always felt something striking against my leg;" adding: "The fact is, it would require an old clothes shop to mend it." It was not seldom such thefts were committed when he stopped in any place.

In the beginning of July, 1756, he went again to Naples. The interests of the Congregation detained him at the court, and he wished to assure himself more and more of the protection of the King, and obtain at length the exequatur of the Apostolic brief. On the tenth of the same month, he wrote to the different houses, ordering a Novena to be made for the success of this affair, and a discipline every evening. On this, as on former occasions, the invitations of curates for Triduos, and instructions for the people, and the convents, left him no repose. He published also at this time a little work, entitled, "Method for the Confessor to exercise his Ministry well." In it he considered the Confessor as a father, as a physician, as a teacher, and as a judge, giving rules of conduct proper to each of these characters. This work was so much admired, that the most learned men went the length of saying that he could not have composed it without the special assistance of his guardian angel. The author of the Dictionary of Illustrious Men, says of it: "It breathes a divine unction, all is charity, gentleness and moderation." And Fr. Zaccharie, in the 12th vol. of his History of Literature, speaks thus of it: "What a precious book! It is an antidote against the poison contained in the Instructions to Confessors and Penitents, published by Occhi; what a difference between these two books! The practice of F. Liguori breathes a divine unction; we see in it but charity, gentleness, and moderation. . . . In it we see the wise man who seeks the salvation of souls. . . . He follows a method just and wisely reasonable, which smooths the way for penitence."

Alphonsus remained at Naples during the following month, but notwithstanding all his endeavors, the opinion of Mgr. Galiani, the Grand Almoner, prevailed; and under pretence that the King, in granting the exequatur to the bull, would not be free to suppress the Congregation, should it degenerate, the petition was refused. But the King, to console Alphonsus, took several opportunities of assuring him that he might rely on his continued protection. At this time Carmin Ventapane, one of the first physicians in Naples, a wealthy and zealous man, proposed to send the missionaries at his own expense into Calabria; the only province of the kingdom which had not been benefited by the labors of the Congregation. Alphonsus, who knew the destitution of these provinces, rejoiced exceedingly, and had the pleasure of despatching a number of his missionaries to Calabria in November, 1756. While they labored successfully in that province, he himself went with fourteen others to give a mission at Amalfi. God blessed it in a most remarkable manner. Among others, there were two suburbs in this town, peopled entirely by women of bad character, who were the ruin of the inhabitants, and a scourge to all strangers. It is attested that every one, without exception, was converted, and persevered in her amendment. Tamborines and guitars were common in the streets, and gave occasion to scandalous dances, which were characterised by libertinism and effrontery. He preached with such force against these disorders, that the young people piled these instruments in front of the cathedral and burned them. God was pleased to concur in a miraculous way in order to confirm the good done in this place. The evening before they left, Alphonsus said in his sermon "We are much fatigued in laboring for you; but to-morrow, as soon as we shall be gone, a devil will come down from the mountain to destroy the fruit of this mission. Listen to me, and look well to it, for you will draw upon yourselves the chastisement of an earthquake." Next day a buffalo was set loose for the amusement of the people, who all ran to the ring; but scarcely was the play begun, when a violent shock frightened the whole town, and the terrified people fled to the church. The Bishop ran thither, and while he recalled to them the prediction of Alphonsus, and the contempt for it which they had shown, another shock was felt, so violent that the flambeaus and the chandeliers were overturned. The Bishop himself became alarmed, and ordered the priests to give absolution to all. Thus a new testimony was given to the truth of the words of Alphonsus.

From Amalfi he was called to Nola by Mgr. Carracciolo, to aid him in the reform of his Seminary, in which the disorders had risen to such a deplorable height, that they seemed too great to be remedied. He went, but for several days he might as well have preached to the walls. The most awful truths of hell and eternity were but subjects of ridicule for many, who amused themselves by imitating the tone of his voice and his gestures. The Bishop was for reforming these disorders by gentle means, but Alphonsus said: "Mgr., do you know how many Bishops are damned because of the Seminaries? This will be your fate, if you do not change your system and employ rigor to banish the evil." He continued to preach, and when the exercises had nearly finished, in spite of the ridicule which still continued, all were suddenly seized with terror. Four of the most turbulent fled, others asked to be dismissed, and the remainder were filled with humility and repentance. A change so unexpected was regarded as the fruit of his prayers and penances. The reform was general; he established morning meditation, visits to the Blessed Sacrament and the Blessed Virgin in the evening, and the practice of Christian mortification. All began to frequent the Sacraments, and even those who had been among the worst, went to communion several times a week. He prescribed Novenas in honor of Jesus Christ and the Blessed Virgin, with other practices of piety, and a day of retreat each month. When the morals were thus reformed, learning began also to flourish, and this Seminary became afterwards eminent for the learning of those educated there. Alphonsus, during his long life, always took a deep interest in it, and, if he could not go in person, sent his missionaries every year to give a retreat.

From Nola he went to the diocese of Cerreto. On arriving at the palace of the Bishop, he requested a servant who was sweeping the saloon, to inform his master of his arrival. The man, seeing an ill-dressed individual with a long beard, continued his work without paying any attention to what he said; and when Alphonsus repeated his request, he began to mutter in bad humor, "I must finish this," and went on sweeping; as he approached where Alphonsus sat, he said: "Don't you see me here, why don't you rise?" Alphonsus rose without showing any annoyance, and when he had finished sweeping, again begged he would inform his master. The servant went and merely said a poor man wanted to speak to the Bishop; he was told to inquire his name, and what he wanted; but when the Bishop heard it was Alphonsus, he got up in a great hurry, calling first to one and then to another for different articles of attire, that he might receive him in a becoming manner. The valet, seeing all this, ran in great fear to hide himself. Alphonsus desiring to say mass, Monsignor sought for the valet to serve him; at first he could not be found, but after being called repeatedly, he came and threw himself at the feet of Alphonsus, asking pardon for what he had done. The Bishop, astonished, demanded an explanation, when the valet with tears avowed what had happened, Alphonsus laughing good humoredly at the whole affair.

From Cerreto he returned to Naples. It was whilst he was staying there that the following example of bilocation occurred. A woman whom he had reclaimed from an abandoned life, was in the habit of coming every Saturday for alms. Being told this time Alphonsus had gone to Naples, she went to the church, sad and disappointed, to recommend herself to God, but while praying, she heard her protector, who called her to the door of the sacristy, and gave her the accustomed alms, beseeching her to remain faithful to God. The woman on leaving the church said to the porter: "How is it that people call you a saint, and you have told lies? you have said the superior was at Naples, and he is here." When the porter denied this, she said: "I know he is here, for he called me just now, and gave me this money;" and she showed what she held in her hand. The porter, stopping the woman, ran to inform the Rector, who came with others of the Fathers to interrogate her, and convinced themselves that while laboring in Naples, he had been at the same time present at Nocera. A similar miracle happened in one of the missions at Amalfi, when he was confessing in the house and preaching in the church at the same moment.

Towards the end of May, the missionaries returned from Calabria, followed by numerous letters of thanks and supplications for more missions. In the month of November he sent again two detachments into the same province, the Prince John Filomarino having besought him to send them to the more remote parts of it at his own expense, to evangelise his poor vassals. Before their departure, the Blessed Sacrament was exposed, and Alphonsus gave them his benediction, almost envying their happiness at being sent on such a mission.

In January, 1758, he went himself with twenty of his companions to Salerno. His voice was too weak to be heard through all the extent of the cathedral, but notwithstanding, the people were dissolved in tears, and the greatest sinners, touched to the heart and deeply contrite, came to cast themselves at his feet. One in particular, sobbing convulsively, exclaimed, "How should I not weep, I who have offended God so much, when I see this holy religious doing penance for me." Long after, when Mgr. Pento had become bishop of Tricarico, he wrote in reference to this mission: "The benefit was great and permanent, the conversions innumerable and astonishing, the aspect of the whole town was changed, beginning with the highest and going down to the lowest. The fruits of this mission were of long standing; I myself owe the grace of being enabled to quit the world, to the light I then received." All agreed that greater effects could not have been produced even by the Apostles themselves.

In the course of this mission, Alphonsus had to bewail the loss of F. Xavier Rossi, the support of the house of Ciorani, and one of his oldest companions. But if he had reason to deplore his premature death, he had more reason to rejoice in his having died the death of a saint. This same Father had formerly been miraculously restored to health by the prayers and faith of Alphonsus. When he was told that the doctors despaired of his recovery, he wrote to him: "Invoke the peace of Jesus Christ, ask him to come and bless this malady and chase it away. I will that you live, and labor for the Congregation." This was sufficient, F. Rossi was cured.

During Lent, Alphonsus was called to Naples, and gave retreats in many monasteries. In that of St. Gaudiosa there occurred a circumstance too remarkable to be omitted. Father Galdieri, who accompanied him, desiring to venerate the blood of the Martyr St. Stephen, which was preserved there, Alphonsus having requested this favor from the nuns, they went in procession to bring the precious relic, and placed it near the tabernacle. Alphonsus incensed it, and two minutes had scarcely elapsed, when the blood liquified and became of a vermillion color, to the great astonishment of all present, for this miracle was never known to occur except on two occasions, the day of the celebration of his martyrdom, and that of the discovery of his relics.

It was about this time, that the same Father being about to sail for Calabria, one evening Alphonsus called him and said: "I wish you would not go by water, especially by this ship, in which you have taken your passage. Wait a little, in a few days some priest or other will arrive who has travelled by land, and you can return on his mule." F. Galdieri obeyed, and in a few days a priest came from Mormanno, and all happened as Alphonsus had said. But this was not all; the vessel in which he had taken his passage, was wrecked in the Gulf of Policastro, and all on board had perished.

A few days after, an event occurred much similar to the foregoing. One evening, when Alphonsus had still to recite his office, and also to correct some proof-sheets which the printer waited for, he was sent for in all haste to assist a certain duchess who was believed to be in extremity, and desired instantly to speak with him. He replied to the messenger: "Go, and tell the duke I am prevented from coming, but bid him take courage, the duchess will recover, and I shall see her to-morrow." During the night, although the case was thought desperate, the duchess recovered.

On account of all these extraordinary gifts, Alphonsus became the object of universal veneration and respect, but he only humbled himself more and more, as the following instance proves. Invited by the Provincial of the Jesuits to dine at their convent, these Fathers were anxious to have something that had been worn by him, and had recourse to the following contrivance. They remarked that his cincture was completely worn out, and brought him another in the hope of retaining the old one, but he, guessing their design, fastened the new one around him, without taking off the old.

Being besought by the inhabitants of Amalfi to preach the novena of the Assumption, he went, and as usual gathered much fruit. One evening, at the end of the sermon, he prayed to the Blessed Virgin for all present, and then besought his auditory to beseech her to bestow upon him some grace; when instantly a bright light, like a sunbeam, darted from the statue of the Virgin and rested on the figure of Alphonsus, who was elevated some height from the pulpit; his face glowed as fire, giving him more the appearance of a seraph than of a man.

About this time he gathered together the most important maxims of our holy religion, in a work entitled "Preparation for death." It met with great success, producing throughout the kingdom the effect of a mission, and causing many remarkable conversions. He gave then also to the public nine discourses with meditations for Advent, and a novena for Christmas, to excite a tender devotion towards the great mystery of the Incarnation and make its grandeur be comprehended, also a novena in honor of the Sacred Heart of Jesus, and considerations for the seven days which precede the feast of St. Joseph, all of which works had wonderful success.

In the year 1758, many of the people of Asia, of the sect of the Nestorians, having opened their eyes to the truth, declared to Clement XIII, their intention to re-unite themselves to the Roman Church, and be instructed in the Catholic faith. The Cardinals of the Propaganda, knowing the zeal of Alphonsus and the devotedness of his missionaries, asked him for workmen to labor for the salvation of these people. He agreed to their proposition, and in July of the same year wrote to the different houses to inform them of the circumstance, asking that those desirous of gaining the crown presented to them by the Lord in this work of so great difficulty, should inform him of their desire. This letter was responded to by all, every one being eager to give his life for Jesus Christ. Thirty of the novices offered themselves also for the work. Some even wrote their letters with their own blood, and Alphonsus was filled with consolation at witnessing such zeal. This project however was never put in execution; the circumstances which interfered to prevent it are unknown.

In the year 1759, Mgr. Lucchèse, Bishop of Girgenti, in Sicily, applied to Alphonsus to have the assistance of his missionaries in his diocese. He had met him previously in Naples, and had it always in mind to claim their services, till the following curious circumstance made him think of it in earnest. A swindling Neapolitan took advantage of the veneration in which Alphonsus was so universally held, to write in his name to different dioceses, requesting pecuniary assistance, and large sums were obtained in this way, for he was careful to inquire regularly at the post-office for the expected supplies. On one occasion, however, he was forestalled by the lay-brother who had charge of their affairs at Naples, and who received a letter from this prelate with twenty ducats. Alphonsus wrote to him to thank him for his bounty, and thus the cheat was discovered; but the correspondence ended in the missionaries going to Sicily.

About this time, Alphonsus undertook, with the aid of his missionaries, another very important work, viz: the reform of a royal hospital for female foundlings at Gaëta, which was by mismanagement reduced to a most miserable condition, both temporally and spiritually, the younger children, about four hundred in number, being entrusted to the care of the older ones, so that every thing about the place breathed only misery and sin; and this establishment, founded by piety, and liberally furnished with every thing from the hospital of the Annunciation at Naples, resembled rather a stable for the body and a hell for the soul. The case being represented to the King, he, knowing the zeal of Alphonsus and his missionaries, charged them with the reform, which had been attempted by different zealous priests, but without success. Alphonsus shed tears on hearing of such misery; he accepted the commission, and arranging a plan, sent the Fathers Mazzini, Fiocchi, and Gajano, as the best qualified to carry it into execution; and, after a work not of months but of years, Alphonsus sending often Fathers who remained there six months at a time, with the aid of four skilful sisters from the hospital of St. Vincent of Paul, at Naples, this asylum was at length converted from abandoned wretchedness into a little paradise, where prayer and mortification, silence and recollection reigned, and all virtues were practised, to the delight of Alphonsus and the great satisfaction of the King.

Always burning with the desire of saving souls, Alphonsus published about this time, 1759, several works calculated to promote this end. 1st, the Great Means of Prayer. This book may be said to be the essence of the soundest theology; it was regarded as a chef-d'œuvre by the most learned theologians of Naples and Rome. He himself says in the preface to it, that he wished to have the means to print as many copies of it as there are men in the world, in order to be able to place one in the hands of each, the neglect of prayer being the cause of the ruin of all the damned. 2d, a learned dissertation entitled, "Of the just Prohibition of Bad Books," in which he demonstrated the necessity of interdicting the sale of dangerous works, and proved that the Church, from her birth, had not ceased to prohibit and destroy them, replying also to the objections of adversaries who refused this power to the Pope. The Marquis Tanucci was displeased that such a work had been printed, and sent immediately the agents of police to the different booksellers to seize all the copies. This persecution vexed Alphonsus, who represented to the minister and other members of the council, that he had published the work only to obviate great evils, and without the slightest intention to give offence to the King. This representation was as water thrown on the fire, and produced immediate benefit. On the other hand the incident made a great noise, and the book, which had been previously little known, was so eagerly sought after, that the booksellers raised the price, and, to supply the demand, secretly printed many more copies in the course of two nights. 3d, the True Spouse of Jesus Christ, published while he was in Naples, during Lent, 1760, and, notwithstanding his weakness caused by excessive fatigues and many infirmities, gave retreats in several convents; an admirable work, useful not only to monks and nuns in particular, but also to seculars. In it he treats of the practice of all Christian virtues, and gives lessons by which all may profit according to their state. 4th, Reflections and affections on the Passion of Jesus Christ, simply stated according to the writings of the Holy Evangelists, a book admirably calculated to imprint deeply in the hearts of the faithful the Passion of Jesus Christ, and to animate them in making it the object of their meditation. 5th, under the title of "Silva of Matters to be preached," he published about this time a collection of instructions extracted from the Holy Scriptures, the Canons, and the Fathers, by means of which ecclesiastics could give the exercises in retreats. In the first and second parts he treats of the sacerdotal dignity, its end and sanctity, and of the virtues proper to the ministers of Jesus Christ. The third part contains the principal rules of popular eloquence, to aid preachers in acquitting themselves with success in the exercise of preaching and giving missions.

All the arrangements necessary for the foundation at Girgenti in Sicily, having now been agreed upon, Alphonsus sent a colony towards the middle of September, composed of F. Blasucci, Superior, and F. Francis Pentimalli, and two others. They embarked under a cloudless sky, and the vessel was soon in sight of Palermo; but at the moment they were about to land, they were overtaken by a violent tempest, and the vessel was thrown back into the Gulf of Naples, where they were forced to run aground. When the sea became calm, they set sail a second time; but again a storm came on, when they were opposite Palermo, which drove them into the Straits of Procida; they made a third attempt; but the more they endeavored to reach the Sicilian shore, the more the powers of hell seemed to set all in motion to oppose them. Again they neared Palermo, when a third tempest was let loose upon the unfortunate boat, which, being tossed about, at length was nearly lost between the Islands of Corsica and Sardinia, the vessel being so much damaged, that the passengers were hopeless of escaping. All this was seen by Alphonsus in spirit, and at the moment of their danger, he was heard to cry, while he raised his tearful eyes to heaven: "My poor children! my poor children!" He approached the window, looked at the weather, and sighed, then turned away, still repeating, "My poor children!" Those who witnessed this scene could not comprehend it, for they believed the Fathers had arrived in Sicily long before, and they said so to Alphonsus in order to calm him, but without success, he still continued to sigh and to repeat; "My poor children!" The tempest lasted more than twenty-four hours. On the third day the vessel with great difficulty reached Baja; their safety was an evident miracle wrought by the prayers of Alphonsus. The terrified missionaries, more dead than alive, took the way to Nocera, and the joy of Alphonsus may be imagined, when he saw his dear children once more in safety.

The missionaries had hardly taken a little breath in safety after their fatigues and dangers, when they were again despatched to embark anew, but another annoyance awaited them. Two vessels from the Levant had been shipwrecked near the port of Messina, and for fear of the plague all communication with Sicily was forbidden. Father Pentimalli, seeing it impossible, for the moment, to proceed, halted at St. Euphemia, his native place; but scarcely had he arrived, when he was seized by a violent fever, which carried him off in three days. This loss afflicted Alphonsus deeply, F. Pentimalli being one of his best missionaries. But this affliction was softened by hearing at length of the safe arrival of the others at Girgenti, and their joyful reception.

After their departure, Alphonsus, like an old soldier who wishes nothing so much as to die sword in hand, went to war against the enemies of God, on the old field of Amalfi. The Lord, in order to show the favor with which He regarded him, performed several miracles through his hands. The town was ravaged by an epidemic which seemed to defy the power of medicine. A canon who had great confidence in the merits of Alphonsus, begged F. Galdieri to give him the shirt the Saint took off after the sermon. He did so, another always being brought in exchange. On being asked what he did with them, he replied: "During this mortal epidemic, all those who have put on one of F. Alphonsus' shirts have immediately been cured." When he went to, and returned from, the church, he was the object of such veneration, that the canons were obliged to escort him to save him from the pressure of the crowd, who precipitated themselves upon him to get his benediction, while some, armed with scissors, cut pieces from his mantle.

The nuns of Conca besought him to come and give a sermon to their community, and during the voyage by sea they passed several fishing vessels, whose crews had been casting their nets without success. The poor people complained bitterly of their ill-luck, and besought Alphonsus to bless the sea, and scarcely had he done so, when the fish appeared in myriads, and their vessels were loaded.

After finishing the exercises at Amalfi, several convents of nuns at Naples besought him to visit them. He accordingly went, and preached with great success. At the convent of St. Marcellina, he found one of the pupils, Catharine Spinelli, dangerously ill; he visited her when she was almost on the point of expiring. "Catharine," he said, "would you wish to live, or die?" "I wish to live," replied the young girl. Alphonsus then made the sign of the cross upon her and said: "You will live, but you must become a saint." She was instantly cured; after sometime, she became a nun, and attained a high degree of sanctity.

He returned again to the capital during the following Lent, when he gave a retreat in the church of Purgatory to a great many students and priests, strangers, as well as

Neapolitans. Inflamed with the desire of seeing priests attentive to the fitting celebration of the holy mysteries, he published, during this visit to Naples, a work in which he showed the necessity of observing the holy rubrics, and gives salutary instructions on the dispositions with which the holy sacrifice ought to be celebrated. He published also a letter addressed to a religious, on the manner of preaching Jesus crucified, with evangelical simplicity, and avoiding the vain ornaments of a florid style. He sent this letter to all the superiors of religious orders, and every one admired the high degree of sacred eloquence which he possessed, and his extreme desire that all should strive to excel in the same, so as to preach Jesus Christ and effectually gain souls for him. Besides this retreat, he preached penance in the barracks, and scandals disappeared. He also gave missions in the different parishes. On one occasion, preaching in the church of the Holy Spirit, he suddenly exclaimed in a transport: "O thou who enterest here, and who flatterest thyself that thou canst be saved in the world as well as in a convent, unhappy that thou art, how far thou art wandering! but ere long thou shalt come to a deplorable end." At that moment, a young Calabrian had entered the church, who, led away by his passions, had long struggled against the grace that had been calling him to a religious life. He applied to himself the words of Alphonsus, and yet he dared to smile at the menace. But a month had scarcely elapsed, when he was killed by a musket shot. When dying, he told his friends what had happened in the church of the Holy Spirit.

CHAPTER XVII.

Alphonsus' Maxims and Conduct in his quality of Founder and Superior of a Religious Order.

ALPHONSUS was now nearly seventy years of age. Laden with infirmities, he believed himself already at the end of his course, but God had ordained otherwise, viz: that he should be raised to the episcopal dignity, and become a perfect model of a fervent and zealous bishop, as he had successively been a perfect model of a fervent and perfect layman, ecclesiastic, and missionary. But before we follow him in this new career, let us relate some of his maxims and actions, particularly relating to his quality of *Superior* and *Founder* of a religious order.

His first care was to inspire his missionaries with a true zeal for the salvation of souls. Therefore he was often heard to say to them: "What have we to do in the world, and for what purpose have we withdrawn into the Congregation, if not to devote ourselves to the glory of God? We are his adopted children, and more than all others ought to fight in the first ranks against his enemies without anxiety for life or death, since he has given His life for us." And again: "The love of Jesus Christ constrains us, irresistibly forces us, to love Him and make others love Him. If sin be not pursued by us, against whom shall we make war? It makes me ready to die, when I see a priest indifferent about any thing that concerns the honor of God." "Our employment," he used to say, "is the same as that exercised by Jesus Christ himself and His Apostles. He who has not the spirit of Jesus Christ, nor the zeal of the Apostles, is not fit for this ministry."

Next he required humility, saying: "It is this virtue which makes us respected by the people; it is this which gains and attracts sinners, however haughty and proud they may be. If the missionary wants humility, he wants all, and I know not whether the evil he will do will not be greater than the good he pretends to do, for how can God aid him who resists Him?" "It is not possible," he said, speaking of the humility and submission due to bishops, and particularly curates, with whom they came in more immediate contact, "it is not possible that God will bless our missions, if we fail in respect and humility towards the heads of the churches, and if we do not put ourselves entirely under them." Having heard, on one occasion, that a missionary had shown a want of submission to a bishop, he punished him immediately, and sent him at once to make the fullest apology for his conduct. He also exacted from his missionaries, humility towards each other, and more especially towards superiors, whose will he would have respected and fulfilled without delay. Every other failing was pardonable in his eyes, but this he considered inexcusable. Resistance on this point was always followed by expulsion. He was willing that every difficulty which he might not have foreseen should be pointed out to the superior, but he required that it should be done simply, without the least intention of resisting. "If obedience is wanting in a religious institute," he said, "all is wanting, for disorders, confusion, and trouble will be the result; a vessel guided by several pilots can hardly escape shipwreck, or at least she will make a very dangerous voyage." It was enough for any one to push himself forward, in order to be forgotten. A Father once complained that it was long since he had been appointed for the principal sermon in the evening. This was enough, he was not allowed to preach at all; and he was so vexed at the possibility of never appearing in the pulpit again, that he abandoned the Congregation.

Another characteristic he exacted from his missionaries, was a spirit of mortification and a love of suffering. Without these qualifications, he considered them unfit to be employed. We have already seen how much he insisted, in missions, on mortification and austerity with regard to food. He gave once a severe reprimand to, and imposed a penance on, Father Villani, for a very slight deviation from the regulations he had established on this point. "Men of the world," he said, "pay more attention to what is done than to what is said, and above all they remark the conduct of missionaries." And again: "They will not fail, when you are in their house, to insist and entreat, they will even appear displeased, if you refuse what they offer, but always decline; they will be edified by your firmness, when they would have been surprised, and perhaps have made you the subject of raillery, had you yielded." He abhorred the slightest appearance of delicacy, above all in him who preached the evening sermon, whoever he might be. At the mission of Salerno they had every day rancid cheese, and a Father took the liberty of asking that his morsel might be roasted. Alphonsus reprimanded him on the instant, although he was an old man, and a most zealous missionary. He distinguished, however, between what was delicacy, and a reasonable care for health. "Health," said he, "is the capital of the missionary; if that fails, he becomes bankrupt." But he charged the Superior to attend to that, and forbade the others to interfere, and rigorously exacted that no discontent should be shown with regard to food or lodging.

He disliked all familiarity and intimacy with laymen, and still less could he endure any species of idle discourse, unworthy as it is of the sacred character of the ministry. "I recommend," he said, "not to seek relaxation with any one whatever. It is necessary to be civil, but also to be serious, with every one, that they may conceive and also preserve esteem for the missionaries, in whom they ought to find men holy and without reproach; this is necessary if we would produce good. When we hold too much conversation with people of the world, and talk of things not spiritual, we let them perceive in us a thousand faults, which hinders the success of the mission. . . . . If any one neglects to correct himself on this point, I will no longer send him on missions." He forbade with the same severity, as well in missions as at home, all species of unnecessary visits,

Preaching being one great means of laboring for the conversion of sinners, Alphonsus was anxious that his missionaries should acquit themselves well in this work. He desired they should in every sermon preach Christ crucified. "He who does not preach Christ crucified," he said, "preaches himself, violates his ministry, and does no good." He required a simple and popular style that every one could understand, and he compared to balloons filled with air, those who, puffed up with their own importance, made fine discourses which they could hardly comprehend themselves. "When the devil wishes to hinder the preaching of the Gospel," he said, "he makes use of such preachers, to paralyze its effects. Miserable wretches, they will be condemned, not for having hidden their talents in the earth, but for having drawn no profit from them." He insisted on reasons and not on words, and clear and solid reasons too. He disliked studied and far-fetched comparisons, but recommended such as were suited to the people. "Jesus Christ," he said, "understood rhetoric better than we, yet to be better comprehended by the multitude, He chose ordinary comparisons in His parables. . . . . . The end the preacher ought to propose to himself is to persuade and to move. If the people be not convinced, (and how should they, if they do not understand?) they will form no good resolutions, and they will not forsake sin. . . . . . What would suit Boccacio, will not suit in a preacher of the Gospel, and many who study Dante and Boccacio will expiate their folly in purgatory." He was himself a perfect model of this apostolic simplicity, as we have already seen, and as is confirmed by the following testimony. Mgr. Carnovale having once been present at a sermon of Alphonsus, while yet very young, he said to himself, when he heard his simple and gentle manner: "This is time lost, F. Alphonsus deceives himself, if he thinks to touch rocks with such mild words." But when the sermon was finished, he beheld thousands weeping and sobbing bitterly; crowds of young men, known for their loose and irregular conduct, were converted by his simple eloquence.

He watched over the young preachers with the greatest care. One Saturday, on his return to Nocera from Naples, he was to preach the sermon of the Blessed Virgin, as he had vowed always to preach in her honor on that day of the week; but being suddenly attacked by fever, the young F. Alexander de Meo was appointed in his place. Not being prepared, he enlarged on several learned subjects not suited to the people, and spoke of the times previous to the birth of Mary, and introduced the Sybils and the Argonauts. When Alphonsus, who had been brought to the choir in spite of his fever, heard these words, he became restless, and leaning towards the others demanded: "Is it thus they preach here!" They knew not what to answer, and F. Alexander went on in the same style. Alphonsus rose, he sat down, he knelt, and said: "I must make him come down immediately. Go," said he to a lay-brother, "and tell him to descend instantly," and almost immediately he interrupted the sermon by intoning the "Tantum Ergo." But this correction did not stop here; on entering the house, the poor Father met Alphonsus on the stairs, and falling on his knees, begged pardon. After having reproved him for the impropriety of his sermon, he condemned him to remain silent during three days, and also to abstain from saying mass.

He exacted from confessors the greatest prudence and the most profound skill, as from their decisions there would be no appeal. He was scrupulous and even rigid in the examination of confessors, and would not confide this to another, but examined them himself, sometimes employing ten or twelve days, interrogating them upon all they had been taught, and if he did not think the candidate fully capable, he delayed giving him faculties. He inculcated upon confessors, as the thing most essential of all, to use the greatest charity and gentleness towards sinners. "The spirit of harshness and rigor," he said, "is what distinguishes the Jansenists, who do much more harm than good, and certainly have neither the spirit of Jesus Christ, nor that of those apostolic men whom we honor on our altars. . . .

An energetic word is sometimes necessary to make the sinner comprehend the gravity of his crimes, but this energetic word must not be repulsive, and before he withdraws, he must be calmed by kind words, so that he be at the same time full of hatred for his sin and of confidence in his Confessor." On another occasion he said: "If it happens that you feel yourself overpowered by bad humor, leave the confessional on the instant, because with your irritability you will cause your penitents to commit more sacrileges than you will do good to them." He could not suffer the least shadow of gallantry towards any woman, and recommended the greatest reserve with them. He regarded as a scandal having respect of persons in the confessional, all the world being equal before God. "Show charity," he said, "but not partiality. Ladies of quality will make way for themselves, but it is not the missionary's business to take care of them, we ought to be equally at the service of all, and ready to receive every body with kindness." Neither would he permit any preference to be given to a gentleman.

When he noticed a Father much sought after in the church, he immediately changed his residence. There was a young Father whom he had been at great trouble to educate, and whom he loved for his excellent talents. When he was authorized to enter the confessional, a great number of young penitents came to him, apparently attracted by his gracious manner. This displeased Alphonsus, who, fearing unpleasant consequences, wished to send him to another house. He resisted; but Alphonsus said: "Either obey, or leave the Congregation." He would not submit, and was expelled.

On the other hand, to encourage the timid, and inspire all with a great desire to help souls by means of the confessional, he said: "The preacher sows, but the confessor gathers the harvest. The confessional is the touchstone of the true laborer; he who loves not the confessional, loves not souls, to whom is applied there the blood of Jesus Christ, and the merits of His grace. In the sacred tribunal we gather fruit for ourselves and for our penitents; it is not so with the pulpit. If we do good by a sermon, a breath of vanity can make the preacher return with his hands empty. It is otherwise in the confessional, vanity does not ente there, but patience is necessary." He could not endure the idea of a confessor being shocked at the thought of hearing a very wicked individual, and who sought pretexts for refusing to listen to such persons. He considered this as a great fault, and insisted that they should willingly listen to all, and that if they could not give them absolution, they should at least point out to them the means of amending, and encourage them to return to them again. He was especially delighted when he saw any of his young priests desirous to seek out those abandoned souls.

He exacted from the priests of his Congregation a profound and continued study of moral theology. "This study," he said, "shows us our own ignorance, and hinders us from erring. The Rigorists and Jansenists of our day are ignorant on the science of morals, hence they are so extravagant and absurd. They wish to be considered masters, although they have never been disciples." A member of the Congregation, a learned and talented professor, fascinated by the opinions of the Rigorists, had constructed for himself a most incoherent system, and hesitated not to combat the opinions of Alphonsus, condemning the wisest authors, and speaking of them with contempt. As confessor, he ruined souls; as professor, he misled the young students. Alphonsus labored long to correct him, but seeing his efforts useless, he took his office from him, sent him to another house, and forbade him to hear confessions. The unfortunate man was offended by the correction, and not having the courage to suffer mortification, haughtily demanded a dispensation from his vows. Alphonsus employed the mediation of others to convince him of his errors, but all in vain. At length he said: "My son, you abandon the Congregation, and you persist in your errors, but tremble, for you will make a miserable end." He departed, but God was not slow in chastising him; in a very short time a horrible cancer appeared in his face, and finding peace nowhere, he ran about the streets, uttering cries of despair. When about to die, he besought with tears to be re-instated in the Congregation, that he might not die in despair. In consideration of his condition, his request was granted by F. Villani, Alphonsus being then bishop.

To inspire all with a true sense of humility, he said: "Humility is necessary in the mission, and it is necessary in the house; my brethren, humility at all times and in all places, if we would please God. . . . . . He who has humility will have sanctity, but without humility all fails." The very name of pride and self-love was odious to him as blasphemy. "This accursed self-love," he used to say, "ruins daily multitudes of laymen, priests, and religious; it sends numbers into purgatory, and many into hell. If this accursed spirit comes into the Congregation, better it would be if it should be destroyed. I beseech God to destroy it, the moment such sentiments are tolerated." It happened one day, that a Father chanced to use the expression, "On my honor." This was worse than heresy in the eyes of Alphonsus. In the next conference he continually repeated, "On my honor!" "Our honor," said he, "is, to be despised, vilified, and to be, like Jesus Christ, the opprobrium of men, and the abjection of the people."

Alphonsus never approved of the indiscretions of excessive zeal; he thought them a cause of unnecessary pain to others, and he dreaded the odium that they might cast on the Congregation. To give an example, there was a diocese which was dissatisfied with its bishop. Father Rizzi's zeal led him to write to the bishop to inform him of what had happened, and to remind him of his duty. When Alphonsus heard of it, he wrote to his Superior: "Tell Father Rizzi, that he has done wrong. He has acted through zeal, but he does not seem to know that we are forbidden to meddle with things out of the confessional, which may cause embarrassment to others. . . . . . He must say three Ave Marias as a penance, and when his lordship comes to the house, let him go to him privately and throw himself at his feet, confessing his indiscretion and asking for forgiveness."

Poverty and obedience were the foundations on which Alphonsus erected the whole structure of his Congregation; he said that if these two virtues always remained therein in full vigor, they would sustain it against all attacks, and that fervor would continue constantly to be on the increase. Although all about them had an air ot poverty and misery, it was still too sumptuous for Alphonsus, who forgot the magnificence and the grandeurs of the world, and had only St. Peter of Alcantara's cave before his eyes. He wished indeed that poverty should reign amongst his sons, but not such a degree of misery as to be contrary to decency. One day, he saw a young cleric in a pair of shoes which were thoroughly worn out; he did not speak, but he cast such looks at the shoes and at the Superior, that the latter immediately understood his meaning; and if he saw any Superior was negligent in procuring what was necessary for the subjects, he became excited by a holy zeal, reprimanded him, and even chastised him for it. He was particularly dissatisfied when he saw a Superior act with indulgence towards himself on this point, and with severity towards others. "Oh," he exclaimed, "how many Superiors will be damned at the Day of Judgment for having themselves violated the vow of poverty, and given a blow to charity and the common life in others."

He heard that F. Fiocchi had caused pewter dishes to be used in the house of Iliceto, in place of earthenware ones: he immediately wrote to him to say that he must sell all these dishes. It was in vain that various reasons for keeping them were alleged, and that he was told that, as earthenware dishes easily broke, and the house was far from a pottery, they occasioned great expense every year. "Poverty," he replied, "thinks of the quality of things, and that which suits it best, is that which is the vilest and coarsest. There is no example of such vanity, even in the less austere orders; he who is poor and professes poverty, ought to be poor in all things." Father Sportelli, when building, asked if he approved of a cornice which had been commenced under the edge of the roof; but Alphonsus blamed this as a luxury; he wished that nothing but the unpolished stones should be seen on the exterior of the buildings. While F. Cajone was Superior at Caposele, the choir of the church was put in order, and a new library was put up. The brother put little cornices on the stalls in the choir, and round the upper part of the library. Alphonsus no sooner heard of these trifling ornaments, than he wrote to F. Cajone, in a tone of great reproof: "You ought to know, that I do not choose to have any ornaments either in the choir or in the library. You must submit to this. If you have put any, you must take them away, and let all be quite simple. Poverty loves what is simple and necessary, but not what is superfluous." Some of the Fathers began to use snuff-boxes of varnished paste-board or of yellow leather; as soon as Alphonsus saw it, he immediately forbade them to do so again, and wished wooden ones always to be used, as before. One day he saw a hat which shone more than the others; that was enough to make him prohibit its further use and consider it as a scandal. Some of the Fathers told him that common cloth was not durable enough for the *mantellas* and *capotes*, and that this material was prejudicial to poverty instead of favoring it, and that the houses of the Congregation would gain by buying cloth of a better quality. "It is we," answered he, "who have made the vow of poverty, and not the houses; and it is we, and not the houses, who must submit to the consequences of this vow. Common cloth humbles and abases, and that is required by poverty." F. Ferrara represented to him several times, that brass lamps would cause less expense than earthen ones, which easily break and cause the oil to be wasted. All these reasons were unavailing, Alphonsus remained firm, because his only motive for not yielding was that brass was a luxury, while earthenware was more conformable to evangelical poverty. The prompt and perfect obedience which he exacted to his own orders, as we have seen above, he exacted also to those of all other Superiors. "It is not wonderful," he often said, "if I am obeyed, but I wish an equal submission to be shown to whoever presides over any exercise, for, whatever may be his personal merits, he holds the office of Superior. If this is not attended to, mischief is done, and we shall see nothing but disorder and confusion." One of the most distinguished of the Fathers, but one tormented at times by a fretful temper, blamed, in a fit of melancholy, some regulations which his Superior had made about a mission. Alphonsus heard of this, and although he felt compassion for him on account of his illness, he nevertheless wrote to him in the following terms: "I have been relieved to hear of your recovery; but I have been distressed to find, that you have given vent to some observations in regard to your Superior which were not at all right. Many things may appear absurd, which it is, however, reasonable to approve, because their motive is not known. If each subject wishes to do what seems to him to be the best, obedience no longer exists. I must, therefore, beg you, when things do not appear to you to be done as they might be at any other time, to state your opinion with simplicity, and then do nothing beyond writing to tell me what you think is wrong."

He was still more alarmed at hearing that the subjects of the Congregation had united together against the will of a Superior, for this was a fault which he never pardoned. "Public murmurs against a Superior," he wrote on one occasion, "are unpardonable faults, and deserve a severe punishment." The lay-brothers once complained of having been deprived of the siesta after dinner during the winter; as their discontent had been public, Alphonsus wished their penance to be so also. He deprived the two chief subjects of the habit for a considerable time, he condemned them to dine on their knees, to do without fruit or meat, and not to receive holy communion oftener than every eight days. Intercessions were made in their favor, but he was inexorable. He was accustomed to say that obedience works miracles, when it is exercised with promptitude and submission of mind; and that, on the other hand, the subject goes astray, when he tries to set himself up to judge of the thing commanded, and to deviate from the will of his Superior.

With regard to the observance of the rule in general, he was careful to see it always kept up in full vigor. He often said that he would prefer to see the Congregation dissolved, notwithstanding all the trouble its establishment had cost him, rather than see any want of discipline in it. When he was importuned by requests to found new houses, he replied: "Why should we wish to found new monasteries? Where there is no family there can be no observance of the rule. What I am anxious for, is to see fervor increase in the Congregation, and not to increase the number of houses." He never consented to any foundation, before he had enough subjects to form a community in which the rule would be perfectly observed. It happened once in the house of Nocera, that some dispensed themselves from assisting in the choir at the public exercises in the morning, either on the plea of not having slept well, or under some other pretext. Alphonsus, who attributed it to idle sloth, and not to any real necessity, ordered the brother infirmarian to take them a cup of tea after prayers, and to reiterate the same thing at every following hour, ordering them not to get up before the doctor's arrival. This had the desired effect, all the ills vanished, and the choir was filled before the time, every morning afterwards.

Speaking one day about the necessity of silence and of interior recollection, he said: "This rule is the rule of rules; if we observe it faithfully, we shall become saints. . . . . . The author of the Following of Christ says that the pious soul profits much by silence and repose; it is through them that she penetrates into the secret things of the Scriptures; it is there that she finds the source of those tears which wash and purify her. My fathers and brothers, let us not complain if we feel ourselves to be imperfect through dryness and want of recollection. Let us speak little to men, so as to be able to converse much with God, and he will act differently towards us, and will raise us up to a state of holiness." "Without recollection of mind," he also often said, "there can be no spirit of prayer, and those who go to the choir in this disposition of mind, go to torture; every instant seems an age to them, they come distracted, and they go away distracted; they lead a miserable life, neither possessing God, nor enjoying the world." In a word, Alphonsus desired that his missionaries should be Apostles in missions, and Carthusians in the house. "When you are without," he said, "you ought to sanctify others, but when within, you must sanctify yourselves."

With regard to tepidity, he one day said: "My fathers, let us drive away tepidity: the tepid soul is an object of disgust to God; she is a burden to the community and to herself. Let us reform ourselves, and betake ourselves to our former fervor, if we wish to please God, to be a comfort to the Congregation, and to live a holy and happy life." When he met with any who were afflicted by this malady, he did all he could to cure them. He called them to him, and warned them, as a father, of their danger. The incorrigibles often caused him loss of sleep. He made use of the spiritual exercises, retreats for some days, and reiterated warnings, and did not give up his efforts, until he saw that the case was a desperate one.

He made use of three methods for delivering the Congregation from these incurables. The first was to torment them by frequent punishments, by mortifications, and penances. When they found themselves treated so severely, these miserable and unenergetic subjects declared that they would not bear such a burden, and asked for a dispense from the oath of perseverance. The second method was to keep them in the house, and to forbid them to practice any apostolic works whatever. "The rebels," he said, "have a stronger desire to labor than the most fervent subjects, not from a zealous wish to win souls to God, but to enjoy greater liberty." The third, and not the least efficacious one, consisted in causing them to change their abode, and in sending them to whatever monastery pleased them the least, because of being either the most incommodious or the least frequented. Besides the constraint which they experienced from this change, they were also subjected to the pains and privations of the first two methods. If they were dangerous and likely to cause trouble in the Congregation, Alphonsus tried the effect of leaving them in a sort of abandonment, by not appearing to take any further care of them; he gave them leave to return to their families, without fixing the time of their return. Thus abandoned, they returned to the world, and themselves renounced the Congregation, to which they had no further desire to return, or else, he let them know after some time, that they had nothing more to do with the Congregation. There was one who caused great torment to Alphonsus, and to several Superiors. Repeated corrections and charitable offices had had no effect upon him. He asked for permission to go and see his relations, and obtained it; after some months had elapsed, Alphonsus pronounced his expulsion from the Congregation, and predicted that he would come to a most miserable end. In fact, after having committed several excesses, the unfortunate man perished a victim to one of his enemies, who caused him to swallow poison at the altar on Holy Wednesday, and on Good Friday, when all the bells were silent, he was buried as an infamous person, and his corpse was exposed to examination in presence of the officers of justice, and a crowd of spectators.

To inspire his sons with a high idea of their vocation, and thus to encourage them to correspond with it and put off the old man, he said, that vocation and predestination were one and the same thing, and that the having been chosen by God to form a part of a rising Congregation, was a grace, which, of itself, required in us a great degree of perfection and holiness. "In calling us to this state," he said, "God has not conferred a merely ordinary grace on us, but one which is as great as it is uncommon. We must therefore pray that Almighty God may cause us to understand the value of this grace, for if we do not correspond to so holy a vocation, we shall run the risk of eternal ruin. God has chosen us to be coadjutors of His Blessed Son, and to rescue souls from the grasp of the devil." "We ought to be most thankful to God," he said on another occasion, "for having taken us out of the world and led us to enter into His house, where the truths of faith are always put before our mind by frequent meditations, spiritual reading, pious discourses, and good examples. All these things are a great help to us in difficult positions; whereas those who are in the world, from only thinking and speaking of the things in the world, have few good ideas and many depraved ones in their imagination which cause them to give way on the least temptation."

When any one of them was on the point of death, the pious Superior felt a mixture of sadness and joy; he wept for the loss of a laborer, but he rejoiced much more at seeing a saint die; he therefore wished that the day of his death should be one of common recreation at table, instead of mourning.

He was not satisfied with ordinary holiness in those belonging to him; he wished them to aim higher. "We know not the secrets of God," he said, "nor on what conditions He may have caused our predestination to depend. He who is called to great holiness does not satisfy the heart of Jesus Christ by a low degree; if we do not aim very high, we shall not easily succeed in reaching the end which God has appointed for us."

If any reverse of fortune had befallen the parents of any of them, he pitied their distress, and wishing to preserve their vocation, he did not hesitate to relieve their families, in spite of the great want under which he himself labored; he did so on many occasions, by giving up to them the fees of their masses. Some of the Fathers thought that such instances of charity were excessive, on account of the poverty of the Congregation; but Alphonsus replied, that charity can never fall into excess, and that God repays all that is given in his name. His affliction was extreme, when he saw one overcome by temptation and ready to fall back. If these combats were caused by temptation, he pitied the subject, and tried to aid him by his prayers and those of others, he even forgave him some impertinence. In such a case he wrote to one most graciously: "St. Paul, the first hermit, said to St. Anthony the abbot, who begged him to open the door, or else he should die on the spot, 'this is a new way of begging, you beg with a menace.' I say the same thing to you. I feel pity in seeing the strife that has arisen in your heart: who ever sent you to Iliceto as a punishment? And then, just observe what you say: 'Otherwise I shall ask for a dispensation.' This is very well, but who will give it to you? Another time I trust you will not be so angry. I repeat that I forgive you, for it is not you who speak, it is temptation. But let us have patience, and wait till this noxious influence has passed away." These words drove away his temptation and restored him to peace. But when he was convinced, that in any one these combats rather proceeded from malice of self-will, and that he had lost the grace of God, and therefore no longer cared for his soul nor for him, Alphonsus did not hesitate an instant to free him from the oath of perseverance, although he did so with great regret, and often accompanied the act by the most fatal predictions; he considered such a dispensation as a very passport to the devil's house, and only gave it in tears.

To one, carried away by excessive attachment to his mother, as nothing succeeded in turning him aside from his purpose, Alphonsus at last said, on seeing his obstinacy, "I give you leave, but you will come to a bad end." The prediction was fulfilled. The unhappy man went away, and returned home, where he became the victim of God's anger and that of man also; he was despised by all priests, and a prey to a thousand contradictions. But his own mother caused him the greatest distress of all; for though he was seriously ill, she turned him out of doors, and he ended his life, deprived of every sort of assistance, in a miserable out-of-the-way hovel.

Alphonsus took no further pains about those who left the Congregation in this way, or who had caused themselves to be expelled from it, and there is no instance of any one of them ever having been admitted again by him. Any further intercourse with these deserters was forbidden, and they were considered as so many heathens and publicans. No reiterated requests to be admitted again, no intercession in their favor, caused their wishes to be granted, the prayers of the most influential persons, such as those of our oldest fathers, or bishops, would not prevail on the holy Superior. One who had been sent away, perceiving what a deplorable state he was in, presented himself before Alphonsus, threw himself at his feet, and all bathed in tears, entreated him to admit him again; but he was immoveable. This Father, knowing that he never refused any thing he was asked in the name of the Blessed Virgin, conjured him to pardon him for the love of Mary. But Alphonsus replied vehemently, "The Blessed Virgin Mary does not wish me to go to hell for you."

The heart of the most tender father could not feel greater love for his children than Alphonsus did towards our students. "We are their fathers;" said he, speaking to their Superiors, "and the Congregation is their mother. Since they have left their parents in order to give themselves to God, it is right that they should be treated with the greatest charity." There were three things which he wished them never to forget in the course of their studies: first, he did not like them to seek to know any thing but what was useful and necessary, and always with suitable moderation; in the second place, he objected to any boasting before others of more knowledge than was really possessed, much more, to setting up for acquirements which one had not; and in the third place, he wished for a continual growth in virtue, and especially in humility. "True knowledge," he said to them, "consists in knowing Jesus Christ well. Of what good will knowledge be to us, if its end is not to seek after God? . . . . . We must study, it is true, as we are laborers; but we ought to be fully persuaded that the one thing needful, and that which Jesus Christ requires above every thing else, is that we should endeavor to be saved as saints. We must study, but our sole object in studying ought to be that of pleasing God, otherwise it will only cause us to be a long time in purgatory, nay, even may lead some perhaps to the torments of hell, which may God forbid. Let your aim then always be the glory of God and the good of souls, and when an opportunity occurs for seeming ignorant, do not recoil from it, for it will not hurt you."

He had also an extreme affection for the young novices. When the noviciate was in the house where he himself lived, he always passed the evening recreation with the novices. In order to inspire faithfulness in following the vocation, and fear of losing it, he was in the habit of saying: "Vocation and perseverance are two distinct graces; God may give us the former even in the midst of our infidelities, but we shall not have the grace of perseverance, if we do not deserve it through prayer and good works. It is this crown which the devil wishes to take from us, and God allows him to tempt us, to try our constancy and to reward us proportionably." Three things he required in the novices, to insure their persevering and triumphing over temptations, viz: humility, obedience, and openness of heart. "He who is humble and knows his own misery," said he, "is all-powerful against the devil, he can never go astray, if he blindly trusts to the guidance of his Superiors, and above all if he is candid in confiding all that he feels to his director. A temptation which is revealed to another is vanquished, or half vanquished, for the devil, who is pride itself, does not suffer his artifices to be disclosed to a creature of earth, such as man is." When he found these dispositions in a novice, he felt sure that there was nothing to fear.

With regard to novices who became sick, his maxim was, that those who were patient and pious in illness, assisted the Congregation by their example, and that as they were themselves pleasing to God, they drew down innumerable graces upon it also. When a fervent novice was at the point of death, Alphonsus was not distressed, for he rejoiced in the assurance that such a novice was happy. If on the contrary a sick person wished to leave us, he only granted it with pain. "If the doctors and remedies we have here," he said, "cannot restore their health, they will not recover it any better in the house of their parents. If God wills that they shall die, it is better for them to die in the Congregation, than in the midst of the world."

Let us close this chapter by giving the wise rules Alphonsus prescribed to himself, which directed his conduct, and caused him to be an eminent Superior:

1st. A Superior ought to lead an exemplary life, for if he does not practice what he teaches, his government will be useless and dangerous.

2d. The Superior ought constantly to labor for God, and to be persuaded that he will often meet with ingratitude from man.

3d. Too severe a Superior makes the subjects imperfect and deceitful, because they will act only through servile fear.

4th. Pride makes a Superior odious to all, it hinders his own sanctification and that of his subjects, as well as the preservation of order in the institute.

5th. The Superior ought to possess heroic patience, he ought to bear all kinds of labor, fatigue, and contradictions, and always appear calm, and affable towards all.

6th. The Superior ought to give every one a reception full of charity and affection, and be all to all on all occasions.

7th. The Superior ought to be careful to cherish the same degree of love towards all, and to assist all alike in their spiritual and temporal wants.

8th. The Superior who does not overcome his antipathies, sympathies, or impressions caused by ill-temper, is hasty in his judgments, and falls into a thousand faults.

9th. The Superior ought not to be so presumptuous as to try to govern the institute by means of his own lights only, he always stands in need of prayers and counsels.

10th. The Superior ought to provide for the spiritual and temporal wants of his subjects, and to relieve them with all the care of a father and a brother.

11th. The Superior ought to be vigilant as to the observance of the rule, he must therefore inquire into every thing with the greatest exactitude.

12th. The Superior must not judge things hastily, but weigh them well, and reflect and inquire into them, before giving any decision.

13th. The Superior ought to punish offences against the rule, but he ought first to give repeated warning, which should always be accompanied by charity.

14th. The Superior ought to be firm with the incorrigible, and he must take care to prevent the contagion of bad example.

15th. The Superior ought to be just, exemplary, prudent, charitable, affable, and vigilant, if he would not undergo a terrible judgment at the tribunal of God.

CHAPTER XVIII.

Alphonsus is chosen Bishop. His journey to Rome and Loretto. His Consecration.

WE are now arrived at that period of the life of our Saint, in which God, in His wonderful providence, placed him on the candlestick, to enlighten all those who were in the house of His holy Church, and that he might labor for His glory by new works, and in new combats The episcopal see of St. Agatha of the Goths, a town situated at the foot of Mount Taburno, between Benevento and Capua in the Abruzzi, built by the Goths on the site of the ancient Saticola, mentioned by Titus Livius, 7th Book of the 1st Decade, chapter 8th, had become vacant by the death of Bishop Flaminius Danza. The succession to it was solicited by at least sixty candidates, amongst whom were bishops, and even archbishops. The Pope, Clement XIII, much embarrassed by the number of competitors, the claims of one not the most worthy, being, besides, singularly favored at Naples by a very high personage, consulted the Cardinals, and Cardinal Spinelli gave the advice to choose a man whose merits surpassed those of all the rest, and proposed Alphonsus, who, from the lustre of his origin, science, and sanctity, enjoyed an esteem as general as it was merited. This advice was followed, as being calculated to put to silence every pretension, and to end every anxiety. The news of the Sovereign Pontiff's decision being spread through Rome, filled all those who knew the future bishop, with joy, and the satisfaction was such that many prelates, and particularly the Cardinals Orsini and Cartelli, went to thank the Pope. Many other distinguished personages, among them, Prince Piombino and D. Gaëtan Buon-Compagno, who had known Alphonsus at Naples, were so rejoiced at this nomination, that they presented themselves in person to his Holiness, and congratulated him on having raised so learned and holy a man to the episcopate.

While this matter was being settled at Rome, the mind of Alphonsus was occupied with anything but this church and bishopric; one day, when conversing with Bishop Nicolas Borgia of Cava, on the mercy of God in rescuing him from the world, he said: "One of the greatest graces that I have received from the Lord, is that of having escaped the peril of being a bishop, a peril which I should have had difficulty in avoiding, had I remained with my family." Thus thought Alphonsus, but God had ordained otherwise. A courier arrived at Nocera on the 9th of March, 1762, with a letter from Cardinal Socatelli, Nuncio at Naples, inclosing one from Cardinal Negroni, which announced to him his election to the bishopric of St. Agatha, in the name of the Pope. On reading them, Alphonsus was thunderstruck; his senses became troubled, and he could not speak. As soon as the community were informed of it, they hastened to his room, and found him agitated, silent, and bathed in tears. After recovering himself, he became tranquil, persuaded that his refusal would immediately end all, and that the election was a mere mark of esteem which the Pope wished to give him. Alphonsus in consequence wrote a letter to the Cardinal-auditor, in which he thanked the Pope for his goodness, and exposed his own incapacity, his great age and infirmities, the vow by which he had engaged himself never to accept any dignity, and the scandal which his consent would give in the Congregation. When the courier was gone, Alphonsus said to F. Corsano: "See, this storm has cost me an hour and four ducats," alluding to the money he had had to give to the messenger, he then added, that he would not give the Congregation for all the kingdoms of the great Turk. He wrote at the same time to Cardinal Spinelli, to let him know the motives which had determined him to refuse the honor offered to him, and to beg him to cause his refusal to be accepted by the Pope. He wrote at the same time to his friend, the Abbé Bruni, who had much influence with the Cardinal. The next day, Bishop Borgia came to see him, and gave him a confidential letter from Cardinal Spinelli, who wrote, that his Holiness wished that he should immediately accept the bishopric, to take him out of his embarrassment, but that he should be at liberty to renounce it afterwards, when affairs should become more tranquil. This threw Alphonsus into new consternation, and greater than the first. Persuaded that the Pope would make difficulty to accept his resignation, he saw that he had no hope left but in God, and he made his brethren pray, that the Lord would deign to exempt him from this punishment, which he always acknowledged to have deserved by his sins. In his sermon on the following Saturday, he recommended himself to the prayers of the people, he redoubled his penances, he condemned himself to a severe fast, he diminished his sleep, and neglected no means to appease what he considered so violent a tempest.

As the time drew near, when the decision was to be given at Rome, the disquietude of Alphonsus increased;

but in spite of his extreme agitation, he was heard often repeating: "May the will of God be done." He remained balancing between fear and hope, but fear had the preponderance. "If the courier comes," he said several times to Fathers Ferrara and Mazzini, "do not let me see him, for he would seem to me like an executioner with the axe in his hand." At Rome, many well qualified personages who were acquainted with the reasons alleged by Alphonsus, hastened to intercede in his favor, especially dwelling on his age and his enfeebled frame. Cardinal Spinelli, informed of the state of Alphonsus, pleaded his cause himself, though with regret. On the evening of the 14th of March, the Pope seemed disposed to accept the resignation, but the next morning he decided to the contrary, without any one knowing why he did so. On the morning of the 18th of March, 1762, the messenger of the Nuncio appeared again at Naples. Fathers Ferrara and Mazzini opened the letters, and when they saw the firm resolve of the Pope, they went to Alphonsus, but before letting him know the truth, they got him to recite an Ave Maria with them. Alphonsus felt his heart beat, and said: "The courier has returned." They confessed it, and told him the Pope commanded him to accept. Upon this he raised his eyes to heaven, bent his head in token of submission, and said: "Obmutui, quia tu fecisti;" then becoming thoughtful, he added: "It is the will of God, God sends me out of the Congregation for my sins." Then turning towards the Fathers, he said: "Do not forget me. Ah! must it be that we shall separate, after having loved each other during thirty years?" On this he was silent, and his eyes became bathed in tears. The Fathers observing that he lacked not friends in Rome, who would cause the motives of his resignation to prevail, "It is not possible," replied Alphonsus, "to make explanations. The Pope has declared himself in absolute terms, which do not permit it: I must obey." At these words, he fell into such convulsions, that he remained speechless for five hours. When he came to himself, he wrote to the

Cardinal-auditor and to the Nuncio, that he was ready to accept, and to submit to the will of the Sovereign Pontiff. The refusal of Alphonsus had caused a great sensation, all Rome was edified, and this edification increased still more, when his unreasoning obedience and complete submission to the will of the Pope became known.

When D. Hercules heard that his brother had accepted the episcopate, he rejoiced, and hastened to offer such services as might be necessary to him under the circumstances. Alphonsus replied as follows: "My dear brother, I have been so stunned by the command of the Pope, that I should accept the bishopric on obedience, that my ideas seem to have left me. . . . . . I thank you for your offer of advancing the money. . . . . . What do you wish I should say? you rejoice; for my part, I can only weep. I have lost my sleep and appetite, I am beside myself, a fever seized me this morning, and this evening, whilst I write, it is not gone. I ask of myself, why my old age is to be afflicted by the painful labors of the episcopate, and how it is that the Pope, who never gives such commands, has adopted a tone of such severity with me? To conclude, may the will of God be done; He desires the sacrifice of the rest of my life, I must submit, whatever I may wish."

It being the custom of the bishops of the kingdom, who came to Naples, to establish themselves in a house according with their high dignity, Alphonsus, having accepted the bishopric, wrote thus to his brother: "As regards th house, I do not want to charge myself with the expenses. I think that when I come to Naples, one or two rooms on the first floor will be enough for me to receive the people in, who may wish to speak to me." To the lay-brother he wrote: "I hope that I shall not return to Naples, but in any case four straw chairs will be enough for me. If I have accepted the bishopric out of obedience, I must follow the example of saintly bishops: do not speak to me, then, about a carriage or livery. What good will it do to me to act the great lord in Naples?" Bishops Borgia and Volpe, and his director F. Villani, having shown him the necessity of his having a carriage, he consented to it, and wrote to his brother: "Yes, I am resolved to buy one, but I wish to see beforehand whether the late bishop has not left a carriage which might do, because I should have that much cheaper. I shall be in Naples this week or next, and then we will speak about it, for the short stay I shall make in that town I have no need to buy a carriage and mules immediately. I will use that of the Cordeliers for the visits I shall have to make there."

Great as was his submission to the will of the Pope, he made so violent an effort, and experienced such internal constraint, that the fever which had seized him on the 20th of March, became so alarming, that his life appeared in danger. "Just are the judgments of God," he exclaimed, "the Lord casts me out of the Congregation for my sins." One thing alone brought him relief, it was the hope of being able to re-enter the order. "I believe it is certain," he said, "that after God's anger is appeased, (and I hope that my prayers and zeal in fulfilling my duties may disarm it in a few years,) I am certain that then the Pope will have pity on my sorrows, and will willingly choose a more worthy person for St. Agatha; then he will send me back here to die within these very walls whence I am now going out." The Pope, rejoicing at the obedience of Alphonsus, wished to testify to him the satisfaction he felt, and in consequence the Cardinal-auditor wrote to the holy man to this effect, signifying at the same time, that his Holiness had consented to his deferring his journey to Rome, on account of the inclemency of the season. Hearing afterwards of his serious malady, the Pope was extremely afflicted, but said: "If he dies, we shall give him our apostolical benediction, but if he lives, we wish to have him in Rome." D. Hercules, hearing at Naples of the dangerous state of his brother, hastened to Nocera, bringing one of the most skilful physicians of that capital with him.

The submission of Alphonsus to the will of the Pope had caused great joy at St. Agatha. The chapter deputed several canons to congratulate him, but their sorrowful surprise on finding him in bed and in danger of death, was as great as their ardent desire of becoming acquainted with him whom God had destined to be their father, and of whose zeal and sanctity they had heard so much. On their return to St. Agatha, this news spread consternation among the inhabitants, and in unison with the clergy they addressed their prayers to God, that he would deign to restore the health of their future pastor. Public prayers were also offered to God in all the houses of the Congregation, each feeling a deep interest in the life of him whom he looked on as his father.

As his mind resumed its calmness, his body also regained its strength, but that he escaped from death, was considered a real miracle. When his humility would oppose itself to the Pope, he was heard to say: "God wills that I should be a bishop, and for my part I will to be a bishop." He was in this disposition of mind when, on the morning of Easter day, finding that he was almost well, he took the sudden resolution of going to his bishopric. He then, without loss of time, entered into one of those miserable carriages which are called *mantice*, and set out for Naples, from whence he had to repair to Rome. He was accompanied by F. Villani. On the Saturday before his departure, he did not omit to preach, according to custom, in honor of the Holy Virgin Mary, and he did it in so pathetic a tone, that he affected all his audience in an extraordinary degree. On leaving his brethren at Nocera, he begged all there present not to forget him in their prayers, in order that the Lord Jesus Christ and the Blessed Virgin might aid him to bear the load which had been placed upon him. After that, he added: "Do not grieve, my dear brethren, because I am going away; I promise that I will return here again to end my days." On passing by the Tower of the Annunziata, he stopped for a few moments, in consequence of a pressing invitation, at the house of the Garganos, a family of which all the members were greatly devoted to him. "I go to Rome," he said to them, "but I am sure that my representations, which have been powerless at a distance, will be more favorably heard when I am on the spot; the holy Father will let me go and die among my brethren, when he finds in me only a miserable carcass." He found fresh subjects of distress on his arrival at Naples. Being obliged to pay his respects to the ministers and magistrates, and finding himself beset at home by the crowd who came to compliment him, he required all his virtue to bear this new mode of life. "Recommend me, and let me be recommended by others very particularly, to Jesus Christ," he wrote to F. Mazzini on the 14th of April, "if I do not lose my senses now, I shall never lose them. Unhappy that I am, I left the world in my youth, and now in my old age I have to begin again to hold intercourse with it."

Very touching was the meeting of Alphonsus with F. Janvier Fatigati. Some years before, Alphonsus, when at Naples, having heard that this, his friend, was going to be elected bishop, went to see him one morning, and met him on the threshold of the door. "F. Janvier," he said to him with ardor, "do not accept the episcopate, if you do, you will be damned." Alphonsus in his turn received, at the time we are speaking of, the visit of his friend, who, more fortunate than himself, had been able to decline the burden. When they met, they were mutually silent, their eyes were bathed in tears, and the features of Alphonsus showed the bitterness which rent his heart, while those of F. Fatigati depicted the compassion he felt for his friend.

The expenditure of Alphonsus, when at Naples, for his equipment, was really extraordinary. His episcopal ring cost only a few carlins, it was adorned with a simple bit of glass; the brilliants in his pastoral cross were also made of false stones. When the jeweller gave it to him, Alphonsus said, "Oh what a heavy cross you bring me!" "What! heavy!" replied the workman with astonishment. "Yes, heavy," answered Alphonsus, bending his head twice, "alas! it is so weighty that I know nothing more overwhelming."

On Monday, the 19th of April, after Easter week, Alphonsus, accompanied by F. Villani, set out for Rome. He went to Cisterna to see Cardinal Spinelli. His Eminence could not help smiling on seeing him; but Alphonsus said at once: "My lord, you have not acted fairly towards me." The Cardinal related what had passed at Rome concerning him, and urged him to undertake the burden of the episcopate courageously, saying: "My lord, be sure of the assistance of God, for your divine vocation is most certain." The first thing which our saint did on arriving at Rome, was to visit the tomb of St. Peter. He remained before the altar in a sort of ecstasy for more than an hour, and he stayed for a long time on his knees before the image of the holy Apostle which is in the Vatican besides. They were so prepossessed in his favor at Rome, that he was welcomed every where with especial marks of esteem. The Fathers of the Congregation of the Pious Workers wished to have him in their house, and the Duke of Sora, Prince of Piombino, D. Gaëtan Buon-Compagno, being at Frescati, and hearing of his arrival, begged him to lodge in his palace, and offered him the use of his carriage. Alphonsus declined the dwelling-place, but accepted the carriage, which his weakness and great age rendered indispensable to him. When the Abbé Bruni came to see him, Alphonsus, who knew that he had taken part with Cardinal Spinelli in his nomination, could not help gently reproaching him by representing his incapacity. "I have no quality which fits me in the least degree for a bishop," he said, "but I submit because the Pope commands, and God wills that I should obey him." "The Pope wills that I should be a bishop," he said to the Abbé Troppi, a professor in Rome, "but I have come to let him see that I am but a machine out of order."

His humility made him quick in finding pretexts for excusing himself courteously from the most of the invitations he received. The Fathers of the Mission of St. Vincent of Paul invited him to dinner one day: "My Fathers," he said to them, "please give my dinner to Jesus Christ's poor for me, in order that He may let me see His holy will distinctly while I am at Rome." Cardinal Orsini invited him to his table. Alphonsus wished to excuse himself again, but it was in vain; he was told that the Cardinal had invited other great personages to meet him. When he was preparing to go to the Cardinal's, he was told that he ought not to present himself there in such a dress, (Alphonsus, even in Rome, gloried in wearing the habit of his order,) but should put on a court-dress. He did not attend to this advice, and when he met the Cardinal, he said to him: "My Lord, I am come as I was." The Cardinal smiled. "I know," added Alphonsus, "that you are ashamed of me." "Well my wish is, that you should shame me," answered the Cardinal; then he embraced him heartily, and led him in his cabinet.

Alphonsus had suffered a great deal at Naples from the numerous visits and compliments, but it was worse at Rome. "The time which must pass before I can leave Rome, seems like a thousand years," he wrote to his brother Hercules, "how I long to be free from all their ceremonial!" On his arrival, he heard that the Pope was at Civita Vecchia, and would not return immediately. He resolved therefore to go in the meanwhile to visit the holy house at Loretto. F. Villani tried to dissuade him from it, to save him from this additional fatigue. "My good mother Mary will strengthen me," he answered; "when will so favorable an opportunity offer itself again? Nothing will hurt me, if I can have the satisfaction of visiting the house where the Eternal Word became man for me." This journey, like that from Naples to Rome, was to him a continual union with God. He commenced before day-break by a long meditation and other prayers; then he said the canonical hours, paid a visit to the Blessed Sacrament and to the Blessed Virgin; he then said the Rosary and Litanies, and wished his servants also to recite the Rosary with uncovered heads. He said many prayers for the souls in purgatory, and passed the most of the time till twelve, in singing pious hymns, and in holy converse with F. Villani. He celebrated Mass every day, and when the hour approached, made his preparation, with a long thanksgiving after it. While he continued his route, he said Vespers and Compline; he then made a long meditation, together with a visit to Jesus and Mary, and recited the Rosary again. On arriving at the inn, he said Matins and Lauds for the following day. His attendants were humility and poverty. He fasted in the morning, and took his evening meal in a strange manner, for he went to the same table as the drivers, as if he had been the poorest of the travellers.

He experienced ineffable consolation, the three weeks he passed at Loretto. He observed, or rather meditated on, the smallest local circumstance. "It is here," he exclaimed in unceasing rapture, "it is here that the Word became man. It is here that Mary held Him in her arms!" One day he told F. Villani to retire, wishing to contemplate at his leisure the mysteries which this cradle of the divine humanity recalled to his mind. During all the nights he passed at Loretto, he never went to bed; he remained constantly on his knees, sometimes without any support, sometimes with that of his bed. These details were given by his servant, who watched him through the crevices of his door. The same servant related also, that for his supper he took only an infusion of sage, ate very little at dinner, and when he was urged to take some dishes which the inn-keeper brought for him, he always declined it adroitly. He never left the house to go to see the town, only going out to celebrate Mass in the morning, and to pay a visit in the evening to the Blessed Sacrament and the Blessed Virgin. The pilgrims came to the saintly man in crowds, and he neglected nothing in order to relieve their misery. One of them coming before him half-naked, he opened his trunk and gave him his best shirt, and a tolerably large alms besides. When he was obliged to leave Loretto, one may say he left his heart behind him on that holy spot. On his return, he did not cease to speak of the great mystery, the very scene of the accomplishment of which, he had been visiting.

A heavy rain fell the night after his departure, which swelled the stream of the river Tarni. The next morning, in leaving Marino in a boat, an awkward evolution nearly upset the barge; Alphonsus fell into the water, and disappeared in the middle of the river; but the servant threw himself into the stream, and miraculously succeeded in bearing him out on his shoulders to the other side. When they arrived at Spoletto, Mgr. Acqua, bishop of that city, being informed of the passage of his saintly colleague, sent his carriage to the hotel for him, being himself confined to bed by gout, and under great uneasiness as to the state of his diocese. He opened his heart to him whose works he admired so much, and told him all his trials. Alphonsus consoled the holy bishop, who passed the greater part of the night with him, blessing God for having been able to converse with a man so full of the Spirit of God.

Alphonsus returned to Rome on the evening of May 8th, 1762; and the Pope arrived almost at the same time from Civita-Vecchia. He went to do homage to him immediately; as he bent to his feet, the Pope hastened to raise him, and embracing him, made him sit beside him; but Alphonsus threw himself anew at his feet, and supplicated with tears to be exempted from a charge which his infirmities, his age, and above all, his incapacity, rendered him unfit for. "Obedience," answered the Pope, "enables one to work miracles; trust therefore in God, and he will assist you." He then made him sit down, and questioned him as to the state of Naples, both in its political and spiritual relations; he kept him for an hour and a half, as he took very great pleasure in talking with him.

When going to visit Cardinal Torregiani, secretary of state, he wished, before making himself known, to wait till all who had asked an audience were satisfied; so he staid humbly in the ante-chamber. But Bishop Molinari, who knew him, happening to enter the ante-room, informed the Cardinal's servant who he was. He had been taken for a mendicant; the Cardinal was immediately informed, and received him with distinction above every one else. The Pope wished often to see him, and conferred with him on many affairs of much importance to the Church. He conceived the highest opinion of his virtues and science from these interviews. He never spoke of him without admiration, so much so that a rumor went about that Alphonsus would be made a Cardinal. Alphonsus himself seemed to confirm these reports, by the terms in which he wrote to his brother Hercules of what had passed between himself and the Sovereign Pontiff.

In one of these visits to the Holy Father the conversation fell upon frequent communion; Alphonsus told him that he had been opposed at Naples on this subject by some men more rigorous than devout, who, by exaggerating the dispositions which this sacrament requires, discouraged the faithful and kept them at a distance from it. He disapproved of the silence of Alphonsus, and charged him to refute his adversaries. Alphonsus consented, and during his stay in Rome composed and published a treatise on this subject, which the Pope received with great satisfaction.

He went to visit the examiners, and when he was asked on what treatises he wished to be examined, he wanted to leave it to their own choice; but as they insisted to the contrary, he named those de Mutuo and de Legibus; but one of them, who knew how much he dreaded the episcopate, wished to propose a question which would please him; it was this: "Is it lawful to wish for the episcopate?" On the eve of the examination, the thought of the burden which threatened him brought on a sick headache, which took away all his rest; he would not eat, and indeed was incapable of taking anything; however, he took a little in obedience to F. Villani, and the next day, in spite of the discomfort he felt, he presented himself for the examination. One of the examiners, having proposed the question, begged him to raise his voice a little, but Cardinal Gallo, turning to the Pope, said: "Holy Father, he does not hear, because he does not wish to hear." The Pope smiled, so did the examiners and persons present. At the end of the meeting, one of the Cardinals suggested to him that he should return thanks to the Pope; but either he did not understand it, or feigned not to understand it, as the Cardinal repeated it a second time. "Most Holy

Father," said he then, "since you have deigned to make me a bishop, pray God that I lose not my soul."

On St. Basil's day, the 14th of June, Alphonsus was consecrated bishop, in the church of Minerva, by Cardinal Rossi, assisted by two bishops. It was an overwhelming day for our saint. He confessed to his director afterwards that he had had two great battles in his life: the first, when he left the world, and had to struggle against the tenderness of a father who clasped him tightly in his arms; the second, when he was forced to be ordained bishop when at Rome. "For then," said he, "I was cast down by fear in thinking of the burden I was loaded with, and the account I should have to give of it to God." After the consecration, some one said to him that if he wished to enjoy the privilege of wearing a cap at the altar, he must obtain a brief: "Oh!" he exclaimed, "what a thing it would be if I should spend money in order to contract a wicked debt towards Jesus Christ!"

Our Fathers, seeing what great harm might happen to the Congregation by his loss, had united to entreat the Pope to grant them that Alphonsus might continue to be superior and rector-major of the institute, and that a vicar-general should govern it in his name. This request was supported by F. Villani, to whom the Holy Father immediately replied with kindness: "I wish that this Congregation should go on and be well supplied with subjects, and I do not intend that it should suffer any harm from the elevation of its founder, for the great good it has effected in the Church and in the kingdom of Naples, is a great consolation to me." Thus his Holiness condescended to grant all their wishes, which helped in no small degree to alleviate the sorrow of Alphonsus, who had believed himself cast out of the Congregation in punishment for his sins.

The Holy Father desired the new bishop to come to his private audience six or seven times; at his last visit, in bidding him farewell, he loaded him with kindness, and seemed unable to separate from him; he recommended the Church and himself to his prayers. He gave him his bulls gratuitously, and Cardinal Antonelli, secretary of the consistory, defrayed the other expenses.

During all the time he staid in Rome, Alphonsus led the most edifying life; he never went out but from necessity, or to visit the sacred places. After his consecration he revisited the tomb of the apostle St. Peter, and placed himself and those committed to his care under his protection. Cardinal Orsini invited him a second time, but Alphonsus declined the honor, excusing himself on the plea of his infirmities. He mortified himself at Rome as elsewhere. The great heat caused him to suffer much from his head; he was asked one day to take an ice which was offered to him, but he refused to accept it, and contented himself with a glass of lemonade, which is called fresh water in Rome. He was always dressed as a missionary, and wore the Rosary at his girdle, and a broad-brimmed hat. A person of high rank could not help telling him: "In not leaving off the habit of your order, you have given a most edifying example to Rome." The Pope himself did not cease to praise his virtues, and said to several Cardinals: "On the death of Bishop Liguori we shall have to honor another saint in the Church."

CHAPTER XIX.

Alphonsus leaves Rome and goes to his diocese. His manner of life as a bishop. He gives the Spiritual Exercises to the Clergy, and a Mission in his Cathedral. Some examples of his severity against hardened sinners.

ON the 21st of June, after celebrating mass at the altar of St. Louis Gonzaga in the church of the Gesù, Alphonsus left Rome. In this journey, as in the preceding ones, poverty was his inseparable companion; though a bishop, he sat at table with the drivers, without suffering any distinction to be made. He arrived at Naples on the morning of the 25th. He visited among others the four ministers, and commended himself most particularly to the Marquis of Marco. "I go into a diocese a little in disorder," he said to him, "and each one will wish to justify his conduct. I pray God that they may all really be able to do so; but I entreat you to regard the honor of God and the welfare of souls." "Do not be distressed," the Marquis answered, "and if you require the King's support, be assured you will obtain it." He was invited to the royal table, and went there; but while he was in the antechamber he was not recognised by the two young chevaliers in attendance. The Canon D. Fabricius Martini made it known that he was Bishop Liguori, and Alphonsus became immediately an object of great attention and veneration. Confused by this, he gently complained to Mgr. Martini for having made him known. In the drives through the town, he always told the coachman not to attempt precedence, but to give way on all occasions. At the gate of the Santo Spiritu, he met a prince's carriage, which seemed disposed to go first. His coachman wished to dispute this advantage, but when Alphonsus perceived it, he ordered him to leave the passage to the prince, and reprimanded the man on his return, enjoining him to give place for the future, even to a groom. The religious of the principal convents, and others, asked him to visit them and to say mass in their churches, but not wishing to prolong his stay in Naples uselessly, he gratified only a few, among them his cousin Francis Cavaliere, who, with the concurrence of the Cardinal, wished him to give the Sacrament of Confirmation to one of his daughters in the chapel of his palace.

Before he left Naples, a priest of Arienzo went to visit him. He thought it meritorious to present himself before his bishop with a worldly affectation of dress; he was perfumed and curled, and wore buckles which covered all his shoes. Alphonsus felt pity on seeing such vanity of mind, and said to him with touching goodness: "My son, these are not the buckles of a priest, and this head-dress does

18*

not suit you at all; if you act thus, you who should be an example to the people, what then will men of the world do?" The poor priest was quite confused, and changed his conduct.

Alphonsus left Naples on the 3d of July. He visited Cardinal Sersale at the Tower of the Annunziata. He received him with the tenderest proofs of friendship, and said smiling: "You are, then, caught." "Obedience so willed it," answered Alphonsus. The Cardinal accompanied him to the stairs, and on seeing his equipage, said jestingly: "But so, you have taken the livery of a Cardinal." "It was not I who ordered it," replied Alphonsus, "it was the work of D. Hercules." Alphonsus had wished it to be of a dingy ash color, but to his great regret, Hercules had made it of crimson on blue ground. Casting his eyes after that on his shoe buckles, the Cardinal said laughingly: "You must have bought these at Rome, and no doubt they cost you a great deal!" They were little iron buckles, which had cost a carlin.

He arrived at Nocera on a Saturday, and preached there according to custom, in honor of the Most Blessed Virgin Mary. On seeing the saintly bishop, the whole audience melted into tears. The Fathers, because of the visits which would be paid to him, did not put him in his ordinary cell, but gave him two in another part of the house, that he might sleep in the one, and receive visitors in the other. One evening passing before his old cell, he exclaimed: "O my cell, formerly thy sight consoled me, now it afflicts me." He was so overcome by regret that he could not banish tears from his eyes.

On the morning of the 8th of the same month, after a tender farewell to his dear monastery of Nocera, he took leave of the missionaries and set out for Naples, accompanied by F. Francis Margotta. "My brethren," he said, when going away, "do not forget me. I go into exile, far from my dear Congregation." He could say no more, for his emotion was extreme.

As it was during the burning heats of summer, and at that period when the weather frequently changes, the doctors of Nocera had given him the advice to defer the journey, but considering it the part of a good shepherd to give his life for his sheep, he braved the inconstancy of the season, and set out immediately to go and unite himself with his church. "A bishop," he said, "ought not to think of his own life, but should sacrifice himself for the souls which are entrusted to him." He was also strongly advised to stop at Arienzo, a town of his new diocese, on account of the comfortable house and more salubrious air he would have found there, but he wished to go to St. Agatha, as the place where God had fixed his abode.

No triumph in the memory of man had ever been seen equal to that of Alphonsus when he entered the diocese of St. Agatha. He wept, being affected at the sight of the crowd of people who filled the road and had hastened from all parts to receive his first benediction. On arriving at the gate of Real-Vale, he was saluted by a discharge of mortars and brilliant fire-works. When passing before the parish church, he perceived an immense crowd, who had hastened from the country, desirous of having his episcopal blessing; affected by this pious eagerness, he got out of the carriage and entered the church, where after a short act of adoration of the Blessed Sacrament, he comforted all the faithful by a simple and pathetic discourse. In passing by Bagnoli, a fief of the see of St. Agatha, he was again saluted by roars of cannon and by a thousand acclamations from a joyous people.

On his arrival at St. Agatha, he received, on descending from the carriage into the court of the episcopal palace, the congratulations and homage of both the secular and regular clergy, and of a number of distinguished inhabitants of the town and diocese. After a moment's repose, when they were making ready to conduct him to the church in procession, the canons discovered that he had no cap or green hat. Not being able to do better, they took that which was placed on the tomb of the deceased Bishop

Danza. After the Blessed Sacrament had been exposed, Alphonsus prostrated himself for a long time with his face on the ground, which he deluged with his tears. The cathedral was so crowded, that spacious as it was, a good many people were obliged to stay at the door. When they had chanted the Te Deum, the bishop descended from his throne, and placing himself on the right side of the altar, he comforted all present by a discourse in which his love and zeal were equally shown forth. All who assisted there shed tears of joy, and thanked God for having given them an angel for their pastor, and when they left the church were heard to repeat: "We have a saintly bishop, we have a saint among us." Such was the impression the first sight of his poverty and humility, and the words of his burning zeal, made on the mind of the people.

During this first sermon, Alphonsus had been suddenly attacked by an obstinate fit of coughing; one of the canons turned to the others, and said in joke: "Make ready, gentlemen, to elect a new vicar-capitular, for if my lord has another such attack, we shall infallibly lose him." Alphonsus, to whom this remark was reported, together with the canon's name, said jestingly in his turn: "He does not know that green pears fall more easily than ripe ones." A short time afterwards, this priest, though in the prime of his life, was carried off by death, the first of all the chapter. The same evening, Alphonsus had occasion to give proofs of his great disinterestedness; several of the most distinguished people sent him a quantity of provisions of great price, for his table; but he sent them all back, giving money to the servants who had brought him these presents, and expressing his gratitude for so much kindness. Some days after, the Provincial of the Dominicans sent him a great quantity of choice dishes, but he refused all, and caused him to be told that he never accepted of such presents. The Fathers Conventual also wished to show him their friendly inclinations, by sending him a basket of little cheeses, with a quantity of sweetmeats, and small wax tapers. Alphonsus took one of the cheeses and sent back all the rest. Others were not more fortunate.

The holy prelate's secretary, Don Verzella, seeing they had several distinguished guests, D. Hercules and others, thought he ought to provide a suitable supper. Alphonsus was dissatisfied, and sent for him and said: "Felix, may God forgive you, what have you done? I am not come here to give sumptuous repasts; I do not wish to treat you harshly, but I cannot understand any excess. When there are so many poor who die of hunger, it does not befit us to make good cheer." Not satisfied with this reprimand, he sent for him again, and fixed the fare for each day; he desired that for his dinner, soup and boiled meat should be prepared; an extra dish was only to be had for those of his household, or for guests.

Though raised to the episcopate, he did not change his manner of life; he even followed a severer rule. Before his departure from Nocera, he had sent a lay-brother to arrange the palace of St. Agatha, and charged him to carry his empty palliasse there, as he did not wish to have any other bed. Not finding this, he complained to the brother, who excused himself by saying that the canons had prevented it, and that they had not been able to procure suitable straw. "Let it be procured," said Alphonsus, "and let it be bought at any price." He had the mattrass removed, and spread the empty palliasse on the boards of the bed, where he passed the night, and the next day was not at rest till he had seen his palliasse arranged according to custom for the following night. He went all over the palace, and chose the most inconvenient and the plainest room for himself, giving the best to his Grand-Vicar, to his secretary, and to F. Angelus Majone, who was to remain with him; he did not go to bed the first evening till he had disciplined himself severely for a long time. He also visited the garden. He found it destitute of trees and vegetables; he sent for the brother, and ordered him to plant a number of kitchen plants, as if it were the month of February. The brother smiled at this order, and represented to him that it was not the proper season. "Do as I tell you," replied Alphonsus. The brother obeyed, and every one laughed at it, but they were much surprised when, a little afterwards, they saw that all without exception throve wonderfully.

From the time of his arrival at St. Agatha, he made a rule of daily conduct, which he continued to follow throughout the thirteen years during which he sanctified his Church. As soon as he arose, he gave himself the discipline to blood each morning. After that, he made half an hour of meditation with his whole household, the Vicar-General alone being free not to assist. The canonical hours followed, and after a suitable preparation, he celebrated Mass; he then heard on his knees that which his secretary or another priest said immediately after. Having thus done his duty towards God, he gave audience to those who had to speak with him, and occupied himself in satisfying the messengers who came from divers parts of the diocese; to spare to all the tedium of the ante-chamber, he told his servant to usher in immediately every person, however poor. The curés and vicars, as well as confessors, had no need of being announced, he wished them to enter at all times with perfect confidence. "These are my privileged ones," he said, "they ought not to suffer any restraint." When no one asked an audience, he began to compose or to dictate immediately after mass, which he never did when he had to attend to the people of his diocese. As soon as there was any one to hear, he directly left his study and did not return till he had satisfied the visitors.

The furniture of his room consisted of little more than a writing table; it was there he placed himself in the morning, with a crucifix and a figure of our Lady of Good Counsel before him, continually engaged in prayer, in work, and in giving audiences and attending to the affairs of his diocese. As his dislike to useless visits was known, no one went to him but for things worthy of notice, and if, after having satisfied them, they did not retire, he said: "Now then, do not let us lose time," or, "Recommend me to Jesus and

Mary." If he had to do with people he could not with propriety dismiss, the constraint he suffered interiorly, on account of the loss of time, of which he was only avaricious for the glory of God and the good of his neighbor, became visible. Every one had free access to him except females; if any one of these asked to speak to him, he desired to be informed first, and generally conversed with them out of his room, and always with a witness. A lady of rank and of a great age wished to speak to him alone: "There is no objection to this brother being present," Alphonsus said to her; (it was brother Anthony,) "he is prudent, depend upon it." Another day, he was seen to give audience in a drawing-room to an old lady who was quite decrepit; he made her sit on a long bench, of which he occupied the opposite extremity, and conversed with her, with his back half turned towards her. When he went to church, he wrapped his right hand in his handkerchief and held the left in the opening of his cassock; if a woman presented herself to kiss his hand, he said: "Kiss the habit, that will suffice."

The habit which our saint had adopted of assisting at all theoffices, was not discontinued when he was a bishop; he liked to preside over all that was done in his cathedral, at the high masses, vespers and canonical hours,—no indisposition stopped him; he was known to officiate pontifically when seized by fever; one day that he had applied a painful remedy to his legs, he officiated notwithstanding, and suffered so much that he was seen to tremble on his throne.

During his meals, he took care to give food to the soul also; each one read in turn. It was generally from the life of St. Charles Borromeo. The time which he passed at table and in recreation did not exceed an hour and a quarter. When the fruit was brought, he conversed with his grand-vicar on the affairs of the diocese, or on some point of devotion, or received those who had not been able to speak to him in the morning, especially if they were poor, or messengers. After dinner he took some rest, which is so necessary in Italy; he was satisfied with twenty minutes, or at most half an hour, and before it he never failed to say the Five Psalms in honor of the name of Mary, a devotion which he had practised from his youth; but often he studied instead of taking this rest. As the example of the saints, as he used to say, encourages us and excites us to do good, he never omitted to employ half an hour each day in reading the lives of the saints, and above all those of holy bishops who had been distinguished by their zeal and contempt of themselves. This was followed by half an hour's meditation, vespers and compline. The rest of the day he gave to business or study. On feast days, and especially in Lent, after vespers, he instructed the children himself, and taught them the catechism. He knew how to attract them by giving them pictures and rosaries; with these little ones, older persons attended in crowds. For visiting the poor, the sick, and those whose consciences were neglected, he went at about five o'clock in the evening; he took care not to forget ecclesiastics who might be ill, making it an indispensable duty to go and comfort them in their infirmities. At half past five, the bell rang for the visit to the Blessed Sacrament, and he himself spoke to the people for half an hour, to inspire them with sentiments of faith and love towards Jesus Christ in this divine mystery. Though the sacristan placed a prie-dieu with a cushion for him, he knelt on the pavement near the altar. It was during this devotion that, wishing to banish profane and improper songs, he introduced hymns full of unction and piety, he gave the tone himself, and repeated the verses in union with the people. A doctor, observing to him that this weakened his chest, he replied: "I must make the people like these hymns, to disgust them with dangerous songs."

When he had returned home, he gave audience and distributed his alms; then, said matins and lauds, which were followed by half an hour's meditation with the lay-brother, and after this, if it were in winter, he worked till nine or ten o'clock, but in summer he immediately assembled all his household, without even excepting the Grand-Vicar, to say the rosary together, the litanies of the Blessed Virgin, and some other prayers. Then came the examen of conscience, followed by acts of faith, hope and charity. All those who happened to be in his house, servants, strangers, and even prelates, had to assist at these prayers; noticing one evening that a bishop who was then in the palace did not assist, he immediately sent to call him; even princes and great lords who visited him were not dispensed from it; and this same severity he practised, wherever he was. When these prayers were ended, supper came, after which he conversed for a few minutes with his Grand-Vicar and other members of the house, on subjects which might concern the diocese; after this every one retired, and Alphonsus resumed his scientific occupations, or was employed in prayer. He did not suffer from this, as he ate so little as to be able to recommence prayer or study immediately. For a long time he took no supper, and only drank a glass of water before going to bed. F. Fabius Buonapane declared, that he regularly employed sixteen hours each day in work and prayer.

Besides the Vicar and Br. Anthony, Alphonsus had a priest with him who filled the offices of secretary, steward, and almoner, one servant, and a watchman, who acted at the same time as groom and cook. His servants were obliged each day to assist at the mass of the Bishop and the Grand-Vicar, and to approach the sacraments at least every fortnight, and on the principal feasts of our Blessed Lord and the Holy Virgin. They were obliged to communicate at the bishop's mass. Every sort of game was forbidden to them, above all, games at cards, where interest might be concerned. Public houses were prohibited to them still more strictly; in a word, he wished the members of his household to edify every one by irreproachable conduct. Though indulgent for every other fault, yet, if holy purity were in question, whoever the culpable one might be, he was dismissed on the spot. He thought he perceived that the cook had some attachment for a woman; not content with sending him away, he wished that he should live in another place; and, as he paid no tattention to his wishes, with the consent of the civil authorities, he charged the constables to arrest him. He also dismissed another, who went out during the night. He made a rule never to receive any servant who was not married, and who had not his wife at St. Agatha. Thus Alphonsus, from the time of his entrance into the diocese, exerted himself to fulfil every duty which is included in the maxim of the Apostle, "He who knows not how to govern his own house, is not fit to rule the Church of God."

Alphonsus found the diocese in a most lamentable condition on his arrival, but on this very account it was a fit field for his apostolic zeal. On the Sunday which followed his entry into St. Agatha, he began to give spiritual exercises to all the clergy, in a retired part of the church, and on the same evening he opened a mission for the people; he preached the principal sermon himself, and committed the catechising to F. Margotta, and requested several able canons to go through the town before the sermon, to give lively exhortations to the people. Floods of tears were shed in the church, and all owned that in the memory of man, St. Agatha had never had an example of such entire devotion and fervor. Grace triumphed over the most hardened sinners. To give complete liberty to consciences, and prevent sacrileges, all the priests of the town were forbidden to hear confessions, and in their stead were summoned the best curates of the diocese. The good done by the mission was incalculable; there were reconciliations and wonderful acts of restitution made; sinners who had been sunk in disorder for years, embraced a new and exemplary course of life, and the spirit of penance infused into their hearts was such, that in the case of two individuals, who died shortly after, their death was wholly owing to their fervor in the exercises of penance. A young gentleman, well known as an usurer at St. Agatha, was so struck with terror, when he heard Alphonsus, with black stole, and torch in hand, pronouncing the malediction against usurers, blasphemers, and above all, against impenitent sinners, that he was seized with fever and carried off in a few days. On the following Sunday, the general communion, for which, Alphonsus had obtained a brief from the Pope granting a plenary indulgence, was so touching, that all those present burst into tears, rich as well as poor, clergy as well as laity. In short, the town of St. Agatha was sanctified; communions became frequent, the Most Blessed Sacrament and the Holy Virgin Mary became the objects of great devotion, and every evening the church was seen filled with fervent worshippers.

So much labor in an old man already burthened with infirmities, filled every one with admiration. "We prayed God," exclaimed a Dean, "to send us a good bishop, and God has heard us favorably, but my lord will exhaust and kill himself." "What are you thinking of," said the treasurer to the Grand-Vicar, "do you not see that his lordship is shortening his days? have you forgotten the tears we shed, and how much it cost us to have him? Curb his zeal therefore; its excess will be fatal to him." And he advised him to speak to his confessor, to enjoin him to put bounds to his immoderate zeal. In this mission, Alphonsus had an opportunity of giving proof of his admirable patience and humility. He had only two teeth, and God permitted, to augment the merits of his servant, that he should feel such sharp pain, in the middle of the mission, that it was impossible for him to take any rest. To the proposition of sending for a celebrated dentist from Naples, he replied: "Are not the dentists in this place as worthy as in Naples? Have we not the barber? let him come, and let us be patient, God wills that I should employ the people of my diocese." They had to wait for the next morning, for the intemperate habits of the barber incapacitated him for work for the remainder of the day. When he arrived, Alphonsus seated himself on the ground, on a cushion, and his secretary advancing to hold him, he took his crucifix from his neck, saying: "What better support can I have than Him who suffered such pain for me?" Then he crossed his arms and pressed the crucifix to his breast, and bore the extraction without the smallest exclamation. Notwithstanding his state of suffering, he did not omit to preach in the morning to the clergy, and in the evening, to the people. There remained one tooth, which, far from being useful to him, only served to incommode him; when the mission was terminated, he had that also extracted by a most painful operation. The barber was obliged to recommence three times, before he could succeed in taking it out. "Oh," Alphonsus exclaimed when all was done, "how firmly this tooth was fixed!" Then turning to the barber, he said gaily: "Master N., henceforth you will have no more of my custom."

Alphonsus had waited, to celebrate pontifically at St. Agatha, until the Annunciation, under which title the Blessed Virgin was the patron of his church, though he had done so in other churches on various feast days. In order to enhance the solemnity of these first functions, he had obtained from the Pope a plenary indulgence to all who should, after having assisted at them, approach the sacraments, or visit the cathedral, the same day. From morning till night the cathedral was filled with the faithful. He had obtained the same favor for the visitations in the diocese. Alphonsus was consoled at the happy success of these, his first labors. "I am well," he wrote to our Fathers at Nocera, "and thanks be to God, our labors are fruitful." On the other hand, he wrote to F. Villani: "I am full of anxiety for my church, this spouse whom God has given me."

However great had been Alphonsus' zeal during the mission and spiritual exercises, he had not been able to convert all. A canon of his cathedral had for many years grieved his superiors and fellow-citizens by the most lamentable behaviour. Supported by the credit of his family, and strong in the protection of one of his colleagues in the chapter, he had not attended to the remonstrances of the preceding bishop, and he despised still more Alphonsus, in whom he only saw a little man, whose humble exterior announced nothing but poverty, and who was bent down under the weight of years; he did not care the least, therefore, for the repeated kind warnings which he gave to him and carried his contempt so far as to use unbecoming expressions. Alphonsus invited him several times to his table; at last, he threw himself at his feet, and taking the crucifix from his breast, he presented it to him, and said with tears: "My son, if you will not do what I ask you in consideration of the character with which I am invested, do it for Jesus Christ's sake, who died on the cross for you and for me:" nothing succeeded; equally indifferent to the name of God, and the entreaties of his bishop, he continued to live as he had done before. Alphonsus, after having, besides, had recourse to the mediation of several good people, without success, at last sent for him, and told him that if he did not repair the scandal he gave, he would crave the aid of the sovereign's arm. This menace made the culprit very angry, and he became so furious, that he nearly used violence towards the bishop.

All the mild measures which Alphonsus used for the conversion of another individual, a beneficiary at Majano, equally failed, and so exasperated the man against the mother of the object of his passion, who had complained to Alphonsus, that on the night of the 4th of August, he fired against the door of the house, killed the mother, and wounded one of the little children. It was then that Alphonsus, seeing no other resource, applied to the King, and an order was despatched to the President of Montefusco, to arrest the two criminals, and place them in the prison of that town. The canon was arrested by the police, in the public place of St. Agatha. There was an extraordinary consternation in consequence, but all were amazed at Alphonsus' zeal and courage.

The relations of the canon used all their interest to conciliate Alphonsus' clemency, and to induce him to keep him in the prison of the officialty. Alphonsus, wishing to pacify them, and prevent further excesses, sought for some one to inform them of the impossibility of satisfying thei request. As the secretary was too dejected to go, and be sides, did not wish to leave the bishop, Alphonsus hurried, himself, to call a chaplain of the cathedral; he met one, who, vested in his choir-dress, came out of the sacristy at the very moment. On seeing him, the bishop said, in a quick and animated way: "Take off these things. . . . ." At these words the chaplain fainted, and fell at his feet. The bishop could not understand the cause of such terror, but the mystery was soon cleared up. He had believed himself arrested like the canon, being also engaged in criminal courses. "Two birds are killed with one stone," said Alphonsus, "the finger of God is here, let us pray him to finish that which he has begun." The chaplain was so frightened at the meeting, that he thought no more of the past, but only of an entire change of conduct, which was so exemplary from that time, that Alphonsus, after some years, allowed him to hear confessions.

The relations of the canon obtained his re-entry into St. Agatha, on condition that they should place two guards at their own expense, to prevent his escape. One day Alphonsus sent for him: "My dear canon," he said to him, "it is not you that I punish, but your sin; I love your soul, and desire that it should not be lost. Remember then, that you have a soul, and remember that there is a God." He had the consolation to see that the canon insensibly began to think seriously; he often sent him books of devotion, figures of our Blessed Saviour on the cross, and of the Blessed Virgin. After one year's imprisonment, the episcopal court condemned him to a three years' seclusion with the Conventual Fathers, and it was not until a long time after, that the canon was enabled to say mass again. The beneficiary, on the other hand, was arrested on the same day at Majano, and kept in the common prison at Hevano, Alphonsus refusing him the privilege of ecclesiastics, as he had never worn their dress. After a long imprisonment he was condemned to ten years' incarceration in a fortress. These two examples of severity produced a salutary fear in many, who hastened to reform their conduct.

Alphonsus' zeal did not manifest itself with less ardor and energy, with regard to the regular clergy and to laymen. Among many others, we will give two examples. There was a monastery in the diocese, consisting of but four religious, including the Superior, who disgusted all reputable people by their scandalous behaviour. After being sent for by the bishop, and admonished, they laughed at it, and did not reform themselves in the least. Alphonsus then cited them before the episcopal court, and informed their provincial of it. He tried to defend his religious. "Your Reverence must send your subjects an order to go," replied Alphonsus, "or I shall give them into the custody of the head of the police." This menace had its desired effect; two of the religious went off with the Superior; as the third was less culpable, Alphonsus was satisfied by his repentance. In the first mission, a married woman, who had lived for a number of years in adultery with one of the first gentlemen of the town, was converted, and went so far as to ask pardon publicly in the church, for the scandal she had given. After this generous confession, she yielded to seduction again, which caused inexpressible sorrow to the pious bishop. He wept over it, and the next morning, before day-break, he sent for the gentleman, represented to him the grievousness of his sin, and exhorted him to penitence; the man, as proud as he was powerful, turned his back upon him with disdain. The bishop, seeing his misconduct, still sent for him again, but the hardened offender, wearied by so many entreaties and reprimands, answered by insults, and even menaces. The bishop was not offended at it, but as he saw that the scandal continued, he informed the King. An order from the Minister of state being sent to the tribunal of Montefusco, a constable went to arrest the nobleman and the woman. Alphonsus was then at Airola; the gentleman, whose passion had made him furious, had come to Airola also, accompanied by a troop of brigands, in order to ill-treat his bishop, and hasten his passage to the other world, as he said, which he would have done, if another gentleman had not succeeded in persuading him to retrace his steps. When Alphonsus heard of this, he said calmly: "He can assassinate me, if he likes:

well! he will give me the crown of martyrdom." When the wretched man recovered from his rage, and saw that he was the object of judicial pursuit, he fled from the diocese and retired into a distant country. The woman was arrested by the constable, bound, chastised, and taken to Montefusco, where she suffered the rigor of justice for many months, and was afterwards banished forever from the diocese. Alphonsus, hearing afterwards that the gentleman had returned, and was concealed in his house, feigned to be ignorant of it, in order to win him over the better, and succeeded in it so well through the medium of persons in authority, that he acknowledged his faults, cast himself at his bishop's feet, and consoled him as much by the sincerity of his repentance, as he had grieved him at first by his scandalous conduct.

The terror inspired by these and other examples of severity, had its salutary effects, not only at St. Agatha and Airola, but all over the diocese and its neighborhood. The same was not less the case with the following occurrence. On the arrival of Alphonsus in the diocese, a young liberated galley-slave was living in crime at St. Agatha. He was first reprimanded, but paid no attention to it. Alphonsus had recourse to the magistrate, who ordered his arrest. He was seized in the house of his accomplice, and as he resisted, he was killed on the spot. Alphonsus wept over the loss of his soul; but to give libertines a spectacle as salutary as it was terrible, he ordered, in concert with the authorities, that his corpse should be placed on a mule, between four lighted torches, and thus carried out of town, and thrown into a ditch. The blessing of the Lord, which was granted to this zeal of our saint, is the most glorious justification of his conduct. Nothing but this divine blessing on the exertions of the saintly bishop could have changed a field full of weeds into a flourishing vineyard.

CHAPTER XX.

Alphonsus commences his Episcopal Visitation. He reforms and regulates the Diocesan Seminary. His zeal, prudence and manner of life during the visitation of the diocese.

ALPHONSUS commenced his episcopal visitation in the town and surrounding country. "Why put off until to-morrow, that which can be corrected to-day?" he replied to some who wished him to defer it on account of the heat, "it is wrong to temporise with abuses." He had convoked the treasurer, Cacciopuoti, the Dominican Master, F. Caputo, the theological canon, D. Evangelist Duddio, and the archdeacon Francis Rainone, all men distinguished for their piety, prudence and knowledge, as well as several curates, with whom he consulted at once, in order to see what would be best suited to procure the good of the diocese. The seminary was the principal end of this first visitation: "It is on the seminary," said he, "that I found all my hope of sanctifying the diocese. If that does not second me, all my trouble will be of no avail." He found a great number of scholars in it, but all were not according to his heart. He therefore ordered a general examination, at which he assisted in person, and afterwards, found an excuse for giving the vacation sooner than usual. When it was ended, he wrote to all the pupils, to tell them that all those who wished to re-enter the seminary, should address a request to him to that effect. Thus he was able to make his choice, and purify the house; this decimation was painful to the relations of the rejected subjects, but, seeing, themselves, their misconduct, or want of aptitude, they began soon to appreciate the wisdom of their bishop. The buildings of the seminary had more the appearance of a prison, than of a house of education, being too confined, and unhealthy for want of air, and subject to a most troublesome multiplication of insects in summer. He sent for two architects from Naples, to remedy these evils, and to repair the interior of the building, directing their labor himself. He conceived at the same time the grand project of pulling down all the old buildings entirely, and raising new ones instead. A plan was got ready, materials were procured, and without delay the work was begun. For the government of the seminary, he established new rules, full of wisdom and prudence, so much so, that many bishops adopted them afterwards for their own seminaries. Don Lucas, who had been at the head of the establishment for more than thirty years, was more than an octogenarian, and, in consequence of this, his advanced age, little fit for the government of it. In order not to hurt this poor old man, Alphonsus confirmed him in his post, and a coadjutor was given to him, in the person of F. Caputo, the Dominican Master. He spared nothing in order to choose good masters, whose knowledge and conduct might serve as models. He abolished the custom of giving the office of prefect to a student, wishing that exemplary priests alone should have the charge. He chose for porter, a diligent man, full of the fear of God. "If death," said he, "enters into us by the windows, it enters into seminaries by the doors." A porter went out one evening, without leave from the president; Alphonsus had him discharged immediately, notwithstanding his tears, and the intercession of several persons.

The autumn vacations were shortened, and replaced by innocent recreations and feasts. "A month's vacation," he said, "is enough to lose all that has been gained with much labor during the year, and which is replaced by sin and vice." He found the terms of the seminary were equitable, but he could not approve that when a pupil went away from infirmity, or any other cause, he was made to pay for the whole six months, and it was with difficulty he consented to the seminary's receiving payment for the month of vacation, as was done every where else. He did not wish any distinction in the provisions for the Superiors, he called it a detestable abuse, and wished to see all treated equally well. They complained that the cook was not skilful; Alphonsus sent his own, several times, to instruct him. Often, at the dinner hour, he went to examine the cleanliness of the dishes, and above all, if the bread and wine were good. Once he found the bread was not of a good quality. The Superior and the housekeeper were immediately sent for and reprimanded, and he ordered that all the bread in the seminary should be immediately given to the poor. When he officiated pontifically, he was in the habit of giving each pupil a small tart, or slice of cake, prepared by his own cook, and was, besides, always provided with sweetmeats for these family rejoicings.

He forbade the dictation of lessons, and wished that printed books should be used. He prohibited Italian poetry, and romances. Before this, Greek had also been taught, but he did not think it necessary, as the students were mostly of the diocese, and destined to supply the numerous churches of the surrounding villages: "Greek is very good in the East," he said, "but for us, who are in the West, Latin is what we want. My diocese requires good confessors, who may aid me in helping the souls of a number of country people." However, he allowed a slight knowledge of it, sufficient for reading and understanding certain passages which occur in philosophical and theological authors. Scholars who returned home for their meals, and to sleep, he would not allow, saying: "They serve as messengers for the seminarists, which is very dangerous for the morals of both." He was in the habit of being present at the lesson twice a week. He took pleasure in hearing the rehearsals, and took part in the discussions. He fixed that once a month, theses should be publicly maintained on philosophy or theology, and, when confined to bed by illness, he wished the meeting to take place in his room. He established also, an exercise for preaching, once a week, at which he made some of the canons, chaplains, curates, and other ecclesiastics assist, also. To cause virtue to dwell in the seminary, he established half an hour's meditation in public, each morning, after mass, and prescribed examination of conscience, in common, twice a day, in the morning, before dinner, and in the evening, before night prayers; and during the morning and evening meals, spiritual reading took place by his orders, as it had not been the custom before. He prescribed, besides, a visit to the Blessed Sacrament and the Holy Virgin, together with the recitation of the Rosary. Usually, on Saturday, he went himself, before going to church, to give them a practical sermon on the beauty of virtue. He introduced the practice of Novenas, in honor of Jesus and Mary, with some mortification, on certain days, recommending them to forego something at table, to eat kneeling, or sitting on the floor, to fast in the ordinary manner, or on bread and water, leading the young people to fly all effeminacy; besides, he exhorted them strongly to the cultivation of humility, of obedience to their Superiors, and of fraternal love, instead of vain friendships, taking rise in sympathy and a spirit of worldly rivalry. He instituted a monthly retreat, and every year, before the recommencement of study, all had to go through the spiritual exercises for eight days. As a kind of relaxation, he gave them a virtuous and zealous ecclesiastic to teach them chanting. He set the hymns he had composed, to music, and had them taught to the young people in relaxation time, and liked to hear them sing them at recreation; he often joined them himself, and was exceedingly pleased to see them joyous and contented. In order to be admitted into the seminary, it was necessary to give certain proofs of exemplary conduct; he inquired if the subject frequented the sacraments, if he assisted at mass in the morning, and at the visit in the evening.

When the seminary was thus regulated, all became edifying there, and although he had not fixed communion every fortnight, as he had done for confession, many approached the sacred altar every week, and others, still more frequently. Charity dwelt amongst them, they studied diligently, and each one advanced in virtue and knowledge. The saintly bishop rejoiced at it, and was accustomed to call the seminaryt he apple of his eye, or the jewel of his diocese. To preserve it in this state, he exerted himself, and solicitously watched to prevent every seed of corruption, establishing secret inspectors, and frequent visits of the rooms. He spared no one; a very orderly young man was surprised reading a Neapolitan poet, Alphonsus made him come down from the course of rhetoric, into that of grammar, in which he had to remain till a new course began. Having heard that some rather loose verses were circulated in the seminary, he ordered immediately a search, and such great terror spread among the pupils, that he who had those verses swallowed them, not having time to get rid of them otherwise. Two were found having forbidden knives, they were immediately dismissed. Three others committed an act of levity, through the windows, towards a woman who had often to pass in the court, he sent all three away on the spot, notwithstanding their submission and promises, and the entreaties of several respectable persons. After many years he admitted one of them to the sub-diaconate, on the representations of his curate, who exposed the wants of his church, and made a protest as to the amendment of the candidate, but Alphonsus thought he perceived other faults in him, though less considerable, so he left him a subdeacon. He perceived a certain vice in the nephew of a professor; he dismissed him the same instant, without any regard to his uncle, who asked in tears for his forgiveness, and who, when he saw the bishop's inflexibility, gave up his class and left the seminary. "What charity! What charity!" he answered to those who wished to intercede on similar occasions, "to pity one individual, and risk the ruin of all the rest? that is not charity, it is cruelty." One example is known of a young man, who, after having fallen, found pardon from Alphonsus. He had not sinned against morality, but being wearied of study, he had run away from the seminary twice, and he found mercy only in consideration of his belonging to a place singularly abandoned, where there was not a single priest.

Alphonsus, though inflexible towards the vicious, had a father's tenderness for those who were worthy of his care. One of these had maintained in a brilliant way, several theses of theology; as he was poor, he gave him several ducats each year; and when he noticed any young man of talent among the children of the inhabitants of small places, he tried to persuade him to embrace the ecclesiastical state, and generously gave him an entrance into the seminary. "The seminaries were only instituted for the help of the churches," he replied to the members of the commission who objected to this charity, "and the pious persons who left their goods in favor of these establishments, could have had no other intention than the good of the inhabitants, and especially of the poor." It was thus, that he procured excellent priests for many villages and country places, of which they had till then been destitute.

For preventing the vacations being of any injury to the morality of the young men, he prescribed that they should make half an hour's meditation every morning in their parish church, before mass; they had to visit the Blessed Sacrament every evening, and on feast days, to be present at all the offices, as well as the instructions of the curate; they were to approach the sacraments of penance, and the eucharist, every eight days without fail, and never to leave the house without the soutane, collar, and cincture. They were not on any account to be present at vintages, and still less at hunts. These rules were sent to the curates of the young seminarists. No one was re-admitted into the seminary who had not an attestation of good conduct from the curate. Several pupils, for having committed very slight faults against these regulations, experienced all his severity.

While Alphonsus labored for the reform of the seminary, he neglected nothing which could be conducive to the end of the visitation. Being informed of the disedifying conduct of several priests, he made some retire into monasteries, and punished others by imprisonment; but the greater number yielded to his charitable remonstrances, and by their after-conduct consoled the heart of their pastor. The sacrifice of the altar and the sacrament of penance were the principal objects of his care during the visitation. He assembled the priests for examination on the rubrics at an altar erected for the purpose; he instructed the least capable himself, and confided several to the care of others. Some he found so inobservant in regard to the most essential rubrics, that he was obliged to suspend them, and he only reinstated them with difficulty and after many months probation. This necessary rigor caused the rubrics to be studied, and mass was celebrated every where with an admirable degree of precision and devotion. He examined also the confessors, but to use the necessary prudence, he called only those before his council who were pointed out to him as relaxed or ignorant, and questioned them in order to know whether he could continue their faculties. In a certain village, he found two in the most complete ignorance; besides prohibiting them from hearing confessions, he forbade them even to say mass; some time after, he permitted them to celebrate, but continued to refuse to let them sit in the sacred tribunal. He found even several curates wanting in necessary knowledge. In the town and suburbs alone he found four completely incapable. He appointed them canons, in order not to injure their reputation, and to avoid the evil which might have resulted to those who would have been alarmed at severities exercised towards men whose functions had acquired their confidence. One of them had deviated so far from rule, that Alphonsus was obliged to propose his immediate resignation. He wished to resist, but was forced to yield whether with good or bad grace. After a scrupulous examination of the town and surrounding country, he commenced the following year to visit the other parts of the diocese. The following facts and ordinances will serve to illustrate his zeal for the glory of God and the welfare of His Church, as also his prudence, wisdom, and firmness.

He met with a curate, well informed and of excellent character, who could not resolve to reside, pretending that his church was too isolated, and that his parishioners were few and scattered about, and who, in consequence, lived in town. The most he did was to say mass on Sundays and feast days. Alphonsus enjoined him to reside in the presbytery; he resisted and was ordered immediately to resign. As he hesitated, Alphonsus said to him: "Decide, give in your resignation, or I will suspend you." Afterwards, by mildness he was able to persuade him, and obtained all he had wished for. Wishing to spare him, he obtained a dispensation from the Pope for him with regard to the fruits of his charge, which he had gathered so ill.

He found that in a rural church there was a door in the interior which gave entrance into the cell of a hermit; he immediately prohibited women from all access to the hermitage, under pain of excommunication ipso facto, and threatened the hermit with three months imprisonment and the deprivation of his hermitage, if he dared to introduce them there for the time to come. He ordered other hermits, in order to prevent them from enriching themselves by the alms of the faithful, to place all that was not necessary for their support in the hands of a canon, to be employed for the benefit of the respective churches.

He met with a priest who had obtained permission from Rome to wear a wig, nevertheless not without his bishop's approbation. Alphonsus wished to see it, and not thinking it suitable, he sent for a vessel of boiling water, into which he plunged the wig, and thus straightened its curls. "This is how it ought to be," said he, "and in no other way." In all ecclesiastics he blamed and prohibited the wearing of curled hair, and the use of perfumes. He forbade them also under pain of suspension latæ sententiæ to wear colored mantles, and prohibited their entrance into the church without the soutane. To remedy the precipitation with which some celebrated mass, he declared that whoever did so in less than a quarter of an hour should incur suspension latæ sententiæ.

He found in a convent a nun, who forgetting her duties as a spouse of Christ, afflicted all the house by her irregularities. She was a Neapolitan. Alphonsus sent her away, and had her conducted back to her home by several excellent priests; but she soon again presented herself at the convent door. The bishop on hearing that she acted with violence in order to enter it, and that she received the aid of her parents, who had accompanied her, went to the convent himself to prohibit her re-entering it.

Finding that a great number of the laity transgressed the commandment of the paschal communion, he charged the curates to insist upon it, and not to give rest to those who refused to amend. He sent for several, to warn them himself and to urge them to perform their duties; to others he sent warnings in writing. It was a custom, or rather a general abuse in the diocese, that after the ceremony of betrothment, the parents received the young aspirant to their daughter's hand into their house. Despairing of being able to prevent these dangerous meetings, except by rigorous measures, he made it a reserved case, and alarmed the offenders by threatening them with excommunication.

Throughout the diocese, the catechising of the children only took place in Lent. He ordered, under very severe penalties, that it should take place every Sunday and feast day, as well as every day during Lent. In order to remedy the ignorance of the people, he recapitulated the most essential points of Christian doctrine, and had them printed on one sheet for their convenience; besides, he ordered that these instructions should be put on a tablet board, and be read by the curates and other priests, on every feast day, at the first mass, and at that at which the most people was present; and he prohibited confessors, under pain of suspension, from admitting any one to the sacrament of penance, in paschal time, who had not been examined by his curate on Christian doctrine, and was not provided with his certificate. Fearing that the sacrament of baptism was not well administered in cases of danger, through the ignorance of the midwives, he examined them himself, and instructed them where there was need of it.

He ordered all women of irregular life to come to him, and in presence of the curate he showed them on one hand his indignation, and on the other his mercy. "If you reform," he said, "you will find in me a father full of charity; but if you remain obstinate in sin, I shall be to you a severe and importunate judge." He advised the curates to watch over them and inform him of their conduct. A great number of these repentant sinners experienced acts of love on Alphonsus' part, but the incorrigible became the objects of his justice and severity, so that he invoked even the civil authority against them.

He established every where, the practise of paying in the evening a visit to the Blessed Sacrament and to the Holy Virgin.

As for the churches, he caused the walls to be whitewashed, the furniture as well as the buildings to be repaired, and ordered to dust every part of the church every week, and to clean the holy water stoups. "The house of God," he said, "demands cleanliness and decency, and too much pains cannot be taken to put it in proper order, for it is difficult for people to pray where their sight is painfully affected by what they see." A cobweb in a church was the cause of a severe reprimand to the curates and sacristans. He forbade images and altars to be preserved which had become disfigured by time, saying: "An image is useless, when it does not inspire devotion." He ordered that all chalices and ciboriums, which had need of it, should be re-gilt in the space of two months. Many unsuitable ones were ordered to be replaced, and ornaments capable of repairs to be put in a good state. A great quantity of albs, chasubles, copes, and missals, &c., were rejected, and great cleanliness in corporals and linen for the altar was exacted. Where they were wanting, he ordered to be procured, canopies for the exposition of the Blessed Sacrament, and for the viaticum, as also remonstrances; and he had the cotton lining in tabernacles replaced by silk lining If little anxiety in making the necessary expenses for these things was shown, he declared that wherever omissions and faults in these points should be found, he would stop the revenues.

At Airola, having been informed of the dissolute conduct of some laics, he sent for them and gave them a paternal correction; but finding them incorrigible, he imprisoned them, and afterwards banished them by the aid of the Prince della Riccia. A nobleman of the first rank, was engaged in a criminal intercourse, and instead of amending, as Alphonsus had succeeded in making him promise, he quarrelled with his wife, and for fear she should denounce him to Alphonsus, he threatened to take her life. Alphonsus immediately ordered his arrest, and had him banished with the prince's aid; and as he continued to live in licentiousness, the prince, at the instigation of Alphonsus, shut him up in a state prison, where he died in impenitence.

While Alphonsus thus performed the visitation of his diocese, God proved him by infirmities and sickness. His asthma tormented him again at Airola, and this torment was soon followed by a fever, accompanied by symptoms which appeared mortal. It was proposed to him to send for some skilful doctor from Naples: "The doctors of Airola will suffice for me," he replied, "have they not studied out of the same books as those at Naples? besides my life is not of so great value." The state in which he was did not prevent the continuation of the visitation; his place was supplied by the Grand-Vicar, whom he ordered to go through the surrounding country, while he himself received accounts of the state of things from the curates and several gentlemen, and gave the necessary instructions and orders.

During this illness he did not fail to communicate each day at a mass said in his own room, and to make his customary meditations in the morning and evening. On the ninth day, the malady got worse, and he asked if there were any danger. The physician knowing the firmness of the saintly invalid's mind, partly avowed the real state of the case. Alphonsus then sent for his secretary, and ordered him to administer extreme unction to him without loss of time. He received it with pious confidence, his face manifested the joy of his soul and his entire submission to the will of God; far from fearing death, he seemed to invite it as a friend, who would deliver him from his exile and lead him to his true country.

The visits which were paid him were burthensome to him; if he did not expressly dismiss the visitors, they were obliged to retire, always finding him meditating or listening to the reading of some pious book, which was not interrupted by the arrival of any one whatever. The doctor cautioning him not to fatigue himself by too much application, he replied: "It is that which relieves me; without it my illness would be too painful to me." His health improved after the fifteenth day, and he was scarcely convalescent, when he returned with ardor to the objects of his pastoral care. He was still in bed, when he examined priests on the rubrics and made them practice under his own eyes, and examined several on moral theology.

In all populous parishes, he established the Congregation of "Cases of Morals" for the Clergy. In order that the same case should be discussed on the same day throughout the diocese, and that no one should find an excuse for not being prepared, he made a choice of several questions himself, and every year he had the list of cases for each week printed in the calendar of the diocese. He also wished that note should be taken of all the decisions and conferences, for future use. The rubrics of mass were also made the subject of special exercises in these conferences. Besides this re-union for the study of morals, he attached a school of moral theology to the cathedral, which had to assemble every week in his palace, he himself presiding at the sittings, whenever he could. This academy was a sweet source of consolation to Alphonsus, and its members were those he most frequently chose for curates.

Besides, as there was a great number of young men unable to maintain themselves in the seminary for want of the means, Alphonsus anxious about their vocation, founded societies on purpose for their benefit, under the management of learned priests, with all necessary regulations, calculated to make them useful for the diocese. He also instituted a society of priests in his capital, destined to give missions. These new missionaries distinguished themselves so much, that Alphonsus attached them to the Congregation known at Naples by the name of the Conference. He established also in many places particular confraternities for gentlemen, for young men, and for girls, who received in them instruction on their duties, and mutually encouraged each other in virtue and goodness. At Arienzo, God was pleased to manifest that he was with the saintly prelate, and inspired him with His holy zeal. One day in a sermon which he preached before the gentlemen he had united in such a congregation, he suddenly fell into an ecstasy, in which he appeared quite transfigured; his face became beaming with so brilliant a light, that the church became resplendent as from the rays of the sun.

He introduced the practice of mental prayer in common in the cathedral, as well as in the other parish churches; at the first mass, a priest, for the aid of the people, read at various intervals, a chapter on the eternal truths, the enormity of sin, or the mysteries of the passion of Jesus Christ.

To remedy several disorders and evils which he observed during his visitation, he composed his little book on hurried mass, with acts of preparation and thanksgiving; also, another practical little book containing an easy and devout method of assisting the sick and dying, which he distributed to all the priests, and especially to the curates and vicars; and lastly, he summed up all the most essential things for the right administration of the sacrament of penance, in one small volume, with all possible clearness, and in the vernacular tongue. He entitled it "The Guide to country confessors." For which work many bishops testified to him their gratitude, for it spread speedily over all the kingdom.

Having terminated the visit at Airola, Alphonsus returned to St. Agatha, and charged his Grand-Vicar to finish the visitation in the other parts of the diocese. As long as he was bishop, he made it a rule to visit it every two years, each year doing half, and he never failed in this.

Humility and charity, penance and disinterestedness were his inseparable companions during these visitations. All the equipage consisted, besides himself, of his Grand-Vicar, his secretary, a canon of the cathedral, and a servant, who waited on them. A wretched hired beast was all his train, the saddle he had borrowed. He was seen seated as women sit, on an ass, the bridle of which was held by a child of ten or twelve years. On the other side was the child's father, who supported the bishop; a sight that caused all who beheld it to shed tears of compassion. As he never omitted any of his ordinary devotions, and never let any poor person pass without consolation, he got on so slowly, that he was often on the road, in the burning heat of the sun, so that the Grand-Vicar often excused himself from starting at the same time, and did not set out till towards evening. At Frasso, a person of distinction, who had prepared for his reception at his house, seeing him arrive on an ass, said: "Why, my lord, do you travel on an ass?" Alphonsus replied with a smile, "hi in curribus et hi in equis, nos autem in nomine Domini." "Some in carriages, and others on horses, but we in the name of the Lord." At Mugnano, a gentleman offered him his carriage, but he declined it and said: "I am so comfortable on this beast, that it is wonderful." At Arpaja the canons exclaimed in their surprise at seeing such an equipage: "What! to travel in this heat, and on an ass!" Alphonsus smiled, and pointing to a vender of poultry, who happened to pass, said: "Look at this poor man, which of us has come more easily, I on this ass, or he on foot, and with this basket on his head." Here is another trait: one day he could not procure enough beasts for all his followers: not wishing to incommode any one, he set out on foot, accompanied by his servant. It was during the heat of the month of August. He had pity on the poor young man, who was bathed in perspiration. "My son," said he, "it is exceedingly hot, take off your waistcoat, and give it to me to hold." The servant at first would not consent, but Alphonsus gave such persuasive reasons for it, that he was induced to give him the waistcoat; he went very nearly half the way on foot, and he would have done so for the whole, if he had not been overcome by fatigue. On the way, he observed always the rule which he had fixed for his journeys, during which he was constantly engaged in saying the Rosary with those who accompanied him, and the litanies of the Blessed Virgin, with other prayers, in honor of his patron, and those of the different places through which he passed.

Once, in going from Durasano to Frasso, being indisposed, he made use of a conveyance, rather in order to please the Grand-Vicar. The coachman, through awkwardness or drunkenness, upset them twice. The second time Alphonsus fell on the Vicar, and dislocated his wrist; he showed no sign of dissatisfaction, and though in great pain, he pursued his journey on a mule. He was to commence the pastoral visit at Frasso, the same evening, and so he would not stop and take rest in St. Agatha, near which he had to pass, but passing through a place called the Steps, a rich merchant forced him to alight at his house, and it was there that a doctor set his wrist. On arriving at Frasso, he opened the visitation the same evening, and as if nothing had befallen him, preached, and was as cheerful as usual. The merchant who had received him in his house, was rewarded for his charity by the miraculous cure of his son, who was ill at the time, and had been given up by the physicians. Alphonsus went to see the dying boy. On approaching him, he made the sign of the cross on his forehead, and then turning to his father and mother, said to them: "Be of good courage, and be assured that your son will recover." Indeed, at the same moment, the child began to get better, and three days afterwards he was walking about.

At Airola, the prince of Riccia had placed his palace at Alphonsus' service, and he had accepted it, not to displease a nobleman who had so powerfully protected him. His steward had prepared a magnificent bed for him in the apartment which the prince was in the habit of occupying himself; when Alphonsus saw it, he praised it highly, but examining afterwards the rooms prepared for his Grand-Vicar, and that destined for his valet, he gave the preference to the latter, saying, "I shall be best off here, for I suffer from my chest; large rooms where there is much air are hurtful to me." At Frasso, convenient rooms had been prepared for him and his Grand-Vicar, but for some reason or other, the Grand-Vicar was very much dissatisfied with his, and disturbed every one on account of it. Alphonsus heard of the thing, and said: "It is nothing, I know how to remedy it." When the Vicar was gone to church, he had his own bed, which was the plainest, moved in the Vicar's room, and that of the Vicar, into his, who, on his return, seemed not to notice any change, and was quiet.

At Real-Vale, God manifested how agreeable His servant's humility was to him: the room which he inhabited in the house of D. Anthony di Martino, had been infested for a great many years, with beetles, and no means of getting rid of them could be found. The Saint passed a night there, and it was entirely freed.

On arriving in a place, he went first to the principal church, where he opened the visitation by a discourse to the people, and announced the plenary indulgence. When the day after his arrival was a Sunday or feast day, he officiated pontifically, if the parish was populous enough, and if the church was not a collegiate one, he sent, at his own expense, for seven canons from the cathedral, or the nearest collegiate church, and also for the seminarists of the place. The second day he commenced the mission in the afternoon, which lasted for eight days. He preached himself every day, and in the evening visited the Blessed Sacrament with the people, which was in itself another sermon. The people were so touched by his words, that at the first sound of the bell, every one hastened to the church, "to hear," as they said, "the Saint who smoothed their way to heaven." He also gave a retreat to the clergy every morning during those eight days, as well as at the convents which were in the town. He assembled the children after vespers for catechism, being anxious to see himself what instruction they received. He instructed also the children for confirmation, himself. He wished that the children should be at least from seven to eight years old, to be admitted to the reception of this sacrament, and that all should be present at the first imposition of hands, recommencing the imposition when others were assembled again. He was so scrupulous on this point, that if any one came too late, he administered the sacrament to him in the private chapel, not to put him off till another year. For the infirm, who were not yet confirmed, he went to visit them, in order that they might not die without the benefit of this sacrament, or be too long deprived of it. On one such occasion, at Airola, he predicted the death of the invalid. He was a young man, to whom he said: "My dear Pascal, be very glad, for in three days you will go to Paradise." The third day arrived, and the sick man seemed far from a speedy death, for he appeared to be better; however, towards the close of the day, the symptoms of fever became more alarming, and before night, young Pascal was dead, as Alphonsus had foretold.

The poor were also the object of his solicitude, in his visitations. He inquired into the miseries of all, from the curates and others. He strove particularly to know those whose houses were irregular, and who made their children sleep, pell-mell, in the same bed. When he was convinced that their indigence was real, he endeavored to supply beds, clothes, and all other necessaries; but he cared most for widows, as also for young women in danger, and spared no expense in aiding them. The sick, above all, the sick poor, were not forgotten, he inquired about them most solicitously, went to visit them himself, and consoled them by his words, and by his alms; and desired their medicines to be furnished at his own expense.

The spirit of mortification also accompanied Alphonsus on these visitations. His table was the same as at St. Agatha, wherever he went, both for himself, and his suite, and he never omitted his seasonings of bitter herbs. Neither did he exempt himself from mortifying himself daily by hair-cloths and disciplines. Once, when setting out, he had forgotten the instruments of penance; he immediately sent his servant to seek for them secretly. The person who made his bed in the morning, when he was at Real-Vale, attested that the sheets were spotted with blood, and small stones were found in the bed. The valet de chambre of Prince della Riccia, at Airola, also attested that at his departure he found nine stones as large as an egg, on the mattress. For a great number of years, and until his infirmities became extreme, he carried the covering of his straw bed about with him, and wherever he arrived, he had it filled with straw, and did not use the bed which had been prepared for him. In the morning, he occupied himself in meditating on sacred things, from the moment of his awaking, and in the evening, after his own prayers, he assembled his family to recite the Rosary, and the other accustomed prayers, in common. His disinterestedness was such, that he always returned from his rounds destitute of money, and burthened with debts; for he scrupulously observed the law he had made to himself, never to accept any present, and besides, reduced the fees of the visitation to nearly nothing. For the members of his household, he recommended them to keep to the maxim of St. Francis of Sales: "Ask for nothing, and refuse nothing."

Such conduct gained him general esteem and respect, so much so, that people thought themselves happy if they could obtain a small piece of his garment. His mitres were several times found without pendants, and one day a piece was cut off his cloak. These relics were very carefully preserved; they were applied to the sick, and every where they related what miraculous cures had been produced by their touch.

CHAPTER XXI.

His Conduct at his Brother's second Marriage. His Zeal for the Preaching of the Word of God by Himself and Others. His Charity during a Famine.

D. HERCULES having become a widower about this time, (1763,) and having no heir, resolved to enter into a second marriage. He imparted his design to Alphonsus, asking him to aid him by his prayers and by saying masses for this intention. With regard to the projected marriage, he answered him on the 9th of November, 1763: "I beg of you to be very careful to choose a young woman of moral habits, not a vain person, or one who would be disposed to take advantage of your advanced age. . . . . . It would be better, as I have already written to you, that she should have less of birth and fortune, than that you should run the risk of some vexatious embarrassments happening to you. Be sure to declare your intention from the first, both to her and her parents, and say to them that you do not like visits, meetings, &c. When the wedding has taken place, try to give your wife good habits from the first; for this purpose take her to Marianella, and make a long stay there." In another letter of the 12th of the same month, he says: "I am rejoiced that such good alliances are offered to you. Use all possible care to choose the wife who will make you least anxious, considering the times in which we live. Be persuaded, that young women have more affection for young men than for those in advanced age as you are. I would warn you of another thing, that now, when you are alone, you ought to take care to send all young female servants away from your house. The devil is always a devil, and with temptation so near, and in the liberty in which you are, I should tremble for myself. Can you not dismiss them for the present, and tell them that you will take them back when you again set up your establishment? You ask me for money, and I would wish that you could lend to me, for this year has been a gulf of expenses. I had to repair two houses, and had to pay to the Nuncio four hundred ducats for the dilapidation of the chapter. I have incurred a debt of four hundred more, to meet the costs of buildings erected at the seminary. . . . . . I sympathise with your pain in having to go to many expenses without having enough to supply for them. The misfortune is, that the episcopate is come to me at the same time as your marriage. Besides, I may say that I too am married, but to a spouse who leaves me no moment of rest." D. Hercules espoused D. Mariana Capano Orsini, of the illustrious house of Nilo, a lady of exemplary conduct and extraordinary piety. Alphonsus rejoiced at her virtues more than at her titles, rendered thanks for it to God, and congratulated his brother.

Alphonsus' great anxiety for his brother, proceeded from a heart, which, though full of charity, was otherwise wholly detached from all which concerned the interests of flesh and blood; of which detachment he gave proof on all occasions. He never had the curiosity to inquire into the state of affairs of any of his relatives, and during the thirty years that he lived in the Congregation, though his journeys to Naples were so frequent, he only entered his paternal house once, when he had to fulfil a last duty to his mother, who was mortally ill. Though his brother lived in the same house in which the hospice of the Congregation was, as we have said before, he never visited him. One day he went to Naples and found the door of the hospice shut; he chose rather to eat a morsel of bread with some fruit in the ante-chamber, rather than to enter his brother's apartment; and when the nuptials were celebrated, as custom seemed to require some present to the bride, Alphonsus, for his only wedding present, gave her a paper print of the Blessed Virgin, inclosed in a little wooden frame. Don Hercules was displeased at this conduct, and returned the little frame almost angrily. "My brother takes offence," said Alphonsus, "I have however more cause than he; what did he expect to receive? I have so

many poor here who die of hunger! yes, so many poor mendicants, and they demand that I should make presents."

Alphonsus held preaching, as among his first duties as a bishop. "This ministration," he said, "is almost the only one that Jesus Christ seems to have imposed on the Apostles, and it is one which he exacts from his bishops; to fail in it is to neglect an express command." So he became remarkable for his assiduity in preaching. When he was at St. Agatha, he never missed preaching every Sunday at the cathedral, after vespers, and on all feast days which fell during the week, he went to preach in the parishes. Every Sunday before the sermon, he catechised the little children, whom he attracted by giving them rosaries, pictures, and sometimes even money. He went also every Sunday to give instructions to the Congregation of nobles, and that of the young girls, which he had established. When he was at Arienzo, as the people could not easily come to the collegiate church, he preached alternately in one of the seven parishes of the town, and as his sermon was always accompanied with exposition of the Blessed Sacrament he furnished the candles on these occasions himself, saying: "I wish, for God's glory, not to burden you with expense." He was accustomed, before the sermon, to sing one of the pious hymns he had himself composed. Every Saturday, as he had vowed, he published also the praises of our Blessed Lady. Not satisfied with doing this himself, he established this devotion in the whole diocese, and according to the convenience of the people, it took place in one town on Saturday, and in another on Sunday, always with exposition of the Blessed Sacrament. At Arienzo and in other populous parishes, he wished it to to be done twice, both on Saturday and on Sunday. Each month he visited a church fixed on beforehand, and made the protestation for a good death there, with a sermon and exposition of the Blessed Sacrament. It is impossible to believe what great good he effected by this exercise.

During the three last days of the carnival, he was in the habit of having public adoration and exposition of the

Blessed Sacrament, to hinder the people from going to public shows, and from otherwise offending God. When he was at St. Agatha, there was a sermon in the morning, at which he assisted, and which was delivered by a deacon of the seminary. He preached, himself, in the evening, and enlarged on the exceeding love of Jesus Christ for man. He fixed that, at Arienzo, there should be in the church of the nuns of St. Philip, a sermon, with exposition, during the Sundays of Lent, after vespers, and this sermon he preached himself, whenever he was in the town; however bad the weather might be, he never failed to go. One Sunday, a furious storm came on, notwithstanding which Alphonsus went, though ill, and urged not to go; he caught a cold, from which he suffered a long time, in consequence. The Conventual Fathers of St. Agatha were in the habit of exposing the Blessed Sacrament every Saturday in March, and had a sermon each time from one of their clerks. Seeing that these discourses were merely an exercise for the young men, and without fruit to the people, he offered to preach there himself; when he had no carriage, he went there always on foot, however severe the weather might be. Before the sermon, he sang his hymn; "O my Jesus," in so touching a manner, that all the people melted in tears. The convent generally gave the young preacher ten carlins; Alphonsus, not to deprive the clerks of this retribution, wished they should continue to fix on some one who could preach in his stead, in case he should be prevented, and give him the same sum whether he preached or not. He also adopted the custom of celebrating the novena of the birth of our Blessed Lord in his cathedral, as well as that of the Assumption and that of St. Joseph; instead of which latter, he celebrated sometimes the seven days which precede the feast of this saint. The panegyric of the Saint, however, he left to one of the Capuchin fathers, not wishing to deprive these religious of the alms attached to it. During Lent, he was in the habit of giving the spiritual exercises to the regular and secular clergy at Arienzo, or at St. Agatha.

As soon as he knew that any particular solemnity would attract a great concourse of people in any church, he was there to preach. He said: "Jesus Christ began to convert souls by preaching, and by preaching this must be continued. Every thing consists in preaching well, Jesus Christ crucified." One feast day, at St. Mary del Vico, he passed before the church of St. Nicholas, and noticed that it was filled by the faithful; he immediately got out of the carriage and entered the church to preach. He did the same on all other similar occasions. There was another reason which prompted him, whether ill or well, to preach on such extraordinary occasions. "There is no festival," he said, "where many sins are not committed," and he wished to contribute, personally, towards the diminution or expiation of those sins. On Easter Monday, the people went in crowds to the convent of the Capuchins, at Arienzo, pleasantly situated on a hill. Many parties of people, of all classes, went there to pass the day in various diversions, "to eat pigeons," as they said. In order to prevent the disorders which might be committed, Alphonsus went to this church after vespers; he had exposition of the Blessed Sacrament, and when the people were assembled together, he preached for hours. "The Word of God;" he was in the habit of saying, "always brings forth fruit, and there is nothing which hell labors more to hinder than preaching." His zeal was especially manifested when he had to preach to men, and particularly to nobles, or the learned; he said: "When the men are converted, piety will reign among women also." He took also advantage of public calamities, to exercise the ministry of the Word. In the spring of the year 1768, there was so great a drought all over the diocese, but principally at Arienzo, that all the wells were dried up. In this general distress he celebrated a Novena in honor of our Blessed Lady, to implore the mercy of God; this exercise became in fact a mission. On the first evening, after having addressed his numerous audience, he assured them, that if they would become truly converted, the Lord would comfort them, by sending an abundant rain on St. Anne's day. He continued to preach on the just punishments which overtake the sinner, and often struck himself severely with a thick rope. He sent two Capuchin Fathers of Naples, through the neighboring country, after the sermon, to exhort people to penance; after this, he kept these two fathers with him, together with some others, to hear confessions. Dry weather continued, and there was no hope of rain; but on St. Anne's day, towards noon, the heavens became covered with clouds, which poured forth an abundant rain, and watered all the distressed country, as he had promised. The consequence of all this preaching, was, that every where piety flourished, sin was done away with, crime disappeared. "Since his lordship's arrival at St. Agatha, we have lost a great deal," said an officer of justice, who had the care of the diocese, to a Neapolitan incumbent, "for his sermons, and those he has caused to be preached, have made the people so peaceable, that there is no longer any disorder to be found."

He was not satisfied with putting his own hand to the plough for the culture of his vineyard; he wished to be assisted by laborers, animated by the same spirit, and provided with necessary science, to aid him in his toils, and hasten the maturity of the fruit. As soon as he entered the diocese, or rather, from the time he accepted the bishopric, he thought of missions. He applied, when at Naples, for laborers, to the Superior of the society of the Apostolical Missions, and of that of the Conferences; he also solicited the Superior of the Congregation of Pious Workmen, as well as the Provincial of the Jesuits, and addressed petitions to the Superior of the Missionary Priests of the church of St. George, and to the Dominican Fathers. In the course of the autumn of 1762, the Superior of the Congregation of the Conference, placed more than five and twenty missonaries at his disposal; Alphonsus sent them to labor in several populous places, and caused the Pious Workmen to preach at Arienzo at this time, and the Jesuits at Durazzano. He repaired to Arienzo himself, "and I also," he said to the Pious Workmen, "I wish to do some-

thing." He gave the spiritual exercises to the gentlemen and noblemen, whom he united in a Congregation. In the sermon on the patronage of Mary, which he preached himself, he spoke with the fire of a seraph; his face was illuminated, and its brightness shed a supernatural splendor in the church: he exclaimed at the same time, carried away in an ecstasy, "See, here is the Virgin coming to scatter blessings; ask her for these blessings; she is ready to grant you every thing." Thus the Blessed Virgin, recompensed, on this, as she had done on many other occasions, as we have seen above, the zeal of her servant for her honor; for it was Alphonsus who had introduced this sermon on the Blessed Virgin, and had made it a rule, that it should never be omitted. After the mission at Arienzo, he went with ten Dominican Fathers from Naples to St. Mary del Vico, a place of more than four thousand inhabitants; he himself undertook the principal sermon. Several times, while weeping over his people's sins, he struck himself in the pulpit most cruelly with a thick rope. The mission lasted twenty-two days, and every one marvelled to see how an old man of sixty-seven, broken down with infirmities, could bear up under so much fatigue. But what astonished them most was, his penitential life; for besides his other austerities, he never departed from the severe rules of diet, which he had prescribed to himself, especially for the time of missions, as we have seen before.

One evening, after the Father who preached to the clergy had ended his sermon, Alphonsus unexpectedly presented himself before them, and said: "If any one has any scruple about having obtained his benefice by simony, let him come to me; I am come here to help him." The fact was, that a young ecclesiastic was in this case, and that, after having been to Alphonsus, he was freed from his scruple and preserved his benefice. At the mission of Airola, he contented himself with being present only, and returned at Christmas to Arienzo, and celebrated pontifically in the collegiate church. During mass, after having received the precious blood, he entered on a sudden into an ecstasy, as many persons attested, and his face beamed with heavenly fire.

After having visited all the diocese, he kept one of the most zealous missionaries with him, and caused him to give a spiritual renewal of the missions. Alphonsus, as we have said above, visited his diocese every two years, and he also caused the missionaries to go through it in the same space of time, and to those who blamed this multiplicity of missions, he answered that skilful husbandmen are accustomed to throw a double quantity of seed into places where the earth is dry and barren, and he added: "It is thus we must do, if we would have an ample harvest. When the seed is sown in abundance, if all does not come up, at least a part of it does. Jesus Christ compares the Word of God to wheat: if it is not sown, neither can it be gathered." Besides these missions, he had also recourse to divers other exercises, as novenas and triduos, in order to strengthen the good, and awaken the sinful. From the first, he also introduced the adoration of the forty hours, at the carnival, and caused, then, the most zealous preachers to ascend the pulpit.

He did not like to employ missionaries of his own Congregation, when he first arrived at St. Agatha, for fear that they might be suspected to be his spies. He founded his hopes on them, however, and in the end, caused some of them to come each year from Nocera, Ciorani, and St. Angelo. The two principal counsels he gave to all these missionaries were: charity towards sinners, and a popular style in preaching, and he was very anxious to see them followed. Once, he spoke very plainly to one of them, whom he knew to be guilty of rigorism. "My father," he said to him, "too much indulgence in a confessor is hurtful to souls, but too much rigor is not less prejudicial; I blame certain rigid spirits, who act not according to knowledge, and destroy rather than edify; with sinners, charity and mildness are necessary. Such was the method of Jesus Christ, and if we would lead souls to God and save them, we must not imitate Jansenius, but Jesus Christ, the chief of missionaries." As to preaching: "When Jesus Christ preached," he said, "He did not use turns of sentences nor rhetorical expressions; all His words were on a level with the people's comprehension; His proofs were natural, and never abstract. He used parables and comparisons, which, by striking the mind and heart, triumphed over the will. The Apostles were instructed by Him, and they imitated Him, and we also must do as they did; otherwise journeys, expense, and fatigue of every sort, will all be useless." One day, when he was present at a mission, he was seen to move about uneasily on his throne, because the preacher used chosen terms and studied phrases. The sermon was hardly ended, before he sent for the preacher, and reprimanded him severely, saying: "That is to betray the people and Jesus Christ; if you only seek to preach yourself, and not Jesus crucified, why did you take the trouble to leave Naples. I do not excuse you from mortal sin."

The expenses of these missions, except those that were provided for by foundations, were all placed to his own account. He paid for the journeys, lodgings, and food, even in case of labors which the missionaries undertook of their own accord. He freed the incumbent and the towns from all expense, furnishing even the oil and candles for the churches, and enabled the missionaries, besides, to give beds and other indispensable things to the poor, whose misery caused them to make their children sleep together, exhorting them to take particular care of necessitous families, converted females, and young girls in danger. Notwithstanding all this, he had sometimes much difficulty in overcoming the obstacles he met with from the incumbents. We give the following example, as it shows at the same time his incomparable forbearance and readiness to forgive. One incumbent had excused himself, saying that he had no house and could not procure one. Alphonsus, who divined his real feelings, answered that he must procure one, at any price, and that it would be defrayed for him. The priest replied in terms any thing but respectful. Indignant at this refusal, the grand-vicar and others wished him to be imprisoned, but Alphonsus blamed their hastiness and pitied the incumbent's weakness, who in the end asked for the mission. On this, Alphonsus far from showing any further dissatisfaction, even begged his pardon. "I do not say," he wrote to him, "that your reverence has put any impediment in the way, but I said that you did not show the anxiety I should have wished; if I have been wrong in this, I hope that now all will be as before. Blessed be God, who has permitted this unpleasantness to arise to you as well as to me."

To cause the Lenten sermons to be as profitable as those of the missions, he also exacted their being in a popular style. As in many localities, the parishioners had the right, founded on ancient usage, of electing the preachers, he had often the sorrow to see elected persons who were far from being according to his own heart. In order to remedy this abuse, he never failed to speak to the most influential persons in each place, to get them to choose subjects who were well known, and according to his wishes, and lastly, he asked and obtained that the preachers should be chosen from among the Capuchin Fathers exclusively. Before giving his approbation to the preachers selected, he obliged them to engage to give the spiritual exercises during Passion week, in the form of a mission, and those who showed repugnance to do so were always refused. He was in the habit of saying to those who nominated the preachers: "The right of election belongs to you, but it is for me to regulate the subject, and the form of the sermons."

During this time of Lent, he was attentive in seeing that the confessors should mutually exchange parishes, providing himself for their food and other expenses by means of the rural deans; and in this way, the Lenten exercises produced general advantage, thanks to the pains-taking care of the vigilant bishop. Besides, when the preachers and confessors presented themselves before him to receive his benediction, he liked to keep them, for some days, with him, and in conversing with them, he judged of their capability and knowledge. The obligations of the sacred ministry, charity towards sinners, and the necessity of encouraging them to penance, furnished him with inexhaustible subjects of conversation, but above all, with the motives for very particular exhortations. Even in panegyrics and sermons, on festivals, he wished, as we have seen, that the preacher should speak simply, in order that the people might profit by them. One day, on the celebration of the feast of the Sacred Heart, at Arienzo, they invited a celebrated preacher, of a well known order in Naples. Alphonsus, too ill to officiate, wished, notwithstanding, to be present, but suffered much in hearing flowery expressions and high flown phrases delivered by the preacher! If he did not quit the church, it was only to avoid creating disturbance in the ceremony. At last he turned towards the altar, and turned his back on the pulpit and preacher, and on reaching his house he sent for him, and in a tone of authority, thus addressed him: "Is it not to wish to betray Jesus Christ and the people, to preach in that way? If I did not make you come down from the pulpit, it was from respect to the habit you wear. What fruit have the people gathered from all the tropes, from all the figures of speech and pompous descriptions with which you ornamented your discourse? All that was only the fruit of vanity, and can only merit the fire of purgatory. Your end ought to have been to touch hearts, and cause tears to be shed; but the people were insensible, because they understood nothing."

In the year 1763, all Italy was a prey to most fearful distress, a famine, which caused our saint to have an increase of sorrow and merits. He predicted this calamity, even before his election to the bishopric; for preaching once in Naples, and becoming more animated than usual, he exclaimed: "Beware, beware, God will overtake us with famine." This he predicted on other occasions, and during the Mission of St. Agatha, he said: "My children, cease to sin, for a great calamity is threatening us," and on another occasion: "Amend your lives, I repeat to you, and recommend yourselves to God, for a great famine will soon afflict you." The same prediction he repeated twice at Arienzo, in the year which preceded the fatal winter of 1763-1764, and expressed himself still more definitely. The people were wearied with these reiterated predictions, and said: "Where is this bishop come from? He only fortells famine and bad seasons." After the harvest of 1763, he ordered his secretary to buy a great quantity of kidney and French beans, and other vegetables. No body understood the mystery, and all laughed at it, the secretary being the first to do so, for the harvest had been at least a tolerable one. But the month of November had not terminated, before the scarcity spread from one end of the kingdom to the other. It is difficult to imagine the holy bishop's sorrow in seeing the multitude of starving poor; they had no bread left, and so all recurred to their common father for aid in their distress. The large hall of the episcopal palace was sometimes crowded with four or five hundred of these distressed people, who in the most suppliant posture, and with tearful eyes, begged for a morsel of bread. Alphonsus tried to relieve them all, saying to the servant: "Make them all go away satisfied, they only ask for what belongs to them." He sent in every direction to obtain corn, and applied to D. Hercules, then governor of Naples, from whom he obtained plenty of corn, though it had already begun to be sold at six ducats the measure. He applied to his rich patrons, and received numerous donations, and was overjoyed at being able to assist his poor children.

He had a large list placed in the great hall, on which all the necessitous families were noted down, alphabetically, and as they presented themselves, they received according to their poverty, a portion of beans or vegetables, together with some money. Besides this, he had arranged a private list of families, who were prevented from coming to his palace through shame or some other cause. But as he soon became destitute of money, he wished to borrow, by paying interest, but was constantly refused, nobody being willing to be satisfied with the guarantee of an old man, asthmatic, and broken down with infirmities. In this extremity he sold the ring, which he had received as a present from Jane Versale, as well as that which he had received from Bishop Giannini, (and which had belonged to his uncle, the bishop of Troy,) with his pectoral cross, only keeping one, silver gilt, for pontifical ceremonies. He ordered also his secretary to sell the little plate he had. Not knowing what else to sell, he was on the point of getting rid of his rochet and watch, but he gave up this idea on its being represented to him, that they were of little value, while to him a watch was indispensable. As the scarcity increased, he resolved to sell his carriage. Being opposed in this by the Grand-Vicar and others, he said: "St. Peter was Pope, and he had no carriage, why should I have one, I, who am not greater than St. Peter?" When D. Hercules interfered, and joined his opponents, he replied: "All these pretexts to induce me to keep my carriage, are only a temptation of the devil, in my opinion. I am old, I have already one foot in the grave; I am burthened with debts, I want a great deal of money, and am distressed to death at being able to do nothing. Do not trouble me any longer about this affair, for I will not answer you any more. You know very well, besides, that when I come to a resolution, after a careful examination, I never go back from it. I cannot bear to see the mules remaining in the stable nearly all the year with nothing to do, while the coachman is wasting his time, and the poor are asking for bread." That which he had resolved on, he executed, and on the 5th of January, sent his carriage and mules to Naples. His brother, D. Gaëtan, not wishing them to pass into the hands of strangers, bought them himself, and at a very high price. When he had nothing more to sell, he thought of getting rid of the plate which had belonged to his predecessors, the pastoral cross, the ewer, and candlestick, as well as the precious stone which adorned the clasp of the cope. But being resisted by the canons, he asked to be allowed, at least, to pledge these things; but this also was denied. This second refusal grieved him so much, that he was seen walking about, alone in his room, weeping and giving way to all the bitterness of his heart. While in this great sorrow, he envied rich bishops, as they had more power to do good. "Oh, that I merited as much before God, as St. Thomas of Villanova," said he one day, "I might find my granaries filled with corn, as he did."

The scourge continuing to increase its ravages, the zealous pastor applied to the Pope, supplicating him to grant him the permission to mortgage all his income, in order to be able to succor the poor. But though the Pope consented to this, the answer did not arrive in time. He assembled, moreover, *all the heads* of the chapels together, and begged, or rather commanded them, to pawn all their plate. This was done, but it was only as a few drops of water cast on a great conflagration. The indefatigable pastor, however, took no rest; he daily assembled the principal gentlemen, canons, and chief functionaries, and consulted with them as to the means of relieving the town, and preventing the death of the poor by hunger. Many refused to give him money, but many others being moved with compassion, placed generous donations in his hands; others supplied him with money under the name of a loan, but, no doubt, never expected to recover the advances they made.

But the pious pastor considered himself as charged with the sins of his people, and offered himself as a victim to the justice of heaven, he bound himself with hair-cloths, and disciplined himself most severely every day, and did not cease to excite the people also to do penance for their sins. One evening, after such a fervent exhortation, on his return home, a woman of the town ran after him, and exclaimed in fury: "Would to God you had never come among us! since you have been here you have only announced calamities, and now you make us eat bread at seven grains the pound." Then raising her hand in a menacing way, she added: "You have plenty of money, you, I say, to eat it at this price." Alphonsus, far from being moved at these violent and undeserved reproaches, gave his blessing to the woman. The sacristan, who accompanied him, began to scold her, and took her by the

shoulder in order to force her to go away; Alphonsus was indignant at this and punished him for it, by four days' imprisonment. "These unhappy people deserve compassion," said he, "it is not their heart, but famine which makes them speak." God, however, did not leave such a wicked act unpunished, and this woman, who had lived in ease before, was soon reduced to the lowest beggary.

Poverty increased, particularly in Naples, to such a degree, that the scourge spared no one; the starving poor were seen, as Alphonsus had predicted, eating the grass of the hedges, and seeking in the country for the nourishment which beasts had refused to eat, so as even to feed on noxious herbs. On seeing thousands of these poor people going about the streets like spectres, Alphonsus was ready to die for sorrow. He confined himself to bread and broth, and one day said to his secretary and grand-vicar: "You see how the people are dying with hunger, it is necessary that we should do without something more; and so you must bear patiently yourself as well as others." In consequence, his table was only supplied with broth and boiled meat, with which every one, without exception, had to be satisfied. He invoked also the superiors of all the convents of the diocese, and not only begged, but commanded them, to contribute to the relief of the poor, by retrenching some part of their ordinary expenditures. He heard that the superior of a wealthy convent was very stingy towards the poor; he sent for him and reproached him for his hard-heartedness. "I am obliged," replied the religious, "to maintain my family; I give what is over to the poor, and no more." This answer pained our saint; he rose from his chair full of indignation, and said: "Do you know what maintain means? It signifies that it is necessary to eat enough to preserve life, and the surplus ought to be given to the poor. When you became a religious, you said that you wished to lead a life of poverty and penance. Do you believe in the Gospel, or are you a Turk?" The religious changed his line of conduct, and the poor of the place were quite differently treated, from this time. He begged also the monasteries in Naples, and his penitents and relations, to bestow gifts on him for the sick.

Thus Alphonsus acted like a true apostle of charity, during this calamity. He was delighted when he could assist the poor, and wept when he had nothing to give them. Every thing was open to them, and there was not a single room in the palace, where one did not see some poor person being comforted or snatched from the grasp of death. One evening, after all had been relieved, the Secretary, in going to bed, saw a man stretched on a bench in the hall, motionless and nearly expiring. Alphonsus, being informed of this, hastened hither, and at the sight of the unfortunate man was filled with sorrow; he sent for vinegar and other things to try and revive him; he ran to his room himself and took a piece of chocolate, which he succeeded with difficulty in placing in the mouth of the dying man. At length by dint of much pains, he had the happiness to see him come to his senses again, and his heart rejoiced at the sight of the poor man thus restored to life.

As St. Agatha was not the only town which suffered from the famine, and as there was a dearth of bread throughout the diocese, all had recourse to him, and he had a helping hand for all. There was no place in the diocese which he did not aid with a quantity of corn and lentils, as well as with money. As bishop, he was lord of the fief of Baynoli; the inhabitants of this domain also demanded his assistance, and more than this, they used menaces. He succeeded in procuring a great quantity of corn from Naples, secretly, and distributed bread to the poor of this estate every day. Thus the diocese of St. Agatha had much less to suffer than the other dioceses, for while, every where, bread was from ten to twelve grains the pound, at St. Agatha, it only cost six and a half.

But however great was his solicitude, he could not satisfy the wants of all. On the 20th of February, 1764, the horrors of famine having become still more felt, the

people rebelled, and chose as the victim of their blind resentment, the syndic Dominico Carvo, the superintendent of provisions at St. Agatha. The mutinous people, desiring to assassinate him, attacked him in his house, and broke down his door. The unfortunate man happily succeeded in escaping, and took refuge in the episcopal palace. The mob having heard of this, hurried thither, and besieged the palace; they penetrated into the interior, and sought for the syndic in order to murder him. Alphonsus, in alarm, appeared before the furious mob, and offered himself as a victim to their anger; he ran into the midst of them, pressed them to his heart, and in tears endeavored to exculpate the syndic. "Life for life," cried the multitude. Alphonsus, not knowing what more he could do to calm their fury, famine rendering them deaf to all his reasons, distributed to them all the meat and bread which he had kept for the most necessitous poor, as also all the bread and provisions of the seminary. This alarm had scarcely ended, when another sorrow succeeded. The court at Naples, being informed of the revolt, despatched sixty horsemen to St. Agatha, to prevent still more serious disturbances; which measure, far from intimidating the people, only served to exasperate them more. Alphonsus, considering this sad state of things, could neither eat nor sleep; he consulted, every moment, with the officers, in order to prevent the soldiers causing inconvenience to any one, while he at the same time negotiated at Naples for the recall of the military. He spoke to the most influential of the populace, to urge them to be peaceful; he procured new stores of corn and vegetables, and his active charity took no rest, until he saw the soldiers depart, and tranquillity re-established.

Assisted by divine light from on high, he often foresaw the misfortunes which would happen, even out of town, and was thus enabled to obviate them. At Arienzo in particular, he saved D. Ciro Lettieri, the first magistrate of this town, from a great disaster. The brother of Ciro was employed by Alphonsus to put the archives of the bishopric in order. It was supposed he would have to be occupied in this, at least a fortnight. But eight days had scarcely elapsed, before Alphonsus suddenly sent for him one Saturday, and said: "I wish you to return to Arienzo this very evening, for your presence will be necessary there." Greatly surprised at such a dismissal, he set out, little satisfied with the bishop's proceedings. On the Sunday morning, being at Arienzo, he heard the sound of the tocsin, he went to the piazza, and found the people collected together, and with arms in hand, proceeding tumultuously towards his brother's house. He understood then what that necessity for his presence was, and he was just in time to save his brother, who but for him would have been killed. He got before the populace, and caused D. Ciro to take refuge in the monastery of the Fathers of St. Augustine, whence, clothed in a religious habit, he fled from the town and escaped from the seditious mob. The tribunal of Montefusco, being informed of this tumult, commissioned an officer to seek for the principal rioters. Thirty fathers of families were denounced by the subordinates; they were innocent, but were all obliged to appear at Montefusco. The governors of the town, out of consideration for the ruin of so many families, applied to their common father. At this news, Alphonsus was filled with grief, and wept over the possible consequences of this denunciation, and, without loss of time, represented to the president of the tribunal the innocence of the accused, and entreated him to stop the prosecution. His representations were so efficacious, that the court granted all that he desired.

As the spring of 1764 advanced, it brought with it new resources, which gradually put an end to the fearful scarcity, and the holy bishop was able to resume the course of his visitation. Many disorders had arisen during the famine; some people had profited by the general misery to practice usury extensively; others tortured their debtors, and constrained them to subscribe to exaggerated claims. He inveighed against these abuses, and used every means to remedy them. He sent for the merchants and moneyed men,

and enjoined them not to deviate from the rules of equity. After having thus contributed to the restoration of order at St. Agatha, and in the neighboring country, he especially enjoined on the parish priests the relief of many sick persons, convalescents, and the most necessitous families, and then set out to visit the other parts of the diocese; he was greeted in all parts with shouts of joy, which showed plainly the delight which the presence of their charitable bishop caused in the hearts of the faithful.

CHAPTER XXII.

Alphonsus presides at a general Chapter of his Congregation. He defends his Moral Theology. He publishes Ordinances for the Regulation of his Diocese. He establishes new Parishes. Becomes dangerously ill. He publishes his Book on the Truth of Faith. Circular to his Congregation.

ABOUT this time, his Congregation had to assemble in a general chapter, and the saintly founder was begged to preside. He accepted the invitation, though he was then overcharged with business. He went, in consequence, to Nocera, towards the end of September. In passing by Nola, he stopped at the seminary, and, at the invitation of the Superior, gave an exhortation to the seminarists, which lasted more than an hour; he also saw Bishop Carracciolo, who, as well as our saint, was an enemy to those pompous titles which were adopted by certain bishops at that time. He related to Alphonsus, that, having been addressed in a letter from one of his colleagues by the title of Excellency, he had not returned the compliment. "You did very right," replied Alphonsus, "I cannot understand what gave rise to this plaguing Excellency. The Council of Trent condescended to grant us the title of Right Reverend, and now they wish to introduce, Most Illustrious. If we had wished for Excellency, we could have staid at home." When he entered the Church to visit the Blessed Sacrament, he was given an arm-chair, which was used by the bishop; he refused it, and placed himself on a bench, saying, "This place befits D. Alphonsus;" wishing to say, that not being in his own diocese, he ought not to usurp any mark of distinction.

The chapter lasted a month. The customs and rules already in vigor, were revised and confirmed. Every thing was done in the most satisfactory manner, thanks to his prudence and wisdom. The chapter was scarcely terminated when he set out again for St. Agatha, where he undertook to combat a new enemy. A distinguished Dominican, F. Vincent Patuzzi, unceasingly criticised the Moral Theology of the saintly doctor. Alphonsus, after his return from Rome, had already published a long and learned dissertation, wherein all the most weighty authorities were brought forward in support of his system, and which was considered as a master-piece. Father Patuzzi, not being willing to give up the combat, had taken up arms again. Patuzzi's work was but a libel, under the name of Adolphus Dositheus, entitled, "The cause of probabilism re-produced after the examination of Bishop Liguori, and again convicted of falsity." Alphonsus replied now in a learned and moderate address, in which he supported his doctrine by the authority of the canons, of the Holy Fathers, and of the most celebrated theologians, principally of St. Thomas. He dedicated his book to his Holiness, Clement XIII, with this declaration: "I protest that in all which I have written on this subject, I had no other intention than to make the truth clear in so grave a matter, on which depends the good or evil direction of consciences, and as I had the honor of dedicating my Moral Theology to the Sovereign Pontiff, Benedict XIV, some years ago, I venture to present and submit to your Holiness, this treatise, which is an appendix to the same Moral Theology, in order that you may deign to look over it, to correct, modify, and cancel all which may be opposed to the rules of Christian wisdom." Alphonsus sent his apology to the bishops and archbishops, as well as to the other theological doctors, who all united with one voice in praising the author's great learning, but not less, the great humility and moderation with which he defended his system, as is proved by many letters of approbation he received on the occasion, the greater portion of which are quoted by Alphonsus himself at the end of his apology. Patuzzi, notwithstanding, sharpened his pen anew, and published another libel, which contained the same abuse as his former writings, only under another form. Alphonsus, without departing from his usual moderation, replied to him on the 16th of January, 1764: "I have received your well meant letter, wherein are mingled praises and counsels, admonitions, reproaches, and menaces." Then, after having apologised for not being able to reply more at length, on account of the business of his diocese, he adds: "You tell me that you are astonished, that, while leading an edifying life, (you had better said that I deceive the public,) I, notwithstanding, profess an erroneous doctrine. My Father, I judge and see precisely the contrary; I see that my life is neither good nor exemplary, but full of faults, and on the contrary, I am sure that my system is very wise and certain." He then continues to overthrow his adversary's objections with admirable skill and learning, supporting his arguments principally by St. Thomas, and other learned writers. F. Patuzzi was conquered, but not convinced, and thus the controversy ended.

When Alphonsus had made himself thoroughly acquainted with the state of his diocese, he informed the Pope that he thought he ought to assemble a synod, in order to remedy numerous abuses, and supported by the approbation of his Holiness, regulate many things which he judged necessary. The Pope heard this determination with pleasure, and to favor his undertaking, he granted, by a brief of the 21st of June, a plenary indulgence to all who, after having confessed, should communicate and visit the cathedral of St. Agatha, on the day of the opening of the synod, and also every year, on its anniversary. But Alphonsus consulting Bishop Borgia, of Aversa, about this matter, as well as F. Fatigati, the founder of the Congregation of the Holy Family, they both disapproved of the project, and their opinion was shared by several bishops who were friends of our saint. After reflecting on their reasons, he said: "I will accomplish what I wished to regulate in a synod, by simple decrees, and thus I shall not have to fear some unquiet spirit preventing my obtaining the royal assent, at Naples." He consulted then several times the most judicious members of his clergy, and thus the articles which he had prepared for the synodical assembly, were replaced by six ordinances, which he promulgated in due form, and caused to be rigorously observed throughout the diocese.

The first referred to the canons, the priests of the cathedral, and the chaplains, concerning the rubrics, the ecclesiastical discipline of the choir, and the conditions of gaining the distributions, with divers regulations, concerning the divine service in the cathedral, and the meetings of the chapter.

The second referred to the duties of the archpriests, vicars, and rectors, throughout the diocese. He renewed the order given after his first visitation, that the summary of the Christian doctrine, composed by himself, should be read twice to the people every Sunday and feast day; and ordered that every Sunday morning, the parish priests should give a detailed instruction on the truths of faith, especially to little children; that the children should be made to know the meaning of the words their lips uttered; and that they should be taught the acts for holy communion, several weeks before Easter, in order that they might understand well the importance of this sacrament, the benefits it procures, and the dispositions it requires; that they should be admitted to this sacrament when nine or ten, or at most, twelve years old. He ordered also, that all who wished to enter into matrimony, should be examined on the most essential points of Christian doctrine, and this indispensably and without distinction of persons, according to the prescriptions of the Roman ritual, and the doctrine of Pope Benedict XIV. In the same ordinance he set before the parochial clergy, their strict obligation to preach every Sunday, reminding them also, that according to the Council of Trent, preaching should be familiar and level to the people's capacity. In order to prevent serious evils, and many sins, he obliged them to receive no promise of betrothal, without the certainty of a speedy marriage, and wished that parents should be repeatedly advised not to receive young men into their houses, who might prove an occasion of scandal to their daughters, this being a reserved case. He also ordered, that no one should be admitted to Easter communion, without having been previously examined by his parish priest, on the things necessary to salvation, and forbade confessors to administer this sacrament to those who were not provided with a certificate of having been thus examined; that those who had not fulfilled the paschal duty, should be warned of the excommunication they would incur, if they did not fulfil it in their parish church, and that if any one had not performed his duty, by Trinity Sunday, the incumbent should then report it to the bishop, without delay. For the young of both sexes, he ordered two general communions, the one on the Sunday after the Assumption, and the other at Christmas. This same ordinance reminded the parish priests, that according to the Roman catechism, they sinned grievously, if they did not administer extreme unction till the dying person had lost the use of his reason. Rectors and other priests were ordered to have a list in the sacristy, in which should be noted, the days, and the altars, at which the perpetual masses ought to be celebrated, and that, when a legacy was left in favor of the church, the payment should be required from the heirs in a month after the death of the testator, and that in case of refusal, recourse should be had to a competent judge, to compel them, or else the bishop should be informed; and besides, informing the bishop before accepting any legacy, that a list of the foundations should be made every ten years, and a copy of it remitted to the heirs, and another deposited in the hands of the chapter.

This same ordinance concluded with several regulations concerning the reserved cases, the distribution of the holy oils, the mass to be said for the people on Sundays and feast days, the residence of the curates, &c.

The third was addressed to all confessors, secular and regular. He reminded them of the necessity they lay under, to study moral theology, and ordered them to join some Congregation for discussing cases of conscience. He wished them to ask parents, whether they sent their children to be catechised, this being a reserved case, and especially, minutely to interrogate those who confessed seldom, or, whose consciences were not known to them. He told them to refuse absolution to backsliding, and habitual sinners, except they gave extraordinary signs of contrition, and to those in occasion of sin, before they had quitted the occasion. He inculcated on them the duty of reminding physicians of the strict obligation which the bull of Pius V, imposes on them, of ordering the sacraments to be administered to those of their patients whom they found, after the third visit, to be in danger, or likely to become so. He condemned the facility with which many confessors granted absolution to venial sins, without being certain that the penitents repented of them, and were resolved to amend. He advised confessors to exhort their penitents to frequent prayer, and to urge them to invoke the sacred names of Jesus and Mary, unceasingly, when in temptation, and above all, to recommend to them, devotion to the Blessed Virgin, the recitation of the Rosary, as well as three Aves, morning and evening, in honor of the Mother of purity and perseverance, and to teach briefly, the exercise of mental prayer to those whom they saw most disposed to piety.

The fourth renewed the pain of suspension, ipso facto, for all those who should finish mass in less than a quarter of an hour, and contained several other regulations regarding the holy sacrifice. He reminded besides, all ecclesiastics, of the suspension, ipso facto, to be incurred by amusing themselves at games of chance, or any other game in public. He equally forbade hunting with a gun, or with nets, without the written permission of the bishop, &c., and lastly, exhorted all the clerics to second their parish priests in the instruction on Christian doctrine.

The sixth, (we shall speak of the fifth hereafter,) provided that which was becoming, in regard to clerical dress and tonsure. These were the principal regulations Alphonsus felt it necessary to make, for the good of his clergy and diocese. He confessed that, in consequence of the circumstances of the times, he had not acted after the rigor of the ancient canons, but he also declared, that in proportion to this indulgence, would be his severity towards transgressors. "Any kind of contempt for myself, does not affect me at all," said he, "on the contrary, I thank God for it; but I cannot suffer any disregard for my ordinances." He was therefore very attentive in watching to see that they were kept, and not satisfied with the reports which were addressed to him by the rural vicars, who were especially bound to attend to what was going on in the different parts of the diocese, he commissioned certain persons, to inform him privately, of all kinds of infraction of these ordinances, and when he saw that the offences were in consequence of contempt of his wishes, he acted with severity, and more than one ecclesiastic suffered an exemplary punishment in consequence. One was deprived of the revenues of his parish; another for having twice failed to be present at the meetings of the discussion of moral cases, was sent for by the bishop, who reprimanded him with severity.

One of the greatest evils which Alphonsus had remarked during his pastoral visitation, was the spiritual abandonment, in which thousands of souls were to be found, who were dispersed through the country, and above all, in the neighborhood of St. Agatha. The population of this town and its environs, amounted to more than twenty-four thousand inhabitants, who were scattered about in a number of villages, hamlets, and farm-houses. In the suburbs and villages, there were not less than two hundred families, who comprised altogether, more than thirteen hundred souls, and formed, what was called, the parish of St. Thomas, divided into several sections, some of which were four or five miles from the church. This occasioned serious inconveniences, for while the heat of summer caused the access to the church to be very painful, winter rendered it nearly impossible; the old and very young, never saw their parish priest. There was no catechising for the young, nor instruction for the adults, and what is worse, nearly all the sick were deprived of the viaticum, and extreme unction. The vigilant bishop, grieving over such a deplorable state of things, determined to divide the parish of St. Thomas, and to form three others, which should be supported by some benefices of free gift, which till then, had only been conferred on clerics, attached to the bishop, or on strangers. The execution of this project was far from being an easy matter, but our saint's zeal and constancy triumphed over all obstacles, and three parishes were established in three ancient churches, at convenient distances.

At Cancello, a place within three miles from Arienzo, there were dispersed about in various estates, a great number of families, dependant on the parish of St. Felix of Arienzo, which being four miles distant, at the least, the inhabitants for the most part, died without any religious aid. Alphonsus resolved to make a parochial chapel of the one to be found there, but finding opposition, he contented himself with establishing there a chaplain, to say mass on Sundays and festivals, for which, the Duke of Maddalon, who possessed large farms on this domain, gave him yearly twelve ducats, to which Alphonsus added six more, out of his own income, in order to induce him to consent to preach, and teach the catechism to the children. He presented to the church, a beautiful missal, and other books, for the celebration of the offices, and promised the priest not to forget him, when a vacancy should occur in the livings. He made the same, or similar arrangements in many other parts of the diocese, so that the word of God was announced in many rural chapels which were distant from the parish churches, he himself supplying what was necessary for the maintenance of these chaplains. Other churches, where the revenues were inadequate, were by his care endowed with rentals and benefices, taken from those which were superabundantly provided. By these means he attracted a number of meritorious priests, who, till then, had been kept at a distance, through fear and distress.

Alphonsus, exhausted with austerity and fatigue, became ill, at the close of the year 1764. The fever made such progress, that his life was soon despaired of, and they hastened to administer to him the viaticum, and extreme unction. It was an affecting sight, to see the bishop of St. Agatha, lie on a bed of straw, between two sheets of coarse cloth, and covered with all the emblems of poverty, with a dying voice, asking the two clergymen who assisted him, to suggest some sentiments of love to him. One of them tried to suggest some holy thoughts, but tears stifled his voice, and he could not utter a single word. "My lord," said then the other, "When St. Martin was near death, he addressed the following prayer to God: 'Lord, if I am still necessary to thy people, I refuse not to work;'" and Alphonsus, who could scarcely move his lips, immediately repeated, "Non recuso laborem," "I refuse not to work." No children ever wept more bitterly, at the death bed of a father, than the inhabitants of St. Agatha did, at the prospect of so soon losing their bishop. Public prayers were had in every place, throughout the diocese, and several religious communities at Naples, offered up Novenas, and other prayers, in order that the Lord would deign to preserve the pastor to his diocese, or rather to the whole Church.

As the invalid's danger had been seen from the first, they proposed to him to send for a physician, to Naples, but he would not hear of it, saying that his life was not worth so much trouble, and that he ought to employ the physicians of St. Agatha, since God had given them to him. Nevertheless, his brother Hercules was no sooner informed of his state, than he came to see him, accompanied by two of the first doctors of the capital. He escaped from death at last, but it may truly be said, that his recovery was a recompense for the tears of the poor, and it was plainly seen, that the Lord wished, for the salvation of his flock, to preserve his life, of which they had still the greatest need. God also manifested his servant's sanctity, during his illness, by a miracle. One day, while he was still in bed, he received a visit from a canon, who brought him some fig-peckers, which he had shot. He was accompanied by his nephew, who, although four years old, could not say a single word. Alphonsus asked the canon what was his nephew's name; the uncle replied, that the child was called Thomas, but could not yet speak, and that they believed he would continue to be dumb. Alphonsus immediately made the sign of the cross on the child's forehead, and taking a picture of our Lady of Power, gave it to Thomas, to kiss, and asked him what this Lady was called. The child kissed the picture, and his tongue being unloosed at the moment, he replied, "The Madonna." Alphonsus turned to the canon, and to conceal the miracle, said to him: "This child is not dumb; it is true that there is an impediment in his speech, but you will see that it will gradually disappear." From that time, the child had the use of speech, in fact, he articulated every sound perfectly, and asked for all he wanted.

The doctors foreseeing the tediousness of his recovery, and fearing that, if he were not entirely set up before the autumn, he would languish all the winter, advised him to go to breathe the salubrious air of Nocera. This proposition alarmed him. "I cannot go far from my residence," said he, "let us place ourselves in the hands of the Lord, and he will do the rest." It required a command from F. Villani, then present at St. Agatha, to cause him to consent to go. From the time that he was among his Congregation again, he never failed, even though not well, to follow all the exercises of the community; he resumed his scientific occupations at the same time, not allowing himself a moment's relaxation. Being asked one day, by a priest, to play the harpsichord, he replied: "What will be said, if I pass my time at an idle instrument, in place of employing it in thinking of my diocese. My duty, and that of every bishop, is to give audience to all, to pray, to study, and never to play the harpsichord." He preached again, each Saturday, in honor of the Blessed Virgin, and from time to time was called on to give familiar instructions to nuns in their convents. The Rector caused him to be treated with some distinction, with regard to food, because of his indisposition; these attentions were a martyrdom to him, he wished no distinction to be made between himself and the rest of the community.

He ate in an upper room, and this was the occasion of a heroic act of mortification for him. As he drank no wine, he once asked for a glass of water, and the brother who was waiting on him, saw a vase, which was full of it, and presented it to him; Alphonsus took it and drank, but a Father who was beside him, smelt a bad odor, and saw that the vase was filled with corrupted water, which had been used for keeping flowers in, a few days before. Alphonsus did not show the least displeasure, or say a word to find fault with one who had waited on him so badly. Here also, God favored him with special graces. Once, when he was saying mass in the domestic chapel of the Mother of Sorrows, and had come to the psalm, "Judica me Deus," he cast his eyes on the Image, and suddenly broke off and stopped in the middle of the verse he had commenced. The Father who served his mass, thinking he was distracted, wished to recall him to the place again, and said the end of the verse a second and a third time, but Alphonsus did not say a word, he was in ecstasy. It was not till the Father had shaken him several times, that he continued the psalm.

Though far from St. Agatha, the holy bishop had the wants of his diocese before him every instant; and as he wished to be informed of every thing, couriers arrived at Nocera constantly, from his Grand-Vicar, the parish priests, and others. One day he received as many as eight, to all of whom he gave an answer, so that one matter was hardly ended, when he began another.

He had been barely a month at Nocera, when he heard that a person, who, for her disorderly conduct, had been sent out of the diocese, was endeavoring to re-enter it. This news tormented him so much, that without regard for his health, he hastened his return, the prayers of the Fathers, and of his friends, being unable to retain him. "God wills," said he, "that I should be at St. Agatha, and not at Nocera, I have overwhelming scruples already." As he had suffered a good deal during the preceding winter, from coughs and affections of the chest, the doctors advised him to reside at Arienzo, as it had a better climate; he yielded, but not without having consulted F. Villani, as he had scruples at leaving St. Agatha, where he had his cathedral, his chapter, and what was of more consequence to him, his seminary. "I wish to have your opinion," he wrote to him, "to take away my fears." F. Villani, as well as bishops Borgia and Volpi, and others whom he had consulted, also wished him to banish every scruple, and go to Arienzo.

When his health was re-established, he recommenced his visitation. F. Villani forbade him to make use of his straw bed during the visitation, in consideration of his age and infirmities, and the numerous maladies which had exhausted his strength. Alphonsus obeyed, but this submission cost him a great deal when he had no fever, for then he thought, that he enjoyed too good health; and he was scarcely recovered, when he recommenced his penances and macerations, but not without the sanction of his director, so he wrote to F. Villani, on the 28th October: "I have not slept on straw again, but the milk diet has quite restored me, and so if you will permit it, I wish to resume the straw bed. . . . . I have begun to wear the chains on the part where the old blisters" (new ones had been applied) "have been taken away. I beg for your blessing." And in another letter: "I have only taken boiled meat at dinner, till now, leaving the first dish untouched; but as I am obliged to eat only once a day, I have consulted F. Majone, and he has told me to take a second dish. In case the boiled meat is sufficient, I wish to ask your Reverence, as my principal director, to allow me to eat the bouilli only. If you do not approve of my request, I will submit to your decision."

Alphonsus' mind was agitated by painful anxieties, at this time. Every day he heard of the great number of evil books, which spread their contagious influence in Europe, and particularly in France, and were clandestinely introduced into Italy by the librarians, who spread them in the provinces. He was constantly protesting against these works at the court, and entreated the Marquises of Marco, and Tanucci, to forbid the importation and sale of them. He enforced on confessors, and preachers, the duty of inspiring a horror of such reading, and especially commanded this to be done, by his missionaries, and those who went through the provinces. Basnage's abominable book, afflicted him very much. He would have liked to enter the lists against this dangerous writer, but being prevented from so doing, he manifested to F. de Meo, his desire to see him labor, to refute his errors, at least, as to matters of religion. He was again attacked on account of his Moral Theology, by Fathers Patuzzi, and Gonzales. "Let them do as they please," he replied on the 7th of January, 1766, to F. Sapio, of the Oratory, who had apprised him of it, "I did not write to gain honor, but only to make truth known. If what I have written is convincing, it is well; if otherwise, I do not wish to be victorious by obstinacy . . . . I regret, that the learned have a prejudice, that he who does not write to defend tutiorism, so in fashion in our days, is not well informed. The ultramontane party has spread in many Catholic countries, it triumphs, and souls go to their ruin. Let us pray to God to put a stop to this. A book has been published, entitled, 'The Realization of the project of Boury-Fontaine,' which shows the Jansenists' intention of overthrowing the Church. This book is important, your Reverence must procure and read it." He also was transported with zeal, against the sect of the Freemasons. "This sect," he said, with tears in his eyes, "will cause evil, not only to the Church, but also to kingdoms and sovereigns. Kings do not attend to them, but they will recognise their fatal negligence, when too late. Free-masons act against God at present, and they will soon attack kings." Besides addressing a great number of letters to the members of the regency, established at Naples after King Charles III, had quitted that town, he also wrote to Cardinal Sersale, to engage him to use all his influence, in order to free Naples, and the provinces, from this abominable sect. He composed his great work, on The Truth of Faith, at this time, against the unbelievers of modern times. And as the infallibility of the Pope was then also attacked, and questioned, particularly by the defenders of the declaration of the Assembly, in Paris, in 1682, he undertook to refute them, in a treatise, which he published, under the title of "Reflections on the declaration of the Assembly of Paris, on the subject of the infallibility of the Sovereign Pontiff."

Another thing caused him much sorrow, and that was the storm raised up throughout Europe, against the Jesuits. He wrote to the F. Provincial de Mattei, as follows: "I have not received any tidings about the affairs of your society: I feel almost as much uneasiness, as if it related to our Congregation. A society is menaced, which one may say, has sanctified the world, and which continues, unceasingly, to sanctify it." "The Jansenists, and all innovators," he said, on another accasion, "would like to annihilate it, in order to overthrow the bulwark of the Church of God. Against such enemies, where shall we find vigorous champions, such as those which the company of Jesus alone can train up?" When Pope Clement XIII, issued a bull, by which he confirmed the company anew, Alphonsus was full of joy, and felt that he must write to the Sovereign Pontiff, to thank him, which he did, in a letter, dated the 19th of June, 1765, to which the Pope answered most affectionately.

Amidst these labors and anxieties, he did not forget his own little Congregation. He wrote a circular, dated the 27th of August, in order to stir up a daily increasing fervor, from his great wish to see it become more and more perfect. He cherished this work as the apple of his eye, and the smallest spot which he observed in it, afflicted him deeply, and always appeared to him considerable. "I perceive with sorrow," said he, in the exaggeration of his feelings, "that fervor is much decayed amongst the subjects of the Congregation, and I beg each of you to watch over himself attentively for the time to come, because I cannot suffer any relaxation in the rule during my life. I am told that there is very little inclination for poverty and mortification. Ah! have we then entered the Congregation to enjoy our ease, and to exclaim against pain? . . . I hear also, that obedience to Superiors is lessened; if obedience ceases, the Congregation will not survive it. . . . . I have told the F. Vicar-General, D. Andrew Villani, to punish public faults by public mortifications, and to expel such as shall show themselves to be incorrigible. The Congregation has no need of subjects: it only seeks for those who wish to become saints. It is enough for it, if ten remain, who truly love God. It is being too ungrateful towards God, to repay him, for the love with which he protects the Congregation, by failings and neglects. Do we wish to become like so many others, who cause the Church scandal, rather than edification? I have told F. Villani, that his government is too weak and mild, and that, for the future, I wish to be better informed of all that occurs of an important nature. . . . . Above all, it is necessary to mortify ourselves and to please God, otherwise God will not aid us, and we shall preach in vain. I bless you all, I mean, all those who are well-intentioned; if there are others, I do not curse them, but God will curse them, and will expel them from the Congregation."

CHAPTER XXIII.

Alphonsus seeks to resign the Episcopate. He establishes at St. Agatha a Convent of Nuns. His great Solicitude in conferring Holy Orders, in giving Jurisdiction to Confessors, and in choosing Subjects for Parishes and Benefices.

ALREADY, in the year 1764, Alphonsus had thought of resigning the burthen of the episcopate, as he had been told, when he was nominated bishop, that circumstances required he should accept, and that he could renounce it afterwards; the Pope had then answered him that he must not think of quitting his diocese, but that ill and infirm as he was, he should govern it. But his infirmities increasing daily, he thought of it again this year, and asked the opinion of several enlightened persons, in order to be sure of the will of God in regard to it. Amongst others, he consulted Mgr. Borgia. This prelate approved of his resolution, but his reasons did not satisfy Alphonsus, nor give rest to his conscience. He wrote to F. Villani on the 14th of January, 1765, ". . . At present I beg you again to speak before your departure to D. Janvier Fatigati, and to the Fathers Alasio, Porcara, and de Matteis. The principal reason for my resignation must not be the desire for retirement, as Mgr. Borgia says, for this cause is rejected in the chap. *Nisi de Renuntiat*, but it ought to be, my advanced age, for I shall enter my 70th year in September, and besides my usual affection of the chest, I was almost constantly ill during the winter, last year; this year, I may say, I have been so even till now. I have been confined to bed, with asthma, for upwards of a month. It is true, (for I must tell all, to prevent scruples,) that I continue to attend to business, and that every thing is done as usual; but as long as winter lasts, I am unable to go about on visitation, or to assist in the choir. In summer, as I am then free from my malady of the chest, I go through my diocese, during three or four months. I feel forced to ask for my dismissal, for I have a host of scruples, at seeing the dissatisfaction that arises from scandals of which I am a witness, and which I ought not to tolerate. I tremble most from the fear, that I have sought for my own ease in this resignation, and not God's glory: this is why I wish to be sure as to what will really conduce to the glory of God." In another letter he said: "I wish that my conscience should be free from a load of disquietudes; I meet with many things to disgust me, but I hear it said to me, '*Si diligis me, pasce oves meas,*' and it matters little, whether I die or succumb. The uncertainty I am in, not knowing whether I am doing the will of God or not, in giving in my resignation, is a greater anxiety to me than all the rest."

Having taken all these opinions, (Fathers Alasio and Poscara having coincided with Mgr. Borgia,) he resolved, at last, to represent his age and infirmities to the Pope in a simple manner, to propose his resignation, and to leave the decision with his Holiness. The Pope was entirely opposed to the holy bishop's wishes, and Cardinal Negroni answered him, in a letter of the 18th of June, 1765: ". . . . The Holy Father thanks God for the great good which you have effected by His aid until now, and he is persuaded that you can continue this good by your authority, your direction, and your example, even should your malady become still more serious, and should your physical weakness become still greater. . . . . His Holiness charges me then, to reply to you, and to encourage you, in his name, to cast aside every scruple on this subject, to be in perfect tranquillity of mind, and to persevere in your vocation, which is most certain, laboring for the good of the souls which are entrusted to you, and for the glory of God, who will assuredly grant you all needful succor."

At the request of the saintly old man, Cardinals Spinelli and Rossi, and Mgr. de Simone, who was Auditor, had supported his request to the Pope, but he answered: "His shadow alone would suffice to govern the whole diocese." Alphonsus did become tranquil, and was content, even if he had to die under the burthen. In the midst of all these anxieties, quite a mysterious circumstance happened to him. From the 1st of June, 1765, he, as well as those who were near him, heard a great number of little blows from the cross he wore at his neck, every time he said the Rosary. They examined to see whether there was some insect there, and made other searches, but they could discover nothing. As soon as he had received the answer of the Pope, the little blows were heard no more. He concluded that there had been a mystery therein, and that God had wished him to understand that he ought to continue to bear the cross with which he had been charged.

At this time Alphonsus succeeded in establishing at St. Agatha, a convent of the nuns of the Most Holy Redeemer. The want of such an institution, wherein young ladies of high family could receive their education, or consecrate themselves to God, was regretted, but no one had yet been able to supply it. The work had been attempted several times during two centuries, but all the plans had remained imperfect. Alphonsus took it in hand and succeeded gloriously. All the other obstacles having been removed, one still remained; there was no sufficient revenue. Alphonsus fortified himself by trust in God, and managed so well that he obtained from the Pope an annual subsidy of ninety-seven ducats, on the ecclesiastical chapels, and a rent of twenty-five ducats from the King, on the lay chapels. The town granted fifty ducats annually for ten years, which being added to the four hundred and twenty-two which the church he had chosen for this establishment already possessed, formed an income of six hundred and ninety-four ducats, which, together with the portions, was sufficient for the support of the convent. He caused the buildings to be repaired; it was an old convent, built a century and a half before, but now abandoned, and destined to lodge the soldiers who might come to St. Agatha; he went to the spot nearly every day to encourage the workmen and hasten the work, saying: "Who knows how much longer I may have to live." He arranged that the religious from the convent at Scala should come there as foundresses, and the Pope permitted him to instal them in the new cloister, in the month of June, 1765. Sister Mary Raphael of Charity, whose sanctity was well known, was chosen to preside over the beginning of this convent; she was accompanied by two other choir-sisters and one lay-sister. Mother Raphael had the consolation of receiving two recruits on the road, the daughters of the family of Speltri de Vitulano.

Alphonsus, filled with joy at the arrival of the religious, persuaded the people to adorn the gates of the town with magnificence and to ornament the streets with wreaths of myrtle, rosemary, and boughs of trees. He advanced, in his pontifical vestments, at the head of the chapter and of all the clergy, to meet them at the cathedral door, while the firing of cannon and the ringing of the bells testified the joy of the inhabitants. After having adored the Blessed Sacrament, they went in procession to the new church of the convent, where the Blessed Sacrament was exposed and the Te Deum solemnly chanted, during which the foundresses took possession of the convent. Alphonsus had taken care to provide every thing which was wanted for the nuns. He sent eatables, already prepared, to the new-comers, for the first eight days. He wished to continue to do so for a month, but the nuns dispensed him from it, wishing to live in the poverty prescribed by their rule. When the new foundation made under the auspices of Bishop Liguori became known in the province, as well as the great regularity which existed there, and, above all, the holiness of its foundresses, the convent was soon filled with pupils from St. Agatha, Arienzo, and Naples.

Soon, two pupils determined to take the novices' habit, with the two recruits mentioned above, and Alphonsus gave them the exercises of the retreat. One of them began to be tormented by melancholy in such a degree, that full of regrets, she unceasingly wept and sighed for her father's house. One evening, after the meditation, Alphonsus called her to the grate, encouraged her, and succeeded in restoring her serenity; he then gave her a crucifix to kiss, and made her promise to take Jesus Christ for her spouse; the young lady immediately experienced a complete change, she returned gaily to the noviciate, and from that time was freed from all thoughts of regret. He did not exercise the same compassion towards another pupil: "We must distinguish," he said, "between temptation and obstinacy." The one of whom we speak, repented of the step she had taken, and lived in a manner little edifying, thus doing harm to herself as well as to others; though she was archdeacon Rainone's neice, Alphonsus silenced all human respect, and sent her back to her parents.

The two young pupils who had joined the religious on the road, were the objects of his peculiar kindness. These young ladies' two brothers were dissatisfied with the part they had taken, and for several years refused to pay their pension. His Lordship, aware of the distress they felt, paid it for them, and amongst other things, supplied thirty measures of corn to the convent: the brothers gave up their opposition, in the end, and they received their portion, and made their profession. Alphonsus, considering this convent as his own work, continued to assist it as far as possible, although he was himself in great poverty. He gave fifty measures of corn to it yearly, and also a great quantity of oil. He even went so far as to promise, that he would maintain the four foundresses, as long as he lived. He very often made them a present of from ten to thirty ducats. He sent them their allowance weekly, whilst he lived at St. Agatha, and let them have it at least monthly, even when he resided at Arienzo. He sent them various little treats on feast days; and when he received any presents from his relations in religion, or others, he bestowed the greatest part on the pensioners and novices.

The most formidable responsibility of the episcopacy, to our saint, was, the imposition of hands. He required learning and virtue from the young Levites. In one of the regulations that he made for the good administration of his diocese, he determined on the points on which the young clerics ought to be examined. Those who received the tonsure, were obliged to give an account of Christian doctrine, and to specify the different parts of meditation which are necessary to reap fruit from it. Those for minor orders, had to know the matter and form of orders, all that appertains to the sacraments, and the Latin grammar. Those for the subdiaconate, had to know the treatises on oaths, vows, canonical hours, censures, as well as on what belongs to orders. Those for the diaconate, the treatises on conscience, laws, human acts and sins, as also the treatises on the theological virtues, on religion and its opposite vices, and on simony. Those for the priesthood, had to repeat, besides the things which relate to this holy order, that which they had already known before, and to know the treatises on the eucharist, the sacrifice of mass, on penance, extreme unction, and marriage, with all that belongs to the commandments of God, and of the Church.

He presided over the examinations in person, and caused all the examiners to assist thereat, as also the other candidates to be present, both to instruct them, and also to show them that there was no partiality, for he always acted as a father, rather than as a superior, speaking to them with so much kindness, that, far from disconcerting them, his presence inspired them with courage. When he reprimanded, he always did it in a way to encourage the subjects to study, and promised that he would not delay in comforting them. The dean told him, that he ought at least to make them stand, during the interrogatories. Alphonsus replied: "I am a father, let us not forget what it is to be examined." A deacon, who had been sent away several times, presented himself at the examination again, but, in spite of the efforts made by one of the examiners, to cause him to pass, by suggesting the answers, he could not succeed. "My son," said Alphonsus to him, "I can do nothing more in this, study well, and with application, and I will ordain you by-and-by." This cleric was the nephew of a priest, whom he esteemed greatly. He came to see him, and Alphonsus let him see how much he was distressed. "Forgive me," he said, "for I am myself distressed about your

24*

nephew; forgive me for the love of God, for my conscience does not reproach me at all. Ask canon Wichella, with what charity we treated him." Another time, a young man of excellent conduct, was attacked by a pain in the chest, which prevented him from learning the treatise, "de censuris." When he presented himself for examination for the priesthood, he was found wanting. "The rules are made to be observed," said Alphonsus to him, "not merely to be posted up in the sacristy." But when the parish priest, whose pupil the young man had been, assured him that he was well acquainted with the other matters of examination, his lordship listened to him, and finding that this was really the case, he made no further difficulty in admitting him.

Of all the orders, the subdiaconate, as being the first of the *major* orders, was the one which caused most embarrassment to the young men, as well as to Alphonsus himself. One priest has affirmed, that he was kept sitting during five hours, at an examination for the subdiaconate. The seminarists themselves, who had already given proofs of their capacity, in examinations undergone in the seminary, in his presence, were still obliged to go through the usual examination before entering into holy orders. If one of these latter were found wanting, and wished to trust to the indulgence of the examiners, imagining that his attending the course of lectures would supply the place of the rest, Alphonsus immediately overthrew his hopes. "I wish," said he, "the thing *done*, and not the thing *to be done*, and in this matter I know of no future tense in my grammar, I know only of the past tense."

From the time of his arrival in the diocese, he had declared, by an edict, that no one need hope to obtain orders or benefices through influence, and that to manifest such a disposition, would be sufficient cause for being excluded, and declared unworthy. The real qualities of the candidate, and the testimony of respectable persons, were the only claims which prevailed; if these were wanting, the case was desperate. A gentleman tried to make him ordain a subject whom he loved, believing Alphonsus would be satisfied with his testimony, and attempted to persuade him with many plausible reasons, on which he enlarged for an hour. Alphonsus listened to him with immoveable patience; at last, when the gentleman had exhausted the matter, and thought he had gained his cause, Alphonsus asked him if he had said all. "I think," replied the gentleman, "that I have wearied you long enough." "Well, that may be," answered Alphonsus, smilingly, "but imagine that you have spoken to a dead man." "What do you mean by that?" replied the gentleman. "A dead person," answered Alphonsus, "could not reply to you. Well, no more can I." Alphonsus had a serious reason for rejecting the candidate, and therefore endeavored to extricate himself in this manner.

The Prince della Riccia, also tried to induce him to admit one of his tenants to the subdiaconate, whom he had previously rejected. "My most honored Prince," he answered him, "I beg you to pardon me for not doing your pleasure, because in conscience I cannot do it. It is a thing which could not be done, without injury to my soul, and I was not made a bishop in order to damn myself." The prince was edified by this proof of zeal and apostolical firmness, and promised not to disquiet the tenderness of his conscience by similar requests again.

Those candidates for holy orders, who presented them elves with dismissory letters from their bishops, were also obliged to give proofs of their learning, in order to be admitted to ordination. A young man having been sent by the bishop of Caserte, Alphonsus did not admit him without making him undergo an examination. The bishop, in retaliation, caused a cleric, whom Alphonsus had sent to him when he himself was ill, to be examined also. This caused dissatisfaction at St. Agatha, but Alphonsus said: "If he has acted so, he has done his duty." The regulars were obliged to pass through the same ordeal, in spite of the dismissory letters of their provincials. In order to make the thing agreeable to them, he sent for two fathers belonging to their order, and caused them to examine them in his presence; but if there was no monastery of the order in the neighborhood, he examined them himself, assisted by his grand-vicar, and a canon. Once, when he was administering holy orders, at the moment he was going to officiate, the master of ceremonies told him that a young religious had just arrived. "That is very well," replied Alphonsus, "but he must be examined." He sent for him, and told him that he was going to question him; the young man replied, that he had already been examined by his provincial. "I am quite persuaded of that," said Alphonsus to him, "but it is I who must impose hands on you, and not the Father Provincial;" and as he was firm in exacting the examination, the young religious thought he had better not expose himself to it, so he took off his surplice, and departed.

Alphonsus wished the candidates to present certificates of good conduct, at least a month before the ordination, and all at the same time, in order to have facility in making his secret investigations in case of need. In order that the parish priests should only give sincere testimonials, he represented the duty of so doing, very strongly to them. He was not contented with a simple attestation, but wished they should testify, on oath, that the candidate had not failed to assist at church, on any Sunday, or day of obligation; that he had assembled the little children, and taught them the catechism; that he had confessed, and communicated, at least, every fortnight; that he had not been seen without a cassock; that he had never played at cards; and that he had never engaged in any kind of sport. He was especially severe towards young men who had studied at Naples. He used every method to be sure of their merits, and never seemed satisfied; he inquired of the master under whom they had studied, and asked if they had been diligent in following the lectures; what persons they had visited, and if they had avoided games and theatres; above all, he wished to know if they had often received the sacraments, and assisted at the congregation of foreign clergy, every Sunday. He never decided, under a considerable time, and did not neglect to charge some friends at Naples, to furnish him with the most exact information about them.

If, after all this information, he was not entirely satisfied as to the conduct of the candidate, he was refused at once. Thus he refused to receive a young man to minor orders, though his conduct was very exemplary, because he sometimes conversed with a suspected priest. He had no more pity for another seminarist, who was several times excluded from orders, as being little studious, and little edifying; and who, despairing of entering into favor with the prelate, laid down the clerical dress, and quitted the seminary. A deacon having walked about during the night, in company with some singers with whom he had amused himself, Alphonsus refused to make him priest, at which the young man shed tears, and got several persons of distinction to intercede for him, but all was useless. A cleric in minor orders, was refused, for a number of years, without being able to be made a subdeacon, because he was fond of wine, although he protested that he had put himself on a regimen of water; nor was he permitted to stay in the seminary. The young man went to another, but in spite of the good testimonials of his new director, Alphonsus always remained inflexible. In order to be sure of his amendment, he made him return to St. Agatha, and did not ordain him until he was convinced of his constant temperance. He who did any thing to cause a shadow of suspicion with regard to purity, was obliged to renounce all hope of ever being a priest; he was not only excluded from orders, but was also obliged to give up the clerical habit. With all this solicitude, Alphonsus had, notwithstanding, two misfortunes to deplore, in regard to ordination. The first was, in regard to a deacon he found in the seminary at his arrival at St. Agatha, who was so distinguished in his studies, that he solved the most difficult questions in theology and philosophy; but Alphonsus heard that he was addicted to wine, and from that time he determined not to admit him to the priesthood. Some person of distinction interfered, but without success. After several years, the parish priest, and other ecclesiastics of the chapter, again endeavored to speak in his favor. Alphonsus resisted for a long time, but at length he could not refuse to yield to the numerous reasons they gave, to assure him of his amendment. "I consent to ordain him priest," said he, "but he will enjoy the dignity but a short time, he will fall back into sin, and die miserably." The deacon was made a priest, but in a little time he took to drinking again. Alphonsus grieved over this; he sent for him one day, and said to him, before his parish priest: "If you do not give up drinking, woe will be to you! Wine will be your ruin." A year after this prediction, the incorrigible man got drunk again, and fell into a ditch, where he lost his life. The other case was that of another deacon, who had been excluded from the priesthood for several years, as he did not appear to possess the requisite dispositions. An ecclesiastic of merit tried to overcome the bishop's repugnance, and represented to him this deacon's regularity in frequenting the sacraments, and his retired and constantly exemplary life. Alphonsus was prevailed on, but he had scarcely ordained him, before his conduct became a source of continual scandal to the diocese; he was soon thrown into prison, but he broke his irons, and banished himself.

He required that those who were to be admitted to holy orders, should also present proofs of a suitable patrimony. He wished them to have five hundred ducats, free from any burden. He examined into the property, as well as the rental, himself, and if the income of twenty-four ducats was not clear, he rejected the case.

Alphonsus was neither too easy nor too cautious in ordaining new clerics, but he admitted all in whom he recognized a real vocation. "It is not our business," said he, "to call any one to this holy state, nor to reject him from it; it is God who calls, and He does it as He pleases." He liked to see young men eager to consecrate themselves to the service of the altar, and if they showed themselves worthy of it, he was happy to receive them. He was particular in observing the degrees of advancement, and only granted a dispensation in cases of necessity. Above all, he never consented to give a dispensation, on account of age, unless there was a real necessity, and for a subject of most exemplary conduct. He attached, also, great importance to the spiritual exercises before ordination, regarding them as the only means of instructing young men in their duties, but he did not allow them to be gone through in a religious house of relaxed observance. He wished them to perform them in one of the houses of his Congregation, or of the Fathers of St. Vincent of Paul. And if he knew any one who was really poor, he himself paid the necessary expenses.

On the day of ordination, Alphonsus was in the habit of assembling the young men in the chapel, beforehand, and of giving them a sermon on the greatness of their state, and their obligation to live in it holily; moreover, during mass, he usually gave them a little exhortation, in order to excite them to receive holy communion with fervor, and he did it with so much unction, that it caused the candidates and spectators to shed tears.

Alphonsus, fully convinced of the wants of the diocese, desired to have the new priests, not only of good character and well instructed, but also truly disposed to aid souls, and to cause religion to be honored. "I do not try," said he, to the examiners, "to approve the candidates, simply that they may be able to say mass, for masses will not be wanting, but in order to have useful workmen for the Church. I wish that, after having ordained them, they may be capable of hearing confessions, and of serving me in time of need, not only in the parishes, but also in the monasteries; and that they may be capable of serving in the missions, and attending to all the wants of my diocese." He himself instructed all the candidates, as to the manner of hearing confessions, and gave them methods of conduct to be used towards habitual sinners, towards the backsliding, and towards those who were living in occasions of sin. When he noticed any among these young priests, of very promising dispositions, he immediately managed to place them as curates. Having found two deacons whom he judged fit to receive the priesthood, and to hear confessions, but, who were poor, and still under the required age, he obtained a dispensation for them, at his own expense.

He gave no one power to celebrate his first mass, if he were not, beforehand, assured that he knew even the minutest rubrics. "When a person begins in a bungling manner," said he, "he never gets right again." He often made young clerics celebrate in his presence. Neither did he allow the first mass to be an occasion of feasting and worldly rejoicing; he even forbade the giving of extraordinary repasts at that time, and the inviting of strangers to them. "Wine has sway at table," he said, "and when wine has sway, sin is not far off." He wished that the young priest should preserve a state of recollection on this day, in order to merit from God the plenitude of graces so necessary in this sublime state. He called this day, that of the solemn marriage of Jesus Christ with the soul, and for this reason, he wished that the mass should then be celebrated in a retired place. He urged, also, the newly ordained priest to make a good preparation before celebrating mass, and to excite in himself good dispositions by repeated acts of faith and charity, so that he might worthily handle so awful a mystery, and recommended him, moreover, not to leave the church without making his thanksgiving. "By the acts which precede," said he, "above all, by those of contrition, the vessel is emptied and purified; and by the acts which follow, it is filled with the gifts of grace." As he detested all precipitation in saying mass, so he equally condemned lengthiness, which is always wearisome to the people. "A mass," said he, "which exceeds half an hour, creates weariness, and not devotion in those who hear it." And he was in the habit of adducing St. Philip Neri's example, who prescribed this rule, to himself, when he celebrated in public. He exhorted them also, to recite the office without hurrying it over. "Mass and the office," he said, "will sanctify us if we go through them as we ought; but they will destroy us, or deprive us of very great graces, if we perform them negligently." Such were, among many others, the measures which Alphonsus took, in order to have well instructed and edifying priests, who might save the people, and console the Church.

Alphonsus was very careful and prudent in giving an approbation to new confessors. The examination, however, was not rigorous, but was conducted with a wise degree of slowness; it was sometimes prolonged for several weeks, during which the subject was obliged to return very often, and to undergo new interrogatories each time. He caused all the questions to be published, and they filled twenty-four pages. If he saw that one was weak and hesitating, he put him off to another time. At times, several were found to be capable who did not receive their powers, or at least, only on condition of returning after two or three months. When the parish priests, or others, came to ask him to give a priest the faculty to hear confessions, saying that their parish was in want of confessors, he admitted no one to examination, without being informed whether he was a man of prayer; whether he made his thanksgiving as he ought after mass, whether he ever failed to visit the Blessed Sacrament every evening, and above all, whether he ever visited suspicious or dangerous people. If any doubt remained on his mind, he was not even admitted to examination.

He was not less severe with the regulars; so that when a regular presented himself to obtain the faculties for confessing, the testimony of his provincial, and letters certifying that he had been a confessor in other dioceses, did not in the least exempt him from the examination. A newly elected abbot of a certain monastery, when he came the first time to see Alphonsus, asked him for faculties for two of his religious. Alphonsus begged to be excused, as he could not acquiesce, without scruple of conscience, before having had proofs of their capability. The abbot insisted and entreated, but all was in vain. When he saw such immoveable firmness, he had not the courage to ask for jurisdiction for himself, and did it through the medium of a person of influence, but this was without success; he was obliged to present himself in person. His lordship acted, however, with prudence; he conversed with him alone, and without formality, and proposed some doubts to him, after the removal of which, he conferred the powers on him. As to the two religious, they did not present themselves, until after they had studied morals for a considerable time. When Abbot Pignatelli, who afterwards became Archbishop of Bari and Capua, went to the abbey of Ariola, Alphonsus, who did not know him well, replied, when asked to give the abbot faculties for hearing confession, that he could not give them if the abbot did not previously answer to the questions which he would put to him. This offended the abbot; he came to visit Alphonsus however, who treated him with every mark of attention, but never spoke of the jurisdiction. The Grand-Vicar, at last, said to him, to do away with his scruples: "Suppose, my Lord, that when the abbot comes again to visit you, we try to make the conversation fall upon theology, and, if he proves his capacity by his answers, you can give him jurisdiction, without fear." Alphonsus agreed to the plan, and put it in execution on the very next visit of the abbot, and the result was completely in favor of the learned religious. Abbot Pignatelli was able to appreciate Alphonsus' impartiality, and had the most sincere attachment to him from that time. Alphonsus, on his part, was convinced of the abbot's merit, and took a great deal of pains to cause him to be nominated archbishop.

It may be said that Alphonsus was as prompt in withdrawing faculties for hearing confessions from those who proved to be unworthy of them, as he was prudent in giving them. Having heard that a religious, at Arpaja, was in the habit of despising the poor, and occupying himself too much with the direction of some devotees, he sent for him, and immediately withdrew his powers. He also suspended several others, and some he even expelled from his diocese.

Convinced of the importance of the duties of parish priests, Alphonsus gave the most scrupulous attention to their election. "A zealous priest," said he, "sanctifies all his people, but an indifferent one does not preserve the good, and can only do harm." He did not require great learning in them, but wished that they should have a sufficiency of information, and, above all, that they should be versed in moral theology, and capable of instructing the people properly. The concourses for the parishes always took place in his presence, and he wished the examinations to be made with severity, and urged the examiners to fulfil their office faithfully, representing to them, how much he sins who co-operates in the nomination of a parish priest who is unworthy of his ministry. An admirable delicacy, also, presided in these examinations. A priest was once rejected by the examiners, for having followed authors opposed to the system of Alphonsus. When he heard of this, he said: "The authors whom he follows, are standard and approved ones; I have no authority to act as a law, in matters of opinion; every one is at liberty to follow his own, when the Church has not condemned it." He thus, undertook the defence of the priest, and the consequence was that he obtained the benefice. At another time, a living having become vacant, a deacon was the one who answered the best among the candidates. Alphonsus witnessed it with satisfaction, but in consideration of the age, and merits of a priest, who was also a candidate, he begged the deacon to be patient for this time, and he spoke to him with so much humility, that the young man was quite confused at it. However, if charity made him give preference to the priest, he did not wish the deacon's rights to be neglected, and the Cathedral parish having become vacant shortly after, the right of election to which belonged to the chapter, Alphonsus immediately wrote to Archdeacon Rainone, to beg that, for his sake, the parish should be given to the deacon, and his request was granted.

He always preferred sanctity to learning; moderate abilities and exemplary conduct were in his eyes sufficient to make a good parish priest. "Those of great talents," he said, "are more solicitous about the dead, than the living. They are full of erudition and speculation only. If they preach, they are not understood; they do not lower themselves to teach children, and will only instruct clerics. I wish the priest to find pleasure in remaining with the dying, and that he should be able to pass his time in talking to one of little capacity, while endeavoring to teach him the Pater noster." He therefore chose subjects who proved themselves humble and submissive, in preference to those who set up for learned; provided, always, they were not wanting in aptness for acquitting themselves of the functions of the ministry. A holy man destitute of energy, or a man whose sanctity did not extend further than to think of himself without anxiety for others, could not, according to him, make a good parish priest.

He wished, from the first, to cause the livings to be considered honorable, so as to have good occupants; and he therefore raised the parish priests to the prebends. It may be said, that, before his time, those who were candidates for parishes, were only the priests who were thought least of, among the clergy, and who, for the most part, were distinguished in no way, and were of no rank; but when the parishes became as the ladders whereby to reach a more elevated position, the first gentlemen labored to obtain them, and in this way the livings were administered with zeal, and to the great advantage of souls.

The holy bishop was still more solicitous, when he had to make the collation to benefices.* Even those which

* Although the diocese of St. Agatha was not so extensive, numbering only 30,000 souls, yet, with the exception of that of Capua, there was not one in the kingdom which had a greater number of benefices. Besides the chapter of the cathedral, there were in it six colleges of canons.

were simple, and without the care of souls, but which required residence, caused him great anxiety. Not satisfied with the good conduct of the subjects, he further wished that they should have great merit, as regarded the Church and the people. "The Church and the people," he said, "are both interested in the collation of benefices." He had a little book, wherein the names of the priests and clerics of the whole diocese were inserted, with the merits and demerits of each, so that when it was necessary to make an appointment, he had usually no need of any further inquiry. A nomination was made without delay; as soon as one incumbent expired, a successor was appointed. When it happened that he could not decide immediately, because he saw good conduct counterbalanced by some defect, or because he had several ecclesiastics of equal merit, he took the opinion of impartial persons, and then weighed the merits and demerits of each in the balance of the sanctuary, and took the matter in consideration, several times, before God. On such occasions, he went often through a real martyrdom, as Archdeacon Rainone, who enjoyed his entire confidence, has declared. One day, Alphonsus said to him: "The anguish which the death of this canon will cause me, is so great, that I would willingly give my life for his; the canon will only die once, while I shall die more than a hundred times." He did not confine himself merely to the town of St. Agatha, when looking for a successor to one who was dead, but searched throughout the whole diocese—and, for the same reason, he never favored any stranger; he would have considered it as an injustice to stand in the way of those of his own diocese.

There is recorded an instance, in which Divine Providence visibly interposed, as it were, in the nomination to a vacant prebend. He had sealed the letter containing the nomination, and the servant was all ready to take it, when a violent storm came on, which kept him in the house, and thus deferred its delivery. Alphonsus received a letter from the archdeacon, during this interval, which informed him of the merits of another candidate. He directly took back his own, destroyed it, and nominated the more worthy competitor who had just been pointed out to him. However, the merits of the second candidate must have appeared to him incontestibly great, for, otherwise, he always remained unmoveably fixed in his first determination.

From the time he had entered the diocese, he had declared, as we have seen above, that no one's influence was to be used in order to obtain livings or benefices, and that all the efforts of the sort which might be made would be so many means of becoming unworthy of them; and, during all the time that he was bishop of St. Agatha, he never listened to the solicitations of persons even of the highest rank. Merit was the only claim in his sight, and even merit vanished when it sought the support of a protector. Out of many examples on record, let the following suffice as an illustration of the strictness with which he adhered to this rule. A prebend became vacant at Arienzo, and Alphonsus decided on giving it to a priest who seemed to surpass the others, especially because he was the only one amongst the canons who had not got some one to intercede for him. He was ready to expedite the nomination, when he saw him present himself with a letter of recommendation from the Prince della Riccia. "God forgive you," he then said to him, "I was determined to give you the prebend, but since you have brought me this letter, I have changed my mind, *indignus quia petiisti.*" He said to the prince, afterwards, that he hoped he would not take his refusal amiss, since, if he gave such a precedent, he would open the way to other and scandalous intrigues. He used to say, that recourse to recommendations, and simony, were twin sisters, and that they had the same devil for their father.

The Marquis of Marco, the king's minister, once wrote to him, quite in a friendly manner, to beg him to confer a living which was vacant, on a young ecclesiastic, whose merits, he said, had caused him to take this liberty; but even this recommendation only served to throw discredit on the protegé. Another living became vacant, and a priest induced another priest, whom he believed to possess great influence with the bishop, to intercede for him; he wrote to tell his friend to ask it for him, for the love of the Blessed Virgin, saying, that if he adopted this method, he would certainly be heard, as the Saint never refused any thing which was asked in her name: but as Alphonsus did not consider him worthy to be appointed because he had procured this recommendation, he replied: "Tell him that I refuse to give him the living for the love of the Blessed Virgin, for our Lady only likes what is good." In several cathedrals, and even in the collegiate establishments, they professed to consider the chaplains as merely the prebendary's servants, which caused the latter to look down on them, and to dislike seeing them raised to their own dignity. Alphonsus, however, who only thought of merit, was always ready to advance such of them, as were worthy of it, to the prebendal stalls, so that the situation of chaplain, being as a ladder whereby to ascend to the prebends, became more honorable. The election of the chaplains of St. Agatha was made by the bishop, and Alphonsus, in order to promote the greater good of the Church, decreed that these situations should be the reward of particular merit. As their office is to chant in the choir, he established meetings for chanting; and in consequence, all the clerics, in the hope of becoming chaplains, applied themselves to the Gregorian plain chant, and the choir was thus greatly improved.

The holy bishop, who had the Church's good and glory alone at heart, obliged the canons to residence as strictly as he had done in regard to priests, (as we have seen above,) and was careful to prevent them from taking upon themselves charges incompatible with their duties. A chaplain was secretary to Count Cerreto, and only went to the cathedral from time to time. A prebend became vacant, and he immediately entered the lists, confident that, as the bishop was just, (so he said,) the prebend would be thought due to him as being the oldest of all the chaplains.

He presented himself, and exposed all his claims. "You are quite new to me," answered Alphonsus, "for I have never seen you at church." "That is true," replied the chaplain with a complacent air, "for I have had the honor of being Count Cerreto's secretary for a number of years." "Well," answered the bishop, "but why did not the count make you a prebendary?" Then he added, in a more serious tone: "You must either give up your situation as secretary as soon as possible, and come and perform your duties at church, or I shall cause you to be no longer a chaplain." "Either quit your new employment," he said to another, who was employed in an important charge which prevented his frequenting the church, "or give up being a prebendary."

Alphonsus' great impartiality and equity in giving benefices naturally displeased candidates of unjust pretensions. He had a great deal to suffer on this account, and was often put in dangerous positions in consequence. They even went the length of insulting him, and saying before his face; "you are unjust, you have neither conscience nor equity, you ought to blush at being a bishop." At such speeches, Alphonsus was never either disturbed or distressed. He pitied their anger, and never opened his mouth except to bless those who cursed him. Such rare goodness and meekness, however, did not always put the unjust pretenders to silence. One individual, who had been unable to get a prebend, to which he had aspired, got angry with him in consequence, slandered him, and even accused him with the king. The sovereign, who knew Alphonsus' justice and impartiality, answered: "I can do nothing; Bishop Liguori exercises his right as a bishop." Another prebend became vacant about the same time, and Alphonsus then forgot his injuries, and bestowed it on the very man who had appealed against him. "If you give to those who oppose you," F. Caputo then observed to him, "you will have no peace, for the future." "That is true," replied Alphonsus, "but at the time of the first gift, I thought the competitor more worthy than the appealer, and at the second, I found that the latter was the most worthy." As F. Caputo observed further, that people would think otherwise, and believe that saying abusive things and appealing against him was the means of obtaining what they aspired to, he answered: "Poor creatures, they do not know what they wish for, and they try to get what they can; but for me, I ought to bear with them, and to do my duty."

Another pretender, having failed, addressed a statement to the king, filled with falsehoods against Alphonsus, whom he designated as unjust. The accusation was sent to the bishop, that he might justify himself; he did so, but so far from seeking to injure his calumniator, he only tried to excuse him. The man was not free from blame for other causes, and people endeavored to get Alphonsus to bring him to justice before his own tribunal; but he not only rejected the advice with horror, but always treated this priest with great kindness from that time. A prebend became vacant after this, and Alphonsus, considering his merits equal to those of another candidate, gave the preference to him who had accused him. In another similar case, Alphonsus was again not only loaded with injuries but also accused with the king by the brother of the rejected pretender, a public notary, who designated him in his libel, as a rebel against the royal will, asserting that he did not make promotions, but let the parishes suffer, in order that they might depend more on the Pope than on his majesty, and asking, besides, that the canons and chaplains should be no longer elected by the bishop, but by the people in public assembly. When this appeal was given to Alphonsus, in order that he might justify himself, he said; "It is true that I cause suffering to the parishes, but all the rest is false." After he had sent in his justification, the king answered through the Marquis of Marco: "The king is persuaded of the wisdom of your conduct, and he trusts in your prudence in the appointments to livings." Alphonsus again took a saintly revenge. One day, when a prebend was vacant, he was, as usual with him at dinner, listening to spiritual reading, and that part of the life of D'Innico Caracciolo, cardinal and bishop of Averso, being read to him, where it is said that he revenged himself for a great offence on the part of a priest, by conferring a large benefice on him; at these words, he said to the reader: "Stop, and repeat what you have just read." When this was done, he sent for the Grand-Vicar, and said: "I have resolved to give consolation to the notary;" and he ordered him to have prepared the necessary papers for conferring the prebend on the brother of the notary. When the Grand-Vicar observed, that, as the king had not yet declared that he was satisfied with his justification, it might be said that he had been intimidated, he replied: "Oh indeed, are we then obliged to attend to all that is said? Let them think and speak what they please; what concerns me is the notary's soul, and not my own glory." And not being able to endure any delay, he sent for the notary, and said to him, as if he had been his intimate friend, "send for your young brother from Naples, I intend to make him a prebendary." Another solicitor, whose pretensions were not complied with, applied also to the king, and slanderously accused Alphonsus of a thousand evil things. One of the greatest causes of offence alleged, was that he despised the episcopal town, and overlooked its citizens in bestowing livings, to give them to other inhabitants of the diocese. The king having again given the accused bishop the power of justifying himself and of replying to these accusations, he sent his justification, in a very elaborate and erudite letter on the ecclesiastical laws concerning the conferring of livings and benefices, which was published, for the first time, at the period of our Saint's canonization.

CHAPTER XXIV.

Alphonsus' solicitude for the Sanctification of Religious. His zeal for the material Churches. The Congregation of Alphonsus is persecuted. He publishes two new works. He goes to Naples for the defence of his Congregation. How he exercises his zeal at Naples.

ALPHONSUS' zeal in laboring for the good of the ministers of the altar, led him, also, to attempt to sanctify the religious, who are more especially consecrated to God. He wished that the ancient monastic regularity should be revived in all the convents, and he tried, at least, to renew their piety, and to prevent their falling into still further decay. "If we succeed in this," he said, "it will not be a trifling thing." In consequence, he sent for F. Villani and other missionaries from Naples, at the time of his arrival in the diocese, to give the spiritual exercises to all the monasteries, and he caused this to be repeated at least once every year. The spiritual exercises were in his eyes the best method, or rather, the only method for sanctifying souls. "A retreat is a fire," he said, "in which the most rusty iron ought to become softened and purified." When he was at Arienzo, he received and entertained the preachers in his palace, in order not to cause any expense to the communities. Moreover, he often seized opportunities of going to visit one or the other of these convents in person, and spent two or three days in preaching, at the grate, on the duties of religious. He by this means caused them to love prayer and mortification, and led them in the paths of the sublimest perfection.

He considered Nuns, in particular, as the most precious portion of his flock, and, following the example of the good shepherd, he neglected no method of saving them from ravenous wolves. Open grates were to him as so many thorns which pierced his heart: "A shut grate, and a sanctified monastery," he said, "an open grate and a relaxed convent." He enjoined the abbesses, and still more the confessors, to watch over this point, and wished to be informed of all disorders, in order to be able to remedy them immediately; relations within the second degree alone had access to the parlor. His vigilance and pains in preventing any one from frequenting the convents, extended to those belonging to his own household. He considered it a great fault for any one, under any pretext, to violate the rule in this respect, the Grand-Vicar alone was excepted. He dismissed, successively, two secretaries from his service for this reason alone, saying, "if the law is not observed by my own household, who then will observe it?"

Alphonsus was also very prudent in his choice of confessors for the convents. No examination was enough to satisfy him; he weighed the gestures, the words, and searched even into the opinions of the subject. He made a new nomination every three years, and, if a lack of confessors compelled him to confirm the same, he only did so with trembling; when, on the contrary, he was able to replace him, all the entreaties of the nuns could not prevail on him to confirm the former one. Frequent conversation with the religious at the grate, was a sacrilege in his sight: "God speaks in the confessional," he said, "but not at the grate." He allowed the confessor to receive some token of gratitude on certain days of solemnity, but he did not suffer him to receive frequent presents, and they were always required to be given by the whole community. He was delighted to hear of any young pensioner who wished to consecrate herself to Jesus Christ. He hastened to assist at the ceremony, and left every other occupation for the purpose. He also accepted every invitation for the profession of even a lay-sister, never omitting to preach on each occasion. He never required the least recompense, on these occasions, or permitted any attention of the sort to be paid to him. "A bishop," said he, "ought to have no other recompense than is necessary to enable him to fulfil the obligations of his ministry." On another occasion, he said: "It is my privilege and it is my duty to consecrate these victims of charity to God."

In order to give the religious every advantage possible, he sent an extraordinary confessor to them, every three months, without their asking for one. He thought, also, that a new confessor ought always to be granted to a religious, when she asks for it. He heard that the nuns of a certain convent could only write to their *ordinary* confessor, through a regulation on that subject, which was in force therein. He immediately sent for the Superior, and desired that this rule should be relaxed, whenever any of them wished to apply to any confessor of well known probity.

In his zeal for the re-establishment of religious discipline, he wished to introduce living in community, in some of the convents, at least, and chose for this purpose, one in which he expected to find the least difficulty. But as soon as he had informed the nuns of his project, they all united against it, and as he saw that more harm than good would result from it, he said: "Calm yourselves, I purposed it for your good, but as you judge otherwise, forget all I have said about it." He had a maxim, that when religious are not all agreed, the discontent of even one will give birth to a party, and, that will cause disorders, and the final ruin of the convent; so, far from being offended at the opposition of these religious, he paid them quite a paternal visit on the following day.

In another convent, the circumstances of the times, and the severity of the rules prevented several points from being observed. "What is the use of preserving a written rule of one sort, if one practises another?" said Alphonsus, and he reformed the rule and caused it to be printed. He acted like another Francis of Sales, in the reforms which he made in these rules, with a rare wisdom, condescending to every want and yet avoiding too great indulgence.

While he endeavored to ameliorate the state of the convents, he also tried to extirpate their abuses. It was the custom among the Franciscans of Airola, that when a young person was clothed or professed, she should remain seated at the door during the rest of the day, to receive the congratulations of her relations and friends. Alphonsus, wishing this day to be one of recollection and thanksgiving rather than of dissipation of mind, ordered, that neither the door nor the grate should be opened after dinner, but that the Blessed Sacrament should be exposed in the church, in order that the new spouse of Jesus Christ might then be able, in a special manner, to obtain abundant blessings. Another abuse had been that the young person dined in the parlor with her relations and friends, and it was all arranged like any worldly entertainment. When Alphonsus saw the preparations for this repast, on the day the two daughters of a noble lady of St. Agatha made their profession, he was indignant, and immediately ordered them to be put an end to. The noble lady and the abbess came to entreat, but he would not yield; the lady's embarrassment was then represented to him, (for she had invited relations and friends from various parts, and had no house in the neighborhood in which she could receive them,) and Alphonsus so far yielded to this consideration as to consent to the repast taking place in the convent, but on condition that the grate and the door should remain shut, and that the keys should be placed in the hands of the abbess.

Alphonsus was once present at the profession of a novice in a convent of Arienzo; at the instant when she was to pronounce the formula of the vows, the master of the ceremonies asked him to pass his hands through the grate. Alphonsus did not understand this mystery, and was at a loss what to do, but as the canon insisted, and said that the novice ought to place her hands in his whilst uttering the vows, interpreting thus literally the direction of the ritual that she should make *the vows* in *the hands of the bishop*, he exclaimed: "Oh, Jesus! Oh, Jesus! What has that to do with the profession? Let her keep her hands to herself, and I will keep mine," and explaining the meaning of the rubric, forever suppressed this strange ceremony.

Figured music, although forbidden to religious by several decrees at Rome, was quite in fashion in another convent. Alphonsus forbade its use in this convent, as well as in others, and prescribed the sole use of the Gregorian chant. "The church is not a theatre," said he, "and religious are no opera singers." He forbade anthems on festivals, with still greater severity, and wished that, if they were ever anxious to sing something extra, it should never be a solo. They were, however, not over scrupulous in following these orders. One evening, a nun was singing the Litany of the Blessed Virgin to figured music, when Alphonsus suddenly entered the church; the nun perceived him, and directly commenced to sing it to the Gregorian chant. He seemed not to take any notice of it at first, but when he came to the grate, he said to the nun: "You wished to deceive me just now, and that was not right; I forbade it because I did not think it proper. Light music is a decoy to young libertines, who do not hasten to it through devotion, but to hear the nun who sings; and who does not see that she is thus the cause of a number of disorders and sins?" Alphonsus made two predictions in regard to singers in this convent. They told him they wished to receive a lay-sister, a young person who was a good musician, to teach plain chant to the novices and young parishioners. "I grant your request," he replied, "but she will not persevere." And so it was; the new lay-sister left the convent a short time afterwards. They solicited him again in favor of another, who also understood music. "This one will not persevere any better," he said with a smile, and the young novice returned home after a few months. "God evidently condemns our duplicity," the religious then said, "since our plans are found out by his Lordship," and they made a firm resolution never to think of having any thing but Gregorian chant for the time to come.

In some convents the entrance of little children was permitted, through an abuse. The Council of Trent forbids it, and Alphonsus immediately confirmed this prohibition, and caused it strictly to be observed.

He took still more pains to prevent the introduction of new abuses, than to extirpate the old ones. The nuns of a convent intended to make new windows, which would open on the street, and which were to be furnished with blinds; they asked permission from Alphonsus, but he refused it. Persons in authority interfered in their behalf, but he let the nuns know, that if they did not desist from their project they would displease him very much, because he could not consent to an improper thing. The religious then followed his advice, and took no further steps in the affair. The Pope granted, from time to time, to cloistered nuns, permission to absent themselves from the convent. Alphonsus, knowing some in the diocese inclined to ask for a similar dispensation, warned them to abstain from so doing. "The Pope refers it to the Ordinary," he said, "and I will never consent to grant it, for I know what a bad reputation these goings out have, and the very least evil which results from them is a very great dissipation of mind." Some nuns complained that he never granted them any thing, and that they had met with three refusals consecutively. "Let them ask me for things that are just and right," he replied, "and I will take care not to refuse them; but whenever they address unreasonable requests to me, they must not expect to obtain any thing.

The material churches were no less the objects of Alphonsus' solicitude than the living temples; and as all that enhances the glory of God's house must be considered amongst the objects of a perfect zeal, Alphonsus also signalized himself in this respect, after the example of King David. "I have loved, O Lord, the beauty of thy house, and the place where thy glory dwelleth."—*Psal.* xxv, 8. When he entered the diocese, he particularly aimed at increasing the magnificence of the churches, and he spared neither labor, fatigue, nor expense, to attain this end. The old church of St. Agnes, at Arienzo, was so much out of repairs, that it was nearly in ruins; Alphonsus at once engaged the canons belonging to the chapter, to restore it, and so inflamed their zeal, that, soon, instead of a low and mean looking building, an edifice of a noble elevation, and with a beautiful roof, was obtained; it was adorned also with statues and other tasteful ornaments, which made the church extremely beautiful.

The church of St. Stephen, also at Arienzo, was likewise in a deplorable state. He caused it to be examined, and ascertained the expenses for the necessary repairs, and, as the incumbent had sold a felling of wood for three thousand three hundred ducats, he sequestered three hundred ducats to be applied to the first third of the payment; with that he repaired the roof, embellished the stucco of the high altar, restored the pavement with taste, and made a large window to remedy the dampness. The principal church of St. Angelus was in a bad state, and presented the appearance of a barracks rather than that of a temple of God, and it would soon have fallen to entire ruin. Alphonsus endeavored to repair it, in spite of the complaints of the incumbent, who cared more for his revenues than for the restoration of the church. The restoration of these two churches was a work of time; but our Saint made arrangements that the labors should continue after his resignation, and it is to his care, that the good state in which they are now to be found is to be attributed.

At Ducento, the church of the Arch-presbytery of St. Andrew had been in a state of abandonment and ruin for a number of years, through the avarice and carelessness of the incumbents; the arch-priest's house itself presented an equally unsatisfactory appearance. All this, added to the unhealthiness of the place, caused the rector of the church to be almost constantly absent, and, in consequence, the faithful of the parish to be neglected. Alphonsus was distressed at this sad state of things, but could find no method of remedying it, when the arch-priest offered his resignation. He thought then that he ought not to nominate another in his place, and he accordingly appointed a priest to perform the duties, assigning him a convenient sum for his support, and reserved the rest of the income of the living for the repairs of the buildings, which were soon completed.

The very large and spacious parish church at Majano was so neglected that it looked more like a barn than a house of prayer. It was said that there was no means of repairing it; but Alphonsus, seconded by the worthy incumbent and aided by the generosity of the faithful, changed this church into a real basilica, worthy to rank with those which are admired in Naples and Rome.

He did not take less pains in beautifying the Cathedral, although it was in a very good state. This church is a magnificent one; thanks to the deceased Bishop Gaeta, who, seeing the ancient Cathedral out of repair, had rebuilt it entirely. Alphonsus found the roof injured in several places, he immediately sent for experienced workmen, and it was put in order; he effected, moreover, a great many other repairs of this kind, without ever flinching from any expense. He spent about four hundred ducats in embellishing the cross pillars of marble, and the horns of plenty of brass. The church had not yet been consecrated; Mgr. Puoti, the bishop of Amalfi, hastened thither at his call, and the consecration took place in the year 1763.

But there is a still more remarkable instance of Alphonsus' zeal for the house of God. The village of St. Mary de Vico, containing more than three thousand souls, was divided into two parishes, the two priests of which had to exercise their respective functions in the same church, which was, moreover, so small that it could not hold more than three hundred persons. As soon as he saw such a state of things, he immediately conceived the bold scheme of building a church capable of holding all the inhabitants. The priests wanted to form two distinct parishes, but he feared that if too much were attempted nothing would be done, and so he decided that there should be established only one, as formerly. He held several meetings, in concert with the two priests, assembling the clergy and gentlemen of the place, and persuaded the two priests to give up their tithes, which might have amounted to three or four hundred ducats, for the benefit of the building; and the parishioners promised to contribute an annual sum of two hundred ducats towards it. Alphonsus, in consequence, sent for two architects from Naples, and had prepared a plan for a beautiful and spacious church. The two priests would have liked to have had the whole of the needed sum in hand, before commencing the building. "If you mean to act thus," said Alphonsus to them, "you will never obtain the desired end; I wish the work to be commenced at once, if it is not, the church will never be finished." A committee of four ecclesiastics and four laymen was formed, and the foundations were commenced. Alphonsus went to the spot to look after it all himself; the circumference of the church appeared to him to be still too small to hold all the people during the time of a mission, so he ordered them to enlarge it. He went full of joy, in pontifical vestments, preceded by his clergy, to bless the first stone of the edifice, in the year 1763. The generous prelate contributed, himself, no small sum towards the expenses of the building. He had only ten ducats at first, yet he furnished money for a work, the cost of which amounted to more than fifteen thousand ducats; his faith did the whole.

The people, encouraged by his magnanimity, aided in the undertaking by spontaneous gifts; the two priests wrote to tell him, that they would be satisfied with retaining, from the two hundred ducats which had remained, only enough for their sustenance, and from the surplice fees, the sum requisite for the food and the clothing of a servant. But troubles did not fail to come, for good things are always opposed. The people grew cold, and as the tithes had been prohibited for the sums they had promised, they applied to the royal council for permission to give up contributing to the expenses. Alphonsus, however, was not at all discouraged; he related all that had happened to the president of the council, D. Balthasar Cito, his friend, and obtained leave for the tithes to be continued until the building was finished, after which other measures could be taken. He also triumphed over many other obstacles, which only served to cause his courage and firmness to be still more admired. He entertained the two architects with their servants and horses at his palace at his own expense, and obtained an abatement of four or five hundred ducats through their generosity. Through his indefatigable energy, he conducted so great an undertaking to a happy termination, and when he left the diocese, there was nothing remaining to be finished but some stuccoing and flagging.

Alphonsus had at heart the interior embellishment of the churches, and the decency which becomes the house of God, as well as the substantial construction of the buildings. He especially wished the altars to be furnished with suitable ornaments. "I have never seen a priest," said he, "make use of dirty and worn-out linen at table; every thing they themselves use is clean, and it is only for Jesus Christ, that dirty things are allowed."

God never granted peace or repose to Alphonsus, but unceasingly exercised him in resignation and patience. The Congregation was in a flourishing state, but an enemy, or to speak more justly, hell, was irritated at the success of this work of God, and could not allow it to go on tranquilly. A quarrel occurred, three years back, between those belonging to the house of Iliceto, and Francis Anthony Maffey, a man of great authority, which caused the greatest difficulties to that house, as well as to the whole Congregation. This person had become engaged in a dispute with the people, about the fief of Iliceto; the fathers, to avoid evil consequences, wished to preserve neutrality, and obtained an exemption from the necessity of appearing at the trial. Maffey got angry at their course of conduct, saying: "he who is not for me is against me," and swore to extirpate, not only the house of Iliceto, but the whole Congregation. Baron Sarnelli, at Ciorani, also felt a secret resentment against the fathers there, on account of some property which his brother had bequeathed to Alphonsus, and which formed the only support of this house. Till then, the fathers had always been able to live in harmony with him, though he had more than once brought forward his designs, but an unintentional mistake, on their part, caused him again to rise up against them. It so happened that some mark of attention, in church, was omitted towards his wife, the baroness, and that was enough to cause the rupture. Maffey seized on the opportunity of exciting the baron, and he became very violent against them. After the flame was once kindled, Maffey accused them, in direct terms, of crimes, to the king, saying that they, to the scandal of the public, had degenerated from what they were when the institution was so much praised by his Catholic Majesty. The minister's offices were daily besieged by letters and claims, and there was not a court of justice in Naples which did not receive some petition against them. The truth only reached the king's ears by slow degrees, and adulterated by falsehood.

Every one may see what grief all this opposition must have caused to Alphonsus. He groaned over it, and humbling himself before God, adored his righteous judgments. He was most moved at Maffey's animosity. "The matter is more serious than you imagine," he said to one of the Fathers. "If D. Maffey is offended, I grieve for the poor house! I know his disposition, and what he caused the venerable Mgr. Lucci to suffer. May God deign to be our Protector." He ordered fasts and prayers in all the houses; he recommended that discretion and charity should be exercised towards their adversaries, and, above all, that nothing should be undertaken against them, even in self-defence, and that recourse should be had to no other arms than those of prayer and observance of the rule. But, notwithstanding, the flame gained ground daily; Alphonsus, therefore, in a circular to the members of the Congregation, wrote: "Behold, my dear brothers, how the Lord has visited us in sending us so many tribulations. . . . It is our negligence in observing the rule which God now chastises—let us hope in the mercy of Almighty God, who will not permit the Congregation to be destroyed; let us now try to appease His anger by our prayers, and by avoiding all voluntary transgressions, especially that of disobedience, because in this respect there is no punishment which we have not merited."

Maffey wished that the Fathers should be deprived of the privilege of possessing the rights of citizens, by a sentence of the supreme court, although he had already robbed them of these rights as far as practice went. They were obliged to appear before the royal council of Sommaria, to which the king had referred the decision, in regard to some pretended claims of trifling value. The royal council were greatly surprised at such grievances, and, finding that the demand for depriving them of civil rights had been dictated by a malicious spirit, they decreed, unanimously, on the 1st of January, 1767, that the members of the Congregation should enjoy the same privileges as the other subjects belonging to the kingdom. Disappointed in this manner, Maffey had recourse to intrigue, and obtained access to the royal council; and the procurator, allowing himself to be prejudiced, forbade the Fathers to administer their property, and the little they possessed was entrusted to a strange commissioner, named by Maffey. Alphonsus' sorrow, on hearing these tidings, and on seeing his children in such distress, may be well imagined. "Let us not cease to pray," he wrote to them, "because all my hope is in God;" and to F. Villani, he said: "Let us behave well, and Jesus Christ will protect us; He does not cease to give us warnings, but if we prove unfaithful He will abandon us."

Things being in this state, Maffey tried by every possible means, to prejudice against them the mind of the king and his ministers, by false or exaggerated accounts and distorted reports, and even by the calumnious accusation that they had excited the people to revolt. And he succeeded so well, that the suppression of the Congregation was spoken of, as well as the chastisement which awaited its members. The same miserable attempts were resorted to, at the same time, at Ciorani. Their conduct was misrepresented; they endeavored to find them guilty of offences against the Sovereign and the state. They pretended to prove that they led a scandalous life, and that they oppressed the people. The Fathers had daily visits from constables and other inferior officers. The work of the missions suffered very much from these interruptions, to the great sorrow of the missionaries, and of all good people.

Alphonsus grieved by such sad events, besides urging the members of the Congregation to penance, and redoubling his own mortifications, solicited the prayers of several monasteries and holy persons at Naples. He also sent a great quantity of wax candles to the hermitage of the Camaldulese Fathers, in order that they might expose the Blessed Sacrament, and intercede for the Congregation with God, and he repeatedly sent large alms to the Capuchin Nuns at Naples, and got them to make novenas and other pious exercises.

His children, fearing as to the result of the accusations at Naples, asked him to go there himself. On this subject he wrote to F. Villani, on the 7th of July, 1767, saying: "I have not gone to Naples, but I have written to the President, D. Cito, in a way that will be very efficacious. If he does not protect me after that letter, a hundred visits would be equally useless. I am prevented from going out, by fever, which is constantly attacking me; the doctors say that the least chill or excessive motion might occasion a relapse, and if I am not cured while summer lasts, there is no chance of being so for the whole winter." Alphonsus, however, was filled with confidence and security, when the tempest was at his height, and, in spite of the peril to which the little bark of his Congregation was exposed, he reposed on the goodness of God, the innocence of his sons, and the king's good disposition.

In this same year, 1767, while the Congregation was thus persecuted, he published his great work for the defence of the Catholic Church, called, "The truths of the Faith;" in which he shows that the Church is of divine institution, and that out of it there is no salvation. To this work, whilst it was in press, he added two appendixes; the first was against Helvetius, or rather against his book, entitled, "The Spirit," which he refuted in two points: First, with regard to physical sensibility, which Helvetius calls the producing cause of our thoughts, and in the second place, with regard to that other proposition of Helvetius, viz: that pleasure and interest form the morality of man, that is to say, that all which increases pleasure is honest, and all which favors interest is just. The object of the second appendix is to refute a French work, entitled, "De la Predication," &c., in which the author attacks evangelical preaching openly, and establishes a distinction between the conversion of the mind and that of the heart, and maintains that the first and not the second is effected through preaching. Alphonsus demonstrates the impiety of this assertion.

This work was received with general applause; a canon of the Cathedral of Naples, said of it in a report to Cardinal Sersale; "Nothing can hinder or slacken the zeal of this apostolical man; in his devotion to the salvation of souls, he enters into the lists with indefatigable courage in order to maintain a generous combat for truth, notwithstanding the double burthen of the episcopate, and of advanced age. One can see that he has purposed in this book to re-establish the integrity of faith and morals amongst the faithful, to avenge the calumnies of the wicked, and to scatter the darkness of error. He completely overthrows all the dreams of materialists, deists, and other impious men." Pope Clement XIII was extremely gratified on reading our saint's work, and he replied to the dedication, which had been addressed to him, by a brief, dated August 4th, 1769, in which the Holy Father testified his esteem for our bishop's learning in very flattering terms.

The ignorance which overspread the diocese, and the wish to aid the people, led Alphonsus to compose an extremely useful work, at this time, which he published under the title of "Instructions on the precepts of the Decalogue, in order that they may be properly kept; and on the sacraments, in order that they may be rightly received." This treatise is short, but its great utility caused it to be highly prized, especially by the parish priests.

The disturbances in regard to the two houses of Iliceto and Ciorani went on increasing, and as the storm became more and more alarming, the Fathers of the Congregation redoubled their entreaties to Alphonsus, to go to Naples in person, in order to hold a conference with the Marquis Tanucci. On this occasion he wrote to F. Villani: "Tanucci has had an interview with Mgr. Albertini; if he has not attached faith to this prelate's words, he would be still less disposed to believe me, who am an interested party. If I see that I can be of any use, I will not fail to exert myself, ... and you ought never to fear that I shall neglect the least thing which I may know would be of use to the Congregation." F. Villani then went to see him, in great sorrow, and in all haste, to inform him that the cause was shortly to be brought before the royal tribunal. At these tidings, Alphonsus sent by his secretary two letters, one to the Marquis of Tanucci, and the other to the Marquis of Marco, begging them to deign to commence the cause in consideration of the reasons which he assigned. But the tempest became still more furious; the alarm of the Fathers was redoubled, and F. Villani, accompanied by some other Fathers, repaired to St. Agatha, and all, with tearful eyes, represented to Alphonsus their adversaries' superiority, and the imminent danger which menaced them; adding, that if he wished to save the Congregation, his presence at Naples was necessary. "What could I do by my presence?" he replied; "that which my letters cannot obtain, I shall be unable to obtain myself." He was moved, however, at seeing their affliction, and ill as he was, he resolved to set out. All his retinue on this journey and all his methods of defence were masses and prayers; confidence in God and hope for protection from on high strengthened his courage. As he had no carriage, he borrowed one from a gentleman, and he arrived at Naples on the 16th of July, 1767.

As soon as he reached Naples, he went to the Cardinal Archbishop. His eminence was at dinner when Mgr. Liguori was announced to him; he immediately arose, and with eyes bathed in tears through joy at this unexpected visit, he hastened to meet Alphonsus, and embraced him, saying: "What has brought you to Naples so unexpectedly?" "My Congregation is passing through a great crisis, your Eminence," answered Alphonsus, "our enemies wish to destroy it, but I hope that God will grant us the assistance of his arm." Before he left, the Cardinal said to him, "Know that you are Archbishop of Naples; you must obtain the victory and dispose of every thing as you wish." Mgr. Liguori's arrival put the whole town in motion. The canons, the superiors of the orders, the chevaliers and ministers came to greet him. Almost all the prelates who were in Naples went to visit him. As for himself, as he had only come for urgent business, he begged every one to excuse him if he reluctantly failed in the duties of civility.

Humility and poverty were his attendants; he lived in his brother's house, but he did not wish to be treated with distinction; and he gave up the room and state-bed which his brother had had prepared for him to his secretary, and selected for himself quite a plain little apartment, which was used as a lumber-room, and had nothing in it but a miserable bed, and some straw chairs. When he had not to officiate in any church, he merely put on the cassock of his Congregation which he had worn every day at St. Agatha, and which was then quite worn out. His shoes were the same he had had made when he went to Rome; he had the same hat, too, which was now no longer in fashion, and which had only cost three carlins when new. His brother, D. Hercules, who was more annoyed at the hat than at any thing else, secretly took it away and substituted a valuable one in its place. Alphonsus was very sorry to be obliged to wear it, but before he left Naples he caused it to be sold, and with the proceeds he bought four more common hats; he kept one for himself, and gave the remaining three to some of his Congregation. As he had no cloak, he made use of a kind of mantilla; but being told that it was not fit for him, he sent it to a pawnbroker in exchange for an old cloak. Some people gave him the title of Excellency. "Excellency," said Alphonsus, "what do you mean by this title? Drop this excellency." He had a singular altercation with a servant in a monastery, on this head, who was continually addressing him by this title. "Come now," said Alphonsus, "give up this word excellency." "But," replied the servant, "why am I not to call you thus? you are a chevalier, and this title belongs to you." "That is enough," replied his lordship, "do not speak to me any more about your excellency." He said this in a tone which made the poor servant hurry to the door as fast as possible. A gentleman observing to him that he carried humility too far: "Humility," Alphonsus replied, "has never injured any one."

Our saint was always preceded by humility, but glory and veneration followed him wherever he went. When he went to the royal palace, to implore the protection of the Prince della Riccia, his majesty's grand equerry, he was received there not as a mere man but as a messenger from heaven. As soon as the prince heard that he was in the ante-room, he hastened to go to him, and respectfully kissed his hand, and when Alphonsus took leave of him he accompanied him to the staircase with affectionate kindness. "I thank God," exclaimed the prince on leaving him, "for having allowed me to see this saintly man once more." The same or similar marks of veneration were given him by the highest personages he had occasion to visit. This veneration was much increased by the manner in which he defended the cause of his children. He managed to justify the missionaries and defend their innocence without injuring those who had calumniated them. He attributed their attacks to interest, and their irritation to passionate temper, and he only sought to procure tranquillity to those belonging to him, and to obtain the prince's protection for the Congregation. Alphonsus' very appearance at Naples put the adversaries of the Congregation to confusion; even their counsel said that the case had an altered aspect, and the advocates, who, till then, believed that they were sure of victory and sought to have the cause brought on, tried now to delay it, and would have liked to suspend it altogether, no longer thinking it expedient to venture further. This delay displeased Alphonsus, and by his solicitations with the ministers he obtained the king's leave to have the affair terminated without loss of time, and the 11th of September was fixed for the discussion of the cause of Sarnelli, at the royal court of St. Clare. It was at this time that our saint met with an accident, which one is tempted to consider the work of the devil, who foreseeing his defeat, wished to cause Alphonsus to perish. He was one day in a carriage with the counsellor, Gaetan Celano; night was approaching, and the rain was falling in torrents, their coachman urged the horses on as fast as possible towards the court of counsellor Pirelli in order to gain shelter, but other carriages had already taken refuge there and he was obliged to turn back; at that moment, another carriage came up at a rapid rate, and struck with such violence against that of Alphonsus that in the fall he was thrown under the counsellor. The windows were broken to pieces, and the coachman was wounded as well as the footman. Alphonsus was not seriously hurt, but the counsellor had his hand cut; they both disengaged themselves from the carriage, but with great difficulty, and took refuge in a grocer's shop more dead than alive. The duchess of Pirelli heard of the accident, and sent for Alphonsus and the counsellor; they rested in her palace for some time, after which the duchess lent them her own equipage to take them home again. In this disaster Alphonsus regretted nothing but his beautiful hat, which was lost in the confusion as well as the wooden stick which he used as a cane.

The proceedings in reference to the cause were at length commenced, but the advocates of the adverse party had not the courage to show themselves. One of them indeed came, but it was only to declare that he had not the heart to speak against a bishop whose sanctity was proclaimed by all Naples. Our enemies' inaction was displeasing to Alphonsus; he sent his secretary to the President Cito, to complain of this disappointment. "He need not be annoyed at seeing his enemies put to flight," replied the magistrate, "let him take courage, and return to his diocese." Such was Alphonsus' success in this visit to Naples. He took leave of all his acquaintances, after a sojourn of two months and three days, and set out for Arienzo on the 10th of September, 1767.

Although Alphonsus only went to Naples on account of the interests of his Congregation, he nevertheless made his visit subserve the glory of God, and fatal to sin and hell. Great disorders had taken place in the convent called "of the Religious of the Wood." These nuns, without respect for the Superior, who tried to unite them, had proceeded to sad lengths on several occasions. Being entreated to lend his aid, Alphonsus went to the convent several times and preached there, and that which others had not been able to effect by their words, was obtained by his humility and mildness. He put an end to all the dissensions which existed in the convent, and was able to re-establish there peace, the love of prayer, and the frequent use of the sacraments.

The Superior of the Congregation of the Propaganda resolved to ask him to preach the Novena of the Assumption of the Blessed Virgin, in the church of the Restitution. The canon fearing that Alphonsus would not be able to grant his request, (as he was ill, and overloaded with business,) it was observed to him, that he had an infallible means of obtaining what he wanted, viz: his authority as Superior; Alphonsus being yet a member of the Congregation. When the humble bishop received this order, he made no opposition, but bent his head and said: "Pray that the Blessed Virgin may give me strength, for I have nothing written, and no time to prepare any thing; you must be satisfied with what God and the Blessed Virgin may deign to suggest to me."

One evening during this Novena, our Saint was obliged to go to the Archbishop's, but the carriage, the one which D. Gaetan had bought, had been sent to be repaired; the servant took another, belonging to D. Hercules, which was rich and handsome. Such luxury alarmed the Saint, and nothing could reconcile him to it. In order to prevent his going on foot, old harness was put on the horses, and an old covering was put over the seat; which mixture of old and new together caused the Bishop of St. Agatha to present a somewhat singular appearance, but satisfied his humility. During the Novena, the church was crowded to overflowing, from the first day, and he preached with such wonderful effect, that floods of tears were shed in the church, and his Eminence, Cardinal Sersale, who made it a duty to assist at this Novena daily with his suite, could not refrain from weeping at the touching spectacle of an entire people in contrition. Canon Sparano declared, that ten missions would not have done so much good nor have effected so many conversions, as God did during this Novena through Mgr. Liguori. Again, on this occasion, pieces of his garments were taken from him in secret; amongst others a piece of his cloak was cut off. Mgr. Bergamo, at that time a priest and afterwards Bishop of Gaeta, thought himself very fortunate in being able to take his hat in exchange for another. He attempted the same thing with his rosary, but Alphonsus found it out; he complained of it, and wished to have it restored to him again on account of the indulgences attached to it.

On the Eve of the Assumption, he went to pay his visit to the Blessed Sacrament in the church of the convent Regina Cœli; while the nuns were chanting vespers, he knelt down before a chair in a corner of the church. Three abbots were officiating pontifically; one of them, who knew him, no sooner saw him in his shabby dress than he turned towards the others and said: "Look what a figure this bishop is! does he not disgrace his character!" The abbot soon found that he was not a good judge. The Prince of Monte Miletto who was present, also saw Alphonsus, and immediately asked his valet who that Prelate was; on hearing that it was Mgr. Liguori, he approached him respectfully, kissed his hand, and held it to his forehead for some time. The Duke of Andria also presented himself to him, or rather cast himself at his feet, and would not consent to arise until after he had received the sign of the cross on his head; some other noblemen also hastened to render him the same homage. The abashed abbots then sent him a velvet cushion by the sacristan, but Alphonsus would not use it.

When the barefooted Carmelite Fathers commenced the solemnity of the Wednesdays in honor of St. Theresa, Alphonsus did not fail to attend, and mixing with the people, he placed himself according to custom on one of the benches in the church. When the Fathers perceived him they wished to show him some token of respect, but Alphonsus refused it. On the following Wednesday they prepared a special chair with a velvet cushion for him, but in vain, for he made no use of it.

Alphonsus had the gift of prophecy, as well as those of knowledge and counsel. A daughter of the Duchess of Bovino, who was on the point of leaving a convent, in order to embrace the state of marriage, still hesitated in regard to her vocation; the duchess went to Alphonsus and begged him to remember her in his prayers. "No, no;" replied he, "she will not marry. God will detach her from the world and draw her to himself." The young lady's mind, up to this time, had been occupied about anything rather than becoming a religious; her mother was therefore much surprised to hear these words from the saintly man, but she was still more so when, on her return home, a note was handed to her from her daughter, stating her intention of taking the religious habit in the convent.

Lady Marianne Cayano Orsini gave birth to a son at Marianella about this time. D. Hercules wished that the ceremony of baptism should be performed by Alphonsus himself, to which he assented. During the ceremony, the priest, in addressing Alphonsus, gave him the title of Excellency, at every instant; he bore it at first, in order not to interrupt the ceremony, but at last he could endure it no longer, and exclaimed: "Rev. Sir, if you wish to call me most illustrious, you can of course do so, but you will oblige me very much by only using the most simple expressions in speaking to me."

Besides the Novena of which we have spoken, Alphonsus also preached a sermon in the church of the Advocate, for the confraternity of the coachmen, footmen, and other domestics. His dear brethren of the chapels, amongst whom was the celebrated Peter Barberese, his former penitent, also heard his holy exhortations once more; he rejoiced in thus being employed for the good of the poorest and most obscure. A head saddler also begged him to come and preach in his chapel, which was situated beyond the gate of Capua, and he went there most willingly. He found a very large assemblage of the lower classes, but as the chapel could not hold them all, he re-assembled them all in the church of St. Onuphrius. These good people assembled together on another occasion, in the hospital of the Annunziata; the Blessed Sacrament was exposed on both occasions, and he exhorted them all to the practice of Christian virtue. He was also asked to preach to them on the Nativity of the Blessed Virgin, and he yielded to their wishes. On the following Sunday he preached to the orphans who were brought up in this hospital, amounting to the number of more than three hundred.

The people were not satisfied with profiting by his words in church, but they hastened in crowds to his house, and as he had not chairs enough for all, they sat on the ground. He rejoiced in being in the midst of this multitude of poor people much more than in receiving the visits of priests, confessors, magistrates, the knights of St. Januarius, the Duchesses, Princesses, and the many others, who not being able to speak to him in the confessional, came to see him, and left him no moment of leisure time until a late hour in the evening; and his loving kindness towards these poor people won him the admiration of all the town of Naples, not less than the fact, that, notwithstanding his advanced age, his infirmities, and the important affairs that had brought him to Naples, he underwent so much fatigue for the glory of God and the good of souls. He visited also the convents of Donna Alvina, of St. Clare, of Sapienza, of St. Marcellinus, of St. Gaudioso, of St. Liguori, of the Blessed Sacrament, of St. Jerome, of Little St. John's, of Donna Romita, of St. Potitus, of St. Andrew's, of the Nuns, and others. He preached in each of them, and returned several times to some of them to hear confessions. Being invited, on the feast of St. Jane de Chantal, to the convent of the Nuns of the Visitation, he went with pleasure and preached there. Nothing, in a word, whereby he could encourage hearts in the practice of virtue and the love of Jesus Christ, was accounted by him as too much.

In all this he never deviated from his profound humility, and though the Cardinal had told him that he was Archbishop of Naples, he never did anything without informing his eminence. A religious asked him one day to hear her confession. He immediately sent to ask for the faculty to do so from the Cardinal, who replied half displeased: "What does Mgr. Liguori want? Did I not tell him that he was Archbishop of Naples? He may confirm, confess, preach, and officiate, and do whatever he pleases, for he has power to do anything?"

Besides the prophecy mentioned above, he made several others in regard to inmates of convents, of which we will only cite the following. Alphonsus' sister, Marianne Liguori, a nun in the convent of St. Jerome, manifested a want of submission towards her director; Alphonsus predicted that she would die mad, and it speedily came to pass. The Princess Zurlo, a pensioner at the convent of St. Marcellinus, had an earnest desire to become a religious; when this young lady's fervor was mentioned to him, he answered: "No, she will not be a nun, but she will return to the world, and lead a saintly life there." And his words proved to be true. At St. Clare, a nun tried to interest him in a niece of hers, whom she wished to get admitted in the convent, although she had already left it. "Leave her alone," said he, "she is not fit for a convent." And so it was; she no longer wished to consecrate herself to God.

Alphonsus made no distinction of persons; he acted just in the same manner towards the convents of women of no rank as towards those of women of noble birth. He willingly consented to go and visit the convents of the Little Rosary, of St. Margaret, of St. Monica, of the Miracles, of Jesus and Mary, of St. Catherine, of St. Joseph, and of St. Theresa; of St. Philip and St. James also, where he gave a sermon on the prodigal son: and his visits were always marked by great blessings, as God assisted his efforts. He also preached several times at the Refuge of St. Clare, and visited the penitents of St. Raphael, as also those of the Crucifix; it was especially edifying to see him return from the most humble and despised places, with still more pleasure than from the convents for the nobility.

He did not omit to gô and comfort a great many infirm nuns, and particularly his old penitents. He evinced his scrupulosity in regard to holy modesty, during these visits. In order to prevent his hands from being kissed, he kept his left across his breast and wrapped up the other in a handkerchief. When asked to make the sign of the cross on a sick person's forehead, he only consented to give her his blessing from a distance, and whenever he entered a convent he wished to be accompanied by a priest, to help him, as he said, but in reality as a precaution; nor did he ever omit to provide himself with hair shirts and iron chains, and to discipline himself to blood.

He also accepted several invitations from different religious societies. The Missionaries of St. Pavone, now called, "of the Conference," wished to hear him speak at one of their assemblies, as a fellow-member. Alphonsus spoke to them of the zeal which every priest ought to have for the salvation of souls, exhorted them to preach in an apostolic style, and declaimed against a far-fetched style. "This is indeed a true apostle," said they, "thanks be to God for having given us a bishop of primitive times in this age." Cardinal Sersale, also, wished the fervor of the young people of the establishment which he had himself founded for the instruction of young clerics *in sacris* in the exercises of the Mission, to be animated by the words of our Saint. He conducted Alphonsus thither, and, concealing his own hands under his arms, made all the young people kiss the bishop of St. Agatha's hand, despite his humility. Alphonsus spoke to them on the practice of sacerdotal virtues, and incited them to devote themselves zealously to the salvation of souls, and to be filled with love to Jesus Christ and the Blessed Virgin. Visits which were only of compliment and useless, he tried always to avoid. The nuns of Little St. John, not satisfied with having seen him at the grate and with having assisted at his mass, solicited him, through F. Fatigati, to repeat his visit; as this, however, was not in order to consult him as their director, he did not accede to their invitation, but answered: "I like much to go to St. John, but not to Little St. John's; they have caused me to lose an hour, and I am scrupulous about time." Although Alphonsus effected so much good in Naples, and although his presence there drew down so many blessings, he never ceased to grieve at being so far from his diocese, but counted the moments, and only longed to return. "If it were not on account of the interests of the Congregation which is persecuted," he said, "and which labors so successfully for God's glory and the salvation of souls, I should believe that I sinned mortally in remaining so long at Naples." It must not, however, be believed that he ever lost sight of the wants of his diocese. Not a day passed on which he did not receive some courier from thence. Being again asked for a Novena, he replied: "What Novena do you wish me to give? I will go and make one in my diocese, where God only knows what disorders I shall find. Jesus Christ no longer wishes me to be at Naples, but at St. Agatha."

Let us give one more instance of Alphonsus' humility, while in the capital. He went to visit the Prince della Riccia, to get, through his protection, a woman, a servant of the Prince's, admitted into the Refuge of St. Raphael;

but the valet remembered that he had received nothing from Alphonsus on his first visit to the Prince, so he said that the Prince was in attendance on the King. A soldier of the Italian guard, who was on duty, said to a comrade, on seeing this old man, whose long beard and neglected exterior seemed unsuitable to his dignity as a bishop, "Look at this shabby lord. He has not a half-penny to be shaved." Alphonsus heard it and smiled. "I thank thee, O my God," he said, "for causing me also to receive the censure of the soldiers." But the guard was soon undeceived when he saw the first noblemen hasten to pay their respects to the holy bishop. He returned a second time to the Prince's palace, and was again dismissed, on some other pretext; he then went a third time, when, on the advice of his secretary, who suspected the real cause of the mystery, he slipt some money into the valet's hand, and the Prince was made visible. Angry at the refusals which Alphonsus had met with, he offered to provide for all needful expenses in regard to the penitent woman, and informed the director of the house that she was one of his tenants; nothing further was required for her admission, and Alphonsus had the consolation to see one more of his sheep in a place of safety.

When he left Naples at last, it was with the firm resolution, if we should not rather call it a prediction, that he would not return there any more. When he visited, for the last time, his dear Mother, in the church of the Redemption where he had received so many graces, he said to her: "My Queen, we shall see each other again in Paradise, but we shall meet no more in Naples." "Tell D. Hercules," he wrote from St. Agatha to a brother of the Congregation who was in Naples, "that he may freely dispose of the apartments which he keeps at my service, for I shall return there no more."

Although Alphonsus was unceasingly, and we may almost say, excessively solicitous for the right government of his diocese, and though his conduct in this respect obtained the admiration of the most distinguished men, and the praises of the Sovereign Pontiff, yet he could not escape the darts of malignity and censure. His reputation for sanctity caused him to be attentively watched, and as his administration seemed rather like that of an angel than of an ordinary man, people fancied that he ought to make sin disappear from the world. As soon as any disorder in his diocese was spoken of, people began to blame and calumniate him; for some were too ready to listen to the discourses of the wicked, and co-operated, through inexcusable credulity, in what others did through malice. A religious, at Naples, found fault with, and condemned things in Alphonsus which he had not seen, but of which he had heard; and Alphonsus, being begged to justify himself, answered: "I have heard of this bad opinion of me. There is no need of writing to him. St. Francis of Sales, F. Torres, and so many others, have not defended themselves. The three who rule, are the Grand-Vicar, who aids me by counsel, Archdeacon Rainone, who performs his duty at St. Agatha, and the Secretary, who governs still less." And in another letter: "Every thing passes through my hands, with the single exception of the ordinary decrees as to temporals, which are under the charge of the Grand-Vicar, and of my Vicar-General at St. Agatha. Tell me where there is a diocese in which there is nothing wanting. As to me, I do what I can, but all ground produces its thorns; one may pluck out one here, but another will spring up elsewhere. I see that I cannot avoid the reproaches made against me; it is enough if God does not complain: however, complaints are of use to me, for my spiritual welfare, by humbling me through the contempt and want of favor which I must meet with from some people. I should be very glad if you would tell Father N. to come and see me, because he may then be enlightened as to the real state of things." The good Father went to him, and was his panegyrist from that time. He liked to be told of all that was said to his dispraise, and never hesitated to make amends if he found he had made a mistake.

An idle person circulated a report through Naples, that they were much dissatisfied with Mgr. Liguori's administration at Rome. It was even added that the Pope was very far from rejoicing at having made him bishop. When F. Villani informed him of this, he replied thus: "You say that the accusation of which you speak, may very probably have been made at Rome; I have heard nothing about it yet. For the rest, and as to the government, I do not know how I could have been more careful than I was. I always note down in writing all that has to be done for the present day and for the following one, and when any business connected with the diocese is in question, I leave every thing to occupy myself about it. All belonging to my diocese may see this plainly; God will do the rest, but this will enable me to get my resignation more easily accepted."

With an inconsistency, which is a characteristic of falsehood, others accused him of governing with too much rigor; but Alphonsus was certain of the good he had done, and cared equally little, for being thought too lenient, or too severe. "Human respect," said F. Raphael de Ruvo, "could never succeed in influencing Mgr. Liguori." One day, in presence of several gentlemen, it was said that people talked a great deal about a priest who, as they alleged, had been banished unjustly. He was guilty of several hidden offences, for which Alphonsus had felt constrained to recur to this punishment, without wishing to publish things against him which were unknown. When he heard that he was censured for it, he got out of the difficulty by a smile, and said nothing to exculpate himself. Some even in the Congregation said, that in the publication of his works he sought for an uncertain good, while he neglected the certain good he could have effected, had he been exclusively engaged in the affairs of his diocese. Being informed of this, he wrote to F. Villani: "In regard to the murmurs relative to my publications, I will say that those bishops who are most celebrated for their great zeal, preached and published works while ruling over their dioceses. . . . . I am always shut up during winter, and converse with no one; besides, every one avoids my conversation, because it is not agreeable. I make meditation three times a day; I make an hour's thanksgiving after mass, as well as a spiritual lecture, at least when I am at liberty. After that I try to profit by all the time remaining to me, in laboring in things which seem useful."

Alphonsus published, about this time, "The Way of Salvation," which is a work of great utility for all classes of men. It is divided into three parts: the first contains meditations for all seasons of the year; the second for divers times in particular: and the third contains a rule of life for a Christian, the practice of virtue, and considerations on the love of Jesus Christ, entitled "Darts of Fire."

CHAPTER XXV.

Alphonsus is visited by sickness and great sufferings. He finishes his work on Dogmatics. His Congregation is persecuted in Sicily. His mode of life and apostolic labors when paralytic. Interest he takes in the education of his Nephews. Circular to his Congregation. His Missionaries abandon Sicily.

WHEN Almighty God wishes to raise one of His servants to great sanctity, the usual course of His providence is to throw him into a sea of troubles and sorrows. Alphonsus, whom God had destined to become a shining pillar in the heavenly Jerusalem, was also obliged to pass through the crucible of tribulation. On the 23d of June, 1768, in the seventy-second year of his age, and the seventh of his episcopate, he was attacked by a fever, which at first seemed so slight that it was believed to be only the consequence of a cold; but it increased on the second and third day, and made such progress that it was taken for a dangerous putrid fever. However it disappeared three day afterwards, and, contrary to all expectation, he was attacked by acute pains in the right side. The doctors called it the commencement of sciatica, arising from rheumatic tendencies; in fact he experienced constant pain in the bone of the thigh, these however were not very severe.

As he had no fever, and his head was free, he never ceased to give audience, nor interrupted his scientific and spiritual occupations. Not being able to visit his diocese himself, he sent his Grand-Vicar into the estates of Trasso and Arpaja, as well as to the village of Forchia. "I continue," he wrote to F. Villani, "to be tormented with internal pains in nearly one-half of my body, and it seems as if the pain would fix in the hip bone. Blessed for ever be God for having sent me this suffering! I shall have difficulty in going out, this year, to make my accustomed visitation." On the approach of the feast of the Assumption, he tried to give the Novena, in the church of the Annunziata; and, notwithstanding his suffering, he succeeded in crawling into the pulpit; but the pain ere long seized him in a most violent manner, and fixed itself obstinately in the hip bone, so as to render it impossible for him to go, on, and a Neapolitan missionary, who had accompanied him, took his place on the sixth day. From this time, the malady made such progress that he no longer knew in what position to place himself: in this state, he was unceasingly occupied in his bed about the affairs of his diocese; he dictated his works, and continued to perform with the members of his household all the accustomed exercises.

However, the fever went on increasing day by day, so that fears were entertained for his life. When it was proposed to him to send for a doctor from Naples, he replied: "Do you, then, think that the doctors in Naples work miracles, or that they have studied other books than the doctors here? I am in the hands of God, and of the doctors he has given me." His two worthy doctors, however, were not of the same opinion, but sent for F. Villani and the Grand-Vicar, and said to them: "We do not wish to bear the responsibility of his lordship's death; we want to have a consultation." A physician was therefore summoned from Naples. Alphonsus said nothing on seeing him, but his face betokened the suffering of his heart.

He affected every one, while in this state, by his ejaculations of love towards Jesus Christ and the Blessed Virgin. He showed great confidence in their merits, but seemed quite confounded at his own conduct, which, he said, had not corresponded to their goodness. A Father of the Congregation was just going to say mass, when he called him, and said with a profound sentiment of humility: "Pray that God may deign to be merciful towards me." Although he had confidence, he still trembled in thinking of the judgments of God. "Non intres in judicium cum servo tuo," he repeated, and, "fac cum servo tuo secundum misericordiam tuam." "Enter not into judgment with Thy servant, O Lord. . . . . Do unto Thy servant according to Thy mercy."

After receiving the last Sacraments on the 26th of August, 1768, he made his will. He would not have had matter for one, if his steward had not received four hundred and twenty-three ducats, some days before, arising from the rents belonging to him. He wished this sum to be placed in the hands of the Arch-priest Romano, and fixed on the number of masses to be celebrated for him at Arienzo, and at St. Agatha; he pointed out what alms he wished to be given to the poor, and ordered that the surplus should be distributed to all who were in his service, as a token of gratitude, two hours after his death; finally, he asked that his body should be taken to the Cathedral of St. Agatha.

The fever, however, visibly abated, although the sufferings were still very sharp. The pains, too, caused by the rheumatism were violent and continual, so that he could find no position in which he could lie in bed, and was obliged, though with great difficulty, to get into an armchair, where he remained as if nailed down by his sufferings. It is easy to imagine how he passed the nights and days, as he could neither move, nor dress himself; his state caused all who saw him to shed tears of compassion.

The rheumatism was constantly making fresh progress, and from the hip bone soon reached the leg, and extended through the nerves of the limbs, which caused a great increase of pain. He bore it with unalterable patience: no groan ever issued from his lips, but that which filled up the measure of admiration in regard to him, was that he never ceased to be still occupied with the affairs of his diocese. The following are some of the lively aspirations collected by one who attended on him: "Lord, I thank Thee for having given me some share in the sufferings Thou didst endure in Thy nerves, when Thou wast nailed to the cross. I wish to suffer, my Jesus, as Thou willest, and as much as Thou willest, only give me patience." "Hic ure, hic seca, hic non parcas, ut in æternum parcas." "Unhappy damned souls! how can you suffer without merit? My Jesus, my hope, the only remedy for all my ills." "Oh, how happy a thing it is to die, fastened to the cross." "A poor person who loves God, dies more contented than all the rich in the world. An hour of suffering is worth more than all the treasures of the earth." "I should like to have a little sleep, but God does not will it, and I do not wish it either." "Oh, my palliass! thou art worth more for one day than all the thrones of the world."

At last, the rheumatism settled in the vertebræ of his neck, and his head was so bent forwards, and rested so much on his chest, that on looking at him from behind he appeared like a body without a head. "Nothing but a miracle," said a doctor, "could have prevented this curvature from taking away respiration altogether." But even this was only a part of his martyrdom. In consequence of this displacement of the head, his chin sank down into the middle of his chest, and his beard being strong and bristly caused a considerable wound there. This could not be seen, and he bore it without any complaint; it did not at first attract attention, but the humor, which soon issued from it, caused the doctors to entertain the most lively fears; they wanted to raise his head in order to examine it, but Alphonsus was obliged to raise his hand, as a sign for them to desist, for any force used in that direction would have broken his neck. They then placed him on a sofa, in a horizontal position, and thus they were able to examine the wound. It was so deep and dangerous, that it had very nearly laid bare the bone of the chest. They, however, succeeded in preventing mortification, and it was soon completely healed.

He began to get better at the end of a few months, but the malignant humor settled on the nerves, the body was contracted, and his head rested on his chest during the seventeen years he lived after this. During the course of this cruel malady he evinced superhuman patience: "Mgr. Liguori," said F. Raphael de Ruvo, the ex-provincial of the religious of St. Peter of Alcantara, "was a true picture of the saintly Job. Though having become, as it were, one mass of pains, he never opened his mouth to utter even the slightest complaint. One look raised up to heaven with some pious aspiration, was the sign of his suffering; he still expressed himself so calmly that he consoled and confounded me, as well as all who were present." One of the first surgeons of the capital, having witnessed his patience at Arienzo, said: "If I had had to endure such torments, I should have become frantic." He could not conceive how the Saint had been able to preserve unalterable serenity in the midst of such terrible sufferings.

At length the invalid was placed on a poor mattress, though not without great suffering, on which he lay in an uneasy and painful position. It was not without difficulty that they succeeded in putting on his cassock, and as he could not undress himself, he remained in this garb night and day, and in the same position. In all these pains, he showed the truth of St. Augustine's words, that he who loves, does not suffer, and wishes to suffer more. "He was fixed on his poor bed," said a canon of Avella, "once, while I was arranging the sheets with Brother Francis Anthony, I saw that he had his large rosary by him, and that there were as many holes in his flesh as there were beads in it. As I attributed this to accident, I told the brother to take it away.

But he answered in a way which made me understand that this servant of God was not satisfied with only bearing his infirmity, but sought to crucify himself still more." His submission to the doctors was no less admirable. "Let us obey them," he often said, "and resign ourselves to die." They had scarcely spoken when they were obeyed; however painful or disagreeable the prescribed remedy might have been, he took it, not through a wish to prolong life, but because he recognized God's will in theirs. One day he said to one of the doctors: "I am nothing but an old man now, what can I hope for, or aspire to? I obey, in order to fulfil your will and that of God." He was not only contented and serene, but he carried his heroism so far as to be quite joyous. One day he said to the same doctor: "You endeavor to hold me up, by means of props and stays, but if you happen to put a new prop some day, and raise it up too much, all the rest will fall, and you will lose your trouble." A priest once asked him how he had passed the night: "I chase flies by day," he replied laughingly, "and I take spiders by night." "There," said he to a canon, slightly moving his head, "that is the ne plus ultra, my head can do no more." Another time he said to the same canon: "They have so often called me crippled, that I am caught at last."

Although reduced to this state of infirmity, he never dispensed himself from any of his exercises of piety. In the evening, especially, he wished all his household to come to his room, together with the Grand-Vicar, to recite the Rosary together, with the Litanies of the Blessed Virgin, and the other accustomed prayers. He passed nearly the whole day in hearing some spiritual reading, which was made for him alternately by Brother Anthony and the priest who attended him. Neither did he, in this state of oppression, forget his flock, but dictated, ordered, and did every thing as if he had been quite well. Thus he caused several noblemen to be written to, touching the reform of abuses, and addressed some Congregations at Naples, and F. Villani, in order to obtain Missionaries, that year, for all his diocese. "That which most astonished me," said a canon, "was, that he not only never ceased to watch and labor for the good of souls and the glory of Jesus Christ, during this excess of suffering, but that he also did so beyond the bounds of the province. Having been informed that a bishop had been guilty of an abuse, which was most prejudicial to souls, he hastened to dictate a letter, which he sent by an express, to inform him of his error, after which he turned towards me and said: 'My dear Benedict, we are obliged mutually to aid each other.'"

It was on this bed of pain that he revised, for the last time, a great work which he published, entitled "The Practice of Love towards Jesus Christ." It manifests the sentiments of his heart, and every where breathes the spirit of the pious author, showing the necessity, and teaching the way, of loving Jesus Christ our God, who ought to be the sole object of the affections of our hearts, and to whom all the actions of our life should be referred.

The convalescence of Alphonsus was very painful, and lasted more than a year. "I continue to be without fever," he wrote to F. Villani, on the 8th of October, 1768, "but the pain is just the same. They make me walk about on crutches, supported however by two people, and this is the sixth day since I began to do this; but I do not see that this or the carriage does me any good. I am awake nearly all the night; nature feels it, but I think that my will is resigned to that of God. Remember me during mass, that God may give me perfect resignation." And, on the 2d of November, "I am in a state which renders me incapable of moving, and fever attacks me from time to time. However, my head is clear, and by God's grace, I am cheerful and resigned."

At this time, a learned man of Naples published a treatise against the authority of the Church, and particularly against her privileges; Alphonsus, though in the midst of such sufferings, did not hesitate to enter the lists. He prepared the manuscript of a refutation, and he would have finished it, but on account of several circumstances, and on the advice of F. Villani, he did not think fit to put the finishing stroke to it. During this convalescence, he also composed and published a treatise on the ceremonies of mass, expounding most clearly all the rubrics to be observed, and urging upon all priests the necessity of making that preparation and thanksgiving which are required by so august a mystery. Whilst he was bringing out this treatise, he received a dissertation against the fees for masses, which was written in an angry spirit, and published at Naples. The author, who wished to abolish masses and the ecclesiastical state altogether, pretended to demonstrate the great disorders, as he said, the sins of simony, the sacrileges, and the scandals which result from the retributions which priests receive from masses. In conclusion he proposed that paid masses should be abolished altogether, and that the custom of the primitive ages should be re-established, of having but one mass, and that the oblations should be made, as formerly, for the support of the priest, and for the wants of the Church and the poor. Alphonsus zealously took up arms and published a learned reply, in which he refutes the impious doctrine of the anonymous author by the true Catholic doctrine. He added this refutation to the aforesaid treatise, of which it forms the third part.

When his Holiness, Pope Clement XIII, passed to a better world, Alphonsus never ceased to pray fervently that God would deign to grant a worthy Pastor to His Church, and immediately enjoined on all priests that the prayer *pro eligendo summo Pontifice*, should be recited in the diocese, and he recommended this matter to all who came to see him. "After God," he said, "is the Pope." When Clement XIV ascended the pontifical throne on the 19th of May, 1769, Alphonsus rejoiced greatly on hearing that the election had fallen on a prelate who was so full of knowledge and zeal. In spite of all the sufferings which had come upon him, he succeeded in finishing his work on dogmatics, which was extracted from the Council of Trent, and against the pretended Reformers, and he hastened to dedicate it to the newly elected Pontiff. This work is one of singular merit, and was applauded even beyond the borders of Italy. The Pope received with pleasure, this new evidence of the zeal of the indefatigable bishop in propagating the knowledge of true religion amongst unbelievers and morality amongst Catholics, to the latter of whom is also shown in this work what attachment they owe to the holy faith they profess. The Pope manifested his satisfaction to him, and thanked him kindly in a brief.

As afflictions are sisters, they always go together; thus in addition to all these anxieties and sufferings, Alphonsus' heart was oppressed by other sorrows. The Congregation had prospered wonderfully in Sicily up to this period. Besides the diocese of Girgenti, the missionaries were welcomed in those of Messina, and Palermo. The bishops of Syracuse and of Massara also wished to have them, though they were not sufficiently numerous to satisfy all these demands. All this prosperity, which consoled them, caused the bishop of St. Agatha to reflect seriously. "If the works of God," said he, "are not contradicted, they are not well rooted." "I am rejoiced," he wrote several times to F. Peter Blasucci, "at the progress of our Congregation in Sicily, and am much comforted by it, but this universal applause makes me tremble." But soon Almighty God, who willed that he should go through a martyrdom of mind as well as of body, permitted a furious storm to be raised up against his dear children in Sicily.

From the month of February, 1767, a Jansenist gloried in accusing them to the Viceroy, as men of corrupt morals, as followers of the Jesuits, and as relaxed probabilists. The calumny was a dangerous one and the missionaries began to be only spoken of as men unworthy of their position. However, they justified themselves with so much energy that the minister was undeceived and assured them of his favor and protection. In October, 1768, Mgr. Lucchesi, who had been their warm friend and benefactor, passed to a better world, and the Prince of Campo-Franco declared himself his heir, ab intestat, and pretended that the hundred ounces annually, which had been assigned to them by the defunct bishop for the work of the missions and for their maintenance, were not validly given, and that the missionaries had no power to make acquisitions. He, in consequenee, proceeded to sequester their revenues, and the Fathers, on finding themselves without provisions, began to make preparations for leaving Sicily. The tidings of these sad reverses reached Alphonsus in the very height of his cruel malady; he was deeply affected, but did not allow himself to be cast down. "I received the disastrous news which you give me," he wrote to F. Blasucci, "but I say wrongly, for nothing that God wills can be disastrous. He wishes to mortify us; may His name be praised for ever. I specially beg you not to lose confidence in Jesus Christ. If you are turned out of your house, try to procure another. It will not do to yield so soon; on the contrary, you must persevere till God shows that he He longer wills you to be at Girgenti. There will be fewer missions, but you will not lack a morsel of bread to keep up life. Wait and see what the deputies will do, what will be done by the new bishop; and, above all, what God's will may be. I believe that God does not will the destruction of this house. I continue to have no use of my body from head to foot, but I am contented, and bless God, and thank Him, for having given me peace and patience."

As Alphonsus heard that his moral theology was also attacked on this occasion, he sent a letter to the bishop of Sicily, to justify his doctrine. He also represented the true state of things to the Marquis of Fogliani, the Viceroy of Palermo, and implored his protection. They both, in reply, did justice to his merit and eulogized his virtue and knowledge.

But a new misfortune, and one more painful than the first, came to increase his alarm as to the fate of his children in Sicily. Mgr. Lanza, who succeeded to Mgr. Lucchesi in the see of Girgenti, discovered in his seminary a traitor, who was a wolf in sheep's clothing, and sought to corrupt both the doctrine and the morals of this holy spot.

He was a chaplain belonging to the Cathedral, and professor of the Holy Scriptures, and gloried in publishing that the Jansenists were the true disciples of St. Augustine, that the Holy Roman Church was contrary to this holy doctor, and that in condemning the doctrine of Quesnel she condemned the doctrine of this and the other holy Fathers, and that the bull Unigenitus was impious. The new bishop no sooner heard of his blasphemies than he dismissed him, and suspended his faculties as a confessor. Now from the time of his arrival at Girgenti, the bishop had chosen F. Blasucci for his confessor and theologian, hence the chaplain thought that this blow could only have come to him through the means of this Father. Though it was the masters of the seminary and the pupils themselves who had complained of him, yet his suspicions appeared to have some foundation, and not being able to lay the blame on the bishop, he thought he had better turn his weapons against the missionaries; and, as his own disgrace had befallen him on account of his doctrine, he tried to assail that held by them. He won over several important personages to his party, and, after having obtained fourteen certificates, he went to Palermo, in February, 1769, and presented himself to the royal junta of the president and to the Viceroy, as having been persecuted by the missionaries on account of his doctrine having been in opposition to that they had spread to the prejudice of souls and of the state.

Mgr. Lanza hastened to represent to the viceroy and the junta how unjust and slanderous these reports were, and to inform them, at the same time, of the errors of the plaintiff, which were rendered public by his obstinacy. Calumny tarnishes what it cannot blacken; and thus, at Palermo, some judged well of the missionaries, others ill, and several hesitated about making a judgment, being embarrassed by the falsehoods alleged against them. These divers sentiments engendered such a confusion, and things wore such an inauspicious aspect, that the suppression of the house of the missionaries and their departure were talked of, to the great dismay of many pious persons, some of whom mortified themselves and fasted on bread and water, in order to avert such a calamity, while others distributed abundant alms, and caused a great number of masses to be celebrated.

When Alphonsus was informed of all this, he adored the judgments of God, and never ceased to urge the members of the Congregation to be humble and respectful towards all, to keep silence and to be patient, and if the truth was to be made known, to declare it without injuring those who had shown such perfidy towards them. "Your Reverence seems much afraid," replied he, full of confidence, to one of the Fathers, "for me, I put all my trust in God, who will protect us, as He has always protected the holy Church, which has also been persecuted throughout all ages. Let us act as we ought towards God, and God will comfort us." However, the storm becoming more and more threatening, in the spring of 1769, F. Blasucci presented a sincere but energetic explanation to the Viceroy, in favor of the doctrine of Alphonsus and that of the missionaries. This apology, notwithstanding an anonymous address full of horrible impostures which it drew forth from the chaplain in whose hand it had chanced to fall, disabused the Viceroy and the other ministers of the monarch, and peace seemed fully restored to the missionaries; but it was only a treacherous calm, as we shall see hereafter.

We have admired the patience with which our saint endured the tedious sufferings of a painful illness, and the energy with which he surmounted them and devoted himself to the cares of the government of his diocese, the labors of controversy, and the spiritual exercises which he had been in the habit of performing: we shall find equal reason to admire the mode of life he adopted as soon as his state became less painful. He generally took only five hours of sleep. The mattress he was obliged to use, as he did not allow it to be shaken, was just like a board. Fastened down to this painful bed, he was ready for every thing, and occupied himself about his diocese, and listened to, and satisfied, every one. After the morning meditation he made his preparation for holy communion, which he never omitted, and assisted at the mass which was celebrated by his secretary. After his thanksgiving, which lasted an hour, he recited the canonical hours, although with great difficulty, and, in the course of the day, performed all his other exercises of private devotion at their appointed hours. He took half an hour's rest, after dinner, which was his only repast; he then made a spiritual reading and a meditation of half an hour each, made a visit to the Holy Sacrament, and the Blessed Virgin, and recited vespers and compline; after that he gave audience, or began to study as in the morning. In fact, he lay on his little bed, surrounded by books, and was occupied without any intermission. "If it has been said of St. Jerome," said a venerable ecclesiastic of Naples who visited him, "that he triumphed over his maladies by not ceasing to read and write, 'perpetua lectione et scriptione superabat;' if there is reason to marvel at seeing all that St. Gregory has written, although he was infirm and in bad health, 'infirma et ægra valetudine:' Mgr. Liguori ought to excite still more admiration, on account of the numerous labors to which he devoted himself when in a worse state than St. Jerome and St. Gregory ever were."

Those who took the greatest interest in him personally, applied to F. Villani, to get him, in his capacity of director, to moderate such great application, that thereby he might not shorten his days. But our saint justified himself mildly, and replied: "I do not think that I ought to remain idle. I could employ myself in reading, without dictating, but my head would gain nothing by that. When I have read for twenty minutes, or half an hour at most, I can do no more; besides, I do not neglect my devotions; . . . . but there are many days which are entirely taken up by the affairs of my diocese, and while the visitation I have commenced continues, all the writings must slumber. I have been anxious to enter into all these details with your Reverence, in order to obtain your blessing."

To take his nourishment caused him extreme pain; he experienced the greatest difficulty in introducing any thing like food into his mouth, and could only drink by means of a quill. It was suggested to him to get a silver pipe made; but he rejected the idea with horror. At first he only made use of a wooden pipe, but the use of hot drinks caused several of them to split. One of the lay-brothers of the Congregation having manufactured another sort of pipe, it had to be thrown away because the rust destroyed it, although Alphonsus did not complain of it. Application was at length made to a silversmith, who made one of silver, but he was obliged to pretend that it was of some other metal.

He was distressed at first at not being able to visit his cherished sick. However, he supplied his place by priests and different ecclesiastics, never neglecting to supply them, or other poor people he heard of, with what they might require, by means of Br. Francis, or his servant. He wished to know about the state of those in greatest suffering, day by day, and what they required in regard to food and medicine. On hearing that a poor cloistered nun had met with an accident which obliged her never to leave her chair, although she could still sew and knit, he assigned her an assistance of five carlins a month.

God also aided him in the exercise of his charity, and several sick persons were cured through his prayers. F. Joseph Morgillo, of the Congregation of Pious Workmen, fell and broke his leg; the bone was reset, but the operation did not suceeed, and he was for ten days in great suffering and unable to take any rest. When Alphonsus heard of his sad state, he sent his servant to him with a little picture of the Blessed Virgin, telling him to have confidence in her, and she would obtain his cure. The Father placed the picture on his face, saying: "My Queen! by the merits of Mgr. Liguori, deliver me from this torment," and he was cured that very instant. F. Morgillo honored this picture as long as he lived, as a relic of the blessed bishop from whom he had received it.

Alphonsus had sold his carriage during the time of the scarcity, as we have already said, and had not since thought of procuring another; but the doctors, on seeing his body so paralyzed, and his mind so devoted to study, ordered him to take a daily drive, in order to preserve a remnant of life. Although he was always anxious to follow their advice, he manifested indifference about it this time, and when the doctors and those of his own household insisted, he answered: "What is the use of these drives? I am well enough as I am, and I do not suffer. The money which a carriage and horses would cost me ought to be employed by me in relieving the poor." On seeing, however, the real necessity of his having it, Br. Francis and others resolved to buy him a poor sort of a carriage, which, together with the horses, caused an expense of one hundred and thirteen ducats. At first he was told that it was a present from D. Hercules, but when he knew how it was, he complained to Br. Tartaglione for having caused so much expense for these things. "You could have economized," he wrote to him, "by buying a carriage and horses of an inferior quality." He also wished the horses to be treated and equipped in a manner conformable to his own ideas, that is to say, as poorly as possible; so his drives afforded great diversion to the gentlemen of Arienzo. "An old bishop," said they, "an old coachman, an old carriage, and old horses."

These drives, though ordered for his relief, often ended in being most painful to him. If the carriage met with any shock by coming in contact with a stone, or from any other cause, it was a martyrdom to Alphonsus, whose head was as it were dislocated by each jolt. One evening, one of the wheels met with such a shock that the spokes were all scattered about, the carriage was upset, and it was a miracle that he was not killed by the blow. Br. Anthony and the servant lifted him up in their arms with great difficulty, but as they were not able to bear such a weight long at a time, they were obliged to put him down on the road, at intervals; some poor women who were going home, perceived him, and in compassion lent him a chair. On other occasions, a shaft or other part of the harness broke, and he had to wait in the middle of the street till it was mended. Moreover, one of the horses had a singular habit; after having gone through various contortions of the head, he would suddenly lie down, and would not get up again until after having been pulled by the ears for a long while. Several times, Alphonsus was obliged to get out of the carriage, in the middle of the road, and to remain there patiently, if he could not be dragged to the palace, supported by those who were with him. The incapacity of the coachman multiplied these accidents, for either he did not see what was in the way, or else, not knowing how to avoid it, he ran up against something or other at every step. Alphonsus was the only one who did not appear to suffer, and he never thought of changing the horses, the carriage, or the coachman. At first he went out in the mornings and evenings, but at a later period he only took his drive in the evening, and always in the country, to avoid the frequent meetings which interrupted him when driving through the town. Not to lose an instant of time, as soon as he was seated in the carriage, he began to recite an Ave Maria to the Blessed Virgin, and then said the Gloria Patri three times in honor of his patron-saints, and the De Profundis for the souls in purgatory. He had then the life of some saint, or some other book on ecclesiastical matters, read to him; as he was a little deaf, they were obliged to read in a very loud tone of voice. He most frequently went to St. Mary de Vico, visited the Blessed Sacrament there, and excited the people to fervor by some holy exhortation. When he left the church, the book was re-opened and not closed again until he re-entered the palace court. After he had gone on with this regimen for nearly two years, he became scrupulous about the expense which the horses and coachman occasioned, and wished the carriage to be sold, that its value might be distributed to the poor. The representations of the doctors, of the Grand-Vicar and the whole household were useless, or moved him but little; but he yielded to the command of F. Villani.

After the evening meditation with his household, he recited matins and lauds with his secretary, and then resumed his studies. All his household assembled again about nine o'clock, and recited the rosary and night prayers. The grand-vicar then went to supper with the rest, while Alphonsus prolonged his studies until midnight, and when they brought him a miserable collation, which generally consisted of a little coffee or milk, or even of nothing but lemonade or pure water, he took it with the watch in hand. "I have witnessed the long sufferings of the saint," said F. Buonopane, "and I have admired his marvellous and truly Christian modesty; this appeared in things almost too undignified to be related; when, for example, he went to bed at midnight, he took off his under garments himself, and after he had got into bed with great pain, he had his stockings pulled off, underneath the clothes."

The celebration of mass was the only thing wanting in the life of Alphonsus. This privation, and it was one which he felt the most, lasted for more than two years, during which time he had been obliged to be satisfied with receiving holy communion from the hands of the priest whose mass he heard. One day he related his distress to F. Marcorio, an Augustinian, who had come to invite him to preach in their church on the occasion of the feast of the Girdle; this Father told him that necessity dispensed him from the less essential parts, and that by placing himself on a chair he could easily take the precious blood. Alphonsus received this advice with a transport of joy, and tried to put it in practice, and after two or three attempts, he had the exceeding consolation to celebrate on the following day. After vespers he went to preach at St. Augustine's, and could not cease thanking him who had suggested such a happy expedient. From this time he celebrated mass every day, and obtained permission from Rome to say that of the Blessed Virgin at all times. As he was most exact in observing all the rubrics, he would bend his knee until he touched the platform, which rendered the genuflexions most painful to him; and when he wished to raise the knee again, it fell heavily back, and he only succeeded in standing up again by the aid of another person, so that when the mass was over, he was in a perspiration, and quite exhausted. But, notwithstanding, the fervor of his devotion was so great that he appeared like an angel, and when he prepared to take the precious blood, his face became inflamed like that of a man ravished out of himself. For his thanksgiving, he heard the mass of his chaplain, or of another priest, sitting down, but at the words "Et incarnatus est," he fell to the ground, full of compunction, and remained there bending profoundly; he did the same at the consecration, and each time he required assistance in sitting down again. All the time he had been unable to say mass, he never forgot his people, but had mass said for them by one or the other of the Fathers of his Congregation.

Such was Alphonsus' condition during all the remaining time of his episcopate; and, all the while, he retrenched none of his austerities or labors. In order to be accessible to all, he caused his bed to be placed in a room where every one might come to him, and this was his only apartment, or to speak more correctly, his sole apartment was his bed: except for the meditation, he had no fixed hours, and wished the door to be open to every body, but the poor were especially privileged. Not a day passed in which he did not receive or dispatch several messages, either for remedying some disorder or to inquire into the state of things. However great had been his vigilance up to this time, it appeared to be redoubled in these latter years, and as he who fears that he will not be able to attain his end hastens his steps in order to reach it, so Alphonsus, always imagining that he did not fulfil his office well, unceasingly redoubled his solicitude in order to accomplish his duties better. As soon as he heard of any disorder, he took no rest; he asked advice, examined into it, and provided for its removal. There was not a single day that he did not cause some priest or episcopal vicar to come to Arienzo, in order to become acquainted with all that could concern him. "You see in what state I am," he said to the priests, "if you are not careful in informing me of all the disorders which occur, you will be responsible for all the mischief, and should you not do so, remember that from this time I accuse you of them before the tribunal of God." When he was informed of any abuse through the medium of some one else, and not by the priest, especially if this latter had kept silence through human respect, he lost all peace, and in spite of all his mildness, he never concealed from any one how much he felt it.

This vigilance had for its objects, as usual, the clergy, the religious, and the laity; and when there was any scandal, and when paternal exhortations were of no avail, he had recourse to the help of the great, and even to that of the king in case of need. When any disorder was to be checked, he did not suffer it to be deferred until the following day, if it could be done at once. "He neither took food nor rest," said his grand-vicar, "until he saw the evil cut down to the roots, and when any matter of this sort was in question, the only meal he took in the whole course of that day was the evening one."

He required to be informed of the way in which things were going on in the seminary, several times a week. He very often caused F. Caputo to come to Arienzo. Sometimes he sent for those students whose conduct and labors were distinguished as being exemplary, and made them give an account of the conduct of the others. He was especially vigilant over those who stayed at home on account of indisposition, taking every possible care to ascertain whether the necessity for thus staying away was real or only pretended, and he particularly recommended them to the care of the priests and episcopal vicars. When he received information of the misconduct of a seminarist, he caused him to be reproved, and if this was not followed by amendment, the subject was expelled; so that the young pupils were much more afraid of displeasing their bishop, when he was paralytic and stretched on his sick bed, than when he was up and well. After the few first years, he had forbidden the vacations being passed out of the establishment; but he wished that all suitable recreations should be afforded in the seminary, and that nothing should be spared which could in this respect conduce to the health of the pupils. The reason of this redoubled severity and vigilance towards the seminarists, as well as towards the candidates for ordination and the faculties of confessors, was, as he said to a canon, that he did not wish to give his successor occasion to weep over sin.

He no sooner gained a little strength than he wished to perform also the ministry of the word, and again went about preaching, wherever any solemnity gave a prospect of a numerous audience. On account of his great infirmities, he required several persons to place him in the carriage, and to aid him in ascending the pulpit. Whilst he preached, his face could not be seen; his arm only moved about towards the people; however, he went on unhesitatingly for hours, and it was uncertain whether his words, or the touching spectacle he himself presented, were the most affecting. He was conducted to the church, every year, when mass was celebrated on Holy Saturday, after which he seated himself at the side of the altar, and announced the Easter feast to the people, endeavoring, by a picture of the resurrection of Jesus Christ, to excite his children to rise to life by a spiritual resurrection, and strongly urged all those who had not yet fulfilled their Easter duty to comply with this holy command. He was particularly watchful in seeing that the priests did not omit to instruct the people and catechise the children.

He opened, in person, the Visitation, on the 2d of July, in the year 1769, in the collegiate church of Arienzo, being assisted thither and supported by his servants. It was a sight which caused all present to shed tears; he preached to the people and to the clergy, and made all the necessary arrangements. He also continued to visit this college and the adjacent villages every year himself, until 1774, a year before his resignation, when his state made it quite impossible for him to do so. He always felt the greatest interest in these pastoral visitations. "However flourishing a graft may be," said he, "if the trunk on which it is grafted is not pruned of its wild shoots, they will be like so many natural branches which will exhaust the graft. The same thing occurs in the culture of souls," continued he, "if one does not cut away all that is wild, that is to say, all that nature produces of herself, the good that one has grafted in cannot fail to perish." As he was unable to go to distant places in person, he supplied his place by the grand-vicar, to whom he especially commended the poor, the widows, and those innocent souls whom indigence exposes to the danger of being lost.

As the observance of discipline in regard to the choir, and vestments, had suffered a little in consequence of his absence from the Cathedral of St. Agatha, he issued an edict, in 1770, renewing the ordinances he had formerly decreed on these subjects. He was informed that a priest had transgressed some of his decrees, especially in regard to some church furniture which he ought to have renewed, whereupon he sequestered twelve ducats from his income, in order to make these repairs, which he entrusted to the management of a canon. He noticed that the church of Bucciano was dirty and too small for the people, and, several times, let the priest know that it required to be enlarged. The priest was afraid of the trouble and expense, and could not resolve to commence the work, but as Alphonsus thought that the holy mysteries could not be decently celebrated in the church, he ordered, in the visitation of 1773, that some adjacent ground should be bought within the space of one month, and he had the satisfaction of seeing a large edifice erected, and one worthy of the purpose for which it was consecrated.

Though he had not sufficient strength to give the spiritual exercises to the priests and religious, as before, he assembled them together at his palace, and during at least three days, reminded them of the duties of their state. Thus Alphonsus, although paralytic, was always vigilant in driving away wolves from his flock, and in procuring the spiritual advantage of his sheep by every possible means. He unceasingly fortified his people by his counsels and the bread of the Word, and sent zealous missionaries wherever he could not go himself. The zeal for the glory of God, which formed a chief trait in his character, actuated him unceasingly, up to the moment when he quitted the diocese. "A hundred bishops put together," Archdeacon Rainone said, "would not have done what Mgr. Liguori alone did, notwithstanding all his infirmities."

We have seen the wise counsels Alphonsus gave to his brother, D. Hercules, on his second marriage; he took, however, a still greater interest in the spiritual welfare of his nephews. D. Hercules had four children by his second wife, three boys and one daughter, and he wished Alphonsus to be the god-father for all four. During D. Marianne's first pregnancy, D. Hercules took her to Arienzo. Both wished that they would obtain a male child; Alphonsus, however, gave a little picture of the Blessed Virgin to Marianne, and said: "You will not give birth to a boy, but to a girl, and I should like you to call her Maria Theresa And this really came to pass. His gift to her, on occasion of the baptism, was a relic of St. Agatha, which he had himself received as a present; it was in a little silver box which did not exceed a few cents in value. D. Hercules then entreated Alphonsus to pray to God to grant him a male child. He went with his wife to Ariola, where Alphonsus then was, during her second pregnancy. When they took leave of him, they again asked of him to pray to God to grant them a son. In reply, he gave D. Marianne two pictures of St. Louis, and told her to be of good courage, and that God would certainly comfort her. Two pictures of the same saint seemed undoubtedly a mystery; but D. Marianne was delivered of twin sons. They were comforted by the birth of a third son after this.

Alphonsus took a great interest in the education of his nephews, that they might imbibe the milk of piety, betimes. The priest, their tutor, related that there came no letter from St. Agatha in which he did not urge his brother to attend to the education of his children. He even composed a short rule for them, which was appropriate to their age, in order that they might pass the day devoutly. In a letter to D. Hercules, of the 4th of December, 1770, he expresses himself thus: "For the love of God often call to mind what I have urged upon you so frequently in regard to the business of your eternal salvation. I am pleased to hear that my little god-sons practice the devotions I have recommended for them. I hope they will be inclined to become saints." When, once, D. Hercules introduced his three sons to their uncle, at Arienzo, he looked at the twins, and said: "If you should lose one of these two, should you be very sad at it?" Alphonsus had prophesied; for after some months, one of the twin-brothers died. The disconsolate and aged father came to St. Agatha to seek for comfort from his saintly brother, when he reminded him of his prophecy. "Do not say any more to me," he said to him, "for your prophecies are too inauspicious." "Fear no more," replied Alphonsus, "for you will preserve the sons who now remain to you, and you will see them live and grow old."

He himself, after having instructed them, gave them confirmation, and whenever they came to see him, he explained to them their duties towards God and their parents, the hideousness of sin, and how much bad conduct dishonors a Christian and a gentleman. He, above all, tried to inspire them with love for Jesus Christ, and a tender devotion towards the Blessed Virgin. When they grew up, D. Hercules intended to place them in the college of the nobility, and communicated his design to his brother, who replied on the 15th of December, 1771, saying: "I cannot approve of your project, because I have not an over good opinion of that establishment; besides, boys are not fit to enter a college until they are at least ten or twelve years of age. In order to prevent their imbibing vice in their very infancy, it is good for them at present to remain with you, and when God wills it, it will be time to think of their going elsewhere; but I repeat, that they ought not to go to the college now. I should like to know where they may best be placed so as to become virtuous as well as learned." He heard that the college of Nunziatella would pass into the hands of the Fathers of the Pious Schools, otherwise called the Tommasque Fathers; he therefore wrote to his brother, saying: "Should this college be under the direction of these Fathers, I should be inclined to wish that my nephews should be entrusted to the management of these good priests, because they are especially pains-taking, from the first, in forming the children who are confided to them properly, and thus your sons would make more progress in three or four years, than they would make elsewhere in twice that time." In another letter, he had said, "The malice of but one is enough to cause the ruin of a hundred. Keep them under your own eyes, and God will provide for the rest, when the proper time shall come. For your part, have their spiritual good at heart, and Providence will take care to supply their temporal wants, without injury to those of the soul."

D. Hercules wished to present his two sons to the king, but Alphonsus wished him not to do it. "If the king were to tell you," he wrote to him, "that he wishes to have them as cadets in the brigade or some other regiment, you will be obliged to make them cadets or soldiers, and thus to risk the loss of their souls as well as that of their bodies. I see that you do not enter into my sentiments as to the way of bringing up these dear little children, and you do the contrary of what I tell you. You are their father, therefore you can do what you please, but I am greatly afraid that you will one day have cause to repent of some misfortune, which you will then be unable to remedy. The love which I bear towards you and your children has made me write thus."

It came to pass that D. Marianne became tormented with scruples, and at last lost her senses. "I sympathize in your sorrow," Alphonsus wrote to D. Hercules, on the 5th of April, 1768, "in regard to the calamity which has befallen D. Marianne, and I beg God to give you patience. Since he has sent you this cross, you must accept it with good courage, otherwise it will become more weighty, and you will be still obliged to bear it." "I beg your reverence," he wrote to F. Villani, on this subject, "to recommend my brother to God, and to write to all our houses to pray for D. Marianne, for my poor brother is in great distress."

D. Charles Cavalieri, the general, and governor of Mantua, a cousin of Alphonsus, died in the beginning of the year 1770, and left to him and D. Hercules sixty thousand ducats. Alphonsus did not hesitate to yield it all without reserve to his brother. He expressed himself in the following terms on this subject, and in regard to all that might happen of a similar sort at any other time: "I do not wish for rents, or possessions, or for any thing else I may have a claim to; even were I to be no longer bishop, I could live on my income from the college of doctors. Be satisfied, therefore, and be not uneasy on this head; it is enough for you to know that I lay no claim to any money from you, either for the past or for the future."

By all this, we see that neither his various and great infirmities, nor his solicitude as a pastor, could stifle the sentiments of tenderness he owed to his nephews. Neither did he forget his dear children of the Congregation. In order to cause virtue and evangelical perfection to flourish, which he had formerly taught by his example, he wrote the following circular on the 26th of February, 1771: "You already know that within a short time God has called several of our companions into eternity; you also know how much the Congregation is persecuted. However, none of all this gives me any alarm. But I am alarmed at seeing some amongst us who have little fervor and numerous faults. St. Philip Neri said that ten holy workmen would suffice for the conversion of the whole world. I write to you this time with tearful eyes, for I hear that several amongst you correspond badly with the end for which God called them into our little Congregation, and that they allow themselves to be governed by a spirit of pride. God cannot dwell in hearts where Christian humility, fraternal charity, and peace are absent. Our sin in not corresponding to God's grace makes me tremble more than the most furious persecutions from men and devils; God will protect us against these enemies, when we live according to His will, and then we can say: '*Si Deus pro nobis, quis contra nos?*' but if we behave ill towards God, He will chastise instead of protecting us. I feel great displeasure when I hear that any of the young amongst you do not live according to evangelical perfection, which is the peculiar duty of laborers of Jesus Christ; but the pain I suffer is still more keen, and the sadness of my heart is still greater, when I am told that faults of insubordination and of non-observance of the rule are committed by the fathers, or by the most aged and most ancient brothers, by those, in short, who ought to serve as models for the younger and those recently received.

"In my letters and my discourses, I have always enforced holy obedience and submission to superiors, who are the interpreters of the will of God here below. On these depend good order, the glory of God, the success of the Missions, and the peace of our souls. . . . Reform and zeal are talked of by some, but no thoughts are entertained by them of reforming their own conduct, which is more evil than that of the rest. . . . God wishes to have obedience and respectful submission to superiors from you, rather than a hundred sacrifices, and a thousand more striking works. God wishes us to be poor, and contented with the poverty we profess; and we ought to thank Him if by His mercy we have bread to eat, and if He provides us with the necessaries of life. He who is not satisfied to lead a life of poverty amongst us, in food and clothing, had better take leave of our society without troubling us further, and can go and live as he likes at home.

"What ought to be the principal aim of him who enters the Congregation, but that of pleasing God and making a good death? and this grace has already been obtained by many of our good brothers, who have now passed into eternity, and who are at present, I feel assured, all occupied in thanking God for having caused them to die in the Congregation.

"Let each of you renounce the vain glory of shining, in preaching the word of God. . . . We must not preach ourselves, but Jesus Christ crucified; we must proclaim His glory, and not display our vanity; I pray God to send His chastisements down on those who preach with vanity; I wish, yes, I wish that they may be rendered unable to ascend the pulpit of truth, and I hope that my desires will be granted. . . .

"I am persuaded that God preserves my life at so advanced an age, in order to remedy the disorders which have arisen, to the detriment of the work of the Missionaries; and I am resolved to remedy them at all costs. God does not require many. It is sufficient if but few remain, if those few be good: a few of this latter sort will do more good than a great number of the imperfect, proud, and disobedient. . . . I say to all who may despise the advice I have just given, that at the judgment day they will find that I shall be their first accuser before the tribunal of Jesus Christ. I have never ceased to give the same warnings to all my brothers, but notwithstanding all that I have said, many turn their backs on God by quitting the Congregation. I shall expect to see these miserable beings, and all who may resemble them, at the day of judgment. . . .

"I advise you all to observe exactly the praiseworthy practices in use amongst us for the promotion of piety and sanctification. I enforce obedience to superiors, and love towards Jesus Christ and His adorable passion. I do the same also in regard to prayer, the spiritual exercises, and the customary retreat. Let him who loves Jesus Christ be obedient, let him be contented with all, and always remain in tranquillity."

It is thus that the saintly founder encouraged his sons, and never let them stand still in the way of perfection. However slight an infraction of the rule might be committed in the Congregation, it did not remain unpunished. "Uncorrected faults," said he, "become an established evil." On hearing that some clerics had become lax in the practice of virtue, and unsteady in the observance of the rule, he was not satisfied with forbidding them to receive holy orders, but wished that they should be sent back into the Noviciate, in order that they might there regain the fervor which was lacking in them, and he did not pardon them until he was assured of their amendment. The exterior trials of the Congregation, however, caused him to act with more circumspection, and he was not so prompt as usual in pronouncing sentence of exclusion, in order not to increase the fire, and cast oil on the flames, by giving the discontented the occasion to join the enemies without. Two subjects were tired of the rule, and no longer took the trouble to observe it; Alphonsus sent for them to Arienzo and spoke to them, but without success. In their blindness they went so far as to say that they would remain in the Congregation in spite even of him, and that if any attempt were made to dismiss them, they would know how to act. Alphonsus, in sorrow that the circumstances of the times did not allow them to be expelled, said that that which he did not do God would do for him; and so it came to pass, one of them asked for a dispensation to go that same year, and the other speedily followed his example. "I know," he wrote to the Superior of Frosinone, "that it is necessary to have the patience of a saint with some, and to go on waiting without gaining what one wishes for; but what can be done? Let us aid the bark as much as we can, and if we meet with scandals, let us not hesitate: let us repress them by the punishments they deserve. It is our duty to punish them, and we must fulfil our duty, let what will happen." And to F. Cajone, he wrote, "I beg your reverence, to govern with all possible mildness, added to great firmness against all attacks against the rule, for they do us more harm than all our persecutions. When it is necessary to use correction, do it privately in the first place, and with charity, and treat every one with affability and kindness."

The persecutions mentioned in these letters were those of which we have spoken above, on occasion of which he had visited Naples; for the enemies of his Congregation had only desisted from their attacks while he was there, resolved to return to the assault at a more opportune time, with renewed strength, and with expedients which it would be more difficult to ward off. Thus they gave a false interpretation to the decision of the king when he said that he did not acknowledge the houses as religious communities, and drew matter for accusation from it, which seemed to furnish them with an engine too formidable to resist. They applied also to the king, and obtained an order to get a copy of the rule which had been approved of by the Pope, in the hope of finding therein arms wherewith to combat the Missionaries advantageously; and then drew up a fresh petition filled with calumnies. As nothing was then talked of but Jesuitism, they took advantage of this and represented the Congregation as forming only a branch of the Jesuits, or rather as being Jesuits in disguise. They thought themselves so sure of success that they considered the Missionaries as already lost. However, all their boasts did not succeed in discouraging Alphonsus. He tried to make his children share in his confidence, and constantly repeated to them: "People say that all will be put an end to, after my death; I maintain that this Congregation does not come from me, and that it does not depend on my existence. It is the work of God, who has preserved it for forty-two years, and he will continue to maintain it. . . . Our stability depends on God in the first place, and then upon our own good conduct; let us therefore be careful to unite ourselves to God, to observe our rules, and to be charitable towards all; let us be contented even with our miseries, and above all, let us strive to be humble, because a little pride may destroy us in the same manner as it has so many other societies." The Fathers of the Congregation had not so much confidence; their fears were founded on the old age and the impaired health of the bishop of St. Agatha. F. Villani went to Arienzo in 1772, accompanied by some of the other fathers, and with tearful eyes implored him to repair again to Naples to appease so furious a tempest. They spoke so plainly that Alphonsus discovered the real cause of their fears, and told them to tranquilize themselves. "Do not be afraid that I shall die yet," he added; but as they continued to urge him still more earnestly, he said to them several times over: "Do not fear for the Congregation, and be assured that I shall live some time longer."

Maffey, at this time, changed his course and his artifices; he applied to the prime minister and left off addressing himself to the minister of ecclesiastical affairs, who had begun to be aware of his character. The prime minister, Marquis Tanucci, looked, or pretended to look on Maffey in a favorable point of view, and attributed all he did to nothing but zeal, the more so as the latter had also gained over some of the minister's clerks by means of his gifts; he therefore ordered the advocate of the king to proceed with the utmost rigor in regard to the heads put forth in the petition, and particularly as to the accusation, that acquisitions had been made by the Missionaries in the kingdom and in the State of Benevento which had been carefully concealed by equivocation, while they ought not to possess anything. When these details were related to Alphonsus, he was not discouraged: "Let us act as we ought towards God," said he, "and He will aid us; for God can do more than man. Let us have recourse to the assistance of prayer. Innocence and prayer are all-powerful." He recommended that prayers should be offered in all the houses, and he never wrote any letters to his friends in which he did not also beg their prayers.

Another cause of distress to our Saint also happened about this time at Palermo. A period of repose had been enjoyed there since the first anxieties that their enemies had caused the Missionaries, though Alphonsus had always feared this calm more than a storm; he had written to them on the 30th of April, 1771, saying: "I feel great consolation at the exercises you have given, I derive comfort from them, but on the other hand these very consolations fill me with fear. St. Theresa said that persecutions are signs that the seed sown produces fruit; you are without persecutions, but here we are plentifully supplied with them; however, God assists us." He was so ill and in such suffering that he signed this letter: 'Brother Alphonsus Maria the cripple.' And indeed this tranquillity was not of long duration in Sicily. Their adversaries returned to attack them with renewed strength; they heaped up calumnies upon calumnies, and stirred up again those which they had already spread against the Missionaries, as being Molinists and Probabilists, dangerous to the State and to the Church, and pursued their persecutions against them even in Naples. When Alphonsus saw affairs take this turn, he did not fail to justify himself and his Congregation to the king and his ministers.

About the same time, Maffey devised a snare into which the Missionaries would have fallen, if Alphonsus, assisted by light from on high, had not been able to avoid it. Maffey got into new difficulties with the people of Iliceto, and tried to secure the Missionaries as mediators between him and his adversaries; there were several influential persons, their friends, who approved of this proposal, and exhorted them to bring the negociation to a satisfactory end; but Alphonsus, being informed of all this, answered: "It would be the means of alienating the minds of the inhabitants from us, without giving any hope of a reconciliation with Maffey; he is an untractable man, whom it is impossible to pacify, besides, what we might say to the people in favor of Maffey would be of no avail; they would all believe that we speak, not because he is right, but to win his friendship. On the other hand, everything makes me believe, that in whatever way one may turn in the matter, right will always be found on the side of the people. . . . I am then decidedly of opinion, that no one belonging to the Congregation must accept the office of mediator on any terms." When Maffey saw that his scheme on the subject of mediation was disconcerted, he endeavored to render the complaints of the people against him ineffectual, by representing the Missionaries as instigators and as the leaders of a party, and the credit he enjoyed with the Marquis of Tanucci influenced that minister in his favor. When Alphonsus saw that the fire was lit at both extremities, he felt that it was time to try and prevent a general conflagration; he therefore recalled his sons from Sicily. "If God wishes us to be there," he said to them, "he will not lack means of procuring our return, and you will then return blessing God and the king." This retreat was a cause of lively distress to Mgr. Lanza. "Who cannot see the triumph of hell therein?" he said. "You will go away from Sicily, but you shall return there again, in spite of hell; and if it is necessary for me to sell my mitre and my cross in order to attain this end, I will sell them for God, for you, and for this work." The most respectable of the people of the town and of the clergy shared in their pastor's sentiments; and though the departure of the Missionaries took place secretly, and during the night, a great multitude accompanied them to the shore, deploring the loss which their departure would be to the town, and the blank they would leave there; and they had scarcely embarked, when the clergy and all the religious orders of Girgenti, the chevaliers and ladies, magistrates and men of letters, united to address petitions to the king to obtain their return. Some of them had also recourse to Alphonsus for the same purpose; and thirty-eight ladies in particular, and twenty-eight chevaliers, wrote to him, saying: "As we have addressed an energetic petition to the king to implore his clemency, the urgency of our spiritual wants also compels us to implore your lordship's assistance."

CHAPTER XXVI.

Alphonsus seeks to resign. He publishes several Works. His Congregation is established in the States of the Church. He publishes still other Works. He assists at the death of Pope Clement XIV. His sentiments on the Election of a new Pope. His Missionaries return to Sicily.

ALPHONSUS, seeing the dangers his Congregation incurred, on one hand, and believing, on the other, that his infirmities and great age rendered him of little use to his Church while he could still be of service to his sons, resolved again to resign the episcopate. He had thought of doing so before, but the differences which existed between the court of Naples and that of Rome in regard to the election of bishops, had made him defer taking any step in the matter, from the fear that his Church would be left without a shepherd for a long time. When the two courts had settled the matter in debate, he represented to the Pope in the year 1772, through Cardinal Castelli, all the reasons which led him to tender his resignation, protesting at the same time that he was far from wishing to do his own will, and that he meant to depend entirely on that of his Holiness, and that he was equally ready to give up the bishopric, or to die under the burden of his office. The Pope was greatly edified by his submission to the head of the Church; but as he was aware of the very great good Alphonsus still effected, he replied to him in a brief, in which he expressed himself in the most consolatory manner, in order to encourage him to continue his administration; and when Cardinal Castelli solicited him to consider the old age of the saintly bishop, and to release him from his burthen, his Holiness replied: "That it would suffice if D. Alphonsus ruled over his diocese from his bed:" and when the Cardinal wanted to show him his incapacity in regard to making his visitations, the Pope answered him: "One simple prayer addressed by him to God from his bed, is worth more than if he went about his diocese a hundred times." Alphonsus, when he heard that the Pope's opinion was contrary to his request, bent his head, and submitted his will to that of the Vicar of Jesus Christ.

The Fathers of the Congregation, and several bishops, his friends, seeing him in such a deplorable state that his very appearance inspired compassion, thought they ought to persuade him to make a formal resignation, but however feeble he felt for so weighty a charge, he would never consent to this. "The voice of the Pope," said he, "is to me as the voice of God, and I shall die content now under the burthen of the episcopate." As they went on to urge him with reasons which seemed to authorize this step, he one day extricated himself from their importunities by answering cheerfully: "The present Pope is a man who does not yield easily; if I were to give him my resignation, he would not accept it; let us be patient, and wait for his successor." At this every one burst out laughing, as Alphonsus was nearly broken down and paralytic, while the Pope was still robust and young, numbering seventeen years less in age. He had prophesied truly, however. Pope Clement XIV, contrary to all expectations, died two years after this, while Alphonsus continued to live on and to labor. Another reason made him afterwards renounce the idea of abdicating, and even caused him to expel the thought of it as a temptation. Numerous candidates aspired to succeed him in the church of St. Agatha, and he heard that the Pope would be obliged, in order to supply his place, to yield to the efforts of a powerful party, who favored a subject who was unfit to govern the diocese. He said on this occasion: "I would rather die the most painful death, than see my beloved sheep in the mouth of a wolf."

In a circular, addressed, about this time, to all the houses of his Congregation, after having exhorted them to a more exact observance of the rule, and a more fervent practice of virtue, in order to merit the favor and assistance of God, he says: "I repeat to you, the tempest rages violently.

Let each one recommend the Congregation to God, and let three litanies be said daily, in common, with three '*De Profundis.*' We stand in need of prayer, and there is no one who will aid us but the Blessed Virgin; but prayers will be of little use to us, if we do not correct our faults. I can do no more; I who am very decrepid, and in bed, all paralyzed. What should I or could I do? It is you, my children, who must support the Congregation, and be assured, that, if we behave properly, God will always assist us, and the more poor, and despised, and persecuted we may be, the more good we shall do, and the greater also will be the reward which Jesus Christ will give us in heaven."

Notwithstanding all the bodily and mental sufferings with which he was laden, Alphonsus did not cease to think and labor for the welfare of the Church in general. In order to impress the sacred wounds of Jesus crucified in the hearts of the faithful, he wrote down the points of his meditations on the subject. The title of this little book is: "Reflections on divers spirtual subjects." It is considered by every one to be admirably adapted to win the hearts of men to that of Jesus Christ. It contains a lively description of the whole passion of our Blessed Saviour, as well as of the most powerful motives to excite us to love Him. Although he had combatted the unbelieving in a dissertation which was published in the year 1756, and had done so again still more recently, in his book 'On the Truth of Faith,' yet in consideration of the ravages they were continually making, he once more attacked them, in a dissertation entitled, 'Reflections on the Truth of Divine Revelation, against the opposing principles of the Deists.' "If the enemies of our religion," said he, "are never satisfied, although they fight against it by thousands of books, which they publish daily, why should the friends of religion get tired of defending it?"

In his zeal which knew no bounds, he also undertook another work, which was intended to be of use to religion, and to separate the true doctrine from the errors which in former ages had endeavored to stifle it. In order to place all the evils which the Church has suffered before the eyes of the faithful, and to show them all the noxious things which error has at all time emitted against her, he put together in three volumes the history of all the heresies which have existed since the birth of Christianity up to our own days. In this work he also animadverts particularly on the innovators of modern times, and shows the contradictions of their doctrine, and the invariable stability of the Roman Church. This history of the heresies was finished in 1772, and published under the title of "The triumph of the Church." The author defends the infallibility of the Pope and his pre-eminence in the Church in a special manner, and combats the errors of Jansenius and his followers, in particular. For this reason, a canon who held the Gallican opinions strongly, did not approve of the work and opposed it, but this opposition was of no consequence; it was printed after the saintly author had written a letter to the ecclesiastical examiner.

Another work caused him more serious embarrassment; it was his collection of Sermons, which he published about the same time. One of his enemies denounced this work to the authorities, as containing things which might be displeasing to the Sovereign, and therefore the publication of it was hindered for nearly a year. But at last when the report of the examiner became known, the intrigue was put an end to, and the work was published, to the satisfaction of the minister, and the glory of Alphonsus. Some letters were added to this book, in the form of an appendix. The first is written to a young student, deliberating on the choice of a state of life. It places before him the great good he may derive from the spiritual exercises made during a retreat. In the second, Alphonsus represents the great utility of missions to a bishop, and settles all the difficulties concerning them; and in the last, which is addressed to a religious, he treats of the manner of preaching with apostolical simplicity.

We have also another very precious little book which the saintly bishop published at this time, under the title of

'The true Happiness of Man, and on his submission to the will of God.' One may truly say that this treatise was inspired, rather than composed. A pious person was so moved by the benefit he had himself derived from it, that he caused it to be printed and gratuitously distributed every where.

In the year 1773, God willed, that, though in the midst of so many troubles, Alphonsus should yet see his Congregation happily augmented by two new foundations, in the states of the Church. Mgr. Sarni, the Bishop of Aquinas, having ardently wished for his Missionaries for many years without being able to obtain them, renewed his entreaties in March of this year. In the following November, Alphonsus destined nine fathers for these missions, under the direction of D. Francis of Paul. The labors of the missionaries, who were divided in two companies, were every where attended with the greatest success, and the fruits of salvation which they produced caused them to be earnestly asked for, to preach also in other dioceses. During the course of these missions, D. Francis, with another father, visited the celebrated abbey of Casamary, of the Order of the Trappists. These religious proposed to them to establish a house of the Congregation, for the advantage of the numerous inhabitants of the neighboring country, at Scifelli, (which is not far from La Trappe,) where there was a church, just then vacated by John Louis Arnaud, who, in his zeal for aiding the villages in these parts, had erected it as well as a commodious habitation for himself, and who had been lately nominated by Mgr. Giacomini, Bishop of Verali, as his Grand Vicar. The bishop, when he heard of this plan of the Trappists, was filled with joy, and agreed with D. Arnaud in wishing for the projected foundation, and wrote to Alphonsus to inform him of the neglected state of the souls in those parts, in order to obtain his consent to it. When the bishop had obtained also the consent of Pope Clement XIV, the foundation was decided on, Alphonsus looking on it as inspiration from on high. "I have consented to let this foundation be made," he wrote to D. Francis of Paul on the 28th of May, 1773. "I have written to thank the Abbé Arnaud for it; it is to him that we are indebted for all concerning it." The fathers were to live with D. Arnaud; so Alphonsus was most anxious that perfect harmony should exist between them and him, and took particular pains in advising F. Francis of Paul, the Rector of the new house, to do all that he could to obtain this end. "Take care," he wrote to him, "not to displease him in things which are not absolutely contrary to the good order of the house. Many things must be yielded for the sake of peace and convenience. He has conferred good on us, and may do so again. Let him see that you esteem him, and listen to his opinions as far as possible. Nevertheless, I advise you to keep up the observance of the rule from the commencement of this foundation. I beg you to do this for the love of God and your neighbor."

Poverty and misery were also the portion of this new house. Alphonsus did not fail to assist it; not, however, with the revenues of his diocese, but with that which he received at Naples from the College of Doctors. "Tell all the subjects in my name," he wrote to F. Francis of Paul, "to remember that this foundation is new, and situated in another kingdom. In all new foundations it is necessary to suffer, and to suffer much, both on account of their poverty, and also because one has to deal with people one does not know. If they wish to please Jesus Christ, let them read what the saints suffered in the first establishments, and how they thereby became saints."

At this period, the Fathers were also laboring to be established in Rome, but Alphonsus did not approve of this project; he replied to him who had made to him this proposition: "I have read your long letter, but I do not approve of your reasons; what is the good of wasting time about these things, since God does not wish for them?" When the Jesuits were suppressed, the Pope, of his own accord, conceived the idea of giving those of the Congregation a convent in Rome. F. Francis of Paul believed that Alphonsus would at length favor his wishes, but he answered him as follows, on the 25th August, 1774: "I am rejoiced at what you tell me about Mgr. Macedonio, and about the Pope's favorable disposition in our regard. But we have cause to thank God that this affair has come to nothing. If the Pope had persisted in such a design, I would have written energetically to him, even if I had had the whole Congregation against me, to try and get him to abandon this project. What have we to do in Rome, let me ask you? The Congregation would be lost, because we should be distracted from the work of our mission, and we should lose sight of the end of our institute. A bastard work would result from this, and that would be all the profit we should derive from it. There are many besides us, who can do all that we have been asked to do in Rome, and in the midst of the great multitudes who inhabit this town, what good can we produce there? . . . . If we are placed in the midst of prelates, lords, and courtly people, adieu to missions, and adieu to the country; we shall become courtiers, greedy after praise and riches. May Jesus Christ deliver us from this. Finally, let us thank God for the good opinion the Pope has of us." He was more pleased with foundations in towns or villages which he saw were destitute and deprived of the bread of life, as was seen, when, about the same time, he was applied to for a new foundation at Frosinone, also in the ecclesiastical States, and in the diocese of Verali. The discalceated Augustinian Fathers had abandoned a church and a hospice which they had had under the title of St. Mary of Grace; these were offered to the Missionaries, and Alphonsus did not hesitate to accept the foundation. Besides, there being a great number of little villages around, which wanted evangelical laborers, there were two other considerations which caused our saint to agree to this proposition. The first was, that in those houses there would be freedom from the persecutions which were suffered in the others, and no obstacle to the exact observance of the rule in all its rigor, which appeared to him as a manifest sign of the will of God. In the second place, he thought, as the two houses were to be near each other, they would be of mutual assistance; however, they were not established there before the 20th of June, 1776.

In the year 1774, Alphonsus gave a new proof how deeply he had been impressed by that saying of the Holy Ghost, "Particula boni doni ne te prætereat," and how faithful he was, (considering *the time* allotted to each man by God to be employed in promoting His glory, to be this good gift,) in fulfilling the vow he had made not to lose any part of it. It was the publishing of his explication of the Psalms, of which he himself says, dedicating it to Pope Clement XIV: "This is a book which I have written in the last years of my life, and at an age when my exhausted strength announces my approaching end. . . . I hope that your Holiness will approve of this work, which may be useful to a great number of the faithful who say the divine office in a language which they do not understand, who are ignorant of the signification of the words, and far more of the sense of the Psalms." This work, which was a difficult one, and composed at such an advanced age, was the admiration of the most learned men at Naples. Of all the eulogiums passed upon it, let the following suffice: "Alphonsus, by his labors," said B. Cervone, who afterwards became Bishop of Aquila, "has shown that he is worthy to rival the holy bishops of the primitive Church; for without speaking of the many other works by which he brought back to the road of virtue many who had wandered from it, or strengthened in goodness many who were already walking in it, had the saintly bishop not written anything else in support of religion and the Church, this work alone would have sufficed to render him worthy of immortality." Alphonsus had added a statement of his system on the rule of moral actions, in an appendix to this work, which he also submitted to the Pope for correction, if any error should be found therein.

The same year, 1774, brought to light his book on the "Triumphs of the Martyrs." In writing which, he had intended to kindle in all hearts a greater degree of love towards Jesus Christ, and a greater zeal for that faith for which the martyrs have so cheerfully given their lives, their blood, their all, and which was, in his time, the object of so many attacks from the mis-called philosophers of the eighteenth century; thus showing himself, as the same B. Cervone expressed it, "full of solicitude for the grand affair, that of salvation, and omitting nothing which could open or facilitate the road to the celestial country, either to himself or to others."

While he was thus occupied for the glory of God and for the good of souls, Baron Sarnelli and D. Maffey never rested, and left nothing undone in order to calumniate his Missionaries with fresh accusations, not seeing any better method of insuring the success of their cause. Laden with infirmity and occupations as was the poor old man, he showed that he still remembered his former profession as a lawyer, and arranged the plan of defence himself. "I have got ready my answers," he wrote to F. Villani, on the 2d of June, 1774, "on the most important point. As this answer must be presented in writing, I will place it in the hands of Advocate Celano, in order that he may arrange it in his own way." However, he was in a state of great uneasiness. "I have caused prayers to be said every where," he wrote in another letter, "I have had masses celebrated, and I know not what more I can do. . . . Get the people to say an Ave before the sermon, and get prayers said in as many monasteries and places as you can." And in another to F. Majone, who resided in Naples: "When the ministers are spoken to, the Congregation must not be named, I only ought to be spoken of, for I am the person principally aimed at in this affair." He recommended also the matter, in writing, to the counsellors of St. Clare, and got some persons of great influence to mediate for them, and especially the Prince della Riccia. He wrote himself to the Marquis of Cito, at that time the President of the royal council, and also solicited Nicholas Vincenzio, the chief minister of the Court della Sommaria, for his intervention in their favor with the President. He addressed also a memorial to the king, in which he, without injuring any one, represented the innocence of his Missionaries, the labor to which they daily gave themselves up for the welfare of the kingdom, and their respectful submission to all the royal decisions; and especially reminded him of the real intentions of his father, King Charles III, who had authorized the four houses in the kingdom. He also wrote a long circular to all the houses of the Congregation, in which he exhorts all to increased fervor in the exercise of all virtues and the observance of rule, as the best means to secure divine protection for the Congregation, of which he says, prophesying its future prosperity: "I am sure that Jesus Christ looks upon our little Congregation with most loving eyes, that he loves it as the apple of his eye, as we see by experience; for in the midst of so many persecutions, he never ceases to protect us and to render us more worthy to labor for his glory in divers countries, by the assistance of His manifest graces. I shall not see it, for my death is at hand, but I feel assured that our little flock will increase more and more, not by becoming richer and more highly thought of by the world, but by procuring the glory of God, and that, through our labors, Jesus Christ will be better known and loved by others. A day will come when we shall see each other again, and be re-united together in that eternal abode where we shall never more be separated; and where we shall also be united to hundreds of thousands of persons, who once lived without the love of God, and who through our means recovered grace, and who will dwell with the Lord forever, and form our glory and joy for all eternity. Ought not this thought alone to stimulate us to love Jesus Christ with all our hearts, and to cause others to love Him also?" He had certainly been favored with some special revelation, which his humility made him conceal, for the same year he wrote to F. Majone, "I am full of joy, because it seems to me that the Blessed Virgin will bring us safe and sound out of this tempest. Therefore let us abandon ourselves into the hands of Jesus

Christ; let us pray to Him, and He will do all for His greater glory."

Alphonsus, who had so many times given proof of his solicitude, not only for his diocese and the Congregation, but also for the Church in general, by the many books he composed and published, as soon as he was aware of a particular want of the faithful, or whenever there appeared a wolf threatening the flock of Christ; could not but be painfully affected by the troubles which disquieted the Church during the pontificate of Clement XIV, and by the misfortunes these troubles forbode to religion: they caused him the greatest alarm, and he continually offered up prayers to Heaven for the peace of the Sovereign Pontiff and of the much persecuted Church. No one can well imagine how he sorrowed over the storm which raged against the Jesuits on all sides; he never spoke of it without the deepest sense of distress. "It is nothing but intrigue on the part of the Jansenists and unbelieving," said he, "if they succeed in overthrowing the company, their wishes will be accomplished; and if this bulwark falls, what convulsions will there not be in the Church and State? If the Jesuits are once destroyed, the Pope and the Church will be in a most disastrous situation. The Jesuits are not the only aim of the Jansenists; they aim at the company in order thereby to be more certain of striking at the Church and State."

Clement XIV suppressed the Society of Jesus, in a brief dated the 22d of July, 1773; this was a terrible blow to Alphonsus. When he received the brief of the Pope, he adored the judgment of God in silence for some time, then he said: "The will of the Pope is the will of God;" and did not utter another word to manifest how much he suffered interiorly. One day, the Grand-Vicar and other persons of distinction wished to cast blame on the dispositions of the Sovereign Pontiff. "Poor Pope," exclaimed the saintly bishop, "what could he do in the difficult circumstances in which he was placed, and when so many crowned heads united in demanding their suppression? As for us, we have only to adore the secret judgment of God, and be at peace. However, I assert, that if but one single Jesuit be left in the world, he alone would be enough to re-establish the company."

No one is ignorant of the constantly increasing troubles in which the Pope found himself after this suppression; the deplorable state of the Church and of its head filled the Bishop of St. Agatha with the deepest sorrow. "Pray for the Pope," he wrote to F. Francis of Paul, on the 27th of June, 1774. "N., who has come from Rome, told me that the Pope is overwhelmed with sadness, and in fact he has cause to be so, for there does not seem to be a shadow of peace for the Church. Pray for the Pope; God knows how I feel for his afflictions!" "Pray for the Pope," he said in another letter, to F. Villani. "For my part I never cease to do so. Pray for the Pope; I have heard that he wishes for death, so great is his distress at all the trials which afflict the Church." In another letter, of the 23d of July, to F. Paul, he says: "The Pope suffers a great deal on account of the pretensions of the crowns, and especially on account of Venice. . . . I do nothing but repeat over and over again, 'Poor Pope, poor Pope, who is tried on all sides!' I pray for him that God may come to his aid." On the 25th of August, he again wrote, saying: "I hear from various quarters that the Pope is in sorrow, that he is shut up and does no business. Let us pray to God to deliver him from this profound melancholy."

On the morning of the 21st of September, Alphonsus, after having ended Mass, threw himself, contrary to his custom, into his arm-chair; he was cast down and silent, he made no movement of any kind, and never articulated a word. He remained in that state, all that day and all the following night. The servants, seeing the state he was in, did not know what was going to happen, and remained up, and at the door of his room, but no one dared enter it. On the morning of the 22d, he had not changed his position, and no one knew what to think of it. However, when the day became further advanced, he rang the bell to announce that he intended to celebrate Mass. At this signal, all the people in the house hurried to him with eagerness. On seeing so many people, the Saint asked what was the matter, with an air of surprise. "You have," they replied, "neither spoken nor eaten any thing for two days, and you ceased to give any signs of life." "That is true," replied he, "but you do not know that I have been with the Pope, who has just died." Ere long, the tidings of the death of Pope Clement XIV was received; he had passed to a better life on the 22d September, at seven o'clock in the morning, the very moment when Alphonsus came to himself.

Cardinal Castelli, well aware of the high reputation for sanctity possessed by Alphonsus, and knowing what a great veneration the sacred college of Cardinals had for the holy man, determined to ask him to write, before the Conclave began, a long letter on all the abuses which ought to be reformed in the various orders of the ecclesiastical hierarchy. The Cardinal wished this memorial to be presented to the Conclave, and that it should serve to determine the election of a Pope capable of remedying all the ills of the Church. Some people who were attached friends of the Saint, were commissioned to make this request to him to overcome his humility. The following letter, of the 23d of October, 1774, was his reply:

"Most Rev. Cardinal:—You ask for my sentiments on the present affairs of the Church and on the election of a Pope. Alas! what sentiments can I worthily express to you, who am but a poor bishop? All I can find to say is, that it is necessary to pray, and to pray much; for in order to raise the Church from the state of remissness and confusion into which all classes have fallen, prudence and human wisdom are insufficient, and nothing less than the powerful arm of God will suffice. There are few among the bishops who have a true zeal for the salvation of souls. Most, if not all, of the communities of religious are relaxed; and in the confusion which surrounds us, observances are destroyed, and rules are despised and treated as if they were not. The secular clergy are in a still worse state, so that there is an absolute necessity for a general reform among all ecclesiastics, in order, afterwards, to be able to reform the conduct and the manners of the laity. Therefore we must pray to Jesus Christ to give His Church a head who has something more than knowledge and human prudence, to give her one who through the spirit of God may be filled with a great love and zeal for His glory, and who may be totally detached from all parties, so as to be able to resist the suggestions of human respect. If we ever have the misfortune to have a Pope who has not God's glory in view, He will not assist him, and things will become worse and worse. Prayer is the sole remedy for such great misfortunes. For my part, I have not only enjoined all the houses of my Congregation to pray with more than ordinary fervor for the election of a new Pontiff, but I have also ordered all the secular and regular clergy of my diocese to say the Collect, '*Pro eligendo summo Pontifice,*' during mass. This is the best advice I can give you; I often pray about this election during the day myself, but what can my poor prayers avail? Nevertheless, I put all my trust in the merits of Jesus Christ and of the Blessed Virgin, and I hope that God will comfort me by letting me see the Church relieved, before my death, which my age and infirmities tell me cannot be far distant.

"I also wish to see all the disorders which exist done away with, and a thousand different ideas come into my mind on the subject which I should ardently wish to communicate to you, if the knowledge of what I am did not take all boldness from me, by convincing me that it is not for me to wish to reform the world. I should also like the future Pope, when he has to supply any vacancies in the College of Cardinals, to select only the best informed and the most zealous among those who may be proposed to him, and that he should request all princes not to present any but men of well-known piety and learning as candidates for a Cardinalship. I should also wish him to exercise firmness, in refusing livings to those who are already sufficiently provided for in all their state can demand; to repress luxury in all prelates, and to fix the number of their servants of all sorts, so that they should only have so many valets-de-chambre, so many other servants, so many horses, &c. This would be a method of putting a stop to the slander and detraction of our enemies. He ought to take pains never to confer benefices on any, but those who have merited well on account of what they have done for the Church.

"I should wish him to be very strict in choosing bishops, and that he should obtain information, on all hands, about those who are proposed as candidates for this high and important office in the Church, and that he should be certified as to the goodness of their character and their doctrine, which are indispensable qualities in ruling over a diocese. It is on these chief pastors that the good of religion and the salvation of souls chiefly depend. I should like him to require all metropolitans, and others, to inform him, in secret, as to any bishops who are careless as to the welfare of their flocks. I should also wish him to threaten with suspension, or the supervision of a Vicar-Apostolic, both negligent bishops and those who are non-resident, as well as those who scandalize the world by the luxury of their attendants, and by the excessive expense of their equipage, their festivities, &c. In some cases it does not do to be afraid of putting these threats into execution; for such corrections not only purify the Church from the corruptions which sully her, but they hinder other delinquent bishops from falling, through the fear of public blame, which admonishes them of their backslidings and causes them to return to a sense of their duty, to the great advantage of their flocks.

"In fine, why should not the future Pope be backward in granting favors which are injurious to the maintenance of discipline; such, for instance, as that of permitting nuns to leave their enclosure to enter into the world without any real necessity for it? He ought not readily to consent to the secularization of religious, on account of the number of evils which result from it, and above all, he ought to constrain all religious whatsoever, to the primitive observance of the rules of their institute, at least, in all the most important points.

"I will not tire you by saying more; I can do nothing further than pray God to give us a Pastor full of His own Spirit. And now I conclude with profound respect, and assure you that I am," &c.

While the saintly bishop was thus occupied for the well-being of the Church at large, for the administration of his diocese, and for the existence of his Congregation, hell too did not slumber, but was on the watch for opportunities of injuring its dreaded antagonist. Up to this time, the enemies of the Congregation had spared its head, and had only fought against its members; but on seeing they could not injure the members while they respected the head, they turned their weapons against him too. As they could find nothing to condemn in his private life, they blamed his doctrine, and raised a cry that his work on Moral Theology was full of decisions of too indulgent a nature, and above all, that it contained the lax sentiments attributed to the Jesuits. This was a sure means of producing a sensation and of exciting suspicion, at that time. Thus the whole Congregation became an object of suspicion, for it seemed impossible for it to escape the taint of the errors of which its founder was accused. But God, who kills and brings to life, caused this same Moral Theology to be approved by the king at the very time that its adversaries expected to see it condemned. Some copies of the work were sent from Naples and reached the custom-house, where they were stopped by the king's procurator-general, who was prejudiced against it, and wished it to be examined with all possible strictness by a Conventual Father. This learned religious assured him in the report, that the doctrine was perfectly sound, and that there was not any proposition which deserved censure. The procurator was rejoiced at this news, and regretted having been obliged to give pain to the saintly old man. It was thus that Heaven frustrated the plots of the wicked, and turned them to the confusion of their authors and the glory of the servant of God.

D. Maffey and Baron Sarnelli, on the other hand, were impatient for the overthrow of the Congregation, and did all they could, in order to accelerate the coming of the day when the debates occasioned by their accusations were to be held in the royal court; and as they flattered themselves with the expectation of victory, they were continually multiplying petitions for hastening this day, which they regarded as that of the Missionaries' defeat. These, and especially F. Villani, again begged Alphonsus to go and cast himself personally at the feet of the king. He replied to them with a smile: "What a figure I should cut before the king in my present state! Would he not take me for a phantom, and order me out of his presence? My brothers, let us place ourselves in God's hands and let us not trust in human means; for the Congregation is a divine work, and not the work of man, who is incapable of supporting it." The adversaries succeeded in fixing the opening of the debates in the royal court for the 24th of December. But while they endeavored to move heaven and earth in order to injure the Missionaries, Alphonsus, on his side, as he was accustomed, did not neglect anything in order to obtain God's mercy. Besides the accustomed penances and mortifications, he had recourse again to the celebration of Masses, the prayers of pious souls, and alms. By his order the Blessed Sacrament was exposed in all the houses, and the psalm "*Qui habitat*" was recited in common in the church, together with an Ave to the Blessed Virgin for the persecutors. Another cause of trouble arose, which was unlooked for. As the Missionaries kept on the defensive, the attacks of the accusation were immediately warded off by their counsel, so that the projectors began to fear that all the plots which they had contrived would be useless, and that the truth would be manifest to the sight of the royal counsellors. They therefore thought of a fresh contrivance; by means of a protector who supported them with the ministers, they managed so that the end of the debate should not take place before the royal council, and that the papers containing the complaints and wrongs, (or rather the calumnies of the adversaries,) should pass through the hands of the commissioner, Ferdinand de Leo, who was to make himself acquainted with their contents, and to make his report of them to the royal court. The appointment of this commissioner took away from the Missionaries all hope; for he was an enemy to all new monasteries in the kingdom, as well as new institutes, and indeed he could scarcely bear the ancient ones. And from some words he had dropped, they could easily conjecture how unfavorable his report would be.

The Missionaries had manifested a wish to come to an amicable arrangement with Sarnelli, for three years, and some mediators had labored to manage so that he should keep the vineyard left to the Congregation by his brother, and give a sum of money in compensation for the pious works his brother had intended to establish, but Alphonsus thought that he ought in conscience to oppose such an arrangement: "I must weigh these matters well," he wrote to F. Majone, on the 4th of December, 1774. "If this conciliatory plan should ever be acted on, I shall have to consult the learned and those versed in spiritual matters, in order to put my conscience to rest;" and to F. D. Matthias Corrado, he wrote: "In case I were to give up the vineyard to the Baron, in return for the equivalent indemnity, my conscience would become uneasy, for I should have interpreted the wishes of the dead man." But there was no need of all this; the Baron, who believed himself sure of victory, wanted to enter into possession of the property without being obliged to give an account of the charitable intentions of his brother's will.

As the Congregation was in imminent danger of being destroyed, Alphonsus was advised to write to Naples in order to gain the patronage of a lady who had great influence with the procurator; but as he entertained some fears that God might be displeased at it, he replied as follows, to F. Majone: "I will never do such a thing; let the Congregation be destroyed rather than become the occasion for even the shadow of any sin."

The tears of the just are never shed in vain, and the Lord, who never permits them to be persecuted except to show forth His mercy and His glory more brightly, also comforted Alphonsus in the midst of these trying circumstances. The inhabitants of Girgenti had never ceased to petition for the return of the Missionaries, as we have already seen. The Prince of Trabbia amongst others, who enjoyed the king's favor, did not forget to intercede for them with his majesty, through the medium of his brother, the bishop. The king gave a favorable hearing to these representations, and permitted them to return to the island, by a royal decree. Their adversaries, on seeing their wishes thus defeated, put an end to their intrigues, and Alphonsus, having, in concert with the bishops, decided on the return of the Missionaries, their departure took place in April, 1775. In order to render their entrance into Girgenti as glorious as possible, Mgr. Lanza had wished them to stop at Aragone, three miles from the town, there to be met and received by a brilliant suite of carriages and a retinue of ecclesiastics and gentlemen, but the Fathers declined this honor. However, several carriages and persons of distinction came to meet them, though they had not announced the time of their arrival; and they were received at the gates of Girgenti by the clergy and the citizens, who were perfectly delighted to see them. When Mgr. Lanza saw them again, he could not help exclaiming with the holy old Simeon: "Now dost Thou dismiss Thy servant, O Lord, according to Thy words, in peace; because mine eyes have seen Thy salvation!" And in fact, on the 23d of this same month of May, this zealous and worthy prelate fell asleep in the arms of the Missionaries, to go and enter into eternal rest. However, God provided them another protector, and one as full of zeal and love for the Congregation, in his eminence, Cardinal Branciforti, who succeeded him in February of the following year, 1776.

CHAPTER XXVII.

Alphonsus' zeal during his Episcopate in reforming his secular and regular Clergy—in removing scandals in general, and preventing sin in all classes of the Laity. How God assists him in his efforts.

HAVING now reached the termination of Alphonsus' episcopate, when he resigned the bishopric and retired into his Congregation, it is not right that we should follow him into his retreat, without giving more in detail an account of his conduct in the administration of his diocese, as otherwise we should omit many particulars and many of his maxims and actions, which will manifest more especially his virtues and his zeal during his government. F. Caputo thus describes the holy bishop's conduct in his endeavors to make his clergy edifying and worthy of the sacred ministry: "His lordship's first reproof was full of sweetness and humility; if he saw no amendment, he gave a second reprimand of mingled sweetness and severity. If after this he found that the person was incorrigible, chastisement soon followed, and in such a case if the king and the Pope himself had wished to interpose in his favor, they would have met with a refusal." Amongst all the sins, drunkenness and incontinence, were those he abhorred the most. He said that the drunkard is not a man, but a brute; that one can even expect more from the brute than from the drunkard; and he looked upon drunkenness as the source of the most infamous vices: it was, in his eyes, even when indulged in only in private, a complete dishonor to a minister of the Church. He had an equal abomination for the vice of impurity, and was in the habit of saying, that he saw no difference between a sow which wallows in the mire, and a man who is addicted to this vice. He compassionated him who had made a false step through weakness, but he could not put up with him who was the voluntary and obstinate slave of passion. He had always salutary remedies at hand for the first, and did not recur to very severe measures with them; his principal mode of causing them to think seriously was the spiritual exercises. But when he saw that the vice had taken root, he did not make any compromise, but used the strongest methods for destroying the evil. One day, not knowing what more to do in order to cure one of these miserable men, he sent for him to speak to him, but took care to place a large crucifix on the floor at the entrance of his room. On seeing this, the wretched man was seized with terror and wanted to draw back. "No," said Alphonsus, "enter and trample it underfoot, it would not be perhaps the first time." He then gave free vent to the ardor of his zeal, and set before him the enormity of his sin. The guilty man was full of confusion and repentance; he burst into tears, and promised to amend; and really did so, giving afterwards full satisfaction to his bishop. When he had in vain exhausted mild measures, in trying to deliver men from these passions, his ordinary remedies were exile and suspension; exile, in order to break through the attachment, and suspension, to avenge the dignity of the sacred ministry. He had also recourse to the aid of the secular power, when there was need, (as we have seen him do in his visitations,) and no personal considerations were ever able to move him, or shake his firmness. His severity in regard to the refractory was so well known, that it soon was a commonly received opinion in the diocese, that if one had begun to be an object of the bishop's watchful observation, there was no further chance of rest for him unless he gave clear proofs of amendment. God also assisted him by exemplary chastisements. One of these weak men he had warned in a paternal manner, but when he saw that he fell back into vice again, he had him shut up in the prison of St. Agatha; even after this chastisement, the miserable man did not amend: "Let him alone," he said then to the episcopal vicar, "God's justice will reach him." He was carried off by sudden death some time afterwards, although he was in the prime of life.

In his dealings towards those whom he had suspended or banished, he never lost sight of the spirit of charity, especially when sin was united to poverty. He once sent for one whose conduct scandalized the people, and kept him for a fortnight in his palace, after which he sent him to the house of St. Angelo, at his own expense. Another, also, was kept for a long while in the house of Ciorani, and supported at his cost. The same course was pursued towards a great many others. Two others, whom he had suspended and banished out of the diocese, received from him two carlins a day for their maintenance; to others, who were suspended, he assigned an adequate indemnification for their fees out of his own revenue, till after a lapse of time, he thought them in a right state of mind, and sent them the pardon, with the power of celebrating.

His inflexibility towards those who remained obstinate in sin, changed into mercy, when he saw that they repented. He had even an admirable degree of charity for those whom he had reproved and who gave proof of real amendment; he received them to his arms with all the tenderness of a father, and put an end to all proceedings begun against them in the ecclesiastical court. One, belonging to a noble and distinguished family, who lived in a scandalous way, had been sent for three times, but he did not deign to give any satisfaction. Alphonsus told his Grand-Vicar to prepare the cause, and gave orders that he should not be shown in if he should come to speak to him, but should be sent to the Grand-Vicar. The culprit not being willing to see his name figure in the courts of justice, hastened to the palace; but being refused admittance, he made a great noise in the ante-chamber, so that Alphonsus, who was making his meditation, in bed, sent for his secretary in order to have silence kept, but at the same moment he entered after the secretary. Alphonsus, on seeing him, told him to go to the Grand-Vicar, but the gentleman fell on his knees at the foot of his bed and said: "I do not know the Vicar, but I acknowledge Mgr. Liguori as my father." At these words, Alphonsus became affected:

"My son,' he said, "I sent for you and you did not come; I was obliged to place you in the hands of justice; you know what scandals you have given." The culprit was ashamed, began to shed tears, and after confessing his faults, said: "Do whatever you please with me." "Since you acknowledge your fault," said then Alphonsus, "and confess the truth to me, I leave you to chose your penance yourself." "I choose the house of St. Angelo for my place of retirement," he answered, sobbing, "and only when God tells me that He has forgiven me, then only will I depart from it." Alphonsus, on seeing that his repentance was sincere, sent for the papers connected with his suit, and said to him while tearing them: "My son, may God do the same in heaven." He went to St. Angelo, and remained there for a month, and was afterwards a source of edification to all.

But if impurity and drunkenness were the two vices which he was the most zealous in extirpating, he was equally an enemy to every other kind of irregularity, and the slightest fault was a considerable sin in his eyes. He took the greatest care to be informed of the conduct of each and all, so that no distance could shelter any one. On one occasion, the culprits finding themselves reproved without being able to discover how Alphonsus had been informed as to their conduct, exclaimed: "It is either an angel or a devil who betrays us, and tells him every thing." By this indefatigable zeal and by the assistance of divine grace, he succeeded in doing away with a great number of scandals in his diocese, and he insensibly worked a reasonable reform among the clergy. A gentleman, on hearing once that he was seriously ill and in danger of death, replied to those who announced these sad tidings to him: "St. Agatha will lose a great deal if Mgr. Liguori dies. Who cannot see what regularity his zeal has succeeded in establishing amongst so many who formerly lived in a state of the most deplorable licentiousness?" As to the regular clergy, Alphonsus said: "Edifying religious are a consolation to bishops and priests, but if they are imperfect and irregular, they are a burthen to their bishops and a misfortune to the people." Therefore when he met with such, he did all he could to amend them: "For if they are not cured, said he, "their malady will be communicated to others; it is with them as it is with fruits—those which are bad spoil the good by contact with them, and in order to avoid the loss of all, it is necessary to throw the bad away." He, therefore, besides private admonitions and reprimands, had recourse to their superiors and provincials, and if speedy amendment did not follow, insisted on their being sent away from his diocese, and showed so much firmness that the superiors had to make up their minds to yield, and the religious had to be transferred elsewhere without loss of time. On one occasion, a religious frequenting a family of high rank too assiduously, Alphonsus urged his superior to send him to another monastery, but in vain. As just considerations prevented his then authoritatively exacting what he had asked, he determined at least to deprive the superior of the faculties to hear confessions, saying to him: "How can you feed the flocks of others, if you allow wolves to ravage your own with impunity?" And he was not satisfied until this religious was out of his diocese. Another, who was a dishonor to his Order, not heeding the paternal admonitions he had given him, was advised to leave the diocese of his own accord. This religious enjoyed the favor of his superior-general, who endeavored to defend him. Other great personages also interceded for him, but Alphonsus persisted, and he had to go away. In the year 1769, when he was at Naples, the Duke of Maddalon came in person to solicit the return of this religious, but he could not succeed. "Even supposing all the reports of his amendment were well founded," he said, "he has not acted in this way for a sufficiently long time, and then he is now so much older. As long as I am bishop," he added, "he shall not enter my diocese."

When the immediate superiors and the provincials would not assist him in thus purging the monasteries from religious who were a dishonour to them, he had recourse to more rigorous measures, and in order not to do any thing to the prejudice of regulars, he applied at Rome to the general of the Order to which the culprit belonged, and when he met with negligence even in the generals, he implored the intervention of the king; many instances in which he had recourse to both of these methods are on record. Thus, in the year 1768 alone, when he especially labored to purify the monasteries, he expelled as many as fifty-two religious, according to the testimony of F. Caputo. "The superiors of the Order, besides, knew him too well," said his Grand-Vicar Rubini, "and often hastened to send away certain subjects who were displeasing to him, of their own accord. I can truly say," he added, "that during his lordship's time, the monasteries of the diocese were as so many gardens, where all breathed forth the sweet odors of innocence and virtue." But on the other hand, he took as much pleasure, in being able to honor by his kindness those religious who proved worthy of their vocation, as he was resolute in punishing those who were dissolute and unworthy. He entrusted them with important employments, and chose them for synodal examiners. It was to them that he confided the care of the convents; he liked to send them to preach during Lent in different places, and often consulted them and rewarded their merit.

Alphonsus waged an equally severe warfare against the laity, whose irregularities were an injury to religion and morality. "I am not merely the shepherd of priests and religious," said he, "they form but a part of my flock. The flock confided to bishops includes all classes; God has committed all these souls to us, and we must render him an account of them." "We may be assured," said a priest on this subject, "that there never was a bishop in the world who employed himself in putting a stop to offences against God, and in procuring the good of the faithful, with more ardor than Mgr. Liguori. He held sin in such abomination that he was implacable in hunting it out, even from its most hidden entrenchments." To this end, he secured to himself the assistance of the magistrates and syndics of the villages, recommending them, with tears in his eyes, to seek after the glory of God and the happiness of families. "You can do what I cannot do," he said to them, "you can remedy every thing, for you are on the spot; you can do more than the king." Besides, he spent a good part of his revenues in making presents to persons who could inform him of existing scandals, and he possessed so much influence with the lords of the places, that he caused chastisements to be inflicted on the guilty persons; they were imprisoned, or sent away from the places in which they lived, and if this did not stop the evil or scandal, he had recourse to the king, to have them banished from the diocese. But before coming to these extremities, he made it a rule to try all the methods he could adopt as a father. He sent, several times, if needful, for the offender, and, whether peasant, or gentleman, reprimanded and threatened him. If that were not enough, he had recourse to the interposition of the friends of the guilty one, or of those who had influence over him; but as soon as he was convinced of the inutility of such correction, he adopted rigorous measures. Of all this we could relate instances by thousands, as such facts were of almost daily occurrence in the life of our zealous bishop. We shall however confine ourselves to a few, in which, one or another of the virtues of the saint, or some other divine favor bestowed on him, particularly shines forth.

He was informed that a physician at St. Agatha had improper relations with the mistress of the hospital; he did all he could to convert him, but on finding that his remonstrances were useless, he wrote to the president of the council and superintendent of the house. He dismissed the doctor from his employment, who thereupon came to the bishop in a fury, and loaded him with a thousand invectives. "My son," said Alphonsus to him, "you brought this misfortune on yourself; remember how many times I reproved you with mildness and charity, but you were deaf to my voice: if I have had recourse to a more powerful arm, it has not been through passion, but on account of the scruples which my allowing you to go on in sin caused me."

A gentleman of high standing, whose conduct was extremely scandalous, on seeing that his lordship thwarted him in his excesses, went to him, and, transported with anger, reproached him for not letting him alone. Alphonsus only answered by still stronger threats, and declared to him that he would inform the king of it; at these words the gentleman got up in a great fury, loaded his bishop with invectives, and made a gesture as if he meant to draw his sword. The alarm which he spread caused all the people of the house to run into the room, where they found Alphonsus perfectly calm before his aggressor. "Ill-treat me," he said to him, "abuse me, if you like, I do my duty: I did not accept the episcopate in order to be damned. Would to God that I might have the honor to die a martyr! My dear child, I pity you! return from your evil ways, but know that I will never leave you at peace in your sin."

A stranger, who was an officer, carried on an adulterous intercourse at St. Agatha, and Alphonsus warned him several times. The officer was tired of these troublesome reprimands, and constantly repeated in vexation, "what does this withered old man want?" He even used menaces, and went so far, that fear was entertained for the saint's life. They informed him of this and of the violent character of the officer; but, fortified with the heart of an apostle, he answered: "I have no cause to fear him; if he wishes to send a ball through my head, I am ready to die, but I am determined that he shall put an end to his excesses." As the scandal continued the same as ever, he informed the chevalier Negroni of it, who caused the woman to be banished, and compelled the officer to submit to the shame of coming to promise amendment at the feet of the bishop.

Being informed that a woman of Arienzo lived in sin, and apart from her husband, he immediately sent his secretary to the governor's house, but not finding him in, the secretary did not take the trouble of going back to him again. After the lapse of a short time, Alphonsus did not forget to inquire into the result of the visit. The secretary wanted to excuse himself, and said that he had not been able to see the magistrate, and had not had time to go to his house again. Alphonsus was exceedingly pained at this negligence: "O Felix," he said to him, with deep sorrow, "when an offence against God is in question, we should leave every thing to put a stop to it." He sent him back to the governor's with all speed, and did not become tranquil again until he knew that the woman was in prison. Another day, the grand-vicar came to him just as he was taking his repast, in bed: "We have bad news," he said to him, "a most suspicious stranger has come to establish herself at Arienzo." "Only one," replied Alphonsus, laughing, "we shall have more than one; adventurers of this sort never come singly." The secretary and the grand-vicar fancied that these tidings had made no great impression on him; but they were mistaken. He had scarcely finished his meal before he dismissed every one, and sent for Br. Francis, to dictate to him a most energetic letter to the Count of Cereto; informing him of the scandal, and begging him to send to Arienzo immediately, that it might be forcibly removed. On the same evening four soldiers drove away the infamous woman.

He expended a good deal of money in similar cases; he had to pay large sums to the inferior people whom he employed, and even to the higher officers, but there was no sacrifice he was not ready to make in order to hinder an offence against God, or to extricate some unhappy creature from sin and misery. Having heard that several soldiers in his diocese gave themselves up to shameful excesses, he immediately wrote a letter, the result of which was, that the regiment's quarters were changed, and that the commanding officer received the strictest orders to take care that none of the men came near that place again. An inhabitant, who had derived benefit from the troops being quartered there, went to complain of their going away and to expose his distress to Alphonsus; he was touched with compassion, and sent for one of the syndics of the parish, and begged him to give the petitioner something in compensation. The syndic replied that he could not take it upon himself, and the others got out of it in the same way, and Alphonsus ended by himself indemnifying the man who had recourse to him, in order not to incur the danger of a return of the military to the place through the complaints and intrigues of interested parties.

Alphonsus, hearing that a prostitute after a banishment of eleven years had come back, wrote the following letter to the priest of the place: "As this woman has come back here again, let her know from me that I will give her six carlins every month if she conducts herself properly; but I must first be convinced as to her persevering." On hearing that a poor widow had caused the ruin of her two daughters, he gave her a severe reprimand; she was converted however, whereupon he assigned to her, as well as to each of her children, a daily allowance of money, besides many alms in furniture, clothes, &c., in order that by adding to these gifts the fruits of their own labors, they might have enough to live on honestly. Another, returning to the diocese after being converted, he let her know that, if she persevered, he would insure her an allowance of fifteen carlins a month. A wicked girl, who had ruined both her body and soul by her debaucheries, when she was reduced to the last extremity, applied to the house of the Incurables at Naples; Alphonsus hastened to recommend her to the notice of several priests, and the unhappy creature at last opened her eyes and wept over her past misconduct. This moved him to tears, and he wrote to one of those priests: "I have sent for the mother, she appears to me to be a good woman, although she is very poor; for this reason I intend to send her to Naples to seek her daughter. I have promised to assist her and to give her a monthly allowance, but I hear that the girl is in the greatest destitution; she must then be clothed from head to foot. Will you have the charity to provide for this at my expense, but with as little outlay as possible? First, procure for her two new chemises, a kerchief for the head, and another for the neck, a serge petticoat, an underdress of canvass, a mantle, a pair of white stockings, and a pair of shoes; but I do not wish them all to be quite new, because that would cost too much. They may be met with at the old-clothes shops, where such things may be found in good condition; if one were to take really old goods, the thing would have to be done over again next day. I should not take the liberty to burthen you with all these commissions, if I did not know your great charity." Who does not admire the true minister of the Lord throughout all these details?

Archdeacon Rainone attested that he spent considerable sums of money, from the time he came to the diocese, in thus aiding a great number whose indigence had led them to crime. Nor were these gifts confined to the towns of St. Agatha and Arienzo alone, he spread them throughout all parts of his diocese without any distinction. The curate of the parish of St. Anthony affirmed that Alphonsus assisted a very great number in that place, and caused them to receive a stipend every month through his hands; other priests and curates affirmed the same of their respective places. When informed that he was often deceived by his goodness; "It matters little if I am deceived," he used to answer, "provided I thwart the plans of the devil: it is no little gain if one can prevent an offence against God, were it but for a quarter of an hour; and besides it often happens that several abstain from their disorders for good." Archdeacon Rainone also one day told him he ought to withdraw the allowance from some whose perseverance was doubtful. "That is not certain," he replied, "but if I abandon them, they may perhaps be led to yield to despair; and besides, if they commit but one mortal sin less, is it not a great thing for God's glory?" Such persons he recommended to the missionaries whom he sent through the diocese, and whom he furnished with all they could require for such purposes. A priest was speaking one day to him of the good dispositions which two of these women manifested, when he replied to him: "I am ready to give my blood and my life for them; and if they act with sincerity, I will not fail to assist them, were I obliged to go without my food to do so." Alphonsus put the finishing stroke to his zeal by causing a great number of these penitents to enter into the married state, and, in order to establish them, he often did not hesitate to contribute from thirty to forty ducats for their portion, but this he especially tried to do in good time; as soon as he heard of any young person's deviating from the right path, he immediately endeavored to get her married, attaching at the same time the greatest importance to its being to her seducer. One day, a Father of his congregation, while on a mission in the diocese, came to see him to settle about six marriages of this sort in one place alone. Besides dispensing in such cases with all his fees, he willingly procured the necessary dispenses at his own expense; and when it happened at times that his own means were not enough for the charity of his heart, he had recourse to the charity of those in affluent circumstances, and to the houses of relief. These unions were generally happy ones. "It is true," he said, "that there are certain kinds of forced unions of which I cannot approve; but of two evils, one must choose the least."

He succeeded also in placing a good number of such penitents in the convents, at Naples, and at Nola, notwithstanding the great difficulties he often had to surmount in so doing, and this was always the greatest consolation to his heart. He was often obliged to go to expense for this purpose; the superior of the asylum of St. Raphael, at Naples, once agreed to such a request, on the condition that he would furnish the applicant with her wardrobe, and he did so cheerfully. Certain missionaries, giving in the year 1765 the mission in the diocese of Bojano, met with a married woman who lived in a state of concubinage. She told them in confession that she belonged to Trasso, which was in Mgr. Liguori's diocese, and added that the child she had with her was by her lawful husband. The missionaries lost no time in informing Alphonsus of all this, and the saintly old man, filled with very great joy at seeing the sincere repentance of this woman and her wish to enter a convent, succeeded in placing her in the refuge of St. Clare, at Naples; where he supplied her with what necessaries she required, and besides many other gifts, assigned her an unusual pension of thirty-six ducats. He had the little child brought up at St. Agatha, and when old enough, maintained him at Naples at his own expense, in order that he might learn a trade. After this woman had been thus supported for five years, her husband died, and she had the opportunity of making an honorable second marriage, and Alphonsus did not fail to assist her to the end with his accustomed generosity.

Besides all this, hundreds of poor girls owed the preservation of their honor to his alms-deeds. Without entering into a detailed account of the assistance he rendered them, we shall confine ourselves to saying that he went so far as even to procure innocent adornments for them, in order to take away from them all temptation to envy or to sin. That which gave him the greatest alarm was, when any engagement of marriage took place between young people whose parents refused to consent to it. When this occurred, he sent for the parents, in order to ascertain whether the grounds of their opposition were reasonable; he united with the priests in doing all that was possible, either to break off engagements entered into rashly, or to overcome the opposition of parents by showing that delay on their part must inevitably lead to sin. It often happened therefore that young people who wished to settle, but were unjustly prevented from so doing by their parents, had recourse to the saintly Bishop, who immediately sent for the parents and managed so well that he obtained their consent. When young people had given public scandal by illicit intercourse, their marriage was preceded by a public penance at the door of the church. He always most carefully tried to stifle evil in its beginning. A troop of actors came to St. Agatha, intending to remain there. He at once entreated for the aid of the Duke of Maddalon's arm against them, and succeeded in getting an order for their withdrawal. They begged for one day's delay, in order to act a play which they said was very good indeed; but there was no reprieve for them, and they were obliged to set out at once. Not being able to prevent, in the time of Carnival, the representation of a play about which the gentlemen of Airola had arranged, he asked that he might at least be allowed to read it, and they were obliged to submit to act it with the retrenchments he made in it. He did not fail to manifest his great displeasure to one of the gentlemen: "You are men of age," he said to him, "and this is the example you give to the young! I do not know how you will be able to think of it at the hour of death." One day, some mountebanks arrived at Arienzo, accompanied by two young female rope dancers, who were dressed up as men. As soon as Alphonsus was informed of it, he applied both to the Governor and to the agent of the Duke, in order that they might be sent away. The players quitted the town, saying they were going to Naples, but they stopped at Airola. "I thought that they had left my diocese," he immediately wrote to the Prince della Riccia, "but yesterday I had the sorrow of hearing that they are at Airola, and that they mean to perform in your excellency's palace. I must entreat you to send your orders to Airola, and prevent its being thought that you consent to this." Nothing more was necessary to cause them to be banished from the diocese.

He dreaded the disorders too common in large assemblages, even those which had religion as their end, and he was therefore in the habit of suspending the confessors for reserved cases, on fetes where there was too great a concourse of people. "This is the way," he said, "to prevent people from coming to unburthen their consciences without any fruit, and then from loading them with new sins through the contempt they show for the sacraments." At Arienzo, on Christmas night, the people were in the habit of going out of the town, with the inhabitants of the adjoining villages, to assist at the offices in the church of the Capuchin Fathers. There was no devotion in this; on the contrary, this concourse of people of both sexes gave opportunity for all sorts of disorders. In order to put a stop to these evils, Alphonsus wished to be present in person, but the doctors opposed this, on account of the obvious danger there was that it might kill him. He then forbade the church to be opened before six o'clock in the morning, and he afterwards issued the same prohibition in regard to all the other churches.

He also looked on himself as the peace-maker of his people, and took all possible pains to reconcile spirits at variance with each other, and to put a stop to discord and prevent its spread in families, and much more so among the clergy. Out of many facts on record, let us relate the two following. One day, at Airola, when on his pastoral visitation, he heard that a young man had been mortally wounded in a combat; he immediately hastened to see the unhappy man, and manifested all the feeling of a tender father towards him, and assured him that he would assist both himself and his family; and having appeased his resentment, he succeeded in obtaining from him the pardon of his murderer. Another day, he heard that two young gentlemen had challenged each other to fight a duel; he instantly sent for both, and represented to them the consequences of their guilty project, and did not dismiss them until he felt sure that his remonstrance had been effectual.

This barbarous custom of duelling caused Alphonsus great grief, and he addressed a memorial to the king to try and get him to be severe in punishing the ferocious practice. He had embodied therein all the various dispositions both of the canon law, and the civil law of different countries, with the arguments from reason, against this detestable custom. His zeal was not unfruitful, for his petition obtained the promulgation of a very severe law against duelling.

Among the vices which Alphonsus combated the most vigorously was that of blasphemy. As the law, which required those guilty of it to be punished at the public square with a bit in their mouths, had been abolished, he enjoined the magistrates to punish them by at least imprisoning them. He had sent several times for a public crier, who, from having been once a novice with the Capuchins, had become a horrible blasphemer—in order to warn and correct him paternally, but he always had refused to come. One day he commissioned his servant Alexis to bring him in the palace, on the pretext of inquiring about the price of corn, but when he saw him, Alphonsus said: "It is not the price of corn, but you that I am anxious about; I hear that there is not a saint whom you do not blaspheme:" he then threatened to have him arrested and condemned to the galleys. The crier was so terrified that he left off his guilty habit, from that day forward. He died shortly after, in sentiments of penitence and resignation.

Another blasphemer, at Forchia, had been excommunicated for several years, and persisted in his impenitence. Alphonsus, unable to put up with him any longer, applied to the Prince of Riccia to have his trial got ready; however, he once more tried to win him by paternal counsels, and sent for him to the palace. As the man did not venture to appear before him, Alphonsus inquired as to the time when he would pass through the street; he then went to the window and called him by his name; then putting his hand on his head, he reproved him kindly, and represented to him the impiety of his words. He was overcome by this excessive goodness, humbled himself and was converted. Alphonsus sent him to confession the next morning, and wished him, in order to repair the scandal he had given, to remain, before being admitted to holy communion, at the church door for three Sundays, with a heavy cross on his shoulders and a large stone hung round his neck. He submitted to every thing, and his return to God was so sincere, that he lived as a good Christian from that time; he approached the sacraments every eight days, and became a member of the Society of the Rosary.

Another, who was not satisfied with insulting the Saints, but went to the length of reviling God himself and of blaspheming against heaven, had already been imprisoned for his blasphemies, but he had begun them again, and was worse than before; after this a monition had been issued against him, without success, by the ecclesiastical court. Alphonsus got the Prince della Riccia to cause sentence to be pronounced against him as an incorrigible. He had therefore to spend many a dreary day in prison, and his purse suffered as well as his person, through the fines he was obliged to pay to justice.

His severity in punishing those who did not fulfil the Paschal precept, was not stopped by any earthly considerations; even the first gentlemen had to submit to see their names affixed to the church door, and if the Church's power were not strong enough to compel them to do their duty, he implored the intervention of the temporal lords. Thus he wrote once to the Prince della Riccia, saying: "For some years N. has not fulfilled the Paschal precept, on a false pretence of insanity, and worse than this, he has prevented his sister from frequenting the sacraments. I know that your excellency is full of zeal for the salvation of your vassals, and therefore I am sure that you will give orders to have this scandal remedied." And in order to lessen the difficulties in the way of the punishment of the culprit, he offered to keep him in prison at his own expense. His request was granted; the pretended maniac was put in prison, and his sister was thus enabled to fulfil her duties with all freedom.

He had ordered the priests to refuse the sacraments to those who gave public scandal or neglected their duties, however noble they might be, and he set them the example himself. All his charitable efforts to cause a gentleman, who was a notorious adulterer, to think seriously, failed utterly, and yet this person presented himself to receive the

Holy Communion on Holy Thursday: Alphonsus, who was administering the Holy Communion to the people, stopped short before him, and said to him: "What! do you not blush to approach the altar? We do not give pearls to swine here. Unhappy man! change your mode of life." At these words he passed on and left him full of confusion.

These are some of the many striking instances of our Saint's admirable zeal, which might at first sight seem excessive, but which was nothing more than the necessary consequence of his ardor for the glory of God and his dread of the awful account he felt he must one day render to him. This thought of the responsibility of a bishop made him really tremble. Mgr. Albertini asked him, one day, how many souls he had in his diocese. "There are forty thousand," Alphonsus replied. "There are as many in mine," said Mgr. Albertini;" upon which Alphonsus bent his head several times, and added: "My Lord, we have each of us a burden of forty thousand hundred-weight on our shoulders; woe to us if one of these souls be lost through our negligence!"

This zeal of our Saint was so pleasing to God that He assisted him in a particular manner by the blessings with which He favored his efforts, viz: by striking punishments inflicted on the incorrigible, and by particular lights from on high. "It was a marvellous thing," said a priest, "that what we were ignorant of, was always known to his lordship. Many times, iniquity was committed at night in the country, or in a distant village, yet the day had scarcely dawned ere we were warned of it at the bishop's house." We will give an example, which happened at his palace at Arienzo. One night, the coachman and the cook tried to perpetrate an abominable act, but at the instant when they were going to commit the crime, they were suddenly seized with fear, and their accomplice, who was as terrified as they were, took to flight, and hid herself. As soon as it was day, Alphonsus sent for his two servants, reproached them with their fault, and exhorted them to confession.

At Arienzo, a woman of bad character, who was unhappily an adept in her trade, taught it even to others and had several women in her service, receiving strangers at her dwelling, particularly soldiers. Alphonsus had several times brought her before the courts of justice, but always in vain; on seeing how incorrigible she was, he once said to her: "Miserable wretch that you are, you will not give over your crimes, but God will know how to put an end to them. You will die in a state of damnation, and in a most tragic manner." This prediction was not long in being verified; for the unhappy creature, in order to escape from a prison, fled from the town, and was obliged to wander about on the neighboring mountains in the depth of winter, and was several times forced to sleep in the woods. Nevertheless, she came near to the town every night to abandon herself to her criminal courses; but the companion of her debaucheries, having also been threatened with imprisonment, one evening determined to have nothing to do with her, and pursued her, casting stones at her. In her flight she fell in a deep ditch, where she died. Alphonsus caused her body to be carried, between three lighted torches, to the trench into which it was thrown, as an example to those of a similar description.

A cleric, who, for his evil courses, had been imprisoned for several years, was at last released and sent by the Prince della Riccia to humble himself before Alphonsus. But, instead of this, he went and bitterly reproached him for the persecutions he had made him suffer. Alphonsus took up his book on the "*Way of Salvation*," and presented it to him, saying: "Read this, and you will be satisfied." But the priest went on in the same tone. Alphonsus made no reply, but looking at him with compassion and grief at so deplorable a state of mind, dismissed him and said: "May Jesus Christ have mercy on you, but divine justice is threatening you." And so it was; he returned to his evil ways, and soon afterwards was shot, and thus perished.

A notary distressed him by his misconduct; after he had reprimanded him several times, and always without success, he said to him one day: "My son, the life you lead will bring you to a deplorable end;" and putting his hand on his shoulder, he repeated, almost weeping: "Yes! you will die a tragic death." This unhappy man went from bad to worse, and at length he was involved in the conspiracy of the Jacobins, and was condemned to lose his head on the scaffold, in the January of 1800. While he was waiting in the chapel for the movement to the place of execution, he said weeping to a monk: "This death was foretold me, in my youth, by Mgr. Liguori." This reflection caused him to enter into himself with serious thought, and, having been hardened till then, he died full of penitence, invoking the saint in heaven.

CHAPTER XXVIII.

Alphonsus' patience in bearing injuries, and great Meekness. His admirable Humility. His Spirit of Poverty, Penance and Mortification.

IN spite of the admiration which his zeal generally excited, those who were its objects were usually offended, and resented its effects with bitterness; and it often happened that in the effervescence of their Italian character, they loaded their good bishop with injuries, and nearly laid hands on him. How undaunted his courage was, we have seen above in similar occurrences, where threats even against his life had been uttered. We are going to relate, among many facts, some in which shone forth an incomparable patience and meekness, united with such charity that often he loaded those who offended him with benefits. "When charity is patient," said he, "it is also kind; if we are really anxious to win over those who do us harm to Jesus Christ, we must do them good."

A priest who had an office in the diocese, fancied himself offended on account of the manner in which Alphonsus treated his brother, and had the impudence to go to him and heap insults upon him. "Do you not see," he said, "that you are unfit to fulfil your duties? How much better it would have been if you had remained at Ciorani to weep over your sins, than to come to St. Agatha to fill the office of bishop." Alphonsus answered with a smile. The grand-vicar asked that this man should be deprived of his post, but he was kept in it, and afterwards was made a canon.

Alphonsus labored to put an end to the scandalous conduct of a certain gentleman; the latter came to the palace full of rage, and asked to see the bishop. The servants seeing a man in a great passion, prevented his being admitted, whereupon he uttered a volley of abuse. This scene became talked of, and reached the ears of the governor, who hastened to put the offender in prison. When Alphonsus heard of it he was greatly distressed, and sent for the governor, to whom he excused the gentleman, and asked for his pardon; nor did he rest until he had got him set at liberty that very day.

One day, when Alphonsus was driving out, he met a villager of bad character, who was full of anger for the correction he had received from him; and who loaded him with abuse and bad language. Alphonsus bore it all in silence. On his return to the palace, the grand-vicar wanted this impudent man to be punished as an example. Alphonsus was indignant at the idea, and positively forbade any thing of the kind to be attempted. However, the grand-vicar informed the governor of it, and the daring offender was imprisoned that same evening. Alphonsus heard of it the next day; he made loud complaints about it, and demanded that the man should be immediately set at liberty: in the evening, having heard that the governor had not yet done so, he sent for the grand-vicar, and manifested his dissatisfaction to him, and as the latter represented to him the dignity of his position, he exclaimed: "What position, if it is necessary for people to be put in prison on my account!" He was not pacified until he had tidings of the release of the offender.

A priest who was convicted of falsehood and serious deception towards his bishop, was so far from humbling himself in consequence, that he even uttered a torrent of abusive language against him. "I am on the point o abandoning my home in order not to be under you any longer," he said to him, amongst many other disrespectful things. From the fear of making him still more angry, the saintly man quietly replied: "My son, what do you wish me to say to you? You are right, and I am wrong; calm yourself I entreat you:" he then made him sit down near him and tried to pacify him.

Another day, a priest came in who set up claims to a prebend, of which he was totally unworthy. Alphonsus gave him a tacit refusal, by saying that he had promised it to another. At these words the priest got outrageously angry, and assailed his bishop with the most abusive invectives. "Is it you they call a saint!" he said. "A pretty kind of sanctity yours is! He only is a saint who knows how to be just." Alphonsus listened in silence, but on seeing that he went on, he said to him gently: "This is too much;" and taking up his pen again, he went on with his work. The other went on abusing him in the same tone, until he had vented all his spleen. The eye-witness of this scene stated that Alphonsus seemed like a marble statue all the time, and that he could scarcely even perceive a faint flush which tinged his face, it was so slight; and he added, that when the priest retired, Alphonsus did not say a word to him about what had just happened.

A layman boldly entered his palace one day, and abused him most violently; he bore it all without saying any thing, and without in the least losing his serenity. When the scene ended, he went to the seminary as if nothing had happened. He visited the different classes, manifested great cheerfulness, assisted at the repetitions, and made the youngest pupils sing a pious song. When he retired the superior followed him, and on seeing him so cheerful, he begged him to diminish the amount of the pension for a young man with whom he was greatly satisfied. The bishop granted him all he asked, with pleasure. When he went away, and the superior heard of the insult he had received just before this visit, he was stupified, and could not sufficiently admire the immovable sweetness of the saintly bishop.

One day he sent the servant to the administrator of the annunciator, to ask his kind assistance in behalf of a poor woman whom he had converted. The administrator was in a bad humor at that time, and sent the bishop, the woman, and the servant about their business. The indignant servant repeated the speech to Alphonsus, and as he blamed the administrator, he said to him: "be silent, he is a holy man. Who knows what was the matter with him? Go back again to-morrow, and you will see that he will give you a large donation." And so it was; the servant went and received more than thirty carlins.

The good bishop's meekness towards those of his household was no less admirable. When they annoyed him in any way, his greatest complaint was to say: "How foolish you are!" or else, "May you become a saint!" If the matter were of more importance, and he saw no way of remedying it, he raised his eyes to heaven and gently said: "Thy will be done;" and if he could not control some emotion, he used to exclaim: "Gloria Patri," &c. A canon related that he always exercised extraordinary mildness towards a priest belonging to his palace, who treated him as if he were his inferior. Every one was indignant at the effrontery and impertinence of this person. Alphonsus alone never showed the least emotion at it.

He one day gently reproved a cleric who was writing under his dictation; the cleric, whether through stupidity or malice, threw the papers down in a heap on the table, and then hastily and angrily retired. When Alphonsus thought he had got calm again, he sent for him and said: "Well, why did you do such a thing? Do you know that you vexed me? now go on writing again."

This calmness in the midst of affronts and insults was not natural to him, however, for he had by nature a fiery and irascible temper. It was the happy result of the violent efforts he made to overcome himself, and to break off all human attachment in his heart. From the moment he left the world, he set the mildness and humility of Jesus Christ before him as a model. Archdeacon Rainone, who was once present when a country priest insulted him, said: "My lord, that is not the proper way to act; it is degrading to your character, and encourages the wicked." "Oh, my dear canon," answered Alphonsus, "I have labored to gain a little patience for forty years, and you want me to lose it in an instant." On a similar occasion he answered to a like remark of the superior of the seminary, with a smile: "I have had no slight struggle to gain a little patience; God knows how much it has cost me. It is the fruit of continued effort, and shall I go and lose it in an instant?"

But this meekness did not prevent him from showing the proper firmness, when, not his own person, but the glory of God, or the welfare of souls was in any way concerned; he became then even terrible as a lion. F. Caputo, who lived in his intimacy, was in the habit of saying, "When this old man wants to manifest his authority, he intimidates and terrifies one." A gentleman, who was rich, but dissipated all his possessions in gaming, had a son at the seminary, and on the plea of poverty, he wanted him to be kept there for the half pension. Alphonsus wished to correct him, so he refused his request. The gentleman then raised his voice and tried to obtain it by intimidating him. Alphonsus, upon this, said to him: "But do you know how unbending I am? He then struck the table with the back of his hand, and added: "When I tell you that I ought not to do the thing for God's sake, you might as well give it up." Another gentleman of Airola went on obstinately in sin; Alphonsus sent for him to the palace and reprimanded him, and on seeing his indifference he got more animated and reproved him more warmly. The gentleman was much nettled, and began to abuse him excessively; this did not move Alphonsus, who merely said to him more than once, while walking up and down: "Sir, you wish me to act as a bishop, and I will make you see that I am one." We could give a thousand instances of this truly apostolical firmness. But it was not without suffering an interior pang that he decided on resorting to firmness or severity. "You cannot imagine," he wrote to one of his penitents at Naples, "how much it costs me to treat certain persons with severity; and I think that one succeeds better by gentleness than by violence." He was once seen to weep, in giving a severe reprimand to a gentleman whose deplorable conduct had not yielded to repeated warnings. At this, the licentious man could not help being affected himself, notwithstanding his being so hardened. Often after uttering words which he thought a little too strong, he would think of some pretext for recalling the person to whom they had been addressed, and giving him some token of kindness. Thus, having on one occasion spoken authoritatively to a doctor, he sent for him on the following day to feel his pulse. "He was very well, however," said the doctor afterwards, "but he made use of this innocent stratagem to show me that he felt no ill-will towards me."

This meekness and the control which he had gained over himself also enabled him to rule over the hearts of others, so that often one word from him sufficed to make all parties agree, and the most obstinate hearts submit. Of this, let us give the following most remarkable instance. One day, the cook, who had forced Alphonsus to give him an assistant for the dirty work, had a dispute with this latter, who carried it so far as to run after him with a knife. The poor servant ran to take refuge in Alphonsus' room, and held the door firmly closed; but the scullion, who seemed determined to kill him, pushed at the door violently from outside. Alphonsus ordered it to be immediately opened, and with a few words succeeded in completely calming the infuriated scullion. The grand-vicar and all the others wished the man to be imprisoned and dismissed; but the saintly bishop only sought to reconcile him to the cook, and he succeeded so well that these two servants were the best possible friends from that time.

In a word, we may say that Alphonsus' meekness was perfect. "There is nothing," said he, "which is more unseemly in a bishop than anger. A bishop who gives way to this passion, is no longer the father of his flock; he is an intractable tyrant, who draws down the hatred of every one." Br. Francis, who lived with our saint for fifty years, and a Father who was in intimate intercourse with him for forty years, attested, that, whether in his relations with them or with strangers, he constantly evinced unutterable sweetness and equanimity, however annoying that intercourse might have been; and a priest, a man whose sanctity made him venerable, never called him any thing but the Francis de Sales of our age.

As the inseparable companion of meekness is humility, so Alphonsus, who was a model of sweetness, rendered himself no less admirable by the low opinion he had of himself. Being entirely detached from the world, wherein he saw nothing but illusion and vanity, he seemed to have forgotten what he once had been, and to seek for nothing but obscurity and contempt during the whole time of his episcopate. He no longer thought of the nobility of his origin, nor of the great achievements of his forefathers, and if any one attempted to speak to him of them, he immediately stopped them. On one occasion, some one talked a great deal about the honors and dignities which his cousin, D. Charles Caralini, had enjoyed at Mantua, as governor of that town; far from taking pleasure in all this, Alphonsus thought it a matter for sorrow, and said: "How much more I should rejoice at hearing him praised for having been full of virtue! How much more cause should I have for pride, had his death been that of a saint." How he hated the title of *excellency*, we have seen above; and his persevering way of rejecting it was such, that every one in the diocese gave it up, in spite of the habit of using it to the bishops who were his predecessors.

As he delighted in serving others, and never in being waited on himself, he was like one of the servants in his house: he made his bed himself, dressed his own issue, and never allowed a valet to come near his person for such services; and although Bishop of St. Agatha, he seemed rather to consider himself the sacristan. "By God's grace," he one day said, "I have never felt vain-glorious. Once only, when I was being incensed on my throne, I felt a sort of pleasing sensation. Now see," he added, "see how the devil tried to tempt me." When he went out of his palace, he never would be accompanied by more than one priest, whoever that one might be; and he very often went out alone, or only accompanied by the sacristan, who was a layman. The canons, on finding out this manner of proceeding, several times complained to the persons belonging to the episcopal house that they were not warned when he went out by the usual ringing of bells; but that was precisely what Alphonsus did not wish for. When he went to church for his private devotions, he went alone; and thus it several times happened that he came too soon, and found the door shut, and waited then patiently until the sacristan arrived to open it. When he arrived alone in this way, he would not allow a cushion to be put on his chair, and when the servant accompanied him, as he knew his wishes, he took care to take it away, if it had been placed there. The slightest mark of deference was distasteful to him; thus, when he went out in the carriage, he would not allow the secretary or any other priest to seat themselves in the front part of the carriage; and he never consented to take the right side unless it were quite indispensable to do so. Even at Naples he made his grand-vicar take it, who, though distressed at such pre-eminence, was obliged to yield through obedience, and in order to avoid vexing his superior. Far from domineering over the clergy, he even manifested submissiveness towards the lowest of his servants, to whom he never spoke but in these terms: 'Do me the kindness.' . . . 'I beg you to do such a thing.' . . . 'Have patience.' . . . 'Please to do that,' &c. No word ever issued from his mouth which denoted command or superiority. He was, above all, respectful in his expressions and conduct towards ecclesiastics. "One day when I was in his room," said a priest, "he did not venture to say to me, 'give me that pen,' but he rung the bell to summon the lay-brother who had to attend to him; he was paralyzed and in bed." Even when he gave an order to a priest relating to his office, he did so in the form of a request. He once said to a priest who gave the spiritual exercises to the nuns at Arienzo: "D. Paschal, the nuns would like to have you for two days more." "Your lordship can dispose of me; you have but to command, and I will obey," was his reply. "Very true," replied Alphonsus, "but a superior ought to be discreet." He was in the habit of saying that a tone of superiority and disdain can only diminish the authority of a bishop. If, however, he were resisted in a thing he had a right to demand, he then remembered that he was a bishop, and changed his love into firmness, but always spoke in a polite manner, and never said any thing offensive. When he wrote to the episcopal vicars and to the priests, he gave them the title of *most illustrious*, and he was as respectful towards those he cited before his tribunal, thus liking to give to others what he would not receive himself. When he had to deal with any superior of a monastery, he almost put himself in the position of a subject. Having gone to the Capuchin Fathers on St. Anthony's day, while he was at Arienzo, and seeing there was a crowd of people in the church, he said to the F. Guardian in the most humble tone: "F. Guardian, if you allow it, I should like to say a few words to these people." He treated all kinds of ecclesiastics in office with the same deference, in regard to the affairs relating to their church; and he addressed the priests, and above all the canons, in the same way, when he wanted to officiate at an unusual time in any church.

He would never allow even the simplest cleric to remain standing in his presence, and all who went to see him were admitted to his table, if they came in the morning. Thus no formal invitation was needed beforehand to enable persons to be admitted to it; every priest, and even every layman who came to see him, might hope to dine with him. He disliked having his hand kissed, and he did not even present it to the clergy, unless they manifested a wish for it, and then he did so unwillingly. He liked to converse with the most vulgar peasantry, and to inquire into their affairs and their wants.

His profound science caused him to be consulted on the most delicate affairs, and recourse was had to him from all parts of Italy, and even from beyond the mountains; yet he never decided any thing of consequence without himself taking advice, and always behaved as if he were incapable of deciding any thing himself. He often took the opinion even of persons of but moderate talents, and he never hesitated in submitting his judgment to that of another, when he thought it more in accordance with the truth. He was the first to condemn himself, if he happened to make any mistake. He did this with joy, and always manifested gratitude for the explanations he had received. But if it happened that he was wrongfully condemned, he was equally sincere, exposed his reasons with candor, and justified himself without blaming others. A commonplace writer, of whom Alphonsus had made an honorable mention in one of his books, not satisfied with having bitterly censured an opinion which he had had grounds for defending, wrote a letter to him, as indiscreet as it was impertinent, in which he did not scruple to call him an impostor. Alphonsus received this piece of impertinence with the greatest calmness, and took care not to complain of it even to a canon, who, as he knew, was a friend of his detractor.

A foreign merchant, who called himself a convert from Protestantism, after having obtained the ordinary letter of recommendation to the diocese from the grand-vicar, wished to speak with his lordship. When he was in his presence he began to talk of the different works which Alphonsus had published, and did not scruple boldly to blame several of his opinions, which he accused of being untenable and scandalous, and went at length so far as to treat him to his face as an ignorant fool. Alphonsus not knowing what to think of such impudence, defended his opinions with humility, without losing his affability. A canon who was present, afterwards said to him: "I cannot imagine how you managed to bear it." Alphonsus only answered by a sweet smile, and then added that very likely he was a Jansenist.

The publisher wishing to give an increased value to Alphonsus' Moral Theology, begged him in January, 1762, to have his portrait taken. Alphonsus answered: "As to the portrait, that would throw discredit on the work; is it fitting for an author to have his picture taken while he is alive? . . . When I shall be no more, let them do what they please with my body; I care but little: but during my life, I wish no notice to be taken of me, and that my name may never be quoted anywhere. I have put it in my books, it is true; but that was to excite the curiosity of people, and to get them to read them, otherwise I should have had them printed without my name." When his secretary, at the instigation of the publisher, made use of some solicitation on this subject, Alphonsus answered: "Do not speak to me more about that, my work would not get more credit, but on the contrary, it would be depreciated in value if the head of such a mummy were put in it." If we have his portrait, we owe it to his servant Alexis and to his secretary, who being pressed by fresh entreaties from the publisher, secretly made a hole in the door of the room where Alphonsus dined; and thus the painter was able to trace his features whilst he took his repast.

The arms of his house were to be seen only in the chapter, they were neither to be found in the church nor in his palace; and the seats which he used, bore no other impression than a cross, or a calvary. There was a magnificent chasuble in the treasury of the cathedral, left there by Mgr. Danza; Alphonsus wanted to have a complete set of vestments of the same sort, and he added some of his own money to what the church funds could supply, and ordered a cope, dalmatics, a humeral veil, and cushions, to match, from Naples. When these things arrived at St. Agatha, the canons fancied that the sight of the arms of Mgr. Danza would be offensive to Alphonsus; they therefore had them immediately taken down, and were just going to send them back to have the arms of Liguori affixed instead, when Alphonsus heard of it and declared that it mattered little that these vestments were adorned by Mgr. Danza's arms, and asked if the ceremonies wherein these would appear, would be of less value on that account. He made them replace every thing as the embroiderer had put it. His brother Hercules made him once a present of a magnificently embroidered piece of cloth, which Alphonsus had made into a chasuble and dalmatics, but he rejected the proposition which the canons made of placing his arms on them; giving as the reason of this refusal, that what he had expended in the making of these things was not out of his personal income, but that he had taken it from the episcopal revenues, of which he did not consider himself to be the owner.

While he thus declined all personal privileges, he also forbade all his household to take advantage of the position they held, in the least degree. The general agent of the duke of Maddalon, said on this head: "In the time of the former bishops, no one dared to bring before the courts of justice any of those who were attached to the bishop's establishments, such as farmers, &c., but in the time of Mgr. Liguori, the horror which he had for all sorts of unjust pre-eminence, caused him to abolish these privileges."

The following is the last proof we shall give of his profound humility. As founder of the Congregation, and Superior General, he had a perfect right to employ any member of it in all his wants as he might please: but it was not thus he acted. F. Villani had destined F. D. Angelo Majone for St. Agatha; but he did not like such a tranquil mode of life, and manifested repugnance to it, so he sent him to give a mission at Gaeto, in order to overcome his aversion, and informed Alphonsus of it. "This news has given me great pain," he answered; "I want an able subject who can assist me in a multitude of difficult cases; for I am surrounded by a thousand difficulties which arise on all sides: but God wills it to be thus, and his will be done. . . . . . Try and get him to aid me willingly; me, a poor old man loaded with trials and cares. Tell him that he will thereby be sure of doing God's will, and that he will do me a great charity. I like him because he leads an edifying and retired life, and does not meddle with any thing that does not concern him; besides, he is a good adviser and a good preacher. I say, *willingly*, for otherwise it would be better for him not to come; for he would then be more burthensome than useful.

The virtues of poverty and penance are the inseparable companions of humility, or rather its most certain outward expressions. We will therefore show how these two virtues also shone forth in our saint during the time of his episcopate. With the exception of one violet suit, he only made use of Mgr. Danza's old clothes, and they were the only ones he wore during the thirteen years he was bishop of St. Agatha. Except when he had to officiate, he always wore the habit of his Congregation, which became dearer to him and more to his taste from its appearing humble and poor; but even this cassock had no fellow. One day, a gentleman coming to see him, found him clothed in violet, and believing that he must therefore be going out, he said to him: "Are you going to officiate?" "No," he replied, "but my cassock is being mended." Another day, as he was passing a monastery of the Dominican Fathers, dressed in an old gown full of patches and in a cassock which was out at the elbows, a father showing compassion for such great poverty, Alphonsus excused himself for it by frankly saying that he had given a commission for four articles of clothing to be bought for him in Naples at the old clothes-shop, but that they had not yet arrived.

He had a cassock which was so bad that the lay-brother was ashamed of it, and determined to take it away from him during the night, and make a new one of the same kind. The next morning while he was assisting him to dress, which he could not then do alone on account of an issue in his arm, the brother adroitly substituted the new habit. Alphonsus did not find it out at first, but on looking at the sleeves, he saw that they were new. "Ah," he said to him, "you have put new sleeves." "Yes," answered the brother, "the others were too much torn." But some time afterwards he saw that it was not his old cassock at all. "I am master," said he then, raising his voice, "I think this cassock is perfectly new." "So it is," replied the brother, "the other was no longer decent for you to put on." "Never mind," he answered in a tone of authority, "go and fetch me the old cassock." "If you will not have this one," said then the brother, "you must do without any, for the other has been given to a poor man." Alphonsus could not help regretting it, and said to the brother: "You always will act of your own accord." His underclothes were of coarse stuff; in summer they were of common cloth dyed black. A tailor said that on receiving a pair of small-clothes to mend, he did not know where to put the needle, and that a beggar would not have taken them. "Although sick and old," said a priest, "he only used hemp shirts, and a wooden rosary was suspended at his neck, similar to those which poor beggars use." The laundress often complained that the shirts were so tattered that the pieces remained in her hands, and wished him to be persuaded to get four new ones. "I undertook the office," said F. Telesca, "and seizing on a good opportunity, which the sight of the rents in the collar of his shirt gave me, I told him that he ought to get new ones." "Old things," he replied with a smile, "suit an old bishop; and then I ought to think of clothing the poor." He was seen in his visitations, mounted on an ass, and with such tattered clothes on that his hair shirt was seen through them. His stockings were of coarse wool; when he officiated he wore spun silk ones, but he never would make use of real silk stockings. The shoes which he had made at his election, were the only ones he wore during the thirteen years he governed St. Agatha, and he still wore them after his resignation, until his death. The walking-stick, which he used for the sole purpose of supporting himself, was of no value, having cost at most, twenty carlins. The little silken twist upon it got so shabby that it looked quite discreditable, and a priest not being able to bear its unsightliness, substituted a simple riband in its stead. When Alphonsus perceived it, he said: "What is that riband for?" Being told who had put it on, he said: "Yes, it could only have been put on by him." His bedstead was of wood, and of coarse workmanship, and he could never be induced to make use of an iron one. He had no curtains, and the sheets were of coarse linen; his blanket in winter was one of coarse wool, like those which the poor use: it was also old and worn out, and however severe the cold might be, he never allowed another to be bought, nor would he have a counterpane, but spread his cloak and his cassock on the bed. "I have admired Naples," wrote the grand chanter of the Cathedral of Girgenti, who had visited Alphonsus at Arienzo, "I have felt admiration for the magnificence of Rome, but the life of Mgr. Liguori has made a much greater impression on me; it has effaced all the beauties of these two capitals from my eyes. I have seen a saintly bishop of the primitive age; he lies on a bed to which he is confined by the most painful infirmities, but his serene countenance betokens the tranquillity of his soul. The glory of God, and the government of his diocese, occupy him unceasingly: in him have I seen extreme moderation in sleep and in food, and such absolute poverty in all things, that the only covering he has on his straw bed is his cassock; his pastoral ring would not excite the envy of a beggar, a false stone is its only ornament; his cross equals it in its simplicity."

At St. Agatha, as well as at Arienzo, he always chose the smallest room in an obscure recess for himself. He had not one valuable chair; those he had were of the sort all the poor use. His table was of unpolished wood, its value consisting in its antiquity, and he had on it a miserable little inkstand of bone. The paper which he used for every thing he wrote was very common, and he was so careful in turning the least piece to advantage, that he used the envelopes of letters for his composition, and for writing to the members of his Congregation. His snuff box was the same that he had used in the Congregation, that is a wooden one, worth only a few grains; in a word, he used nothing which was not very poor and very coarse. The bare floor was his *Prie-Dieu*. The only ornaments which adorned his room, besides his books, were a large crucifix, (which he had received as a present, and which he had always before him,) and a little picture of our Lady of good counsel, which was placed on his table. All the other rooms in the palace also betokened poverty. Mgr. Danza had left handsome furniture, but Alphonsus did not make use of it, and the palace was a mirror of evangelical poverty. With the exception of some common beds for those who might come to see him, some chairs, and deal tables, all the rest evinced distress. There were no valuable paintings, but on all sides devotional pictures of Jesus Christ and the Blessed Virgin. In the vestibule of the house at Arienzo, he placed a cross, which he kissed every time he went in or out of the house. The best piece of furniture for any person of distinction, was a bed which was covered with some old damask cloth, which had belonged to Mgr. Danza; and this was called the bed of state. He had, in a word, such an ardent love for holy poverty, that even the shadow of gold or silver made him afraid. He often went to see, at Arienzo, F. Mascia, the ex-provincial of the Capuchins, and each time he went into his room he tenderly kissed a beautiful parchment picture representing the *Ecce homo*. F. Mascia on seeing this devotion, offered the picture to him, and he accepted it. It was surrounded by the cloth of which the Capuchins make use; he wanted to take it off as a superfluous ornament, but it concealed a little silver frame. He at once returned it, saying he would not deprive F. Mascia of this object of devotion; but when it had left the house, he said to the secretary, "the picture is very beautiful, it is a pity that it has that silver frame."

On the pretext of health, he would only use the commonest sort of bread, which is made of bran with a very small quantity of flour. All the dishes at his table were equally common. He ate only veal or mutton, there being no other kind of meat to be had at Arienzo. "What scandal would it give," he said, "if the people saw one fare daintily." Even when he was ill, he would not allow any thing to be sent for to Naples or elsewhere, saying, "I ought to use the produce of my diocese;" and among the things which were sold in the place, he wished those which were the cheapest to be selected. The secretary one day bought a rare fish; as soon as Alphonsus saw it, he hastened to send it back again, saying, 'let it not be said that the bishop eats the best fish.' If any sort of delicacy were prepared for him during his illness, he said, shaking his head: "I am satisfied with what the others have, I do not wish for any thing in particular." His great maxim in this as in other things was: "All that is superfluous is taken from the poor."

When the Archbishop of Amalfi came, as we have seen above, to consecrate the Cathedral of St. Agatha, the cook thought that this was an occasion on which he could get credit through a grand feast; but when he heard that only two dishes were ordered, he crossly replied: "My lord, the scullion could prepare the dinner which you have ordered." "What do you want to say?" answered Alphonsus, "we received persons of great consequence at Nocera, and we did not treat them differently." "Your lordship was free to do so," boldly replied the cook, who then went out of the room grumbling. "There now," said Alphonsus, "what a passion he has put himself in! God knows all the plans he had concerted." However, the secretary had a third dish prepared; Alphonsus seemed as if he did not observe it while at dinner, but he gave him a severe reprimand afterwards, and said: "A bishop's table ought not to resemble those of the great, it would be a real scandal: poverty does not injure a bishop; on the contrary it does him honor." When Mgr. Albertini, bishop of

Caserto, came to Arienzo with his suite, Alphonsus ordered three more dishes than usual to be prepared; Br. Francis remembered the brilliant reception Alphonsus had received in passing through Caserto, and applied to a Father of the Congregation to obtain some more. The father had a lively discussion with him about it. "I cannot waste money," replied Alphonsus, "which belongs to the poor, in feasts; I am their father and their steward, but not the dilapidator of their possessions. I know not with what face one can eat of dishes prepared with the blood of those unhappy creatures who have no bread." The father managed so that he got some more dishes at dessert, three good dishes having been sent as a present. When Alphonsus saw them he was quite annoyed, and would only allow one to be touched. "The good nuns of the Holy Redeemer," he said to the bishop, "are so poor, we must send them something:" then addressing the other guests, he added, "His lordship does not want any more, he prefers conferring a charity on these poor females;" and he despatched the bearer to St. Agatha that same instant.

His table linen was so common that it looked quite discreditable, and the dishes were in keeping. His only candlesticks were of brass, and the salt cellars of earthenware. On extraordinary occasions, he sent to borrow plates and dishes from the Lords of Lucca, until the brother attendant and the secretary provided them, unknown to him. In conclusion, let us add the following testimony given to his apostolical poverty by a gentleman who went to visit him at Arienzo, in 1769, and who could not help weeping at seeing the great destitution of his host. "I have seen the ideal of poverty in Mgr. Liguori," he said to every body, "what indigence is there throughout the palace! some of the rooms are quite bare, others have three straw chairs made of unpolished poplar-wood in them, the simplest sort of tables, and a bed equally poor. If the saintly bishop required to be moved about, his servant drew him up and down in the room by means of a rope attached to a shabby wheel-chair."

As for the spirit of penance which animated him, he never omitted to discipline himself to blood every day, and the walls of his chamber would have borne constant witness to these macerations, if Mgr. Rossi, his successor, had not had them covered over by several coats of white-wash. It was asserted that his drawers were steeped in blood, as if they had been plunged in it. The prior of the Dominicans at Durazzano once dwelt in the bishop's house, on account of the examinations. The very day they terminated, he wished to set out immediately, (although it was late in the day,) and being urged to remain, he said: "I would return were it midnight, for I have not the heart to hear the flagellations of this poor old man any longer."

In order to obtain an increase of grace from God for himself and his flock, he used generally, on the vigils of feasts, to scourge himself with various cruel instruments, and especially with small cords armed with sharp steel stars. He also redoubled his macerations at the carnival and other profane fetes. Not satisfied with these bloody disciplines, he also mortified his flesh by horse-hair shirts studded with iron points, or by sharp little crosses with which he covered his shoulders, his arms and legs; when he sat down or got up again, his motions betrayed his sufferings. All the particulars of these instruments of penance would have been unknown, if the curiosity of some people had not revealed them to us. "I saw them all secretly," said a canon, who had lived in filial intimacy with him, "in a strong box, of which his lordship kept the key under his bed: I could not help shuddering the first time I opened it." How little he ate, we have seen above. There was a time when he lived on abstinence food entirely; and what was left of his food was so bad on account of the bitter herbs with which he had seasoned it, that not only the poor, but even animals, would not touch it. During the day also, he used to chew these herbs in order to mortify his palate, and he kept such a quantity of them, that one quite smelt them on entering his room.

When he ate any where but at home, he had a thousand stratagems for avoiding partaking of what was before him: sometimes he carved, or distributed portions; sometimes he appeared to be giving his attention to a little dog; at other times, when he thought that it would not be noticed, he mingled bitter herbs with the little that he took. During the whole time he was bishop, he never once complained of any dish being badly cooked, although accidents of this sort were not rare in his house. One day at dinner, he asked for something to drink, and instead of wine, the servant gave him a bottle of vinegar, but Alphonsus drank it without manifesting the least displeasure. A little while afterwards, the grand-vicar also asked to drink, and no sooner had he raised the glass to his lips than he began to scold the servant; but Alphonsus laughed, and excused him. On another occasion, when he was taking his meals in bed, the same thing happened again, and although the vinegar was very strong, he said nothing about it. Only, the next day he said to the servant: "Do not give me the same wine I had yesterday, for I took it for vinegar."

He liked fresh fruit, and used it as a remedy on account of his sedentary life, but, when for this reason D. Hercules supplied him with excellent fruit from Naples, Alphonsus gave it to the nuns of the Holy Redeemer: he did the same when he got rare fish, sweet things, or other delicacies, from his brother, or those nuns who were related to him.

In the midst of the sufferings which continually tormented him, he never sought for any other alleviations than those which were prescribed for him by the physician. One day, when he was oppressed by a very bad sick headache, F. Caputo offered to procure him some of the waters of St. Vincent Ferrer, in the hope that the saint would cure him, or at least relieve him. "Shall we go and apply to St. Vincent for such a little thing?" answered he. "If we want to address him, let us pray to him for the salvation of our souls, and for a good passage into eternity; as to what I suffer, it is nothing."

Although he was sinking under the weight of years and infirmities, he was always careful to mortify his senses. He never indulged in any gratification of the eyes, however innocent it might be. "I am certain," said F. Caputo, "that he scarcely knew that there was such a town as Arienzo or St. Agatha in the world." Another Father, who was intimate with him, said: "Alphonsus was so great an enemy to himself, that he had a universal hatred for all kinds of recreation." "His mortified life," added another, "filled all who saw it with confusion, and sufficed to change their lives." He slept as frequently on the floor as in bed. His bed, besides, was a place of penance rather than of rest, the palliasse being so thin that his body rested on the bare boards. He never had it shaken during all the years which preceded his great infirmity. Let us add one other testimony of our saint's penances during his episcopate; it is that of his grand-vicar, Rubini: "His lordship was as cruel towards himself as he was kind towards others," said he. "I should make you shudder, were I to relate to you all the particulars of his macerations, his abstinences from food, his daily scourgings to blood, of the hair shirts and iron chains which kept his body in a continual state of mortification, his watchings; in short, all which can afflict the flesh was made use of unceasingly."

CHAPTER XXIX.

Alphonsus' charity in relieving all kinds of bodily suffering. His detachment from all self-interest.

TO complete the description of the virtues of our saint during his episcopate, we must add that of his charity towards his neighbor in regard to their bodily necessities. Full of love for all works of mercy enjoined in the Gospel, he said that a *bishop* is especially bound to perform them. The numerous poor of his diocese were therefore the first objects of his charity. His heroic charity during the famine of 17—, and the frequent assistance given to persons in danger of sin, we have seen above. On Wednesday and Friday of each week, he had a general and public distribution of alms; but whenever any assistance was needed, all days were alike to him, none were exempted, even we might say that there was not an hour in the day, in which he could not be seen, purse in hand, giving liberally to all. The grand-vicar, Rubini, affirmed, that after subtracting what was necessary to pay the grand-vicar's salary, and the monthly salary to which the chaplain, the cook and the attendant were entitled, and also the expenses for the table, all the rest of his income was employed in alms, or else to meet the outlays which the suppression of disorders entailed. Archdeacon Rainone said that one day he saw the hall of the palace filled with poor: some asked for salt, others for lard, some for sugar, others for delicacies for their sick relatives at home. He was particularly careful in signing bonds, in exchange for which the apothecary was bound to furnish remedies; and he gave quinine, and other simple medicines with which he was provided to those who required them. The same archdeacon one day represented to him the excess of his generosity, as he was sometimes for whole days without having any thing left to give, (giving usually to each person at least from five to six grains,) and asked him what would remain for himself when he had given all away; reminding him that summer is not unending, and that the wants of winter are still greater. "Providence is never at a loss," replied Alphonsus. A light from on high directed his alms. Alexis, the servant, related that when he announced any poor person, he was in the habit of giving the first time a considerable sum of money; if the same person came back again, he diminished the alms each time, without personally seeing him. But if he were asked for charity for others, he again gave the large sum. During the bad weather in winter, when the poor could not work, his charity became still more striking. He was then in the habit of spending among them six, nine, and even ten ducats a day. "He was so generous in his alms," said a canon, "that he not only deprived himself of what was necessary for himself and for his family, but he did not hesitate even to contract heavy debts for the relief of the destitute." "Repeatedly," said another canon, "I went to borrow fifty, a hundred, and even two hundred ducats for him. When he could find no one to lend him any thing, he had recourse to the liberality of the great, especially of the Prince della Riccia. The Duchess of Maddalon also sent him several hundred ducats at once, which were specially intended for the poor of St. Agatha and of Arienzo. Any expense for purposes not necessary, he did not know, or rather considered as a robbery. We have given his sentiments on this head in several instances above; let us add the following. When D. Hercules came to visit him, for the first time, with his second wife, D. Marianne, the grand-vicar and others told the pious bishop that he ought to think of making some present to his sister-in-law. He consented; but they were much astonished when they saw that this present consisted in a garland of flowers, which he had himself received as a gift, and when the trifling value of the thing he had selected was objected to, he replied: "Do you then wish that I should take away from the poor, in order to make presents to my sister-in-law?" The lady took pleasure in prolonging her stay at St. Agatha, but Alphonsus felt distress at the expenses which this caused him, and for this reason he ingenuously said to his brother: "It would be very pleasant to me to keep you longer, but how can I meet the expenses it would entail? All my money comes from the church, and what one takes from the church, one takes from the poor also."

There are in the diocese sixty-four very rich chapels, of which the bishop has the administration. Alphonsus put aside, out of this, enough to meet the expenses of keeping them up, and for the services in them; and all the rest went for the relief of the poor, whether to the orphans, or to clothe the nakedness of a great number of other indigent persons; nay, he was so lavish in these alms that he sometimes obliged the rectors of these chapels to contract debts. Although several of these chapels were withdrawn from his administration, he did not lose courage, but managed so well with regard to the new managers, that they still distributed many alms according to his wishes. Besides, he was ingenious in turning to advantage every occasion, and in creating new resources for his beloved poor, as for instance, in appointing to offices, &c. Whenever he received any one in his own service, as a secretary, a chaplain, or a servant, he always gave the preference to the poorest, if he were fit for the post. Another instance is the following. A prior of a convent recently elected, sent him some pounds of excellent fish; Alphonsus thought it right to accept the gift, and to manifest his satisfaction at it, especially as he wanted to show that he felt no resentment for an annoyance which he had received from the fathers of the convent some days before. In the spiritual reading of that day out of the life of the Ven. Bartholomew, Br. Francis, who read for him, came to the passage where it is said that the archbishops of Prague were in the habit of sending a certain fish to the king every year, on the occasion of a particular solemnity, and that the venerable Bartholomew resolved to employ the money in the service of the poor, instead. As soon as Alphonsus heard this passage, he said to the brother: "To-morrow there will be a fair at Maddalon; take care to sell the fish, and give the money in charity." It was objected that it was too trifling a thing, and that the payment of the porter would amount to more than the fish was worth; he answered: "I know nothing about all that; do as I tell you."

Not content with assisting the indigent who presented themselves at the palace, Alphonsus took care to anticipate the wants of the bashful poor, and always ordered their priests to make them known to him. "I know," said a religious, "how many entire families he secretly supplied with provisions and clothing; to one he allotted ten carlins a month, to another thirty, and to a third five or six ducats, and even more, according to their station, and the number of individuals to be provided for." A young orphan of rank was destitute of relations, and lived in great misery. When he heard of her situation, he sent her a considerable sum of money through the medium of her parish priest, and then continued to send her a monthly allowance. A lady who had several children was in great distress, on account of her husband being a professed gambler. He supplied her with half a measure of corn every month, unknown to her husband; but he found it out and got some body to go for the alms in the name of his wife, sold it, and gambled with the proceeds. Alphonsus, in embarrassment what to do, sent three measures of corn to the wife during the absence of her husband; but on hearing that he had again got hold of it, he determined secretly to send the poor mother a monthly allowance through the hands of the priest.

Notwithstanding his known dislike to visits, Alphonsus, during his sojourn at Airola, went every evening to see an indigent nobleman, who was the father of a large family. He relieved his poverty, exercising the most refined delicacy in deceiving the very excusable pride of this nobleman.

One of the king's officers, also a stranger, was in want, on account of having a large family whom he was unable to supply with all they required; he informed Alphonsus of his position, and received six ducats a month during the whole time that his regiment remained at St. Agatha.

It was especially in secret alms, that Alphonsus' charity was most remarkable. "He who is a bishop," he was in the habit of saying, "ought to think a great deal about the poor whose tears no one thinks of drying: it is they who are chiefly recommended to us by Jesus Christ." One day when he was with Mgr. Bergame, the bishop of Gaeta, and Mgr. Tosti, the bishop of Fondi, who were both his penitents, he asked them in what way they regulated their alms. "As to that," answered Mgr. Bergame, "I do not believe that I am in fault; thanks be to God, I give largely to all that ask of me." "It strikes me," Alphonsus then said, "that you act as a priest and not as a bishop, you do not understand the meaning of these words of the Gospel: 'Let not your left hand know what your right hand giveth.' I advise you to think of alms-giving in secret, to widows, to families in trouble, and to the poor who conceal themselves."

If Alphonsus was liberal towards all the poor, he was prodigal we might say, when through their poverty they were in danger of offending God. We have already related, above, many facts which abundantly prove this; let us give here some more. A canon relates that one day he heard that a poor old woman had six children, of both sexes, and of a considerable age, who all shared the same bed. Alphonsus was horrified at this, and exclaimed: "O God, send for Br. Francis directly," and he instantly sent the poor woman all that was necessary to remedy this sad state of things. The parish priest of Talanico also found a number of families, who, through poverty, huddled all their children in the same bed; he informed Alphonsus of it, who hastened to procure beds for them all. He bought every year a great quantity of cloth and various kinds of merchandise, that he might clothe the naked in proportion to their wants.

Amongst the privileged poor, as Alphonsus called them, were, besides the nuns of the new convent of the Holy Redeemer, (of his charities towards whom we have spoken above,) the Capuchinesses of St. Peter of Alcantara, and the poor nuns of the convent of St. Philip Neri. Independently of alms in money, he supplied them with a store of oil, corn, and wine, each year.

The money he received in his pastoral visitations, was remitted to the episcopal vicars to be distributed among poor families, for his charity embraced the poor of the whole diocese. If he found a petition from a poor person in the number which came to him from all parts of the diocese, he was accustomed to say in a joyous manner: "Ah, this pleases me, it is a request for charity."

His charity extended even to strangers who were not of his diocese. A priest asked him, one day, for an annuity for a person who did not reside in the diocese. "You know very well," he replied, "that I am bound to assist all the poor in my own diocese; now they are so numerous that I cannot find enough for them. However, tell the canon, Joachim de Cæsare, in my name, to give four carlins a month to the person of whom you speak. I am poor and cannot give more." When strangers came to ask for his charity and he was unable to satisfy them, he said sorrowfully: "Charity must be regulated; if I have not enough to give my own poor, how can I give to others?" The pilgrims also did not ask for his assistance in vain. The following two most extraordinary instances of charity towards strangers are on record. One day, a pilgrim who stated that he was of noble birth, and a recent convert, asked him for alms. Alphonsus told his secretary to give him two carlins; the other refused them, saying that it was not enough. Alphonsus heard this in his room, and hastened to add something to the sum, but on the pilgrim's requiring still more, he ordered all that he had asked for to be given to him. Another indigent person, not belonging to his diocese, often came to ask him for alms; as he was sensible of the distress of this man, who appeared to have sprung from a good family, he was in the habit of sending him from ten to fifteen carlins through Br. Francis. This man loudly complained to the brother one day, and told him that the alms he got were insufficient. Alphonsus happened to come out of his room at this moment, and heard these words of discontent. "My son," he said to him, "I am overburthened with poor, and I know not what more I can sell for their aid; be satisfied with that for the present, and God will provide the rest." However, as the stranger went away murmuring, and with a bad grace, he took compassion on his distress, sent for him again and ordered twenty carlins to be given to him. Another instance of such (we may say) imperious poverty, and of submissive charity, is the following, though this person was of his own diocese. The inhabitants of the village of Cava are almost all attacked with the goitre. A woman of this place came one day to Alphonsus, accompanied by her daughter, (who was afflicted with this disease,) for whom she told him that she had an offer of marriage, but that she did not know how to get a *tonino*. Alphonsus could not make out what sort of a thing a tonino was, so the secretary asked the woman for an explanation of the word, when she replied that it was a collar of small gold beads for an ornament of the neck. The secretary burst out laughing, and said that all the toninos in the world would not be enough to ornament a neck like that. Alphonsus smiled, but touched with compassion, he ordered ten carlins to be given to her, and on her insisting on having more, he added four carlins besides.

Such extended liberality could not fail to be abused, and he was several times in consequence the dupe of the hypocritical poor. Several of their cheating tricks came to the ears of his friends, and they did not fail to warn him of it. Alphonsus replied without any astonishment, "that does me no harm; it is better to give an unnecessary alms and to be cheated, than to run the risk of being reproved for not having given what was necessary."

We have seen above how he supplied with medicine, eatables, and delicacies, those poor whom he knew to be sick; so also he did not fail to send money for their relief. We have seen also in another place, that when five o'clock struck, his relaxation was to go and console the sick who were in the greatest suffering, and he did not forget those whose misery made them repulsive. His solicitude was redoubled in the case of the dying; he left every thing to go and prepare them to make a good end. And there was nothing which he more inculcated on the priests, than the care of the sick, particularly if they were poor and desolate. When his servant Alexis became ill, he went several times to console him by his presence. One day he left four ducats for his wife, and as she was hopeless, the doctors having giving her cause to fear for her husband's life, he said that he would continue her husband's wages to her as long as he himself should live. When he heard that there were any incurable in the diocese, he caused them to be taken to one of the hospitals at Naples, at his own expense, and as he often had not enough wherewith to assist them, he applied to the administrators of the chapels, and to other persons.

The following is the testimony of a priest on this matter. "I was filled with admiration at seeing his lordship practice certain acts of charity, above all, those towards the sick. He numbered seventy-seven years, and although himself infirm, paralytic, and nearly sinking under the weight of old age, he still continued to go about the neighborhood and to visit the sick. To see an old man, all wasted away, his head bent down, so weak as to require not only the aid of my arm in getting in and out of the carriage, but also of that of his attendant; to see, I say, such an old man enter into houses to visit the suffering objects therein, was a sight which filled me with admiration, and I could not contemplate it without shedding tears. I one day asked him how he could still visit the sick, he who daily received the visits of two medical men. 'What sort of charity should I have,' he replied, 'if I were not able to suffer something for the benefit of my children? Oh! how much greater are the obligations of a bishop than those of any other Christian! I will even say, of any other ecclesiastic! The shepherd who wishes to watch over his flock properly, ought not to forget the sick sheep, but must take care of them in proportion to the magnitude of their wants.' His arrival amongst the sick was not without profit to them: . . . he exhorted them to patience, and encouraged them to accept their sickness as a penance sent them by God; he disposed them to receive the sacraments, he filled them with love and confidence towards the Blessed Virgin, whose picture he always gave to them. He inquired into their wants, and did not leave them without giving them an alms."

If any were ill and tormented by scruples, or had met with a fatal accident, he quitted every thing to go to their immediate assistance, and to dispose them to make a good confession. This once gave occasion to a singular mistake. He saw the viaticum being carried to some place in the neighborhood of his palace, at Arienzo, and asked to whom it was taken. Some one replied by the one word: 'Peccatore,' (sinner.) Upon that he was troubled and alarmed, and believing that the sick person was a great sinner, he sent to inquire what signs of repentance he had given. A canon who then saw the mistake said to him: "Peccatore is the name of the sick person; but he is a good man." However Alphonsus could not rest until he had crawled to the house of the dying man, examined into his state of mind, and satisfied himself as to his probity and piety.

On another occasion he heard that a villager had received a mortal wound; he immediately hurried off to see him and induce him to pardon his enemy. He repeated his visits daily while the sick man lived, and sent him provisions for himself and all his family. To the mother of the man, as she cheerfully forgave the murderer, he assigned a pension; but her daughter resisted all persuasions and would not forgive, though he visited her twice, so that he could but abandon her and pronounce the divine malediction against her.

His solicitude became extreme if the illness of an ecclesiastic were in question, and especially if it were that of an ecclesiastic still in the prime of life, and in a doubtful state of mind. When therefore he heard that a priest was in danger of death, he multiplied his visits, until he saw that he was contented and well disposed.

God often deigned to manifest, in a miraculous manner, what pleasure he had in the visits which Alphonsus paid to the bedside of those who were ill. Thus he predicted the death of the brother of the Archbishop of Amalfi, whom he had gone to comfort by his presence, and also that of a lady he went to see; in both cases contrary to the expectations of the medical men, and in the first, even though two celebrated doctors, who had been called from Naples, had held out confident hopes of a speedy recovery. So likewise when Mgr. Albertini was ill at Caserto, Alphonsus having gone to see him, and having heard that two physicians had pronounced him out of danger, knelt down before an image of the Blessed Virgin, and after a short prayer arose and said to the doctors, "It is useless to give yourselves more trouble; his lordship will die." He then entered the sick man's chamber and said to him: "My lord, do not trust to the flattering promises of the doctors; if God were to call you to himself, would you not wish to have received the sacraments?" "Undoubtedly I should, my dear friend," answered Mgr. Albertini, who immediately asked to receive the viaticum and extreme unction. Alphonsus after this said mass for the happy death of the prelate. One of his relations, the Duchess of Cimitile, did not approve of such sad preparations, and the doctors were still more dissatisfied. However, Alphonsus returned to Arienzo. He met the Governor of St. Agatha next day at the church, and inquired about Mgr. Albertini: "He is better," answered the governor, "at least so D. N. writes me word, and the doctors allowed him to take an egg this morning." After this Alphonsus ascended the pulpit, and at the end of the sermon, he said to the people: "Pray for Mgr. of Caserto, who is now in his last agony." He spoke truly, for on the following night Mgr. Albertini passed to another life.

It was just the contrary to this in regard to D. Blase Trossi: the doctor had given him over, and the people in the house told the bishop of the state in which he was, for Alphonsus knew the sick man well, and had often borrowed large sums of money from him. Distressed at such sad tidings, he said mass for him that very day. He then took a picture of the Blessed Virgin and sent it to him, telling him to recommend himself to her, and to be sure that he would obtain a cure. The sick man had no sooner received the picture and kissed it, than his state began to mend sensibly, and the improvement went on so rapidly, that he was quite well again in a few days.

Prisoners were as great objects of commiseration to the charitable bishop as the sick. He frequently visited them, to encourage them and incite them to patience, and if they were poor, he did not fail to relieve them by his alms. He gave six grains to each of them every Saturday. A priest stated that even when Alphonsus was at Arienzo, he sent the same for all the prisoners at St. Agatha every Saturday. But as these latter spent what they received in gambling, he ceased to give them money, and the alms were made in provisions. When there were any prisoners for debt, Alphonsus interceded for them with their creditors, whose claims he often satisfied with his own money. Let us relate the two following instances. At the opening of one of his pastoral visitations at Arienzo, he told the people how much it was his heart's wish to relieve all poor, and that if he could not satisfy all it was not from want of love, but through his own poverty. A man, on hearing these words, turning to a priest near him, said jestingly: "We have at last found our prefect," in allusion to a confraternity which was called, in derision, of St. Misery. When this speech was reported to Alphonsus, he only smiled at it. But sometime after he was told that this same man was in prison for debt, and that his family were starving; he then remembered his joke and said: "He is our fellow-member, we must assist him." He then paid the debt, which amounted to six ducats, and as he owed a great deal more in other ways, he allowed him ten carlins monthly.

A poor man had been in prison for three months for having smuggled salt; being ill besides, he had recourse to Alphonsus, who wrote to the royal administrator of salt at the tower of the Annunziata: "I entreat you to release this man from prison, because he is dying of hunger; he has nothing but alms to live on, for he possesses absolutely nothing of his own. I hope that my request may lead you to have pity on this unfortunate man, and that you will not have the cruelty to let him die in prison. My dear N., do me this kindness, and I will not fail to recommend you to God." The administrator asked him for a medical certificate as a security; Alphonsus wrote to him a few days after: "I send you the certificate you asked me for, and I hope that it will produce the desired effect, and that in reply I shall hear that this poor old man has been set at liberty. Believe me, my dear N., you could not do a better deed. I try to assist this unhappy man by alms, but I cannot remedy his imprisonment; this is why I hope you will kindly give me consolation by releasing him, and spare me the sorrow of hearing that he has died in this mournful prison, and perhaps destitute of spiritual aid."

He also interceded for criminals, and implored the clemency of the barons and judges for them. A soldier in a country regiment having been found carrying prohibited arms, was arrested and put in prison. Alphonsus pitied the young prisoner, and also his aged father, and lost no time in writing to the Duke of Maddalon's agent, to beg him to intercede for him with the commissioner in his name. He wrote also to the governor of the fortress of St. Agatha to the same effect, and obtained what he desired.

This kind of charity by intercession, he even extended to persons out of his diocese. Thus he wrote to the above mentioned administrator of salt in favor of the farmer of salt at Salerno: "I assure you, that this farmer is an honest man, and if he has not satisfied you, it has not been his fault. I therefore earnestly entreat you to leave this man in his farm, and to treat him with all the charity with which your good heart is filled; I shall always be grateful to you for what you will deign to do in his favor."

Compassion often ceases when one has to exercise it at his own expense, but that of Alphonsus knew no bounds. Alphonsus' store of apples once visibly diminished. A canon had suspicions about a person who frequented the palace, and went with Alexis and the commissioner to his house, and found there the missing apples and an iron instrument by means of which the theft had been committed. The magistrate was informed of it, and the thief was put in prison. The canon and Alexis carried the news to Alphonsus, expecting to receive praises for their zeal. But Alphonsus exclaimed: "What! imprison a poor creature for a few apples! go to the magistrate directly, and get him to set him at liberty; and as to the apples, I will buy them." "The apples are your own," replied Alexis. "Well," answered Alphonsus, "do not trouble yourself about that, and make haste and deliver this unfortunate man." Meanwhile, the grand-vicar and several gentlemen came in, and they all told him that he ought to let an example be made of the delinquent. Alphonsus yielded through prudence, but he immediately wrote to the magistrate to beg him to stop all proceedings, and to send him the iron which had been the instrument whereby the offence had been committed. He sent food to the prisoner morning and evening, and even gave something to the guards and the gaoler to cause them to deal well with the poor man; and as soon as he was set at liberty, he sent for him, remonstrated with him, and gave him a large alms. As mass was not said for the numerous prisoners who were confined at Arienzo, whither the country courts also sent their prisoners, Alphonsus managed to get the Duke of Maddalon to allow a chapel to be erected for them.

Among other instances of his procuring the release of prisoners, we will relate only the two following, where one of the immunities of the church, that is, the right of asylum, was in question. The constables met with a man at Arienzo, who was a dealer in tobacco, and arrested him, to examine if it were not the produce of fraud. As this was probably the case, the man had made away with it, not seeing any other means of escape. The constables were irritated at having missed their aim; they bastinadoed him, and wanted to put him in prison. The poor man took refuge in a church, from which they tore him away, and dragged him to prison. When Alphonsus heard of this, he immediately sent for the gaoler, and demanded that the prisoner should be set free. He then turned to the grand-vicar, and ordered him to write out the statement of all that had passed, and he added: "Our immunities are in question; if I had to sell my mitre, I would do so to obtain justice." He was not at rest till the prisoner was released.

Five Albanian soldiers deserted at the bridge of the Magdalene, and had the rashness to turn their arms against the officers who were sent in pursuit of them. Two of them were killed in the mountains of Arienzo, and the three others took refuge in a little country church. The suit was got ready, and application was made to Alphonsus to decide if they might or might not enjoy the privilege of sanctuary. They could not; but as he was in horror at the idea of delivering these men into the hands of justice, to be put to death, he let the allotted month pass without giving any decision, so that the matter might be left to the mixed court, from which he expected a more favorable decision. However, an officer of justice came from Naples for the papers relating to the trial; but on seeing that Alphonsus' decision was not there, he said to him: "My lord, your pity injures the culprits; for now that the mixed court must decide their case, they will assuredly be condemned to death." At these words, Alphonsus became much alarmed, and immediately sent for an officer quartered with a company at Arienzo, and asked him what he could do for these unfortunate men. "Nothing but your intercession can save them," answered the officer. Immediately, that is to say, at six o'clock in the evening, Alphonsus despatched a courier to General Prince Taci, to the Marquisses of Tanucci and of Marco, as well as to D. Anthony del Rio, secretary of war, to ask for the pardon of these criminals, saying that if he were not assured of their safety, his own life would be endangered, for, paralytic as he was, he would then go in person and throw himself at the feet of the king. Alphonsus obtained more than he had asked: the deserters received a full pardon, and all three, by order of the colonel, accompanied by an officer of justice, came to thank their deliverer. On seeing them he was filled with joy; he remonstrated with them in a paternal manner and showed that, not satisfied with having saved their lives, he also wished to save their souls.

Let us cite a last instance of Alphonsus' charity towards prisoners and persons accused. A chanter belonging to the cathedral became an accomplice in a homicide, and was put in prison, but as the evidence was not sufficient, he was set at liberty. As he could not, however, justify himself from having taken some part in the murder, he was suspended. He was very poor, and when Alphonsus saw his misery, he interceded for him with the treasurer, to beg that they would grant him the half of what he would have gained by his presence in the choir. "What you do for this poor creature," he said, "I shall feel as if done to myself." Touched by this request, they gave the unhappy man the whole of it. Alphonsus, still sorrowing over his position, took the opinion of enlightened persons, to know if he could not reinstate him. He sent him to Rome, with a statement of the case, and at his own expense; but as the matter could not be cleared up, he assisted the chanter and his parents by allowing him a pension. He had, moreover, appointed a canon as an advocate in favor of the poor, who was bound to defend them gratuitously in case of need, doing thus by others what he could not do by himself.

Hospitality is numbered by St. Paul among the duties of a bishop, and Alphonsus was also remarkable for that virtue; indeed, his palace was like a hotel, for it was always open. If any one of the clergy went to the palace in the evening, even if he were the lowest of all, he was sure of finding a lodging there. All strange ecclesiastics, and especially the candidates for holy orders who had no acquaintances at St. Agatha or at Arienzo, were also invited to dinner; if they came from a distant place, he made them also pass the night at the palace: and it was the same in regard to the agents of the priests, who daily came in great numbers to see him. When there was a meeting for the election to a living, he used to make the examiners dine at his table, as well as the candidates. "At dinner," he once said to a priest, "I am obliged to give and take of what I destine for the poor, for it does not do to send any of these priests to an inn." During the first period of his residence at St. Agatha, an arch-priest came at the dinner hour, accompanied by two ecclesiastics. He was ignorant of Alphonsus' way of acting, and begged him to receive him into the palace. "By all means," said Alphonsus, and as the two companions were getting up to go to the hotel, he caused them to stay, telling them that the house of a bishop is at the service of all, and particularly of priests.

D. Salvador Tramontana, who did nothing without consulting him, very often came to visit him; he never arrived without bringing either fruit or some cake, but Alphonsus perceived his delicacy and said: "When you come here, do not trouble yourself to bring any thing; a bishop is bound to be hospitable." Another time, he wrote to him: "If you will come here for four days, I shall be glad, but let it be without thinking of paying me for the little bread you may eat; remember that I lodge a great many other people." The grand chanter of the Cathedral of Girgenti, when visiting him, noticed that the table was well supplied, and said laughingly to Alphonsus: "How does this sumptuousness agree with your poverty?" "Hospitality," he answered, "is the daughter of charity, and not of poverty." However, this sumptuousness only consisted in an extra dish; and this was all the difference he made for the Duchesses of Borino and of Salandro, and other gentlemen and ladies who came to consult him, not even excepting his brother Hercules on his first visit after his second marriage. The pilgrims who applied to him, were lodged at the palace, besides receiving provisions for their journey. The members of his own Congregation were always welcome, and he treated them just like strangers, giving them the same kind of food; but he did not allow them any lengthened stay without there being a necessity for it, and when the business in question was terminated, he kindly dismissed whomsoever it might be.

We may also say, that in Alphonsus' time, the episcopal palace was turned into a public hospital. When any traveller fell ill, they appealed to the charity of the bishop. A hermit, who had come to ask his advice, was taken ill. He charitably received him into the palace, often visited him, paid for the doctors and the medicines, and did not let him go away till after a month, when he was entirely recovered. Mgrs. Borgia and Pallante coming once to speak with him, their coachman fell ill, and Alphonsus immediately gave him a bed and a room. The illness became serious, the last sacraments were administered to him, and Alphonsus did not fail to console him frequently by his own presence. The son of the coachman hastened to visit his father, and was received also with the greatest kindness. When the father was convalescent, Alphonsus caused light food to be procured for him, and treated him with the greatest attention. The father and the son remained in the palace for upwards of a month.

Although Alphonsus was so careful in fulfilling the duty of hospitality, he could not escape censure on this score, from those who would have liked to see at his house a splendid table where they might have good cheer and amusement. "They say," Alphonsus wrote to a priest who had informed him of this, "that I do not practice hospitality properly! I know, however, how much it costs me; as Arienzo is a town through which a great many people pass, my palace is almost always full of strangers, for whom I always keep several beds prepared, and the guests are sometimes so numerous that I am obliged to borrow beds."

Alphonsus, who was only economical in order to be liberal, was also admirable in his detachment from all self-interest. He detested the shadow of that cupidity which the apostle anathematises so severely. From the time of his arrival at St. Agatha, he regulated all the fees of the episcopal court according to the customs at Benevento, which considerably lessened the tax on a great many registrations. As to those relating to the ordinations, he wished them to be gratuitous, and when the secretary complained, he answered: "I sacrifice what accrued to me; you can take what is your due." See what he wrote to F. Villani on this subject: "As to the revenues of my bishopric, which are said to amount to four thousand ducats, I should be thankful if I had two thousand two hundred! I have retrenched many of the sums which I formerly received, but which I felt scrupulous about, and I think with reason. I have greatly reduced my income, because I consider it a very good kind of alms to abandon the fees on marriages, especially when there is poverty or danger in the case." When he resigned the episcopate, a canon examined the archives of the church at Arienzo, and said that he did not find a single marriage celebrated for nothing by the preceding bishops, while in Alphonsus' time there were a great many, especially among the poor. He himself wrote to one of his friends: "I often remit considerable sums, and those who serve me know what horror I feel in violently exacting the payment of what is due to me." He moreover generously abandoned all that was due to him for the patents for livings. The sixty-four rich chapels, of which he had the administration, as was said above, were each bound to pay him four ducats at the principal solemnity; but this sum he generally left in the hands of the administrators for the poor.

As to gifts and presents, which formerly formed a large part of the income of the bishopric of St. Agatha, we have seen above how particular he was in refusing them, for he would not receive any other than the dust from the feet of the poor. Let us give some other instances of this. The dean of the cathedral, after his appointment to the charge, sent a present to the bishop, who refused it. The dean on complaining of it, received this answer: "I have only done my duty in making you dean, and no recompense ought to be expected or received for doing what one ought to do." One day in the spring, he wished to have some of the fruits of the season, and knowing that a priest had a quantity of melons, he sent to buy four from him. The priest hastened to send him a dozen. When Alphonsus saw them he asked what they would cost, and the porter replied that it was a present. He immediately sent them back. The priest then came in person, and assured him that these melons cost him nothing. It was quite a contest, in which the priest got the victory, however, as he was set upon it. Alphonsus yielded, in order not to pain him; but he did it with so much regret that he took care in future never to ask for any thing of the sort from this priest or any other. On another occasion, a canon made him a present of three melons; Alphonsus positively determined that they should either be paid for or sent back again. But the canon, in order to get out of the difficulty, told him what they cost him, and said that he left the money in his hands for the poor. This agreement pleased Alphonsus.

He also showed the greatest disinterestedness, or rather liberality, in the farming of the property of the bishopric; and whatever conditions the farmers might have entered into, it sufficed for them to expose their distress and the hardness of the times, to insure their being released from a good part of their rents, especially if they were men who feared God. A great number of them obtained great reductions on considerable arrears. One of the farmers complained one day of the bad harvest, and "Alphonsus at once released him," said F. Buonopane, "from more than two hundred ducats of what he owed him." "In a word," said the grand-vicar Rubini, "he made so many such discounts, that he never had a farmer who paid the full amount of his lease."

Alphonsus dismissed a woman from a house belonging to his see, whom he had been led to suspect of bad character through a false report. The poor woman began a novena to St. Joseph, and went to Arienzo. When she was ushered into his presence, he asked her to what saint she was most devoted. "To St. Joseph," she answered. "Ah well," said he, for he had been previously undeceived, "St. Joseph has been gracious to you, and has told me not to turn you out." The woman encouraged by this good beginning, said that the rent was very high. Alphonsus touched by her poverty, asked her how much she wished to pay him. Her rent amounted to twenty-seven ducats; she offered one and twenty. Alphonsus agreed to this, and she continued to pay the same sum during the whole time he was bishop, though afterwards she had to pay thirty-one instead of twenty-one.

A steward was found to have a deficit of about four hundred ducats; Alphonsus, on seeing him shed tears and confess his negligence, was satisfied with discharging him, and sent him away in peace. Several persons said that he ought to bring him to justice. "What do you say about courts of justice?" said he with emotion, "this man has satisfied justice by confessing his fault. What a thing it would be to see a bishop bring an unfortunate man to justice, to ruin him outright, for the sake of his own interest!"

When he nominated D. Virgil Cimino as his secretary, the grand-vicar thought that as he was of the diocese he might give him only four ducats a month, instead of the ordinary sum of six. "Why be parsimonious?" replied Alphonsus. "D. Virgil is poor, why deprive him of any thing? let him receive what has been given before."

To give a final proof, which is very striking and touching, let us add the testimony of F. Raphael de Nuvo, the treasurer of St. Peter of Alcantara. "I am an old man of ninety," he said, "and yet I never saw a prelate so charitable and disinterested as Mgr. Liguori. His purse was always open to give, and only closed against receiving. Every thing was gratis for others, but he doubly paid what he himself owed."

But though his disinterestedness was so great, it did not go so far as to injure his successors, for he knew how to distinguish between his own individual interests and those of the episcopal revenue. Nay, his vigilance on this point was extreme. On the first Christmas after his arrival at St. Agatha, every priest or rector, even those of the monasteries, presented him with four capons; believing that this was a spontaneous present, he did not wish to receive it. But when Archbishop Rainone had brought the deeds and shown that this gift was not optional but a part of the revenues of the diocese, he not only received them, but even exacted them for the future, and in order to make a capital out of them, he applied to a poulterer each time, in order to know the price, and said to those around him jestingly: "This is a dish for the poor; it is not one for us, who are people of no consequence."

The archpriests, priests, rectors and superiors of monasteries, renewed their protestation of obedience on the Assumption, and according to old custom, they brought the bishop a present as a testimony of their submission. Alphonsus' predecessors had substituted a large sum of money instead of the present, without caring about receiving the accustomed homage; when Alphonsus heard of this, he required that they should renew their promise of obedience, and that in place of the prescribed sum, each one should again make him a little present.

The steward of the episcopal revenue demanded that an archpriest should give to the bishop the fifteen measures of corn due according to the terms of the ancient quit-rent; the archpriest replied that he was not bound to do so, since the payment of tithes had been forbidden. "I am surprised," answered Alphonsus, "that your reverence can thus forget your obligations after having taken an oath to defend the rights of the church. . . . If mild measures are not enough to make you pay what you owe, we will have recourse to the tribunals, because I am determined to receive the tribute which is due to me, at any price." Learning from the priest, in answer to this, that the squire at Arienzo had forbidden his paying the accustomed tithes, he hastened to write to all his priests to tell them to repair to Naples, and to state their rights before the royal council; adding that if the squire or others prevented justice being rendered, he would in that event himself undertake to defend the common law. In spite of his representations, the archpriest would not have recourse to Naples to defend his rights, nor would he pay the rental in question to the revenue. Alphonsus then felt obliged to denounce him to the Metropolitan of Benevento, but the cause remained undecided, as Alphonsus gave in his resignation meanwhile. However, in order not to neglect the interests of the revenue, when Mgr. Rossi went to St. Agatha, he informed him of the reasons which proved his claims. The episcopal income had been lessened by the contribution of wood furnished to the troops quartered at St. Agatha. As Alphonsus was not able to obtain any compensation for this, he appealed to the royal court. He alleged strong reasons in his favor, and the ministers, who were moved by their respect for his person, rejected the claims of the parish. "That which is taken from Mgr. Liguori," they said, "is taken from the poor."

These measures were very painful to Alphonsus, and he only determined to resort to them through necessity; for he was opposed to law suits, and tried, whenever any difficulty arose, to bring things to a happy end by gentle means, saying that a bad accommodation is better than a good law suit. Before proceeding against the arch-priest, he wrote to ask him to come and have an interview with him, and as he did not even deign to answer him, Alphonsus again wrote to him, and humbly said: "If I had a carriage I would have sent it for you long ago; come, I entreat you." It was only when he found that these advances were useless, that he at length resolved to have recourse to the law. A dispute arose between Alphonsus and the Duke of Maddalon, on the subject of the right of pasturage over a fief which belonged to the episcopal revenue, and as these rights had been refused for two years, he defended himself with apostolical courage. "I am obliged," he wrote to the Duke's agent, "to defend the property of the see, which possesses the double right of pasturage and lordship; I beg you to tell the officers of the Duke not to act with violence, because I will only yield to evident reasons for so doing, for I am bound in conscience to defend the revenue. If I am pushed to extremities, I will apply directly to the regency, by whom I hope to be heard. And in another letter, he said: "If I could reconcile it to my conscience, I would yield and say no more about this affair. God knows what a horror I have for law suits; the very name makes me tremble; but how can I yield, after having taken an oath to defend the rights of my church?" He wrote also to the Count of Cerreto, the young Duke's governor, and the affair ended to the advantage of Alphonsus, thanks to his firmness and prudence. The Count had a great veneration for the saintly bishop, who, not to be outdone in civility, placed the case in the hands of one of the Duke's advocates. The Count was satisfied with such a generous proceeding, and wrote to tell the agent to observe the ancient custom, and to pay up the arrears. It was a beautiful sight to see interest and disinterestedness thus struggling together in our saint, or rather to see his justice contending with his charity.

A poor gentleman, who was burthened with a numerous family, owed the revenue about twelve ducats for quit-rent. As he was summoned by the steward, he implored the intercession of a pious widow, who told Alphonsus of the state in which the gentleman was. He forgave him the debt at once, but reflecting on the difficulties in which he was placed, he added: "What shall be done for this man?" and assigned him a measure of corn every month. Nevertheless, in order to prevent the right as to the rent from being injured, he caused the steward to oblige the debtor to appear every year, in order to pay it, and then to give him the money under the title of an alms. He thus preserved all the rights of the revenue uninjured, and was in the habit of satisfying the claims of charity at his own private expense alone.

From the moment he came to St. Agatha, and saw that the see possessed a good deal of property, he took all possible care to prevent its being depreciated in value. Where olive trees were wanting, he caused them to be replanted; he every year had the dead trees replaced, and when any of the ground was uncultivated, he had its value increased by plantations. As one wing of the palace was in a bad state, he immediately ordered the suitable repairs, which cost him more than six hundred ducats. A house belonging to the episcopal revenue being also out of repair, the enant was unwilling to do any thing to it, but he insisted on it. "I feel scrupulous about it," he wrote to a canon, "and I wish to do all that is necessary in order to repair this house thoroughly, rather than diminish the ground-rent." He not only took care that the value of all this property did not become lessened; he even sought to make it still more valuable. As he knew that silk was much sought after, and that a great quantity of mulberry trees were needed for its production, he wished to have a number of plants of those trees, and even inquired as to whether white mulberry trees were more profitable than black ones.

CHAPTER XXX.

Alphonsus resigns the Episcopate. He leaves his Diocese, and returns to Nocera. His manner of life in his retirement.

HAVING thus seen in detail how Alphonsus shone forth in all the duties and virtues of the episcopal state, let us now follow him into his retreat. The successor of Clement XIV was not even elected, ere he again thought of resigning his bishopric; being then an octogenarian and paralytic, the burthen of the episcopate seemed no longer endurable to him. He was not, however, free from his accustomed fears, and as he felt doubts as to the validity of his reasons, he again opened his heart to F Villani, to ask his advice and the assistance of his prayers. He also consulted various zealous bishops, and in particular, Mgr. Borgia, and Mgr. Lusco, bishop of Lucero, and they all thought that he need have no scruples in resigning his office. But he took no resolution until he had received the decision of his director, F. Villani, who, though he had not approved of this resignation at first, yet on account of the state to which Alphonsus was reduced, now advised it, and told him that he ought to resign without any scruples, and that he was even bound to do so as he would abridge his life were he to continue to support the painful burthen. F. Villani, however, doubted whether the Pope would accept the resignation. "There is no reason to doubt about it," he answered to one of the Fathers of the Congregation, "he will accept it, for I am certain that I ought to die in the Congregation, and you will see that I shall die in it as a subject;" and he twice repeated that he must die as a subject. He prophesied, but the mystery was not then understood.

On the 15th of February, 1775, Cardinal Braschi was elected Pope under the title of Pius VI. After the coronation of the new pontiff, Alphonsus' anxiety to be set free from the weight of the episcopate increased. However, during the proceedings which ensued upon this, he still felt his accustomed scruples. "God only knows how I am tormented," he wrote to F. Villani, on the 9th of March. "The fear of abandoning my church in order to escape the cross, disturbs me anew. I should have been very glad if your reverence had spoken to Mgr. Borgia again; I fear that the apprehension of having acted through self-love will torment me during the whole of the short time I may have to live." The following is the petition he presented to the Pope. We give it entire, as it describes perfectly the state of health he was then in, and also gives a short account of the diocese:

"Most Holy Father, I wish to represent to your Holiness that I, the Bishop of St. Agatha dé Goti, in the kingdom of Naples, have attained the advanced age of seventy-nine years. By the aid of God, I have continued to bear the burden of the episcopate for thirteen years; but I am incapable of bearing it any longer. I have many infirmities which foretell a speedy death: I suffer from an affection of the chest, which has several times reduced me to great extremities; the palpitations of my heart have also several times brought me to the brink of the grave; besides this, I have at present such a great weakness of head that I feel often quite stupified.

"Besides all these maladies, I am also subject to divers dangerous attacks, for which I have to make use of bleeding, blistering, and other remedies. I have received the holy viaticum four times, and extreme unction twice, during the time that I have been bishop.

"I must add to what I have just stated, that I have other infirmities which prevent my fulfiling my duties as a bishop. My hearing is much impaired, and my subjects suffer much from it; for when they wish to speak to me of private matters, I cannot hear them unless they raise their voices. The paralysis has made such progress, that I cannot now write a single line; I can scarcely sign my name, and I do it so badly that it is very difficult to read it. I have become such a cripple, that I cannot walk a step, and I require the aid of two people in making the least movement. I pass my time on my bed, or I sit helpless in my chair. I cannot go through ordinations now, nor can I preach, and what is still worse, I cannot now visit my diocese, which necessarily suffers thereby. All this being the case, I think I am bound to beseech your Holiness to accept my resignation of my bishopric, which I formally tender in this petition, because I see that the state in which I am causes me to fail in the duties of my office, and in the right government of my flock. I confidently hope that your Holiness will take pity on me, in consideration of the miserable state to which I am reduced; and that you will console me by accepting my resignation, in order that my flock may be relieved, for they obtain little assistance from so incapable a shepherd, and also that I may be freed from the scruples which torment me when I reflect on my unfitness for government.

"I wish to lay the state of my church before you: The diocese contains about thirty thousand souls; the income amounts to about twenty-six thousand ducats annually, according to a calculation made during the last four years. The cathedral has thirty-one canons, with five prebendaries. In the territory of Arienzo, there is a college which numbers twenty-four canonries. There are three convents of cloistered nuns, namely, those of St. Agatha, those in the town of Airola, and in the territory of Arienzo, and also two asylums where there is also a church in which the sacred functions are celebrated.

"I very confidently look forward to receiving the consent of your Holiness, as well as your blessing, so that I may have nothing else to think of than to prepare myself for death, which will shortly befall me."

He sent this letter to Cardinal Crescensi, who loved him and favored him very much, begging him to consent to present it to the Pope, and to support it by his mediation. He wrote also to the same effect to Mgr. Calcagnini, the Pope's chamberlain, and to Cardinal Castelli. No sooner was it discovered at Arienzo that Alphonsus had sent in his resignation to the Pope, than the news spread throughout all the diocese, and caused general affliction. People consoled themselves, however, by the thought that the present Pope would not accept it any more than his predecessor had done. The superiors of the religious orders wept for the loss of a protector who was both powerful and zealous; the nuns, for that of a father and a comforter; the clergy felt as if in him they lost the soul of the ecclesiastical state, and the seculars, a tender and vigilant pastor: and so they all addressed the most ardent supplications to heaven for the preservation of their saintly bishop.

In the meantime Alphonsus was not idle, but redoubled his exertions and labors for the welfare of the diocese, encouraging the priests to labor for the salvation of souls, and to edify them by their own examples. The students of the seminary were always especially in his thoughts, for said he, "I do not wish to leave my successor overburthened with old debts;" he was therefore, to the last, as kind in rewarding the zealous as he was vigilant in chastising the tepid and expelling the incorrigible. Before he left his vineyard, he was also careful to have it entirely visited throughout by faithful laborers, having applied, from the preceding September, to the various Congregations, in order to have a sufficient number of missioners to preach throughout all the diocese; he had even written to Rome to the general of the Dominicans, in order to obtain a good number of his religious from La Sanita in Naples. Thus he succeeded in not leaving an estate, a village, or a hamlet throughout the diocese, which had not been cultivated by zealous missionaries, having joined, for this purpose, to those of his own Congregation the missionaries he had himself formed at Airola, Arienzo and Durazzano. He himself, from his bed or arm-chair, arranged the smallest details of this great work, even to the providing for the accommodation of the missionaries and all they required. From the following fact, we might almost fancy he was present every where to watch over every thing. On the 12th of April, 1775, he caused his secretary to write to one of the missionaries: "You must be careful in watching N. the lay-brother. You know the convent where he lives, and you must see whether he continues to visit the house of N. to the scandal of the neighborhood. He wishes you to inform him about this as soon as possible, and to come here to him this morning to speak to him by word of mouth touching this monk."

In order that the passion of Jesus Christ should be well impressed on all hearts, he caused a picture of it, as large as life, to be painted in the most moving manner, and to be carried in procession through the church on the last evening of the exercises of each mission. In order also to excite the faithful to compassionate the dolors of the Blessed Virgin, he caused the statue of our Lady of Dolors to be exposed and carried processionally in the same way. Besides, he pointed out in a circular, all that must be done in order to succeed in inspiring the people with compunction through the picture of Jesus crucified, as well as by the image of our Lady of Sorrows, prescribing at the same time the malediction of habitual sinners in all places where corruption or any special vice existed, such, for instance, as blasphemy or licentiousness, and pointing out what was to be observed in order to awaken obstinate sinners.

The Holy Father, knowing too well how to appreciate Alphonsus' zeal and the great good which he was continually effecting in his diocese, was not in the least disposed to accept his resignation. But two fathers of the Congregation happening, after giving the mission in the Abbruzzes, to pass through Rome, and going to pay their homage to the Holy Father, he asked them about Mgr. Liguori. They answered: "Most Holy Father, he is in a state which quite makes one grieve for him: he is deaf, blind, and laden with so many infirmities, that he has no longer even the appearance of a man." The Pope then turning to Mgr. Calcagnini, said: "Do you hear what these fathers say? If this be the case, we must not distress him." Upon this he determined to accept his resignation, though he did so with much regret, and ordered this to be signified to Alphonsus, on the 9th of May, 1775.

This news filled Alphonsus with joy, but in the diocese the lamentations became universal. Archdeacon Rainone, on receiving the letter of Alphonsus which announced it to the chapter, said: "It is a chastisement from God, we have not known how to appreciate him." As soon as the news spread, there was not a single canon or priest who did not go to Arienzo to see him at his palace, and who did not complain of the step he had taken, with tearful eyes; and even those who had experienced his severity were now undeceived, and did justice to his merits, feeling only regret at hearing the tidings of his departure. But the poor were the most afflicted of all. Penitent women, poor girls, and a great number of indigent families who had relied on his assistance, were inconsolable at losing him. These, as well as the infirm, said, weeping, "We shall not have Mgr. Liguori any more, who used to send us comfort or to come and console us himself. Who will now intercede for us with our creditors, and who will plead our cause with the magistrates? His lordship could do every thing, for he was a saint, and every one honored him as such." We cannot forbear quoting here the words of a poor villager, as they show how far Alphonsus' charity went: "When we used to go to the mountain," he said, "we left our children at his lordship's palace, and we felt sure they would be fed; but now that he is going away, to whom shall we have recourse?"

The resignation was formally accepted by the consistory, on the 17th of July; on hearing this news, some one said to him jestingly, that since his resignation had been accepted he appeared to hold his head straighter than before. "Yes," replied Alphonsus, "because the weight of Mount Taburno, (a very high mountain which overtops St. Agatha,) has been taken off my shoulders." After he had thanked the Pope for the great favor he had deigned to confer on him, he asked him to allow him to preserve all the privileges annexed to the episcopate, especially in regard to the portable altar. The Pope granted this request in the fullest sense, and added another favor which Alphonsus had not asked for. "Our Holy Father," Cardinal Giraud wrote to him, "thinks of reserving to you a suitable pension secured on your church, and he wishes to settle as to its amount with yourself." Alphonsus replied that if the Pope deigned to grant him a pension, four hundred ducats would be enough for him. This moderation was extremely edifying to the Holy Father, who, in consideration of his circumstances, graciously assigned him eight hundred ducats, and also released a debt of one hundred and five ducats he owed to the apostolical chamber. He caused him also to be freed from all expenses for the composition and despatch of the letters, saying: "One cannot do enough for Mgr. Liguori." The college of Doctors at Naples decreed also to give him the whole of his pension, just as he had been receiving it up to that time, though he was not entitled to it unless on the condition of residing in Naples.

Mgr. Rossi, bishop of Ischia, was elected as the successor of Alphonsus. Before this election was decided on by the Pope, divers reports were spread about concerning the person who would succeed to the vacant see, the candidates being very numerous. Alphonsus himself inquired as to which of the conjectures on this subject had any foundation; several names were mentioned to him, but he heard them with indifference, until a canon one day said: "Mgr. Rossi, the bishop of Ischia, is talked of as the one who will be elected." "Mgr. Rossi!" replied Alphonsus with earnestness. "My God! My God! I will at once write to Rome to be allowed to reside here until the arrival of the new bishop." He then became more animated, and exclaimed: "My poor church, how long wilt thou have to remain a widow, and without a pastor?" He hastened to write to Rome, in hopes that the Pope would allow him to continue to rule over his church until the arrival of his successor, but, according to a new rule of discipline, a bishop who had resigned was obliged to leave his diocese immediately. Alphonsus had prophesied truly, however, for the clergy of Ischia, contrary to all expectation, opposed the translation of their bishop to the church of St. Agatha, which remained a widow for nearly five years.

As soon as Mgr. Rossi was duly elected by the Pope, Alphonsus, wishing to be useful to his church up to the last moment, wrote to him on the 17th of June, as follows: "When your lordship shall have taken possession of this church, I trust you will do me the favor to come to Nocera for two days, when I will give you full particulars of all that can interest you regarding the bishopric, and of all that I have learned during thirteen years of labor. Two days will suffice to inform you of all. I hope that your lordship, by means of what I will tell you and your own experience, will be able to carry on the government in an excellent manner and for God's glory." Mgr. Rossi went afterwards to Nocera, and Alphonsus informed him of the state of the diocese with tearful eyes.

When Alphonsus was on the point of separating from his dear church of St. Agatha, he wished to visit his children once more in person, although he was so infirm and broken down. In making this visitation of the parishes, he for the last time inculcated on them all, perseverance in well-doing, the avoidance of sin, the frequentation of the sacraments, and above all, the love of Jesus Christ, and devotion to the Blessed Virgin Mary; asking at the same time pardon for his numerous failings, as he called them, and the scandal he might have given, and recommending himself to their prayers, particularly when they should hear of his death. He was every where answered by sobs and floods of tears. How much impression these his last words of exhortation must have made, we may conclude from the following instance. He determined to make a last appeal to a hardened sinner, a surgeon, whom he had imprisoned at Nevano. "Now that I am going away to leave my church," he said to him, "do you also leave off sin." The emotion with which he pronounced these words penetrated the heart of the unhappy man, who before long became converted, and being attacked by a sickness which made him think seriously, he made a public confession of his sins, and died in sentiments of the most sincere repentance, rendering a thousand thanks to Mgr. Liguori.

He visited also all religious communities, of both sexes, reminding them of his paternal lessons and exhorting them to a zealous observance of their rules and a fervent striving after perfection. As he was unable, on account of the fatigue, to go to St. Agatha, in order to make his farewell in person, he wrote a letter to the chapter, the reading of which caused many tears to be shed. As Sister Mary Raphael, the foundress of the Nuns of the Holy Redeemer, could not see him at St. Agatha, she wrote to him a most affectionate letter. Among other things, she said that she hoped he would not forget his daughters in Jesus Christ, and would bequeath his heart to them by will. "Bequeath my heart!" Alphonsus said, when he came to these words, "I have always considered Mother Raphael as a sensible woman, but I have now lost my good opinion of her. My heart indeed! what dish do they want to make of it? It is the soul that has value; as for my body, if they wish to please me, they will throw it away." The present he sent to them was, besides a letter of advice and counsel for Mother Raphael, a simple wooden cross with the emblems of the passion, which he had kept in his room, and which he was in the habit of kissing whenever he entered or went out of it. To the Nuns of the Annunziato, who had asked for a little keepsake, he sent the little picture of our Lady of good counsel, which he had had always on his table—begging them to say a Salve Regina for him every Saturday, and to recite the litanies for him for three days after his death. To the canons, who also asked him for a remembrance, he gave the large cross with the emblems of the passion, which had been on the first landing place of the stair-case, and which he had also been in the habit of kissing whenever he went in or out of the house. To the Capuchin Fathers he left some artificial flowers which had adorned the altar of the Blessed Sacrament in his chapel. To the Seminarists who had come to Arienzo, he gave some books which belonged to him, as well as all his own works. The furniture and valuable goods he left in the palace as belonging to the chapter of St. Agatha, were some few miserable beds and some cooking utensils. The mattress and arm chair he asked to be allowed to take with him as an alms from the two canons who were deputies from the chapter of St. Agatha, who readily granted what he wished for, but shed tears at the affecting scene of such humility and poverty. The other things of which he had made use were carried off as relics. Some asked; others took what they wanted secretly, and as each wished to have something, every thing disappeared, even the little images he had at the head of his bed. A little wooden crucifix was even violently carried off by a gentleman of Arienzo, and as the barber of the house did not see any thing else to take, he asked Alphonsus for a crutch of which he had made use when he had the rheumatism. "Take it," he said, "for it may be serviceable to you some day." In fact, his son's wife being some years afterwards in labor for three days, he remembered the crutch and these words, and taking it, said to her: "This crutch belonged to our late bishop, who worked so many miracles; if you have faith, and will only take it, you will be cured." She had scarcely touched it, when she was delivered and out of danger, though all had despaired of her safety. As to his beloved poor, as soon as his departure had been certain, he had considerably increased his alms to them, and on the day he left Arienzo, the palace was, as it were, besieged by them, and they all had the gratification of sharing in his last donations.

At last, on the 27th of July 1775, after having ruled over the church of St. Agatha for thirteen years and fifteen days, early in the morning, he gave his last blessing in his dear church of St. Agatha to an immense concourse of people; he distributed large alms to a crowd of poor persons who solicited his charity, and amidst the groans of these, as well as the tears of the clergy and the people, he got into his carriage, aided by his household, and accompanied by F. Villani. The sight of the affliction of the people was like a two-edged sword that pierced his heart, and tears began to flow from his eyes. When he saw that the priests, canons and gentlemen intended to follow him, he thanked them and assured them of his gratitude for this mark of their affection, but would not permit them to do so. However, four of the canons were determined to accompany him, as well as F. Caputo and a great number of gentlemen. When they had gone on for some miles, Alphonsus was anxious they should return, and assured them that their presence only increased instead of relieving his distress, but the treasurer and some others would not yield to his entreaties, and accompanied him to Nocera.

On the way he addressed his usual prayers to his saintly patron, and particularly commended the whole diocese to the protection of Jesus Christ and his Blessed Mother; and continued the journey while reciting the rosary and canonical hours with F. Villani. He had not said mass in the morning on account of the emotion which his departure caused him to feel; he therefore went to the Seminary at Nola, and celebrated it in presence of the whole seminary, although he was in a state of great suffering and weakness. Every one shed tears of tenderness at seeing the devotion with which he celebrated the august sacrifice, without omitting the most minute rubric, notwithstanding his age and sufferings. When the mass was ended, he heard that of F. Villani, making his thanksgiving, after which, at the request of the superior, he addressed an exhortation to all the pupils and gave them his blessing. When his arrival had become known at Nola, several gentlemen came to pay him their respects; among these was D. Michael Menichino, whose sight had been so much weakened for upwards of a year through inflammation, that he was no longer able to walk without being led. Various remedies had been fruitlessly tried at Naples and at Nola; and the complaint had got so much worse that he had become at length completely blind. He arrived just when Alphonsus was going to get in his carriage; he threw himself at his feet, and shedding tears, entreated him to make the sign of the cross on his eyes. Alphonsus had no sooner done so, than the blind man recovered his sight.

As soon as he had entered the carriage again, Alphonsus recommenced the recitation of the rosary with F. Villani, and the rest of the time was employed in saying the office and other prayers. When he arrived at Nocera, Mgr. Sanfelice ordered that all the bells should ring out to welcome him. Great rejoicing, though mingled with compassion at the state he was in, was felt by the inhabitants, and tears of emotion were in all eyes. All the clergy and a great number of gentlemen, hastened to kiss his hand and to receive his blessing. When he was on the steps, he exclaimed with transport: "Gloria Patri, &c. The cross which I wear at my breast was very heavy when I ascended the stair-case at Arienzo, but how light has it become today! Gloria Patri," &c. When he reached the choir, he cast himself on his face before the Blessed Sacrament, and was heard to say: "My God! I thank Thee for having released me from so heavy a burden. My Jesus! I could endure it no longer." The fathers in the meanwhile sang the Te Deum, to thank God for having restored their common father to them.

A comfortable room, till then used for strangers, had been prepared for him; when he was conducted there, he observed a piece of tapestry with a kind of black border, which formed the ceiling, and exclaimed: "What, must I live in the midst of ornaments? I will have my old room." He was told F. Villani occupied it, but he would not yield till it was represented to him that he ought to have a room for visitors, when he consented to take two little rooms on the third floor. When he saw that he was lodged as the poor are, he joyfully said to the gentlemen who surrounded him: "O how much better satisfied I am in this cell than in the palace at Arienzo," and taking his little cross in his hand, repeated several times: "This cross has become very light here; but there I sank under its weight." The grand-vicar of Nocera came to see him the same evening, to pay his respects to him as the deputy of Mgr. Sanfelice. In the course of the conversation, the grand-vicar observing that he thought that the diocese was very much displeased at his departure, Alphonsus asked, "why?" "Because it has lost a pastor who did much good," answered the grand-vicar. Alphonsus was disturbed at these words. "Jesus and Mary!" he exclaimed, "what does the grand-vicar say of me, who have done no good at all, none, none, none! If any good has been done, it was God, God alone who has done all." Mgr. Sanfelice came to visit him himself next day, and conferred full powers on him to exercise all authority in the diocese. He received also the visits of the bishops and grand-vicars in the neighborhood, as well as those of all the superiors of the monasteries, and of the nobles and persons of rank of the neighboring places in the diocese, which prevented him from resting for several days.

If Alphonsus' mode of life at Arienzo was admirable and laborious, it was no less so at Nocera. He was only relieved from the burden of the episcopate in order to bear that of the Congregation, as now all had recourse to their common father and left him no rest. "I had hoped to find relief at Nocera," he wrote to F. Majone, on the 26th of January 1776, "but I have met with a thousand thorns, which deprive me of all rest. God be praised! My head is exhausted, and I am forced to have a wet cloth constantly beside me, to prevent giddiness or fainting through the number of letters I have to write. . . . I feel scrupulous in neglecting to write the inspirations which God gives me, for God gives knowledge to superiors which he does not grant to others, and it is this thought which makes me write so many letters." He never omitted to drag himself to the chapel every Saturday, to assist at the chapter, and to animate his sons to greater perfection. "Why are we in the Congregation," he one day said, "if it is not in order to become saints? The end which God had in view in delivering us from the world, is our sanctification; if this had not been his intention, he would have left us in the midst of its dangers."

In consequence of the vow he had made of preaching on the glories of the Blessed Virgin every Saturday, he did not fail to have himself conducted to the church by the lay-brother and his servant on the Saturday after his arrival, though they had the greatest difficulty in placing him in the pulpit. As soon as he appeared before the people, who had hastened in crowds to hear him, they all uttered a cry of compassion, and wept at seeing the saintly bishop broken down by infirmities, but rejoiced also in seeing fulfilled the prophecy he had made of coming to die amongst them. He preached as if he had been quite well, and afterwards did the same on all Saturdays.

A constant concourse of persons of distinction, of priests, and of monks, hastened to be directed by his counsels; and all the bishops who went to Naples or returned from thence, made it a point to consult him on their own necessities, and on those of their dioceses. A congregation of zealous priests, established at Nocera, devoting themselves to the apostolical ministry by giving missions and the exercises of Lent, preaching, and daily hearing confessions in their own church, wished often to have him in their midst to obtain a constantly increasing fervor through his exhortations—and the nuns also wished to hear his instructions; he did not fail to visit both places from time to time, to comply with their wishes and exercise his zeal. He visited also the asylum, called the Carminella. When he first arrived at Nocera, he effected in this asylum what several confessors had attempted in vain. Two of the inmates, though consecrated to God, were living there in a state of scandalous enmity; but one of them, upon merely seeing him, humbled herself, and ran and cast herself at the feet of her enemy, and they both asked each other's forgiveness for their offences. On another day, the mother prioress asked him to remember her in his prayers in order that he might obtain for her the cure of a cancer which she had in her left breast, and which the doctors looked upon as incurable. He encouraged her to bear the malady patiently, by placing herself in the hands of God and embracing the cross. When he returned to the house, he sent her a bottle of pure water, telling her to bathe the diseased part with it; after she had done so, the tumor disappeared, and she was perfectly cured.

One of his rooms served him as an oratory; on the altar there was to be seen a large crucifix, and at the foot of it a beautiful figure of the Blessed Virgin, placed between two others of the divine Shepherd and the Blessed Virgin with the Holy Ghost on her breast. From morning till night, except the time he went, according to the express command of the doctors and F. Villani, to take a short airing in the carriage, he was to be seen before these objects of his devotion, engaged in his exercises of piety, or occupied in reading and in the composition of his works. This room was also adorned by German figures representing the different mysteries of the passion on a grand scale, so that wherever he turned his eyes, they met with objects which served to gratify his devotion. Other ornaments it had none: three or four straw chairs and a little table formed its whole furniture, with the roughly made armchair which he had received as an alms at St. Agatha. It was covered with some old damask silk which the grand-vicar and others obliged him to keep while at Arienzo; but at Nocera this stuff, although torn, was a great pain to him, and as it inflicted a wound on his love of poverty, he several times declared to F. Villani that he could not endure it, and so at last he had it taken off the chair, which he had covered with leather. His bed-room was ornamented with the same kind of pious pictures, with some others of St. Michael, St. Margaret of Cortona, and the seraphic St. Bonaventure; and these were its sole ornaments. The poor were his privileged friends at Nocera also. After he had paid the wages of his servant and his coachman, and for what the keeping of his horses and his own miserable nourishment cost, he gave all the rest to the poor.

He went through all the exercises of the community, and had himself brought, or rather dragged from the third floor to the church, before the Blessed Sacrament, for making his visit there, which lasted often for hours; the way of the cross he performed daily, not in his chair as at Arienzo, but by going to the different stations in a long corridor.

He put the finishing stroke to his book on Divine Providence, that is to say, on the Economy of the Redemption of Man, the year of his arrival at Nocera. He added to this work two treatises, the first, on the love of God, and the methods of acquiring it, the second containing various counsels fitted to encourage a soul in desolation. At this time he took up also the pen against an enemy of the devotion to the Blessed Virgin: "I am determined," he says himself, "to write these few pages from seeing that Abbé Rolli (a Calabrian priest) wishes to throw discredit on the devout prayers and titles commonly given to the Blessed Virgin by the faithful in the litanies and in the Salve Regina—as well as from hearing him call the scapular and the rosary childish devotions, whereas they are most religious practices, and have been dear to me from my earliest infancy."

Alphonsus was full of gratitude to the Holy Father Pius VI, and embraced an opportunity of testifying it to him by dedicating to him his work on Divine Providence, which he sent him together with his last writings. Pius VI accepted this little present, and testified his satisfaction to him by a brief of the 19th of November. Alphonsus, overwhelmed by so much kindness, hastened to offer his most humble thanks to the Holy Father, and recommended his Congregation to him, and Pius VI, who was sensible of his gratitude, replied to him in a new brief dated the 16th of December 1776, saying that his thanks were superfluous both as regarded the augmentation of his pension and the dues which were remitted to him, as he had overpaid for all by the present of his works. "They are," he said, "a fresh and convincing proof to us of your indefatigable zeal in feeding the flock of Jesus Christ as far as lies in your power; so that, although you have resigned the episcopate, you have not, however, renounced the solicitude and the duties of a bishop. As to the protection of the apostolic see which you implore for the Congregation of the Holy Redeemer, you cannot ask us for any thing which is more just, and I will never refuse it to you, whose piety we delight in acknowledging—nor to your Congregation."

There is also another work of Alphonsus', composed after his return to Nocera. It is a treatise on the sacrifice of Jesus Christ on the cross and on the altar, and a short explanation of the prayers used at mass. As there was no lack of individuals who wished to act like free-thinkers, and who therefore designated eternal truths, such as the resurrection, judgment, hell and such like, as mere fables, Alphonsus again attacked them in 1776, in a book entitled 'Dogmatical Dissertations,' in which he sets forth each of these dogmas in all its parts on the authority of the Scripture, of the holy fathers, and of theologians; he also there treats of private judgment, purgatory and antichrist, and speaks of the signs and the circumstances of the end of the world, of the state of the damned, of the blessed, and of infants who have died without baptism.

He had to endure again some opposition from the ecclesiastical examiner at Naples, on account of this work; viz: first, in regard to an assertion that there is no difference between the love of the blessed in heaven and that of the souls on earth, though it is the common opinion of theologians; and secondly, in regard to infants who died without baptism, on which subject the examiner wanted him to prefer the doctrine of St. Augustine to that of St. Thomas. After having written three times to the examiner, he appealed to the archbishop, and thus his opinion in favor of St. Thomas prevailed and the dispute was terminated. He was very ill when he published this work, for he wrote to F. Cajone, at the commencement of 1777: "I cannot now either read or write; I am troubled with a constant headache, and I have been obliged to give up all kinds of study."

CHAPTER XXXI.

The Congregation is bitterly persecuted at Naples. Alphonsus labors in its defence. His anxieties in regard to the houses in the Pontifical States.

THESE were the pious and useful occupations of the saintly bishop in his retreat at Nocera. But he had all the time, moreover, to drink the cup of bitterness which God had prepared for him in the continual persecutions to which his beloved Congregation was exposed. We have seen above, on several occasions, how fierce, how intriguing and obstinate were its adversaries, and that three not over well-intentioned individuals had been commissioned to take information with regard to it and make their reports. The Marquis of Tanucci, on the 3d of October 1775, moved by incessant calumnious petitions, published three ordinances, enjoining it upon those three commissioners, after a compilation of all the proceedings and accusations in the council of St. Clare, that of Sommaria, and in the royal council, and after having examined every thing, to make their opinions known to his majesty, and to transmit all the documents to the chief ministerial council. The suppression of the Jesuits, which had happened not long before, confirmed the forebodings of the speedy suppression of the Congregation; and, besides, very serious difficulties had arisen between the courts of Naples and Rome. The enemies of the missionaries already began to glory in their triumph and in the destruction of the Congregation.

In these critical circumstances, Alphonsus despaired of the aid of men, and therefore, as usual, turned to God with redoubled fervor. He recommended himself again to the prayers of several monasteries, and wrote a circular to all the houses, on the 4th of November, in which, among other advice and exhortations, he says: "My very dear brethren, redouble your fervor in prayer, for our enemies redouble their fury against us. . . . Do not cease to pray, for if you neglect prayer our ruin is certain. If we pray and act as we ought towards God, he will preserve us; if not, we shall assuredly be destroyed. . . . What pains me most is not the seeing one of you ill, or even leaving the Congregation; I wish him well—but to see one commit faults, especially against obedience and poverty, that rends my very heart. I bless you all, one by one. Pray about the persecution which we endure, and which is more intense now than ever; but I trust in Jesus Christ and the Blessed Virgin, who will not abandon us."

Thus Alphonsus was affected by hope and fear, but hope preponderated. "I am quite contented," he wrote to the fathers at Naples, "because I feel sure that our Lady will protect us during this storm." In order to comfort the subjects of the Congregation who were cast down by the constant fear of being turned out of their houses, and the many vexations they were daily exposed to, he used to say: "Persecutions are to the work of God, what a storm is to trees in winter; far from hurting them, it helps them to put forth deeper roots, and renders them more fruitful. There is nothing but the worm which can injure plants. The worms which we ought to avoid are faults and voluntary failures. . . . Let us kiss the walls of our cells, and in proportion to the amount of our persecutions, let us keep all the more closely united to Jesus Christ."

In the meantime, the procurator advocate, one of the commissioners mentioned above, had allowed himself to be persuaded by the adversaries; they also succeeded in acting on the mind of the prime minister by means of intrigue, and this was cause for new shouts of triumph. "The casuistical tribe is extirpated," they exclaimed. "We can see now," said others, "what this Liguori is, and what kind of people he has for disciples." The advocates and the other magistrates on the missionaries' side themselves looked upon their cause as a desperate one when they saw it in the hands of the three persons of whom we have spoken. The fathers therefore were anxious to see Alphonsus in Naples. But he answered, on the 26th of January 1776, to F. Majone, who had solicited him to come: "Your reverence has again written to tell me that it would be a good plan were I to come and speak to the Marquis of Tanucci; but you well know that I am no longer fit for any thing. Last night I suffered from my asthma, and had such palpitations of the heart that I thought I should have died. Yes, certainly, my father, I am ready to give my life to prevent the destruction of this work of God, but it would require an extreme necessity to justify my placing it in evident peril, and that would be the case now."

The adversaries on the other hand, on seeing Alphonsus' impaired health, predicted his speedy death, and every where said that if the Congregation were not forced to come to an end by the weight of their accusations, it would at least become extinct with the life of Mgr. Liguori. "They say," he wrote to the houses of Scifelli and Frosinone, "that when I die all will be ended; I say, for my part, that this Congregation, which is not my work but that of God, will endure after my death, as it has done for forty-four years." To other fathers he said: "Fear nothing, I shall not die yet, God wills that I shall die a subject, and not a chief superior of the Congregation." We have seen that he had already predicted this in the year 1774, and the event will show but too well that he had indeed prophesied.

While things went on thus, some people proposed to Alphonsus to render the houses independent, like those of the Fathers of the Oratory; others, that he should open seminaries for the education of youth, and that they should also preach Latin sermons. But he rejected all these propositions with horror, putting his confidence in God, who would most certainly bless his Congregation if it adhered faithfully to its special vocation, in which it had till then done so much good for the benefit of souls.

The affairs of the Congregation had become still more involved by the two following circumstances. Its enemies by attacking anew the doctrine of Alphonsus, accusing him and his missionaries of laxity, error and malice, and representing his doctrine as opposed to the Gospel and destructive both to church and state, succeeded, (being favored by one of the chief functionaries in the royal ministry,) in making an impression on the mind of the Marquis of Tanucci; who therefore declared that the cause should not be discussed in the royal council, but that it should be rigorously examined in the junta of abuses. This decision was a new signal of triumph to the adversaries, and Alphonsus himself appeared to be disconcerted at it, and considered it as an insurmountable barrier. The other circumstance was that they carried their calumnies so far as to accuse the missionaries of having carried money from the kingdom into the Papal states, in order to elude the restrictions imposed according to the tenor of the approbation given to the houses in the kingdom. This accusation was also of great weight with the Marquis, who was already prejudiced by the former calumnies, and it was no sooner made than commissioners were sent with urgent despatches, to go through the houses of the states and make inquiries about the purchases of property which, according to the adversaries, (who had gone so far in their efforts against the Congregation as to corrupt inferior agents by means of money,) had been made there. Alphonsus considered this last circumstance as the principal grievance, and the only one which could hurt the Congregation. "It seems to me," he wrote to F. Majone on the 26th of January, "that we must justify ourselves before Tanucci regarding the acquisition as soon as possible, and that we must labor unceasingly for this. Whilst he is persuaded that we have acquired possessions contrary to the decree of his Catholic majesty, we shall only sail against the wind, for he will always look on us as transgressors, and in that case what good can we hope for? It is, I believe, through this false impression that so many despatches have been issued against us." "The président himself," he says in another letter, "believes us guilty, as he told the Cardinal Jerrale, and the cardinal did not know what to reply. His eminence wishes to support us, and to speak to Tanucci, but he must be informed of all the answers to the general as well as to the particular accusations. I am ready to write to Mgr. Guttilieri (the queen's confessor,) but first it will be necessary for the cardinal to have spoken to the queen." By this we see that Alphonsus did not neglect human means, though he put all his trust in God as we have seen by the many prayers he offered himself, and by his asking those of the Congregation and of others.

As an answer to these multiplied prayers, may be considered an unexpected return of good fortune for Alphonsus, viz: that on the 16th of October 1776, the king allowed the Marquis of Tanucci to retire, and the Marquis of Sambuca was made prime minister in his stead, who had the most favorable opinion of Alphonsus, and was as favorably inclined to the Congregation as Tanucci was to its enemies. This gave Alphonsus and the Fathers courage, without, however, lessening that of their adversaries.

The report of the Procurator Leon was at length presented to the throne, on the 13th of February 1777. As nothing equalled the animosity of the procurator, the sword of opposition had become doubly formidable in his hands; he had styled the missionaries *rising Jesuits*, and had sworn to have the Congregation suppressed and the missionaries ruined. This report, a master-piece worthy of the age in which the Society of Jesus was suppressed, was as a thunderbolt which cast terror into the hearts of all the members of the Congregation as well as of their friends. Alphonsus immediately had recourse to his anchor of daily safety; he recommended himself to the prayers of many devout souls, especially of various convents of religious, both at Naples and in the provinces, and ordered that besides prayers and masses in all the houses of the Congregation, the discipline in common should be continued every Monday, and that Saturday should be kept as a fast in honor of the Blessed Virgin. He inculcated on the rectors that they must especially watch closely over the observance of that same rule which the adversaries chose to aim at. He several times sent alms to the Capuchinesses at Naples, as well as wax candles to the Camaldolese Fathers, that they might have prayers for his intention and exposition of the Blessed Sacrament.

When the bishops heard of this state of things, those who had the greatest interest hastened to present petitions to the king, attesting the probity of the missionaries, the poverty in which they lived, their disinterestedness, their submission to orders from those in authority, and the good they effected in the provinces and their respective dioceses.*

*An authentic record shows that from the end of 1777 until the month of May, 1778, thirty-five missions were given with benefit and satisfaction to the bishops. The holy exercises were given to eight clergymen, seven seminaries, and nineteen convents, in the dioceses of Caserto, Avuso, Capua, Benevento, Cerreta, Avellino, Nari, Aurenza and Matera, besides a great many triduos during the Carnival, the devotion of the forty hours, and the time of Advent. Alphonsus said: "Redeemed souls ought to be the advocates of our cause," and he therefore caused his sons to redouble their efforts and zeal to win souls to Jesus Christ.

Alphonsus also addressed letters of supplication to the new prime minister, and at last, through the intervention of Cardinal Branciforte, the Bishop of Girgenti, who was then at Naples, and Mgr. Filomarino, the Bishop of Caserto, obtained, that the cause, after it had been examined by the minister, should be sent back to the royal council. This consoled Alphonsus much, and he gained new strength at seeing this dispensation of Providence. "I can do nothing," he wrote to D. Francis de Paul, "but thank Jesus and Mary for all the many blessings they have conferred on me during these last days of my life. . . We have good news from Naples of the action with Sarnelli, for it has been remanded to the royal council. . . These matters have now an altered appearance. Blessed for ever be Jesus and Mary."

As one of the chief points of the opposition referred to his Moral Theology, he therefore wrote a long pamphlet, in which, appearing both as a theologian and a canonist, he justified it fully; he resumed also his former spirit of a lawyer, and without abandoning that of Jesus Christ, he digested an ample defence in reply to all the accusations. Every one was affected by this petition of the venerable old man, the talent of which was no less admirable than its moderation. He also addressed letters to the ministers of the royal council, to the Prince of Riccia, to the President Cito and the Marquis of Marco. Being again asked by the Fathers to go to Naples in person, he replied, on the 2d of September: "he who could see to what a miserable state I am now reduced, would not, I think, have the courage to require me to repair to Naples. My arrival would only serve to attract the hootings of a crowd of children, who would be curious to know if the man in the carriage were dead or alive. It is a thing which cannot be thought of, because I cannot do it; and besides, my presence would not make the cause succeed. . . . The weakness of my head prevents my being able to express my thoughts clearly, and I cannot now pronounce my words promptly. . . . Let us place ourselves in God's hands; he will know better than we how to defend this cause, which is more his than ours."

Although matters appeared now under a favorable aspect, Alphonsus did not wish the cause to be immediately discussed in the council; his adversaries, on the contrary, aware that delay would certainly be disadvantageous to them, were eager in demanding this discussion. They had made all their preparations; there were no less than seven advocates appointed to assist them in the council. They visited all the officers of the ministry, and the procurator himself, who was jealous of his honor, went round about every where making comments on his famous report. The cause was, however, deferred until the month of August 1779, when the Marquis of Marco wrote to Alphonsus as follows: "I stated to the king the representations of your lordship against the allegations tending to the destruction of the Congregation which you direct. His majesty has commanded me to reply, that as the Catholic king, his august father, permitted the missionaries of whom your lordship is the head to give missions and to live in the four houses of Ciorani, Nocera, Caposele and Iliceto, and prescribed the means and conditions under which this great undertaking might be maintained, his majesty also consents to there being a superior in the four above named houses, to watch over the internal order therein, and to see that the other offices are properly distributed; and as it was the intention of the deceased Catholic king that this salutary work should never cease to exist, his majesty also approves of young men being received and taught those things which shall be needful to enable them to supply the place of those who have become incapacitated through great age or any other reason."

Alphonsus rejoiced at this act of clemency on the part of the sovereign, thanked God for it, and exhorted his brethren to do the same by offering up prayers and masses. The procurator advocate, on the contrary, was enraged, with his whole party, and felt it most keenly. "If the Grand Duke of Tuscany had come here in person," he said several times, "he would not have obtained from the court what this handful of upstarts have got." Thus God, who never forsakes his children, protected Alphonsus and his Congregation from the wicked designs of its enemies, even whilst the debate and the particulars regarding the offences alleged against the Congregation were before the royal council.

It was evidently the same kind Providence which, after all the calumnies spread concerning the doctrine and the practice of Alphonsus and his sons, had already some time before inspired the king to adopt a new course, which had, not less than this decision, filled their enemies with confusion and the procurator with dejection. The king had obtained leave to celebrate the jubilee in his kingdom, from Pope Pius VI, on the 21st of November 1777. His majesty principally selected Mgr. Liguori and his missionaries to announce the attendant spiritual graces. In consequence, on the 22d of October of the following year, the Marquis of Tambuca wrote to him as follows: "In consideration of the constant labors of the missionaries of the most Holy Redeemer, which tend to instruct the people and to their being led to true piety, and of the solicitude with which they disseminate good principles which are calculated to form virtuous Christians and faithful citizens, his majesty has determined to make use of your Congregation to publish a jubilee, the only object of which is the salvation of the faithful, and the good of the state. Therefore the king has commanded me to let your lordship know, that in return for the happy success which will attend the labors of your missionaries in this respect, he will not fail to give you proofs of his royal gratitude." Alphonsus seconded the piety of the king by his own zeal, and addressed his sons, on the 8th November, in a circular, in which he sets forth the excellence of this work and its utility for the good of souls, and exhorts them to prepare themselves with all possible zeal, as being nothing less than the accomplishment of the very end of their institute. He was at the same time full of gratitude for all these blessings of Divine Providence, and wished therefore that due thanks should be offered to God for them. In consequence, he wrote, on the 24th of January 1779, to all the houses, to direct that every evening the following prayer should be recited in common, and repeated three times, adding each time a Pater, an Ave, and Gloria Patri: "What have I desired in heaven or on earth but thee, oh thou God of my heart and my portion for ever? My Jesus, I devote myself wholly to thee; I wish for nothing but thee; I wish for nothing more." "Prayer," said he, unceasingly, "is all-powerful with God."

The honorable preference which the king bestowed thus on the missionaries, and particularly the promise of future liberality, filled their adversaries, and especially the procurator, with dismay and the bitterest sorrow. "Strange fancy!" exclaimed the procurator; "it would seem as if scandal is to be made lawful, and even rewarded, although it causes ruin to the State and to the Church." He lost courage, as did also the commissioner, but they made one last effort in despair of gaining their cause; they entreated the royal council for a new appeal, hoping that at least the baron might then be able to recover the property left by his brother, and that they might thus escape entire confusion. But neither the one nor the other saw the end of this affair. They were both prematurely cited before the tribunal of Jesus Christ: the one died on coming out of a bath, without being able to have the sacraments administered to him, and the other was found dead in his carriage. As the other supporters of the baron disappeared also, he had no longer any heart or strength to go on with his wicked prosecution.

Having thus shown at length all the anxieties, troubles and labors occasioned to our saint by the persecutions raging against his Congregation up to this time, let us relate his other occupations and doings in the meanwhile, that is, from the commencement of the year 1777, when we left him. He was applied to by Cardinal Banditi for the establishment of a house of his missionaries at Benevento. After this town had been given up to the Pope, on the entrance of the Neapolitan army on the 5th of February 1774, various petitions were addressed to the Holy Father, to expose to him, (the see being vacant,) the spiritual necessities of the people. When Mgr. Banditi, the Bishop of Montefiascone, was elected archbishop of this town and made cardinal, the Holy Father Pius VI charged him to suggest some expedient by which he might further the glory of God and the good of souls at Benevento, and supply the void which the Jesuits had left there from the time of their suppression. Cardinal Banditi consulted the canons of the Cathedral and the nobles of the town, and all agreed to give up the church and college of the suppressed Jesuits to the Redemptorist Fathers, as well as all the rentals attached to them. The Cardinal applied to Alphonsus, who declined the offer with thanks, saying that Benevento already possessed a great many eminent religious who could supply the spiritual wants of the people, while his missionaries were more profitably engaged among the poor in the country.

Neither the clergy nor the nobles of Benevento would give up the point, and as they were unable to prevail on Alphonsus, they addressed themselves to F. Villani; who, being moved by the reasons exposed to him by the Cardinal, succeeded in persuading Alphonsus, (who was himself forced to acknowledge the justice of these representations,) no longer to refuse to acquiesce in the foundation. When Pius VI was informed of it, he rejoiced greatly, and in a letter written with his own hand, on the 22d of April 1777, he granted to the missionaries the said church and college, and on the feast of the Sacred Heart of Jesus, the 6th of June of the same year, they entered in possession of this house.

The other two houses in the Pontifical States were in great poverty and distress, and in consequence were a source of solicitude and anxiety to Alphonsus, the more so as he thought and said: "In the event of a tempest these houses will be our refuge." We will confine ourselves to transcribe some passages of the many letters he wrote to them during this year. "The house of Frosinone," he wrote to F. de Paul, on the 7th of July 1777, "interests me more than that of Girgenti, because that house is independent of the kingdom. The persecutions we endured at Naples have not yet terminated, and I attach the greatest importance to maintaining this foundation, for which we are indebted to the Pope:" and on the 17th of September: "I have again been suffering from one of those catarrhs which will one day deprive me of life. . . . If it be God's pleasure, I should like to live until I can succeed, through my pension, in completing the affair of the patronage of the church, and in finishing the building now commenced. Tell me what state the little rooms near the church are in. For the present I can only dispose of about ten carlins; but I hope to receive some money from St. Agatha shortly. Do not doubt that I will send you as much as I can." Alphonsus attached weight to each subject's having his own room: "Without that," said he, "a religious is a most miserable man." "I will do all in my power," he said, in another letter, "to assist you as soon as possible. . . Father Landi has just written to tell me that they are in the greatest misery at Scifelli; I have been obliged to divide the small sum of which I have been able to dispose by causing six ducats to be borrowed. . . . I have a great many debts. I am in continual distress, from seeing that I cannot assist Frosinone and Scifelli as I should wish. . . . I have been begging alms, and I have got thirteen ducats, which added to the other twenty-seven, amount to forty." "F. Constant," he says in another letter, "has twice reproved me sharply for not having sent him more than two hundred ducats, whilst he was four hundred and fifty scudi in debt. Yes, it is true that I told him to procure some money by borrowing, but I meant that it should be a moderate sum. . . . If I do not take some money from the pension, where shall I find any? Even were I to sell my cassock I should not obtain twenty carlins. I will beg and provide for it as well as I can."

"I have never dispensed you," he wrote to F. de Paul, who had entered into some agreement about the patronage of a chapel at Frosinone, "I have never dispensed you from giving me information of what you do. Thank God, I am not yet dead, and have not lost my senses. On the contrary, I have been an advocate and a bishop, and I have several times had to do with such things. I am now superior-general; what reason can there be for not informing me? . . . For the future, I wish to be informed of every thing that takes place. . . . There is perhaps no house which has given me more trouble than that of Frosinone. God be praised!" "Do not arrange about any mission," he wrote to the same Father, on the 15th of October, "without having previously informed me all about it; you must excuse yourself to the bishops who ask you for missions, by saying that you cannot allow them without my leave. . . . I wish the missions to be conducted with all possible prudence and edification, and in quite an apostolical spirit." Thus we see how Alphonsus' solicitude extended itself to every thing; and above all, how anxious he always was about the great work of the missions, never being satisfied with all he said about them in his works, and in the many instructions, circulars, and letters which he never ceased to write about them.

In order to increase still further the good produced in them, by the happy influence of those graces which are accorded by the head of the church, he addressed, on the 12th of September 1777, a detailed recital to Pope Pius VI, of the origin and progress of the Congregation, its labors and sufferings, as well as of the good which the missions effected, and entreated his Holiness to communicate to him the graces, privileges, and indulgences which had been granted to the Passionist Fathers; and he obtained all that he had asked for.

"I have heard that your reverence," he wrote on the 12th of September of the same year to F. D. Diodates Crisenoli, "has accepted an exercise for Lent in the diocese of Sora, and that F. de Paul has done so at Atin, in the diocese of Aquino. . . . I do not wish your reverence, or any one else, to agree to undertake such exercises, especially in the kingdom. Our institute forbids it, and it would become a cause for jealousies. In any event, your reverence must try to excuse yourself to Mgr. de Sora, and F. de Paul to the bishop of Aquino, by representing my prohibition to them, and the observance of rule which I require. I wish you to be solely engaged in missions; they are what God wishes from us, and not Lenten sermons. Obey, however great be the solicitations of parishes and bishops. To F. de Paul, who had asked to be allowed to preach during Lent in the college of Frosinone, and to accept the remuneration for it, he answered: "As for preaching this Lent, it is true there are some reasons for so doing on account of our extreme want, but I will not have the rule broken which expressly forbids it. Leave all to our good God. If we labor for Him, He will never allow us to want what is necessary." "You know," he wrote on the 12th of October to the same F. de Paul, "that I keep up these houses in Romagna to see the rule vigorously attended to. Manage so that the fathers make the accustomed retreat, or if they are ill, at least a part of it." "You tell me," he said in another letter, "that the house might very well be inhabited, but the doctor thinks that it ought not to be used before October, and I will not endure remorse for having caused the death of some one of my brethren."

When the necessary buildings were finished, he wrote as follows: "I send you thirty ducats as a subsidy for the house of St. Cecily, (at Frosinone.) I do not wish them to be spent in building, but only for the maintenance of the subjects. Extraordinary expenses must not be incurred for the church, nor for pictures, statues, chasubles, or other rich ornaments without my permission. On solemnities, decorations and illuminations must be spared, even if others are willing to bear the cost. I also forbid every kind of adornment of the altar, such as decorations in silk or any other rich material; let it be ornamented with garlands, candles, and flowers: these are befitting the stat of poverty in which we are at present." "I have always felt as much affection for Frosinone as for Scifelli," he says in another letter, "but there are a great number of young men at Scifelli who are now in want of bread, F. Landi has written me word. Foundations in their commencement occasion distress, confusion, contradiction, and misery; but if we remain entirely resigned to the will of God, he will remedy every thing. Let us behave properly, and Jesus Christ will protect us." "I entreat your reverence," he wrote to F. de Paul, then superior at Frosinone, "to be humble towards your companions and affable towards all, especially in mission time, and to treat your brothers with all possible consideration, remembering that they are far from their country and their family, and that thus they have a right to have the exercise of charity redoubled in their regard."

CHAPTER XXXII.

Alphonsus exerts himself incessantly for the welfare of the Church at large, and for the general promotion of piety. His efforts to maintain discipline in the Congregation.

SUCH was Alphonsus' admirable solicitude for the well-being and perfection of his subjects in the pontifical states, while in his retreat at Nocera, amidst the unceasing persecutions in the kingdom. It was in the same retreat, and about this time, that he composed a work, entitled, "The fidelity of subjects towards God is a sure pledge of that which they have for their prince." "They deceive themselves," said he, speaking of monarchs, "they will never have any peace, if they have not the prevention of immorality at heart; where religion does not reign, iniquity triumphs, as well as perfidy; admit sin, and all is in peril; but if they make their subjects faithful towards God, they will find that they will be equally faithful towards them." When he wrote this work, he said to one of the fathers in a transport of zeal: "Have as many missions as you please; but if I gain one sovereign, it is worth more than a thousand missions, for the good which a sovereign who is touched by the grace of God can do, could not be effected by a thousand missions. He sent several copies of this work to Cardinal Castelli, and through him to all the ministers of foreign powers. He also applied to Canon Henry Hennequin to get it conveyed to the august Maria Theresa, to the electoral Princes of Cologne and of Treves, as well as to the archbishops and bishops of the empire who had temporal possessions. He also transmitted it to Prince Charles, the governor of the Netherlands, to the kings of Spain and Portugal, to the king of Turin, to the duke of Parma, and to the grand-duke of Tuscany; in a word, to all the Catholic sovereigns and principal ministers. None of the answers of these personages to Alphonsus are in existence, for, according to custom, he sacrificed them to his humility. The work became so celebrated that it was translated into French and sold in different kingdoms. "This work," said the translator, "is the voice of a soul which thirsts for nothing but the glory of religion, the spread of morality, and the happiness of sovereigns and their subjects, and which has no other ambition than that of leading men to virtue and rendering them happy." By this, as well as by his other publications, Alphonsus has shown a zeal as universal as ardent. It was this zeal also which caused him to weep bitterly at seeing what progress infidelity and libertinism made in France, through the fatal influence of the writings of Voltaire and Jean-Jacques Rousseau; the more so as their contagion had begun to penetrate into Italy, and the works of Voltaire formed the fashionable reading at Naples, so that even ladies made them the pastime for their idleness. As his age and infirmities no longer left him strength enough to combat them, he unceasingly encouraged different literary friends of his at Naples to labor in their refutation. In the midst of this grief, a refutanon of the errors of Voltaire by he Abbe Nonnote fell into his hands;

he was full of joy at this, and could not cease to thank God for having raised up a man who braved the spirit of the age, and occupied himself for his glory with such courageous devotion. Animated by holy zeal, he wrote a letter of congratulation and encouragement to him on his having dared to undertake the refutation of the most impious of blasphemers. No tongue can express with what consolation this letter filled the heart of the worthy priest of Besançon, who, as we shall presently show by his own words, found little encouragement in his own country, though he so zealously and triumphantly fought the battles of the Lord. He testified his gratitude to the saintly bishop, in a letter dated the 21st of April 1778, in the most glowing terms: "I am accustomed," he says among other things, "to appreciate nothing except in conformity to the spirit of God; it is an unspeakable pleasure to me to meet with men who also value the things of God alone, and who being in themselves greater than great dignities could make them, cause one to be in doubt whether most to admire in them the gifts of genius which they possess or the bright lustre of the greatest virtue. I have often sought for such men; I had not found any such, when your letter arrived to inform me that there is one in Naples. . . . All who have read your excellent and very celebrated work on Moral Theology congratulate me on my having received such a flattering letter from so learned a prelate, and I congratulate myself in turn for having received the approbation of so distinguished a man for my works."

In order to encourage this generous confessor to strive more and more against these impious and furious enemies of the church, Alphonsus undertook to present a petition to the sovereign pontiff to obtain an apostolical brief in favor of the Philosophical Dictionary of Religion. "It is with unspeakable pleasure and gratitude," Abbe Nonnotte wrote to him, "that I have heard that you have resolved to address a petition to the sovereign pontiff, to ask him for an approbation of my dictionary, such as Clement XIII deigned to give to my book called 'The Errors of Voltaire.' It is indeed a thing which I most ardently desire, and for this reason I sent him my works, but have not received any answer, although Cardinal Pallavicini told me that he had transmitted them to the sovereign pontiff. Have I then to believe that my work has been despised by this great pope? . . . You exhort me to attack and to combat unceasingly all the new sophisms which may again be brought forth by the followers of this infernal philosophy. . . . I have already undertaken to do all that you wish for and hint at, nay, I have even completed it; but the want of suitable and necessary assistance has prevented me from publishing what I have written. . . . I should have been exceedingly glad to have this work printed at Paris . . . but every one here is so full of wild admiration for Voltaire, or rather, the fear which this extremely sarcastic man inspires is so great, that I have not been able to succeed in finding a friendly examiner; on the contrary, even the archbishop of Paris himself told me that I should never find a censor of this kind. . . . I shall perhaps be obliged to cause a book which I have written in defence of religion to be printed at Geneva, because Catholics have not courage to do it. . . . For upwards of twenty years I have been constantly under arms to fight for the Lord, and I have never received any aid from man; on the contrary, I have been loaded with invectives from the impious."

This reply of the Abbé filled Alphonsus with sorrow and regret. "O God!" exclaimed he, "at Paris, where there are so many Christian orators, there is not any one to be found who will oppose this monster who is so great an enemy to the Church and to religion, and this defence must be published at Geneva! Miserable beings that we are! This is the authority the Church has at Paris! She cannot face an infidel and reprove his audacity! Poor archbishop! Poor church! This abuse will undoubtedly not remain unpunished! Poor France! I pity thee, and I pity the many innocent people who will be involved in thy disgrace!" Let us remember that these words were uttered only eleven years before the catastrophe of 1789, that is, the first French revolution, with all its horrors and expiatory rivers of blood. Alphonsus would have liked to send letters to the king. "But how could I effect at a distance," said he, "what the archbishop and so many good bishops cannot obtain although they are on the spot?"

A ray of false consolation came for a moment to soften the grief of the afflicted old man: in the May of this same year, 1778, there was a report that Voltaire had retracted his errors and blasphemies, and that corresponding with the influence of grace, he had declared himself to be a sincere Catholic. It is impossible to express what joy Alphonsus felt when he heard of this conversion. Animated by fresh zeal, he at once wrote a letter to congratulate him on his return to grace, and on the great good which his conversion would confer on the whole church, and at the same time to encourage him to write something as a refutation of his errors and sophisms, or if possible to use his pen against another modern writer, Rousseau; promising earnestly to pray to God to give him strength, if not to write, at least to dictate (Voltaire suffered then from his eyes) something against the unbelievers of those times. But soon Alphonsus received the tidings that the rumor of Voltaire's conversion was unfounded, or rather grew out of one of his many hypocritical simulations of conversion, and that he persisted in his obstinacy. He was on the point of sending his letter, but had to keep it back. "Such conversions," he then said, "are not ordinary graces; they are the effects of divine mercy, but not of a common degree of mercy. God only grants blessings of this sort to those whose errors have not arisen from a bad intention, like those of St. Paul. But all is very bad in Voltaire." On the 30th of May, in this same year, 1778, Voltaire passed out of this life, having died in impenitence and despair. On the 2d of July following, his colleague in evil, J. J. Rousseau, also died a sudden death. "I received the tidings of the death of the unhappy Rousseau," Alphonsus wrote to a friend, on the 13th of September: "God be praised for having delivered the church from two of its greatest enemies in so short a time."

Alphonsus had one source of consolation about this time, however. Let us hear himself speaking of it in one of his works; ("Spiritual Reflections;" p. 2, p. 25) "may I be permitted here to manifest the great joy I have lately experienced. I have been positively assured, that the celebrated Abbé P. Metastasio, after having received so many praises for his poetry throughout Europe, which is all the more dangerous from its being so very beautiful, because his tender and ardent expressions are thereby all the more calculated to kindle the flames of impure love in the heart, (I only allude to his profane poems,)—I have been assured, I say, that he is going to publish a little book in prose, wherein he protests his profound repentance for his dangerous poetry, and the wish he has, if possible, to withdraw this kind of works from the hands of the public, at any price whatever, even at the expense of his own blood. . . . It is also said that he leads quite a retired life, spent in prayer and devotional exercises. This has given me unspeakable consolation, because this public declaration and the great and good example he gives, will cause many misguided young people to think seriously, who have tried to gain a name and glory through amorous poems of a similar description. . . . Thus, whilst I formerly detested the vanity which made him glory in producing such compositions, I cannot now cease to praise him, and, were it in my power, I would kiss his feet on seeing him become the censor of his own works, and professing a wish to stop their circulation in the world, even at the price of his own blood, as he himself said."

Let us give here another instance of the horror Alphonsus had of all amorous poetry, which is so pernicious to youth, and with what joy he was filled when any remarkable composition of sacred poetry came before him. He was so much pleased with the compositions of X. Maffei, that he was always praising the labor of this distinguished man. "If all occupied themselves thus," said he, "we should see lascivious poetry banished from the lips of the young." Maffei, full of gratitude for Alphonsus' praise and esteem for him and his works, did not forget to offer his thanks to him in the preface to his translation of the Psalms. On the 30th of November 1774, Alphonsus replied to him as follows: "It gives me great comfort to receive your little work on the Psalms, and I keep your much esteemed letter before me whilst I am composing my work, (also on the Psalms.) This is fitted for the learned as well as for the ignorant, because it both instructs and pleases, while mine is only for the ignorant, and has nothing attractive. Your translation has been applauded by the literary men throughout all Italy, and I may even say throughout all Europe; what I have done is scarcely able to please even a small number of devout persons. I see what progress you make as a lawyer, but how much I should have preferred to see you continue to make use of the great talents and knowledge which God has given you by exercising them for the good of His church. However, even in the position in which you are, you can do a great deal for the service of religion, since every one takes upon himself to speak of theology and of the Holy Scriptures, and to put forth whatever propositions he pleases."

In the year 1779, Alphonsus' humility made him become, like another St. Charles Borromeo, a public penitent. For six months, that is to say, from the 16th of December 1778, the heavens had become like brass, and there had not been a drop of rain. The whole country was in distress, fearing the loss of the corn and the fruit. Alphonsus was moved at the sight of such a scourge, and wept over the sins of the people. One Sunday, (it was the 13th of May 1779,) notwithstanding his weakness, he undertook to make a penitential procession, in order to obtain God's pardon and the favor which was so much longed for. After having put on his purple vestments, which he was never in the habit of doing, he covered himself with ashes; and accompanying his sons with a rope around his neck, he resolved to go and place a large cross in the parish church.

The way was long, but all efforts to dissuade him from going were useless. It was with great difficulty that he was persuaded to go half the way in a carriage. He was determined to go the rest of the way on foot; and as his state of exhaustion no longer allowed him to walk without support, the lay-brother and others aided him in performing this painful pilgrimage.

All the inhabitants assisted at this ceremony—the church and the square were crowded with people. In order to satisfy all, the pulpit was placed at the church door, and as Alphonsus was not able to ascend it, he was carried up to it. He preached for upwards of an hour upon the punishment which sinners deserve, and exhorted all his hearers to do penance. His words, added to such a touching spectacle, made a general impression, and on that very evening the salutary effects were seen by the great number of those who went to cast themselves at the feet of the confessors. But heaven appeared to be insensible. The next day, after vespers, when Alphonsus was returning from his accustomed drive, and had nearly reached the house, he ordered the coachman to turn back, and to go to the chapel where the month of Mary was celebrated. He entered the church, and went and prostrated himself before the altar of the Blessed Virgin. This drew a crowd together, and Alphonsus caused the image of Mary to be exposed, and exhorted all present to have recourse to their divine Mother. After he had prayed in silence for some time, he again turned towards the crowd: "Continue," said he to them, "to recommend yourself to our Lady with confidence; confess and communicate this week, and you will have rain on Sunday." And so it was, for on the predicted day, just when it was least expected, and when the impatient people were murmuring and saying that he was mistaken for this time, a sudden change was perceived in the atmosphere, and the rain fell in such great abundance that all the country was deluged. It was impossible not to see the favor which the Blessed Virgin had granted to the prayers of her servant; but as to Alphonsus, it seemed almost a cause of confusion to him, and he said, when he returned: "The words I addressed the people are taken as a prophecy: they merely escaped from me by chance, however, for I am no prophet."

We have seen above how the persecutions to which the Congregation had been so long exposed, ended in this year, 1779. The greatest evil resulting from them had been a certain interior derangement and relaxation in the regular observance of the rule; some taking advantage of these troubles to have their own way, and in many instances, the superiors, to their great regret, being forced to bear with this, or at least to be very careful when they gave any reprimand, and in the expulsion of an incorrigible subject finding still more difficulty. But as the pilot, after the tempest, causes all the damages which the vessel has sustained to be repaired, and gets the rigging renewed, so Alphonsus, after the storm of these persecutions, occupied himself in remedying the injuries which the observance of the rule had sustained. He became inflamed with zeal, and rigorously required that discipline should be respected. "In the Congregation," said he, "one must either edify, or go." Therefore he wrote a circular to all the superiors of the houses to encourage them and enkindle in them the same zeal for regular observance, and he set himself, without respect of persons, to correct what was wrong, and to give both verbal and written warnings to the rectors, as well as to the subjects. He insisted on this point, and never rested until he was satisfied; he was resolved to dismiss all the rebellious spirits from the Congregation, and he unceasingly prayed to God for this end. Several of those to whom the yoke of the religious life seemed too heavy, returned into the world, and Alphonsus, whilst he deplored their misfortune, was more consoled at their departure than at the reception of those who were fervent.

Some had taken the liberty to retire to their homes on frivolous pretexts. Alphonsus had complained of this to F. Villani before his resignation, but during the troubles this father had to shut his eyes to a great many things. As soon as peace was restored, Alphonsus took the most efficacious means to cause all the subjects to return to their respective houses. One of them would not obey, and got several persons to intercede for him. Alphonsus delayed action for a while, but on seeing that he was incorrigible, he ultimately sent him away, saying: "I pity this unhappy man; God knows how to punish these wilfully deaf persons, who set no value on their vocation." And as if he had prophesied, this subject was afterwards miserably assassinated, on account of the crime of usury, which he had practised in favor of his nephews, for the love of whom he had become unfaithful to his vows.

Although circumstances thus forced Alphonsus to act with severity, he did not fail to use at the same time all possible circumspection and prudence: "I have let all the subjects know," he wrote to a subject who also was absent, "that they must each return to the house assigned to them within fifteen days. I have sent this announcement to all, couched in the same terms, and in the same form. However, as I have a peculiar degree of esteem for you, I take the trouble of addressing a separate letter to you, different from the others. I do not write to tell you that you must positively return in the space of fifteen days; I only beg you to let me know what necessity there is for your reverence's remaining with your relations. . . . My dear D. Bartholomew, your reverence is one of the oldest fathers, your example will therefore cause the more harm and will be a precedent for others. . . . I beg you at least to write and tell me the reason which keeps you in the world, because I shall exercise all possible indulgence towards you provided it be a reasonable one, and I must give some kind of reason for your absence. I have for some time wanted to beg you to come and remain with me at Nocera, where I am superior, in the midst of difficulties, and in continual need of some prudent person whose advice I can ask."

In the following letter we will see an instance of his firmness: "Your reverence," he wrote to a rector, "must give Father N. a sharp reprimand; I have not wished to dismiss him, as he has deserved, as a punishment for his fault and also for his habitual obstinacy, but tell him in my name, that I shall be obliged to do it the first time he again commits a fault of a similar nature. I think it arises from his going out too much. Your reverence must therefore not send him out any more, nor allow him to go out again unless you have my written consent for it; and you must not continue his faculties, because he must have forgotten the little he knew by going about from place to place in this way without ever studying moral theology, and this makes me afraid to allow him to continue as a confessor." On hearing that a subject entertained too loose opinions, he positively forbade him to hear confessions, and he was so strict with him that he himself asked to be released from the vows. He also dismissed another in a similar manner who would not conquer a certain levity of conduct.

As we have already seen, in Alphonsus, firmness was never severed from prudence. On hearing that a certain subject disliked going on missions, he did not give him any definite order to do so, as he feared a refusal; but once when this subject was in his room with others, he dexterously began to speak of the value of obedience, and of the injury which he who is intractable inflicts on himself; this caused him to reflect seriously, and he of himself offered to do what was wished. In general, whenever the resistance proceeded rather from nature than from the will, Alphonsus had compassion on the weakness of the man, and tried by his gentleness to soften the bitterness of his command. "I have received your letter;" he wrote to the superior of a house, "in one part you console me, and in another you distress me. I find therein certain words which I did not expect from your submission and your love of obedience. You say, 'I am resolved to return to the kingdom.' I pity you, for I see that you wrote these words in distress of mind. . . . My letter could not have provoked such language, because I wrote it with all the affection I have ever felt towards you. And then, you say, some think that you are of a peevish temper, as F. Villani has told you. But did not your piety demand that you should have received this mortification peacefully, and the more so because you know how much I esteem and love you? F. Villani gave me a similar reprimand myself; but, thank God, I received it quietly, and it has caused me to be more moderate and humble."

On the 8th of September 1779, D. Hercules expired, of a disease which was as violent as it was unexpected. Alphonsus had had a presentiment of it three months before, though his brother was then robust and in perfect health. One day when he was meditating according to custom, he suddenly turned towards F. Costanzo and said: "Hercules will cause me sorrow this year." Alphonsus was always united to the will of God, so he received the tidings with calmness. "Good God!" he exclaimed; he then clasped his hands and was silent. When he heard that D. Hercules had left the advocate, D. Peter Gavotti, as tutor to his children, but under his authority and that of counsellor D. Nicholas Vespoli, their relation, he felt comforted, and instantly dictated a letter to the former, not so much in order to secure the temporal interests of his nephews, as to urge him to attend to their religious education. D. Gavotti replied: "I am quite at your service, and I will devote myself as far as I can to the good of your nephews, but your Lordship must pray to God to deliver me from the headache which continually afflicts me." "Take care of these little children," Alphonsus replied to him, "and be sure that God will relieve you." Don Gavotti has attested that when he received this letter, he felt instantly cured, and he never suffered again from this malady as long as he lived.

Alphonsus felt the greatest interest in the welfare of D. Theresa, his niece, who was sixteen years of age at this time, and a pensioner at the convent of St. Marcelline. His only wish was to see her consecrated to Jesus Christ, as she had manifested a desire to that effect some time before. He wrote to her to remind her of her former resolution, and exhorted her to be faithful to God, who had inspired her with this desire. "If any one advises you to leave the convent," he wrote to her in one of his letters, "and to go and throw yourself down a precipice, that is to say, to marry, do not listen to such counsel, for you will certainly repent of it the second day. . . . Take the advice of a good confessor, and of some nun of exemplary life." He prayed most fervently for this object, and he wrote to his cousin, Antonia Liguori, also a nun, to beg her to watch over her, as also to D. Gavotti, to urge him to attend to her vocation. "I have begged her confessor," he wrote to him, "to be most careful in directing her so that she may become a nun, and I also beg you to assist him in this, because if she marries in this corrupt age I shall look upon her as lost."

Alphonsus obtained what he so ardently desired. D. Theresa soon declared that she wished to embrace the religious state; Counsellor Vespoli and D. Gavotti opposed her on the ground that she was yet too young, but she insisted upon it, and Alphonsus did not fail to second her. When she had to leave the convent, according to custom, before entering on the noviciate, he feared to entrust her to her relations, saying: "If we place her in the house of her parents, she will incur a thousand dangers; there will be parties, theatres and soirées; this will be quite enough to cause her to lose her vocation." In consequence, he applied to his penitent the Duchess of Bovino, who willingly consented to receive her into her house. Whilst with the Duchess, the only recreation D. Theresa asked for was to go to Nocera to kiss the hand of her uncle.

Although the visits of ladies were usually disagreeable to Alphonsus, that of his niece was an exception, and gave him the greatest pleasure. The duchess and her daughter stayed three days at Nocera. The presents he gave them were confined to copies of the Visits to the Blessed Sacrament, and of the Preparation for Death, with a relic, in a little box of no value. D. Theresa had been suffering from a wound in her leg for six months. When Alphonsus heard of it, he was much distressed; and when she knelt down and asked him for his blessing on taking leave of him, he said to her: "*I bless you as your uncle, and as a bishop.*" This took place in the morning, and in the evening when the wound was unbandaged at Naples, the surgeon, the duchess, and the other members of the household found, to their great admiration, that it was entirely healed.

On the 16th of June 1781, D. Theresa returned to the convent. After her noviciate, she begged Alphonsus to assist at her profession. "Your last letter," he replied, "has given me such great comfort, that I have been unable to restrain my tears: I am sad at being unable to comply with your wishes. If God had granted me power to witness your sacrifice, I should certainly have done nothing but shed tears of joy; but he has not granted me this consolation." It was necessary to give a present to her, and he did not fail to do so. "I send you this picture of the Blessed Virgin," he said to her, "to remind you to thank her, and unceasingly to implore her protection."

Alphonsus manifested as much indifference regarding the establishment and marriage of his nephew, D. Joseph, (the eldest of the two,) as he had shown interest in his niece's entrance into religion. Some years back, when the boy was not yet thirteen, and D. Hercules, anxious to see him settled before his death, had begun a matrimonial negociation for him with the heiress of Counsellor Vespoli, Alphonsus was distressed at it, and exclaimed in a sorrowful manner: "Ah! my little Joseph is going to lose the grace of God. . . . If but one of the servants hears of it, that will be enough to cause little Joseph also to know it soon himself. The children of the great are lost through servants, through valets de chambres and coachmen—they will now say to him, 'good news, little Joseph, papa has found a pretty young lady for you,' and a thousand other improper remarks; it is thus that children get irremediably corrupted." He was so uneasy that he commissioned one of the fathers who was then about to go to Naples, to tell his brother how much he was displeased, and to represent to him that he ran a fearful risk of causing his son to be out of the favor of God. After his father's death, when the son was of an age to marry, Alphonsus entirely referred the matter to Counsellor Vespoli and to D. Gavotti, confining himself to advising them not to constrain him, but to choose a wife for him of exemplary conduct and of suitable birth. When D. Joseph went himself to inform him of the decision about his marriage, Alphonsus received the news with indifference; he then gave him his blessing, and said to him: "I pray God to bless you also;" adding some good advice, and sent him away satisfied.

It was about this time that Alphonsus finally revised his Moral Theology, taking the greatest care to avoid either too severe or too lax opinions. As upright intentions are always accompanied by the blessings of heaven, this work, like all the other works of its saintly author, obtained such a high reputation among all the most civilized nations that it was spread throughout Europe. Even during his lifetime there were seven editions of the Moral Theology published at Naples and at Venice; and it was spread not only throughout Italy, but also in France, Germany, Poland, Spain, Portugal and Switzerland, and even beyond the bounds of Europe, and every where it met with applause. With regard to the Visits to the Blessed Sacrament, he himself lived to see twenty-two editions of it at Naples and Venice alone, (besides those in other places,) and to see it translated into most of the modern languages. The most of his other works, whether dogmatical, polemical or ascetical, were during his lifetime translated in various languages, and published in Poland, France, Germany, Spain, the Netherlands, and elsewhere, to the great advantage of souls.

The last work he published was that entitled "The fidelity of subjects towards God," &c , of which we have spoken above. The authority of his director, F. Villani, was needed in order to make him put an end to his composing and publishing. However, he published yet some little treatises which he composed, as he assured F. Villani, by way of relaxation, and which he had distributed during the course of the missions. He had summed up in them, in a few pages, these two counsels, viz: "The necessity of prayer, and of the intercession of the Blessed Virgin Mary." He composed further in the same way some other little treatises on various spiritual subjects. All his works, the most important of which have been mentioned by us at the several dates of their first publication, make up, in the two most complete editions of them, (one of Monza, and the other of Turin,) seventy-two volumes, in small octavo. They will be an eternal monument of his profound learning, tender piety, and ardent zeal, as well as of his fidelity in keeping the vow he had made not to lose a moment of time.

CHAPTER XXXIII.

The Congregation, through the treachery and intrigue of some of its members, is threatened with complete disorganization. Alphonsus exhibits through all these trials entire submission to the will of God.

ALPHONSUS had, on two different occasions, predicted that he should die as a subject, and not as superior. The time of the fulfilment of this prediction was now drawing near, the Lord having pre-ordained that he should not finish his long career in peace, but that as one of the living stones of the heavenly Jerusalem, he should be perfected by the stroke of the chisel to the last. As the devil had not been able, by persecutions from without, to gain the victory over the Congregation founded by our saint, he sought to stir up treason within, in order to cause it to be ruined through itself.

The rule was approved and confirmed by the Pope, but it had not been sanctioned by the government, and this had been one of the chief arguments put forward by its enemies, as we have already seen. When, through the decree of the 24th of August 1779, the royal approbation had been obtained on different points, it was thought to be a favorable moment to ask for a general approbation which would at last put an end to all further troubles. Mgr. Testa, the grand-almoner, who was applied to, did not hesitate to promise his protection, provided the rule were transcribed, and the part which was opposed to the royal decrees regarding the acquisitions and the rentals of the houses were left out. Alphonsus agreed to this; and the affair was entrusted to F. Majone, one of the consultors-general. This father, under the pretext that if they should receive a refusal from the king and the thing should become known to its enemies, it would be a blow to the Congregation, proposed that the whole matter should remain secret between the consultors, and that they should all take an oath to preserve secrecy in regard to all that might be done in the course of this affair. Alphonsus and the other members of the council all agreed, and took the oath in consequence. But under the cover of this secresy, F. Majone and the consultor who had been associated with him made the most arbitrary changes in the rule, adding to it, modifying it, or abridging it, entirely according to their own fancy.

Notwithstanding the precautions of F. Majone, suspicions were awakened as to his intentions; a report became current among the subjects that innovations were about to be made in the rule, and general alarm ensued. Protestations were addressed to Alphonsus expressive of these fears, and of the wish not to have the rule altered. The poor old man, who had no reason to suspect any treachery of the kind, endeavored to reassure every one. This however did not satisfy the subjects, (though F. Majone boldly denied every thing,) and the dreaded innovations being specified as relating to poverty and life in community, unceasing protests were addressed to him and to

Alphonsus. Alphonsus persisted in believing in the sincerity of F. Majone, and assured all that there was nothing to fear. "I assure you," he one day said, taking the little cross he wore on his breast in his hand, "that nothing is being done against the rule; what is to be retrenched relates only to the acquisitions, because the king does not choose to have them and we must obey him."

So many appeals, however, aroused the attention of Alphonsus, and in order to become more fully acqainted with the real state of the case, he wrote to F. Majone, and plainly told him that some innovation in regard to poverty and life in community was suspected, and that he would never agree to that. F. Majone reassured him as to his conduct, saying: "As for what you say to me touching life in community, to wish to do away with this regulation would be to wish to destroy the Congregation. I hope that Divine Providence will punish all those who thus spread discord." His intrigues did not end here. He came to Nocera, and with audacious effrontery, presented the regulations he had made to Alphonsus, assuring him that with the exception of what related to the acquisitions all the rest was in conformity with the rule. The poor old man could not read it himself, the writing being small and illegible and covered with erasures and interlinings, so he gave it to F. Villani to be examined with care. F. Villani saw that the vows had been done away with, and that holy poverty had also been injured. "The king does not wish to have vows," F. Majone said to him. "Besides, it is not for us to make the laws; we must receive them from the almoner, and if some slight changes must be made in order to obtain the approbation of the rule it matters little." F. Villani had not the courage to oppose either F. Majone or his colleague, and fearing to overwhelm Alphonsus by by such sad tidings, he told him that all was going on well; Alphonsus believed this and became tranquil in the expectation of a happy termination, no longer doubting that the mistrust felt by the subjects was the work of the devil.

F. Majone returned to Naples, and there consummated the work of iniquity. On the 1st of January the affair was proposed to the royal council. F. Majone did not find it difficult to obtain all that he wished; the favor of the king, and the venerated name of Alphonsus, smoothed all before him. As they were ignorant of his deceitfulness, the grand-almoner and all the council of state entered willingly into what they thought would be agreeable to our aged saint, and the king most graciously gave his approbation. The whole being thus settled, F. Majone, in order to confirm his work, managed that two copies of the said regulations should be sent to the office of the ministry by royal authority, one of which was intended for the procurator-general, and the other for the royal council.

On the 27th of February 1780, the mutilated rule reached Nocera, accompanied by an official letter from the grand-almoner. As soon as this was known, the whole house was in a state of anxiety. But F. Villani, who was vicar-general and superior, did not open the papers, as Alphonsus was too ill for it. But the fathers managed so that they got the statutes into their hands the same evening and copied them. Before daybreak, they went to awaken Alphonsus to tell him of the havoc that had been made, and to ask for justice. At these sad tidings the poor old man was in the greatest distress; he asked for the fatal pages, he looked over them, and in sorrow of soul, he exclaimed: "It cannot be! it cannot be!" Then turning to F. Villani, he said to him: "D. Andrew, I did not expect such deception from you." He then addressed the community, and said: "I deserve to be dragged at a horse's tail, for I ought to have read every thing myself, as I am superior." He then turned to the crucifix with his eyes bathed in tears, and exclaimed: "My Jesus, pardon me, I trusted to my confessor; on whom could I have better reposed confidence?" "You know," said he, addressing the community again, "how much it costs me to read even a line." He then gave way to his tears: "I have been deceived," he said with sobs, and then was silent,

He passed the whole morning in profound silence, and in such a state of dejection that sorrow seemed to have overpowered him; he would hardly consent to take any nourishment, and what he ate he mingled with his tears. "Ah, Lord," he repeated, "punish not the innocent, but punish the guilty one who has destroyed thy work." His heart was pierced with the most poignant anguish; he no longer slept, and his life was soon in danger. Not knowing what course of action to resolve upon, he was constantly sending first for one subject and then for another, in order to obtain the assistance of their advice. On the 10th of March, he wrote to F. Corrado, who was then at Naples: "My dear D. Bartholomew, I am in danger of becoming delirious, for I find that the new regulations made by Majone are quite contrary to my opinion. The young men here are clamorous about it. I entreat you to leave every thing and to come and see me, if you do not wish me to lose my senses and to die of grief."

F. Majone, on seeing what opposition he met with, put on the semblance of zeal, and feigning to pity Alphonsus, represented him to the grand-almoner as sinking under affliction in the midst of rebellious subjects. The latter therefore immediately intimated to the Congregation in an official letter of March 1st 1780, an order to follow the new regulations in every particular. The following was its conclusion: "Your Lordship, as founder and superior-general of the Congregation, must inform each member in my name, that this regulation must be put in force from this time without any alteration or retrenchment whatsoever, for it is now the only rule and is binding in all its parts on all the members of the Congregation present and future, on superiors, priests, students, and lay-brothers, without any room for reply or opposition."

It may be imagined how this letter served to increase the flame in all the houses. Whilst Alphonsus endeavored to allay it, he did not wish for the death of F. Majone, who was the cause of all these evils, but rather that he should be converted and dwell always among his children.

Though every one was bent on his ruin, he neglected nothing in order to save him; he wrote to him at Naples, and without speaking of his treachery, he begged him to retire into the house at Ciorani, or if that did not please him, into any other he should choose. "Let us forget the past," he said, "and pass over all that has been done. You will continue to be consultor-general as formerly, and you will give your opinion in all important affairs of the Congregation. As for your honor, place that in my hands, I will not cease to defend it in the Congregation and to strangers." It was thus that he acted towards him with all mildness, "because such is the will of Jesus Christ," he wrote to another father on the same day, "and it is thus he inspires me to act. I shall continue to act thus in his regard until God restores peace to us." But far from yielding to such loving measures, F. Majone became more and more inflamed with indignation against the Congregation, and against Alphonsus himself. On seeing his designs thwarted, he resolved to address a petition to the king, to get him to constrain the subjects to embrace the new regulations under pain of being expelled from the Congregation. This news supplied fresh fuel to the fire already enkindled, but caused him also to become still better known; so Alphonsus hastened to prevent the consequences of such a step, and instantly wrote to Naples on the 12th of April to take away from him the procuracy and to transfer it to F. D. Bartholomew Corrado, charging the latter to inform the grand-almoner of every thing. "If Mgr. Testa," he said, "is not convinced as to the deceit which has been practised we can obtain nothing from him, because he will always say that he has granted me all that I have wished for. . . . If the regulations are to be maintained I am afraid that several will lose their vocation. Try and make him understand the state of our Congregation; tell him that we have more than a hundred young men who have finished their studies in it, and who would have honorably distinguished themselves at the Sorbonne or at Louvain, but that F. Maione would destroy them all in order to attain his end.

Tell him that I have not become imbecile, as F. Majone would wish him to believe; my head is still of use to me, although this father labors to make me lose my senses." On the same day he wrote to the grand-almoner himself to represent to him the treachery of which he was the victim, and to inform him of the spirit which actuated F. Majone, who in order to increase his own power as consultor-general had tried to take away all the faculties of the superior-general, and had added to the regulations all that his own fancy suggested to him.

The subjects, on finding themselves called on by reiterated letters from the grand-almoner to follow a rule which they had never promised to observe, protested against the consultors, and even against Alphonsus himself, for having kept the thing a secret. Their dissatisfaction was so great that they lost that veneration which they had always cherished and manifested towards him; so that he did not know where to steer in such a stormy sea, and did nothing but groan in silence at the foot of the crucifix. He again wrote a long letter to the grand-almoner; and he sought to obtain the aid of D. Joseph Cantore, (one of the first clerks in the ministry,) as also that of D. Januarius Fatigati, superior of the Chinese College, and Mgr. Bergame, bishop of Gaeta—all of whom he knew had some influence with the grand-almoner. But the latter, who had himself taken part in the composition of the new regulations, was far from acceding to his wishes, and maintaining that the regulations were excellent, refused to annul what he had done, as he said, with the consent of the parties. He was, moreover, beset by F. Majone, and instead of condescending to hear the prayers of Alphonsus and his excellent friends, he urged the execution of the regulations.

Alphonsus had foreseen all this calamity as far back as the 25th of January 1780. One day he aroused himself from a profound meditation, and said: "I foresee that the devil will do all in his power to overthrow us this year." "Your reverence must, therefore," he said, writing on the same day to F. Cajone at Benevento, "cause the short prayers marked in the enclosed paper to be recited every evening in common, from the month of February until the end of May."

Alphonsus, in order to re-establish order and peace in the Congregation without incurring the displeasure of the Pope or of the king, suspended the execution of the regulations, and after he had recommended the matter to God and implored the protection of the Blessed Virgin during several days, he decided that, on the return of the Missionaries from their excursions, a general assembly of two subjects out of each house should be held, and the result of the deliberations be presented to the king. He consulted several persons at Naples on this subject, and they all assured him that these measures would be attended by the most happy results. He informed the grand-almoner of this resolution, and begged him to lend his support; as he received no answer, he charged a father in Naples to let him know that "if he will not hear us," (these are the words of his letter,) "I will go to him myself, all paralyzed as I am. . . . In conclusion, if he will not hear you, I will send a thousand letters to the Marquis of Marco, and a thousand petitions to the king." When the grand-almoner saw the real state of things, and the general dissatisfaction he had produced, he showed a disposition to favor Alphonsus, who hastened to communicate the news to all the houses, and to announce the general meeting on the 1st of May, urging them all to be tranquil in the meanwhile.

While Alphonsus thus sought to remedy the evil and extinguish the flames enkindled in the houses, the devil was not backward in improving this opportunity of increasing the fire more and more in order to bring every thing to ruin. The house of Frosinone, in the pontifical states, contained amongst its members one of those restless and factious characters who are always a burthen to communities. His superiors were constantly obliged to remove him from one place to another; these changes were very displeasing to him, and he got indignant against the saintly founder, and took advantage of the circumstances of the times to create discord between the houses in the states and those in the kingdom. He concealed his perfidy under the mantle of a lively zeal, while he suggested the raising of the standard of rebellion against Alphonsus, and the effecting a separation which would render the missionaries of the pontifical states independent. In consequence of this, steps were taken to have a council held at Rome on the 3d of February, at which Alphonsus was denounced as an accomplice to the scheme regarding the innovations, and was deprived of his dignity as superior: it was also decided that the Pope should be informed of this, and that he should be entreated to convoke a general chapter of the houses in the states, to pronounce their separation from those of the kingdom, and to give them power to elect another head.

Alphonsus' circular ordering the meeting of which we have spoken was far from being welcomed by those in the states; as they believed that the object was to constrain them to adopt the new regulations, they did not even reply to it. So he felt obliged, contrary to custom, to issue an order to them to send their deputies to this chapter by virtue of holy obedience. When these deputies of the houses of the states arrived at Nocera, they were accompanied by the subject of whom we have spoken, and whom we shall designate as the procurator. He was the deputy of the house at Frosinone, and came filled with thoughts of insubordination and discord, firmly resolved to carry out the separation he had projected. The chapter was opened on the 12th of May, when flames burst forth on all sides. The greater part were prepossessed against F. Majone and his colleague, whom they considered as the enemies of the Congregation, and wished to expel them from it, or at least to depose them; on seeing such exasperation, Alphonsus regretted having convoked this meeting, which only seemed to forbode disastrous consequences. On the one side he saw the partizans of a dangerous novelty, and on the other the friends of the rule who were ready to revolt against him, and the procurator bent on increasing the discord. With a sense of the impossibility of reuniting them, he pressed his crucifix to his heart, and shed tears of bitterness, saying: "On one side I see the disciples of Jesus Christ, and on the other the instruments of the devil."

When F. Majone saw the impossibility of escaping, he strove secretly to thwart the measures which were adopted at Naples in regard to the grand-almoner, though Alphonsus had all the while been endeavoring to save him and his colleague and to prevent any thing being done against them. General dissatisfaction was felt in the assembly at this course towards F. Majone and his colleague, and at the compassion with which F. Villani and another consultor had treated them, and, led away by the semblance of holy liberty, they audaciously went beyond their prerogative, and, on the 20th of May, deposed the six consultors and forced Alphonsus to resign his office. The saintly old man submitted unresistingly to all. He would have liked to be the only victim of the tempest, to restore calm to the troubled sea and to save all his sons from shipwreck. After many difficulties, they proceeded to a new election on the 26th of May: Alphonsus was re-elected as superior-general, but of the six former consultors, only the fathers Villani and Mazzini were reinstated in consideration of their previous valuable services, and F. Corrado was nominated vicar-general instead of F. Villani. As F. Corrado did not wish to take such a charge upon himself, Alphonsus wrote to him, saying: "I entreat you to accept and fill the post; if it be necessary I cast myself at your feet, and I hope you will not refuse me." He had to oblige him to accept the office under pain of great sin.

As Alphonsus had been unable to preside at this assembly, they adopted the most arbitrary decisions, in contempt of the rule as well as in its favor. In a word, the rudder was without a steersman, and the Congregation was like a vessel without a pilot in the midst of rocks during the height of the tempest. During the twelve days this contest lasted Alphonsus was aimed at by all: his neutrality in regard to the parties was looked upon as the cause of all the evil; some reproached him as well as the consultors, for having kept the secret, others for not having listened to the general complaints, and instead of admitting the validity of his reasons, they forgot the respect due to his person and loaded him with reproaches: "You have founded the Congregation," they said to him, "you have destroyed it. We know not whether God will forgive you this fault." Alphonsus suffered all in silence, attributing every thing to his sins; far from complaining, he only replied to every one with words of respect and kindness, and however bitter were his sorrows, he received all as from the hand of God, and submitted patiently to drink of that chalice, of which the dregs were not even yet fully exhausted.

After the assembly was dissolved, he found no longer in the Congregation the spirit of submission which had existed in it before. Division of opinion had produced that of hearts, and even in the houses of the kingdom several parties arose, and each one constituted himself judge of what had been done and what was to be done. When F. Majone saw the evil he had done, and the sorrows Alphonsus had to endure in consequence, he had not the courage to return amongst his brethren. After having recalled him several times, Alphonsus signified to him that if he should not return within a given space of time he would be looked upon as excluded from the Congregation. The unhappy man, in his blindness, preferred to devote himself to the service of a baron of rank, as his secretary. It was there he terminated his days by a premature end, shedding tears over the ills he had caused, and over his own unhappy fate.

In the midst of this confusion, the F. procurator did not lose sight of his criminal designs. As he had been unable to succeed in his unjust pretensions, he had withdrawn from Nocera with his partizans with a mind filled with wicked thoughts. In order to attain his ends, which were to mortify Alphonsus and to divide the Congregation, he hastened to go to Rome and to present himself before the Holy Father. With a great display of zeal he stated to him what injury the rule approved by Benedict XIV had sustained in the kingdom, and begged the Pope's protection for himself and the houses of the states, representing Alphonsus as caring little for the decrees of the Holy See. Pursuing his perfidious designs, he got also into favor with the members of the Sacred Congregation, and thus obtained on the 12th of June 1780, a decree, by which the Pope charged Cardinal Banditi of Benevento to inform the members of the said Congregation who were in the two houses of his diocess, that his will was that they should strictly observe the rule and constitutions approved by Benedict XIV, that they should obtain a copy of them, and take care that they might undergo no alteration. A similar decree was despatched to Mgr. Giacobini, the bishop of Veroli, in regard to the houses of Scifelli and Frosinone.

This decree gave courage to Alphonsus. "God be praised," he exclaimed, "by this order of the Pope the subjects of the states are deprived of the liberty to make changes in the rule. My Jesus! bless the work, for it is thine own." As soon as the decision of the sovereign Pontiff was known in the houses of the kingdom, a great number of the subjects who were faithful to the rule went into the houses of Benevento and St. Angelo, through fear of being obliged by the grand-almoner or the king to observe the new regulations. This was in contempt of Alphonsus; however, his resignation was always perfect, and bowing his head, he only blessed the hand which struck him. He wrote to Cardinal Banditi to entreat him to protect the Congregation, and to act with freedom without regard to any thing which had been written or done in the assembly. "Even if your Eminence wishes," he added, "to deprive me of my office of superior-general, I say do as you think right before God. I have no other wish than that of seeing peace restored to my poor Congregation, and I know of no one but your Eminence who can succeed in doing this. * * * I have ordered all the subjects to obey your Eminence blindly."

Not satisfied with all he had done, the procurator pursued his measures without anybody's being able to resist him. He pretended that the new elections were null and void, and demanded in consequence, that the houses in the states should no longer be subjected to the authority of Alphonsus. His representations were such that, on the 4th of August, an order was expedited in the Pope's name to Cardinal Banditi and to Mgr. Giacobini, to the effect that no obedience was to be paid to the superiors of the kingdom in any thing, and that no subject was to be permitted to leave the houses of the states. When Alphonsus learned that the Pope had made arrangements in regard to the houses of the states, he immediately sent for the most ancient fathers of Benevento and St. Angelo, to inquire about it, but they replied to him that they were not bound to obey him as he was no longer their lawful superior. These words were as a sword which pierced his heart; the interior conflicts which they caused him to endure twice endangered his life. His soul, however, was inseparably united with the will of God, and he awaited death with calmness; but the Lord, in order to crown his servant more gloriously in heaven, had prepared still severer trials for him on earth.

After the procurator had gained the favor of the Sacred Congregation, he, (without making known any of the reasons which excused Alphonsus,) drew up a petition on the 4th of July in the name of the four houses of the states, to obtain the convocation of a chapter, or at least the nomination of a president for these houses; but this wise assembly, acting with its usual prudence, before adopting these extreme measures, wished to examine most thoroughly into the state of affairs, and instructed the internuncio at Naples secretly to inquire into the matter, and to make a faithful report thereupon. Alphonsus in consequence received an order from Cardinal Caracciolo, the prefect of the Sacred Congregation, to remit all the acts which were drawn up at the last assembly to the Sacred Congregation, with an exact account of all that had taken place. But this order threw Alphonsus into the greatest perplexity. The court of Naples had at that time most strictly forbidden any intercourse whatever to be held with the court of Rome. Not knowing what to do in these critical circumstances, he replied to the cardinal on the 24th of August, that he would send two of his fathers to Rome the following November, to give all the wished-for information by word of mouth. In order however that his having sought for delay might not be found fault with at Rome, he wrote once more to the cardinal to set before him a summary of the critical conjuncture in which he was placed, the unhappy nature of the attendant circumstances, and his total want of power to remedy them.

The procurator did not fail to cause the delay which Alphonsus asked for to pass for a piece of chicanery, made use of by him in order to gain time and to elude the orders of the Holy See. He multiplied his petitions, exaggerated the pretended offence of Alphonsus, and representing the injury which the absence of a head would occasion to the houses of the states, he redoubled his solicitations that a superior should be given to them. He was supported especially by those of the house of Frosinone; for which house Alphonsus (besides all he had done for it in common with the other houses in the states, as we saw above,) had, four months before, sold his four services, and had wished to sell his carriage and even to deprive himself of actual necessaries. The procurator was listened to, and through the misunderstanding which at that time existed between the courts of Naples and of Rome, he succeeded in defaming Alphonsus so much that Pius VI, ill-informed, at last declared that the houses of the kingdom should no longer form part of the Congregation. He stripped Alphonsus of his authority, and appointed F. D. Francis de Paul superior of the houses in the states. This fatal blow was inflicted on the 22d of September 1780. The procurator went farther, and obtained a rescript from the sacred penitentiary, to the effect that the Congregation was abolished in the kingdom of Naples, and that no petition coming from a redemptorist missionary out of the Roman states should be received; and he caused a paper to be circulated among the other congregations of cardinals, in order to get a similar declaration from each of them.

As Alphonsus did not know how far things had gone, he sent two fathers to Rome. They arrived there on the 25th of September, but it was too late; every thing had been decided on the 22d. The procurator received the fathers with feigned sorrow, saying he had done all that had been in his power to undeceive the holy father, and to prove the innocence of Alphonsus to every one; but at last he took off the mask, and showered forth torrents of abuse against Alphonsus. "He has been disappointed of canonization," he one day said with a triumphant air, as if he wished to dishonor the saintly founder even beyond the tomb. The two fathers could do nothing in Rome; the Sacred Congregation was closed, and the cardinals had gone to their country houses. When they returned to Nocera, F. Villani informed Alphonsus of the decison adopted against him, just as he was preparing for communion and to hear mass. This fatal blow quite disconcerted him at first, but he soon rallied, and adoring the Divine Will as manifested in that of the Pontiff, he said with a profound inclination of his head: "I wish for God alone; it is enough for me to have His grace. The Pope wills it thus. May God be praised!" He said nothing more, but he quietly went on with his preparation, heard mass, and strengthened himself with the eucharistic food. After the thanksgiving, he went out in the carriage, when the devil assailed him with a horrible temptation: he set before him the ruin of the Congregation as his own doing and as a punishment for his sins; he tried to persuade him that God had abandoned him, and that he had no further hope of salvation. During this painful conflict he humbled and abased himself, and strove to open his heart to confidence; but his humility seemed to him as if it were false, and his hope as presumption, and he saw nothing before him but despair. He hastened to return to the house, and no sooner had he reached the threshold of the door than he burst into tears, and exclaimed in a heart-rending tone of voice: "Aid me, the devil wants to make me despair; aid me, for I do not wish to offend God." At these cries F. Villani and the whole community hurried to him, but he did nothing but repeat: "Aid me, the devil tempts me to despair. My sins have caused God to abandon the Congregation; aid me, for I do not wish to offend God. The devil wants to lead me to despair." Fathers Villani and Mazzini at last succeeded in calming him. When the temptation was dissipated, he turned towards the crucifix and a figure of Mary, and repeated several times: "My mother, I thank thee; thou hast aided me now; aid me at all times, my dear mother. My Jesus, my hope; I shall never be confounded." This temptation returned to him from time to time, but he overcome it each time by his confidence in Jesus and Mary.

In all these troubles he never uttered the slightest complaint. Whenever the fathers began to speak of the injustice done to him he silenced them, and said: "The Pope has thus decreed it. God be praised! The will of the Pope is the will of God." The following Saturday he went to the church, though he was so ill, in order that he might magnify the Blessed Virgin according to custom, and ask for the prayers of the people. F. de Paul was touched with compassion in thinking of the sorrow which Alphonsus must feel at seeing the Congregation divided and placed under another head, and represented to him that he felt sorry to be constrained to displease him through the mandate of the Pope. To this Alphonsus replied as follows: "By God's grace I have never lost my judgment; I rejoice that your Reverence is appointed superior; all is right, and you must accept every thing because it is the Pope's will." In fact he was so indifferent as to his deposition, that when a certain religious came to visit him to console him for the division which had taken place, and testified his great displeasure in regard to the election of the president, Alphonsus heard him in silence and made no other answer than this: "I care little about my dignity as rector-major being taken from me; it is enough for me that they have not taken Jesus my Saviour and my mother Mary away from me." But he was not so indifferent as to the breaking of the bond of charity between the subjects of the kingdom and those of the states. "I strive to instill a spirit of charity into all my brothers," he wrote to F. de Paul, "your Reverence must do the same thing on your side, for God loves those who love charity." When Mgr. Bergame heard of the distress of his venerable friend he instantly went from Naples to see and console him, for he had all the tenderness of a son towards Alphonsus. Full of compassion for the saintly old man, he resolved to go to Benevento to see Cardinal Banditi, and to consult with him as to the manner in which the work of the missions was to be maintained in the kingdom of Naples. He went accompanied by one of the fathers. The cardinal was not a little distressed on hearing the sad and true state of things. He grieved over it; but he thought that it was not then expedient to take any steps at Rome in the matter.

Not satisfied with having submitted his will to that of the Pope, Alphonsus also wished to put himself under obedience to the new superior, the president de Paul, and he made up his mind to go and live as a simple subject in the house at Benevento. When F. Villani, in order to get him to give up his determination, told him that as the rule had not been abandoned the Congregation would always continue to exist in the kingdom, his answer was: "Whatever be the state of things, the Pope no longer recognizes these houses as forming part of the institute." One reason alone caused him to desist from his project, and that was the disturbance which such a step would cause at Naples at a time when the king was not on good terms with the court of Rome, and the consequent annoyance to the Pope likely to follow from it. However, he hastened to write to the new president, to assure him of his entire obedience, and of his readiness to repair to whichever house in the states he should point out to him, and he did not regain his tranquillity until after F. de Paul had commanded him to remain at Nocera, with the assurance that he should always form part of the Congregation.

The measures of the Pope were as a thunderbolt to the houses of the kingdom. Many of the subjects retired into the houses of the states. Those who had the most respect for Alphonsus went to ask his advice, but received no other answer than this: "Obey the Pope." Some, without regard to him, abandoned him without even so much as previously warning him of it, and there were others who made shipwreck in the storm and returned to the world again. So that on this more than on any other occasion, was fulfilled in regard to the children of the holy founder what our Saviour said to the apostles after the last supper: "Behold satan has desired to have you that he may sift you as wheat." In all this Alphonsus was insensible to his own humiliation, and only thought of the desolation of his disunited children; what distressed him the most was the displeasure which this afflicting separation caused to the sovereign Pontiff, and the cruel thought that he himself had fallen into disgrace with him, though he hoped always that he would be able to inform him of all in due time and to regain his favor. In his distress he had again recourse to the protection of Cardinal Banditi, begging him to represent to the Pope the serious difficulties of his position, as well as that of so many of his children who were deprived of his favor. He himself composed an abridged history of the vexatious vicissitudes which had agitated the poor Congregation from its very beginning, and he sent this memorial to his Eminence, that he might confirm it and remit it to the Pope. To this recital, he added a statement of all the good that his missionaries had done in the two kingdoms of Naples and Sicily, in which every year six or seven companies of them gave upwards of fifty missions within the space of eight months. He caused a novena to be made at Nocera by the whole community for the good success of this letter; he also sent to Naples to have a novena begun by the capuchins of St. Francis, and caused a mass to be sung in every house in the kingdom.

The cardinal signed this letter and sent it as if it came from himself; but as truth approached the pontifical throne, calumny strove to repel it. When the procurator heard that the letter had been handed to the Sacred Congregation, he was filled with fresh fury, and invented a thousand falsehoods to render Alphonsus more and more odious. When Alphonsus saw that his hopes were again disappointed, he wrote again to the cardinal, and also to the president de Paul, to know what he should do in these circumstances, (when every communication with Rome was forbidden without the previous authorization of the chamber and the king,) in order to satisfy the Pope, and obtain again the faculties and the privileges necessary to the good success of the missions, of which they were deprived in the kingdom by the decree of separation. During all these severe trials Alphonsus always behaved admirably, never putting his own interpretation on the will of the Pope. Several of the fathers said: "If the Pope speaks of those who have abandoned the rule, how can we, who have always observed it, be of the number of those whom he has condemned." The argument was plausible, and it was assented to by the bishop of Troy, and Mgr. San Severino, the king's confessor, but Alphonsus wished for unconditional submission. "It is not for us to judge," he several times said, "we cannot judge the Pope in our own cause; let us humbly bow our heads in submission. If the Pope has cast us down by one decree, he can raise us up by another; we must obey, and not put interpretations of our own on what he does." Mgr. Carafa, when one of the fathers complained to him at Rome of having been so unjustly deprived of the favor of the Holy See, said: "But what has he done to you? The Pope did not, and could not have you in view:" and on another occasion, to two other fathers: "You are theologians; how could that touch you?" Relying upon his name, several of the fathers wished to take advantage of these answers; but Alphonsus never would listen to them. "Mgr. Carafa's words prove nothing," said he, "those of the Pope alone are those which we ought to attend to." He was chiefly distressed, because the privation of pontifical favors in regard to the exercises of the missions acted to the injury of souls. "At Rome," he wrote to the president de Paul, "they endeavor to make me hope that the Pope thinks of restoring to me the office of superior-general; but the blow which has struck me is not that; it is the loss of faculties for the missions, of those faculties without which we can be of but little assistance to souls." He then went on to commission him to use his influence to regain them, and he also begged F. Cajone to have the kindness to go to Rome to arrange this affair. However, though things were in such a state, Alphonsus did not neglect the missions. "We have not ceased to labor for the good of souls in the kingdom," he wrote to Cardinal Banditi on the 15th of January 1781, "we have given a great many missions. That of Foggia may be counted as four, for it will last a month and a half; that of Nola will soon take place, and will continue for a month; similar ones will also be given at Nocera and elsewhere."

Whilst the servant of God thus manifested such earnest solicitude for the work of the missions, the affairs of the Congregation grew daily worse and worse; thanks to the calumnies of the procurator. Alphonsus and his missionaries were now only looked upon in many places as a reproach among men, and as loaded with the indignation and the censures of the Holy See. Several bishops took them for schismatics, and refused their missions, and if the priests or the people asked to have them, they were refused. Alphonsus' only consolation in the midst of so many troubles and humiliations consisted in meditating on the passion of Jesus Christ, or on the truths of eternity, and in reading over and over again the life of St. Joseph Calasanctius, the founder of the regular Clerics of the Pious Schools, whose old age had also been afflicted by a similar cruel persecution from three of his subjects. Except when he spoke to the fathers what it was necessary to say, he maintained continual silence, and kept himself closely united to God. His sight being much weakened, he was to be seen for hours together with his forehead almost resting on his book. He adored the will of God in that of the Pope, and did all he could to prevent the smallest complaint being uttered against it, and was still more anxious that nothing should be done to cause him the slightest displeasure. On hearing that several of the fathers thought of soliciting the king's protection, and fearing that that would occasion trouble between the courts of Rome and of Naples, he entreated the vicar-general, F. Corrado, expressly to forbid it.

CHAPTER XXXIV.

Unavailing efforts of Alphonsus to bring about a re-union between the houses of the Pontifical States and those of the Kingdom. Signs of Alphonsus' approaching dissolution. His zeal for the salvation of souls continues unabated.

AMIDST this thick gloom, a ray appeared to console Alphonsus and his children. He remembered the promise of the king to recompense the services of his missionaries, whom he had appointed to publish the jubilee in 1779. He determined to ask that it might be made lawful for the subjects of the Congregation to make an oath to God to lead a life in community according to holy poverty, and to remain in the Congregation until death. He came to this conclusion because the grand-almoner would not allow of vows; and Innocent II having in 1664, (in the case of the clerics of St. Joseph) commuted the vows of poverty, chastity and obedience into so many oaths, he thought that his plan would be approved by the Sacred Congregation and the Pope, and that thus there would no longer be an obstacle to a reunion, and the consequent enjoyment of the favors and privileges dependant upon it. When the president de Paul was informed of this project, he entered warmly into it, thinking that if the king should grant the favor, the troubles would be ended and a re-union brought about. But whilst Alphonsus thus made use of human measures, he grounded again all his hopes in prayer. Amongst other things, he ordered that the Blessed Sacrament should be exposed in each house for the adoration of the community, every evening for nine days, and that various prayers should then be recited. All the members, besides, adopted a spirit of penance; many masses were celebrated for this intention, and large alms were distributed among the poor. He then again had recourse to his old friend the Marquis of Marco, who laid the petition before the king and supported it. The king graciously granted all that was asked for. "His Majesty," the marquis replied on the 24th of February 1781, "is full of gratitude for the indefatigable labors of your missionaries, and the success they have obtained in the publication of the jubilee, and so he has deigned to grant you all the favors you have asked for. He therefore permits, 1st, the missionaries of your institute to make the oaths of a life in common and of poverty; 2dly, that the said missionaries may take the oath of perseverance in the Congregation, from which oath they may be dispensed by the superior-general for lawful reasons; 3dly, he also consents that the missionaries may ask for some assistance from their friends and benefactors in the time of the wheat and olive harvest."

These tidings filled Alphonsus with joy; he fancied that every thing was now put to rights. Considering it a miracle of the Blessed Virgin Mary that he had obtained this favor, he exhorted all, in notifying it to all the houses, to offer up, before the Blessed Sacrament during its exposition, fervent thanksgiving for this blessing to Almighty God and to the Blessed Virgin. Great was the joy in all the houses, as well as among the friends of the Congregation; the inhabitants around Iliceto even made bonfires in rejoicing.

As soon as the decree was published, Alphonsus sent a copy of it to Cardinal Zelada, (who presided over the Sacred Congregation as prefect, on account of the death of Cardinal Caracciolo,) again explaining to him how he had been deceived, and showing that the wound was healed through the oaths, so that there was no longer any obstacle to the re-union so much wished for on both sides. He wrote also to the procurator himself to entreat him to co-operate for this re-union, or at least not to oppose it. "I pray your Reverence to remember," he said, "that if you persevere in wishing for the separation, and obtain what you wish, you will, as I believe, spend the remainder of your days in sorrow, especially when you shall see that it is too late to remedy it. I entreat you by the love of God, to consider this point at the foot of the crucifix." Alphonsus also once more begged Cardinal Banditi to speak favorably for him to the Holy Father. Every thing seemed to foretell a happy termination of affairs, but the iniquity of the procurator, who had been insensible to the entreaties of Alphonsus, triumphed once more. "Mgr. Liguori's pretensions are too numerous," he said, on presenting himself before the Sacred Congregation, "he wants to act as Pope, or at least not to take any notice of the Pope. The oaths are another alteration he wishes to make in the rule. But besides this, the rule is altered from one end to the other. We wish to have the rule of Benedict XIV, and not the reform of Mgr. Liguori." He took special care to make his passion appear like zeal, and to render Alphonsus inexcusable in the eyes of the cardinals; and taking advantage also of the misunderstanding between the two courts, which prevented Alphonsus from pleading his cause before the Sacred Congregation, he had no difficulty in dissuading the cardinals from all measures of conciliation. Cardinal Zelada, who had an extreme veneration for our Saint, and knew his inviolable attachment to the Holy See as well as his innocence, proposed to the Sacred Congregation, that they should respect his person and make some arrangement in favor of re-union; but he was alone in this proposition, and all the other cardinals, especially Cardinal Ghilini, the reporter of the cause, were of a contrary mind. The Pope was again misinformed, and, beset by the procurator, far from granting any thing, he confirmed all the previous decisions. When Alphonsus heard of it, he said: "I wish for what God wills. The will of God makes all things straight." Although his affliction on hearing of his fresh defeat at Rome was very great, Alphonsus did not despair of regaining the favor of the Pope. He begged F. Corrado to go to Benevento, there to meet the president de Paul, in order that they might consult together as to the measures to be adopted to effect the re-union.

On the 3d of April, the fathers Corrado and Constance, of Nocera, F. Augustin, the rector of Caposele, F. Carmin, the rector of St. Angelo, and F. Tannoja, of Iliceto, arrived nearly at the very same hour at Benevento. The meeting was providential, for they had not preconcerted it. They were all of one mind, and settled on the measures to be adopted for the re-union with the F. president. Amongst other things, it was decided that two provinces should be established, and that that of the states should be under his direction; they also determined on sending two fathers to Rome, to settle this matter with the Pope. But the procurator, irritated at this pacific interview, and dissatisfied with the F. president, threatened to upset every thing in the kingdom and in the states. The hatred he had conceived against Alphonsus increased day by day. He swore that he would never permit a re-union to take place: "This is a satisfaction," said he, "which Mgr. Liguori and his adherents will never obtain from me." "If Mgr. Liguori had me in his power," he said on another occasion, "he would ruin me outright." Thus fear of some mischance happening to himself had entered the heart of this unhappy man, and together with his hatred against Alphonsus, made him act as if he were quite desperate, and all the hopes of Alphonsus and of all the other fathers were frustrated again.

After Easter, the Pope was to go to the Pontine Marshes; hence Alphonsus begged Cardinal Banditi to go there in person, in order that he might see his Holiness, and inform him of the real state of things. He made the same request to

Mgr. Bergame, the bishop of Gaeta. But the mind of Pius VI was quite prejudiced against Alphonsus and his houses. To all they said, he only answered: "Let them then come and state all that has been done, for it is not well to change the rule of a religious Congregation without the sanction of the Holy See;" and, "I know that Alphonsus is a saint, and that he has hitherto been obedient to the Holy See; but on this occasion he has not adopted the same course:" and again, "Let them come and tell me of all that has been done with sincerity." In consequence of this, Alphonsus at the end of May sent two fathers to Rome, ordering at the same time prayers and masses to be said, and exhorting the houses of Benevento and St. Angelo to co-operate in furthering the success of this matter.

In the midst of these troubles, Alphonsus had one more source of distress. Through his love of holy poverty he had made a vow to depend on the local superior, just like any other subject; but the rectors in the kingdom not being at this time lawful superiors of the houses, he did not know to whom to apply, and was continually afraid of sinning against his vow. He had therefore charged one of the fathers who had been sent to Rome to speak about it to the Pope—to inform him of his uneasiness, and to entreat his Holiness to cause him, in all his doubts, to submit to the will of the superior or his confessor. The father did not apply to the Pope, but to the cardinal grand-penitentiary, who was filled with admiration at the saint's delicacy, and at the vow he had made in regard to poverty, which was so new a thing in a superior. "Let him submit to his confessor," was the answer of the cardinal.

The proceedings at Rome in regard to the re-union had not the fortunate results which had been expected. The procurator again managed so, that all that had been done at Benevento and the negotiations with the Pope at the Pontine Marshes came to nought. The following answer to the petition of Alphonsus was given on the 22d of June: "Let the procurator-general of the Congregation present at court be heard." The fathers stated all the reasons which were in their favor, and the procurator also presented his statement on the 9th of July. His words had little in them calculated to produce conviction, but there was such a prejudice in his favor that he once more gained his cause; and in the report which was presented to the Holy Father, quite the contrary was asserted of that which he had heard from Cardinal Banditi and Mgr. Bergame, so that his dissatisfaction with those in the kingdom was converted into indignation. He therefore sent them an answer on the 24th of August 1781, to this effect: "*Standum in decisis per Sanctissimum sub die* 13 *Septembris* 1780;" that is, "let all previous decisions stand;" and as a double victory for the procurator, it was added: "*Et amplius non admittantur preces,* "and let no farther petitions be received." This confirmation of the preceding dispositions was a final triumph to the procurator's unceasing endeavors to humble and grieve Alphonsus by calumniating him personally and destroying his work. "He has failed as to his canonization," he exultingly repeated over and over again, to the disgust of the bishop of Narni, to whom he said it.

The fathers returned from Rome in November; when Alphonsus heard of the decision which had been adopted, he exclaimed, with all the calmness of perfect resignation: "For six months I have asked for nothing from God but that his will might be accomplished. Lord! I only will what thou willest." Thus did he make a perfect holocaust to God of that work which he had maintained for forty years amidst numberless difficulties, and for which he had sacrificed his repose, his honor, and his reputation. He adored the unfathomable judgments of God, by which he, who had in so many ways manifested his zeal, submission, and respect towards the Head of the Church, should nevertheless be looked upon by him with an eye of severity, and treated with rigor. It is true, that when they proceeded to the examination of his virtues in the Sacred Congregation of rites with that scrupulous exactness always practised there, the calumnies were discovered, and his innocence was brought to light. It is true, that when the Holy Father was thus at last undeceived, he wept at having grieved a saint, and did not hesitate to declare in a solemn decree of the 29th of April 1796, that Alphonsus had always been most submissive towards the Holy See, "as his words, his actions, and his writings have often testified." It is true, that the same Holy Father even imposed perpetual silence on this subject, so that during the course of the process of the canonization no farther allusion to the faults of which he had been supposed to be guilty could be made. But all this happened after his death. God willed that he should die without the satisfaction of seeing his innocence brought to light, and of being justified in the eyes of the world.

It was at this time that the Pope established a house of the missionaries of the Congregation in Rome in the Church of St. Julian, not far from that of St. Mary Major; and not satisfied with granting them this favor, Pius VI gave them fresh proofs of his esteem and protection, by founding two houses at Gubbio and Spello, in the diocese of Foligno, in order to supply the necessities of his states. The F. president de Paul and those of Rome informed Alphonsus of this. So far from remembering his own humiliations, he experienced the greatest joy at these tidings, and although he had before been opposed to an establishment in Rome, now that the will of the Pope was plainly expressed on the subject, he testified as much satisfaction as if it had been his own work, and as if he had been recognised as superior. He wrote several letters of congratulation to those in the states, testifying how much he rejoiced at their progress, as well as at the flourishing state of their noviciate. "I hope," he said in one addressed to the F. president, "that God will make use of you to increase his glory, and I will not cease to pray to him for this end. I thank you for the *Ave Maria* which you recite every evening for me; apply it specially for a happy death." He finished by offering some advice suggested by his zeal, as to the importance of the sermon on prayer and that on the Blessed Virgin, in the missions, no less than on all other occasions.

Those at Rome, whilst rejoicing at the opening of the two new houses, wrote word to Alphonsus that the missionaries had also been demanded at Ravenna. "Our brothers in the states," he said thereupon, "are well pleased, because they have got a new field of action. I am glad that they are to have one at Ravenna; may they do that which God wills; but you will see that Ravenna will not take root. To conclude, I shall find pleasure at seeing the progress of the affair." That which he predicted came true; all the negotiations as to obtaining Ravenna were useless."

All this was very consoling to the heart of Alphonsus, but it could not but increase the sorrow he felt at seeing the houses of the kingdom cut off from the Congregation. That this sorrow filled his heart entirely, might be gathered from what he uttered during the delirium of a fever, brought on by a vomiting of blood caused probably by so many domestic misfortunes. "What," said he, "are we not of the Congregation of the Most Holy Redeemer? Do we not acknowledge the rule of Pope Benedict XIV? If we submit to the rule of the Pope, why are we out of the Congregation?" At other times he said: "We have the rule of the Pope, we have taken the vows and we keep to them; therefore why do we not belong to the Congregation?" and again: "Perhaps they doubt whether we do observe this rule, and this is why we are now rejected; God wills it to be thus, let us have patience!" As his state excited great compassion, he was told, in order to calm him, that they were really Redemptorists; he then became silent and tranquil. It was observed that during these deliriums he never uttered a word indicative of the slightest dissatisfaction at what the Pope had done, or against any one whatever.

During his recovery, several of the fathers, on their return from a mission, went to get his blessing; Alphonsus who had always this same idea before his mind, said on seeing them: "I cannot make out how it can be said that we do not belong to the Congregation of Redemptorists, since we receive the rule of Benedict XIV, and this rule has been always kept by us, and is so still." "There can be no doubt on the subject," responded one of the fathers, "both the Pope and the king designate your lordship as its founder." "I do not wish to be spoken of any more in this world," he replied, "but I wish it to be known that the rule which is observed by us is the very one which we received from the Pope, and from which we have never departed." On another occasion, having been told that it would always be acknowledged that the Congregation existed in the kingdom, and that the rule which Mgr. Liguori received from the Pope was observed there, he replied with agitation: "What does my name signify? what I care about is that it should be known that we are subject to the Pope. Let us bless God for all that he has done."

However deplorable was his situation, Alphonsus always rose above his misfortunes, and never ceased to hope for happier days for the Congregation. Once when they tried to persuade him that it would never be re-established again as before, he answered: "I assure you that God willed and still wills that the Congregation shall subsist in the kingdom; I founded it for the kingdom, and it is for that God has given me the vocation." He even, however he might be cast down himself, unceasingly inspired the fathers with fresh courage, by the assurance that they should one day be re-united again, and that the Pope would restore his favor to them. "Do not lose courage," said he, "Lazarus arose on the fourth day; be faithful towards God, who can do all things; let us pray and be resigned."

In the year 1783, it pleased the Lord partially to console his servant, by the restoration of the privileges and favors for the work of the missions. When the houses of the kingdom were deprived of the favor of the Pope, the bishops shared in their sorrow. They were alarmed at seeing themselves deprived of a congregation of workmen who took such a part in their solicitude, and so most of them felt it a duty to represent Alphonsus' innocence to the Pope, to Cardinal Zelada, or to Mgr. Carafa, and to tell them the sad consequences which would result to their dioceses if His Holiness had not the clemency to restore these favors to the missionaries of the kingdom as before. Mgr. the pro-nuncio also, who had been charged to take secret information, (though he had been very slow in acquitting himself of his office, through an excess of prudence,) had presented his report to the Sacred Congregation on the 17th of October 1782. After having represented the painful position of the Congregation, which was in imminent danger of being suppressed, he manifested the deceit of which Alphonsus had been the victim, and clearly exposed his entire innocence. "I believe," said he, "that Mgr. Liguori acted in such a manner that his conduct does not deserve the censure which the plaintiffs belonging to the houses of the states have attempted to cast upon it; it must therefore be worthy of approbation." He finally represented that the preservation of the missionaries was indispensable to the kingdom and to the welfare of its population; and that several bishops and other respectable persons had assured him of the zeal and utility of this Congregation. "I think it my duty," concluded he, "to beg and implore the kind interest of their Eminences the Cardinals, in favor of the re-establishment of union and harmony in this Congregation, that it may continue to do the good for which it was instituted by Mgr. Liguori, and which has caused it to merit the protection of the sovereign."

This report of the pro-nuncio, and the petitions of so many bishops, could not fail to make an impression on the heart of Pius VI. When therefore, Alphonsus himself, strong in his innocence and confiding in the clemency of the Pope, addressed a petition to him to obtain the restoration of the favors and privileges, the privation of which had caused him the most distress on account of the loss resulting to souls, His Holiness at once granted what he prayed for. The petition was as follows:

"Most Holy Father: Mgr. Alphonso Maria Liguori prostrates himself at the feet of your Holiness, and humbly entreats you to grant to his missionaries all the graces, faculties and privileges conceded by the Holy See to the Venerable Congregation of Redemptorists in the Pontifical states," &c.

This petition Alphonsus addressed to the Pope in March 1783, and on the 4th of April following, the Holy Father granted to Alphonsus and the present and future members of his Congregation, all the indulgences and spiritual favors which the Redemptorist missionaries in his states enjoyed during mission time, and in all other exercises of their ministry. This rescript wounded the very heart of the procurator. Not knowing how else to thwart this favorable decision, he forged a petition under the name of one of the fathers of the kingdom, and presented it himself to the Pope. It contained several questions, and a prayer that the graces conferred should be specified. By this means he hoped considerably to reduce those powers and favors; but this time his intrigue failed, and he was told that the matter did not admit of explanation. Shortly after this, God granted Alphonsus another consolation, viz: that of seeing himself exculpated before the royal council, and justified from all the calumnies and accusations with which the procurator-advocate and the other adversaries of the Congregation had loaded him. The senators declared the missionaries free from all contravention of the royal decrees, which had been the most serious point; and as to the contested property claimed by Baron Sarnelli, after having repeatedly heard the respective advocates, they all with one accord agreed to represent to the king that there was no ground for admitting the pretensions of the baron. The royal council in consequence addressed to the king on the 4th of February 1784, a report, by which they acquitted the missionaries of all the charges against them; and a royal decree approved of this decision, on the 10th of April of the same year, after the tribunals at Naples had been occupied about these affairs for no less than nineteen years.

These two favors on the part of the Pope and the king, following one another so closely, filled Alphonsus' heart with unspeakable joy, and raised up the courage of his desolate children. He desired that special thanksgivings should be offered to God and to the Blessed Virgin in all the houses for what he called a great miracle; and a miracle in truth it was, but it was the fruit of the prayers and penances of this great servant of God, and his unlimited confidence in the protection of Mary.

When matters were thus tranquillized, various things happened which were calculated to divide the houses of the kingdom from those of Sicily, and these latter again from those of the states. A chapter was convoked on the 15th of October 1783, in the house of Scifelli, with the consent of the Pope, and the F. president de Paul was elected rector-major. Those in Sicily declared against those in the kingdom, and nominated F. D. Blasucci rector-major for themselves. Thus all hope of reconciliation was entirely lost. Those in the kingdom, on the other hand, fearing that they would lose their principal support by the death of Alphonsus, also held a chapter in the same month at Ciorani, and elected F. Villani as the coadjutor and future successor of Alphonsus. In the midst of all these new difficulties, Alphonsus never lost the hope of seeing the Congregation re-established under one head; he often repeated on different occasions: "Act uprightly towards God, and God will not abandon the Congregation; matters will be settled after my death." One day he said to one of the fathers: "I should have liked to have seen things settled before my death; I have asked for it, and continue to ask for it of the Blessed Virgin; but it is not the will of God. Things will be arranged, but that will be after my death."

What he had predicted came to pass four years after he had gone to receive his reward in heaven, through the very orders of Pius VI, in concert with King Ferdinand IV. The latter by an edict of the 29th of October 1790, decreed that the missionaries in the kingdom should observe the rule of Benedict XIV, and that their houses should be reunited to those in the states. Pius VI, on his side, restored all his favors to them on the 5th of August 1791, and wished that after the re-union one rector-major should be elected by common consent in a general chapter.

When things were arranged as we have seen above, there were a great many subjects who repented of their former conduct, and addressed repeated petitions to be allowed to return to the kingdom, and two of them in particular, who had been the most obstinate in maintaining the separation, protested that they wished to return and were content to take the lowest place. They met with so many imitators, that the president, on seeing that his houses were becoming depopulated, asked the Pope if he could in conscience permit these transmigrations, and received a negative answer. This last verdict was as the dregs of the bitter chalice which Alphonsus had to drain; though he received it with the most perfect resignation. "If the Pope thinks so," said he, "I also wish it. The holy will of God turns all that is bitter into sweetness; the will of the Pope is the will of God."

But as God is not accustomed to leave his servants for a length of time in tribulation without any consolation, so he did not fail to console Alphonsus at this time. Two distinguished subjects of Germany, John Clement Hofbauer and Francis Hübel, who came from Vienna, were admitted into the Congregation at Rome as novices. What had made them decide to join the Congregation, was the edifying conduct of its missionaries, and especially the reputation of its founder, Mgr. Liguori, well known in Germany for his sanctity and his learning. These good Germans burned with a holy zeal, and ardently wished to see a house of the Congregation established in Vienna. The ardor of their zeal was so great that they could perceive no difficulties in the way, and looked upon the thing as if already accomplished. This projected German house was laughed at amongst the fathers. But when Alphonsus heard of the pious object of the fervent novices he thought differently, and it caused him extreme joy: "God," said he, "will not fail to spread his glory in that country by their means. The suppression of the Jesuits has caused those populations to be nearly abandoned. The missions, however, ought not to be like ours; instructions are more useful there than sermons, as the people are living amidst Lutherans and Calvinists. At the commencement they should be made to say the *Credo*, and then the faithful should be prepared to abandon sin; these good priests will do good, but they will require greater lights than they have. I would write to them, but God does not will that I should have any thing to do with it. My Jesus! humble me more and more, and reap therefrom thy glory."

Partly in consequence of the last decree of the Pope, and partly because he had not yet felt it right to acknowledge the Congregation in the kingdom as forming an ecclesiastical body, in proportion as the houses in the states became more flourishing, those in the kingdom seemed to decay. Whilst Alphonsus was consoled at seeing the prosperity of the former, he could not see the others languishing and in lack of subjects without sorrow; and this sorrow was increased by their great poverty. F. Villani represented to him that the house of Iliceto was no longer capable of maintaining the students, and that the other houses being in poverty and distress could not give any assistance. "Now," at last said Alphousus sighing, "all our houses are falling into ruin. Ah! Lord, thy will be done, let the consequences be what they may."

Alphonsus' humiliation and that of his houses was not enough to satisfy the hatred of the procurator. The saint's kind way of acting towards him did not avail to soften his heart; in order to humble and distress Alphonsus still more, he asked the Holy Father to specify in a brief the number and the names of the true houses of the Redemptorists. He succeeded, and in a special brief of the 17th of December 1784, the Pope declared that the only houses of the Congregation of the Most Holy Redeemer were those of Benevento, of St. Angelo, of Scifelli and Frosinone, of Spello and of Gubbio, and also the hospice at Rome near the church of St. Julian. At the solicitation of the procurator, His Holiness also declared that the house of St. Julian should be regarded as the general and pricipal house of the whole Congregation. The procurator had had something still further in view in this petition. He was pained at seeing the number of graces and privileges which the Pope had restored to Alphonsus. He determined on taking the cardinal whose office it was to draw up the brief by surprise, and, presenting him all the decrees previously issued against the houses in the kingdom, he wished to cause him to insert all that they contained to their disadvantage in this last one, that is to say, that the houses in the states were confirmed in the possession of the favors of the Holy See, and those of the kingdom were deprived of them as refractory. He had already written to inform a great many friends of it, and had represented those in the kingdom as having become objects of the abomination and anathemas of the Holy See; but some how or other he got afraid of being discovered, and gave up this piece of deceit. Nevertheless he did not cease to try to make people believe that Alphonsus was imbecile, and even that he was out of his mind. "Poor old man," he answered to a prelate who being ignorant of his sentiments asked him how Alphonsus was, "he is in a pitiable state; his mind is so impaired that he is no longer a man but a child; and what is worse he falls into extravagances. When he is spoken to about the Pope and the affairs of the Church, he replies with emphasis, that the Pope is the Pope, and the Church is the Church; in a word, he has so lost his senses that he has become quite a child." He even went so far as to wish to deprive Alphonsus of the title of founder of his Congregation; and not satisfied with words and false assertions, he tried to introduce into the Congregation of Rites the cause of the canonization of Bishop Falcoja, (who had died in the odor of sanctity and had also worked miracles,) hoping to be able during the proceedings to secure the glory of founder to this servant of God, who had been the chief adviser of Alphonsus at the time of the foundation. Such was the conduct of Alphonsus' persecutor, and his sentiments were not changed whilst the saint lived. His hatred even followed him beyond the tomb; at the very time when God glorified his servant's sanctity by miracles, the implacable persecutor wished to prevent his canonization, but his odious conduct excited the indignation of the whole court of Rome against him. Pius VI perceived, but too late, the hypocrisy of this impostor, who went so far as to seek to divide the cardinals and disquiet the Pope himself; however, he was at length unmasked and seen through; he was forbidden to approach the Vatican any more, or to enter the Congregation of the bishops and regulars. This unhappy man's change of fortune did not produce a change of heart or conduct. Alphonsus had predicted, on seeing his prosperity, that he would one day receive a great chastisement from the hands of God. In fact, he fell ill in the year 1801, and death overtook him suddenly, on the very day when the sons of Alphonsus celebrated the festival of the Most Holy Redeemer. He would not have any advice, for in his madness he fancied he was quite well, and when it was proposed to him to receive the viaticum, he answered that it was not necessary; there was scarcely time to administer extreme unction to him before the agonies of death came upon him, and he died striking his hand violently against the bed, a prey to all the torments of despair, without uttering a single word which could give reason for hope as to his eternal salvation.

Some time before the fatal catastrophe of 1780, Alphonsus was reduced, as we have seen, to a state of extreme weakness, and seemed to have arrived at his last moments, but after the blow which separated him from the greatest part of his children, we may say that his life was nothing but a prolonged death. Until this time he had never ceased to preach to the people every Saturday on the virtues of the Blessed Virgin, as also during the novenas before her feasts, and on the evening of Holy Thursday to describe the passion of Jesus Christ to the people in a most touching manner. On all these occasions crowds hastened to hear him, and to gather, as they said, the last precious pearls which fell from the lips of the pious bishop. In order to put a check on this admirable zeal, which could not but shorten his days, the express orders of the doctors and of his director, F. Villani, were necessary. But for all this he did not cease to take the greatest interest in all that concerned his missionaries and their labors; his solicitude appeared even to redouble itself with the increase of his afflictions. We have seen proofs of this above. When the missionaries came home, he received them with open arms, and his delight was to hear them give the recital of the good they had done, and of any extraordinary conversions. "And I!" he exclaimed in tears on one such occasion, "what do I? I am useless, nay, I am even a burthen to the Congregation." "The others labor," replied one of the fathers, "and as you are their founder, you take part in their labors." "Founder, founder!" he replied with vivacity, "what am I but a poor miserable creature! I can only do evil; it is God who has founded the Congregation. God alone is its founder, and I have only been a worthless instrument in his hands." Admirable humility united to such an ardent zeal! The same interest he took in the general welfare of the Church. When any person came to see him from Naples or elsewhere, he forgot all his pains to inquire into the state of religious affairs in all Catholic countries. He was inconsolable when he heard that religion was despised, or the Church persecuted, or morals corrupt. "Unhappy Naples," he one day said on hearing of the disorders of this capital: "The Lord whom thou hast offended will not forget to punish thee. God will not bear for ever, and if his mercy is disdained, it is changed into malediction." He often offered himself up in sacrifice to stay the anger of the Lord. He felt such keen sorrow when the misfortunes of the day were spoken of, that F. Villani was obliged to forbid the fathers to speak to him of such subjects, especially of the disagreement between the Pope and the states.

One of his principal occupations was to read those authors who avenged the cause of religion and undertook its defence, thanking God for the zeal with which he inspired them, as also for having caused him to be born in the faith and in the pale of the Church, in Europe, and in that part of Europe which is the centre of faith. He was deeply grieved when he heard of any who were disposed to become infidels, and his distress at hearing of the triumph of the *zealous* Jansenists, as he called them, was still greater. But not less great was his joy on hearing that the Jesuits were established in Prussia and Russia, and he did not cease to offer up thanksgivings to God for it, as well as to magnify the hospitality of the Empress Catherine. "People assert that they are schismatics," said he, "but they talk nonsense. I know that the Pope recognizes them as members of the Church, and protects them. Let us pray to God for these holy religious, because their institute is a work which is calculated to promote the good of souls and that of the Church also. Schismatic! What does that mean? Pope Ganganelli was God's instrument to humble them, and Pius VI is also God's instrument to raise them up. It is God who kills, and brings to life again; let us pray to him, and he will not fail to bless them."

He heard that a religious of a strict order, who was imbued with the spirit of Anthony Arnauld, was depriving the faithful of holy communion, even for the space of several years, on the specious pretext of want of sufficient advancement in perfection; and that he taught his doctrine publicly, and was supported by others, and that he had won over several priests and confessors to his side. This news not only made him shed tears but enkindled also his zeal, and as he was unable to do any thing to remedy this himself, he did all in his power to get his missionaries to disabuse those who had been thus deceived, especially the confessors; he even wished that the Archbishop of Amalfi, in whose diocese this had happened, should be warned on the subject in his name.

Although Alphonsus' zeal was fettered by his numerous infirmities, yet he did not remain entirely idle. When the spiritual exercises were given to the people in the house, he was in the habit of having himself carried to the church on the last day, that he might encourage the faithful to persevere in the grace of God. On one occasion, he determined to give his accustomed counsels, although he had been bled in the morning: he expatiated on the love of Jesus and Mary, and preached quite a sermon which lasted for an hour. At the end, he gave the benediction to the people with a large crucifix. The effort he made in this re-opened the wound, and the blood flowed in abundance whilst he gave the blessing. While retiring, as he did not perceive the accident, and it was not observed by those who supported him, all the way as he went to his own room was covered with blood. The faithful hastened to collect it, with religious respect, striving to steep their handkerchiefs in it. There were some free-thinkers there, and two in particular, who were the sons of a notorious infidel, repented of their evil thoughts, and imitated the eager crowd, carrying home even the very earth which was reddened with the blood of our saint. He was also in the habit of sending for the seculars or ecclesiastics who might be in retreat in the monastery, and of going through some spiritual reading with them. He then tried to inspire them with piety and to confirm them in their good resolutions, and he especially excited them to devotion towards the Blessed Sacrament and the Blessed Virgin: "If all those who come here," said he, "only carry away a devotion to our Lady when they leave us, that will suffice to save them."

He yielded also sometimes, as we have already seen above, to the wishes of the nuns, who were always most eager to hear him. He went to the Convent of The Purity for the last time in the month of June 1781. He spoke to them of the detachment we should have in regard to earthly things, of the love we owe to Jesus Christ, and the filial trust we ought to have in the Most Holy Virgin. His sermon lasted for nearly two hours; but it seemed to these pious nuns as if but for a moment. When he left, they presented to him a nosegay of flowers, which he refused, till he was told that he could offer it to the Blessed Virgin, when he consented to accept it.

At the time of the indulgences of the Portiuncula in the convent of the Poor Clares, he went there in order to gain them. The religious asked him to give them an exhortation, and he spoke to them at length and with great fervor, on love towards the Blessed Sacrament and the Blessed Virgin Mary, and especially extolled the religious vocation and the strict observance of rule.

He was also anxious to maintain fervor among his own sons, and seized every occasion to exhort and encourage them, and never ceased to repeat and inculcate the maxims of the spiritual life and of perfection, as he had done with so much earnestness during his whole life. "It is certain that God wishes you to be saints;" he said one day to the young clerics who had come from Iliceto to Nocera to receive his blessing; "I recommend two things to you, obedience and poverty: obedience, were it even to the cook; obedience is that which preserves us; he who wants obedience is wanting as regards his duty to God, and God will drive him out of the Congregation; I also recommend poverty to you, for it is that which unites us to God. I regard faults against obedience and poverty as capital offences." Besides, as we have seen above, his infirm state did not prevent his holding the ordinary conference with the subjects of the house every Saturday. The last he gave was in the month of November 1780.

CHAPTER XXXV.

Alphonsus suffers great interior trials. The favors and graces by which God attested his sanctity.

SUCH were some of the exercises of the ardent zeal of Alphonsus in his retreat at Nocera. But whilst he had the holiness of others so much at heart, his special labor was to sanctify himself. He was constantly engaged in meditation and reading, and he was specially occupied with the life of his advocate, St. Theresa, and with the actions of the first heroes of the reform of this saint; and when he came to any passage which he thought particularly worthy of attention, he communicated it to those who went to sit with him after supper, so jealously anxious was he, as he had been all his life, to turn every moment of time to profit, and never to lose one minute. Indeed, constancy and perseverance were distinctive characteristics of our saint, no less than a burning zeal for the good of souls. Thus he was always most constant and punctual in performing the exercises of the community and his private devotions, as well as in the observance of all the rules he was yet able to observe: "I do not want great things," he often said; "let them be little, provided they be but constant."

His greatest trial under his infirmities was the anxiety they might cause to others. If he asked any one to do him some service, he made his request in the humblest terms. As he fancied that it was an inconvenience to the community for him to take his meals in his own room, he determined to take them with the others in the refectory, and would not yield to the reasons that were alleged against his so doing, till he was told that his slow way of eating would be inconvenient to the community.

He went out in the carriage up to the year 1784, as the doctors, and much more the community, were most anxious to prolong his life. But on the 19th of September of this year, being then eighty-eight years old, an internal rupture took place, which got worse by the shaking of the carriage, and obliged him to be taken out of it and to have recourse to the charity of a poor person who received him into her house; he was placed on a bed, and remained there as if he were quite dead. The surgeons succeeded in replacing the intestines; but he was brought back to the house in a most alarming state. The doctors were convinced that he required some exercise, and ordered that he should go out in a sedan-chair. As soon as he heard of this, he found a thousand pretexts for dispensing with it; but as the rector told him that it was the doctor's order, he consented. The day after the first essay, he opposed a second trial so much that the rector and the fathers united together in vain in endeavoring to persuade him to use it again. "What!" he said to them with tears, "must I be carried on the shoulders of these poor men! The thought of this made the going out yesterday more painful than salutary." The fathers replied that people of this sort were used to such labor, and that they gained their bread by it; but he testified so much repugnance on the subject, that the doctors, in order not to distress him, made him get a wheel-chair to go up and down the corridors.

When he was thus freed from the necessity of going out in the carriage, he sent the horses to Naples to be sold, and on the 24th of September he wrote as follows to F. Hilary: "As for the horses I send you, I do not want to have any scruples about them: mention therefore that one of them suffers in the jaws, and cannot eat either hay or oats; the other, that is to say, the oldest of the two, suffers from giddiness, and throws himself on the ground from time to time, and his ears must be pulled in order to make him rise again. Explain all this, as I wish to be free from scruples." His horses therefore were not, as we may see, over-expensive ones. One of them was sold for four ducats, and the other for twenty-two carlins. Such was the end of Alphonsus' pompous and superb equipage.

During this same year God deprived Alphonsus of his greatest consolation, that is to say, he became unable to say mass any longer. The celebration of the holy mysteries had been most painful to him, especially as he would observe the most minute rubrics, and make the genuflections to the ground. As F. Villani saw that he became daily more and more infirm, and that he had several times been nearly unable to go on, he told him that it was the will of God that he should abstain from celebrating the holy sacrifice any more. As soon as he heard that it was the will of God, and that of his director, he bowed his head in submission, and on Friday the 25th of November 1784, he celebrated mass for the last time. But though incapable of celebrating himself, he did not therefore dispense himself from assisting at the divine mysteries. Every morning after he had heard mass in his oratory, received holy communion and made his thanksgiving, he went down to the church with the assistance of his servant and Br. F. Anthony, and was placed at the side of the altar: he staid there without moving from his chair for several hours, and heard as many as five or six masses. During the day he was again conducted to the church, and prayed for several hours before the Blessed Sacrament. Br. F. Anthony declared that he remained before the altar for at least five or six hours every day. But it is impossible to describe what pain he felt at not being able to celebrate mass.

Fresh torments however were reserved for him, for God, who wished to prove him as gold in the crucible, gave him up, as he did holy Job, to all the malice of the enemy of our salvation. I allude to distress of mind, to scruples, terrors, and perplexities, the martyrdom of privileged souls. A torrent of iniquities came to alarm his heart; he saw nothing but sin and offences against God; and he was the sport of the temptations and illusions of the devil to such an extent, that he lost all his peace and serenity, and thick gloom overspread his mind. "Who knows," said he weeping, "who knows if I am in a state of grace, and if I shall be saved? Ah, Jesus, do not let me be damned! O Lord, do not send me to hell, because in hell I cannot love thee." "Ah, Lord, punish me as I deserve; but do not cast me out from before thy face." He had at the same time to endure the rebellion of his senses, and continual thoughts of vanity, presumption, and incredulity. "There is not one of our holy mysteries," said F. Mazzini, "against which he had not temptations. At one time the devil would attack him on one point, at another on something else; but that which most excited my compassion, was to see him attacked on several points at the same time. I have been terrified at his temptations, and delighted at his courage in surmounting them." His confidence in Jesus and Mary caused him to invoke their names unceasingly when he was tempted by distrust. His temptations against purity were especially overpowering. Concupiscence became at times so enkindled within him, that he was no longer able to distinguish the feeling from consent, and he then used to break forth into loud groans and strike his feet against the ground. During this time a priest who went one day to see him, said to him: "My Lord, you seem to me to be melancholy, you, who used always to be so cheerful." "Alas," replied Alphonsus, "I endure the torments of hell." As he was often unable to resist so many assaults alone, and was afraid of sending for the fathers Villani and Mazzini too often, he was sometimes to be seen dragging himself to their rooms, descending from the upper corridor to the lower one in search of some relief, and when he could not find either of these two confessors, he went to the first father whom he happened to meet with. Very often, in the middle of the night, when he was unable to sleep through his temptations, he awoke the servant or the brother who assisted him, that they might aid him in dissipating his terrors; and sometimes they were so violent, that he went to speak to F. Villani.

His only relief was in prayer; but he often found no support even in that. "I go to God," he one day said to F. Villani, "and at every word I say, he seems to reject me. A fresh storm assailed me this morning. I said 'My Jesus, I love thee,' and I heard a voice, which answered: 'That is not true.'" On another day when F. Villani tried to console him, Alphonsus replied: "I hear a voice which says to me, 'thou hast abandoned thy God, and he has abandoned thee.'" His chief reason for thinking himself lost, as we have seen above, was because he could not remember having ever done any good work and had been so very unfaithful to God. "I have trodden under foot all my obligations," he one day said to F. Villani, "I no longer say mass, I no longer say the office, I do not do any good works; my senses are rebellious, and I eat like a wolf; I cannot tell how God can bear with me any longer." However, he never ate without regret: "In the circumstances in which I am," said he to F. Villani, "I ought to be vigilant in mortifying my senses and my appetite." Many times, the fear of sinning made him suddenly put down his knife and fork and stop eating. At other times he could not make up his mind to take any thing.

His scruples and disquietude were especially great just as he was going to communicate. His love for Jesus Christ made him long to be united to him, and the fear of being in an unfit state made him draw back. The celebrant was often obliged to tranquillize him, and to wait till he had recovered his composure. Several times he would not have communicated if F. Villani had not arrived just in time to make him do so. One day when he was greatly disturbed, he remained irresolute until it was twelve o'clock; but when the cloud was at length dispersed, he exclaimed weeping, "Give me Jesus Christ." But as all had said mass, it was necessary to carry him to the church to enable him to have the happiness of communicating. On a similar occasion, after the storm, his desire of receiving his God became so ardent, that in order to console him it was necessary to take the Blessed Sacrament to his room. "When will you come?" he then kept exclaiming, "when will you come, my dear Jesus?" Thus it was, that although rejected by God, as it were, he was therefore only more eager to receive him, and to converse with him in the Blessed Sacrament. When he was the most assailed by his ordinary temptations, he redoubled his entreaties to be carried to the church, and he told Br. Anthony that the devil left him in peace whilst there.

Whilst in this state of desolation, he did not cease to welcome and console people who came to see him in order to consult him in their troubles. One of his cousins, who was a religious at Naples, was tormented by scruples and temptations at this time, and wrote to ask his advice; Alphonsus said in reply: "Your Reverence tells me that there are times when you believe that you are lost; let us console one another, for I am under a similar trial. Although I am so near death, temptations do not leave me, and like yourself, my only resource is to gaze on the crucifix. Let us then embrace the cross, and remember always to keep our eyes fixed on Jesus Christ dying. In this way we have ground to hope that he will not send us to hell, where we should be separated from him, and unable to love him any more, which would make the hell of our hell. Let us therefore continually say to him, 'Lord, cause me to love thee, and then send me where thou wilt. I deserve all sorts of trials through my sins; chastise me as thou wilt, but do not deprive me of the happiness of loving thee.' . . . . Although you are amid all these disquietudes, do not forget always to recommend poor sinners to Jesus Christ at the end of your meditations."

Alphonsus continued for upwards of a year in this deplorable state, during which time, according to the testimony of F. Villani, his blind obedience and self-abandonment in the hands of God never once quitted him. He had such faith in obedience, that as he could not always have F. Villani in person when he wanted advice, he used often to send his servant or the brother to tell him of the object of his uneasiness. What consoled him the most was to abandon himself to the goodness of God. One day when he was tempted as severely as possible, a father said to him, "My Lord, look at the crucifix, and say with me: '*In te Domine speravi.*'" Alphonsus had no sooner done so than he regained his peace of mind, and he went on repeating: "*Non confundar in æternum.*" "My only resource amid my distress," he himself said to F. Villani, "is to cast myself into the hands of God; he alone can give me peace; I do trust that Jesus Christ, through a pure effect of his mercy, will not send me to hell." It is true that he recovered his serenity at certain intervals, but they were very short. However, this interior desolation never caused him to omit his devotional exercises; nay, his whole time was consecrated to prayer and spiritual reading. He took at this time particular interest in the life of St. Gregory Nazianzen, and in that of St. Francis of Sales, as they had both gone through the same trials.

The devil, not having succeeded in shaking our saint's faith and virtue by all these temptations, strove to cause him to fall into his snares by presenting himself before him under the form of strange phantoms. One day he sent for F. Corrado in the greatest haste, and said to him in extreme alarm: "An enemy has been here who has thrown me into a state of great distress; he said that I have no faith, and that I shall be damned. I have not attached any faith to all that he wished to make me believe, and I have not really doubted. I believe all that the Holy Church teaches, and I hope to be saved through the merits of Jesus Christ and those of the Most Holy Virgin Mary." When F. Corrado related this to F. Mazzini, he told him that Alphonsus had for some time been tormented by similar apparitions, sometimes under one form, and sometimes under another.

One day the devil appeared to him under the form of a Napolitan missionary; he began to converse with him about his numerous works, and told him that every one was always praising his writings, and was full of admiration at the good they every where effected. At these words Alphonsus humbled and abased himself, saying: "I have done what I could, but all the good is the result of the assistance of God." "That is true," replied the pretended missionary; "but it will always be said that they are your works, and that you are the author of all this good." Alphonsus upon this feeling some temptation to self-love, humbled himself still more; he recurred to God by prayer, and made the sign of the cross, which caused the phantom instantly to vanish.

The devil went to him on another day under the form of a priest, and said: "After all your labor in composing so many works, what have you gained? All that you have said and written is useless as regards yourself; you will be damned notwithstanding all this, for there is now no hope of your salvation. Something besides books and missions is necessary." Alphonsus humbled himself interiorly and replied: "I have done and could do nothing good of myself; I have no merit before God, save the merits of Jesus Christ and the Most Holy Virgin Mary." Upon this the phantom immediately vanished.

One day when he was tormented by the thorn of the flesh, the devil came before him under the appearance of one of the fathers. Alphonsus confided his temptation to him: "O that is nothing," replied the impure spirit, "those are natural feelings, to which one need not attend." Alphonsus was seized with horror, and invoked Jesus and Mary with so much agitation that he nearly fell from the chair, and thus put the tempter to flight.

Another time he appeared to him under the form of a gentleman who had been in his confidence, and for whom he had great esteem, and endeavored to lead him to despair. Alphonsus, who felt no reason to distrust him, acknowledged his faults, but nevertheless said that he hoped in the merits of Jesus Christ. "But what can you hope for?" said the supposed gentleman, "or what have I to hope for myself, if we are among the number of those unhappy beings who are destined for hell?" "Even in hell I will love Jesus Christ;" replied Alphonsus, "I do not put my trust in my works, but in the merits and passion of Jesus Christ." This put the devil to confusion; he was obliged to manifest who he was and to disappear.

But this generous soldier of Jesus Christ did not fail to receive the consolations of the Lord from time to time, even in the midst of all these alarms. His ecstacies and ravishments were in fact more frequent than ever. A father who happened to be at Nocera in the October of 1784, and had several times the opportunity of observing him before the Blessed Sacrament, testified that he some times fell into such raptures of love that he made the most animated gestures, in spite of the weakness of his body. At other times the fathers perceived a ray of light which issued from his forehead, and shone upon the book which he held in his hands. A father once passing along the corridor before his room heard him utter a loud cry. He went in to know what was the matter, and saw him in an ecstacy, with his arms extended and his eyes fixed on the crucifix, and instead of the ordinary paleness of his face, it appeared like that of a seraph.

Alphonsus had a supernatural instinct which plainly told him of the presence of Jesus Christ in his heart after holy communion. F. Garzilli, who was ninety years old, had communicated him one day as usual, but as soon as Alphonsus commenced his thanksgiving, he said to the brother: "F. Garzilli has not consecrated this morning." The brother, astonished at this, hastened to inquire about it from Alexis who had served the mass, and he found that the father had inadvertently passed from the memento of the living to that of the dead.

On the evening of holy Wednesday, Alphonsus was in bed and alone, when the servant, who was outside his room, heard him exclaim ten times over in a transport of joy: "To-morrow is the feast, to-morrow is the feast of the blood of Jesus Christ." Br. Anthony went in and found him continually repeating in his joy: "To-morrow is the feast of the blood of Jesus Christ." "That is true," the brother said to him, "to-morrow is Holy Thursday, when commemoration is made of the body and blood of Jesus Christ." Alphonsus did not then say another word, finding that he had been overheard. The wonder in this was that for some time he had been unable to distinguish any of the months of the year, and much less the weeks and the days.

One day he seemed quite joyous, and sending for the students after dinner, he asked them for an explanation of a stanza of a hymn by St. John of the Cross. No one was able to understand it, when he explained it to them with so much unction and such knowledge, that all the fathers and clerics who were present were filled with admiration.

Another day, when he was sitting in silence in his chair, a brother who was in the room observed that in an ecstacy he darted forwards towards the altar as if he wanted to take or embrace something, and that he did so several times. Br. Anthony then came in, and perceiving that his eyes were turned towards the figure of the Blessed Virgin, which was on the altar, he immediately took it and presented it to him. Alphonsus seized it with holy impetuosity, and kissed it with a thousand acts of love. After some time he exclaimed in rapture: "I cannot, I cannot separate myself from the love of Jesus Christ."

Whilst he was being taken round the corridor, he was unceasingly reproaching himself, fancying that he did not satisfy his obligations. A father feeling compassion for the state he was in, went up to him once to tell him that his age and infirmities dispensed him from all, and that he could supply every thing by one act of love. "By an act of love!" Alphonsus repeated with emotion, "Teach me then how to make this act of love." The father went close to him and said: "My God! I love thee with all my heart." And Alphonsus immediately repeated: "My God! I love thee," but with such a sudden motion of his head, that it struck against the father's chin, which was inclined towards him.

An architect from Naples came one day to Nocera, and Alphonsus asked him if the theatres were frequented in Naples, and if his nephew, D. Joseph, attended them. When the architect said that they were a good deal in fashion, he was silent for some minutes, and then asked with still more interest: "Are the chapels much frequented?" "Yes," answered the architect, "and you cannot imagine what good results from this; a crowd of people of all classes go to them now, and we have saints even among the coachmen." At these words, Alphonsus, who was lying in bed, jumped up suddenly and exclaimed: "Saintly coachmen at Naples! *Gloria Patri*, &c.," and he repeated this three times. The joy which these tidings gave him prevented him from sleeping the following night, and calling sometimes for the servant, sometimes for the lay brother, he kept continually repeating: "Saintly coachmen at Naples! what do you think of that! You heard what the architect said: *Gloria Patri!* there are saintly coachmen at Naples."

Such were some of the holy ardors and the celestial favors with which the Lord comforted his servant in his trials. He was moreover also pleased at times to manifest his holiness. During an eruption of Mount Vesuvius, the mountain of Somma, which is close to Pagani, threatened some fresh disaster, to the great injury of the town. It was seen emitting torrents of fire. The fathers were alarmed at this sight, and hastened to inform Alphonsus of it. The poor old man immediately dragged himself to the window, and appeared filled with sorrow. They begged him to bless the mountain, but he resisted; however, on their reiterated entreaties he raised his hands, and said: "I bless thee in the name of the Father, and of the Son, and of the Holy Ghost." He had scarcely done speaking ere the danger ceased; the torrents took another direction, and the volcano emitted its fire and stones into the gorge of a valley near by.

Theresa Desiderio of Nocera had a child of about eight years, who had suffered from various serious maladies for several years. A relation of hers took it to Alphonsus, and told him how much it suffered. Alphonsus blessed the child, and told him daily to recite three *Aves* in honor of Mary. The child was cured that very instant; he continued to have good health, and afterwards became a priest.

A gentleman of the diocese of Nola had a son who was deaf. He one day took him to Alphonsus to beg him to bless him: Alphonsus did so, and the child returned home entirely cured.

Whilst Alphonsus yet went out in the carriage, mothers used to press forward on the road to meet him and to present their sick children to him, praying him to bless them. His great charity caused him to stop the carriage, and while the servant held the children he laid his hands on them and said some prayers, after which he restored them to their mothers safe and sound, saying to them: "Recommend them to Mary." When these drives ceased, they brought their children to the house; the servant then took them to Alphonsus, who imposed his hands on them as before, and they were healed instantly. Alexis, the servant, and Br. Anthony declared that he effected thousands of such cures.

He often also prophesied during these latter years. "Our Congregation will sustain a great loss soon," he one day said to the fathers, and shortly after F. Alexander de Meo was struck with apoplexy in the pulpit, while preaching at Nola, and died in the church.

A young Neapolitan, having come to Nocera for the recovery of his health, went to see Alphonsus one day and begged him to recommend him to God that he might obtain a perfect cure. Alphonsus only said these few words to him: "Pray to the Blessed Virgin to assist you to die well." The young man understood the meaning of the words too well; he returned to Naples, and in a few days had ceased to live.

One day Alphonsus suddenly aroused himself from a profound meditation, and exclaimed: "A great calamity will befall Naples in the year '99, and I thank God for sparing me from witnessing it." He had foretold the entrance of the French army into Naples, and the misfortunes which ensued.

Another day a gentleman came to Nocera, accompanied by one of his sisters, who said she had been possessed by the devil, and wished Alphonsus to come down to bless her and to recommend her to God. When he was asked to go and comfort her, he several times cast his eyes on the crucifix and the figure of Mary; and then with a sigh said to the Father who had come to speak to him about her: "Possession! possession! Tell her to make a good confession." The young lady did so, and the evil spirit which had tormented her remained in the confessional.

One day he said to the fathers, as if he were awaking out of a deep sleep: "There is a wicked intercourse being carried on near this," and he repeated this several times with signs of the greatest uneasiness; but no one understood what he meant. He immediately sent for the priest, and complained to him of what was taking place in his parish with impunity. The priest was confounded, and said: "That is true, it is a hidden disorder which I have not yet been able to do away with." No one, however, in the whole neighborhood knew any thing about it.

As Alphonsus' body became visibly weaker day by day, his soul only became thereby stronger and his fervor in the exercises of all virtues more admirable; let us give some instances of it. He was always submissive to the will of God, suffering all his ailments without ever murmuring, and the crosses, with which he was so heavily laden, never caused him to commit the slightest act of impatience. One day when he asked F. Villani some question, he was not able to catch his answer: "What can I do," said he, "if God has also visited me with deafness? Blessed be his name for ever!" One evening when he could not read a passage of Scripture, he said in a cheerful tone: "When one once gets old, one loses his sight and his hearing: if this be the will of God, our best remedy is patience."

His humility seemed to increase as he approached his end. Some sick persons presented themselves before him one day to beg him to heal them. "If I were a saint," he said to them, "and if I knew how to work miracles, I should cure myself, who am so crippled and worthless." During his last years he used sometimes to go to the door of the convent to get a little air; several persons used to take advantage of this opportunity to ask his blessing; this alarmed his humility, and he consulted fathers Villani and Mazzini to know whether he ought to give it. They replied that as it was a bishop's office to bless, it would not be proper for him to refuse. One day a number of young children came and ranged themselves before him. "Look at these young sparrows around an old owl," said Alphonsus cheerfully. Canon D. Gabriel Genga, the superior of the Propaganda at Naples, went to see him one day: when the canon asked for his blessing, he said "It is you who ought to bless me, for I am your subject, and you are my superior." The contest was quite a serious one; at length the canon yielded, but only on the condition that he would bless Alphonsus as superior, and that Alphonsus should bless him as bishop.

A spirit of obedience naturally springs from true humility. He, therefore, although a superior and a bishop, always depended on the local rector, or, in his absence, on the minister, in regard to all his actions and wants. He did not like even to move, I may say, without a permission. F. Mazzini, when he was rector, had exhorted him not to undertake vocal prayers. After this Alphonsus once felt disposed to recite some prayers for the souls in purgatory. "Go," said he to Alexis, "and tell D. John to bless as many *Pater Nosters* as I want to apply to the souls in purgatory; but tell him that I want to recite a great many, and ask him to bless them all." But he carried his submission to others much farther, so that Br. Fr. Anthony and Alexis really made him do all they wished.

As he had taken holy poverty for his spouse, any thing contrary to it made him tremble. In consideration of his episcopal character, the rector of the house had allotted a silver fork for his use, but Alphonsus only used it with regret. He employed some little address in order to get rid of it, and tried to prove that it was not sharp enough. He complained of it so often that it was at last felt necessary to give him a steel one, "a sharp and good one," as he said. He was quite pleased at this, and made use of it till F. Villani, not thinking it suitable for a bishop, especially before strangers, forbade him to go on with it. Alphonsus did not say a word in remonstrance, but it was perceptible how painful it was to him to make use of a silver fork.

One day when going round the house in his wheel chair, he was taken into the library, where he saw a harpsichord and asked what it was. "It is your harpsichord;" was the answer: "It is the one your brother gave to you." "*Your* harpsichord!" Alphonsus replied in great alarm, "I have nothing of my own: it was not given to me, but to the community." If the food was not quite plain, he became uneasy, and even refused to eat. He would have no other fish than sardines at Nocera, as at Arienzo, because they are of little value. "I am poor," said he, "and I ought to eat as the poor do." One day when a rare fruit was served up to him, which he had heard was sold at a very high price in Naples, he took it in his hands and looked at it, but nothing the servant could do could persuade him to eat it. One day, it was the 25th of October 1786, he ate nothing at all; as he had had no relish for any kind of nourishment for some time, a mullet was prepared for him. He asked what it was, and the servant afraid of the consequences of telling him, replied, "It is some fish." Alphonsus did not venture to touch it in such uncertainty. "Tell him it is a mullet," said one of the fathers, "and then he will eat it." It was just the contrary; at the very name, he exclaimed "Take away this dish—take it away, it is not fit for the poor." The servant cut it in pieces and put vinegar with it, and then served it up to him as another dish; but Alphonsus discovered it and sent it away. He was then given some blanc-mange, under the pretext that it was a dish which the poor use. Alphonsus tasted it, but finding what it really was, he also sent that away; and as it was a Wednesday, he would not eat any fruit either, so he remained fasting. Another time, as it was observed that he had scarcely eaten any thing, a little piece of Spanish bread was presented to him; he looked at it, but would not take it; and as the servant urged him to take it, he replied: "I never ate it even in the world, and do you wish me to eat it in the monastery!"

Far from making any complaints when he was badly served, he even then returned thanks with humility. As he fancied it was a trouble to the brother and the servant to draw him about in his wheel chair, he never used it without regret. He wanted to dispense with this comfort altogether, but the orders of the doctors and of F. Villani prevented his doing so. He also thought that the noise of the wheels might incommode the others during the time of silence and study, and so he was not satisfied till the wheels were covered with leather.

As to modesty, he was so particular in this regard, that he would not even allow his nails to be cut, and it often required the express orders of the doctors and of his director to make him consent to have his wounds dressed. When he used to go to the church, whenever people pressed around him, he took care to wrap his handkerchief around his hand to prevent women from kissing it; and as to his eyes, one day when he was conversing on purity with the missionary priest established at Nocera, (whom he went sometimes to visit, as we said above,) he said to him: "Even I, old as I am, am obliged to walk with my eyes down in coming merely from St. Michael's, in order to prevent temptations against holy purity. Some use no control over their eyes, and yet they wonder that they are tempted."

With regard to mortification, Alphonsus cherished it to his last days. One day he had unthinkingly manifested a wish to have some little cakes; the brother at once had them procured for him, but nothing would make him eat them when they were brought to him. The doctors ordered raisins to be put in his soup, but as he liked them, he carefully put them aside when he found them; he even forbade them to be served up to him again, but F. Villani commanded him to take them. On Wednesdays, Fridays, and Saturdays, he did all he could in order to abstain from meat, although he had a dispensation to eat it from the doctors and his confessor. One day some livers of fowls were served up to him; as he thought it to be Wednesday, he wanted to send them away, pretending he had no relish for them, and saying: "Meat does not suit my stomach." When the brother urged him, he said: "It is Wednesday to-day, and I keep it because I wear the scapular." The brother told him he was mistaken, it being Tuesday; he then began to eat them, and his stomach felt no further repugnance. He also had made it a rule not to eat fruit when it first came in season, and he never touched it even when a nonagenarian. Some cherries just ripe were one day put before him, but as it was on a Saturday he had a double reason for abstaining from them; he examined them, and put them down again, saying: "I will not eat them, they are not ripe"—and when efforts were made to get him to eat them, he said: "I will not, they might disagree with me." So he did with the first of grapes and other fruits. From the time he entered into religion he never drank any thing on Saturdays, either at meals, or throughout the whole course of the day; and he kept this practice up until he was eighty-eight years of age. At this period, the doctors ordered that he should daily take a cup of cold chocolate. He would not take it on Saturdays, and it was necessary to have recourse to F. Villani.

All dishes were insipid to him if they were not seasoned with the salt of mortification. His pocket was always filled with bitter herbs, which were dried and often reduced to powder, and it was with these aromatics that he continued to season all his food, as he had done throughout his life; he even put the fruit he took in salt, in order to mortify his palate. For some years he had been in the habit of taking two small glasses of wine before going to bed, in order to obtain some rest; but latterly he did without it, and in order to conceal this mortification, he said: "A little water is better than all the cordials in the world." In fact, he had such an avidity for mortification that he was constantly complaining, saying that he led an easy life and did no penance. "It is not thus the saints lived," he often said with sorrow. As he could not crucify his flesh by instruments of penance as he would have liked to do, he found an expedient by which he could do continual penance; it was the motionless position in which he remained in his chair from morning to night. The servant one day seeing him placed in an uncomfortable manner, said to him: "Move a little, my Lord, for you are in an awkward position." But Alphonsus replied; "What is the use of my moving? I am always crooked." His apparent insensibility while in this attitude caused him to appear more like a block of marble than a living being; and he practised this heroic act of penance during the twenty years his illness lasted.

Charity, also, that noble bond which unites all virtues together, was in Alphonsus both the foundation and the summit of his perfection, and in all his actions he only had union with God in view. "By the mercy of Jesus Christ," he one day said to F. Villani, "I do not feel attached to any thing." His transports of love towards God were so frequent, that it seemed as if he formed but one act of love from morning till night. Notwithstanding all the weakness produced by his maladies, he still always performed the smallest practices of religion; he never even took the least nourishment without blessing it. His respect for the holy sacrifice always impelled him to cast himself on his knees at the consecration, until F. Villani forbade him to do it. After he had communicated, he lost all control over himself; he entered into a sweet ecstacy, and often repeated in an audible tone, "My love, my God! O my Mother, love him for me." His delight in his retreat at Nocera was, as we have seen above, to remain almost all day before the Blessed Sacrament. In October 1784, on the last day of the novena of St. Theresa, which he had made with the people, he entered into a long ecstacy, and continually repeated: "O eternal love, I love thee." As F. Villani saw with regret that these transports of love attracted general attention, he tried to persuade him that his health no longer permitted him to go to the church. He submitted; but this privation was the greatest he had to endure. When the time when he had been accustomed to be taken there arrived, he testified the most incredible desire to go as he had been used to do: he dragged himself to the staircase, and tried to descend it, and not being able to do so went away again quite in affliction. When he made his visit in his oratory, it was with lighted candles on the altar, though the Blessed Sacrament was not kept there; and his heart supplied him with the most tender sentiments of adoration, love and confidence, which he expressed in a loud voice.

When he was taken round in his chair, he often said: "Let us go to the church, let us visit Jesus Christ;" and he had often quite animated disputes on this head with the servant and the brother. Even in his sleep he dreamed only of the Blessed Sacrament and the Most Holy Virgin, and made the most affecting aspirations. A cleric once entered his room whilst he was asleep, and found him dreaming and saying: "How lovely art thou, O Mary! how beautiful thou art, O Mary! how beautiful art thou, my Jesus!" Another time he heard him repeat: "I wish to please God, even if the whole world were to be overthrown; I ever wish to please my God."

One evening when he was in a fever, he exclaimed in his delirium: "I cast myself into the arms of Jesus Christ, I die without uneasiness, and I believe that I shall be saved by the merits of Jesus Christ and my Mother Mary; yes, I hope to go to thank them in Paradise." His affection for Jesus crucified was very ardent; his image was always before his eyes, and his acts of love towards Jesus on the cross never ceased. The way of the cross, as we said above, he daily performed in a corridor of the house; he continued this devotion say to the age of eighty-eight, when he was forbidden to practice it any more, and after that he never omitted to perform it in spirit in his room before a large crucifix. In a word, his meditations never had any other object, he himself asserted, than the passion of Jesus Christ.

His love towards the Most Holy Virgin Mary became more ardent than ever in his latter years. He never neglected an opportunity of rendering homage to her. As long as he was able to walk, he could be seen making an offering of two fowls to the Blessed Virgin during the Octave of Easter and on the last Sunday of July, when the miraculous statue called *of our Lady of the fowls* was carried in procession; it being the custom at Nocera to carry it about at that time, and to deposit fowls at its feet. He never omitted to say an *Ave* before his meals and his other actions, as well as when he heard the clock strike. After the *Angelus*, which he never omitted, he always remained for some time absorbed in the contemplation of the grand mystery. If it were on Saturday or Sunday, he took care to recite it standing; and when others tried to persuade him to remain seated, he answered: "One does not gain the indulgences, if one does not stand." The same thing took place in the evening when the bell rang for the *De profundis* for the dead. He continued to say this until the eighty-ninth year of his age, when F. Villani, in consideration of the great difficulty he had in making these acts, ordered that he should no longer be informed when they took place.

As the rosary had always been his special devotion, he recited it several times a day with the servant or Br. Fr. Anthony, whilst they took him up and down the corridor, never omitting to meditate on the mysteries. But when F. Villani, in order to relieve him from all uneasiness, commuted all his vows into the recitation of the rosary, he was to be seen with the beads in his hand from morning to night. It was touching to hear the altercations he daily had with the brother or the servant, sometimes because he had not made the intention properly, sometimes because he had not distinguished the mysteries carefully, or they had not suggested them according to the day of the week, and then he insisted on recommencing afresh. One day when dinner was ready, he fancied he had not finished his rosary, and he resisted going to it, saying: "An Ave Maria is worth all the dinners in the world." Another day when he did not remember having recited it, the brother told him he had done so;—"But," said he, "you forget that my salvation depends upon it." One day in 1784, when he was in a profound lethargy, Br. Fr. Anthony said to him, by the advice of F. Villani: "My Lord, we have still to recite the rosary." At the simple word rosary, he moved, opened his eyes, and began "*Deus in adjutorium*," &c.

He was, besides, always, up to the last, careful to recommend devotion to the Blessed Virgin to all who came to see him, strangers as well as those of the Congregation, especially the novices and young clerics. "Be devout to the Blessed Virgin," said he to them; "he who is devoted to her will be saved." He recommended every one to visit her images, to recite the rosary, and to fast in her honor on Saturday and on the vigils of her feasts.

In conclusion, we might say there was not even a sigh which he did not consecrate to God by solemnly offering it to him; so that the whole life of our saint was truly full of good works and virtues. To give a last proof of this wonderful fullness, let us mention the number of good acts which he used to make before going to sleep; they would have remained unknown, had he not caused Br. Fr. Anthony to write them down one day in 1784, for fear of forgetting them. They are as follows: Ten acts of love; ten acts of confidence; ten acts of sorrow; ten acts of conformity to the will of God; ten acts of love towards Jesus Christ; ten acts of love to the Blessed Virgin; ten acts of love towards the Blessed Sacrament; ten acts of confidence in Jesus Christ; ten acts of confidence in the Blessed Virgin; ten acts of resignation to suffering; ten acts of abandonment to God; ten acts of abandonment to Jesus Christ; ten acts of abandonment to Mary; and ten prayers to do the will of God.

To his love of God he did not fail to unite, up to the last, as he had done throughout his whole life, that of his neighbor. When he heard that any one of his fathers was ill, he was sensibly distressed; he immediately caused himself to be conducted to him in his chair, and as it could not be taken into the room, he himself was carried in and conversed with the sick person for some time. He inquired about his maladies, exhorted him to patience, but above all recommended union with God and conformity to his will. He manifested this solicitude for all, and as much in regard to the lay-brothers as to the fathers. Besides, he constantly prayed for the perseverance of the just and the conversion of sinners; he was seen to burst into tears for the latter, and to offer himself a victim to God for them. In order to see him look young again, it sufficed to tell him of some extraordinary conversion. He started on hearing it, and the satisfaction of his heart was then depicted on his countenance; and it sufficed to say the words "the glory of God" and the "salvation of souls," to reanimate him and give him fresh strength. But, on the other hand, he was greatly distressed when he heard of scandals and offences against God. Mgr. Bergame, the bishop of Gaeta, being about to set out for Naples after a visit to our saint, Alphonsus said to him: "Now that you are going to Naples, I entreat you to send for Father N., and to tell him from me not to ill-treat souls, which have been redeemed by the blood of Jesus Christ." This was a Jansenist zealot, who caused him the greatest uneasiness.

We ought not to omit to record here two most precious confessions which in these latter years fell from his own lips. One day he was heard to exclaim: "Lord! thou knowest well that all that I have thought, said, done, and written, has been for souls and for thee;" and on another day, conversing with F. Villani, he let these words escape: "I am a bishop, and I ought to tell the truth; I do not remember having ever uttered a deliberate falsehood even when I was a child."

CHAPTER XXXVI.

Alphonsus' last illness and Death.

ALPHONSUS was now in his ninetieth year; and the rectitude of his judgment and his presence of mind continued to be admirable, although his humility and detachment from all earthly affections made him sometimes assume an air of puerile simplicity. This was the case especially in visits of mere civility, which now more than ever were insupportable to him. When he was obliged to receive such visits from persons of distinction, he knew how to get rid of them speedily, whatever might be their rank, by manifesting weariness, or making his deafness an excuse for keeping silence, so that imagining he was imbecile, or in a state of second childhood, they soon took their leave. He acted however very differently with religious people who conversed with him about things which merited his attention. Two conventual fathers visited him in these latter days. He was told that one of them, who had recently been ordained priest, wished to kiss his hand. At the word priest, Alphonsus exclaimed: "A great dignity, a great dignity is the sacerdotal dignity!" The priest then recommended himself to his prayers. "I am a miserable creature," said Alphonsus, "you must pray God for me, who am on the eve of making the great journey from time to eternity, and of presenting myself before the tribunal of God." He said these words with such an expression, that the two religious retired in terror, saying: "If his lordship trembles, what will become of us?" Two young fathers of the Congregation, on being raised to the priesthood, went to him to thank him and kiss his hand; but Alphonsus, through respect for the dignity with which they had just been invested, kissed their hands, exclaiming; "Oh what a great dignity! Oh what a great dignity it is to be a priest! you are now exalted above sovereigns, kings, and emperors." Counsellor Gaetan' Celano came to see him in October 1786, with his wife and the Marquis of St. Lucia. He received these distinguished guests with all due consideration, especially as he considered himself under great obligations to the counsellor, who had always supported him and his Congregation at Naples under the most embarrassing circumstances. He turned the conversation, to render it profitable to them, upon the duties of the marriage state, and strongly exhorted them to have but one will, assuring them that their happiness depended upon it.

He showed a great degree of strength of mind and memory in all the most important and difficult affairs of the Congregation, as well as in other affairs about which he was consulted or on which he had to decide, of which many instances are on record. Nor did the Lord cease to communicate his favors to him. In December 1786, D. Fr. Tortora, his physician, being taken ill, sent to beg him to recommend him to God. He said an *Ave Maria* to the Blessed Virgin and recited the litanies, after which he said at once without any hesitation: "he will die." The illness did not appear to be mortal, but three days afterwards D. Francis Tortora, though contrary to all expectations, had passed into eternity. The F. Master Caputo, the president of the seminary at St. Agatha in Alphonsus' time, was taken ill at Naples. Alphonsus was informed of it that he might recommend him to God. Some days afterwards, on the 8th of October 1786, at about four o'clock in the afternoon, Alphonsus suddenly turned round towards Br. Fr. Anthony, and said: "the F. Master is dying." And so it was; this same day at about eight o'clock in the evening, he passed into eternity after four hours agony. God also revealed to him about this time the approach of his own deliverance, that is to say, the time of his death. In the month of September 1786, a Carmelite father came to see him, as he was in the habit of doing every year, when Alphonsus said to him: "F. Joseph, we shall not see each other again next year." At a later period, on the 16th of July 1787, he turned to Br. Fr. Anthony, and said to him in quite a joyful tone: "Brother, I have a new function to perform." He spoke of his death and funeral. The mystery was understood when he was attacked by a violent dysentery during the night of the 18th of the same month. On the morning of the 19th, after he had assisted at mass and received the holy communion, he was attacked by a fever. In the after part of the next day, he fell into such a state of weakness and prostration, that he seemed as if he were just going to expire. He was, however, able to take some nourishment, and after having recovered some strength, he slept during a part of the following night. As soon as his death drew near, all his scruples vanished, and his serenity never again left him throughout the whole of his painful illness.

Towards eight o'clock on the morning of the 22d, as he was still in full possession of his intellectual faculties, he was asked if he would like to hear mass and to communicate; he replied, "Make haste." When he was told that mass had commenced, he made the sign of the cross as usual and repeated: "Make haste." At the reception of the blood he was no longer quite himself, but being told that he must then communicate, he recovered his senses, communicated, and continued to make acts of love towards Jesus in the Blessed Sacrament. He was quite calm and serene until the evening, but fever then seized him again, and he became delirious. He became worse on the night of the 23d. As soon as it was day-light, he was told that it was time to hear mass and to communicate. "Let them make haste," he replied in a state of great prostration. On seeing that there was a delay, he repeated several times over: "Will they not then give me communion?" but when the time arrived for giving it to him, he had lost his senses. The doctor was summoned, who gave him over. He was then told to prepare for exteme unction; but he answered: "I do not understand." At length, as he saw that he did not receive communion, he said and repeated: "I wish to have his body." His wishes were not satisfied, for fear that he had not sufficient consciousness. After extreme unction had been administered to him, F. Villani told him to bless the whole Congregation; but although he repeated it over to him, he did not understand him. F. Villani then told him that he must bless the Congregation as bishop and as superior, in obedience to the names of Jesus and Mary; on hearing the word obedience, he became quite collected, raised his hand and gave the wished-for benediction.

When the extreme danger in which Alphonsus was had become known in the town and neighboring villages, gentlemen, religious, and priests hastened to visit him daily; Mgr. Sanfelice especially, never once omitted to come: and prayers were offered for him in all the monasteries and all the churches. When the sad news was received in the houses of the Congregation, it caused general lamentation, and all the rectors, accompanied by all the subjects who were not wanted in the houses, set out to see him and receive his blessing. They all arrived within three days, even those of Benevento and St. Angelo. As soon as the saintly old man perceived them he maifested much pleasure, and blessed them with the sign of the cross.

On the morning of the 27th, as he seemed a little relieved, a second mass was celebrated towards seven o'clock in order to communicate him, but it was perceived that all his physical strength had abandoned him, though on hearing that mass was being celebrated and that he was going to receive Jesus Christ, he had testified extreme joy. After some time, he himself asked for his rosary, and he felt about with his hand here and there as if to find it. It was given to him, and although he had lost his senses, he went through it in a stammering way, but what he said was unintelligible. As he continued in the same state, the doctors wished him to swallow some bark with lemonade; after he had taken two or three spoonfuls, he did not want to have any more. But he was told that the doctor required it, and that he must take more under obedience. At the words doctor and obedience, he instantly opened his mouth; he then held out his hand to the doctor, who had asked to feel his pulse, saying: "Here I am, O my God." He also wished to feel his feet, but as soon as he perceived this, he exclaimed: "Do not touch me," and drew back his legs. Although he was burning through the extreme heat of the weather, his love for modesty never allowed him to be at all uncovered: one day when the covering was a little displaced in order to wash him, he exclaimed in a tone of complaint to the servant Alexis: "They have uncovered me, is not that sinful?"

As he was every where held in very great veneration, when it became generally known that he was dying, it would be difficult to believe how many demands for relics of him were made even from distant places. The linen which was sent to be washed at this time was either not sent back to the house, or was returned only in fragments. Handkerchiefs full of rosaries and other objects of devotion were brought continually, with the request that they might touch his body.

His state underwent little change during the 23d. As it was observed that his mind seemed more alive in the evening, he was asked if he wished for communion. At this proposition he started for joy, and when he was told that the time was come, he joyously exclaimed several times: "Come, my dear Jesus." He also made many acts of desire, and manifested a saintly eagerness by his gestures. He wanted the acts of thanksgiving to be suggested to him: this was done, and he listened and stammered them out, but without any body's being able to make out the words. He was then asked to bless all who were present in the name of Jesus Christ; he then raised his hand and blessed them all in a perfectly collected manner. He became delirious again later in the evening.

Several votive masses were said in his room on the morning of the 24th. Very early in the morning he repeated with great urgency: "Give me Jesus Christ." The acts of desire which he made, and his impatience to be soon consoled, drew tears from the eyes of all who were present; he was satisfied, and after having communicated he remained in a state of recollection, and made acts of love and thanksgiving. As fever came on again, his strength was once more prostrated, and he lost the use of his faculties, but when a father suggested to him to recite the *Ave Maria* and to have recourse to the Blessed Virgin, he moved his lips and recited the angelical salutation by himself, and turned to the father to know if he had said it properly; he then continued to stammer through the rosary.

When it became known at Naples that Alphonsus was dying, the grief was general. All the nuns interested themselves about his state, and many religious followed their example; amongst others, the fathers of the Oratory, of the Pious Works, and of the Holy Family. The superior of the Congregation of Apostolical Missions, in concert with the superior of that of the Conference, hastened to inform all their subjects of it. The town and the diocese of St. Agatha also displayed their attachment to their former bishop. Prayers were said for him throughout the diocese, and the Blessed Sacrament was exposed at mass in the cathedral on the morning after the news had arrived. Several bishops who were his friends, also offered up the holy sacrifice and got their flocks to pray for him.

D. Joseph had at once left Naples and come to see him, accompanied by his wife and her uncle, the Prince of Polleca. They asked for his blessing, but there was much difficulty in making him understand who they were and what they wanted; however, he raised his hand and blessed them. D. Joseph asking him to give him some good advice, he answered: "Save your soul." On seeing they did not go, he said to them: "Be satisfied, it is finished; you can go now."

The devil could not leave Alphonsus in peace. On the morning of the 25th, whilst mass was being celebrated, he said: "He who sins is the enemy of God." As the father saw he was tempted, he interrupted the mass and exhorted him to confide in the merits of Jesus Christ, and to have recourse to the Most Holy Virgin Mary; he then breathed freely again, and regained his serenity. He was tempted again towards the evening, and said: "Do you wish to make me despair?" The same father immediately reminded him of the passion of Jesus Christ and of Mary. When he heard of the merits of Jesus and Mary, he opened his eyes and listened attentively, and repeated distinctly the acts suggested to him. He then asked, "What can I do in order to merit?" and receiving for answer: "Do the will of God," he remained silent, and at intervals was seen to fix his eyes on the picture of our Lady of Sorrows.

Such great faintness came on about seven o'clock, that it was believed that the hour of his agony was approaching. The prayers for the dying were commenced, and he received the absolution. Whilst this took place he recovered his senses, gave his blessing, as he had been asked to do, to the doctor, the brother, and the servant, as also to all the houses and subjects of the Congregation. He was also reminded of the houses in the states which had caused him so much sorrow, and he raised his hand twice and blessed them also; and, as if the devil, like a skilful tactician, had seized this opportunity of assaulting him, at the end of half an hour he opened his eyes and said in a loud voice, so as to be distinctly heard in an adjoining room: "I bless the houses in the states." After an interval he was asked to bless the diocese and the nuns of St. Agatha, and he moved his hand to signify that he blessed them, and afterwards he said in a loud and intelligible tone of voice, of his own accord: "I bless the king, all the generals, the princes, and the ministers, and all the magistrates who administer justice."

The rector of the house then asked him if he wished to receive Jesus Christ. Full of joy at this, he replied: "Give me communion; yes, give me communion;" and as it was some time before they brought the Blessed Sacrament from the church, he several times repeated: "Is communion coming?" On hearing a sound he opened his eyes, and seeing the priest with the holy ciborium, he appeared as if in an ecstacy, and began to make many acts of love, exclaiming in the transports of his devotion: "My Jesus, do not leave me." Some time afterwards a picture of Ven. Br. Gerard, to whom he had a special devotion, was presented to him; after having recognized what it was and looked at it for a moment, he said: "God does not will that he should cure me." Mass being afterwards commenced, he made the sign of the cross three times according to his custom, and distinctly pronounced the words the third time. Afterwards, a picture of the crucifixion being shown to him, he made a sign with his trembling hand that he wished to have it. He then put it to his lips, kissed it, and held it thus for some time, after which the delirium returned again.

The large wound near his throat, from which he had suffered so much at Arienzo, re-opened during his illness, and rendered his condition an intensely painful one; but through his patience and resignation this accession of suffering only served to increase the splendor of his crown. Whilst in this painful state, God was pleased to glorify him by a miracle. A canon, who had been suffering from a complaint in the knee for three years, so as to be unable to walk without crutches, came to see him on the 24th, but he had scarcely taken leave of him when he felt that he was completely cured, and said to two priests he met at the door: "I came here a cripple, and I go away perfectly healed; I secretly applied his lordship's scapular, which was on his bolster, to my leg, and now I am cured." Up to this time he had tried several remedies, but without any success.

On the morning of the 25th, the invalid was much better; he heard mass and communicated at day-break, after which two more masses were said for him, but in the middle of the second he became perturbed. Some acts of love and confidence in Jesus Christ were suggested to him, and he became calm again. Late in the evening of this day he appeared to be so faint that he was thought to be dying. The fathers hastened to aid him in his passage by their prayers, and began to say mass about two o'clock on the morning of the 26th. Holy communion was proposed to him, but he did not answer. At the *Sanctus* bell during the first mass he opened his eyes and looked at the celebrant; he aroused himself again at the elevation, looked at the altar and moved his lips. He had a fresh attack at three o'clock; absolution was given to him, and the prayers for the dying were commenced, but he regained his senses at the end of the litanies. At a later period, as he manifested an ardent desire for communion, it was given to him, and during the following mass he continued to make his thanksgiving, although he was extremely faint. Some time afterwards he asked for his rosary; it was given to him, and his lips were seen to move while he recited it.

Among the many gentlemen and ecclesiastics who came constantly to visit Alphonsus, was a great friend of his, F. Samuel, ex-provincial of the Capuchins at Arienzo. As his efforts to obtain the benediction of our saint had been in vain, he took his hand and raised it upon his head, making the sign of the cross with it; he touched also one of his ears which was diseased with it, and it was immediately healed. F. Buonapane, of his own Congregation, had suffered from an abscess in the throat for two days, and much apprehension was felt as to the consequences; in the evening he applied a little piece of linen, which had been used in bandaging Alphonsus' wounds, and the next morning the father was cured.

The 27th was a day of suffering to Alphonsus. At about seven in the morning he was suddenly seized with such a severe colic that he could not find any rest, and exclaimed: "Aid me. . . . Unbind me. . . . put me on the ground." During the violence of these attacks, he several times fixed his eyes on the picture of the Most Holy Virgin Mary and said in a faint voice, "My Jesus." Mortification had already commenced. A poultice being applied, when he felt that he was touched, he said in broken accents and with tears in his eyes, "They have touched me." On the 28th, being interrogated as to whether he wished to hear mass and to communicate, he seemed quite joyous, and made a sign in the affirmative. He made the sign of the cross before communicating, and also made his preparation. He heard two masses during his thanksgiving. When afterwards preparations were made to rub him, he said quickly, "Do not touch me;" but he at last submitted through obedience.

As his mind was weakened and he was exhausted, he wished holy affections to be suggested to him from time to time; he took pleasure in them and repeated them in a faint tone of voice. Mortification went on increasing, and as his sufferings became greater they brought on frequent spasms, which caused the fathers who assisted him to stop speaking and to look on in compassion and silence; but dissatisfied that the aspirations were not suggested to him as before, he asked with a remnant of strength which his love gave him: "Have you no more holy thoughts to suggest to me?" His weakness increasing, the blessed candle was lighted and the prayers for the recommendation of the soul were commenced. He recovered however his senses, and a picture of the Blessed Virgin being given to him, he opened his eyes, and joining his hands in a praying attitude he kissed the picture, and recited an *Ave Maria* in a distinct voice. After this he seemed to be agitated, and putting his hand to his forehead he said: "My thoughts. . . . . Will you not let me rest?" At seven o'clock in the morning he seemed again dejected: the crucifix was presented to him; he took it, raised it to his lips, and holding it in his hands often opened his eyes to contemplate it. A picture of Holy Mary was also given to him, and he was told to place his life and his soul in her hands; he then extended his arms to signify that he made the offering, and looking at the picture, he pronounced some words which were not understood. The following night he was better than before, and he slept quietly. However, on the following morning, the 29th, he was not in a state to communicate. Whilst mass was being said before him, he exclaimed: "What a number of foreign enemies?" The death of Jesus Christ being afterwards recalled to his mind, and it being suggested to him to make an offering to him of his own death, he listened attentively, raised his hands, clasped them together and moved his lips for some time. He turned then his eyes to a picture of the Blessed Virgin, and it being suggested to him to invoke her, he said an *Ave Maria* in a distinct voice. A picture of St. Joseph being also presented to him, he looked for some time at it, and recognizing it, he began to pronounce some words whilst keeping his eyes fixed on the picture of the spouse of Mary.

A father beginning to suggest holy thoughts to him, Alphonsus said of his own accord: "Give me the picture of our Lady." When he had it in his hand, he began to pray to her. The death-rattle then commenced, which never ceased till he was dead. A picture of the Blessed Virgin being again placed in his hands, he kissed it, and slowly and with difficulty pronounced the words of the *Ave Maria.*

His beard had become very long, and caused him great discomfort. A brother cut it off as well as he could, and Alphonsus seemed relieved. When the operation was over, these few hairs were eagerly sought for and kept as precious relics. He was extremely ill during the whole of the 29th, and nearly unconscious; about nine in the evening it was believed that his agony had commenced. The whole community surrounded his bed, and the prayers for the agonizing were commenced; but he came to himself again. He was again asked to bless all the Congregation, and as he could no longer raise his hand, he moved his head in acquiescence. On the morning of the 30th, several masses were celebrated, and it seemed that he wished for communion. F. Villani, however, would not allow it, as he feared that he was unable to swallow the Sacred Host. A Carmelite father came during the day to give him the last indulgence of the scapular. It sufficed to remind him of the sacred names of Jesus and Mary, or to give him a picture of his holy patrons, to make him quite collected. That of St. Michael being presented to him, he took it in his hands and kissed it, and gazing on it, moved his lips and recommended himself to the archangel. He also opened his eyes and was heard to murmur whilst the acts of faith, hope and charity were suggested to him. He also took in his hands a crucifix which was presented to him, pressed it with love, and three times endeavored to raise it to his mouth, but as he was unable to do it, a father assisted him to kiss it. At about eleven o'clock he took some spoonfuls of milk; after that he refused all that was offered to him. He preserved the use of his faculties during all that day and the following night, although so very weak, and was seen to assent to the holy affections which were suggested to him, either by opening his eyes or moving his lips.

At about two o'clock on the morning of the 30th, as his agony was near at hand, masses were begun to be said in his room, in the church, and in the oratory. A crucifix was offered to him; he opened his eyes, looked at it, and took it in his hands. A picture of the Most Holy Virgin was also presented to him, and he looked at it with devotion. At about seven o'clock the crucifix being again presented to him, he looked at it with tenderness. At about twelve he himself took into his hands a picture of the Blessed Virgin which he had at his breast; he kissed it and pressed it to his heart; he took it up again at about two, and held it for nearly a quarter of an hour. A fresh attack came on at three; it was believed to be the commencement of the agony, but he again came to himself.

The Blessed Virgin did not fail to assist and to console him in his last moments; it was a favor which he had ardently desired during life, and had unceasingly prayed her to grant him. His prayer was heard. He became worse every instant, but his peace and serenity were unalterable. At about six o'clock, when he was being attended by two fathers and held a picture of the Blessed Virgin in his hand, his face suddenly became inflamed and resplendent, and a sweet smile overspread his lips. The same thing happened again before seven. A father put a picture of the Most Holy Virgin before him, and suggested to him to invoke her that he might have a good death; as soon as he heard the sweet name of Mary, he opened his eyes and looked at the picture, and seemed again to have a mysterious interview with the Queen of Heaven.

He was in a state of complete prostration throughout the whole of the following night, but he was always tranquil and serene. He was quite recollected, and listened with pleasure to the holy affections which were suggested to him. When the crucifix was presented to him, he endeavored to kiss it. On the morning of the 1st of August, when some compresses were applied to him, he caught hold of the sheets in order to cover himself.

Masses were unceasingly celebrated, in the church, in the oratory, and in his room, from one o'clock in the morning, his children trying to do a holy violence to heaven to obtain special assistance for the last moments of their common father. He grew worse at half past nine. From the early part of the evening he clasped the crucifix, and as every one wished to have a crucifix which had been for some time in his dying hands, a fresh one was constantly substituted. The fathers continued to arrive from all the houses, and, as he had always wished to die among his dear brethren who would aid him to die well, Alphonsus, like another Jacob, entered into his last agony surrounded by his numerous children who were his joy and his crown. He seemed not so much to be struggling with death, as to be conversing with God in a prolonged ecstacy. No change was observed in his body, no oppression of breathing, no painful sigh; but whilst holding a picture of the Blessed Virgin in his hands, and amidst the prayers and tears of his sons, Alphonsus gently and sweetly expired, or rather he tranquilly fell asleep in the arms of the Lord and of the Most Holy Virgin Mary, at the very moment when the bell was rung for the *Angelus*.

CHAPTER XXXVII.

The Ceremonies of the Interment. Many Miracles are wrought through the intercession of Alphonsus. The process of his Canonization.

ALPHONSUS Maria de Liguori died on the 1st of August 1787, at about eleven o'clock A. M., and at the age of ninety years ten months and five days. He was of middle size, with a rather large head, and of a fresh complexion. He had a full forehead, pleasing azure blue eyes, an aquiline nose, a small mouth and smiling lips. His beard was thick and his hair black; he kept them short, and often cut them himself. He was short-sighted and made use of glasses, but never in the pulpit or when he spoke to women. His voice was clear and sonorous; however spacious the church might be, and however long a mission might last, it never failed him, and it continued thus until his last infirmities. He had an imposing mien; his manners were grave and gracious at the same time. His judgment was subtle and penetrating; his memory prompt and tenacious; and his mind precise and methodical. He was of a passionate temper, but through virtue he became a model of sweetness. His whole life was one continual application; but he was never occupied about indifferent things, nor even about matters which were more curious than useful.

No sooner had Alphonsus rendered up his pure soul to

God, than the fathers foreseeing the enthusiasm of the people, applied to the commander of the royal cavalry, before ringing the knell, to have a detachment of horse to keep order at the door of the house. When the body was properly placed on a bier, which was surrounded by a great many lights, in the part of the church destined for the confraternity of gentlemen, his death was announced by a little bell, to which all those in the other churches echoed, as Mgr. Sanfelice had ordered. The whole town was immediately thrown into a state of agitation, and crowds of people flocked to the church; nobody was allowed to enter, and all had to be satisfied with having their rosaries, scapulars, and other objects of devotion applied to the saintly body. Several persons brought baskets of flowers, which they had strewed on the body, and then carried them away to distribute them as so many relics.

When the fathers of the Congregation had paid their last homage to their common father by the recitation of the office for the dead, the fathers of St. Francis de Paul and the Carmelite fathers sang the *Libera* together. The missionary priests of the town then united together to chant the office in their turn, which was also followed by the *Libera*. During this time, a great number of gentlemen from the high town of Nocera arrived, with the commander and his staff. It was seven o'clock in the evening, yet they had the greatest difficulty in shutting the door.

Mgr. Sanfelice had already made preparations to have the funeral conducted in the most solemn manner possible. He had settled that besides the chapter of the cathedral, the seminarists and clergy of Pagani, and all the religious and confraternities, should be invited to accompany the sacred remains in procession through the town, with military escort, to the Convent of the Poor Clares which is near the high town; and that after having consoled these religious, as well as those of the Purity, by chanting the *Libera* in their respective churches, the funeral procession should return by the same streets and with the same pomp: but the inhabitants of Pagani or the lower town, suspecting his lordship meant by some pious stratagem to transport Alphonsus' remains to his cathedral, strongly opposed the execution of this design. When he was returning to the palace in the evening, they stopped his carriage, and protested that they would not allow such a translation. The bishop solemnly asserted that they were wrong in their suspicions; but they did not believe him, and at eight o'clock in the evening the crowd were still assembled and in a state of great disturbance, and their minds became tranquillized only when the fathers themselves went to them and assured them that no such project was in contemplation. His lordship, however, fearing some tumult in which the venerated body might suffer, altered the arrangements he had before made, and determined that no invitations should be issued, and that the funeral should be conducted in the simplest manner possible.

On the morning of the 2d of August the door could not be opened until after the arrival of a detachment of twenty soldiers. An immense concourse of people of all classes flocked from the adjacent places; they all ranged themselves before the house, protesting that they wished to render homage to the saintly bishop and to have some of his relics. Besides Mgr. of Nocera, the chapter of the cathedral, the seminarists, the clergy of Pagani, the priests, and, amongst the regulars, the fathers of St. Francis of Paul and the Carmelites, arrived all of their own accord to honor the memory of Alphonsus. The ceremony was commenced by the clergy of Pagani, who sang the *Libera*, in which the canons of the cathedral and the regulars joined. During this time, as a number of altars had been erected on the preceding evening, a great many secular and regular priests offered up the holy sacrifice of the mass.

When all was ready, Mgr. Sanfelice arranged the procession. It was decided that it should not enter the town, but that it should go out by the door of the house, make a semi-circle before the monastery, and then return to the church; the precious burden being carried on the shoulders of the rectors of four houses of the Congrgegation, preceded by all the clergy, and followed by Mgr. of Nocera, while the gentlemen and troops of the town made up the rear. When the body was deposited in the church, the canons chanted the office, Mgr. of Nocera assisting, and mass was celebrated by D. I. B. Villani, who was canon and vicar-general. D. F. Pinto, a canon and patrician of Salerno, afterwards bishop of Tricarico, preached the funeral sermon. As the church was too small to contain the crowd, care had been taken to place the pulpit near the door. The catafalque was not very high, as the church was too low to admit of it; the body was raised about six palms only from the ground, and this made it possible, after the office, to allow people to satisfy their wish to kiss it, to touch it with rosaries and to strew it with flowers. Br. Fr. Anthony and the servant Alexis stood at each side of the catafalque, and many mothers presented their children to them that they might touch the saint's body. As they could not seize on any relics of it, it being surrounded by soldiers, every one enriched himself by carrying away some flowers or rosaries which had touched it.

At this time a celebrated painter from Naples came to take the likeness of Alphonsus, without the fathers having sent for him. It was about eleven o'clock when he wished to form the cast, and there was the greatest difficulty in shutting the church. The body had preserved its bloom and appeared as if alive. When the cast was taken off, a part of the skin of the left nostril adhered to it, and a quantity of bright blood issued from it, which was eagerly collected in handkerchiefs. When the operation was over, the church was re-opened; and in the mean time a multitude of gentlemen of the neighboring places had arrived, so that all the ground in front of the house was crowded with carriages. There were also whole communities of regulars who formed part of the concourse. The fathers were insufficient to distribute to all these devout persons pieces of the linen which Alphonsus had made use of; it was said that more than ten thousand people came to do honor to the ceremonies of this funeral.

At about seven o'clock in the evening, as Mgr. Sanfelice saw what a multitude of people there was, and feared some disagreement between them and the military, he ordered the interment of the holy body, but it was not without much difficulty that the soldiers succeeded in emptying the church. Several gentlemen solicited the honor of taking the body down from the catafalque. It had remained there for thirty-three hours, and yet, notwithstanding the heat of the weather, and the mortification which had reached the flesh, the limbs remained flexible and emitted no unpleasant smell. Mgr. of Nocera wished that an attempt should be made to draw blood from the body. It was done, first at the right arm, then at the head, and then at the jugular vein; but without success, as Alphonsus had foretold long before his death: for, when it was related before him, that as the body of F. D. John Rizzi after his death would give no blood, the rector commanded it to flow, upon which the blood at once flowed—he smiled at the recital and said: "When I am dead, such wonders need not be attempted, for I will yield no blood."

The holy remains were deposited in a leaden chest, which was sealed with six seals; four of the town of Pagani, and two of the Congregation. It was shut with three different keys: one was given to the Prince of Polleca, who assisted in the name of the nephews of Alphonsus; the second to the regents of the town; and the third remained in the hands of the rector of the house. After these precautionary measures, the chest was deposited at the left side of the high altar, and the door of the vault was closed by a single slab of marble with the following inscription:

"*Hic jacet corpus—Illustrissimi et Reverendisimi Domini—D. Alphonsi de Liguorio—Episcopi S. Agathæ Gothorum—et Fundatoris Congregationis—Sanctissimi Redemptoris.*"

On the following evening a fresh concourse of people and persons of distinction arrived, from Nola, from Salerno, and other distant places; even from Ariano, which is two days journey from Nocera. As they found that the body was already placed in the vault, they collected some remains of the mortar which had been used in fastening the stone, as if they were precious relics. Others, went away satisfied with having been able to touch the stone with their scapulars or rosaries. A great number of little children did homage to Alphonsus' sanctity, by kneeling down on it and kissing it with humility and devotion.

God was not long in glorifying his servant: signal favors were obtained through his intercession on the very day of his funeral. D. Angela Tortora had suffered violent and frequent tooth-ache for a great number of years; when Alphonsus was exposed on the catafalque, she applied a little piece of his vestment to her mouth, and she was instantly cured. Another woman had been nearly blind for some months; she had specks on her eyes and a great many pimples on her eyelids; she invoked Alphonsus while the funeral rites were being celebrated and was instantly cured. There was a woman who had suffered great pain in her side for three days; she had recourse to the saint, and, after having applied a morsel of his raiment to it, she was healed. The Abbot of Montevergine had a diseased liver; he applied to his body a piece of the saint's clothes and was also relieved. A lay sister in the Convent Della Purita had a sore on her leg, which had begun to mortify; she made use of a relic of Alphonsus, and was immediately in a state to wait on the community. In the village of Cartoli, there was a lady who had been for several years afflicted with a tertian fever, accompanied with pains in the whole body and obstinate vomitings, and she too was cured by the mere touch of his relics.

Angela Oliviero, a nun at Naples, who was a former penitent of Alphonsus, and who had a great devotion to him, was inconsolable when she heard of his death. But whilst she was thus sorrowing, Alphonsus appeared to her in glory to console her.

When his death became known at St. Agatha, the inhabitants of this town also resolved to fly to his patronage. A woman of this place who had been tormented by pain in the side for three days, had recourse to Alphonsus and was instantly cured. Another woman who suffered most acutely from tooth-ache, applied a thread of the saint's vesture, and became perfectly free from all pain. Canon Lucca, who had suffered from violent colics, had no sooner made use of a letter of the saint than his pains disappeared. For some days the brother of a poor woman had been confined to bed by a high fever; he was ordered to take quinine, but as she could not command the sum it would have cost, in her distress she cast herself down on her knees and exclaimed: "My Blessed Lord, come to my aid, for I cannot aid myself." Animated with confidence, she took some threads of linen which the saint had used and caused her brother to swallow them. The fever instantly ceased, and two days afterwards he was laboring in the fields.

We pass over many other similar prodigies, and confine ourselves to the relation of the following striking miracle which took place in the church at Nocera during the celebration of the funeral rites. For ten days Joseph Maria Fusco, a child of rather more than a year old, had been suffering from a violent fever accompanied with dysentery, and all hope of saving him was abandoned. His aunt resolved to take the boy to the church, and she did so in spite of the opposition of her brother, of another relation, and of the mother, who feared that the sick child would die on the way. At first, the saintly body was touched with a rosary which was afterwards placed on the dying child, and then the mother, who had followed it, suddenly became filled with great confidence, and begged Br. Fr. Anthony to let her son's face touch the body, which was scarcely done ere the child was cured. On the evening of Friday, the 3d of August, his uncle D. Gaetan Fusco, who was a priest, came to the house of the fathers and informed them of the miraculous cure of his nephew. They had just then received some pictures of Alphonsus from Naples, and they gave one of them to D. Gaetan. Having carried it home, he sent for his nephew and held it out to him. After the little child had looked at it with attention, he seemed to be raised out of himself, and suddenly exclaimed: "Alphonsus is in heaven!" His parents were filled with admiration; the little child became more animated and joyous, and repeated, while pointing to the picture: "Alphonsus! Alphonsus! The saint! the saint!" then after again raising his hands and eyes to heaven, he exclaimed: "The saint is in heaven! the saint is in heaven!" This unanswerable testimony from the mouth of a child who had never before spoken, and was not even old enough to do so without a miracle, contributed greatly to spread Alphonsus' renown every where; and as God daily glorified his servant by fresh prodigies, crowds were seen coming to his tomb to implore his powerful intercession, or to make offerings to him in token of their gratitude.

Thus the Lord had begun, (according to the promise: "I will glorify him who hath glorified me,") to glorify Alphonsus in this world from which he had only wished to receive contempt; and he ordained that he whose whole life had been devoted to promote the Divine glory, should receive this kind of reward in full measure. Besides the solemn rites celebrated for him in the houses of his own Congregation, in the kingdom, in the pontifical states, and in Sicily; magnificent catafalques were erected, and obsequies, more like feasts than funeral rites, were celebrated in a great number of churches and dioceses where he had either personally given proofs of his apostolical zeal, or was only known by fame and his writings. Cardinals, archbishops, bishops, archpriests, canons, religious and nuns without number, vied with each other in causing magnificent funeral preparations to be made in their respective churches, and in procuring the most renowned preachers to deliver discourses on the virtues and merits of the saintly apostle whom God had called to his reward; and on such occasions, the concourse of the clergy, the magistrates, the nobility, and the people in general, was every where immense, not to say prodigious. At Amalfi alone, the expenses of this ceremony amounted to more than a hundred crowns. These solemnities, at which nothing was spared to enhance their pomp, were in many instances illustrated by miracles; God himself wishing thus to contribute to the glory of his servant. Among others, at Caposele, a lady who had suffered from a cataract for ten years, and had entirely lost her sight, caused herself to be led into the church from the desire to obtain her cure. She was full of confidence, and raising her voice before all present, she exclaimed: "Alphonsus, I will not believe that you are a saint and in heaven if you do not obtain this favor for me." Her prayer was heard, and she returned home glorifying him who had restored her sight. At Girgenti, in Sicily, there was a man who had been suffering from a great many infirmities for a long time, and having heard that the obsequies of the saintly bishop were being celebrated, he caused himself to be conveyed to the church, as he could not go on foot; when there, he recommended himself to the saint, and obtained a complete cure on the spot, which was visible to all present.

Persons of all classes and from all parts eagerly sought to possess something of which he had made use. As soon as he had expired, his room was completely pillaged: gentlemen and persons of the highest rank did not scruple to carry off various things which their piety caused them to covet. The cloak which was torn into pieces at Amalfi; the shirts and other articles of dress which were taken from him there as well as in other places, and for which new ones had been substituted; the many pieces which had on innumerable occasions been rent off from the borders of his garments, when passing through crowds; beds in which he had slept; the rooms he had occupied—were all religiously regarded as precious relics, and God worked by their means a great many miracles. Among others, Mgr. Puoti, Archbishop of Amalfi, preserved a simple girdle which was quite worn out, but which Alphonsus had made use of when celebrating mass, as a valuable treasure; and as St. Anthony made use of the dress of palm leaves of St. Paul the hermit on solemn festivals, so the Archbishop made use of this girdle only when he officiated pontifically. Canon Genga of Naples obtained one of the shirts of the saint, and his house was from that time frequented by such a great concourse of people that the relic was soon divided into a thousand pieces, as each one wanted to have some portion of it. Amongst others, the Prince of Scilla carried off the collar as a precious treasure. Sister Mary Michael Grimaldi, a Dominicaness and one of Alphonsus' penitents, of Lorrento, wrote the following lines to the fathers of the Congregation: "All those who are ill beg for some threads of his soutane, as the famished poor entreat for a morsel of bread, and miraculous cures are every where effected by them."

The town of St. Agatha being inconsolable at not possessing the mortal remains of its holy bishop, by way of amends a mitre of which Alphonsus had made use was given to the cathedral chapter. When the people saw it being taken there they all knelt down with uncovered heads; then they hurried to the church to kiss it, being full of veneration for their precious relic. All the canons and the clerks received it with the same respect: and the chapter returned the most grateful thanks for this inestimable treasure; which they preserved with the greatest care, in memory of their saintly prelate, and in the certain hope that it would one day become the relic of a canonized saint, who would deign to be the special advocate before God of the town, the chapter, and the whole diocese.

A print seller, by name Nunzio Petrini, anticipating the great sale of likenesses of Alphonsus which would take place at his death, had taken pains to procure one of his portraits beforehand; so that immediately after the decease of the servant of God, the town of Naples and all the kingdom were full of prints of him, which were every where sought for with a holy avidity. The shop-keepers of Naples alone, asserted that more than sixty thousand were sold by them. The same eagerness for relics and pictures was manifested out of the kingdom, especially in the Roman states. Even at Varsovia, F. Hofbauer, wishing to satisfy the great number of persons who wanted to have these pictures, got several new plates engraved after the original at Naples. The same thing was done at Venice, where every one wished to possess a likeness of this servant of God. At Rome, several cardinals were eager to procure copies, which they honored as those of a saint. Cardinals Zurlo and Banditi were as eager as the rest, and placed his picture at the head of their beds, as that of a powerful protector. The sovereign pontiff, Pius VI, was presented by Cardinal Buoncompagno with a copy of the funeral sermon, composed by Joseph Cavallo of the Congregation of Pious Workmen, accompanied by a picture of the saint. When the Holy Father saw the picture, he kissed it with devotion, and held it to his forehead for some time with the greatest respect, saying: "He is a saint, and I doubt not that he is now in the enjoyment of the glories of heaven;" he then thanked the cardinal for the sermon and said: "I will read it with much pleasure." It was marvellous to see how as soon as one plate was worn out, another was instantly engraved in a different style. Tramontana, the priest, alone, had a dozen of these portraits taken at his own expense, each one more beautiful than the last.

The miracles we have already related were but the beginning of prodigies without number, by which God, in recompense for the charity his servant had exercised on earth, deigned to glorify him by bestowing innumerable blessings through his intercession. We will relate some of the most striking of them. F. Francis d'Ottajano, of the reformed order of St. Francis, at Palermo, had been suffering since the month of November 1786, from a burning fever and a painful cough. In spite of all remedies the fever got worse, and the sick man had already begun to spit blood and matter; and four of the first physicians of Naples, who were consulted, agreed in saying that he was in an incurable consumption. On seeing that no hope of his recovery was entertained, and that every one was afraid of coming near him on account of his contagious disease, he went to the house of an old aunt of his. He placed himself under the care of two doctors, who declared, in the month of July 1787, that he was in the last stage of consumption. To this serious malady was added a retention of urine. When reduced to this extremity, the dying man, being animated by the account of the numerous miracles of Alphonsus, had recourse to his intercession, and said: "If you are really dear to God, and if you enjoy beatitude in Paradise, obtain for me that I may not die of this malady, which renders me an object of horror." He promised also to offer up to him a pound of wax every year, and to carry it himself to his tomb. He had scarcely finished his prayer, when he felt a sudden change; and whereas all food had before caused him to feel nausea, he now ate with relish. After this he had a quiet sleep, and, on awaking, he was perfectly cured. This was juridically deposed at Nocera, at the time the process was arranged; and for a number of years the religious continued to enjoy good health, and every year, in all weather, was to be seen bringing his offering to the tomb of his benefactor.

In the same monastery, there was a religious who laughed at the confidence which F. Francis had in Alphonsus, and often teased him on this subject, going so far as to ask how much the wax cost, and what use was made of it by his saintly advocate. Alphonsus was displeased at this conduct; he appeared to him one night, and said to him in an indignant tone: "Audacious man! when will you cease to laugh at my servant?" The religious, seized with terror, replied that he had not done it with a bad intention, and that what he had said was nothing but a jest. "People do not jest in this manner," answered Alphonsus, and in a threatening tone of voice, he added: "Go now to confession, and never have the boldness to speak in this way again." The religious was terrified; he instantly jumped out of bed, and ran and cast himself at the feet of his confessor; the next morning he informed all the community of what had happened to him, and took good care never to repeat his jests again.

In the year 1787, Vincent Cocca, a joiner at Foggia, was wounded in the chest by a knife. The injured part was cut away, but the wound remained incurable. He suffered for more than a year, and there was no further hope of his cure, as the doctors said that he was in a consumption. F. D. Joseph Stella went to see the sick man, gave him some threads of Alphonsus' cassock, and assured him that if he had confidence in him he would be cured. The mother of the joiner, animated by a lively faith, took off all the bandages of the wound, and applied to it some threads of the holy garment. It was again uncovered a short time afterwards, when it was found to be healed, and the skin had grown over the holy relic; the sick man was quite cured, and recovered his former health.

D. Catharine Biscotti, a Benedictine nun in the town of Diana, in the province of Salerno, was attacked by a bloody flux which caused her to suffer severely. After fourteen months suffering, the malady got so much worse that she had no rest day or night, and the doctor was much afraid that mortification had commenced. While in this state, she invoked Alphonsus and said: "Alphonsus Liguori, show me that you are really a saint, as is every where proclaimed. You must deliver me from this malady; and as the process of your canonization will have to be drawn up, I promise you to bear witness to my cure juridically, and to have a mass and *Te Deum* sung in thanksgiving." After this prayer the nun fell asleep, and on awaking, she found that she was perfectly cured.

For fourteen days, D. Julian Jourdain, procurator-advocate at the tribunal of Lucere, had suffered from a malignant fever, and from the ninth day he had been unceasingly tormented by hiccough, and his death was expected every instant. His disconsolate sister entered her chamber, and there before a picture of Alphonsus began to pray, saying with faith: "My countryman," (the family of Jourdain came from Nocera,) "I, a poor stranger, have recourse to you. You must spare my brother to me: I wish to obtain this favor." After that, with greater confidence still, she took the picture and brought it to her brother, who took it, and placing it on his forehead, said: "My Lord, succor me." At the same instant the fever ceased, and the crisis was succeeded by a complete rocovery.

At Foggia, D. Louisa Palatella, the wife of the lawyer D. Francis Xavier Massari, had been pregnant for eight months, when her child died in her womb. On hearing of the sad state she was in, a father of the Congregation exhorted her to have recourse to Alphonsus with confidence. She did so, and on applying a picture of him to herself, she promised to offer him a pound of wax, and to support an abandoned girl, if he would heal her. Her delivery was pronounced to be, humanly speaking, impossible, and symptoms of death appeared after three days, but she did not lose confidence, and continued to hold the picture close to her. The said father encouraged her more and more, and at length she was delivered without the least accident.

At Benevento, there was a poor woman who was very often afflicted by violent convulsions, which were so severe that one night she fell out of bed, and as she was alone in the house, she was unable to rise again. She had a picture of Alphonsus at the head of her bed, and she invoked him with confidence, as well as the Most Holy Virgin Mary. At the same moment, she saw the saint enter her room, accompanied by a most beautiful lady, who lifted her from the floor and laid her in bed again with the greatest compassion. Alphonsus then sat down beside her and said: "See, we have come to assist you, but you must go to confession to-morrow, your pains will be redoubled until then; but when the confession is finished, they will cease." At these words the lady and Alphonsus disappeared. When the morning had arrived the poor woman sent for F. Anthony Corrado, who found her in a very suffering state; but when the confession was finished, she was entirely free from pain.

For thirty-four years Leopold Marino Rousseau, of Foggia, was tormented by a dysentery, which had reduced him to a mere skeleton. The malady grew worse and worse, and the doctors declared he could not live, and ordered extreme unction to be administered to him. When D. Paschal Rousseau was informed of the state his brother was in, he sent him two pictures, one of the Blessed Joseph of the Cross, and the other of Alphonsus. In the evening, they lit a lamp before the two pictures, and recommended the dying man to the two saints. At midnight, a bishop appeared before him clad in a rochet and an almuce; he was little and bent; he inquired what was the matter with him. The sick man replied: "I have no strength, and I entreat the saints to pray to God to grant me deliverance from my wretched state." The bishop then assumed quite a joyous manner, and answered: "Have confidence;" and as the sick man's entrails were supported by bandages, he went on to say: "Take off this handkerchief, and you will feel better." "How can I do so?" said the sick man, "I have not strength for it;" but as the bishop again told him to undo the bandage, he tried to do it, and perceived that it was already done; as he felt instant relief he called his daughter, and asked for a light, but he saw the bishop no more. The next morning he cast his eyes on Alphonsus' picture, and said: "It is he who has cured me." When the physicians came they found him quite recovered and free from fever.

We will now mention a miracle of another kind, which happened to F. Louis of St. Catharine, apostolical missionary in the Roman states. He wrote to the superior-general of the Congregation of the M. H. Redeemer: "I tried in vain to convert a great number of sinners who were living most obstinately in vice, and who told me they could not separate from the object of their passion; I persuaded them to recite an *Ave* to Mary Immaculate, praying her to extinguish these impure flames in them through the merits of Mgr. Liguori, who had exalted her so highly. After that they all came to me again, giving extraordinary proofs of conversion; they are now reformed and have led exemplary lives from that time. I had also the consolation of seeing this same method succeed with other sinners who nourished inveterate hatreds."

We forbear relating any more of the miracles wrought by the intercession of our saint, for they would fill volumes; we may say without the least exaggeration, that they may be numbered by thousands. Indeed, the Lord was truly lavish with such favors towards his servant, in order, undoubtedly, the sooner to illuminate the Church, his house upon earth, by causing Alphonsus to be placed on her altars as a shining and burning light.

No sooner had Alphonsus gone to receive his immortal crown than two verbal processes were drawn up by the ordinary judges; the one at St. Agatha, and the other at Nocera, in order juridically to confirm his heroic virtues and the miracles wrought through his intercession. The acts of these processes were forthwith sent to Rome, to obtain the introduction of the cause of the beatification and canonization. About the same time there were sent to Rome and duly registered, (without counting those that came too late,) four hundred and eight petitions, from cardinals, archbishops, bishops, vicars capitular, chapters of cathedrals, collegiate establishments, religious bodies, magistrates of the highest rank, and from the king Ferdinand IV, earnestly entreating the Holy See for the commencement of the process. By a decree of the 9th of July 1794, the sovereign pontiff selected Cardinal Archinto as the reporter of the cause, D. Gaetan Cardone, of the Congregation of the M. H. Redeemer, being its postulator. On the 30th of April 1796, another decree was issued in order that the cause might be introduced. The calamities of the times and the exile of the Holy Father, it might have been expected, would have put a stop to all proceedings, but it was not so. As early as the 27th of March 1802, Cardinal Caraccioli, who, in consequence of the death of Cardinal Archinto, had been substituted by Pope Pius VII on the 6th of the same month as reporter of the case, issued a decree in favor of the validity of the apostolical process on the reputation of sanctity enjoyed by the servant of God. On the report of Cardinal Saluces, who took the place of Cardinal Caraccioli, the Sacred Congregation of Rites decided, on the 14th of May 1803, after a theological examination, that nothing was to be found in the printed or manuscript works of the venerable Alphonsus Liguori which was worthy of censure, and that therefore the proceedings might be continued. On the 25th of June 1803, the Pope granted a dispensation from the decree of Urban VIII, which forbids any proceedings with regard to the special examination of the virtues of a servant of God to be entered upon until fifty years after his death, only sixteen having elapsed since the death of Alphonsus. The *anti-preparatory*, the *preparatory*, and the *general* Congregations of the Cardinals having previously been held at the Quirinal palace; on the 7th of May 1807, the feast of the Ascension, after having celebrated mass in his domestic chapel, and having assisted with the cardinals at the solemn mass in the basilica of St. John Lateran, the Holy Father published his solemn decree on the virtues of the servant of God; proclaiming that Alphonsus Maria Liguori had possessed the theological and cardinal virtues in a heroical degree. The extraordinary anti-preparatory Congregation for the examination of the miracles was to take place on the 25th of September 1809, but the captivity of the Pope, the dispersion of the cardinals, and the invasion of the Roman states, suspended the proceedings. They were resumed on the 28th of February 1815, and on the 17th of September of the same year, the day on which the feast of our Lady of Sorrows was celebrated throughout the whole Catholic Church for the first time, (this day having been selected on account of the great devotion of the servant of God for the sufferings of the Blessed Virgin,) the Pope, after having offered the Holy Sacrifice in his domestic chapel of the Quirinal, published his decree, by which he recognized two miracles of the second class, (related hereafter,) which had been effected through the intercession of the venerable Alphonsus Maria Liguori. On the 21st of December 1815, the feast of St. Thomas the Apostle, the Pope Pius VII, after having celebrated mass in the chapel of the Quirinal, published the decree which permitted the proceedings regarding the solemn beatification of the venerable servant of God to be continued; and on the 26th of September 1816, he signed the brief of the beatification, conferring the title of *The*

49

Blessed on the illustrious Bishop, declaring that he is most assuredly in possession of the celestial glory, and that his relics and images might be exposed to the veneration of the faithful, authorising at the same time the dioceses of St. Agatha and of Nocera, as well as the Congregation of the Most Holy Redeemer, to celebrate yearly the mass in honor of the beatified. The ceremony of the beatification itself took place nine days afterwards, in the basilica of St. Peter, the whole being conducted with great pomp and splendor, only twenty-nine years and a few days over two months having elapsed since the blessed death of Alphonsus.

God, who willed that his servant should be still more highly exalted, was not long in manifesting his will through fresh miracles worked by Alphonsus. Many new and illustrious solicitations were addressed to the court of Rome, requesting the continuation of the process for the canonization of the servant of God; they were assented to by the Sacred Congregation of Rites, and, on the 28th of February 1818, Pius VII signed the decree which introduced the cause of the beatified for canonization. After this, Leo XII succeeded to Pius VII, and Pius VIII to Leo XII, F. Joseph Montone, the general procurator of the Congregation of the Most Holy Redeemer, succeeded to the deceased Vincent Andrew Giattini, as postulator of the cause, and Cardinal Odescalchi to the deceased Cardinal Caraccioli, as reporter; and, after due examination of the two fresh miracles (selected for that purpose amongst a great many others) in the extraordinary anti-preparatory, preparatory, and general Congregation of Cardinals, prelates and consulters, his Holiness Pius VIII approved and confirmed, by a solemn decree of the 3d of December 1829, (the feast of St. Francis Xavier,) which was published the same day in the church of the Jesuit fathers, the judicial declaration of the same two miracles, which are related hereafter. On the 16th of May 1830, the 5th Sunday after Easter, after having celebrated the Holy Sacrifice in the chapel of the Quirinal, his Holiness declared that the solemn canonization of the Blessed Alphonsus Maria de Liguori could be safely decreed, and ordered that this declaration should be published, and preserved among the acts of the Sacred Congregation of Rites, and that the apostolical letters should be prepared for the canonization, to be celebrated in due time in the basilica of the Vatican. The storm which Pius VIII had predicted in an encyclical, soon burst forth throughout all Europe; and this pontiff dying some months afterwards, Gregory XVI succeeded him, on the 2d of February 1831. To the political reasons which still existed and acted as hindrances to the canonization, was added the outlay which is entailed by the magnificent ceremonies which must always accompany the canonization of the saints; but various subscriptions were set on foot to meet the expenses of the *fête* of the five saints who were to be canonized together, and at length the 26th of May 1839 was selected as the day for the canonization of these servants of God, Alphonsus Maria de Liguori; Francis of Jerome, of the Company of Jesus; John Joseph of the Cross, of the reform of St. Peter of Alcantara; Pacificus of San Severino, a reformed Minor; and Veronica Juliana, a Cupuchiness: which took place accordingly on the said day with the utmost pomp and solemnity. Here follows the Bull which was given on the occasion.

Bull of the Canonization of St. Alphonsus.

GREGORY,

Servant of the Servants of God, for a perpetual remembrance:

PREFACE.—§ 1. Sanctity and knowledge, ought, in the judgment of the Apostle of the Gentiles, so to adorn every bishop, to whose care the salvation of souls is entrusted, that, by the holiness of his life, he may be to the sheep committed to him as a shining light for running without stumbling the way of salvation, and may be able also to exhort them according to sound doctrine, and to convince the gainsayers. We know, that, from the earliest ages, there have been most excellent bishops, illustrious in both these respects, lively images of the Good Shepherd, who, "being made a pattern of the flock from the heart," have carefully and wisely watched over its safety, and, as a light set upon a candlestick, were no less by the examples they gave of a spotless life, than by the excellence of their doctrine, the glory of the Church of God.

§ 2. Alphonsus Maria Liguori appears to have been given by God to the Church in the last century, in order to renew this admirable example of a holy prelate. As he had from his early youth applied himself to the practice of the Christian virtues, and especially as he possessed sacred knowledge in an eminent degree, he was called to fill the office of the episcopate, a charge by far the most weighty of all, in order that his labors in the field of the Lord, in which he had already, as a priest, shown himself a diligent laborer, might be yet more abundant and fruitful in good. But, by no means content that this his zeal for spreading the divine glory should be confined within the narrow limits of his own life, in order that he might leave successors in this ministry of salvation to the most distant ages, he founded a Congregation of priests, who, inflamed with the same zeal, should devote all their labors and care to the furthering the salvation of souls. And, as it has been clearly shown, that the admirable virtues of Alphonsus, which have been examined with the usual judicial severity, reached the highest degree of Christian perfection, and it appears that the miracles, by which God, the author of all good, has manifested the sanctity of his servant, have been duly verified; by virtue of the apostolical authority which has been divinely committed to us, though unworthy, and on the advice of the fathers the cardinals of the Holy Roman Church, as also of the patriarchs, archbishops, and bishops, who were present in Rome at that time in great number, we have judged, and do by the present letters ordain, that the honors paid to saints be rendered to the Blessed Alphonsus Liguori, by the whole Church, and that his intercession with God be invoked.

§ 3. Alphonsus was born at Naples, of noble parents, on the 5th day of October 1696. Being endowed with a wonderful vivacity of mind, he applied himself, when he had scarcely ceased to be a child, to the classics, then to the higher sciences, and afterwards to the study of the law, and had so happy a facility in learning, that he had hardly entered the sixteenth year of his age, when, after the usual examination, he received the degree of doctor of civil and canon law with great distinction. In deference to the wishes of his father, he entered into the profession of the law, in the discharge of which though he led a pure and upright life, yet, because he found it to be full of cares and dangers, he determined to leave it, and entered into the service of the Church. Despising, therefore, a very splendid matrimonial alliance, and voluntarily and cheerfully renouncing, in favor of his brother, the ancestral fortune which belonged to him as the eldest son, he put utterly away from himself all care about earthly things.

§ 4. Then being admitted to holy orders, and invested with the sacerdotal character, he exerted himself with all his strength to extend the glory of God everywhere, to sow in the hearts of men the seeds of virtue, and to root out the vices. As he was persuaded that no one will ever reap much fruit from his apostolic labors unless he practise as well as teach, he proposed to himself in the beginning as a thing to be insisted upon, that by the exercise of every virtue he should show himself as a minister of God and a dispenser of his mysteries. He most vigilantly guarded that chastity which he had long before vowed to God, constantly having in view, in every motion of his mind and body, the preserving it free from the slightest stains, and, in order that he might be sure to succeed in this aim, he placed it with perfect confidence under the protection of the Mother of God. His love of God was so ardent, that he kept his mind continually fixed upon him, and he seemed to take delight in nothing but in thinking and speaking of him. It is easy to understand with what ardent charity for his neighbor one so inflamed with the love of God must have burned. Wherefore, he never declined any labor or fatigue, when there was question of bringing back to the bosom of God men plunged in vice and laden with crimes. Hence, he very frequently visited the hospitals, in order to wait on the sick, and especially that he might be ready to assist those who were in danger of death: he heard confessions with the greatest patience, and often spent almost the whole day, and even the greatest part of the night, in this employment: he frequently preached to crowds of auditors, in language so earnest, that he triumphed over the obstinacy of the most abandoned, and, exposing to them the turpitude of the crimes in which they had become hardened, he excited in the hearts of his hearers such lively feelings of sorrow as to bring them to tears, and frequently the sacred edifice resounded with weeping and groanings. As he allowed himself no respite, day or night, but exerted all the powers of his mind and body in laboring for the salvation of his neighbor, becoming at length weakened and broken down by these great and incessant efforts, he fell into a dangerous illness, from which, however, having recovered, by a signal favor from heaven, he again applied himself to his labors of charity, with more alacrity than ever.

§ 5. As soon as he knew that he was called, in the providence of God, to be the founder of a new religious Congregation, that there might be no lack of industrious laborers in so plentiful a harvest, he suffered himself to be deterred by no obstacles, however great, from hastening the accomplishment of his undertaking, destined to be of such service to the Church. Relying, therefore, upon the divine assistance, he undertook the work, and happily succeeded in frustrating the designs and arts of the infernal enemy, striving to prevent the execution of his plans. Having united with himself twelve men of eminent piety, he laid the foundations of his religious Congregation, to which the name of the Most Holy Redeemer was given; and he proposed to the members as their chief aim, the bringing back to the way of virtue, as well by their words as by their examples, the profligate and abandoned, especially those among the peasantry who lived dispersed throughout the country. As the Congregation spread in a short time, and in a wonderful manner, throughout the cities and provinces of Italy, he obtained from our predecessor, Benedict XIV, its confirmation, by virtue of his apostolical authority, and, being appointed rector-major, he excited his companions, by his own example, to the exercise of all virtues, in a manner truly wonderful.

§ 6. He excelled, in an especial degree, in the virtue of humility; although every one had the highest opinion of his sanctity, and he was honored by the esteem of the most distinguished men, yet he ever preserved a lowly opinion of himself, and deemed himself unworthy of all honor and consideration. He loved the Virgin Mother of God, as a son his mother, with a piety truly singular. He had the most ardent sentiments of love and veneration for the Most Holy Sacrament of the Eucharist, and often passed whole hours in succession in adoration before it, his soul, meanwhile, being filled with an ineffable sweetness. In order that he might, after the example of the Apostle, bring his body into subjection to the spirit, he continually treated it as a domestic enemy, and crucified it by all kinds of torments.* He allowed himself so little food and drink, that it seemed scarcely sufficient to keep up his strength and support life, and even the wretched nourishment he took he was accustomed to season with the most bitter herbs, in order utterly to take away every occasion of sensual gratification. Moreover, he always wore the roughest hair shirts, and constantly afflicted his body with iron chains; he was accustomed to scourge himself with disciplines armed with sharp points, and that so severely, that the blood, flowing copiously from his mangled flesh, sprinkled the floor and the walls of his cell; he took great pains, however, to efface these bloody stains, that they might not lead to the discovery of his self-macerations.

§ 7. But what is especially worthy of admiration, is, that, notwithstanding his constant labors in the apostolic ministry, and the extent to which he chastised and weakened his body by every kind of torture, he was able, nevertheless, to find so much time for, and to apply with so great alacrity of mind to, the study of sacred things, as greatly to enrich the Church by the production of many equally learned and laborious works. Indeed, that he might consecrate himself and his whole life to the divine service, he made the very difficult and till then almost unheard of vow, never to allow even the least instant of time to pass idly by, but to employ every moment usefully. Thus he was enabled to produce a great number of works, having for their several objects the support of morality, the more perfect instruction of the ministers of the sanctuary, the establishing the truth of the Catholic religion, the asserting the rights of the Holy See, and finally, the awakening piety in the hearts of Christians. In these productions we must admire the unusual fervor, the richness and variety of attainment, the striking proofs of the pastoral solicitude, and the ardent zeal for the interests of religion, which he discovers. But this is specially worthy of note, that, although he wrote so vast a number of works, it has nevertheless been found, upon the strict examination which has been instituted in regard to them, that they may be read by the faithful without the least fear of finding the smallest error in them.

§ 8. As Alphonsus possessed so great a reputation for holiness and learning, he was raised to the episcopal see of St. Agatha of the Goths, by Clement XIII. The holy man dreaded the being loaded with so heavy a burden, and made use of every means to escape it; but when he had perceived the will of God in that of the Pontiff, he concluded, with a ready and undaunted mind, to submit, and to undertake, confiding in the divine assistance, the charge, which his humility made him feel was beyond his strength.

§ 9. It is indeed difficult to express with how great care and earnestness he strove to fulfil all the pastoral functions of his office: he watched assiduously over the flock which had been committed to his charge, and took every pains, that not even one of the sheep entrusted to him should perish. Neither did he relax, in any respect, his very austere mode of life, on account of his new dignity: he avoided all sumptuousness in food and clothing; there was nothing in his palace, nothing in his furniture, which was superfluous or luxurious. He loved the poor with singular affection, and profusely distributed to them food, clothing, and alms; he even did not hesitate to sell, on one occasion, his golden cross and episcopal ring, in order to relieve their distress. He was in the habit of giving dowries to young women, out of his own income, to enable them to marry, and of maintaining at his own expense such young clerics in the study of the liberal arts, as, on account of their humble birth, were suffering from poverty. He opened convents for virgins wishing to consecrate themselves to God, and houses of refuge for poor women who were in danger of losing their innocence. Not being deterred, in the visitation of his diocese, by any difficulties of the roads or inclemency of the season, he sedulously visited the little towns situated on the tops of mountains, and the people dispersed throughout the country, and with words full of ardor he excited them to the love of virtue, and he withheld them from the commission of sin. But it was with regard to priests and young men preparing for the sacred ministry, that he took especial care. With what great diligence did he not labor, that they might grow up in piety while yet in early youth, and be rightly imbued with the sacred sciences especially, so as to become, at length, fit instruments for the ministry of the altar, and for the guidance of the faithful. But it must be said, that it was the life of their saintly pastor which had the greatest effect in enkindling their minds, inasmuch as, beholding his manner of living, they had before their eyes the most illustrious examples of continency, of religion, of poverty, in a word, of all those virtues with which a priest should be adorned and enriched, if he would contribute any thing to the common good of the Church.

§ 10. After having for thirteen years given an example of all pastoral solicitude and vigilance in the government of the Church which had been confided to his care, as he was now laden with years and become infirm, he resigned (having several times besought our predecessor, Pius VI, for, and at length obtained, permission,) the charge which he found so heavy. But having betaken himself, thus free from the duties of the episcopate, to the society of the brothers of his Congregation, he devoted the remainder of his life, not to a well-earned repose, but to fresh cares and labors, even in his most advanced age. Thus, he was always engaged in writing something which he knew would be of use to the faithful, and never ceased preaching, that he might reform the morals of men, and, as far as lay in his power, inflame them with the love of virtue.

§ 11. When he had at length reached his ninety-first year, pressed down with the weight of his age now rapidly approaching its term, he fell grievously ill. Having endured with incredible patience the excruciating pains of his disease, and most earnestly exhorted the members of the religious Congregation of which he was the founder to the utmost zeal in the pursuit of virtue, he was refreshed with the viaticum of the Most Holy Eucharist, and fortified with extreme unction. After he had most devoutly received these sacraments of the Church, his soul filled with joy and gladness, and desiring nothing more ardently than that, loosed from the prison of the body, it might be with Christ, fled, in perfect peace, into the bosom of its God.

§ 12. As soon as the report of Alphonsus' death was spread abroad, an immense concourse of people flocked to his coffin, mourning for the loss of one so dear to them, and striving, through devotion and veneration, to possess themselves of something which had been used by him during his life. Nor was there wanting the fame of miracles, by which the almighty and good God manifested in the sight of all the exceeding sanctity of his servant. Which prodigies being made known far and near, the high reputation his virtues had for a long time won for him became increased in a wonderful degree, and several princes and other persons high in dignity, as well as a great number of religious orders, earnestly besought the sovereign pontiff, Pius VI, that judicial proceedings might be commenced regarding the saintly life of Alphonsus. The process having been gone through with in the usual manner, and the works which he had published having been most carefully examined and scrutinized with the greatest severity, Pius VII, our predecessor, after hearing the opinion of the Sacred Congregation of Rites, published a decree, on the nones of May 1807, in which he declared, that it was certain that the venerable Alphonsus Maria Liguori had practised, in a heroic degree, the theological and cardinal virtues, together with all which depend on and spring from them.

§ 13. After this, they proceeded, in the said Sacred Congregation, to the examination of the miracles which were said to have been wrought by Almighty God, at the intercession of the venerable Alphonsus. Among this number there were two, in particular, of the second class, which were judged certain and incontestible: that is to say, the instantaneous cure of Magdalene of Nuncio, who, being at the point of death, a great part of her breast having been amputated by reason of a gangrenous ulcer, invoked the aid of Alphonsus, upon which she arose, contrary to the expectation of all, perfectly healed, and her breast became quite whole again: the other was the cure, likewise instantaneous and perfect, of Francis of Octajano, of the order of Reformed Minors of St. Francis, who was in the last stage of consumption, and utterly exhausted, so that his recovery was despaired of; but after he had prayed to the venerable Alphonsus for several days, he was suddenly cured, and every trace of his former malady disappeared. However, Pius VII, of holy memory, judged that he ought to delay pronouncing any decision in a matter of so great importance, in order to implore more additional light from God by more ardent prayers. At length, on the 16th of the kalends of October 1815, the day consecrated to our Lady of Dolors, the memory of whose sorrows Alphonsus had ever affectionately and piously cherished during his life, the same pontiff pronounced his judgment, and issued a decree, in which the two above related cures were declared to be true miracles. Finally, after having heard the opinion of the same Sacred Congregation, he issued, on the 12th of the kalends of January 1815, pontifical letters, in which he ordained the beatification of the venerable Alphonsus Maria Liguori, which was celebrated with the greatest pomp and splendor, in the basilica of the Vatican, on the 16th of the kalends of September 1816.

§ 14. But after the honors of public veneration had been rendered to the venerable Alphonsus, many others experienced his aid in present danger, and it was clearly seen that God had willed, in his goodness, to reward the faithful steward of his house with a measure of honor among men, proportionate to the greatness of the care and pains taken by the holy prelate to extend the glory of the divine name. Being struck with the greatness of these miracles, Ferdinand I, the most pious king of the two Sicilies, and many other princes, together with the most of the cardinals of the Holy Roman Church, of the archbishops and bishops, as well as the religious orders, and especially the Congregation of the Most Holy Redeemer, which justly glories in having Alphonsus as its founder, earnestly besought Pius VII that the Sacred Congregation of Rites might commence at once the process of the canonization of the Blessed Alphonsus. The same pontiff, our predecessor, received their entreaties most favorably, and an inquiry was instituted concerning the authenticity of the recent miracles; and, after a long deliberation, two were found to be without all doubt: namely, the sudden and perfect cure of Antoinette Tarsia, who, having fallen, loaded with a heavy burden, from an elevated place, was brought to the point of death, in consequence of the very grievous injuries she received in the abdomen, but, after having earnestly implored the aid of the Blessed Alphonsus, suddenly arose perfectly cured, to the utter astonishment of all who were present. The other was the instantaneous cure of Peter Canalis, a professed lay brother of the Congregation of Camaldules; he was suffering most severely from a deep, hard, and mortified ulcer, which every remedy seemed only to irritate more and more, so that, having abandoned all hope of recovery, he was expecting death every hour. When he had for several days besought the Blessed Alphonsus to deliver him from a death which seemed inevitable, he obtained his desire, recovering on a sudden (without the least trace of the ulcer remaining) his health, the loss of which he had so long deplored.

§ 15. The truly wonderful cures we have cited having been judicially confirmed, our predecessor, Pius VIII, issued a decree on the 3d of the nones of December 1829, acknowledging their authenticity. Afterwards, when it had been discussed in the usual manner in the Sacred Congregation of Rites whether the solemn canonization of the Blessed Alphonsus could safely be proceeded with, and whether none of the conditions, which, according to the custom of the Holy See are required, were wanting, the same sovereign pontiff, Pius VIII, declared, after having celebrated the Holy Sacrifice in the chapel of the palace of the Quirinal, on the 17th of the kalends of June 1830, being the 5th Sunday after Easter, that the aforesaid canonization might be proceeded with in safety. Being desirous to put this decree into execution, and readily yielding to the wishes of the Congregation of the M. H. Redeemer, we first conferred upon the matter with the whole college of our venerable brothers the cardinals of the holy Roman Church, in a secret consistory held on the 4th of the ides of December 1838, who unanimously agreed that the honors paid to saints should be conferred on the Blessed Alphonsus Maria Liguori. We afterwards assembled a great number of our venerable brothers the archbishops and bishops, for the deliberation of this important matter, and submitted to their judgment the whole series of acts comprising the virtues and miracles of the Blessed Alphonsus, which we did by word of mouth, in the public consistory, in which our beloved son Anthony Maria Cagiano d'Azevedo, the advocate of our consistorial court, defended the cause of the beatified, and also in writing, that is to say, by presenting to them an accurate account of the acts taken from the authentic records of the Sacred Congregation. After that, we convoked before us, on the 8th of the ides of May, a semi-public consistory, to which we summoned not only our venerable brothers the cardinals of the holy Roman Church, but also our venerable brothers the patriarchs, archbishops and bishops, who were then present in Rome, and asked them whether they were of opinion that the Blessed Alphonsus ought to be inscribed in the catalogue of the saints. As they unanimously replied in the affirmative, and even expressed the most lively wish to see this honor conferred upon the Blessed Alphonsus, we ordered that a public instrument of this their verdict should be made by our beloved sons, the notaries of the Apostolic See, and that the suffrages of our venerable brothers, after having been committed to writing and signed by themselves, should be preserved in the archives of the Roman Church. Nevertheless, we thought it right still to defer pronouncing a definitive sentence in so weighty a matter, until, having fixed on days for solemn feasts in Rome, and also pointed out churches in which the faithful might offer up prayers to God, we should obtain from the Father of lights more abundant rays of his wisdom.

§ 16. The 7th day of the kalends of June having been at length fixed upon for the solemn canonization of the Blessed Alphonsus, and also that of the Blessed Francis Jerome, of the Society of Jesus; John Joseph of the Cross, of the order of the Discalceated Minors of St. Peter of Alcantara; Pacificus, of St. Severino, of the order of Minors of the Reformed Observance; and Veronica Juliana, Abbess of the Capuchinesses, we repaired with solemn ceremony to the Vatican, accompanied by the whole of the secular clergy and the religious orders, by the dignitaries and officers of the Roman court and of our palace, finally, by the aforesaid our venerable brothers, the cardinals of the holy Roman Church, the patriarchs, archbishops and bishops. Before we ascended the altar to celebrate the holy mysteries, our blessed son Aloysias Lambruschini, cardinal priest of the holy Roman Church, of the title of St. Callistus, again most humbly presented to us by the advocate of the consistorial court, the prayers of the Christian princes, prelates and people, that the Blessed Alphonsus might be placed in the number of the saints, and prostrating ourselves, we implored the choirs of angels and all the heavenly court to assist us; then, upon the iteration of the same prayers aforesaid, we ardently besought the Holy Spirit, that he would by his divine power strengthen us, now about to pronounce our final decision. Finally, upon the prayers of the postulator of the cause being repeated for the third time with great earnestness, and much more in consideration of the wishes of the whole Church, and of the suffrages which the prelates, aided by God had given, after the very rigid examination which had been instituted in so important a matter, we, by virtue of the apostolical authority, which, notwithstanding our unworthiness, has been given us as successor of St. Peter, the prince of the Apostles, in the supreme government of the Church, to the praise of the holy and indivisible Trinity, for the honor and glory of the Catholic faith and of religion, pronounced our solemn and definitive sentence, and placed the Blessed Alphonsus Maria Liguori, so distinguished for the lustre of his Christian virtues and the splendor of his miracles, among the number of the holy confessor-bishops, and appointed the 4th of the nones of August for the celebration of his memory by the Universal Church. Moreover, we have accorded to those who shall visit on this day the tomb of St. Alphonsus, and, on the appointed days the bodies of the other saints, an indulgence of seven years and as many quarantines.

§ 17. We then offered up to God the Father the Immaculate Lamb, on the great altar of the basilica of the Vatican. Finally, having affectionately given to the assembled multitude, from the height of the upper balcony of the same basilica, our solemn benediction, we granted in the Lord, a plenary indulgence to all the faithful, as well those present at the bendiction, as to those who had assisted at the ceremony of the canonization.*

*Besides this special indulgence for the canonization, the Holy Father granted the following in perpetuity:

GREGORY XVI, POPE,

For a Perpetual Remembrance.

Among the brightest lights and ornaments of the Catholic Church, St. Alphonsus Maria Liguori shines forth pre-eminently, who, renowned for his doctrine and sanctity, and inflamed with an ardent charity, having in view, in the admirable examples he gave of all virtues, and in his very numerous works which are replete with learning and piety, only the glory of God and the spiritual welfare of his fellow-men, having received the crown at the end of a most holy life, possesses now the palm of glory, and triumphs with God in heaven. In order therefore to increase the piety and devotion of the faithful towards this great saint more and more, we have most willingly consented to unlock the ecclesiastical treasures of the Church. Wherefore, yielding to the request of our beloved son John Camillus Ripoli, priest and rector-major, as we are assured, of the Congregation of the Most Holy Redeemer, founded by this saint, and trusting to the mercy of Almighty God and in reliance on the authority of his Blessed Apostles Peter and Paul, we grant in the Lord, to each and all of the faithful of Christ, of either sex, who, being truly contrite shall, after having confessed and

§ 18. It is therefore meet and right that we give up our hearts to sentiments of rejoicing, and that we render worthy thanks to Almighty God, who does not cease to give his Church fresh examples of virtue, in order that we may be excited by them to walk with more ardor in the way of salvation. Wherefore, encompassed as we are by so many and so great perils, and assailed on all sides by so many malicious enemies, let us implore St. Alphonsus to be our intercessor with God, that, by the divine assistance, we may one day obtain in heaven the palm of victory prepared for those who conquer, and that crown of glory which fadeth not away.

§ 19. In order that the memory of this most happy event may never be obliterated by any length of time, we have recorded and confirmed it by these apostolic letters, ordaining that copies of them bearing the signature of a public notary, and the seal of some dignitary of the Church, shall have, when shown, the same authority as these present letters themselves.

§ 20. Let no one, therefore, impugn or rashly gainsay our will and decree, set forth in these letters. But if any one should have the presumption to attempt to do so, let him know that he

received Holy Communion, devoutly visit any one of the churches of the said Congregation of the Most Holy Redeemer, on the feast of the said St. Alphonsus Maria Liguori, from the time of the first vespers, or on any one day, at choice, within the octave of the feast, and shall there offer up prayers to God for concord among Christian princes, for the extirpation of heresy, and for the exaltation of our holy Mother the Church, a plenary indulgence and remission of all sins, once every year, which may be applied by way of suffrage, to the souls of the faithful departed. The present concession is made in perpetuity, notwithstanding all obstacles.

Given at St. Peter's at Rome, under the seal of the Fisherman, on the 10th of January, 1840, in the ninth year of our pontificate.

A. LAMBRUSCHINI.

This is a faithful copy of the original,

JOHN CAMILLUS RIPOLI,
Rector-major of the Congregation of the Most Holy Redeemer.

We have seen it, and allow it to be published. Given at Liege, on the 7th of April, 1840.

† CORNELIUS, Bishop of Liege.

By order, E. BREMANS, Secretary.

will incur the indignation of Almighty God, and of his Blessed Apostles, Peter and Paul.

Given at St. Peter's at Rome, in the year of the Incarnation of our Lord, 1839, on the 7th of the kalends of June, in the ninth year of our pontificate.

Besides the special indulgence for the canonization, the Holy Father granted in perpetuity, on the 10th of January 1840,* to each and all of the faithful of both sexes, who, being truly contrite, shall, after having confessed and communicated, devoutly visit one of the churches of the Congregation of the Most Holy Redeemer on the feast of St. Alphonsus, from the time of the first vespers or on any one of the seven days following, a plenary indulgence and remission of all sins once every year, which shall be applicable to the souls in purgatory, provided they pray for unity amongst Christian princes, for the extirpation of heresy, and the exaltation of their Mother the Church.

His Holiness, Gregory XVI, by a decree of the 10th of Sept., 1839, not only allowed, but prescribed, that the feast of St. Alphonsus should be celebrated throughout the world by all those obliged to say the breviary, and by the faithful in general, under the rite of *duplex minor;* inserting his name in the ecclesiastical calendar.

The inhabitants of Naples, moreover, entertaining the most lively desire of numbering this new hero, their former townsman and apostle, as one of their saintly patrons, on the 4th of July 1839, the authorities, in answer to a petition of the fathers of the Congregation of the Most Holy Redeemer presented on the 25th of June of the same year, declared him patron of the said city. This decree received the sanction of the sovereign, with the consent of the ecclesiastical authorities, and the syndic was authorized to make the needful arrangements. In consequence, according to the decrees of the Sacred Congregation of Rites, a *fête* took place in the church of the Congregation of St. Anthony, which, (after the first ceremonies were gone through

* See Note, p. 590.

on the 15th of August 1840) commenced on the following day, and lasted for nine days. On the 24th of the same month, a silver statue containing a relic of the saint, presented by the Congregation to the town, was carried in procession to the cathedral, with extraordinary pomp and solemnity, where, after all the ceremonies had been gone through, it was placed with that of St. Januarius, the first patron of the town, on the altar of the chapel of the treasury; the fathers of the Congregation of the Most Holy Redeemer being authorized to come in procession for the statue of their saintly founder each year on his feast day, after giving an assurance that they would bring it back again in the same manner. It is impossible to find words to describe the prodigious concourse of people that assembled together to witness this religious pomp; they filled the streets, the public squares, the balconies and even the roofs of the houses. The king and the queen, the queen mother, and all the royal family, saw the progress of the procession from the balcony of the royal palace, with most religious attention. The eminently religious spirit of the king had led him before to the foot of the altar of Alphonsus. He went thither privately on the first day, accompanied by his august spouse, and heard two masses, to the great edification of all present; he returned again on the last evening, accompanied by the queen and his royal highness the count of Aquila. Her majesty, the queen's mother, also visited the church to honor in person the hero whose triumph was being celebrated; she went there on the 17th, the 19th and the 22d, and on the last occasion she was accompanied by the princess royal. On the same day, their royal highnesses the prince and pirncess of Salerno, and their august daughter, came to crown this religious homage with their presence.

Were it allowed to desire any further addition to the glories of St. Alphonsus, it would be that of seeing him declared *Doctor* by the head of the Church; to the obtaining of which title our saint appears to have fulfilled the necessary conditions. The following are the conditions,

50*

which, according to Benedict XIV, the Church requires for this honorable distinction, viz: eminent knowledge, great sanctity, and the declaration of the Church. Now, who can fail to perceive that Alphonsus had all these qualifications necessary for obtaining the honor of this title? Benedict VIII says that eminent learning is proved by combating heretics victoriously, by clearing up obscure and doubtful questions, and by setting forth Holy Scripture with clearness. Have not the works of Alphonsus on heresies and against heretics, all the pages of his Moral Theology and his commentary on the Psalms, (not to speak of his numerous ascetical writings,) perfectly fulfiled these conditions? and have not the sovereign pontiffs themselves, several times declared that the learning and sanctity of this servant of God were carried by him to an eminent degree? It rests therefore only with the Vicar of Jesus Christ to add this additional glory to the crown of the new confessor pontiff.

THE END

A Catechism of Scripture History, compiled by the Sisters of Mercy, for the use of the Children attending their Schools. Revised and corrected by M. J. Kerney, Author of a Compendium of Ancient and Modern History, First Class Book of History, Catechism of the History of the United States. Second American, from the last London Edition......................18mo. 50 cts.

The object of this Catechism is to render children early acquainted with the truthful and interesting events recorded in the Sacred Scriptures; to familiarize them with the prophecies relating to the coming of the Messiah, and lead them to regard the Old Testament as a figure and a foreshadowing of the New.

In its style and arrangement, it is happily adapted to that class of learners for which it was designed. It was originally compiled for the use of the pupils attending the schools of the Sisters of Mercy, in the city of Limerick, Ireland. The first edition was published under the supervision of the Rev. Dr. O'Reilly, of Maynooth, and shortly after its appearance it acquired an extensive circulation among the Catholic schools of England and Ireland. Its merits soon extended to this country, and in a short time it became extensively used in our Catholic Institutions. Heretofore, however, our schools have been supplied from the English press, but in order to meet the increasing demand for the work, the publishers have deemed it expedient to issue an American edition.

Advantage has been taken of the present favorable opportunity, of having the work carefully revised and improved. Experience had shown that the *answers* were generally much too long for a work in the catechetical form, and consequently the task of committing them to memory was rendered unnecessarily difficult. To obviate this objection many of the answers have been divided and sub-divided by the introduction of additional questions, thus rendering the labor of preparing the lessons much easier for the pupil.

Just published, in 1 vol. 12mo., price 50 cents.

Elementary Algebra, by B. Sestini, S. J., Professor of Natural Philosophy and Astronomy in Georgetown College.

To render the Science of Algebra intelligible to pupils whose minds are yet unaccustomed to such studies, is not an easy task. For should the instructor subject every principle, as it is announced, to a rigorous demonstration, he will very probably not be comprehended; while, on the other hand, inconclusive reasoning is worse than none at all.

To obviate this difficulty has been the main object of the present treatise. The beginner will here be furnished with such proofs as are suited to his capacity; examples will afford new light to what might be otherwise obscure; with regard to operations founded on higher principles he will, for the present, content himself with merely practical rules, exemplified in the same manner.

With a mind thus gradually led on to strict mathematical discussion, he may then resume his course with profit, and by the aid of a treatise now in preparation, which is intended as a sequel to the present, complete his study of Algebra.

NEW WORKS IN PRESS.

The People's Edition of Lingard's England.

Will be ready early in December, in a beautiful 8vo volume of nearly 700 pages, with a fine Portrait and Memoir of the distinguished Author. Price, in embossed cloth, $2; Library style, $2 50.

The Primacy of the Apostolic See Vindicated. Fourth Revised Edition. By the Most Rev. Francis Patrick Kenrick, D. D., Archbishop of Baltimore.

The Genius of Christianity; Or the Spirit and Beauties of the Christian Religion. By M. De Chateaubriand. A new and beautiful translation, with a Memoir of the Author.

This work will be issued in an elegant and attractive style, at an early day.

A New Historical Tale, by the Author of "*Bertha, or the Pope and the Emperor.*"

Florine, a Tale of the First Crusaders.

This highly interesting Tale will be issued in a neat and attractive form, at an early day, from advance sheets furnished by the distinguished author.

GERMAN PRAYER BOOKS, &c., *published by* MURPHY & Co.

The following German Prayers are published with the Approbation of the *Most Rev. Archbishop of Baltimore.* They have been compiled with the greatest care by gentlemen of experience, under the immediate superintendence of the Rev. Superiors of the Society of the Holy Redeemer, in Baltimore, with a view to their adaptation to the wants of the German Catholics of this country.

Der gute Same, ein katholisches Gebetbuch. Herausgegeben von der Versammlung des allerheiligsten Erlösers. Mit Gutheissung der Obern. Mit 36 feinen Kupfern und Holzschnitten verziert...32mo. Leder-Einband. sheep 25
Dasselbe in Corduan.... roan 38 ....Saffian, imit. turk. 75
....mit Goldschnitt, roan, gilt edges 50 türk. Saff. mit Gold., turk. sup. ex. 1 25

Gelobt sei Jesus Christus. Ein Gebetbuch für fromme Christen. Enthaltend kurze Belehrungen über das Gebet, die heilige Messe, Beichte und Communion, und die ammthilligsten Gebete für diese heiligen Handlungen, nebst einer Vesper-Andacht, mit beigefügtem lateinischen Texte, den Buss-Psalmen, Litaneien, &c. Herausgegeben von der Versammlung des allerheiligsten Erlösers. Mit Gutheissung der Obern. Leder-Einband.....sheep 38
Feinem Papier, in Corduan, roan.. 50 .... Saffian, imit. turkey 1 00
Goldschnitt und Platten, ru. gt. ed. 75 fein. türk. Saff. Gold., turk. sup. ex. 1 50

The Glories of May, in German, a new and beautiful edition.

Die Herrlichkeiten Marias. Von dem heiligen Alphons M. Von Liguori, Bischof von St. Agatha und Stifter der Versammlung des Allerheiligsten Erlösers.—Aus dem Italienischen übersetzt. Herausgegeben von der Versammlung des Allerheiligsten Erlösers. Erste Americanische Ausgabe. Mit Approbation Geistlicher Obrigkeit. The Glories of Mary, in German, translated from the Italian of St. Alphonsus M. Liguori.—A new Edition; with Devotions for Mass, Confession and Holy Communion. 18mo. roan 1 00
...... Arabesq., Goldschnitt, &c., 1 50 .... imit. gt, edges 2 00

It is deemed superfluous to add any of the numerous testimonials in favor of this book. The name of Saint Liguori is sufficient to recommend it to every pious Catholic. This edition is comprised in an 18mo. volume of nearly 800 pages, printed and bound in a style of unsurpassed elegance and neatness. It has been carefully revised by one of the Redemptorist Fathers, and can be recommended with confidence, as one of the cheapest and best books ever offered to the German Catholics.

Besuchungen des Allerheiligsten Altars-Sakramentes, &c. (Visits to the most Holy Sacrament, and a complete Prayer Book combined,) und Begrüssungen der allzeit unbefleckten Jungfrau Maria; für jeden Tag des Monats. Von dem heiligen Alphons Maria von Liguori, Stifter der Versammlung des Allerheiligsten Erlösers. Nebst einem Gebetbuche. Neu herausgegeben von einem Priester derselben Versammlung mit Genehmigung des Hochwürdigsten Erzbischofes von Baltimore..............18mo. Leder-Einband, sheep 63
Corduan............. ......roan 1 00 Saffian...........turkey morocco 1 50
...mit Goldschnitt, roan, gt. edges 1 25 feinem türk. Saff., turk. sup. extra 2 00

To this edition of the Visits to the Most Holy Sacraments, by St. Liguori, all the *Prayers* and *Devotions* used on *ordinary occasions*, have been added, which renders it *a most useful and complete Prayer Book* for the use of devout persons. It is well printed on good paper, and sold at a very low price.

GERMAN SCHOOL BOOKS.

Biblische Geschichte des Alten und Neuen Testamentes, [The History of the Old & New Testaments, for the use of Cath. Schools,] zum Gebrauche der katholischen Schulen.—Herausgegeben mit Genehmigung und Erlaubniss des Hochwürdigsten Erzbischofs von Baltimore :....12mo. Halb-Franzbper doz. 2 00

Katholischer Katechismus. [Catholic Catechism.] Verfasst von Johann Nep. Neumann, Bischof von Philadelphia. Zehnte Auflage. Mit Genehmigung des National Conciliums von Balt ....18mo. Halb-Franzb, per doz. 1 50

Kleiner Catechismus. [Small Catechism.] Verfasst von Johann Nep. Neumann, Bischof von Philadelphia. Zehnte Auflage. Mit Genehmigung des National Conciliums von Baltimore. ....32mo. Per hundred, 1 00

A, B, C, und Buchstabir und Lesebuch. [Primer and Spelling Book, for the use of Catholic Schools.) Nach der Buchstabir und Lautir-Methode eingerichtet. Zum Gebrauche in den kathol. Schulen...Halb-Fr'zb. per doz. 1 00

Alle deutschen Bücher von Murphy & Co. sind mit Gutheissung der Obern herausgegeben.

CPSIA information can be obtained at www.ICGtesting.com
Printed in the USA
LVOW131429200412

278496LV00003B/15/P